INDEPENDENT TRAVELLERS

USA

THE BUDGET TRAVEL GUIDE

Managing Editor: Barbara Radcliffe Rogers

Thomas Cook
Publishing

Published by Thomas Cook Publishing,
a division of Thomas Cook Tour Operations Limited
PO Box 227
The Thomas Cook Business Park
15–16 Coningsby Road
Peterborough PE3 8SB
United Kingdom

Telephone: 01733 416477
E-mail: books@thomascook.com

ISBN 1 841574 98 8

Head of Publishing: Chris Young
Production/DTP Editor: Steven Collins
Project Administrator: Michelle Warrington
Cover design and layout: Studio 183, Thorney, Peterborough
Maps by RJS Associates, Lovell Johns Ltd
Editorial and layout for 2006 edition: 183 Books, Thorney, Peterborough
Editor: Deborah Parker
Project Manager: Stephen York
Proofreader: Stuart McLaren
Country map and city maps: Lovell Johns Ltd, Witney, Oxfordshire
Route maps: Pixel Cartography and Studio 183
Locator maps: Studio 183, Thorney, Peterborough

Text typeset in Book Antiqua and Gill Sans using QuarkXPress
Printed and bound in Italy by Legoprint S.P.A.

Help Improve this Guide

This guide is updated each year and we welcome reports and comments from our readers. Similarly we want to make this guide as useful as possible and are grateful for any comments.

A free copy of this guide will be sent to all readers whose information or ideas are incorporated in the next edition. Please send all contributions to the Series Editor, *Independent Travellers USA*, Thomas Cook Publishing at PO Box 227, The Thomas Cook Business Park, Coningsby Road, Peterborough PE3 8SB, UK, or e-mail books@thomascook.com.

First edition (2000) written and researched by:
Tom Bross; Ann Carroll Burgess; Tony Kelly; Tim Nollen; Barbara Radcliffe Rogers; Lura Rogers; Kirk D. Schneider; Roberta Sotonoff; Wendy Wood

Updating for 2006 edition:
Tom Bross; Ann Carroll Burgess; Tom Burgess; Ethel Davies; Fran Folsom; Tim Nollen; Eric Parks; Barbara Radcliffe Rogers; Stillman Rogers; Lura Rogers Seavey

Transport information:
Peter Bass, Editor, and **Reuben Turner**, *Thomas Cook Overseas Timetable*

Managing Editor:
Barbara Radcliffe Rogers

INDEPENDENT TRAVELLERS

USA

THE BUDGET TRAVEL GUIDE

Other titles in this series include:

Independent Travellers Australia
The Budget Travel Guide

Independent Travellers Britain and Ireland
The Budget Travel Guide

Independent Travellers Europe by Rail
The Inter-Railer's and Eurailer's Guide

Independent Travellers New Zealand
The Budget Travel Guide

Independent Travellers Thailand, Malaysia and Singapore
The Budget Travel Guide

SHARE YOUR EXPERIENCE

Have you had a great, interesting or even awful experience while travelling in the USA? Or do you have a helpful tip to pass on, that no guidebook seems to mention? We'd love to hear from you – and if we publish your experiences in the next edition we'll be happy to send you a free copy of the guide!

Write to the Series Editor, *Independent Travellers USA*, Thomas Cook Publishing, PO Box 227, The Thomas Cook Business Park, 15–16 Coningsby Road, Peterborough PE3 8SB, UK, or e-mail books@thomascook.com.

The Authors

Barbara Radcliffe Rogers is the New Hampshire-based author or co-author of more than a dozen travel guides and other books about places from New England to South Africa. She is the former President of the Travel Journalists Guild.

Tom Bross is a Boston-based freelance travel writer with 20 years' experience covering New England destinations and attractions for US and Canadian magazines and newspapers.

Ann Carroll Burgess, travel writer, editor and broadcaster, has travelled North America and Europe extensively. She is the author of *Atlanta Alive* and *Secret Portland* and member of the Travel Journalists Guild.

Tom Burgess started serious travelling while in University, driving his MG TD from Vancouver to San Francisco and Reno, and has been writing about his travels for 20 years.

Ethel Davies is a freelance photographer and journalist who makes her living travelling around the globe. She has spent the last year exploring the USA in a campervan (RV) with a copy of this guide constantly by her side.

Fran Folsom is a New England-based travel writer whose articles have appeared in *The Boston Herald, AAA Horizons, Christian Science Monitor, New York Post, Boston Globe* and *Toronto Sun*. She is a member of the Travel Journalists Guild.

Tony Kelly took up travel writing after teaching English in Sudan and China. Among his recent books are guides to Mallorca, Catalonia and New York City.

Tim Nollen hails from Washington, DC, though he has frequently fled the US for extended stays in Europe. His guidebooks and articles cover destinations from Prague to Philadelphia.

Kirk D. Schneider is a travel writer based in Northern California. Schneider is editor of *California By Train, Bus & Ferry* and contributed to *Thomas Cook's International Air Travel Handbook.*

Lura Rogers Seavey is the author of books about Switzerland, Spain, the Dominican Republic, as well as *Fun With the Family in New Hampshire and Vermont*. She also wrote about New England in Frommer's *America on Wheels.*

Roberta Sotonoff is a confessed travel junkie whose favourite mode of transportation is a 747. To support her habit, she became a Chicago-based travel writer.

Wendy Wood, intrepid adventurer, studied at Oxford. She has a great love of America, particularly Arizona, and has written and researched for several Thomas Cook publications.

Photographs

The following are thanked for supplying the photographs (and who hold the copyright):

Colour section pp. 96/97: Ethel Davies except Niagara Falls, Spectrum Colour Library
pp. 240/241: Spectrum Colour Library except Bar Harbor and Portland Indoor Market, Ethel Davies; Jefferson Memorial, Index Stock/Alamy; Inner Harbour, Stillman Rogers; Charleston inset, Image Select
pp. 352/353: Spectrum Colour Library except bison inset and Old Faithful, Image Select
pp. 496/497: Maxine Cass except Grand Canyon; Natural Bridge, Bryce Canyon National Park; Las Vegas, ImageState/Alamy; Gaslamp Quarter, San Diego Convention & Visitors Bureau/Brett Shoaf; San Francisco cable car, Stillman Rogers

Cover photograph
Grand Canyon at sunset. George H. Huey © Corbis

The authors and Thomas Cook Publishing would like to thank the following for their help during the production of this book:

Robert A. Gregory; Ralph Walden; Charlie Pepe; Glenn Faria; Bill DeSousa; Rick Hoeninghausen; Tom Mesereau; Cheryl Slaughter; Lucy Arnold; Paul Haught; Josh Nickerson; Andrew Maraniss; Nicky Short; Ellie Shelton; Matthew Dolling; Christopher Kieper; Dee Dee Poteete; Joan Jenkins; Tim Thompson; Nina Laramore; Charlene Williams; Linda Fish and Kristen Zissel.

CONTENTS

GENERAL INFORMATION

ROUTES & CITIES

CONTENTS

INTRODUCTION

The United States is a huge, dynamic, exciting, varied and often puzzling place to visit. Just as you think you know it, you can travel to another region and find an entirely different atmosphere, culture, climate, topography and even a different way of speaking the English language.

Forget about trying to understand what makes America and its inhabitants tick. Americans are as varied as the peoples of the world, partly because they *are* people from all over the world. No other country on earth contains so many people whose national ancestry is so short. Apart from the relatively few Native Americans (the correct term for those who used to be called Indians), Americans are all sons and daughters of immigrants. Descendants of the first families – those whose ancestors arrived on the *Mayflower* and other early ships – are still immigrant in origin.

People from every corner of the earth have settled here, bringing some of their ways and discarding others, blending with neighbours from other places into the rich soup that is the uniquely American heritage. The soup is far from bland, and it contains hearty chunks of cultures that have been preserved intact, or mostly intact. Americans have come to value their ethnic roots, and are fond of celebrating the customs and traditions of homelands, even ones they never knew, in holidays and festivals throughout the year.

Americans are proud of their rebellious history, and cling to a stubborn independence, especially in rural areas and small towns.

History is everywhere, especially along the coasts, where the first settlers built cities and the pivotal events of America's early history took place. To explore America's past and find the most significant sites of its early history, see the Timeline on pp. 68–69. But whatever your quest in America, take time to enjoy its variety, to lose yourself in the zest of its lively cities, to explore its quiet rural corners and to see some of the monumental natural attractions that decorate and shape its land. Don't expect to understand it, but do expect to have fun trying.

Barbara Radcliffe Rogers

PRICES

The price indications given below (in US dollars) have been used throughout this book. Please bear in mind that prices do fluctuate – these symbols have been given for guidance. Occasionally we do mention accommodation, food and highlights that are very expensive (shown $$$$+) but these are included in this budget guide if the attraction is an unmissable one or in case you want to splash out on a special treat.

Accommodation

$	=	under $50
$$	=	$50–90
$$$	=	$90–150
$$$$	=	over $150

Based on standard double room, no meals but including all taxes.

Food

$	=	under $10
$$	=	$10–15
$$$	=	$15–25
$$$$	=	over $25

Based on the price of a mid-range main course.

Highlights

If an admission charge is made:

$	=	under $7
$$	=	$7–15
$$$	=	over $15

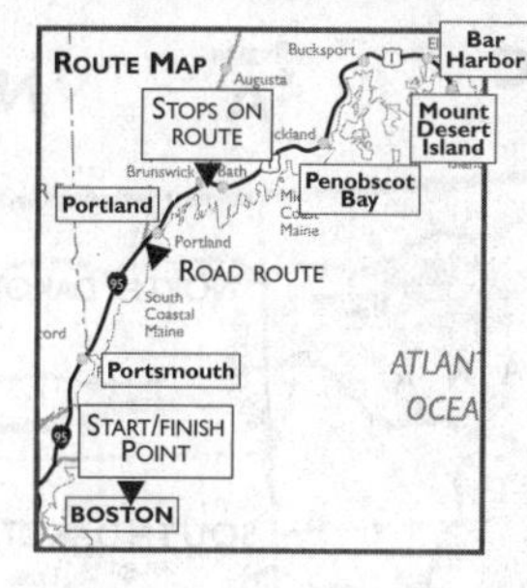

Independent Travellers USA presents over 75 different routes, cities and regions, each in its own chapter. Reflecting the tremendous variety of the United States, as well as its almost daunting size, these chapters vary in their approach, each featuring the best way to see and enjoy that part of the country. Some routes take advantage of the rail routes that connect major cities across the land. Others use cross-country bus, local bus and train lines, or even boats, to show you the best of a smaller region. In other areas the routes are best explored by hired car, and these detail the exact driving routes, town by town. In each case, stopovers and the most important attractions are described. The remaining chapters feature cities or attractions which are worth longer stops, each including information on how to get there, get around and make the most of your time there. All chapters give suggestions for budget-friendly accommodation and places to eat, as well as local entertainment.

The vast expanse of the United States has been divided into seven characteristic areas with introductions and maps, highlighting regional history, culture and cuisine. These area groupings are the Northeast, Middle Atlantic, the South, Midwest and Plains, Southwest, Northwest and the Far West.

Most chapters are accompanied by a map, showing the route or city or its environs and the stops described in the text. Each also has a route description or a summary of ways to get there: either a table showing bus and train times or a list of driving approaches, and sometimes both. Throughout the book you will see notes and tips in the margins. These provide added information, suggest places to stop en route or day trips from the main destination, tell you about interesting boat trips or walking tours, and suggest an onward route connecting this with other chapters.

PUBLIC TRANSPORT DETAILS

Timetables for the routes (e.g. see p. 98) have been extracted from *Thomas Cook Overseas Timetable* (OTT); see p. 58.

Symbols used in timetables:

①	Monday
②	Tuesday
③	Wednesday
④	Thursday
⑤	Friday
⑥	Saturday
⑦	Sunday
ex	except
s	set down only
u	pick up only

KEY TO ICONS

- Rail Services
- Car
- Bus Services
- Ferry Services
- Airports
- Information
- Accommodation
- Food and Drink

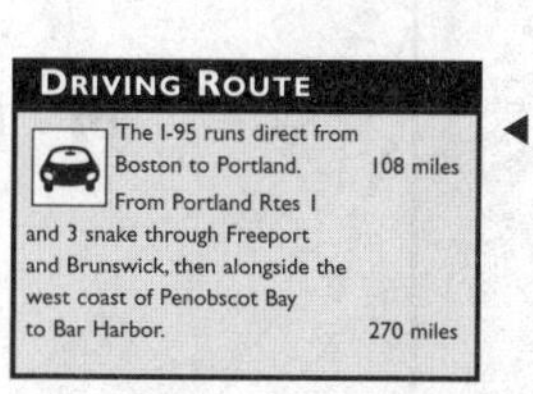

ROAD DETAILS
Route details and approximate cumulative mileages given.

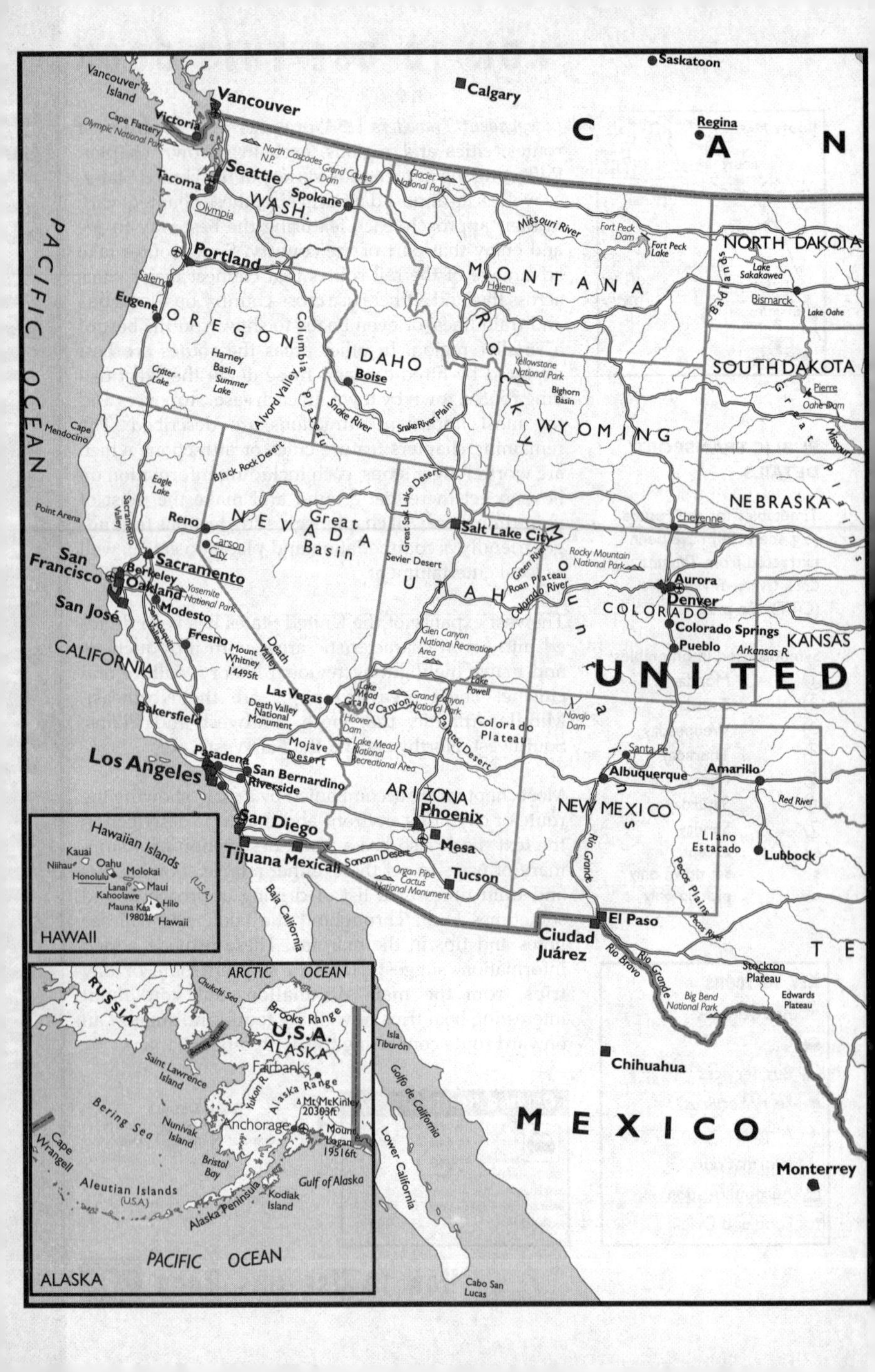

Saskatoon
Calgary
Regina
CANADA
Vancouver Island
Vancouver
Victoria
Cape Flattery
Olympic National Park
North Cascades N.P.
Grand Coulee Dam
Glacier National Park
Seattle
Tacoma
Spokane
WASH.
Olympia
Missouri River
Fort Peck Dam
Fort Peck Lake
NORTH DAKOTA
Lake Sakakawea
Bismarck
Lake Oahe
Badlands
PACIFIC OCEAN
Portland
Salem
MONTANA
Helena
Eugene
OREGON
Columbia Plateau
IDAHO
Boise
ROCKY MOUNTAINS
Harney Basin
Summer Lake
Crater Lake
Alvord Valley
Snake River
Snake River Plain
Yellowstone National Park
Bighorn Basin
SOUTH DAKOTA
Pierre
Oahe Dam
Great Plains
Missouri
Cape Mendocino
WYOMING
Black Rock Desert
Eagle Lake
Great Salt Lake Desert
NEBRASKA
Point Arena
Sacramento Valley
Reno
NEVADA
Great Basin
Salt Lake City
Cheyenne
Carson City
Sevier Desert
Green River
Rocky Mountain National Park
San Francisco
Sacramento
Berkeley
Oakland
Yosemite National Park
UTAH
Roan Plateau
Colorado River
Aurora
Denver
San José
Modesto
COLORADO
San Joaquin Valley
Colorado Springs
KANSAS
Pueblo
Arkansas R.
CALIFORNIA
Fresno
Mount Whitney 14495ft
Death Valley
Glen Canyon National Recreation Area
UNITED
Lake Powell
Las Vegas
Lake Mead
Grand Canyon
Grand Canyon National Park
Death Valley National Monument
Hoover Dam
Navajo Dam
Bakersfield
Colorado Plateau
Painted Desert
Mojave Desert
Lake Mead National Recreational Area
Santa Fe
Pasadena
Los Angeles
San Bernardino
Riverside
Albuquerque
Amarillo
ARIZONA
Phoenix
NEW MEXICO
Red River
San Diego
Mesa
Llano Estacado
Lubbock
Hawaiian Islands
Kauai
Oahu
Niihau
Honolulu
Molokai
Lanai
Maui
Kahoolawe
Mauna Kea 19803ft
Hilo
Hawaii
(U.S.A.)
HAWAII
Tijuana
Mexicali
Sonoran Desert
Organ Pipe Cactus National Monument
Tucson
Rio Grande
Pecos Plains
Pecos River
Baja California
El Paso
Ciudad Juárez
Rio Bravo
TE
ARCTIC OCEAN
RUSSIA
Chukchi Sea
Brooks Range
U.S.A.
ALASKA
Bering Strait
Saint Lawrence Island
Fairbanks
Alaska Range
Yukon R.
Mt McKinley 20303ft
Bering Sea
Nunivak Island
Anchorage
Mount Logan 19516ft
Cape Wrangell
Bristol Bay
Aleutian Islands (U.S.A.)
Alaska Peninsula
Kodiak Island
Gulf of Alaska
PACIFIC OCEAN
ALASKA
Stockton Plateau
Edwards Plateau
Big Bend National Park
Isla Tiburón
Golfo de California
Chihuahua
Lower California
MEXICO
Monterrey
Cabo San Lucas

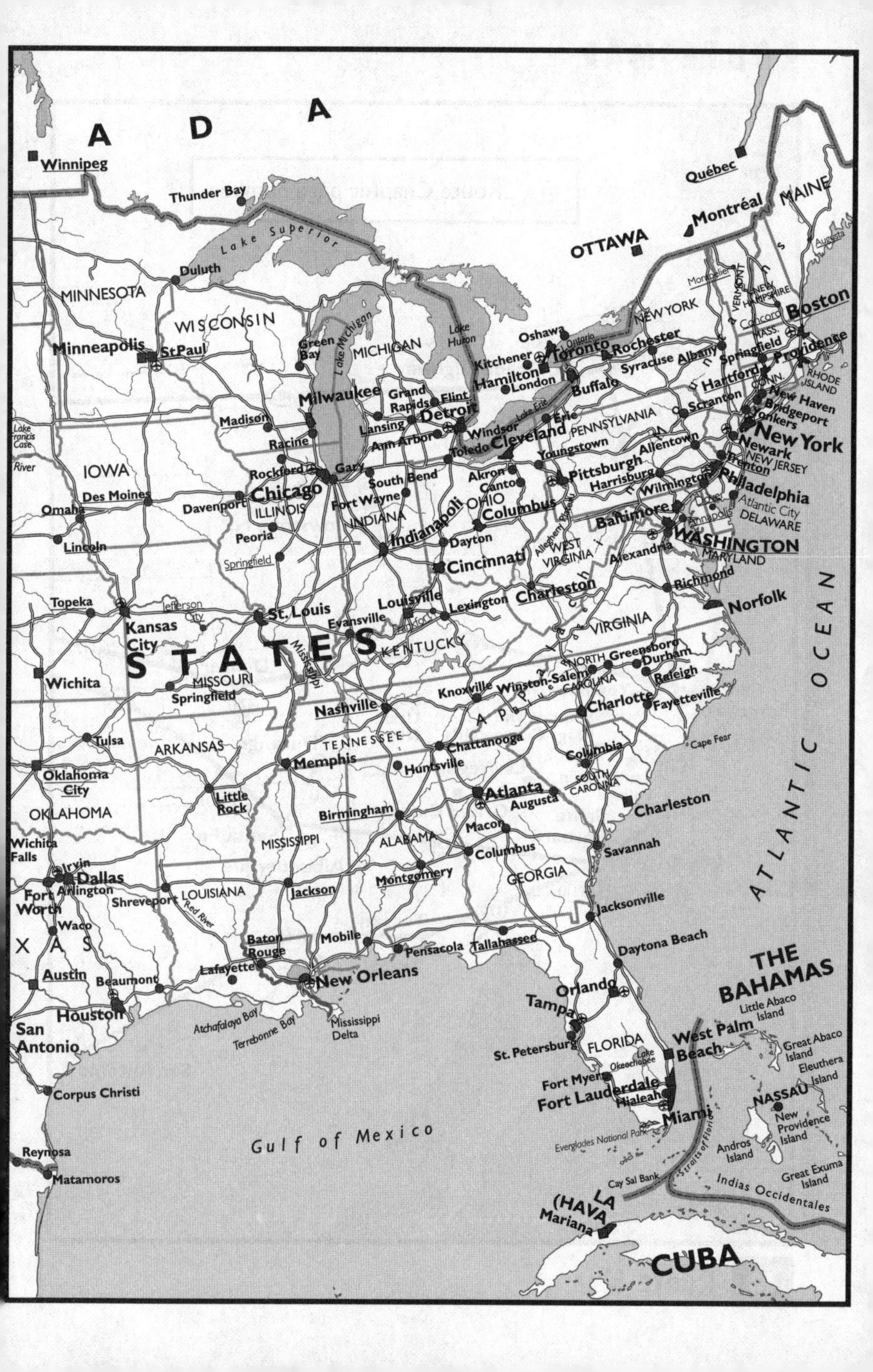

A D A
Winnipeg
Thunder Bay
Lake Superior
Duluth
MINNESOTA
WISCONSIN
Minneapolis
St Paul
Green Bay
Lake Michigan
MICHIGAN
Lake Huron
Milwaukee
Grand Rapids
Flint
Lansing
Detroit
Madison
Racine
Ann Arbor
Windsor
Lake Erie
Toledo
Cleveland
Erie
Québec
Montréal
MAINE
OTTAWA
Augusta
Montpelier
VERMONT
NEW HAMPSHIRE
NEW YORK
Concord
Boston
MASS.
Oshawa
Ontario
Toronto
Rochester
Kitchener
Hamilton
London
Buffalo
Syracuse
Albany
Springfield
Providence
RHODE ISLAND
Hartford
CONN.
Scranton
New Haven
Bridgeport
Yonkers
New York
PENNSYLVANIA
Youngstown
Allentown
Newark
NEW JERSEY
Trenton
Pittsburgh
Harrisburg
Philadelphia
Atlantic City
Wilmington
Dover
DELAWARE
Annapolis
Baltimore
WASHINGTON
MARYLAND
Lake Francis Case
River
IOWA
Des Moines
Omaha
Lincoln
Rockford
Gary
Chicago
Davenport
ILLINOIS
Peoria
Springfield
South Bend
Fort Wayne
INDIANA
Indianapolis
Akron
Canton
OHIO
Columbus
Dayton
Cincinnati
Allegheny Plateau
WEST VIRGINIA
Alexandria
Charleston
Richmond
Norfolk
Topeka
Kansas City
Jefferson City
St. Louis
Evansville
Louisville
Frankfort
Lexington
VIRGINIA
KENTUCKY
STATES
Mississippi
MISSOURI
Springfield
Wichita
NORTH CAROLINA
Greensboro
Durham
Winston-Salem
Raleigh
Knoxville
Nashville
Charlotte
Fayetteville
Appalachian
Tulsa
ARKANSAS
TENNESSEE
Chattanooga
Cape Fear
Memphis
Huntsville
Columbia
SOUTH CAROLINA
Oklahoma City
OKLAHOMA
Little Rock
Atlanta
Augusta
Charleston
Birmingham
Macon
MISSISSIPPI
ALABAMA
Savannah
Columbus
Wichita Falls
Irving
Dallas
Arlington
Fort Worth
Shreveport
LOUISIANA
Red River
Jackson
Montgomery
GEORGIA
Jacksonville
Waco
X A S
Baton Rouge
Mobile
Pensacola
Tallahassee
Daytona Beach
Austin
Beaumont
Lafayette
New Orleans
Orlando
Houston
Atchafalaya Bay
Terrebonne Bay
Mississippi Delta
Tampa
San Antonio
St. Petersburg
FLORIDA
Lake Okeechobee
West Palm Beach
Fort Myers
Fort Lauderdale
Hialeah
Miami
Corpus Christi
Gulf of Mexico
Everglades National Park
Straits of Florida
Reynosa
Matamoros
Cay Sal Bank
LA (HAVA
Mariana
CUBA
ATLANTIC OCEAN
THE BAHAMAS
Little Abaco Island
Great Abaco Island
Eleuthera Island
NASSAU
New Providence Island
Andros Island
Great Exuma Island
Indias Occidentales

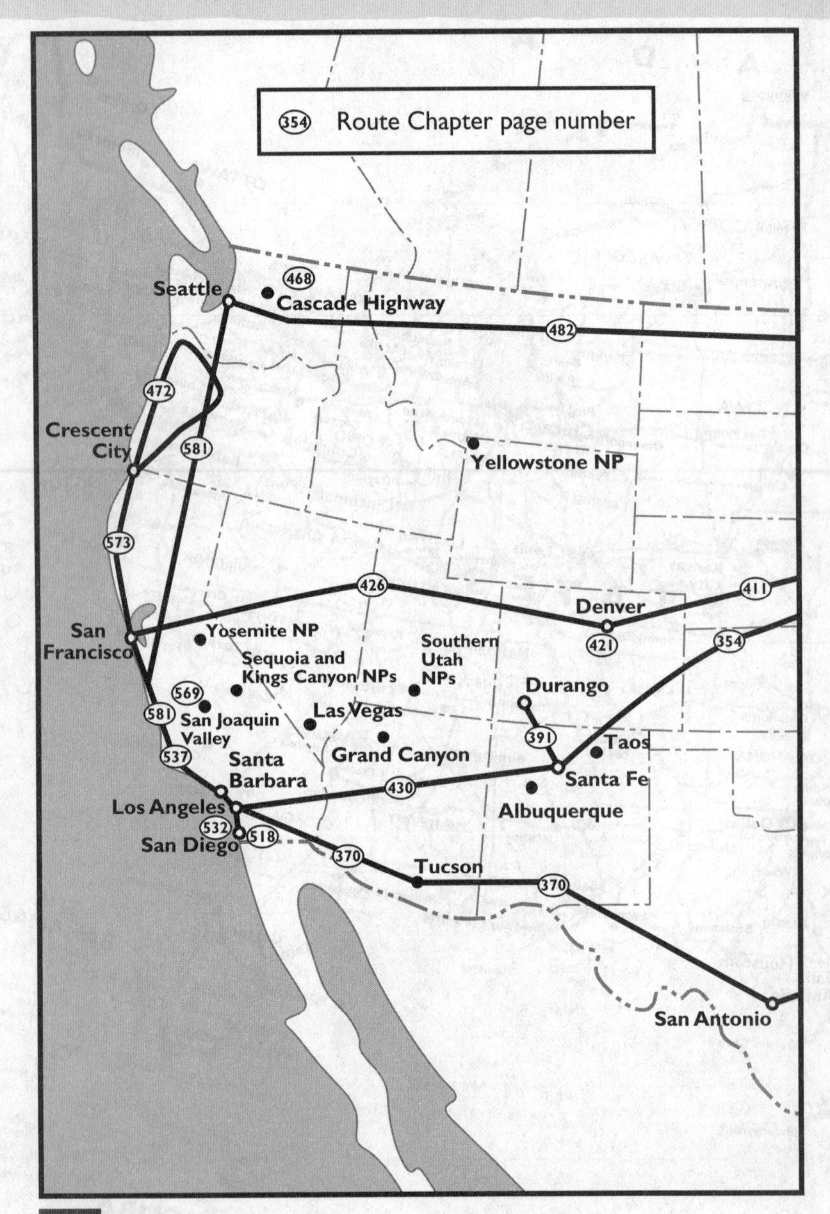

354 Route Chapter page number
Seattle
468
Cascade Highway
482
472
Crescent City
581
Yellowstone NP
573
426
411
Denver
421
354
San Francisco
Yosemite NP
Sequoia and Kings Canyon NPs
Southern Utah NPs
Durango
569
581
San Joaquin Valley
Las Vegas
391
Taos
537
Grand Canyon
Santa Barbara
Santa Fe
430
Los Angeles
Albuquerque
532
518
San Diego
370
Tucson
370
San Antonio

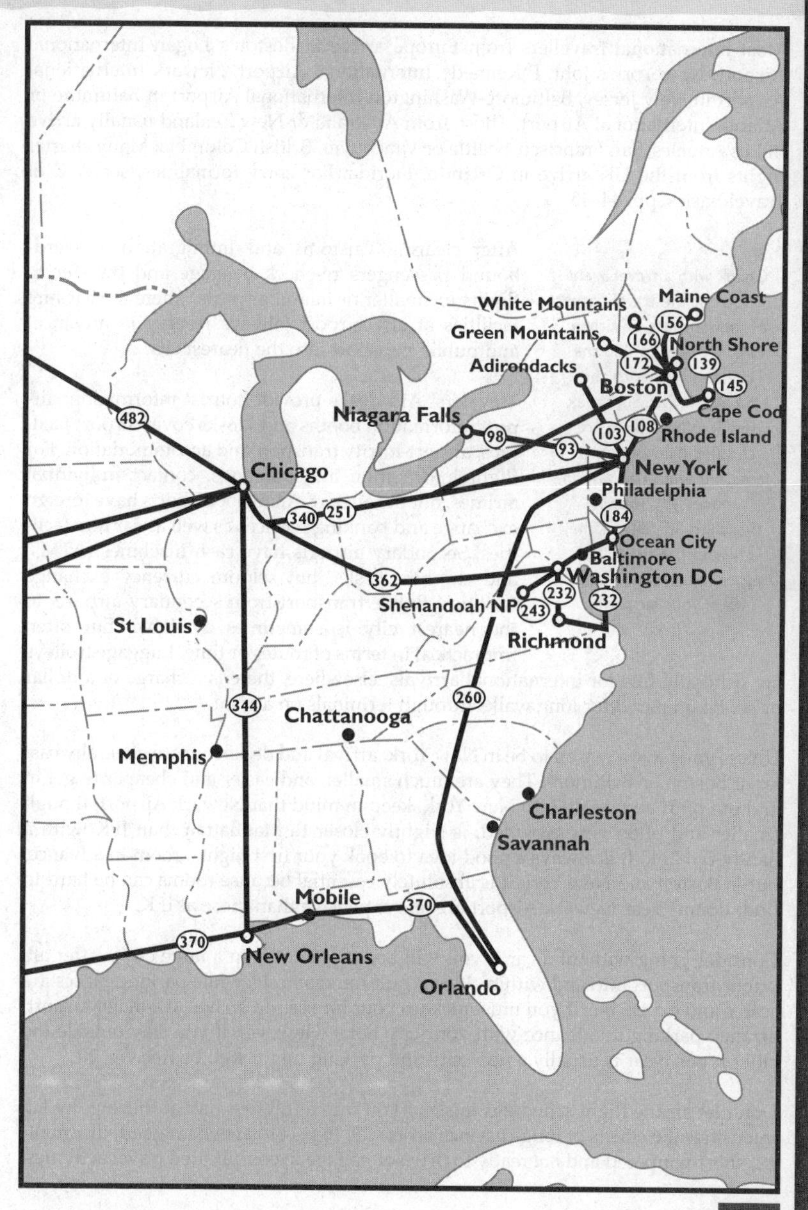

White Mountains
Maine Coast
156
Green Mountains
166
North Shore
172
139
Adirondacks
Boston
145
Cape Cod
Niagara Falls
98
103
108
Rhode Island
482
93
New York
Chicago
Philadelphia
340
251
184
Ocean City
Baltimore
362
Washington DC
232
232
Shenandoah NP
243
St Louis
Richmond
344
260
Chattanooga
Memphis
Charleston
Savannah
Mobile
370
370
New Orleans
Orlando

REACHING THE UNITED STATES

Most international travellers from Europe arrive at Boston's Logan International Airport, New York's John F Kennedy International Airport, Newark International Airport in New Jersey, Baltimore-Washington International Airport in Baltimore or Atlanta International Airport. Those from Australia or New Zealand usually arrive in Los Angeles, San Francisco, Seattle or Vancouver, British Columbia. Many charter flights from the UK arrive in Orlando, Florida. For entry formalities, see A–Z of Travel Basics, pp. 44–45.

Check with a travel agent or look at the travel pages of newspapers or airline internet sites to find the cheapest flights to the USA. Apex, Pex, Superpex and Standby tickets are cheaper than Economy fares, but what you save in money you lose in flexibility. In general, the cheaper the ticket, the more restrictions placed upon your air travel.

After clearing Customs and Immigration, onward-bound passengers re-check baggage and transfer to flights to smaller or inland airports. There are car hire facilities at any airport (always reserve in advance) and public transport into the nearest city.

Travelers' Aid desks provide tourist information; airport information booths and kiosks cover airport facilities, airport-to-city transport and accommodation. For flight information and bookings, contact individual airlines, not the airport. All major airports have foreign exchange and banking services as well as car hire facilities. Secondary airports have cash machines (ATMs) and car hire desks, but seldom currency exchange facilities. Public transport from secondary airports to the nearest city is sometimes available, but often impractical in terms of routes or time. Luggage trolleys are generally free for international arrivals; elsewhere, there is a charge of a dollar or so. Be prepared for long walks through terminals on arrival.

Unless you have a reason to be in New York, arrival and departure are generally easier at Boston or Baltimore. They are much smaller, and easier and cheaper to get in and out of. If you do fly into New York, keep in mind that Newark Airport, though smaller and often very crowded, is slightly closer to Manhattan than JFK, with a handy rail link. It is always a good idea to book your first night's room in advance, but in Boston and New York it is absolutely essential because rooms can be hard to find. Rooms near Newark Airport are less expensive than those at JFK.

Consider going without a car if you will begin your stay in a large city – after all, public transport into and within cities is quick and simple, while parking places are scarce and expensive. If you must pick up your hire car on arrival at a major airport, arrange parking in advance with your city hotel. However, if you stay outside the city proper, a car is usually a necessity and parking might well be free.

Don't let airline flight schedules mislead you into a full first day of touring. Jet lag intensifies the effects of long-distance air travel. Expect to arrive fatigued, disoriented, short-tempered and *not* ready to drive or engage in complicated travel activities.

Night-time flights seem to offer an extra day of sightseeing upon arrival. Resist the temptation. Most travellers do better by timing their flights to arrive in the late afternoon or early evening, then getting a good night's sleep before tackling the sights. Since many airport-area hotels and motels offer a free shuttle service to and from the airport, you can take a shuttle to the hotel, recover from the flight and pick up the rental car the next morning at no additional cost.

Many fly-drive programmes offer what looks like an easy first-day drive, e.g. Los Angeles International Airport to the Disneyland area in Anaheim. Although this should be a 45-min jaunt, it can stretch to hours in heavy commuter traffic. Better to spend the first night in an airport-area hotel and hit the road refreshed in the morning – especially if you're not accustomed to urban traffic or driving on the right-hand side of the road. In general try to avoid 'rush hour' traffic around large cities by travelling after 0900 and before 1600.

On your return, don't plan a tight schedule that gets you into a city and on to the airport just the requisite two hours before an international departure. Unexpected volumes of traffic can leave you stranded on a highway as your plane takes off overhead. Airlines won't hold an entire flight for a carload of passengers flying on non-refundable bargain fares, but they will happily allow you the privilege of paying full fare for single tickets home on the next available flight. Allow a safety margin by spending your last night near the departure airport.

Travel Arrangements It is a great temptation for independently minded travellers to make all their arrangements separately, instead of locking into a packaged plan. However, the many types of air ticket and the range of temporary deals available on busy routes make it advisable to talk to your travel agent before booking to get the best bargain.

In fact, taking a fly-drive package such as one of Thomas Cook's own, or one of the many others offered by airlines and tour operators, can be more economical than making all your own arrangements. All include the air ticket and car hire element; some also follow set itineraries which enables them to offer guaranteed and pre-paid en route accommodation at selected hotels. Flexible tailored holidays such as Thomas Cook Signature's America allow you to put together an individual trip to suit your taste with the benefits of booking the airline ticket at an advantageous rate and then choosing from a 'menu' of other items, often at a discounted price, such as car hire, hotels and other extras such as excursions.

Insurance

Experienced travellers carry insurance that covers their belongings and holiday investment as well as their bodies. Travel insurance should include provision for cancelled or delayed flights and weather problems, as well as immediate evacuation home in the case of medical emergency. Thomas Cook and other travel agencies offer comprehensive policies. Medical cover should be high – at least $1 million.

TRAVELLING AROUND THE USA

The most difficult thing for travellers planning trips to the USA is to remember just how big it is. Once you leave the smaller states of New England and the Northeast, it can take an entire day's driving to cross just one state. And since your purpose is to see something while you are there, you won't want to spend all your time moving from point to point. However you decide to travel, beware of planning to cover too great a distance. It is better to see one area of the country, enjoy it and get to know it a little, than to flit from place to place without time to see any of them.

If you arrive in the eastern USA and plan to visit the west coast, flying is the most practicable way to get there unless you have plenty of time for overland travel. Transcontinental train and motor coach travel is slow, cramped and unpredictable, although Amtrak operates popular north–south coastal services. Air travel is even more cramped, but travel time is counted in hours rather than days and timetables are almost always accurate.

TRAVELLING BY AIR

The US domestic air service is extensive and cheaper than within Europe. There are shuttle flights into Boston and other eastern cities every hour from New York's LaGuardia Airport and from Baltimore, plus regularly scheduled flights from cities all over the USA and Canada. Southwest Airlines (tel: (210) 617-1221) has revolutionised domestic air fares with its 'no frills' flights at prices that rival bus and train fares, and forced other airlines into competitive pricing. That said, it is still advisable to compare these to VUSA rates (see p. 17), which must be purchased outside the US.

Bumped Off

Being 'bumped' from your flight can throw your travel plans into chaos – or it can be profitable. If you are flying on a busy route, and could just as easily take a somewhat later flight, you could find yourself with a coupon towards a future ticket. To best position yourself for voluntary bumping, check in early, then go to the gate and sit close to the desk. If the flight over-fills, you can be the first one at the desk when the call for volunteers comes. The initial offer is usually a $200 certificate towards another flight and a guarantee of a seat on the next flight to your destination. Wise travellers usually accept this offer, even though a larger reward may be offered later. The coupon is issued immediately, so you can use it whenever you like, usually within one year.

Cover major cross-country routes by air – at least one way – and you can save days for sightseeing at your destination. Many American carriers include options for additional flights within the USA at reduced rates or even include free stopovers; and local airlines, as noted above, often have special fares. These are arrangements you should make well in advance, however, since special fares often apply

Air Passes

A number of major airlines offer VUSA (Visit USA) air passes which can be purchased by those travelling from outside the US when booking a flight to the US. These passes, which offer good value if you are going to stick to an itinerary, pre-pay your air travel within the USA. Conditions and restrictions vary depending on the carrier – you usually have to pre-book all your flights before you reach the US, and may not be allowed to alter these arrangements. Check with the airline or enquire at your travel agent before booking your transatlantic flight.

only to a certain number of seats on each flight. In general, the closer you are to flight time, the rarer bargain seats become. Within the last seven days, rates are rarely reduced. Amtrak has arrangements with United Airlines to combine cross-country train travel with a return by air, under their Air Rail scheme.

In making air arrangements, keep in mind that return air fares are cheaper than single tickets. If you are only travelling one way by air, always give a return date, and as far in the future as possible, to take advantage of the lowest rate. Do not tell the ticketing agent that you do not plan to use the return portion, however; agents are not allowed to sell you a return ticket if they know it won't be used.

In the wake of the 2001 terrorist attacks on the USA, security measures in airports have been tightened considerably. These are not altogether consistent, but for the latest official word, consult www.faa.gov, the website of the Federal Aviation Agency. For the latest packing tips and other information on security procedures and requirements, visit the Transportation Security Administration website, www.tsa.gov. A tip worth noting is to leave your check-through bags unlocked in order to avoid locks being broken for inspection.

TRAVELLING BY TRAIN

Amtrak is the official passenger train transport company in the United States: tel: (800) USA RAIL or (800) 872-7245; www.amtrak.com. Main routes along the west coast run from California to Portland, Seattle and Vancouver. Along the east coast, principle routes run from Boston to Miami, through New York, Philadelphia, Baltimore and Washington DC and through Atlanta to New Orleans. Four major routes travel east–west across the USA: one just south of the Canadian border, one along the Gulf coast and Mexican border, and two across the centre: north–south is Chicago–New Orleans. A map of the Amtrak routes can be found on their website at www.amtrak.com/pdf/national.pdf. John Pitt's *USA by Rail*, published in the UK by Bradt Publications and distributed in North America by the Globe Pequot Press, is a good guide to long-distance routes; website: www.USA-by-Rail.com. **VIA Rail** handles passenger traffic in Canada; tel: (888) 842-7245; www.viarail.ca. Trains do not stop at each town.

AMTRAK PASSES

Amtrak passes allow unlimited train travel for 15 or 30 days, valid for peak season (28 May–6 Sept and 16 Dec–2 Jan) or off peak (all other times). Passes pay for travel (supplements are payable for sleeping accommodation and on Metroliner and Acela Express services), but reservations must be made on most routes.

Route	15/30-day	Peak (2005)	Off Peak (2005)
National Rail Pass	15-day	$440	$295
	30-day	$550	$385
West Pass	15-day	$325	$210
	30-day	$405	$270
Northeast Pass	15-day	$211	$191
	30-day	$247	$232
East Pass	15-day	$325	$210
	30-day	$405	$270

For prices in sterling, contact (in the UK) The Travel Bureau, tel: 0800 698 7545, fax: 01902 324333, e-mail: leerailtours@thetravelbureau.co.uk.

Train times for many Amtrak, VIA Rail and local services are published in the *Thomas Cook Overseas Timetable* (see pp. 58–59). Amtrak sells a range of rail passes – details of the main ones are shown in the box opposite. Its National Rail Pass covers the entire USA and nearby Canadian cities. Other passes cover the entire west (from Chicago), the north-east (from Virginia to Montreal) and all points east of Chicago. A five-day Northeast Pass costs $175 peak season, $149 off peak. These passes are available in the UK through The Travel Bureau; for contact details see the Amtrak Passes box. Even with a pass, you will still need a reservation, which you can only make at a station or through a travel agent.

Other passes are the California Rail Pass, valid on all Amtrak trains and Amtrak Thruway buses, and the North America Rail Pass, valid on Amtrak and Via Rail. These can be purchased from agents. Note that Amtrak Thruway buses should always be reserved in advance.

Remember, however, that these passes are only economical if you will be spending many days within that period on the train. If you plan to spend several days sightseeing at each of several destinations, you may well do better to buy single tickets. All long distance and several of the New York–Boston trains require advance reservations even if you have a pass. Other discounts, including 15 per cent reductions for travellers over 62, passengers with disabilities, and students with a pass ($20) and half fare for children aged 2–15, can bring individual ticket rates lower than passes for those who qualify. Children aged 2–15 and seniors may also get 10 per cent off the cost of a 15- or 30-day pass, however. Current offers are shown on the Amtrak website: www.amtrak.com.

Keep in mind, however, that return fares (called round-trips in the USA) usually cost the same as one-way fares and that advance reservations make fares even cheaper. Consider this, too, when deciding between bus and train. Return bus fares are usually simply double the one-way rate. Since most comparison charts use one-way as a base, these charts are not entirely reliable. Always ask for both single and return fares. Train travel is somewhat less useful as a way of connecting closer destinations, except along the well-used coastal routes.

Amtrak offers dining and snackbar service on long-distance trains and on some shorter runs, but prices tend to be high. You can save substantially by taking a picnic meal on board. Stations no longer have facilities for leaving luggage while you tour; a complete list of station facilities is shown in Amtrak's National Timetable. In many places, Amtrak carries passengers from central railheads to nearby destinations by special shuttles or coach. Arrive one hour early if you do not have a ticket, to allow for security checks, and have your passport available.

TRAVELLING BY BUS

Bus (coach) lines serve many more destinations than do the railways. Bus lines also cover the same long-distance routes as trains, often in the same time. The Boston–New York bus trip, for example, is comparable to the train in both duration and price, unless you use the pricier high-speed trains.

Greyhound Bus Lines (tel: (800) 229-9424 from the US; www.greyhound.com) provide long-distance bus services between cities (and stops en route) nationwide. Trailways, an association of independent operators, provide a complete connected bus network in many areas, and in some parts of the US are the major operator. Greyhound offer discounts for seniors (over 55), disabled travellers and their helpers and children (under 12) riding with a full-fare paying adult. The International Ameripass offers special discounts for adult travellers not resident in North America.

GREYHOUND PASSES

Passes have to be presented to the station/terminal ticket agent for validation before travel.

AmeriPasses
(bought outside the US or in New York, NY)

4 days	$179
7 days	$239
10 days	$289
15 days	$349
21 days	$419
30 days	$479
45 days	$529
60 days	$639

Greyhound's (International) AmeriPass, like rail passes, may not necessarily be a lower price than individual tickets, especially if you reserve and buy individual tickets at least three days in advance. Because these are not 'flexi-passes' they are not good for those who are only travelling for a short time and visiting a few destinations. But for long-distance travel, they are a very good buy. The Greyhound pass is valid on most other operations including Trailways. Seats are not guaranteed on Greyhound buses. It is best to turn up 45 minutes before departure, but if a bus is full another bus will usually be laid on to take the overflow. In the UK, passes are available from Trains Europe Ltd, 4 Station Approach, March, Cambridgeshire , tel: 01354 660222.

USEFUL ADDRESSES AND TELEPHONE NUMBERS

Greyhound Bus Lines, Customer Service, PO Box 660689, MS 490, Dallas, TX 75266-0689; tel: (800) 229-9424; www.greyhound.com.

For telephone numbers of other regional bus lines and local commuter, bus and ferry systems, consult the appropriate table in the bi-monthly *Thomas Cook Overseas Timetable* which contains timetables and much more additional travel information.

If you're buying tickets locally enquire about the **North America Discovery Pass**, which, depending on distance travelled, may be more economical (but slightly more expensive if bought within the US). Local transport companies listed in the telephone directory under individual cities and towns provide a local service, or consult the *Thomas Cook Overseas Timetable*.

The (International) CanAm Pass allows travel in all US states except Alaska and in all Canadian provinces except Newfoundland (15-day $399, up to 60-day $679). The (International) Regional CanAm passes are for use in a limited number of states and provinces: the Eastern Pass (10-day $285, 21-day $385) and Western Pass (10-day $285).

TRAVELLING BY BOAT

The USA has very little regularly scheduled boat travel, except on short ferry connections. Long-distance boat trips, such as steamboat trips on the Mississippi and coastal travel, are by cruise packages of several days to a week. These tend to be luxury holidays, too pricey for budget travellers.

TRAVELLING BY CAR

Possibly one of the most difficult things for non-Americans to understand about the United States is how important a car is for getting to places. Public transport is quite good between cities of any size, passable between many smaller cities, but generally inadequate for smaller towns and rural areas. It serves the needs of commuting workers, but not of travellers. Because so many of the 'sights' of the USA are away from cities, often (especially in the west) remote from settled areas, getting to them without a car can be quite challenging, even impossible. In the east, many of the best places to go are lovely scenic rural areas, such as New England's small towns and villages or the great plantation houses of the south. Other attractions, such as museums and living history villages, may be miles from anywhere. Being without 'wheels' puts you at the mercy of erratic local buses or expensive and crowded rush-through tours.

Being without a car also leaves you little option in accommodation. In the USA, most budget accommodation (other than fleabag boarding houses and by-the-hour hotels) is outside city centres, along the Interstate highway or other approaches to a city. Here you will find rows of budget chain motor inns offering plain but clean and comfortable rooms at a tiny fraction of their in-town counterparts in the same range. The saving in hotel rooms alone can pay for car hire.

If you plan to spend days sightseeing in the city, it is often easiest to stay in hotels on the outskirts and drive to a nearby free commuter car park at a railway or bus station. You will usually be travelling during 'commuter hours', when buses and metro systems run frequently and in the right direction. For example, the area around Concord and Acton, Massachusetts, has several nice budget hotels, and is served by commuter rail that takes you right to Porter Square in Cambridge or into North Station, both stops on the city's subway system.

SOME US DRIVING AND SIGN TERMS

Big Rig – a large lorry, usually a tractor pulling one or more trailers

Connector – a minor road connecting two freeways

Cop – slang word for police officer. The proper form of address is 'officer'.

Crosswalk – pedestrian crossing

Curve – bend

Divided Highway – dual carriageway

DUI – driving under the influence of alcohol or drugs, aka drunk driving. Drink-driving laws are very strictly enforced.

DWI – driving while intoxicated

Expressway – motorway (called 'throughway' in the west)

Fender – bumper

Flat – puncture

Freeway – motorway (in California)

Garage/Parking Garage – car park

Gas(olene) – petrol

Grade – gradient, hill

Highway – trunk road

Hood – bonnet

Interstate – main road between states, shown as 'I-95'. Road signs are a red, white and blue shield with the number in the centre. Maps show the number in a shield

Motor home – motor caravan

Pavement – road surface. A UK pavement is a sidewalk.

Ramp – slip road

Rent – hire

Rotary or Traffic Circle – roundabout

RV (Recreational Vehicle) – motor caravan

Shift(stick) – gear lever

Sidewalk – pavement

Sig-alert – an official warning of unusually heavy traffic, usually broadcast over local radio stations

Shoulder – verge

Switchback – serpentine road

Tailgate – driving too close to the vehicle immediately in front

Tow Truck – breakdown lorry

Tractor Trailor – large lorry

Traffic cop – traffic warden

Trailer – caravan

Truck – lorry

Trunk – boot

Turnpike – trunk road or motorway

Unpaved Road – rough gravel or dirt road – check car hire restrictions on driving

Windshield – windscreen

Yield – give way

Many budget travellers plan to spend their days in the city, returning to the outskirts at night to find dining in the budget restaurants that often surround 'motel row' or in small suburban village centres where more upmarket restaurants congregate. A car gives you this flexibility.

GETTING FROM HITHER TO YON

The extensive US Interstate highway system brings car traffic smoothly into and around cities, travelling across and up and down the entire country. The best of US roads, these are dual carriageway, limited-access highways carrying two, three, four or more lanes of traffic in each direction. Most major cities have circular 'beltway' highways, also part of the Interstate system.

Although they don't all run north–south or east–west, you can generally tell the principal direction of an Interstate highway by its number. Odd two-digit numbers run north–south, even two–digit numbers east–west, and three-digit numbers are either connectors or beltways around cities. Washington, DC, for example, is linked to New York and the south by I-95, while I-66 leads west. I-495 circles the city and I-295 and I-395 are short connector routes.

Some Interstate highways are toll roads, others are free. Some have toll segments and free segments. Interstates are the quickest, most direct routes but offer little to see. Petrol stations, restaurants and motels generally cluster at exits, off the highway; rest stops between some exits offer parking and often toilet facilities. Rest stops along other, non-Interstate toll roads offer petrol and food as well.

Most major bridges charge tolls, as do scattered small private bridges, but the latter are becoming more rare. These tolls usually range from less than $1 to $4; most expensive is the bridge-tunnel across the mouth of the Chesapeake Bay, about $10. Some toll highways use a card system, giving you a card as you enter and tallying the correct toll as you exit, based on how far you have travelled. Some (the bane of through-motorists) stop you every so many miles to collect a small fee. Some of the pay points (called toll plazas) are manned, others use a collecting machine that signals with a green light when the money is received.

It is wise to carry a small change purse filled with 25-cent pieces (quarters) and smaller change, as well as $1 bills, enabling you to choose the exact change lane at toll plazas. A common failing of these is not advising motorists of the exact toll until changing lanes becomes more difficult; this cache of small change assures that whatever it is, you will have it handy.

CAR HIRE One of most important decisions that must be made well in advance is whether to rent a car, and if so, where, what kind and from whom. In general, it is cheaper to include car hire (called rental in the USA) as part of your flight package, although this might require that you pick the car up at your destination city, which might not be the best choice. If, for example, you plan to arrive in New York, see the sights, and move on to see Providence, Newport and Boston before touring northern New England, you might prefer to pick up your car as you leave Boston, using public transport where it serves the best.

Car categories vary, but most hire companies offer sub-compact, compact, economy, mid-sized, full-sized, luxury and sport utility (SUV) vehicles. The larger the car, the faster it accelerates and consumes petrol. Standard features usually include automatic transmission, air conditioning and unlimited mileage.

Recreational vehicles, or RVs (camper vans and caravans), are an increasingly popular way to travel, with the higher cost of hiring and operating an RV offset (in theory) by savings on accommodation and meals and the convenience of not packing and unpacking at every stop. Although most tour operators can arrange RV hire, it is better to work with an independent agent that specialises in RVs and is able to find the best rate by choosing among various companies. Hemmingways arranges a package that includes insurance and necessary accessories, such as bedding and cooking utensils, at a pre-paid rate; tel: 0870 742-2673, www.hemmingways.co.uk. Make sure that you are given operating manuals and a full demonstration for all systems before leaving the hire company. In planning your itinerary, allow extra time for shopping, cooking and cleaning. For more details on RVs as an accommodation alternative, and for useful contact addresses, see Accommodation, pp. 32–36.

It is often cheaper to pick up a vehicle at an airport than in the city centre (and it's also easier to leave town from one). Be sure to ask when reserving and compare costs. A surcharge, or drop fee, may be levied for dropping the vehicle off somewhere other than the place of hire. If considering an RV, ask about one-way rates if you aren't planning to arrive at and leave from the same place. Most car hire companies require a credit card deposit, even if the hire has been prepaid. Before accepting the car, be sure you have all necessary registration and insurance documents and that you know how to operate the vehicle. To minimise safety problems, try to spend the first night in a hotel near the airport rather than jump from an exhausting international flight into a strange car.

Many states require third-party liability insurance cover of at least $15,000 for death or injury to one person, $30,000 for death or injury to more than one person and $5000 for property damage. US and Canadian drivers may be covered by their own insurance, but other drivers are strongly advised to take out their own cover or buy the collision damage waiver (CDW), sometimes called loss damage waiver (LDW), offered by hire companies. Without the waiver, hirers are personally liable for the full value of the vehicle. CDW is often required as part of fly-drive packages. It is wise to compare the costs of pre-booking and pre-paying in the UK or working directly with a US car hire in advance. The cost of CDW in the US can more than eat up any saving. Be sure to ask about this charge when enquiring.

Your home country driving licence is valid in the USA, but you must have the licence in your possession while driving. The minimum driving age is 16 in most states, but most car hire companies require that all drivers be at least 25. Be sure to have the vehicle registration and proof of liability insurance handy at all times.

PICKING UP YOUR HIRE CAR A few car hire companies have desks near luggage claim areas of major airports, but for most you have to take a coach to an off-airport facility to pick up your hire car. Follow terminal signs for Rental Cars to the proper coach or van loading area. Once there, have your booking number, passport, credit card and driving licence ready. Everyone who might drive the vehicle must show his or her driving licence and be listed on the rental contract. If an unlisted driver has an accident, you will probably have to pay for repairs yourself.

If hiring an RV, ask the hire company about airport pick-up and drop-off when making your booking. Most hire companies provide free or low-cost transport to and from their offices, which are usually located some distance from the airport.

Driving Before you leave the car park, take a 'tour' of your car: test the gear lever (although most US hire cars have automatic transmissions), and find the headlight and other light switches – it doesn't help to reach for the wrong lever in an emergency! Be sure you know how to operate windscreen cleaning systems to avoid being suddenly blinded by a splash.

The most immediate problem will be for those used to driving on the left (using right-hand drive controls), such as the UK and South Africa. The operating equipment will be on the other side from where you expect it. When you are in normal traffic, driving will begin to seem natural as you follow other drivers, but at roundabouts (called rotaries or traffic circles in the USA) or on dual-lane highways, it becomes more difficult, because your natural instincts give you the wrong signals. Be especially alert and continue to remind yourself of this danger.

The most difficult time for some is in starting out in the morning on a road without other traffic. You can sometimes drive for some distance without realising that you are on the wrong side of the road. To solve this, attach a card to your keys, with the words 'Drive Right!' printed in large letters. Whenever you leave the car, and need to pocket your keys, this will be in your way. Remove it and tape it to your steering wheel. That reminds you as soon as you enter your car, at which time you return the card to your keys. A roll of tape is a small price to pay for avoiding a head-on collision.

In most places in the US, it is permitted to turn right on a red light after stopping first, unless signs prohibit ('No Right Turn on Red').

RVs drive more like lorries than cars and are treated as lorries by traffic laws. In most places, the RV highway speed limit is 55 mph, as opposed to 65 mph for cars. Be cautious while driving. RVs are blown about by the wind more than cars and are more subject to rollover. They are also taller and wider than cars, which can create hazards at petrol stations, toll booths, car parks and low-hanging trees or signs.

It's wise, but not obligatory, to leave headlights on at all times for safety. Headlights must be used from dusk to dawn, or whenever conditions such as rain, fog or snow require. In some states, including California, it is illegal to drive with only parking lights illuminated.

In many states the driver and all passengers must wear seat belts. Nearly everywhere, children under the age of four or weighing less than 40 lb must ride in approved child safety seats. Safety seats can be hired with a car, or bought for under $100 at a discount store. In an RV, passengers riding behind the driver's seat need not wear belts, but should be safely seated.

No single set of rules governs driving in the USA. Each state makes its own laws, which may vary. As you cross a state line, slow down to read any signs by the roadside that inform you of ways in which laws differ. For example, most states require that you come to a complete stop whenever a school bus (indicated by a sign or its bright yellow colour) is loading children. While its flashing red lights are illuminated, all traffic, in both directions, must stop. Bus drivers can report violators.

FUEL Petrol (called gasoline) and diesel are sold at petrol stations in US gallons (there are about 4 litres to the gallon). Most vehicles take unleaded petrol, which comes in regular, premium and super grades. Buy regular unless the car hire company specifies otherwise. Most stations are self-service, although some offer a higher priced full-serve alternative. Pump prices include all taxes. Petrol stations generally accept credit cards and a rare one might take $20 traveller's cheques but will not take $50 or $100 bills in case they are counterfeit.

PARKING Parking garages and parking lots (car parks) are usually, but not always, indicated by a white P on a blue background. Prices are posted at the entrance. Some city centre garages charge $20 or more per hour, especially for short-term stays.

Kerbside parking time is usually limited, either by posted signs or by coin-operated parking meters. Costs range from nothing to several dollars per hour. Kerbs in some places may be colour-coded. In California, for example, *red* means no stopping or parking at any time; *white* is for passenger loading/unloading only; *green* means limited time parking (usually 10 mins); *yellow* is a commercial loading zone; *blue* is handicapped parking. The general rule is that if the kerb is painted, don't park there. In most places, parking is not allowed within 15 ft of a fire hydrant, within 3 ft of a disabled kerb ramp, at bus stops, zebra crossings (crosswalks), or on freeways. Fines vary from a few dollars to several hundred. Fines levied against hired cars are charged against the hirer's credit card.

DRIVING CONDITIONS The United States has almost every difficult driving condition imaginable, sometimes just an hour or two away from each other. Here is a survey of those you may encounter.

DESERT TRAVEL For desert travel, be sure that air conditioner and heater are both in good order. Carry extra water, food, warm clothing and a torch in case of trouble. If the car breaks down on a highway, one person should walk to the next phone box and call for help, then return to the car to wait. On secondary roads, raise the bonnet. Either way, *always stay with your vehicle*. It's the only shade in sight and the breakdown lorry will be looking for a stranded car, not someone on foot. Sandstorms can reduce visibility to zero. If visibility drops, pull off the road onto a spot higher than the surrounding terrain and wait it out.

WINTER DRIVING Blowing snow can reduce visibility to zero in minutes, not only on mountain roads, but on Interstate highways. Many passes over the Sierra Nevada mountains are closed late Nov–June, and even in northern New

England some mountain roads close Nov–Apr. In the mountains of the west, highways that remain open frequently require the use of chains. If you're planning mountain driving in winter, ask the car hire company to include chains or buy your own (under $50). When chains are required, petrol station attendants and roadside workers will install them for about $20. For any long-distance winter driving, carry warm clothing and food in case of traffic delays and always keep the petrol tank at least half full. Useful items include an ice scraper and a small shovel.

Avoid driving in snow or on icy roads; listen to weather predictions and plan your route or activities around the weather in winter. Be especially cautious when temperatures hover just around freezing and it is raining. The road may be wet one minute and icy the next.

OTHER HAZARDS In California, fog and blowing dust are frequent hazards, causing massive chain-reaction collisions in the Central Valley each year. When visibility drops, *slow down* and turn your headlights on low beam. High beams blind oncoming drivers and reflect back to reduce your own vision. Fog can be a problem in any coastal area, more so at night.

Driving across the long, flat, straight roads of America's midlands, the greatest hazard may be falling asleep. Be sure to have someone else awake in the car, keep the radio on and carry small boiled sweets (hand candies) or fresh fruit to eat. Stop often and, if necessary, get out and jog on the spot beside the car.

Most state highway maps have a number to call for information on conditions, including road closures, and roadside signs often give call numbers of dedicated radio reports for motorists. Local radio stations also broadcast weather and driving information. In urban areas, most stations have regular traffic reports during morning and evening rush hours, which is why you may sometimes see a helicopter hovering overhead as you sit in a traffic jam.

SPEED LIMITS The speed limit on Interstate highways is 65 mph for cars (55 mph for trucks and RVs) unless posted otherwise. Some rural freeways have a limit of 70 mph. In town, the speed limit is usually 25 or 30 mph unless otherwise indicated. If driving conditions are poor, drivers are required to keep to a safe speed, no matter how slow. Police use radar, lasers and planes to track, stop and ticket speeders, but highway traffic normally flows at least 10 mph above the limit.

Police signal drivers with flashing red or blue lights, sirens and loudhailers. Pull off the roadway as quickly as possible, turn off the engine and roll down the driver's side window a few inches. Stay inside the vehicle unless asked to step out. Have your driving licence and vehicle registration ready for inspection. Officers occasionally let drivers off with a verbal warning. If they issue a ticket – a citation – arguing will only make a bad situation worse.

It is sad but true that some localities support their police departments with 'speed traps', where signs are misleading, or where speed limits are deliberately lower than conditions require. Often these are just as you leave or enter a town, when a low speed limit continues far outside a congested area. Drivers resume normal speed, believing that they have simply failed to see the sign indicating higher limits. If stopped there is little you can do but pay the fine quickly and leave town. Arguing will usually lead to a court appearance several days or weeks hence. Although speed traps are becoming less frequent on major roads, you may encounter them in the south, and in small communities anywhere. The best rule is to watch speed limit signs carefully and obey them, however odd they may seem.

IN CASE OF TROUBLE If your car breaks down, pull as far off the road as possible, turn on the flashing hazard lights and, if it is safe to get out, raise the bonnet and return to the vehicle. Do not split passengers up. Change tyres only when out of traffic. Emergency phone boxes are placed every half-mile on some highways; otherwise, dial 911 from any telephone for police or medical assistance, but not for a tow truck (breakdown lorry). Lights on emergency vehicles are red or red and blue, so do not stop for flashing white lights or flashing headlights. Ask directions only from police, at a well-lit business area, or at a service station.

AAA or other auto club membership is especially valuable in case of breakdown. Membership usually includes free towing service to the nearest garage for repairs. Most hire car companies either pay for repairs directly or reimburse the cost shown on repair receipts. If a hire car will be out of service for more than a few hours, ask the hire company for a replacement vehicle.

If you are involved in a collision, stop. Call the highway patrol or local police if there are injuries or more than minor scratch damage to either vehicle. Show police your driving licence, vehicle registration, proof of insurance and contact information, and exchange the same information with the other driver. Get the names and addresses of any witnesses. Accidents must also be reported to your car hire company.

In most states (and the responding officer can tell you) collisions resulting in death, injury or property damage over $500 must be reported to the state's Department of Motor Vehicles (DMV) within ten days. DMV offices are listed in the telephone book white pages. In some states, such as Nevada, property damage amounting to only $350 or more must be reported to police.

Driving under the influence of alcohol, or any other drug, is illegal. The blood alcohol limit is 0.01 per cent in most states and strictly enforced. Drivers suspected of drunk driving have the choice of a breath, blood or urine test; refusing the test is an admission of guilt. Police establish random checkpoints and frequent roads near wine-tasting rooms and popular roadside restaurants.

ROAD SIGNS European-style road signs are widely used, but not universal. *Red* signs indicate stop, do not enter, or wrong way. *Yellow* signs are warnings or direction indicators. *Orange* means road repairs or detours. *White* shows speed limits and distances, almost always in miles. *Brown* indicates parks, camping and other recreation opportunities. *Blue* gives non-driving information such as services in a nearby town.

VEHICLE SECURITY AND SAFETY Try not to accept a vehicle with a hire company sticker or logo visible – it's an advertisement for theft. You probably can't hide the hire company advert on an RV, but the rolling homes are obvious targets already. Whether you have an RV or a car, lock your vehicle when you're in it as well as when you leave it. Check for intruders before getting in, especially at night and in RVs at any time. Never leave the engine running when the driver isn't behind the wheel and always park in well-lit areas.

Ask car hire counter personnel to recommend a safe, direct route on a clear map before you leave with the vehicle. Take all valuables with you if possible; if not, lock all valuables and luggage in the boot or glove box so that nothing is visible to passers-by or other drivers. Don't leave maps, brochures, or guidebooks in evidence – why advertise that you're a stranger in town?

Always keep car doors and windows locked. Do not venture into unlit areas or neighbourhoods that look seedy. Do not stop if told by a passing motorist or pedestrian that something is wrong with your car, or if someone signals for help with a broken-down car. If you need to stop, do so only in well-lit or populated areas, even if your car is bumped from behind by another vehicle. At night, have keys ready to unlock car doors before entering a car park. Check the surrounding area and inside the vehicle before entering. Never pick up hitchhikers.

In general, you and your car will be far safer in rural areas (except possibly in the South) than in and around cities. Millions of people travel in the USA each year without incident or danger, but not knowing the territory does put you at risk anywhere. You can minimize that risk by being well informed, aware, cautious and alert.

TRAVELLING ON FOOT

While walking remains the best way to see most cities, and is practical in parks, nature reserves and other wilderness areas, it is not generally a good way to tour in the USA. Long-distance walking paths are rare, and routes often involve long stretches of roadside. But within local areas, especially those with considerable parkland, such as the White and Green Mountains of New England, walking and hiking are the only way to see many of the natural wonders such as waterfalls and mountain views.

The same cautions that apply anywhere else are good in the USA, particularly in mountain and wilderness areas. Know the route; carry a map, compass and basic safety gear; carry food and water. Stay on marked trails. Wandering off the trail, easy to do in the forest, adds to erosion damage and increases the danger of getting lost.

HITCHHIKING

In an earlier, more trustful era, hitchhiking was the preferred mode of travel for budget travellers. Today, hitchhiking or picking up hitchhikers is asking for violent trouble, from theft to physical assault and murder. Don't do it.

For wilderness travel, US Geological Survey topographic maps show terrain reliably; they can be purchased in sporting goods stores in each area. For hiking along the Appalachian Trail, which runs the length of eastern USA, get maps and guidebooks from the **Appalachian Mountain Club**, 5 Joy St, Boston MA 02108; tel: (617) 523-0636 – indispensable. In remote areas of the west, logging companies sometimes provide the most accurate and up-to-date off-road maps, available through travel information centres and timber industry information centres. But getting lost in the wilderness is a genuine possibility even with the best of maps in hand, so if you are thinking of driving off the beaten track, always carry a topographic map and compass in addition to any other maps and guides. Sierra Club and Wilderness Press publish the most up-to-date and reliable maps and guides to more remote areas. Outdoor supply shops and good booksellers stock maps of this kind as well.

Before leaving civilisation behind, compare every available map for discrepancies, then check with forest or park personnel. Most are experienced wilderness enthusiasts themselves, and since they're responsible for rescuing lost hikers, they have a vested interest in dispensing the best possible information and advice.

TRAVELLING BY BICYCLE

Cycling is popular for countryside day touring – less so for overnight trips, due to geography. Bikes can be hired by the hour or the day in most country and urban areas as well as in major parks.

For serious bicyclists, biking tours are available at all levels, from easy day trips to arduous pulls over the Cascades or Rockies. On-your-own bike tours are also possible, but beware of unexpected distances and make plans based on topographical maps that show mountains between towns.

Many highways have narrow or non-existent verges, which can make cycling a nerve-racking experience as well as dangerous in heavy traffic. Local law in many places requires cyclists to wear protective helmets while riding. Sensible cyclists always wear them, whatever the law says.

CROSS-COUNTRY ROUTES

Remember how big the USA is before planning to see it from coast to coast. If you have only a week, don't even think about it. If you have two, you will spend most of it in a bus, train or car unless you fly the cross-country routes. But if your schedule is longer, you might want to travel one or both ways by land, just to get a fuller sense of the great expanses that lie between the two oceans.

By Train To plan a cross-country return train trip, consider making a giant loop, going through the northern cities westbound, and southern destinations eastbound, or vice versa. In the chapters that follow, several train routes are detailed, describing the attractions of the routes and the cities they pass through. By connecting those that appeal to you most, and filling in the spaces between them with through-train travel, you can create a custom-tailored itinerary. Be sure to do it with a copy of the *Thomas Cook Overseas Timetable* at hand, to ensure that you arrive in stopover cities at an appropriate time of day and travel the most scenic stretches by daylight.

Chicago, at the base of the Great Lakes, is the central point through which all but one east–west rail route passes, so unless you plan to see the Deep South, your routes can begin and end there. If you plan to travel both ways by train (or bus) you could choose different routes on each side of it, forming a huge figure 8.

For example, your northern east–west route from New York or Boston to Seattle via Amtrak might stop at Niagara Falls, Chicago, Milwaukee and Glacier Park. Possible side trips, using VIA Rail and Amtrak Thruway bus connection respectively, could take you to Toronto and Vancouver. You can get to Chicago from New York or Boston on the *Lake Shore Limited*, following the shores of three Great Lakes and the Erie Canal, whose locks you can see from a seat on the right. This is also the side to be on for the route along the Hudson River if you begin in New York. If you begin in Boston you'll pass through the Berkshire Mountains in western Massachusetts. Or you could travel the portion of the trip from New York to Niagara on the *Maple Leaf*, for more stops along the way. This train continues on to Toronto, just across the border in Canada.

You can continue to Seattle from Chicago via the northern route on the *Empire Builder*. This route goes through seldom-visited Milwaukee and the twin cities of Minneapolis and St Paul. Milwaukee is a German city, with good museums, parks and festivals. (Both the Amtrak station and the Greyhound terminal are in unsafe neighbourhoods, so take taxis to the city centres.)

The *Empire Builder* continues through the wide open spaces of Montana and Glacier National Park, over the Rockies, and follows the Columbia River Gorge to the Cascade Range before dropping dramatically to Puget Sound.

The southern route, from Chicago to Los Angeles, goes through the heart of the Wild West. Dodge City, the Santa Fe Trail, Grand Canyon – some of the most famous

The *Sunset Limited* runs three times a week along the southern edge of the US. The 3000-mile trip, from Orlando to LA, crosses eight states.

names of the west are along this one route. Stop in Lamy, New Mexico, to visit Santa Fe, and at Flagstaff, Arizona, to see the Grand Canyon. Leaving Chicago on the *Southwest Chief*, the boring parts of the corn belt are mostly travelled through at night, so there is daylight to see parts of the original Santa Fe Trail.

A middle option goes from Chicago to San Francisco. One of the most scenic rail routes in the west is followed by the *California Zephyr*, through Omaha, Denver, Salt Lake City and Reno, Nevada. The best of the scenery is west of Denver, and climaxes as the train follows the Colorado River along a succession of canyons, crossing and recrossing it. Before arriving, the train has to cross over the Sierra Nevada mountain range, along a canyon and through Gold Rush country. Or you can choose a route through the south-west, from Chicago to San Antonio. Amtrak's *Texas Eagle* takes you deep into the heart of Texas, passing St Louis at 2100 and 0809, but with a great view of the huge arch. The ranchlands and flower-filled fields of Texas are seen by daylight.

The *Coast Starlight*, Amtrak's most popular train, connects the west coast cities of Seattle, Portland, San Francisco (via Thruway bus from Emeryville) and Los Angeles, offering some stunning views from the northern forests and Cascade mountains, California's fertile valleys to the shoreline of the Pacific.

On your return, perhaps Amtrak's most scenic long route in the eastern USA is the trip from Chicago to Washington on the *Cardinal*, which leaves Chicago in the evening, saving daylight hours for the trip through mountainous West Virginia. You can see the New River Gorge, and its bridge hundreds of feet above the river.

By Bus Cross-country bus travel can follow much the same routes, although bus travellers have more flexibility in varying the stopover cities and can add destinations not accessible by train. Plan for a slightly longer trip crossing the country by bus, but for a greater choice in schedules.

By Air Unless you have a lot of time to spend travelling both ways by train, you may wish to opt for a compromise - travelling one way by land, the other by air. Southwest Airlines, and often others, spurred by Southwest's and Jet Blue's competitive rates, offer fares so low that they often beat train or bus travel. This is ideal for anyone who tires quickly of flatlands, cornfields and amber waves of grain, and wants to see both coasts. In a few hours, instead of a few days, you can move from Baltimore/Washington International Airport (a major east coast hub) to Santa Fe, New Mexico - or any of several other western destinations. If you decide to opt for this, look into Amtrak's return flight agreement with United Airlines, which discounts tickets for passengers who don't wish to take the train both ways.

A–Z OF TRAVEL BASICS

This chapter contains useful information for planning your travels across the USA. As travellers may consider crossing the northern border – Amtrak's North America Rail Pass allows travel on the VIA rail network in Canada and the Greyhound Ameripass includes services to Vancouver, Montreal and Toronto – information useful for visitors to Canada has been included.

ACCOMMODATION

The United States offers accommodation of every style and price level imaginable, from five-star hotels and posh resorts to youth hostels and campsites. Local tourist offices can provide accommodation lists and telephone numbers, but many cannot make bookings. Most room prices are quoted for two people, unless followed by 'ppdo' (per person, double occupancy).

HOTELS AND MOTELS At chain hotels and motels, even with budget prices, expect a clean, comfortable, relatively spacious room with either one or two double- or queen-sized beds and a private bathroom. Some independent hotels and motels provide a lower standard, but others have good quality facilities plus charm and character.

Motels are often the best bet, especially if you travel by car. Literally 'motor hotels', motels are one- to three-storey buildings with a modest version of a hotel's accommodation and facilities. Most belong to nationwide chains which enforce service and safety standards. Motels fill up fast during high season, but last-minute rooms are usually available in the off-season, especially during the week.

Motels often line major roads and advertise availability with 'vacancy' signs, as well as signs advertising special rates or offers. Most chains have toll-free reservation telephone numbers that can be reached from anywhere in North America (see p. 52). Motels occasionally offer a mediocre continental breakfast.

> Hotel and motel rates, unless otherwise noted, are quoted for single or double occupancy; children usually stay cheaply or for free with parents. Advance bookings generally require a voucher or credit card number to guarantee the booking. When checking in, always ask if there's a cheaper room rate than the one you pre-booked. It's often cost effective to find accommodation day by day, especially in off-peak seasons (see Seasonal Pricing, p. 36). Also ask about any discounts (see p. 36).

Budget hotels are sometimes acceptable, but those in cities, especially close to railway or bus stations, tend to be dim, dirty and dangerous. Look for a motel or youth hostel instead.

Bed-and-breakfasts (B&Bs) can be a homelier alternative, but they are seldom such a bargain as their British cousins, especially in cities or in highly visited areas, such as

New England or California wine country. The accent is more often on luxury than on value. The typical urban bed-and-breakfast is a refurbished room in a Victorian mansion, complete with chintz curtains, down quilts, fireplace, bric-a-brac atop antique furniture, and private facilities. If 'Victorians' are in short supply, any ordinary mansion will do, even a converted garage or barn, so long as it's suitably luxurious.

Bed-and-breakfast accommodation in smaller towns and rural areas may be much closer to the original concept, a tidy room with antique furnishings and handmade quilts in a restored 19th-century home or a comfortable bedroom in a farmhouse. Bathroom facilities may be private or shared. Usually the owner lives in the house, but some B&B owners live in an adjacent house. By their very nature, each is as different as its owners and the home they share; some join guests for a glass of wine in the evening, others keep a discreet distance.

Breakfasts vary, but the standard includes fruit juice, coffee or tea, an egg dish, and home-made bread. Some, however, serve these only at weekends, serving a continental breakfast of fruit or juice and home-baked breads on weekdays.

Non-smokers should specify 'non-smoking room' when reserving.

Country inns are a very fine line away from B&Bs, but most offer charm and personal attention. A small inn might have the look and feel of a B&B, but with more rooms and breakfast choices. Bigger inns typically include a full restaurant with hearthside dining, a wide porch with rocking chairs for relaxing, and higher prices.

CAMPING Camping means a tent or a recreational vehicle (RV) in a rural campsite. Those in state or national parks and forests are the quietest and most primitive, with firewood available but facilities sometimes limited to pit toilets and cold showers. Most of these, however, do offer hot showers. Private sites usually offer more facilities but may be filled with RVs, with pitches crowded close together.

Kampgrounds of America (KOA) is a private chain of RV parks that accepts tents (address p. 34). Many other campsites are public; most are operated by federal, state or provincial authorities. Overnight fees range from $7 to more than $20, depending on location and season. Standard facilities include a fireplace for barbecues, food storage locker (where bears are a problem), tent site, nearby showers/toilets, and, during high season, daytime guided hikes and evening educational programmes around a large campfire.

The latest introductions in camping are the yurt – a permanent fixture modelled on traditional Mongolian nomad tents – teepees, and covered wagons. All three are available at selected parks in the north-west through Reservations Northwest, tel: (800) 452-5684 or (503) 731-3411. As a guide, expect to pay around $25 per yurt per night for up to five people, including beds, mattresses, table and lights.

A–Z OF TRAVEL BASICS

At many state and provincial park campsites, a place can be reserved in advance. Nearly all private campsites accept reservations.

Campers and RVs The freedom of the open road, housekeeping on wheels, a tinker's delight: an RV, caravan or motor home provides kitchen, sleeping and bathroom facilities, all integrated atop a lorry chassis.

Fly-drive holiday packages usually offer the option of hiring an RV. This additional cost can be offset by the economies of assured accommodation for several people, space for meal preparation and eating, plus the convenience of comfort items and souvenirs stored nearby. However, RVs are cramped, designed to stuff you and your belongings into limited space. The economics work only if advance planning assures that the pricey spur-of-the-moment allure of a hotel shower or unplanned restaurant meal doesn't overcome you too often. You should also add in the cost of petrol – an RV guzzles three to four times more than a medium-sized car. And remember that you will travel more slowly than a car on long hauls, especially over mountain roads. After all, you are hauling your house around; remember the turtle!

RV travel information for planning your trip can be obtained from: **Recreation Vehicle Industry Association** (RVIA), Dept RK, PO Box 2999, Reston VA 22090-0999; tel: (703) 620-6003. To plan RV camping, request *Go Camping America* from Camping Vacation Planner, PO Box 2669, Reston VA 22090; tel: (800) 477-8669, covering the USA and Canada.

Camping clubs offer RV information for members: some, including the Good Sam Club, PO Box 6060, Camarillo CA 93011; tel: (805) 389-0300, offer roadside assistance for breakdowns and tyre changing. Many camping clubs publish magazines or newsletters with tips on operating and driving an RV. For a hilarious insight into RV travel, find a copy of *Out West*, 9792 Edmonds Way, Suite 265, Edmonds WA 98020; tel: (206) 776-1228; fax: (206) 776-3398; e-mail: outwestcw@aol.com, a periodic tabloid with bizarre pictures of signs and stories about Western characters. The publisher packs his family and computer into an RV for several weeks at a time, and they deliver a flavourful picture of the best and the worst of home-on-wheels travel.

Campsite directories and state/provincial tourist office guides list private RV park locations, with directions and details of facilities. Directories cover parks in the USA and Canada. Popular directories include: *Trailer Life Campground & RV Services Directory*, TL Enterprises, 2575 Vista del Mar Dr., Ventura CA 93001; tel: (805) 667-4100 ($19.95); *Woodall's Campground Directory* (Western Edition), 13975 W. Polo Trail Dr., Lake Forest IL 60045; tel: (800) 823-9076 ($13.70); *Wheelers RV Resort & Campground Guide*, 1310 Jarvis Ave, Elk Grove Village, IL 60007; tel: (708) 981-0100 ($15.50); and *Kampgrounds of America (KOA) Directory*, PO Box 30558, Billings MT 59114-0558; tel: (406) 248-7444 ($3 or free at KOA campsites).

Booking Ahead

Although you may not want to lock into an itinerary by making advance reservations for every night, it is comforting to know that you have a bed waiting for you at the end of each day's travel. Thomas Cook or any other good travel agent can handle room bookings when you purchase air tickets, as well as car or other local transportation. All-inclusive fly-drive arrangements, and 'do-it-yourself packages' can provide hotel coupons, exchangeable at a range of hotel chains, which guarantee a pre-paid rate at participating chains, although they do not guarantee rooms – it's up to you to phone ahead as you go, or take a chance on availability. It is particularly important to pre-book the first and last night's stay to avoid problems when connecting with international air flights.

It is also important to confirm pre-booked rooms by telephone if you will arrive after 1800. Many hotels and motels automatically cancel bookings at 1800, especially during high season, even if rooms have been guaranteed with a credit card. The best time to make the reconfirmation is 1600–1800 on the day of the late arrival.

If you do not want to book so far ahead, it is still worth carrying the toll-free numbers for hotel and motel chains with you. This way you can stop at midday, when you have an idea of how far you are likely to travel that day, and call to secure a room at your destination. Several tips may make that easier:

If you don't know what is available in the area you need, call the toll-free number of major chains to locate the nearest ones (see Travel Directory, p. 52).

Begin with the chain nearest to your ideal budget and work upwards.

Take a map to the telephone with you, since operators in a central reservations office rarely know what other towns may be nearby.

If you belong to an automobile club with AAA affiliation, a call to AAA's central reservations office can often turn up a room even when they are scarce – and with a member discount.

If the central reservations office tells you that a hotel is full, ask for the local number of the hotel. If you fail to find a room from any other chain, it is worth calling the individual properties, since they often keep a room or two for 'regulars' and may also put your name on a waiting list in case of 'no-shows' or cancelled reservations.

Have your credit card handy when you call, so you can immediately reserve a room.

If all else fails, go to the hotel anyway and ask to see the manager. A good manager will often try to find a room by calling managers of other establishments or local B&Bs you might never have found.

If you are truly desperate, ask permission to sleep in your car in the hotel parking lot. This often procures a room when nothing else does.

When staying in a chain hotel, always ask for a copy of the chain's directory of properties to take with you. A collection of these will be helpful as you travel and you can discard them before flying home.

Local tourist offices also provide accommodation lists and telephone numbers, but generally cannot make bookings. Where available, local services are noted in each chapter.

YOUTH HOSTELS Youth hostels are much less common in the USA than in Europe; many cities have none. Most US hostels provide a dormitory-style room and shared bath for $10–$20 per night. Some have family rooms; all offer discounts to local attractions. However, when two or more people are travelling together and can share a room, budget motels may be even cheaper than hostels. In accommodation listings for each location in this book, prices given for hostels are based on beds for two people, to allow comparison with double room charges in the other listings. For information on hostels in the USA and Canada, contact the Youth Hostel Association in the UK, tel: (08708) 708808, or visit www.iyhf.org or www.HIhostels.com; in the US, contact American Youth Hostels, 733 15th St NW, Suite 840, Washington DC 20005; tel: (202) 783-6161. Hostelling International offers free online booking at www.hostelbooking.com and free call booking at (800) 909-4776 from US phones only.

SEASONAL PRICING Accommodation may be hard to find in major tourist destinations during high season – Memorial Day (end of May) to Labor Day (early Sept). In Vermont, New Hampshire and western Massachusetts, the hardest time to find a room is foliage season (mid-Sept–mid-Oct); many inns and hotels are completely booked a full year in advance by return clients. At ski resorts, high season prices arrive with the first good snowfall. In Florida and other winter havens, high season is Dec–Mar.

Expect to pay as much as 60 per cent over low season rates during the high season, and even more at beach resorts. It is sometimes possible to avoid the higher tariffs by travelling during the 'shoulder' season, one or two weeks before or after high season, when crowds are smaller and rates lower. It is also possible to travel out of season, but many attractions, especially in smaller towns, close when high season ends.

DISCOUNTS Like everything else, accommodation has its deals. Senior and disabled persons should ask if discounts apply. Members of automobile clubs may find discounts through affiliated clubs in the USA. Military personnel (even foreign) on holiday may get special rates, as they do at Super 8 Motels. Other chains, such as Holiday Inn, give children free meals in their restaurants.

CHILDREN

Whether at home or abroad, travelling with youngsters is rarely easy, but nearly always rewarding. Preparation helps. Children become bored and cranky on long drives. Pack favourite games and books, and pick up a book of travel games. A traditional favourite is to count foreign, i.e. non-local, licence plates. The winner – always a child – gets a special treat later in the day.

If the children are old enough, suggest that they keep a detailed travel diary. It will help them focus on where they are instead of what they might be missing back home.

A diary also helps them to remember details later to impress friends and teachers. So does collecting anything from postcards to admission tickets, dropped into the child's own backpack and pasted into a diary each evening. Even children too young to maintain a diary can enjoy this visual record of the places they have visited.

Instead of focusing your travel on made-for-children attractions, such as theme parks and amusement parks which are much the same everywhere, aim for places that are unique to the area or to the USA, but with plenty of activities aimed at the young. Living history museums and restoration villages nearly always have special events, hands-on experiences, tours, and even activity-filled guidebooks for children. Look for aspects of a place that will delight your children, and find themes for them to follow wherever they go, such as how many different kinds of transport they can ride on. Older children may gain more from a trip if they read books set in some of the places they will visit; a librarian can help you discover these. From museums to transport, check for children's rates, often segmented by age. A student card must be shown to use student rates.

Most hotels and motels can arrange for babysitters, though the price may be steep. Many motel chains allow children under 12, 14, and sometimes up to 18, to stay free in their parents' room. A rollaway child's bed, usually called a cot, should come free or at low cost. At mealtimes, picnics offer flexibility, as does a small cooler filled with cold drinks and snacks. Most towns have roadside restaurants with long hours, cheap children's menus and familiar names. If your children like fast food at home, they'll like it in California or Maryland.

CLIMATE

Climate is what you expect; weather is what you get. Being so big, the USA can harbour several major weather systems all at once, which you can see moving about weather maps on TV evening news programmes, or by tuning to special weather channels. To find these from your hotel room, consult the directory that usually accompanies the television set, or call the reception desk. In looking at a weather map, remember that most storm systems and high and low pressure areas move west to east, with others moving northwards up the Atlantic (east) coast. New England occasionally suffers from storms moving down the coast from Canada.

While the climate is variable nearly anywhere in the USA, some trends prevail for each region. Mountains and the sea are the primary geographical features that affect weather, as are the Great Lakes. Although no one weather pattern governs the entire country, most have great variations within short periods. Especially in the north-east and in the Great Plains (between the Appalachian and Rocky Mountains), conflicting air masses may bring changes of as much as 50°F/10°C within a few hours.

New England's weather is known more for changeability than for extremes. In general, expect cold and snow from December to March, and warm days and cool nights from June to September. Depending on locale, daytime temperatures in summer are in the 70s or 80s F/20s or 30s C; July and August usually bring short spells of uncomfortably humid weather with temperatures above 90°F/32°C. Winter snows are heaviest in the mountains of Maine, New Hampshire and Vermont. Snowfall is generally light in southern New England, except for occasional big storms, with temperatures in the 20s or 30s F/-6 to -1 C. September and October can be the most pleasant months, with daytime temperatures from the 50s to 70s F/10 to 26 C, and leaves turning colour dramatically.

The middle Atlantic region, around Chesapeake Bay, has hot, sunny summers, a balmy spring and autumn, and fairly mild but crisp winters with little if any snow. Intermittent storm systems bring rain, and occasional freezing rain around the Chesapeake. The closer you are to water, the less likely it is to snow. Average coastal temperatures in July and August rarely exceed the low 90s F/32 C, but it can become much hotter in Washington DC, where city pavements and buildings absorb and store the heat. All along the east coast, September is hurricane month. In severe storms coastal regions are evacuated, but travellers can easily learn if one is brewing further south and heading their way. A good sign of an approaching hurricane, if you haven't tuned to the weather forecast, is when you see locals hammering large sheets of wood over their windows.

The climate warms noticeably in the southern Atlantic states, becoming almost tropical in Florida. Summers don't get much warmer than in the Washington DC area, but they last much longer. Florida, surrounded by water, has a more moderate climate, warmer in the winter and cooler in the summer than neighbouring southern states. Snow is rare in the south, but summer thunderstorms are frequent. Florida is the sunniest state, particularly in the winter.

Mid-west winters are cold and summers quite warm, with frequent droughts and heatwaves. Snow can be heavy, especially in the north, where blizzards sweep down from the Arctic without mountains to divert them. Generally the eastern part of this region is rainier than the west, but throughout, the area tends to be sunny much of the time. Average daily temperatures hover around the freezing mark in Chicago, where summer averages range from the mid-70s to the low 90s F/mid-20s to low 30s C. To the south, the Gulf states (Alabama to Texas) have similar weather without the winter snows, and with longer (but not significantly hotter) summers.

In the north-west, you can expect grey skies west of the Cascade Range and blue skies to the east, but weather can change abruptly on either side of the mountains. Rain and snow are more likely between October and April, but don't be surprised by a downpour in August. Fog is common along the coast all year. Portland, Seattle and Vancouver are known for cloudy skies and rain all year round, but the sun shows itself for at least a few minutes on most days from May to September. Sunshine is a treasured experience on the western side of the Olympic Peninsula, where tall mountains wring rain from prevailing winds off the Pacific Ocean. The San Juan Islands, sheltered by those same mountains, are much drier and sunnier.

The Pacific Ocean moderates temperatures west of the Cascades. Expect greater extremes east of the range, colder in winter and hotter in summer. Summer is also fire season. Forest fires may be allowed to burn unchecked unless human lives or major property damage are threatened. Regular burning is a natural renewal mechanism and necessary for the regeneration of many forest species. If a patch of forest has not burned in several years, deliberate fires, called controlled burns, are set during wet weather to burn out accumulated dead growth and prevent later conflagrations. Smoke-jumpers – airborne fire-fighters who parachute into remote areas to fight fires – and water bombers are at their busiest in late summer.

In the south-west, expect sunshine in southern California, fog along the coast, and heat inland. However, uneven terrain creates a patchwork of weather patterns. Summer fog can hang heavily or burn away to reveal deep blue skies and a blistering sun. Winter temperatures generally drop with altitude and distance north, with snow above 6000 ft. In summer, expect increasing heat inland and to the south.

Tornadoes and Hurricanes

Tornadoes, although rare, can occur anywhere in the USA, especially in the general area of Kansas, Oklahoma and Nebraska, where they are called cyclones or twisters. They are highly unpredictable, and are most frequently accompanied by thunderstorms. These rotating air masses can generate wind speeds of 300 mph inside their vortex, and move along the ground at speeds of 30–40 mph. Some are visible on the horizon as a long cone-shaped cloud with its point moving along the ground.

Weather reports include warnings when these storms are expected or known to be in the vicinity, so if you are driving through areas of thunderstorm disturbance it is wise to keep your radio tuned to a local station. If you know a tornado is coming, the best place to take cover is in a cellar or a low cement or other sturdy building, as close as possible to the ground. As with earthquakes, stay clear of windows. If you approach an area where any heavy wind or storm has felled trees on the road, look very carefully at power lines overhead before proceeding. Live wires may be hidden in the fallen foliage and can be lethal.

Hurricanes, unlike tornadoes, give ample warning, and you should have had any evacuation notice. Hurricane season is June–Sept, most frequent Aug–Sept.

CUSTOMS

Personal duty-free allowances which can be taken into the USA by visitors are: 1 litre of spirits or wine, 120 cigarettes and 100 (non-Cuban) cigars, and up to $100 worth of gifts.

Personal duty-free allowances which can be taken into Canada by visitors are: 1.14 litres (40 fl oz) of spirits or wine or 8.5 litres (300 fl oz, 24 bottles/cans) of beer or ale, 50 cigars, 200 cigarettes and 400 g (14 oz) of loose tobacco.

The value of goods allowed on your return home varies with each individual country, and a separate allowance of tobacco products, alcohol and perfume is usually added. You can check these allowances by contacting your own customs authorities before leaving home.

DISABILITIES, TRAVELLERS WITH

Access is the key word. 'Physically challenged' is synonymous with disabled. Physical disabilities should present less of a barrier in the USA than in much of the world. Federal and state laws, particularly the Americans with Disabilities Act (ADA), generally require that all businesses, buildings and services used by the public be accessible to handicapped persons, including those using wheelchairs. Every hotel, restaurant, office, shop, cinema, museum, post office and other public building must have access ramps and toilets designed for wheelchairs.

In practice, however, many small 'mom and pop' restaurants and diners do not comply with this law (there are certain exceptions), so it is wise to call ahead. Also, buildings designated as historic properties, such as Colonial homes which are now museums, do not have to comply if to do so would damage or change their historic architecture or integrity. They are protected by another law which grants special status to historic preservation properties. Some of these protected properties may be hotels or may contain other public facilities, so if in doubt look for the wheelchair symbol or call in advance. Some places can accommodate wheelchairs with temporary ramps, but only with advance notice. Most cities and towns have ramps built into street crossings and most city buses have some provision for wheelchair passengers. Even many parks have installed paved pathways so disabled visitors can get a sense of the natural world.

The bad news is that disabled facilities aren't always what they're meant to be. Many older facilities do not yet comply with the standards. Museums, public buildings, restaurants and accommodation facilities are usually accessible, but historic homes and properties often are not. Special controls for disabled drivers are seldom an option on hired vehicles.

Airlines are particularly hard on disabled passengers. Carriers can prevent anyone who is not strong enough to open an emergency exit (which weighs about 45 lb or 20 kg) or has vision/hearing problems from sitting in that row of seats - even if it means not allowing them to fly. Commuter airlines sometimes deny boarding to passengers with mobility problems on the grounds that they may block the narrow aisle during an emergency.

Some public telephones have special access services for the deaf and disabled.

Broadcast television may be closed-captioned for the hearing impaired, indicated by a rectangle around a double cc in a corner of the screen.

Two helpful organisations are:

RADAR, 12 City Forum, 250 City Rd, London EC1V 8AF; tel: (020) 7250 3222; www.radar.org.uk.

SATH (Society for Accessible Travel and Hospitality), 347 5th Ave, Suite 610, New York, NY 10016; tel: (212) 447-7284; www.sath.org.

DISCOUNTS

Reductions and concessions on entrance fees and public transport (including most Amtrak services) for senior citizens, children, students and military personnel are common. Some proof of eligibility is usually required. For age, a passport or driving licence is sufficient. Military personnel should carry an official identification card. Students will have better luck with an International Student Identity Card (ISIC) from their local student union, than with a college ID.

The most common discount is for automobile club members. Touring guides from AAA (Automobile Association of America) and CAA (Canadian Automobile Association) affiliates list hundreds of member discounts throughout the country. Always ask about 'Triple A discounts' and 'CAA discounts' at attractions, hotels, motels and car hire counters. Most recognise reciprocal membership benefits; ask your AA at home for a reciprocal card before you travel. At hotels, ask for their best promotional discount before mentioning the AAA, since these are often cheaper. Some cities will send high-season discount booklets on request, which may cover shops, restaurants or accommodation.

If you are visiting more than four or five national parks, monuments or historical sites for which entrance fees are charged, purchase a Golden Eagle Passport for $50, which covers the holder and one other person. Blind and disabled travellers can request a free-of-charge Golden Access Passport upon arrival. These passes usually include discounted prices at campsites. Canada has a similar scheme for its national parks, Canada's Great Western Annual Pass, costing $35 per person or $70 per family, from individual parks or Parks Canada Service Centre, Rm 220 Canada Place, 9700 Jasper Ave, Edmonton, Alberta T5J 4C3; tel: (800) 748-7275.

Another programme to consider is Entertainment Guides: this provides books of coupons and discounts purchased annually (about $40–$65) that allow half-price rates at hundreds of hotels. While the 50 per cent discounts are usually at higher priced hotels and are based on the 'rack' rate, not any special seasonal or promotional rates, they still bring prices down noticeably. Budget chains, such as Days Inn, Comfort Inn and Econo Lodge, take 20 per cent off their regular rates for Entertainment members. Reservations for all rooms must be made in advance. To learn more about these, contact Entertainment Publications, Book Order Dept, 2125 Butterfield Rd, Troy, MI 48084; tel: (248) 637-3999; www.entertainment.com.

ELECTRICITY

The USA uses 110 volt 60 Hz current. Two- or three-pin electrical plugs are standard. Electrical gadgets from outside North America require plug and power converters. Both are difficult to obtain in the USA. Beware of buying electrical appliances in the USA: few gadgets on the US market can run on 220 volt 50 Hz power. Exceptions are battery-operated equipment such as radios, cameras and portable computers – or a few dual-voltage models of electric shavers and hair dryers.

North American video equipment, which uses the NTSC format, is not compatible with the PAL and SECAM equipment used in most of the rest of the world – prerecorded video tapes sold in the USA and Canada may therefore not work with other equipment unless specifically marked as compatible with PAL or SECAM. Blank videotapes purchased in North America, however, can be used with video recorders elsewhere in the world.

E-MAIL AND INTERNET ACCESS

Most public libraries, located in towns and cities across the USA, have free internet access. Internet cafés and public access points are not as common in the United States as they are in other parts of the world, partly because so many homes have access. While waiting lines may be long to use library internet in larger cities, those in smaller cities are usually readily available. As a rule they will be less busy during the day, before the close of school (about 1500). Although many smaller hotels do not have access for their guests, B&B owners will sometimes let you check your e-mail or will make reservations or other arrangements for you via the internet. Larger hotels often have in-room data ports, but these are rare in budget chains.

EMBASSIES AND CONSULATES

US EMBASSIES A good source of information about US (and other) embassies in your own country is www.embassyworld.com. The following websites connect to specific US embassies and consular offices.

Canberra, Australia: http://usembassy-australia.state.gov/consular/index.html
Melbourne, Australia: http://usembassy-australia.state.gov/melbourne
Perth, Australia: http://usembassy-australia.state.gov/perth
Sydney, Australia: http://usembassy-australia.state.gov/sydney
Nassau, The Bahamas: http://nassau.usembassy.gov
New Delhi, India: http://newdelhi.usembassy.gov
Pretoria, South Africa: http://usembassy.state.gov/pretoria
Republic of Ireland: http://dublin.usembassy.gov
Wellington, New Zealand: http://usembassy.org.nz

UK (includes London, Belfast, Cardiff and Edinburgh embassies): http://www.usembassy.org.uk

Australia	**Embassy:** 1601 Massachusetts Ave NW, Washington DC 20096; tel: (202) 797-3000.
	150 E 42nd St, 34th Floor, New York, NY 10017; tel: (212) 351-6500.
	1 Bush St, 7th Floor, San Francisco CA 94104; tel: (415) 362-6160.
Canada	**Embassy:** 501 Pennsylvania Ave NW, Washington DC 20003; tel: (202) 481-1740.
	Plaza 600, Suite 412, Seattle, WA 98101; tel: (206) 443-1372.
New Zealand	**Embassy:** 37 Observatory Circle NW, Washington DC 20008; tel: (202) 328-4800.
	2461 Warrenton Dr., Houston, TX 77024; tel: (847) 384-5497.
	1 Maritime Plaza, Suite 700, San Francisco, CA 94111; tel: (415) 399-1255.
	Box 51059, Seattle, WA 98115; tel: (206) 525-0271.
Republic of Ireland	**Embassy:** 2234 Massachusetts Ave NW, Washington DC 20008; tel: (202) 462-3939.
	655 Montgomery St, San Francisco, CA 94104; tel: (415) 392-4214.
	Chase Building, 535 Boylston St, Boston, MA 02116; tel: (627) 267-9330.
	400 N Michigan Ave, Chicago, IL 60611; tel: (312) 337-1868.
South Africa	**Embassy:** 3051 Massachusetts Ave NW, Washington DC 20008; tel: (202) 232-4400.
	50 N La Cienega Blvd, Suite 300, Beverly Hills, CA 90211; tel: (310) 657-9200.
	200 S Michigan Ave, 6th Floor, Chicago, IL 60604; tel: (310) 939-7929.
UK	**Embassy:** 3100 Massachusetts Ave NW, Washington DC 20008; tel: (202) 462-1340.
	820 First Interstate Center, Seattle, WA 98101; tel: (206) 622-9255.
	Suite 850, 1 Sansome St, San Francisco, CA 94104; tel: (415) 981-3030.
	Suite 2110, Sun Trust Center, 200 S Orange Ave, Orlando, FL 32801; tel: (407) 426-7855.

EMERGENCIES

To telephone **police** in an emergency, ring 911. The USA has no national police force, and there are many different police jurisdictions within any area, each with its own force. Even locals don't know whether state, county or town police have jurisdiction in any given situation, but 911 emergency personnel will see that the proper help is sent at once.

In case of **medical emergency**, also **ring 911**. Ambulance, paramedic, police, fire brigade or other public safety personnel will be dispatched immediately.

Hospital emergency rooms are the places to go in the event of life-threatening medical problems. If a life is at risk, treatment will be swift and top-notch, with payment problems sorted out later. For more mundane problems, doctors' offices, 24 hr walk-in health clinics and urgent care units are available in urban areas and many rural communities.

In Canada, government-run programmes provide health care for all, including visitors. Non-Canadians must pay for treatment, but prices are a bargain compared to most other industrialised countries. This is not so in the USA.

ENTRY FORMALITIES

For travellers from British Commonwealth countries, entry into either the United States or Canada is generally routine. Customs and immigration officials are paid to take their jobs very seriously, and those at entry points into the United States are known for being particularly thorough. Both Canada and the United States have had problems with illegal immigration: quite often visitors overstay tourist and student visas. Don't view this as inhospitable, just as standard precautions.

If it's any consolation, customs and immigration lines are just as annoying to US citizens returning home as they are for visitors. Officials can ask any question, search anyone or anything, and do it as they see fit. In reality, most inspectors are polite to a fault, but the only defence against an inspector who got out of the wrong side of the bed is to have passport, visa, proof of support and return ticket in order.

PASSPORTS AND VISAS

All non-US citizens must have a valid full passport and, except for Canadians, a visa, in order to enter the United States.

Visitors requiring a visa must obtain one from the US embassy in their country of residence in advance. Citizens of Britain, New Zealand, Ireland and 18 other countries may complete a visa waiver form, which they generally receive with their air tickets if the airline is a 'participating carrier'. Only travellers using a machine-readable passport may get a waiver. Provided nothing untoward is declared, such as a previous entry refusal or a criminal conviction, which would require a full visa, the waiver exempts visitors from the need for a visa for stays of up to 90 days. It also allows a side trip overland into Mexico or Canada and return. In the UK, your local

Thomas Cook branch can advise on obtaining a US visa (which lasts for the life of your passport). In order to use the visa waiver, however, you must have a machine-readable passport. If your passport is an older one, you may need to get a new one before applying for the waiver.

Documentation regulations change frequently and are complex for some nationalities; you should confirm your requirements with the nearest US embassy or consulate at least 90 days before you plan to depart for the USA.

Take a few passport photos with you and photocopy the important pages and any visa stamps in your passport. Store these safely, together with a note of the numbers of your traveller's cheques, credit cards and insurance documents, separate from the documents themselves. If you lose your wallet, you will have some identification, and replacing the documents will be much easier. Apply to your nearest consulate (see Embassies and Consulates, p. 42) to replace your passport.

A valid passport is required for entry into Canada, but no visa is required for citizens of Australia, New Zealand, Republic of Ireland, South Africa, the UK or the US. Citizens of countries other than Canada and the US who plan to return to the USA after visiting Canada should check with US immigration officials that their visa, if one is required, permits a return.

Although brief crossings into and return from neighbouring Canada are generally permitted, they can be time consuming if an official targets you for a car search. If you're not carrying illegal drugs, alcohol, firearms or agricultural products, and if your documents are in order, you should have no difficulty. But expect long delays at border crossings on your return to the US.

There are generally no restrictions on taking hire cars across the border in either direction, but check when making your initial booking and again when picking up the vehicle. It is also important to ensure that vehicle insurance purchased in one country is valid in the other.

Both the USA and Canada prohibit the importation of weapons, narcotics or certain non-approved pharmaceutical products. Carry doctors' prescriptions with documentation (such as a doctor's letter) to prove that medications are legitimate.

Rules are Changing

Be aware that heightened security in the US is causing entry requirements and policies to change quickly, and may make it more difficult for UK and other citizens to enter. Be sure to check the latest regulations before planning your trip or purchasing tickets. You can do this by checking at the US embassy in your home country, which you can locate at www.embassyworld.com.

FOOD AND DRINK

American meal portions tend to be large, beginning at breakfast, which may include thinly sliced bacon, eggs cooked to order, fried potatoes, toast and endless refills of coffee. Or it may be a plate heaped with pancakes or French toast (bread slices dipped in egg and fried). Crumpets (confusingly called English muffins), waffles, bagels, fresh fruit, yogurt, porridge and cereal are other possibilities. A 'continental breakfast' is juice, coffee or tea and bread or pastry.

For most Americans, midday lunch includes light dishes, such as soups, salads and sandwiches, although most restaurants also offer dinner-type main courses (known as entrées), usually at prices lower than in the evening. Evening dinner menus offer appetisers, salads, soups, pastas, entrées and desserts. While pasta may be listed as a separate course, most Americans (especially those not of Italian descent) order it in place of a meat entrée.

Sunday brunch (usually 1100–1400) is often a self-service buffet piled high with hot and cold dishes, which can be good value for teenagers and other hearty eaters, or can be the day's main meal, with only a light supper to follow.

You will be surprised not only at the number and variety of places to eat nearly everywhere, but also at the wide span of price ranges. Small-town family-style restaurants, diners and self-service cafés are usually at the lower end of the scale, while on the other hand resort dining rooms and trendy city watering holes can become quite pricey.

Restaurant Tipping

Service charges are not added to bills and tipping is expected and part of the waiter's pay, which is proportionately lower to allow for it. Expect to add about 15 per cent of the tab, and up to 20 per cent for exceptional attention. In luxury restaurants, also be prepared to tip the *maître d'* and sommelier a few dollars, up to 10 per cent of the bill. If the service is terrible, leave only small change as a lesson, instead of no tip at all, which might be interpreted as an oversight. In bars and pubs (you do not serve yourself at the bar here) tips should be about 10 per cent when drinks are all that's served at a table, or $1.00 to the bartender.

For hearty eating, try a steak house where salad, baked potato and beans accompany a thick steak. Italian restaurants may serve pizza, pasta and hearty dishes with tomato sauce or they may be upscale northern Italian eating places. Mexican cooks use thin wheat or corn tortillas as the base for beans, rice, cheese, tomatoes, spicy sauce and other ingredients. The Chinese cuisine offered in most restaurants is Cantonese with bean sprout chow mein and fried rice. More authentic Chinese dishes can be found with regional variations, from spicy Hunan to rich, meaty Mandarin. Japanese, Vietnamese and Thai food are other easy-to-find Asian cuisines although Japanese restaurants tend to be very pricey.

The melting pot of cuisines in major cities includes Basque, French, German, Spanish, Cuban, Ethiopian, Salvadoran, Indian and a hundred others. 'Fusion' is the key word these days, describing the cuisine of the 'New American' restaurants, where talented chefs blend ingredients and techniques from the entire world. At these restaurants, your sandwich of Maine lobster may be seasoned with Japanese pickled ginger. The brightest and best chefs are not confined to big-city culinary capitals; look for them in country inns and in small cities, too.

America made fast food an international, if dubious, dining experience. Fast meals on the road can be found at the abundant chains where food is ordered, paid for and picked up from a service counter, all within a few minutes. At some fast-food outlets the driver can pull up to a window, order from a displayed menu, pay and get the meal, all without leaving the vehicle. Hamburgers, hot dogs, tacos, fried chicken and barbecue beef are common offerings. Fast-food chains include Arby's Roast Beef, Burger King, Carl's Jr, Del Taco, Domino's Pizza, Jack-in-the-Box, KFC, Little Caesars Pizza, McDonalds, Pizza Hut, Subway and Taco Bell.

> Americans still enjoy the first foods the Pilgrims met – turkey, pumpkin (or similar winter squashes), cranberries, seafood and maize (corn). So close are these to the hearts of most Americans, that they are essential to the dinner menu for the national feast of Thanksgiving Day in November.

Chain restaurants are ubiquitous, with pre-measured portions and the same menu in Miami as in Seattle. Chains include Friendly's (ice cream, sandwiches and simple meals), Bertucci's (Italian), Boston Market (roasted chicken) and International House of Pancakes (IHoP), which serves all-day breakfast plus safe, unexciting lunch and dinner choices. They are hardly the best America has to show of its culinary talents, and they are not necessarily a bargain. Far better to sample what each region has to offer at a locally owned eatery where the chef is also the owner.

Expect to pay $5–$8 per person for breakfast (much more at hotels), $5–$12 for lunch and $10–$25 for dinner (plus drinks).

You can keep to your budget by having breakfast at local diners or family restaurants (instead of hotel dining rooms), and lunch at carry-outs (takeaways) and little cafés, or as picnics. If you stay in B&Bs or inns with giant-sized breakfasts, you may decide to skip lunch and take advantage of the 'early-bird specials' that many restaurants offer between 5 and 6 pm.

Each region of the USA has its own traditional foods, based on its climate and growing season, its proximity to the sea, its ethnic mix and a dozen other factors. Although some dishes are unique to certain regions, many regional dishes have become favourites far beyond their home town. With the advent of refrigerated air cargo, it is almost as easy to get fresh Maine lobster in San Diego as it is in Wiscasset. Lobster is the main event at clambakes and shore dinners along New England's coast, and you can eat it in fine dining rooms or from picnic tables on the wharves where the lobsters first saw land. Another of New England's favourite treats now enjoyed everywhere is fried clams. These are dipped in a crumb coating (sometimes a batter, to the despair of purists) and deep fried. Delicious and virtually indigestible.

If you want to start a fight in the north-east, get residents of different states talking about chowder. The real thing, whether it's clam, fish or corn chowder, besides the main ingredient, will have chunks of potato and onion suspended in a savoury cream base seasoned with salt and pepper. 'Manhattan style' has tomatoes, not cream, and to New Englanders it's not chowder at all, but a poor excuse for fish-flavoured vegetable soup.

Americans have puddings such as bread pudding or Indian pudding (milled maize with molasses), but the sweet course is always called dessert. Desserts are often a way for a chef to show off with a dinner-plate-sized arrangement, and it is perfectly acceptable to order one to share. The same is true of appetizers; ask your server how big the portion is.

Americans are fond of food festivals, usually celebrating a local crop. In rural areas at various seasons you may find strawberry festivals, apple festivals, or those celebrating blueberries, mushrooms (in Pennsylvania) and even garlic (in California). These are filled with fun and food, and a good place to meet people in a relaxed and friendly local setting.

ALCOHOL Some small restaurants without liquor licences allow you to bring your own wine – the term for this is BYOB – but most are licensed. Beware that occasionally you will encounter a 'dry' town where restaurants are not allowed to serve wine or beer and you must bring your own from a neighbouring town. Buying alcoholic drinks by the bottle varies by state; wine and/or beer may be available in grocery or convenience stores. In some places, alcohol cannot be sold on Sunday. Not only do these laws vary by state, but by municipality as well, so if in doubt, ask whether a restaurant is licensed when you make dinner reservations.

BEVERAGES Coffee has become something closer to a religious experience than a hot drink in the Pacific north-west where espresso carts are a way of life. Motorists stuck in traffic jams jump out for a quick shot of espresso to speed the drive home, while petrol stations sell pseudo cappuccino and latte alongside the motor oil and road maps. Drive-through espresso stands have become common in some urban areas. Espresso is the basic brew at these. Latte is similar to cappuccino, without the foam or the spice dusting. Most coffee bars offer more than a dozen flavours, from vanilla and hazelnut to banana and coconut. Apart from the West Coast coffee bars, the majority of places still serve 'American coffee', a tad weak for most European tastes.

Two centuries after the Boston Tea Party, Yankees are again drinking the beverage they once boycotted; in some places they've readopted the proper way of preparing it, forgoing the teabag-in-a-cup-of-warm-water travesty for the real stuff, and even enjoying fine blends in place of the once ubiquitous orange pekoe. But don't expect good tea most places: you still have to look hard. American tea drinkers usually carry their own premium-brand of teabags with them when they travel, and you might wish to follow their example. Twinings teabags are readily available in most grocery stores.

Don't be surprised if your classy B&B or inn offers you afternoon tea perhaps with all the accompaniments. Two cautionary notes, however. 'Tea Room' does not necessarily mean that afternoon tea is served. More often, it is simply a restaurant retaining an old-fashioned name for a spot where respectable ladies would feel comfortable dining. It may be a centre for psychic readings, as in tea leaves. Remember also that Americans often drink their tea without milk, so before you pour, be sure to check and make sure you have not been given a jug of cream, a distinction non-tea drinkers sometimes fail to make.

Bottled water is popular, but rarely necessary for health reasons. However, water from streams and ponds in natural areas should be avoided. Soft drinks (called soda or tonic) and fruit juices are available in stunning variety.

DRINKING AND THE LAW

You must be 21 (and able to prove it, so keep your passport handy) to drink – anywhere, at any time. In most states you cannot carry an open container of any alcohol – even wine or beer – in the car. In many towns you cannot drink in public places, such as parks or beaches, so be careful about picnics with a bottle of wine.

HEALTH

The USA is basically a healthy place to visit. No inoculations are required and commonsense is enough to avoid most health problems. Eat and drink normally (or at least sensibly) and avoid drinking water that didn't come from the tap or a bottle. Most ground water, even in the high mountains, is contaminated with giardia and other intestinal parasites. Be sure to drink plenty of non-alcoholic liquids, especially in hot weather. Too little water is a particular problem when travelling from the coast to the dry interior.

HEALTH INSURANCE When considering travel insurance that covers your return home in case of illness or accident, it is important to remember that the United States does not have a socialised medical system. As a traveller there, you are responsible for paying for your own medical treatment, just as American citizens must do. This is often quite expensive, so it is important that you purchase medical insurance before leaving home. This should, in fact, be one of your first concerns, right up there with visas and airline reservations.

Sexually Transmitted Diseases The best way to avoid AIDs or other sexually transmitted diseases (or STDs, as they're usually called) is to avoid promiscuous sex. In anything other than long-term, strictly monogamous relationships, the key phrase is 'safe sex'. Men should use condoms in any kind of sexual intercourse – they're very strongly encouraged by prostitutes plying the sex trade. Condoms can be bought in drug stores, pharmacies and supermarkets, and from vending machines in some public toilets.

Rural Hazards The following advice covers some of the hazards you might encounter, especially if you are camping or hiking, and precautions you should take.

Wildlife Seeing wild animals in their natural habitat is a rare thrill, one most Americans never experience. But for those who plan to hike or camp, especially in the western parks, it is a good idea to know how to deal with the various creatures you might meet.

Cougars (also called bobcats, mountain lions and pumas) would rather run than fight, but can be vicious if defending a den or accidentally cornered. Avoid hiking alone and never let small children run ahead or fall far behind. If you meet a cougar, never try to run or hide – you won't escape and either behaviour signals that you're prey. Instead, be aggressive. Stand your ground. Try to appear larger by raising your arms or opening up a jacket. Should the cougar approach, shout and throw sticks or stones. And if attacked, fight with all you've got. Prove that you're not an easy target, and it will probably look for something easier – like a hare.

Bears are a more serious threat. They're large, strong, fast-moving, always hungry, and smart enough to connect humans with the food they carry. Parks and campsites have detailed warnings on how to store food safely to avoid attack. When possible, hang anything edible (including toothpaste) in bags well above the ground or store it in metal lockers. Never feed bears, as they won't know when the meal is over. Shouting, banging pots and throwing stones usually persuade curious bears to look somewhere else for a meal.

Few people in the northern USA ever see **snakes** outside a zoo. The poisonous rattlesnake is found in drier areas east of the Pacific Northwest. They, along with other poisonous snakes, grow more common in the woodlands and wet areas further south. Rattlers are harmless if left alone (as all snakes should be). Most, but not all, rattle a warning. In the wild, look where you're walking; don't put hands or feet on ledges which you can't see; and check your seat before sitting down.

The **squirrels** and **chipmunks** that haunt many parks may look cute, but it is not uncommon for those trying to hand-feed them to end up being bitten instead. Rabies is endemic in the USA, so if bitten by an animal, try to capture it for observation of possible rabies, then go to the nearest emergency medical centre. You must seek immediate treatment – if left too late the disease is untreatable and fatal. Squirrels and chipmunks also carry fleas that transmit serious diseases.

Tick-borne Diseases Don't wear shorts for hikes through the inviting grasslands, forests and mountains. Instead, cover up with long trousers, long-sleeved shirts, and insect repellent. The risk of contracting **Lyme disease** from ticks which thrive in moist climates is rising by the year, as the deer ticks that carry it spread northwards. Lyme disease is frequently misdiagnosed and usually mistaken for rheumatoid arthritis. Typical symptoms include temporary paralysis, arthritic pains in the hand, arm or leg joints, swollen hands, fever, fatigue, headaches, swollen glands, heart palpitations and a circular red rash around the bite up to 30 days later. Early treatment is effective; late treatment often fails. Symptoms may not appear for three months or longer after the first infected tick bite, but the disease can be detected by a simple blood test.

In the west, ticks also carry **Rocky Mountain spotted fever**, **Colorado tick fever** and **tularemia**. All are treatable, but it's easier to avoid the diseases in the first place. Cover up while hiking and check skin for ticks at midday and again in the evening. Look for tiny dark dots. Ticks especially like to hide in hair on the head and at the back of the neck.

Poisonous Plants The most common hiking problem in the west is **poison oak**, found primarily in southern Oregon and north along the coast into Washington but also in California. This oak-like plant is usually a shrub, sometimes a creeper, and always a trailside hazard. Variable leaf shapes make the plant difficult to identify, although the leaves always occur in clusters of three and usually look like rounded oak leaves. Leaves are bright, glossy green in spring and summer, bright red in autumn, and dead in winter – but not forgotten.

In the east, watch for **poison ivy**, also with three shiny leaves that turn reddish in the autumn. It is a low-growing plant, often creeping across the ground.

The two plants have similar effects on those who brush against them. All parts of the plant – leaves, stems and flowers – cause an intense allergic reaction in most people. The most common symptoms are red rash, itching, burning, and weeping sores. The best way to avoid the problem is to avoid the plant. Second best is to wash skin or clothing that has come into contact with the plant immediately in hot, soapy water. If you are afflicted, drying lotions such as calamine or products containing cortisone provide temporary relief, but time is the only cure.

HOTEL AND MOTEL CHAINS

In the following list, numbers given are for use in the USA and Canada. Telephone numbers with area codes 800 or 888 are preceded by a 1 and are free calls from pay telephones, although not from in-room phones in most hotels.

HOTEL AND MOTEL CHAINS

Best Western
(800) 528 1234
www.bestwestern.com

Budgetel Inn
(800) 428 3438
www.baymontinns.com

Clarion
(800) CLARION
(800) 268 1133
www.hotelchoice.com

Comfort Inn
(800) 228 5150
www.choicehotels.com

Days Inn
(800) 325 2525
www.daysinn.com

DoubleTree Inn
(800) 222 8733
www.doubletree.com

Econo Lodge
(800) 424 6423
www.hotelchoice.com

Embassy Suites
(800) 362 2779
www.embassy-suites.com

Fairfield Inn
(800) 228 2800
www.marriott.com

Fiesta Americana
(800) Fiesta
(800) 343 7821
www.fiestamericana.com

Friendship Inns
(800) 424 6423

Hampton Inns
(800) 426 7866
www.hamptoninn.com

Holiday Inn
(800) 465 4329
www.holiday-inn.com

Hostelling International
(202) 783-6161
www.hiusa.com

Howard Johnson
(800) 654 2000
www.hojo.com

Hilton
(800) 445 8667
www.hilton.com

Inter-Continental
(800) 327 0200
www.ichotelsgroup.com

Marriott
(800) 228 9290
www.marriotthotels.com

Motel 6 (not toll-free)
(505) 891 6161
www.motel6.com

Novotel
(800) NOVOTEL
www.novotel.com

Quality Inn
(800) 228 5151
www.choicehotels.com

Quality Suites
(800) 228 5151
www.hotelchoice.com

Radisson
(800) 333 3333
www.radisson.com

Ramada
(800) 854 7854
www.ramada.com

Red Carpet Inns
(800) 251 1962
www.redcarpetinns.com

Red Lion Hotels and Inns
(800) 547 8010

Red Roof Inns
(800) 843 7663
www.redroof.com

Rodeway Inn
(800) 228 2000
www.hotelchoice.com

Sheraton
(800) 325 3535;
1 (800) 325 1717
(hearing impaired)
www.sheraton.com

Sonesta
(800) SONESTA;
(800) 766 3782
www.sonesta.com

Suisse Chalet
(800) 524 2538

Super 8
(800) 800 8000
www.super8.com

Travelodge
(800) 578 7878
www.travelodge.com

Venture Inn
(888) 483 6887

Westin
(800) 228 3000

MAPS

The best one-stop sources of maps are the American Automobile Association (AAA) and Canadian Automobile Association (CAA), which distribute their maps through local affiliates. State, regional, county and city maps are available free at all association offices, but only to members. Fortunately, most motoring clubs around the world have reciprocal agreements with the AAA and CAA to provide maps and other member services. Be prepared to show a membership card to obtain service. AAA offices may be closed at weekends.

The most detailed road maps are produced by Arrow Map Inc., 50 Scotland Blvd, Bridgewater MA 02324; tel: (508) 279-1177. Wire-bound and folding Arrow maps are sold at booksellers, news-stands, souvenir shops and airports. Detailed inland maps are available from DeLorme Map Co., Rte 1, Freeport ME 04032; tel: (207) 865-4171.

Rand McNally road maps and atlases are probably the best known of the ranges available outside the USA, in the travel section of bookshops and more specialist outlets. Each state produces a road map of its own, good for travelling within the state, but chauvinistically ending with its own borders, often without indicating so much as the route number of a road continuing on the other side. Like other information you will be sent, these vary greatly in quality and detail. The most detailed, not surprisingly, is the Rhode Island map.

Handy in cities – especially difficult-to-navigate ones like Boston and San Francisco or the enormity of New York – are *City in Your Pocket* maps and map booklets. Sharply contrasting colours and type make these easy to read and their size is convenient. Order from Global Graphics, www.mapbiz.net.

MONEY AND BANKS

Try to arrive with a few dollars in US currency and coins. Luggage trolleys are sometimes free in the international arrivals area but must sometimes be paid for. Some trolley stands accept credit cards, usually Visa or Access/Mastercard, but others require cash – and currency exchange facilities are located outside the arrivals area.

International airports have currency exchange facilities in the international terminal which are usually open at times when overseas flights are arriving. Domestic terminals and smaller airports have no exchange facilities at all. But nearly all will have automatic cash dispensers or ATMs.

ATMs offer the best currency exchange rates and never close. Star and Cirrus are the most common international ATM networks, but check with your card issuer before leaving home to ensure that you have the proper four-digit PIN (personal identification number) for US outlets. Expect to pay transaction fees to both the bank which owns the ATM and your own bank for each transaction, but also expect to get the best rate of exchange for that day, since electronic transfers use the commercial exchange rate.

For security reasons, avoid carrying large amounts of cash. The safest forms of money are traveller's cheques and credit or debit cards. Both can be used almost everywhere.

US dollar traveller's cheques from Thomas Cook and other major issuers are often accepted, but traveller's cheques in other currencies must be cashed at a bank, and not just any bank, either. Except in large commercial and city banks, expect, at the very best, delays as staff telephone the main office in search of exchange rates and procedures. In smaller cities and towns you may not be able to cash traveller's cheques in foreign currencies at all. Eurocheques and personal cheques drawn on banks outside the United States are generally not accepted. Don't even bother trying to exchange coins: it costs banks in both countries more to collect and process them than they're worth.

A number of Thomas Cook locations offer MoneyGram, a quick international money transfer service. To contact Thomas Cook offices while in the USA, tel: (800)-CURRENCY (toll-free).

If possible, bring at least one, preferably two, major credit cards such as Access (MasterCard), American Express or Visa. Nearly all US shops accept both MasterCard and Visa. Plastic is the only acceptable proof of fiscal responsibility and car hire companies require either a credit card imprint or a substantial cash deposit before releasing a vehicle, even if the hire has been fully prepaid. Hotels and motels also require either a credit card imprint or a cash deposit, even if the bill is to be settled in cash. But you cannot travel entirely on plastic: some shops, cheaper motels, hostels, small local restaurants, and low-cost petrol stations require cash.

CURRENCY US dollars are the only currency accepted in the USA; Canadian dollars are used in Canada, but shops in border towns will usually accept American dollars, sometimes at a favourable exchange rate.

US banknote denominations are $1, $2 (rare), $5, $10, $20, $50 and $100. All banknotes are the same colour – green and white – and the same size, so take great care not to mix them up. The only differences, apart from the denominations marked on them, are the US presidents pictured on the front and the designs on the back. Very confusing at present are the new bills which have been issued to foil counterfeiters. Their new designs are still unfamiliar to many people.

There are 100 cents to the dollar: coins include the copper 1¢ piece, 5¢ nickel, 10¢ dime, 25¢ quarter, 50¢ half-dollar (rare), and a seldom-seen Susan B Anthony dollar which is almost identical to the quarter, and an even rarer Sacagawea dollar.

Canadian banknotes come in $1, $2, $5, $10, $20 and $100 denominations, all the same size but each a different colour. The $1 and $2 bills have been replaced by coins: $1 coins are popularly called 'loonies' after the image of the loon, a native bird, on the original issue; $2 coins, a small silvery disk surrounded by a golden disk, are popularly called 'toonies'. There are 100 cents to the dollar: coins include the copper 1¢ penny, 5¢ nickel, 10¢ dime and 25¢ quarter. Size and weights of US and Canadian coins are slightly different and seldom work in the other country's vending machines or coin-operated telephones.

FINANCIAL EMERGENCIES

If you lose your Thomas Cook traveller's cheques, tel: (800) 223-7373 (toll-free 24-hr service). In the event of loss or theft of a MasterCard, or for assistance with other card-related emergencies, call MasterCard Global Service at (800) 307-7309 (toll-free 24-hr service). Thomas Cook locations also offer replacement and other emergency services if you lose a MasterCard.

MoneyGram provides money transfer by telegraph, with locations all over the USA and around the world. If you need to have funds sent to you in an emergency, call (800) 926-9400 (toll-free).

OPENING TIMES

Office hours are generally Mon–Fri 0900–1700, although tourist offices also keep short Saturday hours all year, and weekend hours in summer. Most banks open from 0900 or 1000 to 1700 or 1800; a few stay open Sat 0900–1300. Cash dispenser machines are ubiquitous and open 24 hrs. Petrol stations generally open from early morning until late at night; a few stay open 24 hrs on major travel routes.

In major cities, big stores, supermarkets and shopping centres open at 0900 or 1000 Mon–Sat and close at 2000 or 2100, with shorter hours Sun. Small shops keep standard business hours. Sunday opening hours for many stores and businesses are slightly shorter.

Many restaurants, museums and theatres close Mon, but most tourist attractions are open seven days a week in summer. Many tourist attractions are closed Sept–May, corresponding with the normal school year, but some are open during school vacations, which vary from state to state.

PACKING

What you will need travelling in the USA depends largely on what you plan to do, where you plan to go, and when you will be travelling. It's an old rule, but still a good one, to bring half as much clothing as you think you will need, and twice as much money. Of the two, money is the lighter to carry. Porters don't exist outside even the most expensive hotels, and luggage trolleys (baggage carts) are rare outside airports. Luggage has to be light enough to carry.

Luggage must also fit into the car or other form of transport. North Americans buy the same cars as Europeans, Australians and the rest of the world, not the enormous 'boats' of the 1960s. If it won't fit in the boot at home, don't expect to cram it into a hire car.

Absolutely everything you could ever need, except your own personal teddy bear, is available, so don't worry if you've left anything behind. In fact, most North American prices will seem low: competition and over-supply keeps them that way. Pharmacies (also called drug stores but never chemists) carry a range of products, from medicine to cosmetics to beach balls. Prepare a small first-aid kit before you leave home with tried and tested insect repellent, sunscreen cream, and soothing moisturising lotion. Carry all medicines, glasses, and contraceptives with you, and keep duplicate prescriptions or a letter from your doctor to verify your need for a particular medication, as well as the note of its generic name – brand names will vary.

Other useful items to bring or buy immediately upon arrival are a water bottle, sunglasses, sunhat or visor with a broad brim, umbrella and light rain gear, Swiss Army pocket knife, torch (flashlight), padlock for anchoring luggage, money belt, travel adaptor plug, string for a washing line, alarm clock and camera. Those planning to rough it should take a sleeping bag, sheet liner and inflatable pillow. Allow a little extra space in your luggage for souvenirs.

A small daypack that is easy to carry can be handy for picnic lunches, guidebooks and daily use items, and can double as a spare bag for souvenirs on the trip home. On the way over, it can be folded flat in your suitcase.

Because the USA is such a big place, where you go will govern what clothes you will need. In general, if you plan to spend most of your time in cities, you will want dressier clothes, especially if you plan to attend the theatre and concerts. But if you plan to hike or ski during your trip, space will quickly be filled with sturdy boots and heavier clothing. The biggest problem comes in packing for multi-activity trips that include a little of everything or a number of different climates.

In any season, take plenty of layers, from shorts for the beach and interior valleys to jumpers and jackets for the mountains. Cotton and wool, worn in layers, are the traveller's favourite fibres. One layer is cool, several layers are warm. Adding and removing layers makes it easier to stay comfortable no matter how many times the weather changes in a single day. Umbrellas and lightweight rain gear are indispensable along the coast.

Informality is the norm throughout the USA, with the exception of a handful of elegant city restaurants which require jackets and ties for men. Trainers (sneakers), sandals and hiking boots are far more common than conventional shoes and high heels, even in fancy hotels. When in doubt, leave it at home. US clothing prices are cheaper than almost anywhere outside the Third World, so if you suddenly realise you need something you left at home, you can quickly replace it. But do take good, broken-in walking shoes.

POSTAL SERVICES

Every town of any size has at least one post office. Hours vary, although all are open Mon–Fri, morning and afternoon. Major US Postal Service branches are open Sat, and only a select few Sun. Stamps may be purchased from machines in some pharmacies and convenience stores. Some hotels sell stamps through the concierge; large department stores may have a post office; and some supermarkets sell stamps at the checkout counter. Stamp machines are installed in some stores, but a surcharge may be included in the cost.

Poste restante is available at any post office, without charge. Mail should be addressed in block lettering to your name, General Delivery, city, state, postal code, and USA or Canada. Mail is held for 30 days at the post office branch that handles General Delivery for each town or city, usually the main office. Identification is required for mail pick-up.

Postal rates are lower in the USA than in Canada. Letters and cards with correct postage may be dropped in blue boxes outside postal branches or on street corners; parcels weighing more than 1 lb must be handed to a postal clerk, for security reasons.

Post everything going overseas as air mail (surface mail takes weeks or even months). If posting letters near an urban area, overseas mail should take about one week. Add a day or two if posting from remote areas. All US mail must include the five-digit zip code (also use the four-digit suffix if you know it).

PUBLIC HOLIDAYS

North America's love affair with the road extends to jumping in the car for holiday weekends. Local celebrations, festivals, parades or neighbourhood parties can disrupt some or all activities in town. This works both ways, either keeping shops and businesses open longer hours or closing them earlier. Local museums which are normally open only on certain days will often open during local festivals.

The Fourth of July (Independence Day) is celebrated in every city and town with cookouts, concerts and fireworks. Memorial Day (last Monday in May) and St Patrick's Day (17 March) are occasions for parades, which may tie up traffic for a few minutes or a few hours, even on those numbered routes that become the main street of small towns they pass through.

The following holidays are celebrated nationally:

New Year's Day	(1 Jan)
Martin Luther King Jr Day	(third Mon in Jan)
Presidents' Day	(third Mon in Feb)
Memorial Day	(last Mon in May)
Independence Day	(4 July)
Labor Day	(first Mon in Sept, unless Mon falls on 1 Sept)
Columbus Day	(second Mon in Oct)
Veterans' Day	(11 Nov)
Thanksgiving Day	(fourth Thur in Nov)
Christmas Day	(25 Dec).

On these days post offices and government offices close, as do many businesses and shops. Large department stores stay open and may hold huge sales. Convenience stores, supermarkets, liquor stores and petrol stations generally remain open (sometimes with curtailed hours). Nearly everything closes on New Year's Day, Thanksgiving Day and Christmas Day. If you find yourself without a place to eat on Christmas Day, look for the nearest Chinese restaurant, which very likely will be open.

Some states have special holidays. Massachusetts celebrates Patriot's Day on 19 April and Boston celebrates Evacuation Day on 17 March, the day the British troops left Boston. (In practice, however, it is celebrated by Irish-heavy Boston as St Patrick's Day.)

Canadian national holidays include New Year's Day (1 Jan); Good Friday and Easter Monday (Mar or Apr); Victoria Day (late May); Canada Day (1 July); Labour Day (early Sept); Thanksgiving (mid-Oct); Remembrance Day (11 Nov); Christmas Day (25 Dec) and Boxing Day (26 Dec).

Call in advance before visiting an attraction on a public holiday as frequently there are special hours. National and state park campsites and accommodation must be reserved in advance for all holidays. Easter, Thanksgiving and Christmas are family holidays, so accommodation is usually available and may even be discounted (to fill hotels and motels). On other holidays Americans are 'mobile', so book early.

READING

Referred to throughout this guide as the **OTT**, the *Thomas Cook Overseas Timetable* is published every two months, price £10.50 per issue. Indispensable for independent travellers using public transport in the USA, it contains timetables for all the main rail and bus services in North America, plus details of local and suburban services. It is available from UK branches of Thomas Cook or by mail order, phoning (01733) 416477 in the UK. In North America, contact SF Travel Publications, 3959 Electric Rd, Suite 155, Roanoke, VA 24018; tel: (800) 322-3834; e-mail: sales@travelbookstore.com;

website: www.travelbookstore.com. A special edition of the *Overseas Timetable* is available from bookshops and from the outlets given above – the *Thomas Cook Overseas Timetable Independent Traveller's Edition* includes bus, rail and ferry timetables, plus additional information useful for travellers. Please note that the OTT table numbers very occasionally change – but services may easily be located by checking the index at the front of the *Overseas Timetable.*

If you are considering spending more than a couple of days in a city or region of the USA, then it may be worth obtaining a localised guidebook. Most guidebook series include separate volumes covering the major cities and regions of the USA, and may issue titles that cover more remote areas that are beyond the scope of this guide.

SAFETY AND SECURITY

Despite well-publicised incidents of street violence, millions of people travel (and live) in perfect safety in the USA. So can you if you follow commonsense precautions. Throwing caution to the winds is foolhardy at any time, and even more so on holiday.

The best way to avoid becoming a victim of theft or bodily injury in the USA, as in any other part of the world, is to walk with assurance, and try to give the impression that you know where you are going and are not worth robbing. Sightsee with a known companion, or in a group. Solo travel, in urban areas or in the countryside, is not recommended.

Never publicly discuss travel plans, or money or valuables you are carrying; keep to well-lit areas; do not wear or carry expensive jewellery or flash rolls of banknotes. Use a hidden money-belt for your valuables, travel documents and spare cash. Carrying a wallet in a back pocket or leaving a handbag open is an invitation to every pickpocket in the vicinity. In all public places, take precautions with anything that is obviously worth stealing: use a handbag with a crossed shoulder strap and a zip, and in restaurants wind the strap of your camera case around your chair or place your handbag firmly between your feet under the table.

Never leave luggage unattended or with strangers, no matter how pleasant and trustworthy they appear. At airports, security officials may confiscate unattended luggage as a possible bomb. In public toilets, handbags and small luggage have been snatched from hooks, or from under stalls. Airports and bus and train stations usually have lockers. Most work with keys; take care to guard the key and memorise the locker number. Hotel bell staff may keep luggage for one or more days on request, sometimes for a fee – be sure to ask for receipts for left luggage before surrendering it.

Concealing a weapon is against the law. Some defensive products resembling tear gas are legal only for persons certified in their proper use. Mugging, by individuals or gangs, is more of a problem in larger cities than in smaller ones and rural areas. If you are attacked, it is safer to let go of your bag or hand over the small amount of obvious money, as you are more likely to be attacked physically if the thief meets with resistance. Never resist. If you do encounter trouble, dial 911 on any telephone for free emergency assistance from police, fire and medical authorities. Report incidents immediately to local police, even if it is only to take a copy of their report for your insurance company or to show authorities should your passport be included in the stolen property.

EARTHQUAKES

Earthquakes are a fact of life in California and not unknown further north in Washington State and Oregon. If you feel a mild earthquake, treat it like an amusement park ride. If items start falling from shelves, lamps sway or it becomes difficult to walk because of a quake, take cover. Crawl under the nearest solid table for protection against falling objects. If there's no table handy, brace arms and legs in an interior doorway. Stay away from windows, bookcases, stairs or anything else that could fall or break. Don't run outside – glass, masonry and live power lines could be falling.

If you are driving, pull off the road and stop – it's almost impossible to control a vehicle when the road won't hold still. Once the quake is over, treat it like any other civil emergency. Make sure everyone is safe and provide all help possible to the wounded. And get ready for the next shake: there are always aftershocks.

SHOPPING

Airports do not have duty-free shopping for incoming travellers, but it's no great loss. Prices for alcohol and other duty-free items are almost always lower in supermarkets and discount stores than in duty-free shops. The same goes for other goods. Airport prices are generally higher than in similar shops nearby and the selection is smaller. Remember that all purchases must fit into your luggage for the trip home.

SMOKING

Be careful about lighting up. More often than not, smoking is forbidden in public buildings and on public transport; in several states it is prohibited by law in all public places. All plane flights in North America are non-smoking, and some hire cars are designated as non-smoking. Most hotels/motels set aside non-smoking rooms or floors; bed-and-breakfast establishments are almost all non-smoking. Restaurant dining regulations vary by locality: some forbid all smoking; others permit it in the bar or lounge only; some have a percentage of the eatery devoted to smokers. Smoking is prohibited in most stores and shops. Always ask before lighting a cigarette, cigar or pipe. When in doubt, go outside to smoke.

TAXES

There is no value added tax in the USA, but many other kinds of sales taxes can raise the cost of your holiday. Sales taxes vary with the state; a few do not have them at all. Cities can also add sales taxes to each purchase, although various items are usually exempt, including food in most jurisdictions. Nearly all states add taxes on accommodation and on restaurant meals. There may also be special taxes or fees on rental cars. None of these is refundable on departure.

TELEPHONES

Public telephones are located on street corners or inside restaurants, hotels and other public buildings, indicated by a sign with a white telephone receiver depicted on a blue background. Enclosed booths and wall-mounted or free-standing machines are all used. If possible, use public phones in well-lit, busy public areas. Dialling instructions are in the local white pages telephone directory. Phone numbers are always seven digits, preceded by a three-digit area code when calling outside the local area. In some places (Maryland is one), you must dial the area code even if it is a local call. For all long-distance calls, precede the area code with a 1, or with 0 if calling collect (i.e. reversing the charges).

Like all long-distance numbers, the free 800/855/866/877/888 area codes must be preceded by a 1, e.g. (888) 123-4567 must be dialled as 1 (888) 123-4567. Some telephone numbers are given in letters, i.e. (800) VAN-RIDE – telephone keys have both numbers and letters. A few numbers have more than seven letters to finish a business name. Don't worry: US phone numbers never require more than seven numerals, plus three for the area code.

Information

For local number information, dial 411. For long-distance phone information, dial 1, the area code, then 555-1212. Dial 0 for an operator, but remember that operator-assisted calls will be more expensive. There will be a charge for information calls. Phone numbers with the 800/855/866/877/888 area codes are toll-free. Those with a 900 area code charge the caller for information or other services, often at high per-minute rates.

The North American telephone system is divided into local and long-distance carriers. Depending on the time of day and day of the week, it may be cheaper to call across the country than to call 30 miles away. After 1700, Mon–Fri, and all weekend, rates are lower. A local call usually costs $0.35; a computer voice will come on-line to ask for additional coins when needed.

Pre-paid phone cards are gaining popularity and may be purchased at pharmacies, news-stands and grocery stores.

Many hotels and motels add a stiff surcharge to the cost of a call from a room; nearly all charge a service fee of $0.50–$1.50 per call for local calls and those using a credit card, even to toll-free 800 or 888 numbers. Nearly every hotel, however small, will have pay telephones in the lobby.

Before you travel, ask your local phone company if your phone card will work in North America. Most do, and come with a list of contact numbers. However, remember that the USA has the cheapest overseas phone rates in the world, which makes it cheaper to fill pay phones with quarters than to reverse charges. A credit card may be convenient, but is usually exorbitant.

INTERNATIONAL DIALLING

Dial 011 – country code – city code (omitting the first 0 if there is one) – local number. Some country codes are:

Australia	61
New Zealand	64
Republic of Ireland	353
South Africa	27
UK	44

So to call central London, for example, dial: 011-44-207-local number.

Dial an international operator on 00 for enquiries or assistance.

TIME

Continental USA is divided into four time zones:

Eastern Time: GMT -5 hrs
Central Time: GMT -6 hrs
Mountain Time: GMT -7 hrs
Pacific Time: GMT -8 hrs.

If you are crossing into Canada, there is Atlantic Canada Time (GMT -4 hrs) and Newfoundland (GMT -3.5 hrs) to bear in mind. Daylight saving, when all clocks are advanced one hour, runs from the first Sunday in April until the last Sunday in October – something not to forget if you are travelling at these times of the year and have a train or a plane to catch.

TIPPING

Acknowledgement for good service should not be extorted. That said, tipping is a fact of life, to receive, to repeat, or to thank someone for service.

Hotel porters generally receive $1 per bag; a bellperson who shows you to the room expects several dollars; in luxury properties, tip more. Room service delivery staff should be tipped 10–15 per cent of the tariff before taxes, unless there's a service charge indicated on the bill. Expect to hand out dollars for most services that involve room delivery. Pay $1–$5 for valet parking each time your car is delivered. Some hotels have a chambermaid name card placed in the room: it's a hint for a tip of a few dollars upon your departure, but is never obligatory. The pricier the hotel and the more services it offers, the more you will be expected to tip.

For restaurant tipping, see p. 46

Ushers in legitimate theatres, arenas and stadiums are not tipped; cinemas seldom have ushers, nor are tips expected. You are not expected to tip petrol station attendants. It *is* expected, however, that you tip taxi drivers; in New York if you do not, you risk injury or at least verbal abuse.

Toilets

'Restroom' or 'bathroom' are the common terms in the USA, and 'washroom' in Canada; 'toilet' is acceptable. Americans do not usually recognise 'WC'. Whatever the term, most are marked with a figure for a male or a female; 'Men' and 'Women' are the most common terms. Occasionally, a restroom may be used by both sexes. Restaurants sometimes use supposedly cute terms or pictures to replace the standard 'Men' and 'Women' signs, often to fit in with the theme of the establishment, and these can be confusing. Common in seafood and waterfront eateries are 'Buoys' and 'Gulls'; 'Colts' and 'Fillies' are popular in places with a Western theme.

Most businesses, including bars and restaurants, reserve restrooms for clients. Petrol stations provide keys for customers to access restrooms. Public toilets are sporadically placed, but well marked. Public toilets are not common along city streets, but roadside rest stops often have them. Hotels, museums and other tourist attractions have them too, of course, as do department stores and shopping malls. Small shops usually do not.

Tourist Information

In the USA, each state is responsible for its own tourism promotion. Ask for information to be sent to you well in advance to allow time for overseas shipping of large packets. While travelling in the USA, you can call tourist information offices to ask questions or seek advice, although many state offices are not able to recommend accommodation. They can, however, steer you to local chambers of commerce or information offices.

Local tourist information centres (TICs) are not all government-run bureaux, but are often staffed by volunteers. While some have regular hours, others vary with the day of the week or season. Often those run by local chambers of commerce are open 0900–1700 on weekdays, but not at weekends For links to many of the following groups, and many others, visit www.seeamerica.org.

Alabama Bureau of Tourism and Travel, 410 Adams Ave, Montgomery, AL 36117; tel: (205) 242-4670 or (800) 252-2262; www.touralabama.org.

Arizona Tourism, 1100 West Washington, Phoenix, AZ 85007; tel: (602) 542-8687 or (800) 842-8257; www.arizonaguide.com.

Arkansas Dept of Parks and Tourism, 1 Capitol Mall, Little Rock, AR 72201; tel: (501) 682-7777 or (800) 643-8383; www.arkansas.com.

California Division of Tourism, 801 K St, Ste 1600, Sacramento, CA 95814; tel: (916) 322-2881 or (800) TO-CALIF; fax: (916) 322-3402; www.visitcalifornia.com.

Colorado currently has no tourism office; contact the regional Grand Circle Association, PO Box 987, Page AZ 86040; tel: (520) 645-3232; www.colorado.com. This agency provides information on the entire south-west mountain country.

Connecticut Office of Tourism Department of Economic and Community Development, 505 Hudson St, Hartford, CT 06106; tel: (800) CT-BOUND; www.ctbound.org.

Delaware Council for International Visitors, PO Box 831, Wilmington, DE 19899; tel: (302) 656-9928; www.visitdelaware.net.

Florida Tourism, PO Box 1100, 661 E Jefferson St, Tallahassee, FL 32302; tel: (904) 487-1462; fax (904) 224-2938; www.flausa.com. In the UK: ABC FLORIDA, Box 35 Abingdon, Oxon, OX14 4TB; tel: (0891) 600555.

Georgia Department of Industry, Trade and Tourism, PO Box 1776, Atlanta, GA 30301; tel: (404) 656-3590 or (800) 847-4842; www.georgia.org.

Idaho Parks and Recreation Dept, 5657 Warm Springs Ave, Boise, ID 83720; tel: (208) 334-4199; www.visitid.org.

Illinois Office of Tourism, 620 E Adams St, Springfield, IL 62701; tel: (217) 782-7500; www.enjoyillinois.com.

Indiana Division of Tourism, 1 North Capitol 77, Indianapolis, IN 46204; tel: (317) 232-8860; www.in.gov/enjoyindiana.

Iowa Department of Economic Development, 200 E Grand Ave, Des Moines, IA 50309; tel (515) 281-3100 or (800) 345-4692; www.traveliowa.com.

Kansas Department of Commerce, 700 South West Harrison, 1300, Topeka, KS 66603; tel: (913) 296-3481 or (800) 252-6727; www.travelkansas.com.

Kentucky Department of Travel Development, 500 Metro St, Frankfurt, KY 40601; tel: (502) 564-4930 or (800) 225-8747; www.kentuckytourism.com.

Louisiana Travel Office, PO Box 94291, Capitol Station, Baton Rouge, LA 70804; tel: (504) 925-3800 or (800) 633-6970; www.louisianatravel.com.

Maine Publicity Bureau, PO Box 2300, Hallowell, ME 04347-2300; tel: (207) 623-0363; Maine Office of Tourism: www.visitmaine.com.

Maryland Office of Tourism Development, Department of Business and Economic Development, 217 E Redwood St, Baltimore MD 21201; tel: (410) 767-6270; www.mdisfun.org.

Massachusetts Office of Travel and Tourism, 100 Cambridge St, 13th Floor, Boston, MA 02202; tel: (800) 447-MASS, ext 300; www.massvacation.com.

Michigan Travel Bureau, 333 South Capitol, Suite F, Lansing, MI 48909; tel: (517) 335-1876 or (800) 543-2937; www.michigan.org.

Minnesota Office of Tourism, 100 Metro Sq., St Paul, MN 55101-2112; tel: (612) 296-5029 or (800) 657-3700; www.exploreminnesota.com.

Mississippi Division of Tourism, 1301 Walter Siller Bldg, 55 High St, Jackson, MS 39209; tel: (601) 359-3414 or (800) 647-2290; www.mississippi.org.

Missouri Office of Tourism, PO Box 1055, Jefferson City, MO 65102; tel: (573) 751-4133 or (800) 519-0900; www.missouritourism.org.

Montana Travel, PO Box 200533, Helena MT 59620; tel: (406) 444-2654 or (800) 541-1447; www.visitmt.com.

Nebraska Department of Economic Development, PO Box 94666, Lincoln, NE 68509; tel: (402) 471-3796 or (800) 228-4307; www.visitnebraska.org.

Nevada Commission on Tourism, PO Box 30032, Reno, NV 89520; tel: (702) 687-4332 or (800) 638-2328; fax: (702) 687-6779; www.travelnevada.com.

New Hampshire Office of Vacation Travel, PO Box 586, Concord, NH 03301; tel: (603) 271-2666; www.visitnh.gov.

New Jersey Division of Travel and Tourism, 1 W State St, Trenton, NJ 08625; tel: (609) 292-2470; www.visitnj.org.

New Mexico Department of Tourism, 491 Old Santa Fe Trail, Santa Fe, NM 87501; tel (505) 827-0291 or (800) 545-2040; www.newmexico.org.

New York State Division of Tourism, 1 Commerce Plaza, Albany, NY 12245; tel: (518) 474-4116; www.iloveny.state.ny.us.

NYC & Company, 42nd St at Times Square, New York, NY 10036; tel: (212) 484-1200; www.nycvisit.com.

North Carolina Travel and Tourism Division, 301 N Wilmington St, Raleigh, NC 27601; tel: (919) 733-4171 or (800) 847-4862; www.visitnc.com.

North Dakota Promotion Division, Liberty Memorial Bldg, Capitol Grounds, Bismarck, ND 58505; tel: (701) 224-2525 or (800) 437-2077; www.ndtourism.com.

Ohio Office of Travel and Tourism, 77 S High St, PO Box 1001, Columbus OH 43215; tel: (614) 466-8844; (www.ohiotourism.com) www.discoverohio.com.

Oklahoma Tourism and Recreation Dept, 500 Will Rogers Bldg, Oklahoma City, OK 73105; tel: (405) 521-2409 or (800) 652-6552; www.travelok.com.

Oregon Tourism Commission, 775 Summer St NE, Salem, OR 97310; tel: (800) 547-7842 or (503) 986-0000; fax: (503) 986-0001; www.traveloregon.com.

Pennsylvania Office of Tourism, 453 Forum Bldg, Harrisburg, PA 17120; tel: (717) 787-5453. In the UK: 11–15 Betterton St, London WC2H 9BP; tel: (0171) 470 8801; www.experiencepa.com or www.padutchcountry.com.

Rhode Island Tourism Division, 1 W Exchange St, Providence, RI 02903; tel: (800) 556-2484 or (401) 222-2601; www.visitrhodeisland.com.

South Carolina Department of Parks, Recreation and Tourism, 1205 Pendleton St, Columbia, SC 29201; tel: (803) 724-0122; www.travelsc.com.

South Dakota Division of Tourism, 221 South Central, PO Box 1000, Pierre, SD 57051; tel: (605) 773-3301 or (800) 843-1930; www.travelsd.com.

Tennessee Department of Tourist Development, PO Box 23170, Nashville, TN 37202; tel (615) 471-2158; www.state.tn.us/tourdev.

Texas Division of Tourism, PO Box 12728, Austin, TX 78711; tel (512) 463-8586 or (800) 888-8839; www.traveltex.com.

Utah Travel Council, 300 N State St, Salt Lake City, UT 84114; tel: (801) 538-1030; www.utah.com.

Vermont Department of Tourism and Marketing, 134 State St, PO Box 1471, Montpelier, VT 0560-1471; tel: (802) 828-3236; www.travel-vermont.com.

Virginia Division of Tourism, 901 E Byrd St, Richmond VA 23219; tel: (804) 786-2051. In the UK: 1st floor, 182–4 Addington Rd, Selsdon, Surrey CR2 8LB; tel: (0181) 651 4743; www.virginia.org.

Washington DC Convention and Visitors Association, 1212 New York Ave NW, Washington DC 20005; tel (202) 789-7000; www.washington.org.

Washington State Division of Tourism, Box 42500, Olympia WA 98504; tel: 800-544-1800 or (360) 753-5630; www.experiencewashington.com; www.tourismwa.gov.

West Virginia Division of Tourism and Parks, State Capitol, Charleston, WV 25305; tel: (800) CALL-WVA; www.callwva.com.

Wisconsin Division of Tourism, 123 W Washington St, PO Box 7606, Madison, WI 53707; tel: (608) 266-2161 or (800) 432-8748; www.travelwisconsin.com.

Wyoming Travel Commission, College Drive, Cheyenne, WY 82002; tel: (307) 777-7777; www.wyomingtourism.org.

Canada also has active federal tourism promotion offices, usually located in Canadian consulates around the world.

WEIGHTS AND MEASURES

Officially, the USA is converting to the metric system. In truth, few people have changed and metric measures are rarely seen. (A few road signs show both miles and km.) The non-metric US measures are the same as imperial measures except for fluids, where US gallons and quarts are five-sixths of their imperial equivalents. See conversion tables, opposite. Canada has long since joined the metric world. Clothing sizes are the same as or very close to imperial sizes for menswear, tights and children's clothing. Women's sizes are quite different. Shoe and hat sizes are close enough to be confusing, but not close enough to fit!

WORKING IN THE USA

As in most countries, non-citizens must get special documentation to work in the United States. To find out about visa requirements for working, contact the nearest US embassy or consulate or visit http://travel.state.gov. For placement listings, tips and information on working abroad, take a look at www.gapyear.com. Job bulletins, information on working holidays and a directory of helpful links is at www.payaway.co.uk.

DISTANCES (approx. conversions)

1 kilometre (km) = 1000 metres (m) 1 metre = 100 centimetres (cm)

Metric	Imperial/US	Metric	Imperial/US	Metric	Imperial/US
1 cm	⅜ in.	10 m	33 ft (11 yd)	3 km	2 miles
50 cm	20 in.	20 m	66 ft (22 yd)	4 km	2½ miles
1 m	3 ft 3 in.	50 m	164 ft (54 yd)	5 km	3 miles
2 m	6 ft 6 in.	100 m	330 ft (110 yd)	10 km	6 miles
3 m	10 ft	200 m	660 ft (220 yd)	20 km	12½ miles
4 m	13 ft	250 m	820 ft (275 yd)	25 km	15½ miles
5 m	16 ft 6 in.	300 m	984 ft (330 yd)	30 km	18½ miles
6 m	19 ft 6 in.	500 m	1640 ft (550 yd)	40 km	25 miles
7 m	23 ft	750 m	½ mile	50 km	31 miles
8 m	26 ft	1 km	⅝ mile	75 km	46 miles
9 m	29 ft (10 yd)	2 km	1½ miles	100 km	62 miles

24-HOUR CLOCK

(examples)

0000 = Midnight	1200 = Noon	1800 = 6 pm
0600 = 6 am	1300 = 1 pm	2000 = 8 pm
0715 = 7.15 am	1415 = 2.15 pm	2110 = 9.10 pm
0930 = 9.30 am	1645 = 4.45 pm	2345 = 11.45 pm

TEMPERATURE

Conversion Formula: (°C x 9 ÷ 5) + 32 = °F

°C	°F	°C	°F	°C	°F	°C	°F
-20	-4	-5	23	10	50	25	77
-15	5	0	32	15	59	30	86
-10	14	5	41	20	68	35	95

WEIGHT

1kg = 1000g 100 g = 3½ oz

Kg	Lbs	Kg	Lbs	Kg	Lbs
1	2	5	11	25	55
2	4½	10	22	50	110
3	6½	15	33	75	165
4	9	20	45	100	220

FLUID MEASURES

1 ltr.(l) = 0.88 Imp. quarts = 1.06 US quarts

Ltrs.	Imp. gal.	US gal.	Ltrs.	Imp. gal.	US gal.
5	1.1	1.3	30	6.6	7.8
10	2.2	2.6	35	7.7	9.1
15	3.3	3.9	40	8.8	10.4
20	4.4	5.2	45	9.9	11.7
25	5.5	6.5	50	11.0	13.0

MEN'S SHIRTS

UK	Europe	US
14	36	14
15	38	15
15½	39	15½
16	41	16
16½	42	16½
17	43	17

MEN'S SHOES

UK	Europe	US
6	40	7
7	41	8
8	42	9
9	43	10
10	44	11
11	45	12

LADIES' CLOTHES

UK	France	Italy	Rest of Europe	US
10	36	38	34	8
12	38	40	36	10
14	40	42	38	12
16	42	44	40	14
18	44	46	42	16
20	46	48	44	18

MEN'S CLOTHES

UK	Europe	US
36	46	36
38	48	38
40	50	40
42	52	42
44	54	44
46	56	46

LADIES' SHOES

UK	Europe	US
3	36	4½
4	37	5½
5	38	6½
6	39	7½
7	40	8½
8	41	9½

AREAS

1 hectare = 2.471 acres

1 hectare = 10,000 sq. metres

1 acre = 0.4 hectares

Timeline of American History

Before 1500	Native Americans inhabit most of North America, some as nomadic hunter-gatherers, others in agricultural villages.
1492–1535	Early European explorers make first contact with native populations.
1539–42	Spanish explorers De Soto and Coronado claim Pacific coast for Spain.
1565	Spanish establish first permanent European settlement in St Augustine, Florida.
1603	Samuel de Champlain begins exploration and colonisation of what is now eastern Canada for France.
1607	First British colony established at Jamestown, Virginia.
1609	Henry Hudson explores Hudson River, leading to Dutch trading colony of New Amsterdam, later New York. Santa Fe founded by Spanish.
1620	Pilgrims land at Provincetown, then settle at Plymouth, Massachusetts.
1675–76	King Philip's War between native tribes and New England colonists.
1692	Witch trials begin in Puritan colony of Salem, Massachusetts, bringing European practice of witch-hunting to New World.
1700–90	Population of the 13 original colonies increases from 260,000 to 3,900,000.
1754–59	French and Indian War, ending with the fall of Quebec to the British and the end of French control in North America.
1763	Britain gains Florida and all lands east of the Mississippi by treaty, ending all Dutch and Spanish control in eastern North America.
1765	Colonial Stamp Act Congress meets to protest against taxation without representation and British trade restrictions. Sons of Liberty and other 'subversive' groups form.
1773	Protesters attack taxation and trade restrictions at 'Boston Tea Party' and similar incident in Annapolis, Maryland. Rebellion brews.
1775	First shots of the American Revolution (War of American Independence) fired at Lexington and Concord, Massachusetts, followed by Battle of Bunker Hill in Boston.
1776	British evacuate Boston; Declaration of Independence signed in Philadelphia on 4 July.
1777	British army under Burgoyne defeated at Saratoga, New York.
1781	British leader Cornwallis surrenders at Yorktown, Virginia, ending Revolutionary War.
1787	Constitution signed in Philadelphia.
1789	George Washington inaugurated as first president.
1790	Industrial Revolution begins in Pawtucket, Rhode Island, and elsewhere; inventors' rights protected by copyright law.
1803	President Jefferson buys most of central continent from Napoleon.
1804–06	American explorers Lewis and Clark explore the north-west.
1812	War with Britain to establish American shipping rights.
1831	Northern Abolitionists begin serious crusade to end slavery.
1836	Texas wins independence from Mexico, becoming a state ten years later.

1845–48	Through treaty and war with Mexico, USA acquires lands to Pacific, creating borders almost as they stand today.
1848	Gold discovered in Sacramento Valley, beginning California Gold Rush of 1849.
1850s	Immigration soars to 400,000 a year, with 40 per cent from Ireland; the Cotton Kingdom reaches its height in the south.
1860	Lincoln elected president; southern states secede from Union, precipitating Civil War in 1861.
1865	Civil War ends at Appomattox, Virginia, after Confederate capital falls to Grant's army.
1869	Railroad spans the nation from ocean to ocean, meeting at Ogden, Utah.
1870s–1900	Industrialisation of both north and south heals divisions of Civil War. Telegraph, radio, and electric power spur continued growth and westward expansion.
1898	Battleship *Maine* sunk in Havana, Cuba, beginning Spanish-American War. USA acquires Philippines, Guam, Hawaii and Samoa in Pacific and becomes a power in the Caribbean.
1903	Wright brothers succeed in first aeroplane flight at Kitty Hawk, North Carolina. Automobile manufacture begins in earnest.
1917	USA joins European allies and enters World War I.
1918–29	Post-war economy booms through the Roaring Twenties. Prohibition of liquor.
1929	Stock market crashes, beginning the Great Depression. The economy grinds to a halt.
1933	President Roosevelt begins New Deal to provide relief and begin economic recovery.
1941	Japanese attack Pearl Harbor, Hawaii, bringing USA into World War II.
1945	Atomic bomb dropped on Hiroshima, Japan, ending World War II.
1947	Marshall Plan aids European postwar recovery.
1950s	Interstate highway system begins under President Eisenhower.
1954	Racial discrimination banned in all US schools.
1961	Alan Shepard, first American man in space, launched from Cape Canaveral, Florida.
1963	President John F Kennedy assassinated in Dallas, Texas.
1963	Civil rights movement, with massive rallies in Washington DC and elsewhere.
1964–73	Protest at home grows as US intervention in Vietnam escalates; US involvement ends.
1969	*Apollo 11* puts first man on the moon.
1972	President Nixon opens relations with Communist China.
1974	President Nixon resigns in Watergate scandal.
1980	Mount St Helens explodes in a violent volcanic eruption.
1999	Impeachment proceedings against President Bill Clinton fail a majority vote in Senate.
2001	On 11 September ('9/11') radical Islamic terrorists crash passenger jets into the Twin Towers of the World Trade Center, New York, and the Pentagon, Washington DC.
2003	President George W Bush orders US attack on Iraq despite UN opposition.
2004	Dictator president Saddam Hussein of Iraq captured by US military.

TIMELINE OF AMERICAN HISTORY

THE NORTHEAST

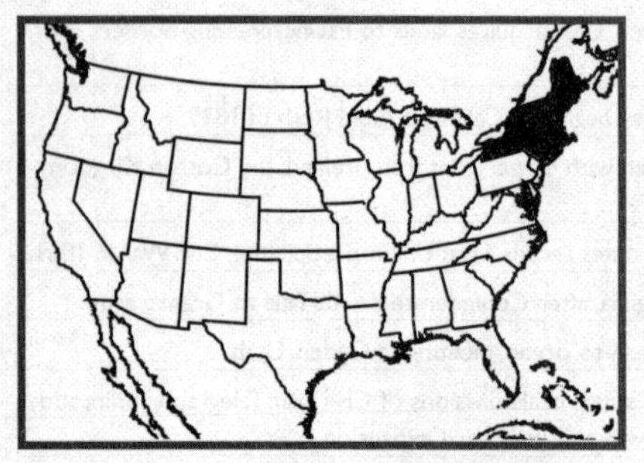

Many foreign visitors never get beyond this small, but attraction-packed corner of the United States. Visitors from the UK and Europe feel especially at home here, in a landscape that echoes their own compact arrangements, without the vast wide-open spaces of the western part of the country.

Although it is an area very much of its own, the Northeast – the six New England states (Maine, New Hampshire, Vermont, Massachusetts, Rhode Island and Connecticut) and New York – is in many ways a microcosm of the rest of the United States. Geographically, it has a little bit of everything, except desert. While it doesn't have the Rocky Mountains, it has several smaller ranges that are part of the Appalachians. It has a respectable sea coast, ranging from rocky cliffs and tiny cove beaches in the north to the dunes and long sandy strands of Cape Cod.

Socially, it is the epitome of the American melting pot. Nearly all the early immigrant groups arrived on the east coast, and the ancestors of many of the people you will meet here began by working in the mills that once lined nearly every river in the Northeast. These people powered the Industrial Revolution that catapulted the United States into its early position as industrial and financial leader of the world.

Although they have woven into the fabric of American life – indeed they are the fabric of America – many of these groups still preserve customs, foods and lifestyles brought from their homelands. In the Northeast you will find towns and neighbourhoods that bear the definite stamp of various ethnic communities that predominate. In Massachusetts, for example, New Bedford is largely Portuguese, as is nearby East Providence, Rhode Island. Boston has a heavy Irish influence and both Boston and Providence have good-sized Italian neighbourhoods. Boston has an active, though small,

Chinatown. Manchester, New Hampshire and Woonsocket, Rhode Island, have large populations of French Canadians and active Franco-American churches and community clubs. Dutch names and architecture are common along the Hudson Valley in New York, and in New Hampshire you can find the onion-shaped domes of Russian churches in both Claremont and Berlin. And, of course, New York City has ethnic neighbourhoods that reflect its historic role as America's foremost port of entry for immigrants.

Wherever you find these ethnic enclaves, you will find the corresponding food, which makes travelling in the Northeast especially enjoyable. While this ethnic diversity is common on the west coast, too, you will find less culinary variety in the rest of the country. New England food has taken a bad rap, often portrayed as bland and uninteresting. When you hear that, you will know that the person who says it has not travelled there within the past decade or two.

Boston and Providence are major dining-out cities, offering the variety and panache of New York's restaurant scene with neither its prices nor the trendy favourite-of-the-month mindset. New York continues to have the largest concentration of eating places, which range from celebrity-studded hot spots and pricey gourmet palaces to tiny diners and neighbourhood eateries of every possible ethnic and regional origin. In the city, you don't just go for Chinese food, you can choose a province.

But fine dining in the Northeast is not confined to its cities. Many highly trained chefs, tiring of the city life, have moved to small inns throughout the region, or to smaller, lively cities. And the constant stream of new immigrants keeps the ethnic traditions alive, so you may find Guatemalan food in Rhode Island or a West African restaurant in Vermont.

The Northeast is full of other surprises, too. In defiance of its reputation as staid and reserved, New England is filled with lively, often outrageous festivals. Newport seems to have one going all the time, and major events highlight more remote places like Keene, New Hampshire, which finds its way into the *Guinness Book of World Records* with the grandaddy of all pumpkin festivals, featuring thousands of carved and lighted jack-o-lanterns.

Can you just visit the Northeast and say you've seen the whole USA? No, but you will see a wider sampling of it in a smaller area than you could do in any other part of the country. You will also have a good feel for some of the characteristics that are the most

American. The fierce sense of independence, for example. Remember that it was New Englanders who fired the first shots of the American Revolution at Lexington and Concord. And although it was fought further south, the Civil War was largely fired by New England abolitionists in their outcry against slavery.

You will also see a good sampling of communities of all sizes, from mind-boggling New York to tiny villages in Maine and New Hampshire, only a few houses clustered around a white-spired meeting house. Many are too small to have even a general store or any commercial activity at all. You will see miles and miles of rolling farmlands in the green valleys of Vermont and upstate New York. You will see seaports that look much as they did a century ago, except that the tall masts and furled canvas have given way to engines.

You can travel here by train, air, bus, bike, boat, or on foot, but the best way to see what makes the Northeast unique is to explore it by car. This takes you into remote and rural areas and lets you sample the variety and savour the experiences you will find only here. Roads are good, even those which climb over the mountains. A few of these are closed in winter because they are too steep and narrow to keep clear of snow. But they are well marked, both on maps and by road signs, so you can easily pick alternative routes.

Which brings us to the big question: when to visit. The Northeast has considerable charm in almost every season except early spring – 'mud season' the locals call it. But that's the only season when you can watch 'sugar bushes' at work, gathering sap from maple trees and boiling it into sweet syrups and candies. It's also a good time for 'fair weather skiers' who enjoy the longer days and warmer temperatures of spring on the many ski trails of the Green Mountains, White Mountains and Adirondacks. Midwinter is cold, but most of the north will be covered in a white mantle of snow. Winter sports are in full swing, as is the cultural season. Concert venues and theatres are busy, and the cities are alive with activities.

In the summer things slow down a bit in the cities, but pick up in rural and resort areas, with water sports, beaches, festivals and summer resorts going strong. Summer and autumn are the best seasons for outdoor sports, such as hiking, cycling, kayaking and sailing. As summer melts into autumn, or 'fall', days become crisper and the leaves begin to change colour until all New York and New England seem to have been painted in shades of red and gold. It's a glorious display of brilliant colours set off by ample stands of dark evergreen trees such as fir and pine.

While New England is at its most beautiful then, fall's glories are hardly a secret, so expect attractions and roads to be more crowded, and be sure to make reservations for accommodation very early. Many people reserve their autumn weekend rooms for the next year before leaving their inn or B&B. The colours move from north to south, changing in northern Maine as early as mid-September, and finishing off in the Litchfield Hills of Connecticut in late October. Weather has an influence, so you cannot be sure when the height of colour will be. But the entire autumn is beautiful, and even if you miss the so-called 'peak' you will certainly not be disappointed.

Cultural Destinations of New England is a unique group of the region's foremost historical and cultural attractions, matched with notable nearby lodgings. Destinations such as Mystic Seaport (see p. 112), Plimoth Plantation (p. 147) and the Shelburne Museum (p. 176) are included in their custom-designed itineraries; some member inns add discounted admissions to other local attractions to the packages; tel: 00-1-800-0466-0466 from Europe, (802) 878-3863 or (800) 207-4951 in the US. For tourism information on New England in the UK, contact their representative on (09065) 588555.

OUR CHOICE

New York neighbourhoods: Chinatown, Little Italy, Greenwich Village

Statue of Liberty and Ellis Island

View from the top of a skyscraper

Niagara Falls

Mystic Seaport

The Freedom Trail

Harvard Square and the Harvard museums

Boston Duck Tour or harbour cruise

Old Sturbridge Village

Salem

Plimouth Plantation

Newport mansions and Cliff Walk

The Old Man of the Mountain and Lost River

Mount Washington Cog Railway

Acadia National Park

Penobscot Bay

Ferry or cruise to a Maine island

Shelburne Museum

Smugglers Notch and Stowe

HOW MUCH YOU CAN SEE IN A ...

WEEK (7 DAYS)

Boston, Cape Cod and Newport or Nantucket

Boston, the White Mountains and lower Maine Coast

The Berkshires, Green Mountains and White Mountains

New York, the Hudson Valley, Green Mountains and Berkshires

New York, Mystic Seaport, Newport and ferry to Block Island

Portsmouth, the Maine Coast to Acadia and the White Mountains

Boston, Old Sturbridge Village, the Berkshires, Hudson Valley and southern Green Mountains

New York, Mystic, Newport and inner Cape Cod, with a stop in Providence

New York, Finger Lakes via the Hudson Valley, and Niagara Falls

FORTNIGHT (14 DAYS)

Boston, Providence, Newport, Cape Cod and the islands, maybe with a short excursion to the White Mountains or lower Maine Coast

Boston, the Maine Coast, White Mountains, Green Mountains and Old Sturbridge Village

New York, the Hudson Valley, Green Mountains, White Mountains, Berkshires and western Connecticut coast

New York, western Connecticut coast, Mystic, Newport and Cape Cod with one island

New York, Mystic, Newport, inner Cape Cod and one island, with a day or two in Boston

New York, the Hudson Valley, Green Mountains, Finger Lakes and Niagara Falls

NEW YORK

New York can claim, with some justification, to be the capital of the world. Not only is it the home of the United Nations but of immigrants from every corner of the globe. Ever since Dutch settlers established their first trading post on the southern tip of Manhattan in 1626, buying the island from local Indians for a few dollars' worth of trinkets, New York has been a mecca for everyone wanting to share in the great American dream.

The sheer energy of the Big Apple is exhilarating. It is felt in the manic pace of the city's street life, the creativity of its artists and designers, the skyscrapers which rise ever higher. At first, New York can be exhausting and the tension impossible to escape; after a while you get used to it and everywhere else seems dull by comparison.

New York City consists of five boroughs – Manhattan, Brooklyn, the Bronx, Queens and Staten Island – but to most outsiders New York simply means Manhattan. Wall Street and Broadway may be household names across the world, but Manhattan is really just a collection of neighbourhoods, each with its own personality. Harlem and Chinatown are as different from Greenwich Village as New York is from the rest of America.

Must See/Do In New York

Take a clip-clopping horse-and-carriage ride through Central Park
Stroll across historic Brooklyn Bridge, with Lower Manhattan's skyscraper skyline as a backdrop
Gaze at the panoramic views from the Empire State Building's observatory
After nightfall, see the pulsating neon-lit extravaganza surrounding Times Square: American commercialism at its excitingly gaudiest
Pay your respects at Ground Zero for an emotional reminder of September 11 2001 ('9/11'), when terrorist-piloted airplanes slammed into the World Trade Center's twin towers
Inside Beaux-Arts Grand Central terminal, look up at the concourse's vaulted ceiling twinkling with starry constellations

GETTING THERE

Air International flights arrive at John F Kennedy (JFK) Airport in Queens or at Newark in New Jersey. There's a flat taxi fare from JFK into Manhattan (about $55 including bridge and tunnel tolls and a tip). Uniformed dispatchers will guide you towards the licensed taxi stand; avoid the 'gypsy cabs' which tout at the airport. The New York Airport Express Bus, tel: (718) 875-8200, runs to the PATH bus terminal every 15 mins, 0615–2310, taking about an hour; it also runs to Grand Central Terminal and Penn Station, similar timings. SuperShuttle New York, tel: (800) 258 3826, runs a 24-hr on-demand shared shuttle service to hotels between Battery Park and 227th. The cheapest option is the free bus to Howard Beach station, then an A-line subway train.

Taxis from Newark start at around $50; the transit bus to Port Authority Bus Terminal or Grand Central Terminal, or the Gray Line limos, are about $15. Best bet is the new train from the airport to Penn Station, $11.50.

Some US domestic flights arrive at La Guardia in Queens, the closest airport to Manhattan. Again, a minibus into Manhattan (about $10) is about half the cost of a taxi, but the cheapest way into town is on the M60 bus, with links to the various subway lines along 125th St.

ORIENTING YOURSELF

New York is relatively simple to navigate once you know a few basic facts and the lingo that goes with them.

From 14th St to Central Park, the **streets** run east–west and the **avenues** north–south.

Fifth Avenue divides Manhattan into **East Side** and **West Side**.

Uptown is an area – from the 60s up – as well as a direction, of ascending street numbers.

Downtown is the lower (southern) part of Manhattan, and also the direction of descending street numbers.

Midtown is the middle part of Manhattan (between 14th and 59th Sts).

RAIL/BUS Amtrak long-distance train services from elsewhere in the USA and Canada arrive at Penn Station, close to Midtown Manhattan and with connections to the subway network. Greyhound buses arrive at the Port Authority Bus Terminal on West 40th St, a short walk from Times Square – though a taxi would be advisable if you are arriving late at night.

ROAD I-95 runs up through New Jersey and crosses briefly into Manhattan on its way to New England. Of several exits to New York, take the I-78 at Jersey City to enter Lower Manhattan through the Holland Tunnel; the I-495 at Union City for Midtown Manhattan via the Lincoln Tunnel; or cross the George Washington Bridge into Manhattan and take the Henry Hudson Parkway down the west side of the island. Once you are settled in Manhattan, park your car securely in a garage and get around by public transport. Driving in New York is a nightmare and is not worth the hassle.

GETTING AROUND

New York is a great city for walking, and Manhattan's grid system makes it easy to get about. The only real exception to the grid system is Broadway, originally an Indian trail. Allow one to two minutes per block if heading up or downtown, 5 minutes across town between avenues, and you won't go far wrong.

Two of the most scenic and enjoyable bus routes are the M5 from Greenwich Village, skirting Central Park on its way to Riverside Drive, and the M4 from Penn Station and the Empire State Building, which crawls along Museum Mile and then up Broadway on its way through Washington Heights to the Cloisters, replicating medieval architecture in the far north of Manhattan. Change between these two routes where they meet up on Broadway and you have an enjoyable bus tour of Manhattan for a fraction of the cost of an organised tour.

The quickest way to go longer distances is by **subway**. Operating 24 hrs a day, it is both easy and safe to use once you have mastered the map (see inside back cover). Remember that 'express' trains only stop at certain stations and if you want one of the stations in between you need to catch a 'local'. Better than single-ride fares ($2) is to buy a magnetic MetroCard which can be 'loaded' in advance with multiple rides; if you plan to use the subway a lot, a seven-day unlimited MetroCard, also valid on buses, is even better value. Be sure to check posted subway maps for temporary closures and changes.

Buses are slow but they can be a good way of seeing the city. A single flat fare (exact change only) takes you anywhere in Manhattan, so if you need to change buses ask your driver for a 'transfer'.

Open-top bus tours are operated by a number of companies, including **Gray Line**, tel: (800) 669-0051. A single ticket is valid for two days, allowing you to hop on and off as you choose. The standard 4-hr city tour ($$$$+) includes all the main sights. A Harlem gospel tour ($$$$+) includes a visit to a Sunday gospel service as well as two days' unlimited travel on the Uptown tour route. Tickets are available from the visitor centre at 8th Ave and 47th St or on the bus.

Taxis are fine if you are in a hurry, but an unnecessarily expensive way of getting about. Always use a licensed yellow cab - you can hail them on the street - and make sure that the driver switches on the meter.

Visitors staying in hotels near JFK may find the Long Island Railroad useful for getting into the city, although you need to access it via bus to Jamaica.

INFORMATION

DISTRICT & TRANSPORT MAPS – inside back cover

NYC & Company, 810 7th Ave at 53rd St; tel: (212) 484-1222; open Mon–Fri 0830–1800, Sat, Sun 0900–1700, is the official tourist office and offers maps, brochures, metrocards, attractions tickets, and discount coupons for Broadway shows. Check their **NYC Guide** for off-price coupons, as well. Another useful source of information is the **Times Square Visitor Center**, 1560 Broadway; open 0800–2000 daily, which also has a theatre booking service and free internet access. The kiosk outside Grand Central Terminal has a wide range of leaflets; there are also tourist information desks in the major department stores. For information on events, pick up a

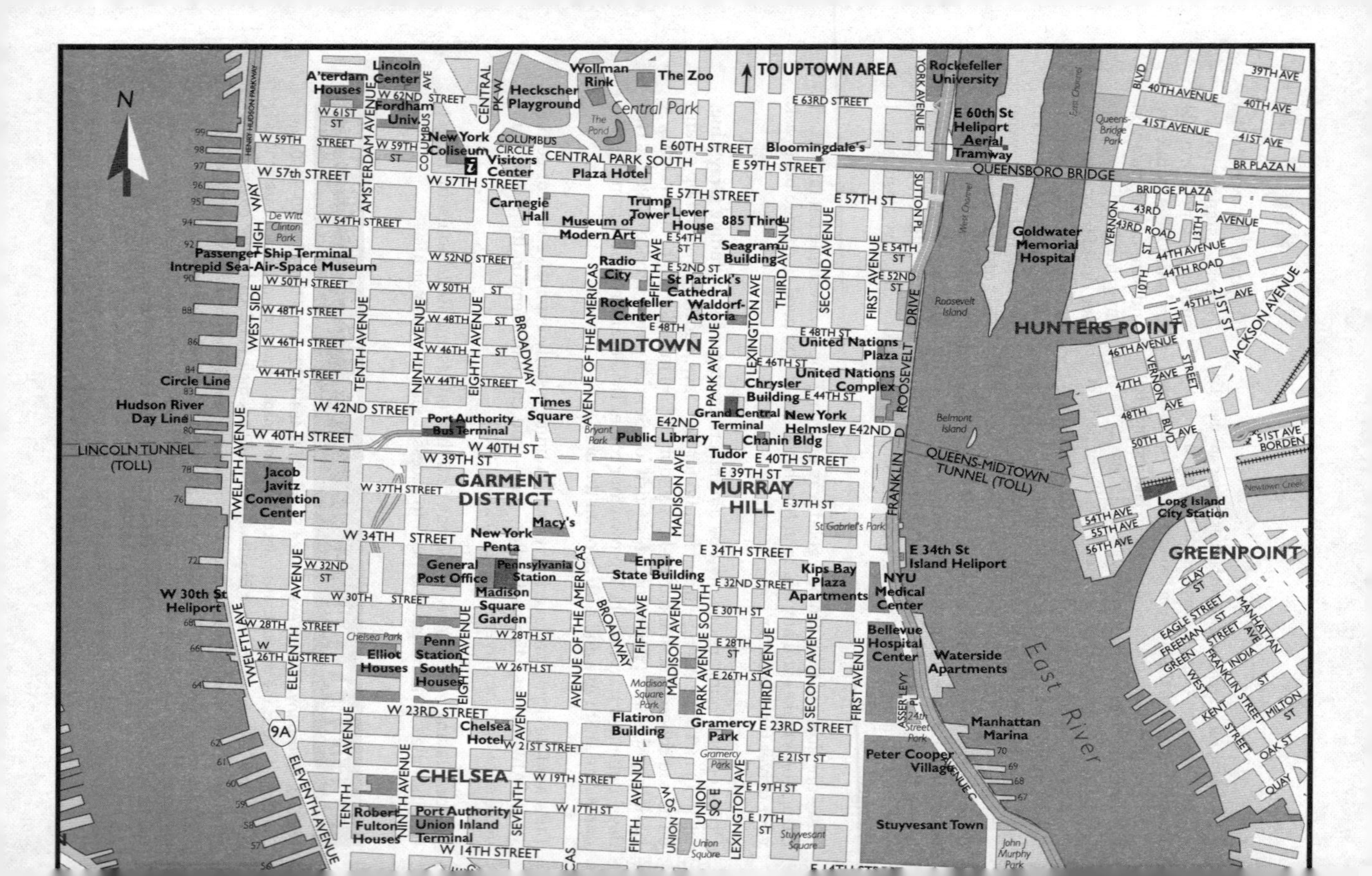

TO UPTOWN AREA
N
Lincoln Center
A'terdam Houses
Fordham Univ.
New York Coliseum
Visitors Center
Wollman Rink
Heckscher Playground
The Zoo
Central Park
The Pond
COLUMBUS CIRCLE
CENTRAL PARK SOUTH
Plaza Hotel
Bloomingdale's
Rockefeller University
E 60th St Heliport
Aerial Tramway
QUEENSBORO BRIDGE
Queens-Bridge Park
Carnegie Hall
Museum of Modern Art
Trump Tower
Lever House
885 Third
Seagram Building
Radio City
St Patrick's Cathedral
Rockefeller Center
Waldorf-Astoria
MIDTOWN
United Nations Plaza
United Nations Complex
Chrysler Building
Grand Central Terminal
New York Helmsley
Chanin Bldg
Tudor
Public Library
Bryant Park
Times Square
Port Authority Bus Terminal
Passenger Ship Terminal
Intrepid Sea-Air-Space Museum
De Witt Clinton Park
Circle Line
Hudson River Day Line
LINCOLN TUNNEL (TOLL)
Jacob Javitz Convention Center
GARMENT DISTRICT
MURRAY HILL
Macy's
New York Penta
General Post Office
Pennsylvania Station
Madison Square Garden
Empire State Building
Kips Bay Plaza Apartments
NYU Medical Center
E 34th St Island Heliport
St Gabriel's Park
W 30th St Heliport
Chelsea Park
Elliot Houses
Penn Station South Houses
Chelsea Hotel
CHELSEA
Robert Fulton Houses
Port Authority Union Inland Terminal
Flatiron Building
Madison Square Park
Gramercy Park
Union Square
Stuyvesant Square
Bellevue Hospital Center
Waterside Apartments
Manhattan Marina
Peter Cooper Village
Stuyvesant Town
John J Murphy Park
Goldwater Memorial Hospital
Roosevelt Island
Belmont Island
West Channel
East Channel
QUEENS-MIDTOWN TUNNEL (TOLL)
HUNTERS POINT
Long Island City Station
GREENPOINT
Newtown Creek
East River
FRANKLIN D ROOSEVELT DRIVE
YORK AVENUE
SUTTON PL
FIRST AVENUE
SECOND AVENUE
THIRD AVENUE
LEXINGTON AVE
PARK AVENUE
PARK AVENUE SOUTH
MADISON AVE
FIFTH AVE
AVENUE OF THE AMERICAS
BROADWAY
SEVENTH AVENUE
EIGHTH AVENUE
NINTH AVENUE
TENTH AVENUE
AMSTERDAM AVENUE
COLUMBUS AVE
ELEVENTH AVENUE
TWELFTH AVENUE
WEST SIDE HIGHWAY
HENRY HUDSON PARKWAY
9A
E 63RD STREET
E 60TH STREET
E 59TH STREET
E 57TH STREET
E 57TH ST
W 57th STREET
W 57TH STREET
W 59TH STREET
W 62ND STREET
W 61ST ST
W 54TH STREET
W 52ND STREET
W 50TH STREET
W 48TH STREET
W 46TH STREET
W 44TH STREET
W 42ND STREET
W 40TH STREET
W 40TH ST
W 39TH ST
W 37TH STREET
W 34TH STREET
W 32ND ST
W 30TH STREET
W 28TH STREET
W 26TH STREET
W 28TH ST
W 26TH ST
W 23RD STREET
W 21ST STREET
W 19TH STREET
W 17TH ST
W 14TH STREET
E 54TH ST
E 52ND ST
E 48TH ST
E 46TH ST
E 44TH ST
E42ND
E 40TH STREET
E 39TH ST
E 37TH ST
E 34TH STREET
E 32ND STREET
E 30TH ST
E 28TH ST
E 26TH ST
E 23RD STREET
E 21ST ST
E 19TH ST
E 17TH ST
UNION SQ W
UNION SQ E
ASSER LEVY PL
24th Street Park
AVENUE C
VERNON BLVD
JACKSON AVENUE
21ST ST
BRIDGE PLAZA
BR PLAZA N
39TH AVE
40TH AVENUE
40TH AVE
41ST AVENUE
41ST AVE
43RD
43RD ROAD
44TH AVENUE
44TH ROAD
45TH AVE
46TH AVENUE
47TH AVE
48TH AVE
50TH AVE
54TH AVE
55TH AVE
56TH AVE
51ST AVE BORDEN
CLAY ST
EAGLE STREET
FREEMAN ST
GREEN STREET
WEST STREET
FRANKLIN STREET
MANHATTAN AVE
INDIA ST
KENT STREET
MILTON ST
OAK ST
QUAY

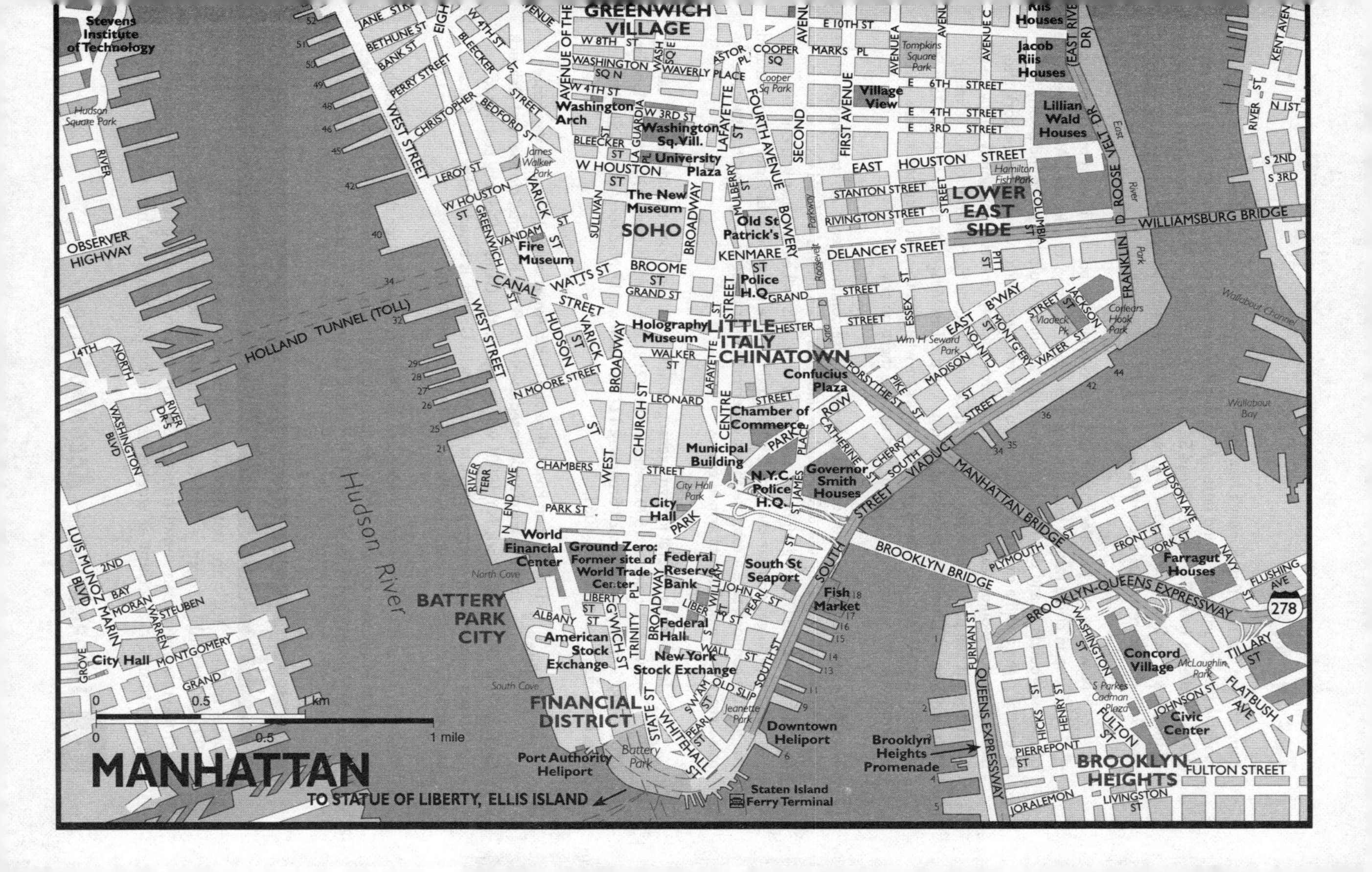

MANHATTAN
TO STATUE OF LIBERTY, ELLIS ISLAND
0
0.5
1 km
1 mile
GREENWICH VILLAGE
SOHO
LITTLE ITALY
CHINATOWN
LOWER EAST SIDE
FINANCIAL DISTRICT
BATTERY PARK CITY
BROOKLYN HEIGHTS
Hudson River
East River
Wallabout Channel
Wallabout Bay
North Cove
South Cove
Stevens Institute of Technology
Hudson Square Park
City Hall
Washington Arch
Washington Sq.Vill.
University Plaza
The New Museum
Fire Museum
Holography Museum
Old St Patrick's
Police H.Q.
Confucius Plaza
Chamber of Commerce
Municipal Building
N.Y.C. Police H.Q.
Governor Smith Houses
City Hall Park
World Financial Center
Ground Zero: Former site of World Trade Center
Federal Reserve Bank
Federal Hall
New York Stock Exchange
American Stock Exchange
South St Seaport
Fish Market
Downtown Heliport
Port Authority Heliport
Battery Park
Jeanette Park
Staten Island Ferry Terminal
Brooklyn Heights Promenade
Village View
Tompkins Square Park
Cooper Sq Park
Riis Houses
Jacob Riis Houses
Lillian Wald Houses
Hamilton Fish Park
Wm H Seward Park
Vladeck Pk
Corlears Hook Park
James Walker Park
Farragut Houses
Concord Village
McLaughlin Park
Civic Center
S Parkes Cadman Plaza
HOLLAND TUNNEL (TOLL)
WILLIAMSBURG BRIDGE
MANHATTAN BRIDGE
BROOKLYN BRIDGE
BROOKLYN-QUEENS EXPRESSWAY
QUEENS EXPRESSWAY
FRANKLIN D ROOSEVELT DR
(EAST RIVER DR)
OBSERVER HIGHWAY
WEST STREET
SOUTH STREET
SOUTH STREET VIADUCT
278

copy of *Time Out New York*, Sunday's *New York Times* or *Where New York*, a free monthly magazine available from tourist offices and hotels. Also visit www.nycvisit.com. In Lower Manhattan, visit the **Downtown Info Center**, 25 Broad St; open Mon–Fri 1100–1900. Situated one block south of the New York Stock Exchange, it is a key resource for maps, brochures, events schedules and even 9/11-related reconstruction updates.

SAFETY New York is a lot safer than it was – 'zero tolerance' policing has led to a dramatic drop in crime rates – but as in any large city it still pays to take care. Always be aware of your surroundings and don't look too much like a tourist. Avoid the parks and poorly lit streets at night, and if a situation is starting to feel tense, just walk away. Treat New York after dark just as you would treat London or Paris, avoiding lonely streets or obviously seedy neighbourhoods. It still pays to be wary at night of: Central Park; the Port Authority Bus Terminal; Midtown west of Times Square; east of Avenue A in the East Village; Harlem north of 125th St and the Financial District. A good general rule, as anywhere, is to shun deserted streets unless you know exactly where you are going and can get there quickly.

It is safe to use the subway after dark so long as you use common sense. At stations, stay in the 'Off Hour Waiting Area' by the ticket window until your train arrives or head for the section on the platform marked 'During off hours train stops here': this will ensure that you can be seen and also that you get on near the centre of the train, where the conductor's carriage is situated. For greater comfort, take a cab. The threat of terrorism has made subways and transport terminals safer, with the addition of armed guards.

MONEY Travelex has several foreign exchange offices which are open outside normal banking hours. The office at 1590 Broadway, tel: (212) 265-6063, is open 0900–1900 Mon–Sat, 0900–1700 Sun. Others are at 29 Broadway, 1271 Broadway, 317 Madison Ave and 511 Madison Ave. For details, tel: (212) 265-6063.

POST AND PHONES The General Post Office at 421 8th Ave is open 24 hours a day. Poste restante letters addressed to Name, Poste Restante, c/o General Delivery, General Post Office, New York, NY 10001 will be kept at the General Delivery counter for 10–30 days. The Bowling Green Station, in the Financial District, is based in the 1921 Cunard building at 25 Broadway; open Mon–Fri 0800–1800, Sat 0800–1300.

New York has two telephone area codes, 212 for Manhattan and 718 for the outer boroughs. For calls within Manhattan, omit the area code and simply dial the final seven digits of the number. When using a public phone, deposit $0.25 for a local call and have a stack of further quarters ready.

ACCOMMODATION

Hotels in New York are notoriously expensive – even 'budget' hotels charge over $100 for a double room – and to make matters worse, the rates quoted usually exclude taxes. You can sometimes get the cost down by asking for the 'corporate rate' or negotiating a discount at weekends, but the fact remains that accommodation is going to eat up a sizeable chunk of your budget in New York. If you are flexible about where you stay, you could try calling one of the discount agencies who book up rooms in advance and can usually offer a discount of 20 per cent or more. Two of the biggest are **Take Time to Travel**, tel: (212) 840-8686; fax: (212) 221-8686; and **Hotel Reservations Network**, tel: (214) 361-7311; fax: (214) 361-7299; reservations (800) 964-6835. For a list of hotels, with contact information, visit www.nycvisit.com.

If you don't mind sleeping in a dorm it will work out a lot cheaper to stay in one of the city's hostels. Another option is bed and breakfast in a private apartment, usually shared with the host. For a completely different experience, **Homestay New York** offers accommodation with Brooklyn families from about $90 for a double room including dinner, breakfast and a MetroCard. Tel/fax: (718) 434-2071.

DOWNTOWN (BELOW 14TH ST)

Larchmont $$$–$$$$ 27 W 11th St; tel: (212) 989-9333; fax: (212) 989-9496; www.larchmonthotels.citysearch.com. Small, arty boutique hotel on a tree-lined street in Greenwich Village.

Off SoHo Suites $$$–$$$$ 11 Rivington St; tel: (212) 979-9808; fax: (212) 979-9801; www.offsoho.com. Smart new apartment suites with kitchen and bathroom for two to four people. The Lower East Side location is good for bars and clubbing, but can get a little dodgy at night.

Washington Square Hotel $$$$ 103 Waverley Pl.; tel: (212) 777-9515; fax: (212) 979-8373; www.wshotel.com. The location is everything at this old-fashioned hotel, where both Bob Dylan and Joan Baez stayed while busking in Washington Square. A bonus is the free breakfast.

MIDTOWN (14TH ST TO CENTRAL PARK)

Gershwin $$$–$$$$ 7 E 27th St; tel: (212) 545-8000; fax: (212) 684-5546; www.gershwinhotel.com. Bohemian hotel with pop art on the walls and some private rooms with baths. The rooftop terrace is good for parties.

Herald Square Hotel $$$–$$$$ 19 W 31st St; tel: (212) 279-4017; fax: (212) 643-9208; www.heraldsquarehotel.com. Clean, basic, budget hotel in the original *Life* magazine building.

Hotel 17 $$$–$$$$ 225 E 17th St; tel: (212) 475-2845; fax: (212) 677-8178; www.hotel17ny.com. Super-hip and slightly seedy establishment where Madonna posed in her knickers for *Details* magazine. In the swanky Gramercy Park vicinity.

Hotel 31 $$$–$$$$ 120 E 31st St; tel: (212) 685-3060; fax: (212) 532-1232; www.hotel31.com. The sister establishment of Hotel 17; Murray Hill location.

Wolcott $$$–$$$$ 4 W 31st St; tel: (212) 268-2900; fax: (212) 563-0096; www.wolcott.com. Popular budget hotel near the Empire State Building.

Chelsea Hotel $$$–$$$$ 222 W 23rd St; tel: (212) 243-3700; fax: (212) 675-5531; www.chelseahotel.com. This Edwardian-era national landmark with florid cast-iron balconies and art-filled lobby dates from 1884 was the hangout of Dylan Thomas, Brendan Behan, Thomas Wolfe, Eugene O'Neill, Tennessee Williams, Bob Dylan, Andy Warhol and Sid Vicious. Living here, playwright Arthur Miller wrote *Death of a Salesman*, *The Crucible* and *A View from the Bridge*.

Comfort Inn Manhattan $$$$ 42 W 35th St; tel: (212) 947-0200; fax: (212) 594-3047; www.choicehotels.com/hotel/ny410. Small, family-oriented hotel close to Macy's and the Empire State Building. The free continental breakfast adds to the value.

Gramercy Park Hotel $$$$ 2 Lexington Ave; tel: (212) 475-4320; fax: (212) 505-0535; www.gramercyparkhotel.com. Old-fashioned European style in a quiet area of Manhattan. Guests receive a key to the private park in the square.

Pickwick Arms $$$$ 230 E 51st St; tel: (212) 355-0300; fax: (212) 755-5029. Clean and comfortable Eastside hotel with good views from the rooftop garden.

The Sherry-Netherland $$$$ 781 Fifth Ave at 59th St: tel: (212) 355-2800, (800) 247-4377; fax: (212) 319-4306; www.sherrynetherland.com. In the heart of Midtown on Central Park, this architectural landmark has been the haunt of everyone from Ernest Hemingway to David Bowie. It's definitely a splurge, but what a way to spend it! Summer weekend specials bring rates down a notch.

Uptown (Above 59th St)

Beacon $$$$ 2130 Broadway; tel: (212) 787-1100; fax: (212) 787-1100; www.beaconhotel.com. Friendly hotel in a lively Upper West Side district, close to Central Park and Zabar's deli.

Excelsior $$$$ 45 W 81st St; tel: (212) 362-9200; fax: (212) 721-2994; www.excelsiorhotelny.com. The suites are good value for families at this cosy Upper West Side hotel, where the rooms are decorated in art deco style.

Hostels

Chelsea Center $$ 313 W 29th St; tel: (212) 643-0214; fax: (212) 473-3945; www.chelseacenterhostel.com. A small, friendly hostel with dorm beds and garden courtyard. Breakfast included.

Chelsea International Hostel $$–$$$ 251 W 20th St; tel: (212) 647-0010; fax: (212) 727-7289; www.chelseahostel.com. This good-value hostel also has a few smaller rooms that come with private baths.

Hostelling International New York $$–$$$ 891 Amsterdam Ave; tel: (212) 932-2300; fax: (212) 932-2574; www.hiayh.org. The most popular budget place, with 500 beds in dormitories. Upper West Side near Columbia University. Discounts at nearby dining.

YMCA Vanderbilt $$$–$$$$ 224 E 47th St; tel: (212) 756-9600; fax: (212) 752-0210; www.ymcanyc.org. Somewhere between a hostel and a hotel, the Y has single and double rooms, some with bath, as well as a swimming pool.

YMCA Westside $$$–$$$$ 5 W 63rd St; tel: (212) 875-4100; fax: (212) 875-1334; www.ymcanyc.org. The larger of the two Ys is situated close to Central Park.

Bed & Breakfast Agencies

The following offer rooms in both hosted and unhosted apartments, in the $$$–$$$$ price range.

Bed & Breakfast (& Books): tel/fax: (212) 865-8740 during office hours.

City Lights Bed & Breakfast: tel: (212) 737-7049; fax: (212) 535-2755.

New World Bed & Breakfast: tel: (212) 675-5600; fax: (212) 675-5600 or (800) 443-3800.

Also try the websites www.bbonline.com/ny and www.yahoo.com, New York City link, lodgings.

FOOD AND DRINK

Generations of foreign immigrants have brought their cuisines to New York and it is easy to try a different style of cooking each day. Chinese, Italian and Moroccan are all popular and good value; the more adventurous can seek out Brazilian, Russian and Colombian cuisine. If you're looking for something authentically New York, the best bet is one of the delis which serve essentially Jewish food, such as doorstop-sized pastrami sandwiches with pickles on the side. Another symbol of New York is a toasted bagel spread with cream cheese and lox (smoked salmon).

Some of New York's restaurants may leave a severe dent in your credit card limit, but it is perfectly possible to eat both cheaply and well. Pushcarts on every street corner sell bagels, pretzels and the ubiquitous hot dogs. Look out, too, for diners, serving huge portions of pea soup, burgers and fries in unpretentious surroundings; fill up on a diner breakfast and you won't need to eat again all day. Chinatown is full of cheap Asian eateries where a bowl of rice noodles will set you back less than $5. Other good hunting grounds for inexpensive food include Little India (centred on E 6th St between 1st and 2nd Aves), Harlem and Greenwich Village.

For picnic food, pick up a sandwich to go and a ready-made salad from one of Manhattan's high-class delicatessens. The best of these, like Balducci's in Greenwich Village (424 6th Ave) and Zabar's on the Upper West Side (2245 Broadway), have mouthwatering displays of breads, cheeses, fresh pasta and ready-to-eat dishes. New Yorkers use them when they are giving a dinner party at home; it's worth wandering in just to look around, but snack food in these places isn't cheap.

FINANCIAL DISTRICT

Café World $ 50 Trinity Pl; tel: (212) 269-4355. A typical deli just three blocks from Wall St.

McDonald's $$ 160 Broadway; tel: (212) 385-2063. This McDonald's has doormen, waiter service, a Wall St trading bulletin and a piano.

GREENWICH VILLAGE

Moustache Pitza $$ 90 Bedford St; tel: (212) 229-2220. Funky Middle Eastern specials like Lebanese salads and pitta-based 'pitzas'.

Pink Teacup $$ 42 Grove St; tel: (212) 807-6755. A long-time Village favourite, serving Southern soul food and a huge weekend brunch.

Tea and Sympathy $$ 108 Greenwich Ave; tel: (212) 807-8829. Quaint Cockney café serving comfort food like sherry trifle and scones.

Knickerbocker Bar & Grill $$–$$$ 33 University Pl.; tel: (212) 228-8490. Old-time West Village steak house. Popular for celebrity-watching, famous for New York-style cheesecake. Live music Fri–Sat.

Casa $$$ 72 Bedford St; tel: (212) 366-9410. Home-style Brazilian cuisine – the house special is *feijoada*, a casserole of chorizo, bacon, black beans and salted beef.

THE NORTHEAST

CHINATOWN AND LOWER EAST SIDE

Bo Ky $ 80 Bayard St; tel: (212) 406-2292. One of several restaurants in Chinatown offering filling rice and noodle dishes. Always packed out at lunchtime.

Katz's Deli $$ 205 E Houston St; tel: (212) 254-2246. Presidents and film stars visit this legendary deli, seen in *When Harry Met Sally*.

Lombardi's $$ 32 Spring St; tel: (212) 941-7994. NY's original pizza parlour, on the edge of Little Italy. Look for other Italian restaurants along Mulberry St.

McSorley's Old Ale House $$ 15 E 7th St; tel: (212) 473-9148. New York's oldest pub (circa 1854), serves snacks and home-brewed beer.

Veselka $$ 144 Second Ave; tel: (212) 228-9682. Noisy, comfortable café serving pirogi (wild mushroom is superior) and other Ukrainian and Polish favourites.

Café Charbon $$–$$$ 168 Orchard (at Stanton); tel: (212) 420-7520. Lower East Side bistro which may look pretentious, but is lively with DJ music and superb food. Cash only.

MIDTOWN

Empire Diner $$–$$$ 210 10th Ave; tel: (212) 924-0011. Meet a cross-section of the city in this classic chrome-and-steel 24-hour diner.

Pete's Tavern $$–$$$ 129 E 18th St; tel: (212) 473-7676. Pub grub and home-brewed beer in a 19th-century inn.

Carnegie Deli $$$ 854 7th Ave; tel: (212) 757-2245. Legendary for queues and skyscraper-sized sandwiches; near Central Park.

Café Fonduta $ 120 E 57th St (nr Madison Ave); tel: (212) 935-5699. A tiny eatery for hearty pasta dishes and pizza, at scant tables or to take away.

Grand Café $ 230 Park Ave (45th St); tel: (212) 883-6769. Tucked into a passageway corner, with a few tables and take-away. Full-meal sandwiches, filling $3 breakfasts, no NY attitude.

Grand Central Oyster Bar $$$ Grand Central Terminal, 42nd St; tel: (212) 490-6650. Seafood and oysters beneath the railway station concourse with a cheap lunchtime counter as well as more formal dining.

BELLINIS AT GRAND CENTRAL

Try a Bellini cocktail (dry sparkling prosecco wine and white peach juice) on the balcony of Cipriani Dolci at Grand Central Terminal, $$. It's a treat!

UPTOWN

Tom's $ 2880 Broadway at 112th St; tel: (212) 864-6137. Greasy-spoon diner popular with students and for its role in the *Seinfeld* TV series.

Drip $$ 489 Amsterdam Ave; tel: (212) 875-1032. A coffee bar/dating agency that's a hot venue in the West Side singles scene.

Londel's Supper Club $$$ 2620 Frederick Douglass Blvd; tel: (212) 234-6114. Trendy Harlem restaurant and jazz club serving a modern version of soul food.

Sylvia's $$$ 328 Lenox Ave; tel: (212) 996-0660. The original Harlem soul food restaurant, popular with locals and tourists, offers up giant portions of fried chicken and sweet potato pie.

Café Pierre $$$$ Pierre Hotel, 2 E 61st St; tel: (212) 940-8185. *The* place to take afternoon tea, in an art deco rotunda with painted murals. Not cheap, but worth doing once.

Tavern on the Green $$$$ Central Park at West 67th St; tel: (212) 873-3200. Over-the-top decor and a Central Park setting make this a favourite with anyone out to impress a date. Amazingly, it serves more meals than any other restaurant in the USA.

BROOKLYN

Grimaldi's $$–$$$ 19 Old Fulton St; tel: (718) 858-4300. If you've trekked over the Brooklyn Bridge, it's worth queuing for some of the best brick-oven pizza in New York at this waterfront hideaway beneath the bridge.

Peter Luger Steak House $$$$ 178 Broadway, Brooklyn; tel: (718) 387-7400. A Brooklyn institution, serving, many say, the best steaks in NYC. The porterhouse is charred outside, pink inside, best served with hash brown potatoes. Booking advised.

HIGHLIGHTS

When Frank Sinatra sang 'New York, New York', he was not just getting carried away with the name – New York, New York is the official name for Manhattan. To most people, New York *is* Manhattan and this is where you will inevitably spend most of your time, though a day in one of the outer boroughs – Brooklyn, the Bronx, Queens or Staten Island – will show you a very different side to the city. In fact, there is no better place to start than by leaving Manhattan to walk over **Brooklyn Bridge**. This was the world's longest suspension bridge when it opened in 1883 and it continues to provide one of the most iconic images of New York. John Travolta danced over it, Hart Crane immortalised it in poetry and numerous New Yorkers have leapt from it to their deaths. The views back to Manhattan, through a tangle of cables and a neo-Gothic archway, are spectacular.

For more views, stroll to **Brooklyn Heights Promenade**, from where Manhattan appears as a forest of steel and glass, vividly reflected in the East River. The view is especially attractive at sunset and early evening, when the lights glimmer across the river.

New York City's skyline was changed forever on 11 September 2001, when the twin towers of the World Trade Center (WTC) were attacked from the air by Islamic terrorists and collapsed. Yet some features remain the same: indeed, the Empire State Building

BOAT TOURS

A Circle Line boat tour around Manhattan is a great way to get your bearings and see the skyline from every angle. Full island cruises, lasting 3 hrs, depart Mar–Oct from Pier 83 at the Hudson River end of W 42nd St; $$$$. A 2-hr cruise ($$$) around the southern half of Manhattan operates year round; there are also sunset cruises in summer. For bookings and timetable, tel: (212) 563-3200; www.circleline.com. If you don't want to fork out for a cruise, take the free Staten Island Ferry instead.

and the Chrysler Building have regained their position of dominance as landmark features of New York's architecture.

Ground Zero, as the site of the former WTC is called, now looks forward to a new phoenix rising from its ashes. In February 2003 the *Freedom Tower* design by architect Daniel Libeskind was selected out of over 400 designs from around the world to revitalise the site, both a memorial and a symbol of new hope. It will preserve some visible remains of the tragedy – parts of the slurry wall – and will incorporate a September 11 memorial and museum in what is being called the 'bathtub' area of the site. Reaching for the sky will be a brand new 1776-ft-high spire, way taller than the other new buildings to rise on the site, providing an exciting new feature on the Manhattan skyline. Note that heavy security prevails in the immediate vicinity of the New York Stock Exchange at the Wall St/Broad St intersection. There are ongoing amendments to the subway routes in the area and visitors should be prepared for changes as construction progresses.

The area surrounding Ground Zero is also making a strong comeback and some notable attractions are open to visitors. **Trinity Church**, located on Broadway at the head of Wall St, reopened to visitors in February 2002. This church was the tallest building in New York at the time of its construction in the early 18th century. **St Paul's Chapel,** a 1776 landmark close to Trinity Church, located between Fulton and Vesey Sts, has a moving exhibit that shows the work of the chapel as a place of refuge for workers at the World Trade Center site; open Mon–Sat 1000–1800, Sun 1000–1600. The **New York Stock Exchange** is open on a limited basis to visitors (check www.nyse.com for times). The **Federal Reserve Bank**, 33 Liberty St, is open for tours daily.

DOWNTOWN **Battery Park**, at the southern tip of Manhattan, is the departure point for the **Staten Island Ferry**, one of the most romantic experiences in New York. The ferry (free) runs 24 hrs a day and is probably best at night with the lights of Manhattan twinkling in the distance. Boat trips to Ellis Island and the Statue of Liberty also leave from Battery Park. **Ellis Island** was New York's immigration centre from 1892 to 1924, when more than 12 million newcomers from many countries passed through its doors. It is now a museum of immigration, telling the moving story of some of those who arrived – the names included Bob Hope, Irving Berlin and Golda Meir – and those who were turned away. Sailing through New York Harbor, all of them would have seen the massive female figure of the **Statue of Liberty**, with a shining torch in her hand and broken shackles at her feet. More than a century later, the statue remains a powerful and slightly kitschy symbol of 'the land of the free'. Most people content themselves with a close-up look from the boat, especially as access to the statue has been limited since 9/11. Guided tours now operate to some parts of the monument for which a timed pass is required (www.statuereservations.com), but wandering the grounds of Liberty Island is free with no booking is required. Admission to Ellis Island and the Statue of Liberty is included in the cost of the boat trip ($$, see www.statueofliberty.org.)

The **Skyscraper Museum**, 39 Battery Place, tel: (212) 968-1961, www.skyscrapermuseum.org, is in Battery Park at the southernmost tip of Manhattan island. Focused on Manhattan, the 'vertical city' – history, development and design of high-rise buildings during the 20th/21st centuries. Open Wed–Sun 1200–1800, $.

CITYPASS

If you're planning to visit most of the major sights, get hold of a City Pass which can save you 50 per cent on admission as well as cut down on queuing times. The pass is valid for nine days and gives entry to the Empire State Building, Metropolitan Museum, Museum of Modern Art, American Museum of Natural History and Intrepid Sea Air Space Museum. You can buy it at any of these sights.

North of the Financial District, the skyscrapers gradually disappear and give way to a succession of small neighbourhoods. **SoHo** (the name means South of Houston St) is a centre of the New York art scene, where vacant loft spaces and cast-iron factory buildings have been turned into trendy avant-garde exhibition spaces. Saturday morning is the best time for gallery hopping here. Nearby **Greenwich Village** (east and west), with its ivy-covered mews cottages and tree-lined streets, has long been popular with writers, bohemians and the gay community. **Washington Square**, in the West Village, is a great place for people-watching, with buskers, rollerbladers, dog-walkers and open-air chess matches.

Across town, the USA's largest **Chinatown** is slowly taking over the **Lower East Side**, traditionally the first port of call for European immigrants. This area has a strong Jewish flavour, with kosher bakeries and shops selling religious items, but these days many of the residents are Hispanic and the area is becoming known as Loisaida. North of here, the **East Village** is grungy and ultra-hip, with funky clothes shops, alternative theatres and an edginess rarely seen elsewhere.

MIDTOWN Above 14th St, the grid pattern takes over as you move into **Midtown**, the quintessential Manhattan of crowded sidewalks, speeding yellow taxis and long, straight avenues hemmed in by skyscrapers. This is where the noise never seems to stop and the sheer energy of Manhattan hits you in the face. At the centre of all this activity is **Times Square**, the neon-lit crossroads at the heart of the Broadway theatre district. Once a seedy haunt of pushers and pickpockets, Times Square has been cleaned up in recent years as a model of the new, tourist-friendly image which the city has been able to promote. The theme stores have moved in, the hookers have moved away and many New Yorkers complain that Times Square is losing its soul.

Pick up a free leaflet in the lobby of the GE Building (570 Lexington Ave) for a self-guided tour through some of New York's best art deco art and 'moderne' architectural areas.

The Midtown skyline is dominated by two buildings, each of which was once the tallest in the world – the gleaming art deco spire of the **Chrysler Building** and the elegant **Empire State Building**, Fifth Ave at 34th St,

WALKING TOURS

Look in the *Weekend* section of Friday's *New York Times* for details of weekend walks. The **Municipal Art Society**, tel: (212) 439-1049, has a number of interesting tours with an emphasis on the architecture of different neighbourhoods. Walking tours that delve into Harlem's Afro-Hispanic social history are organised by **Harlem Spiritual Gospel Jazz Tours**, tel: (212) 391-0900, **Braggin' About Brooklyn**, tel: (718) 297-5107, and **Brooklyn Attitude**, tel: (718) 398-0939. Ask at the Belvedere Castle visitor centre in Central Park about guided nature walks in the park. See also For Free, p. 89.

observation deck ($$) open daily 0930–2400. To either side of the Chrysler Building are two more structures which in their different ways represent aspects of New York. **Grand Central Terminal** was once the gateway to the nation, the romantic railway station from which passengers would board the *Twentieth Century* to Chicago each evening. After falling into disrepair, it has been thoroughly restored and now conjures up the glory days of the 1930s once again. Nearby, beside the East River, is the complex of buildings which make up the headquarters of the **United Nations**. Tours run every half hour, $$, 0915–1645 daily; under 5s not admitted.

Fifth Avenue is the pulse of Midtown and the most famous shopping street in America. Starting at 49th St and continuing to Central Park, its ten blocks epitomise a consumer paradise where upmarket department stores mix with designer boutiques, jewellers and theme stores devoted to sports and Mickey Mouse. Don't miss Trump Tower, a spectacularly over-the-top shopping mall built by the property tycoon Donald Trump on the corner of 57th St – the street where many of New York's most exclusive designers have their shops. Also on Fifth Ave, facing **St Patrick's Cathedral**, is the **Rockefeller Center**, a 'city within a city' built by billionaire financier John D Rockefeller Jr in the 1930s.

At Columbus Circle on Central Park's south-west corner, the new mega-big high-rise multi-use TimeWarner Center includes CNN's New York broadcasting operation, with studio tours ($) available. For details: www.cnn.com/insidecnn.

The **Museum of Modern Art**, at 11 W 53rd St, has one of the best collections of 20th-century paintings anywhere, with works by Picasso, Matisse, Dalí, Monet and Warhol. Following a multi-million-dollar expansion project, MoMa is now double its original size, dominated by a six-storey gallery building designed by Yoshio Taniguchi; augmented by the enlarged Abby Aldrich Rockefeller sculpture garden. The winter 2004–2005 reopening celebrates the museum's 75th anniversary. Open Thur–Tues 1030–1800 (Fri to 2030); $$, children free; free entry Fri after 1630.

If you don't mind breaking the bank, or can share the experience with three others, you can take a horse-drawn carriage ride around Central Park. The starting point is from outside the Plaza Hotel on 59th St and the rate should be negotiated with the driver in advance. It's a little schmaltzy, but still a magical experience, especially at night.

AERIAL EXPERIENCE

If a real helicopter ride is beyond your budget, you could always try the simulated helicopter flight inside the Empire State Building instead. For another cheaper thrill, take the cable car across the East River from E 60th St to Roosevelt Island.

There are more museums along Museum Mile, the stretch of Fifth Ave which borders Central Park. Must-sees include the **Frick Collection** ($$, 1 E 70th St; open Tues–Sat 1000–1800, Sun 1300–1800; under 10s not admitted), a collection of European Old Masters in the mansion of a 19th-century industrialist; and the **Guggenheim Museum** (1071 5th Avenue at 89th; open Sun–Wed 0900–1800, Fri–Sat 0900–2000; $$, children free and free entry after 1800 Fri), where modern art is displayed inside a spiral white building by Frank Lloyd Wright which critics have described as 'an inverted oatmeal dish'. The single most important museum, however, is the **Metropolitan Museum of Art** (1000 Fifth Ave at 82nd St). The collections include everything from an ancient Egyptian temple to a Chinese scholar's garden and a series of American period rooms, plus 30 galleries of Old Masters and another 20 devoted to 19th-century European art – you could easily spend two days here and still not have seen it all. Open Tues–Thur and Sun 0930–1730, Fri–Sat 0930–2100; $$, children free.

UPTOWN **Central Park** (www.centralpark.org) is Manhattan's green lung, where New Yorkers come to let off steam, walk, jog, rollerskate, picnic, row boats, take carriage rides and fall in love. Parts of it, like the wooded area known as the Ramble (popular with

NEW YORK ON TWO WHEELS

To visit ethnic neighbourhoods, scenic viewpoints and historic sites few tourists see, join a tour with **Tours by Bike**; tel: (201) 941-0100; www.toursbybike.com. Bicycle trips use paved cycle paths and streets in low-traffic areas, in the city and surrounding countryside.

FOR FREE

Stroll through the quiet streets of Greenwich Village, beside the Hudson River and up to Central Park, where numerous free events are held throughout the summer. Get there before 1300 to queue for free tickets for **Shakespeare in the Park**, a summer festival which often attracts big-name actors. Look out too for free concerts in the plaza of the Lincoln Center (Broadway and 64th St), New York's premier performance venue.

Take advantage of 'pay-what-you-wish' evenings at several of New York's museums, including the Museum of Modern Art and the Guggenheim Museum (both Fri) and the Whitney Museum of American Art (945 Madison Ave; free Thur after 1800). The **National Museum of the American Indian**, at 1 Bowling Green in down-town Manhattan is free; open 1000–1700 daily (Thur until 2000). This is just a short walk from the New York Stock Exchange, where entry to the viewing gallery is also free (see p. 86).

Kids and techno-freaks will enjoy **Sony Wonder Technology Lab**, a free interactive museum of technology.

For Free cont.

Madison Ave and 56th St; open Tues–Sat 1000–1800 (Thur until 2000), Sun 1200–1800.

Free **walking tours** leave from the Fifth Ave entrance of the Empire State Building (Thur at 1230; 1½ hours) and from the Whitney Museum at Philip Morris, 42nd St at Park Ave (Fri at 1230; 1½ hours).

The best bargain in New York is a walk around one of the city's neighbourhoods with a volunteer 'greeter' specially chosen to match your interests. The service is free and tips are not accepted. Call **Big Apple Greeter**, tel: (212) 669-8159, www.bigapplegreeter.org, about a week before your visit to fix things up.

Visit www.nycvisit.com, clicking 'Visitors' and 'Things to Do' for many more free activities.

birdwatchers), are still virtual wilderness, but on a summer Sunday other parts can be as crowded as Times Square. Children take rides on a vintage carousel, storytelling takes place beside Conservatory Water, and there is even a small zoo with snow monkeys and polar bears. Look out for free events in summer, which include performances by the Metropolitan Opera and Shakespeare in the Park.

At Columbus Circle on the park's southwestern edge, new high-rise, multi-use **Time Warner Center** includes international CNN broadcasting operation, with studio tours ($) available. For details: www.cnn.com/insidecnn.

Beatles fans will want to pay respects at **Strawberry Fields**, the garden memorial to John Lennon, located in Central Park. Enter from Central Park West at 72nd St, opposite the Dakota Building, his home and the site of his murder.

Across the park, the **American Museum of Natural History** has a world-class collection of dinosaur skeletons as well as dioramas featuring African, Asian and American mammals in their natural habitats. The giant-screen IMAX® theatre shows wildlife films, and a new Earth and Space Center called the **Rose Center**, including the Hayden planetarium, is now open. $$, open Sun–Thur, Fri–Sat 1000–2045. The museum is situated in the **Upper West Side** (Central Park West and 79th St), a fashionable area with an arty, alternative feel, lots of bookshops and cafés, and streets which seem designed for strolling. **Riverside Park**, overlooking the Hudson River, is quieter than Central Park and leads into Morningside Heights, where you find **Columbia University**, the oldest and most prestigious in New York, as well as the unfinished **Cathedral of St John the Divine**, which should one day be the largest in the New World. The cathedral hosts regular concerts and art exhibitions and is also an outspoken supporter of radical causes – as witnessed by the chapel for AIDS victims on the south side of the nave. In December 2001 a fire broke out in the Cathedral's gift shop. Fortunately, the main sanctuary was spared. Two of the Cathedral's 12 Barberini tapestries were seriously burned and only portions have been saved. The building is once again open for limited concerts and exhibitions.

From here it is a short walk to **Harlem**, an area described by Nelson Mandela as 'the capital of the black world'. Despite its recent history of poverty and race riots,

Harlem does not deserve its fearsome reputation and during the day it makes a pleasant place to stroll, with handsome brownstone houses in elegant tree-lined streets. The streets of Harlem echo with the sounds of black American culture, and nowhere do you feel this more than at the **Apollo Theater** (253 W 125th St), whose Amateur Nights have been the making of performers from Ella Fitzgerald to Michael Jackson and are still the best place to catch the hip-hop and jazz stars of tomorrow.

SHOPPING

People travel halfway around the world just to do their Christmas shopping in New York. The fashion boutiques and posh department stores are spread out along Madison and Fifth Aves, but it can be just as much fun to seek out the wacky, alternative shops in areas like Greenwich Village, the East Village and the Upper West Side. Also worth exploring are Manhattan's fleamarkets, such as the one that takes place in SoHo on the corner of Broadway and Grand St every Saturday and Sunday – a good place to pick up vintage Americana and second-hand clothes. For listings look in Friday's *New York Times*.

Shopping: The Big Ones

Century 21, 22 Cortlandt St. Discount designer store in the Financial District with a huge range of jeans, clothing and shoes.

Macy's, Herald Sq. (Broadway and 34th St). Billed as 'the world's largest store', with ten floors of clothing and household goods.

Virgin Megastore, Times Sq. The world's biggest music store is open late into the night and features a cinema as well as live performances.

Greenmarkets were started in 1976 as a way of bringing city dwellers into contact with farmers, and they are now a great source of organic food, including bread, cakes and snacks as well as fresh produce. They are held weekly at more than 20 sites across the city, but the biggest is at Union Sq. It takes place four times a week (Mon, Wed, Fri, Sat), beginning at around 0800.

New York has some great bookshops. **Barnes & Noble** superstores, like the one on Union Sq., stay open late into the evening, with live music, author readings and trendy cafés which have established a reputation as sophisticated pick-up joints. The **Gotham Book Mart**, 41 W 47th St, is a wonderful old-style bookshop founded in 1920, with new and second-hand books and a heavy literary atmosphere. **Strand**, at 828 Broadway, has 8 miles of new and second-hand books including lots of books about New York. The store sells half-price review copies and has discounts on most new books.

NIGHTLIFE

For comprehensive listings of theatres, cinemas, music and clubs, the best sources are the weekly *Time Out New York* and the radical free newspaper *Village Voice*.

To see a Broadway show, go to the TKTS discount ticket booth in Times Sq. (Mon–Sat 1500–2000, Sun 1100–1900, Wed and Sat 1000–1400 for matinées), which offers reductions of up to 50 per cent on the day of the performance. No credit cards. If you don't mind paying full price plus a booking fee, the ticket desk inside the visitor centre in Times Sq. is helpful. Alternatively, some theatres sell cheap standby tickets immediately before the performance. Visit www.ilovenytheatre.com for discounted tickets to Broadway shows and nearby attractions.

For drama, ballet, opera and concerts, go to the Lincoln Center for the Performing Arts, Broadway, between W 62nd and W 67th Sts; www.lincolncenter.org.

Manhattan's club scene is constantly on the move and the best way to find out what's hot is to pick up a copy of the monthly style magazine *Paper*. Chelsea and Greenwich Village are good for gay clubs and bars.

Some of the biggest names in jazz play the **Blue Note**, 131 W 3rd St, tel: (212) 475-8592, and **Village Vanguard**, 178 7th Ave, tel: (212) 255-4037, both in Greenwich Village, while **SOBs**, 204 Varick St, tel: (212) 243-4940, highlights Brazilian and Afro-Cuban bands. The covers at these places might be steep, but there are smaller bars and clubs all over Greenwich Village where you can hear live jazz and blues. Jerry Rose of **ET Tours**, tel: (212) 875-7019, offers evening tours ($$) of some of the lesser-known jazz clubs. Alternatively, head up to Harlem on a Wednesday, when Amateur Night at the **Apollo Theater**, 253 W 125th St, tel: (212) 531-5300, provides some of the best entertainment in town for around $20.

WHERE NEXT?

From Midtown, cross the Hudson River to New Jersey aboard an NY Waterway ferryboat ($3); www.nywaterways.com. Lower Manhattan skyline views are stunning from Jersey City's riverfront walkways. Turn-of-the-last-century brownstones have been lovingly restored in Hoboken, Frank Sinatra's home town. During springtime, millions of cherry blossoms burst into bloom in Newark's Branch Brook Park. The new Hudson-Bergen light-rail connects those three 'North Jersey' cities efficiently and inexpensively. For accommodation featuring skyline panoramics, consider the 250-room Hyatt Regency Jersey City $$$-$$$$ 2 Exchange Pl.; tel: (201) 469-1234; fax: (201) 432-4991; www.hyatt.com.

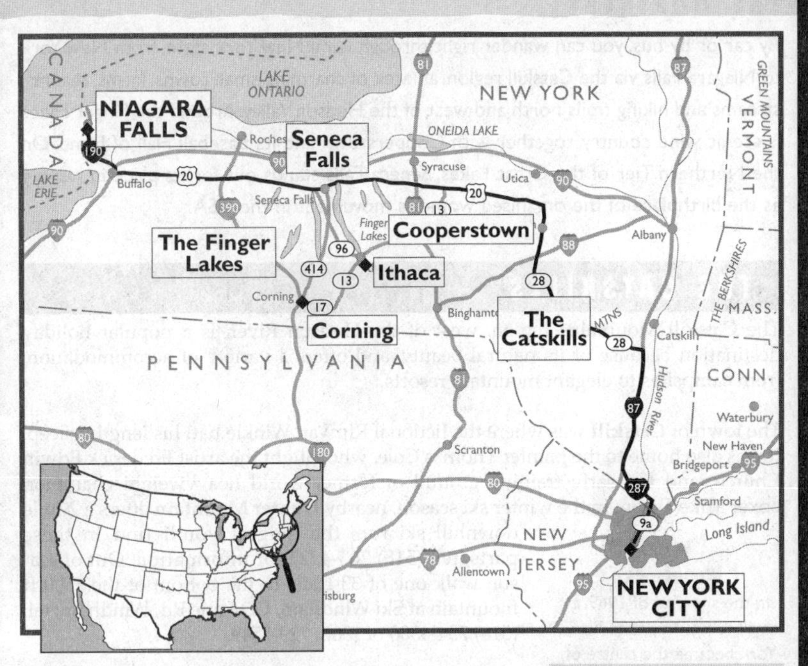

Driving Route

From central New York City take the Henry Hudson Pkwy (Rte 9a), which becomes the Saw Mill River Pkwy through Yonkers.

Take Exit 20 onto the New York State Thruway (I-87) north, which will join I-287 west. — 18 miles

Cross the Hudson River via the Tappan Zee Bridge; 17 miles west of the bridge, join I-87 north (the New York Thruway to Albany; toll payable). Do not stay on I-287. — 60 miles

At Kingston, turn onto Rte 28 through to the Catskills and Cooperstown. — 140 miles

Continue on Rte 28 to join Rte 20 westbound to Seneca Falls. — 240 miles

Rte 20 continues through Finger Lake country to Buffalo and Niagara. — 370 miles

Notes

Greyhound, Adirondack Trailways, New York Trailways, Chenago Valley Bus Lines, Hudson Transit Lines, The Short Line, Trentway-Wagar Inc. and Capitol Trailways run connecting bus services from New York and Boston to this area. OTT tables 532 and 533.

The Northeast

By car or by bus, you can wander right through rural New York state, from New York to Niagara Falls via the Catskill region, an area of charming small towns, farms, resorts, streams and hiking trails north and west of the Hudson Valley. Around the Finger Lakes is scenic wine country, together with Cooperstown and its Baseball Hall of Fame. On the Northern Tier of the Great Lakes, Seneca Falls stands out for its place in history as the birthplace of the organised women's movement in the USA.

THE CATSKILLS

The Catskill Mountains region, west of the Hudson River, is a popular holiday destination because of its natural beauty, and offers a variety of accommodation, from campsites to elegant mountain resorts.

The town of **Catskill** was where the fictional Rip Van Winkle had his lengthy sleep. It was also home to the painter Thomas Cole, who taught the artist Frederick Edwin Church, and the early training ground of former world heavyweight champion boxer Mike Tyson. In the winter ski season, nearby **Hunter Mountain** offers a 2-mile downhill ski run, the longest you'll find in these parts; tel: (518) 263-4223 for information. Out of season walk one of 33 trails to the bottom of the 1600 ft mountain at Ski Windham, CD Lane Rd, Windham; tel: (518) 734-4300 or (800) 729-7549.

The region includes a 287,989-acre forest preserve, the **Catskill Game Farm** (12 miles off I-87, exit 21) and legendary rock music haven **Woodstock**. Access to Woodstock is from I-87, exits 19–21; from Rhinebeck via Rte 9 to 199 to 28; or via Rtes 23 to 23A.

i **Greene County Tourism**; tel: (800) 697-2287; www.greene-ny.com. **The Ulster County Tourism Office**, tel: (800) 342-5826; www.co.ulster.ny.us, has information on Woodstock and the surrounding area.

North-South Lake Campground $ County Rte 18, Haines Falls; tel: (518) 589-5058 or (800) 456-CAMP.
Redcoat's Country Inn & Restaurant $$ Dale Lane, Elka Park; tel: (518) 589-9858 or 589-6379. Owned by Tom Wright, who was a chef on the *Queen Mary*. Closed Apr–May.
Mohonk Mountain House $$$ 1000 Mountain Rest Rd, New Paltz; tel: (914) 255-1000. A landmark resort, built above Lake Mohonk in 1869.

Woodstock

In the summer of 1969, a small town in upstate New York became the centre of the universe for 500,000 young rock and folk music enthusiasts – and groupies of every stripe. They hit the road from all over America to camp under the stars, listen to music and protest against everything from the war in Vietnam to drug laws. All the greats were there, from Joan Baez and Arlo Guthrie to The Who and The Grateful Dead. Today these former 'Flower Children' are leaders of business and industry – and not one of them will ever forget Woodstock.

In Woodstock, Tinker St, the main street, has an abundance of good restaurants, cafés and bakeries.

Blue Mountain Bistro $$$, just outside Woodstock, tel: (845) 679-8519, junction of Rtes 212 and 375. Luxurious eating.

Catskill Rose $$ on Rte 212 outside Woodstock, tel: (845) 688-7100. Good home cooking.

New World Home Cooking Company $, 424 Zea Rd, tel: (845) 246-0900, for very cheap Caribbean and Creole cuisine.

Rasher's $ 13 Tinker St, Woodstock, tel: (845) 679-5440, for a cheap drink and simple snack.

COOPERSTOWN

Tiny Cooperstown has a surprising tourist pull, largely thanks to the presence of its three museums: the Farmers' Museum, Fenimore House and the National Baseball Hall of Fame. The town gets its name from one William Cooper, landowner and also father of James Fenimore. **Fenimore House** ($$, which was also the home of Edward Clark, of the Singer Sewing Machine Co.) houses memorabilia of James Fenimore Cooper, and has seen its popularity much increased since the film of his best-known novel, *The Last of the Mohicans*.

Baseball associations began with another resident, General Abner Doubleday, who was falsely credited with inventing baseball here in 1839. The connection has stuck and Cooperstown is home to the most popular sports museum in the USA. The **National Baseball Hall of Fame and Museum** is baseball's national shrine. It is home to all the important artefacts: signed hats, uniforms and balls, plaques honouring the players and photos of memorable moments. The museum has its own cinema and library. $$, Main St; tel: (607) 547 7200; open 0900–1700 (until 2100 May–Sept).

i **Cooperstown Chamber of Commerce**, Higgins Cottage, 31 Chestnut St; tel: (607) 547-9983 or (800) 843-3394; www.cooperstownchamber.org.

The closest campsite is the **Cooperstown Beaver Valley Campground** on Rte 28; tel: (800) 726-7314.

Otesaga Hotel $$$ on Otesaga Lake; tel: (607) 547-9931 or (607) 547-9931. Open summer only.

Try Main St where the restaurants between Chestnut and Fair Sts serve family-sized portions at a cheap price.

Otesaga Hotel $$$ (as above). The elegant interior frames the view of the lake.

THE FINGER LAKES

One of New York state's most scenic and rural destinations, the Finger Lakes region is is divided into Northern and Southern 'tiers'. Stretching between the two are the long, thin lakes that give the region its name, interspersed with hills dotted with vineyards.

Most of the vineyards around the Finger Lakes region are open throughout the year and offer an excellent way of taking in the hillside scenery and learning some of the history of the region, while enjoying some of its most famous produce. After California, New York is the second largest wine-producing state in the USA, with annual sales topping $300 million. Here the topology of the region, created in the Ice Age when glaciers carved out the lakes and hills, very much lends itself to the production of grapes. The result is a superb collection of wineries, linked by 'wine trails': look for giveaway signs of bunches of grapes by the roadside to point you to your stop.

The **New York Wine and Grape Foundation** is an excellent source of information on all the Finger Lakes wineries and on promotional events throughout the summer, which include jazz festivals and route picnics. 350 Elm St, Penn Yan (Northern Tier); tel: (315) 536-7442.

ITHACA AND CORNING

An easy loop detour from Rte 20 can be made to visit the Southern Tier towns of Ithaca and Corning. Rte 13 leads to Ithaca, Rtes 13 and 17 to Corning and Rte 414 returns to Rte 20 at Seneca Falls.

The university town of Ithaca is at the southern end of Lake Cayuga, surrounded by countryside that provides ample offerings at the town's farmers' market. Further south, on the Chemung River, is the town of Corning. It is known as the home of the Corning Glass Works, although the company moved to Brooklyn after the Civil War. The pretty market street area has been carefully restored to look as it did in the 19th century. The **glass museum**, tel: (607) 937-5371 or (800) 732-6845, is just west of Rte 17 on Cedar Street, and houses glass objects from as early as 1400 BC to the present day. $$, open 0900–1700 (to 2000 in summer).

Ithaca/Tompkins County Convention and Visitors Bureau, 904 E Shore Dr., Ithaca, tel: (607) 272-1313 or (800) 284-3352, has information about the town and region; www.visitithaca.com.

Taughannock Falls State Park, Rte 89, Trumansburg; tel: (607) 387-6739 or (800) 456-CAMP; open mid-May to mid-October; north on Rte 89, 8 miles from Ithaca.
Lando's Hotel $ William and Bridge Sts, Corning; tel: (607) 936-3612. A convenient base for the town and glass museum.

Colour Section
(i) New York (pp. 75–92); inset: the Statue of Liberty
(ii) Niagara Falls (pp. 100–102); New England fall colour
(iii) Boston (pp. 113–130), the Old State House; inset: Quincy Market
(iv) Cape Cod (pp. 145–155), Falmouth Lighthouse; Woods Hole

MetLife

Hanshaw House Inn $$ 15 Sapsucker Woods Rd, Ithaca; tel: (607) 257-1437 or (800) 257-1437.

La Tourelle Country Inn $$$ 1150 Danby Rd, Ithaca; tel: (607) 273-2734 or (800) 765-1492.

Medleys $ 61 E Market St, Corning, tel: (607) 936 1685.

Moosewood Restaurant $–$$ 215 N Cayuga St, Ithaca; tel: (607) 273-9610. One of the USA's most famous vegetarian restaurants, and justly so.

The Upstate Tuna Co. $$ 73 E Market St, Corning; tel: (607) 936-8862. Provides chicken teriyaki or fish kebabs and lets customers cook for themselves.

John Thomas Steakhouse $$$ 1152 Danby Rd, Ithaca; tel: (607) 273-3464. One of the town's best.

SENECA FALLS

Seneca Falls is situated on Rte 20 a few miles west of Cayuga Lake, and was the home of Elizabeth Cady Stanton, who in 1848 put together the proposal for a 'Declaration of Sentiments', proclaiming all men and women to be created equal. Her home, **Stanton House**, 32 Washington St, has been restored and includes some original furniture; entry is free.

Seneca Falls Chamber of Commerce Visitors Center, 2020 Routes 5&20 West, tel: 315-568-2906 or (800) 732-1848; www.senecachamber.org. Sited in a complex housing Stanton House and the remains of the Wesleyan Chapel, home of the first Women's Rights Convention.

Cayuga Lake State Park $ tel: (315) 568-5163. Seven miles outside town, and offers cheap camping May–Nov.

NY Pizzeria $ 74 Fall St. tel: (315) 568-4131. Wholesome pizzas by the slice.

WHERE NEXT?

Rte 20 provides many interesting detours. Rte 390 can take you to Rochester, a town built on the Genesee River, home to the George Eastman House International Museum of Photography and Film, and bordering Lake Ontario. Continuing westwards will take you to Buffalo on the eastern tip of Lake Erie, a short distance from Niagara Falls *(see pp. 100–102)**.*

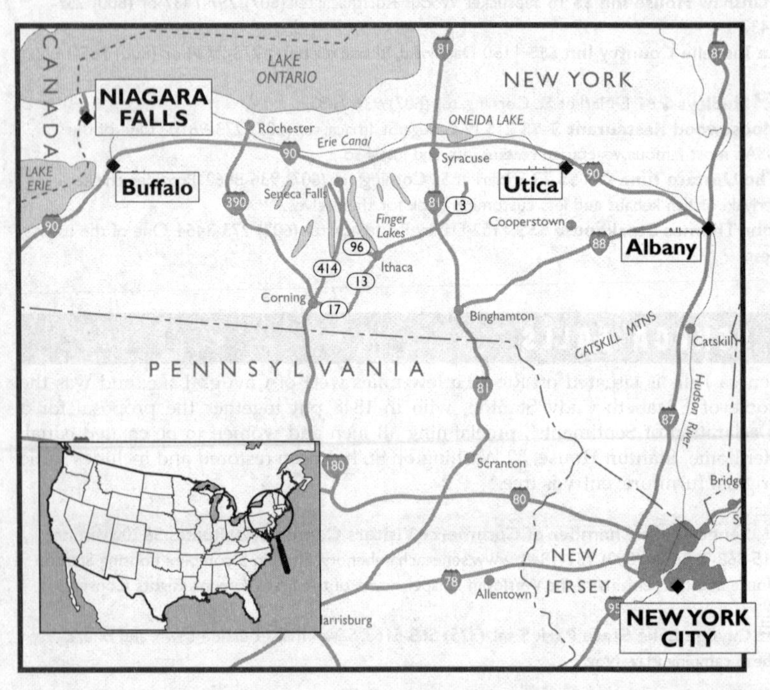

NEW YORK — NIAGARA FALLS

OTT Tables 182/300/301/532/615

Service	RAIL	Bus	Bus	RAIL	RAIL	Bus	Bus	RAIL	Bus	Bus	Bus	Bus
Days of operation	Daily	Daily	Daily	⑥⑦	ex⑥⑦	Daily	Daily	Daily	Daily	Daily	Daily	Daily
Special notes	C			E	E			E	A	B		B
New York d.	0715	0730	0845	0945	1045	1115	1300	1345	1430	....	1930	....
Albany d.	1000	|	|	1225	1325	|	|	1625	1715	2135	|	0035
Utica d.	1139	|	|	1402	1504	|	|	1804	....	2325	|	0205
Buffalo d.	1456	1630	1830	1721	1826	1915	2100	2126	....	0405	0315	0635
Niagara Falls a.	1610	1745	1945	1845	1950	2025	2215	2250	....	....	0415	....
Toronto a.	1944	1945	2120	....	....	2210	2359	....	....	....	0555	....

Special notes:
A–Additional trips: 0001, 0700, 0830, 1030, 1130, 1330, 1530, 1630, 1730, 1830, 2000, 2330.
B–Additional trips: 0035, 1115, 1330, 1645.
C–The Maple Leaf.
E–Empire Service.

On the 'Empire'

The Amtrak 'Empire' service from New York to Niagara Falls winds across New York state via the Lower Hudson Valley, Albany and the Erie Canal. Take the route northbound, where the stunning scenery can be appreciated in daylight, and sit on the left-hand side of the train for superior views of the Hudson Valley.

Notes

The bus services from New York to Niagara Falls are operated by Greyhound, Adirondack Trailways and Trentway Wagar Inc.

The service goes via Syracuse and takes 7hrs 40mins to Buffalo and 1hr–1hr 30mins from Buffalo to Niagara Falls.

Past a bevy of elegant mansions and the military academy of West Point, the train chunters to a halt in Albany, the state capital. Moving on through the Mohawk Valley, the train eventually arrives at its destination, the international boundary between the USA and Canada and the magnificent Niagara Falls. These can be viewed from almost any angle and means, including boat, platforms or aerial tramway; the brave can even venture behind the falls for an inside-out perspective.

ALBANY

New York state's capital city, Albany, began as a Dutch fur trading centre and fort on the Hudson River in 1609. It boomed with the opening of the Albany–Buffalo Erie Canal in 1825, but more recently author William Kennedy's novels, including *Ironweed*, have shown its grittier side. The main sights cluster around the massive, 96-acre **Empire State Plaza**, built by Governor Nelson Rockefeller and derided as 'Rockefeller's Edifice Complex'.

Free attractions in the city include the late-19th-century **New York State Capitol**, between Washington Ave and State St, tel: (518) 474-2418, where the state legislature meets; it has tours Mon–Fri 1000–1500. **New York State Museum**, on the plaza, features the original sets for *Sesame Street*. Open daily 1000–1700; tel: (518) 474-5877.

i **Albany County Convention and Visitors Bureau**, 25 Quakenbush Sq.; tel: (518) 434-1217 or (800) 258-3582. Visitor centres are at Broadway and Clinton Ave; tel: (518) 434-0405; www.albany.org.

The Amtrak station is located in Rensselaer, a short walk across the Hudson on Rtes 9 and 20 from Albany.

Pine Haven B&B $$ 531 Western Ave; tel: (518) 482-1574.
Crowne Plaza $$$ State/Lodge Sts; tel: (518) 462-6611 or (800) 227-6963. For comfort and luxury.

Restaurants to suit a range of tastes can be found at the intersection of Western Ave and Quail St.

The Ginger Man $$ 234 Western Ave; tel: (518) 427-5963. Named after J P Donleavy's novel, features sketches and quotations from British authors on the walls. Reservations recommended.

NIAGARA FALLS

From the USA you will first see on your right the **American Falls**, then the smaller **Bridal Veil Falls** and ahead, to the left, the larger and more famous **Canadian Horseshoe Falls**. This is the most visited scenic attraction in North America and one of the world's great natural wonders, formed when the waters of Lake Erie chiselled out an exit channel towards Lake Ontario at the end of the last Ice Age. Daredevils, sightseers and honeymooners (a trend started by Napoleon's brother) have all been drawn to see the awesome power of the foaming water as it thunders 170 ft into the Niagara River.

Amtrak stops at Lockport Rd and 27th St, just north of the centre of town. In town, connect on to the highly publicised 'people mover', a system of green air-conditioned motorcoaches travelling an 18-mile circular route from just above the Falls (Rapids View parking lot) to Queenston Heights. They operate approximately every 20 mins, with stops at all major sites. One ticket gives you a day's unlimited travel. $, open late Apr–mid-Oct.

Most of the area near the river and around the American Falls is part of the **Niagara Reservation State Park** – take an immediate right turn from the Rainbow Bridge; tel: (716) 278-1796. From **Prospect Point Observation Tower**, you can see the view from

EN ROUTE

Pageantry is rich at the US Military Academy at **West Point**, on the west bank of the Hudson River, just outside Newburgh. There are great river views, and fine weather brings out the cadets on parade in the spring and autumn. West Point Tours ($) gives tours of the academy daily, and a visitor centre, at Thayer Gate, is open daily 0900–1645; tel: (914) 446-4724.

ERIE CANAL

Farmers, axemen, ex-slaves, Irish labourers fresh off the boat – about 3500 'canawlers' – cleared land and dug the Erie Canal for a period of seven years. Climbing and descending 688 vertical feet over a distance of 363 miles, it linked the Great Lakes to the Hudson River and, thus, the American frontier to the port of New York City. After it opened in 1825, thousands more men, women, boys (known as 'hoggees') and mules helped move the freight barges up and down the canal. Today, waterways along the route of the original Erie Canal have been reborn for leisure, not work. Marinas, restaurants, inns and historic sites dot the banks, and nature preserves, parks and campsites have replaced mills and factories. The historic corridor, an engineering milestone that opened a path to the settlement of the West, is now a playground. For information on recreation, cruises and boat rentals, contact the New York State Canal Corp., tel: (800) 422-6254.

above the Gorge and for less than a dollar take an elevator down to the base of the American Falls.

For more than 150 years visitors have cruised to the foot of the Falls on the *Maid of the Mist* excursion boat, 5920 River Rd; tel: (905) 358-5781 or (716) 284-8897 (NY). Rain gear is provided, as it is for the **Journey Behind the Falls**, in which elevators descend 125 ft from Table Rock Complex for a self-guided tour behind Horseshoe Falls. $, open from 0900 year round. Alternatively, venture to view the Falls from high on the observation decks located at the **Skylon Tower**, 5200 Robinson St, $, and at the **Minolta Tower**, 6732 Oakes Dr., $.

The Falls are illuminated nightly, by garish multicoloured lights on the American side and by a soft rose glow on the Canadian side. On Fridays in summer there are free fireworks displays at 2200.

Niagara has some more unusual attractions away from the Falls. **Oakes Garden Theatre** is an outdoor amphitheatre at the foot of Clifton Hill (on the Canada side), with free live entertainment 1900–2100 (mid-June–Sept). **Oh Canada, Eh?**, 85 Lundy's Lane, tel: (905) 374-1995, $$$, is a fun dinner-theatre musical celebration of Canada, with a log cabin décor. There are more quirky entertainments on Clifton Hill, including **Ripley's Believe It or Not Museum** and the **Guinness Museum of World Records**. At Pyramid Pl., the **IMAX® Theatre and Daredevil Museum**, 5400 Robinson St, tel: (905) 374-4629, $, presents the history of the Falls from Native legends to modern-day daredevils on a six-storey-high screen.

The quieter nature lover can try **Niagara Parks Greenhouses**, Niagara Parkway, south of Horseshoe Falls, tel: (905) 371-0254, open from 0900; free. Nightlife, on the other hand, is not forgotten, and **Casino Niagara**, 5705 Falls Ave, tel: (905) 374-3598 or (888) WINDFALL (946-3255), features 3000 slot machines, 123 gaming tables, and snack and restaurant facilities.

NIAGARA AND THE DAREDEVILS

Fame and fortune have lured many to the Falls: some lost their lives, but almost all went away empty-handed. One of the first recorded to risk life and limb in an attempt to gain celebrity status was a schoolteacher, Mrs Annie Taylor, who in the early 1900s decided to travel over the Falls in a padded barrel. She jarred and bounced the whole way down, eventually losing consciousness. Seventeen minutes later, her barrel was retrieved and the bleeding and bruised Mrs Taylor was removed, alive enough to be triumphant about her success. Sadly her fame was short-lived and she died destitute 20 years later.

i On the US side, the **Niagara Falls Convention and Visitors Bureau**, 310 4th St, tel: (800) 421-5223, will provide you with a free guide. Alternatively try **Orin Leham Visitor Center**, Niagara Reservation State Park, tel: (716) 278-1796; open daily 0800–2215 in the summer; www.nysparks.com.

On the Canadian side, the **Niagara Visitor and Convention Bureau**, 5115 Stanley Ave; tel: (905) 356-6061 or (800) 56-FALLS, is open daily 0800–2000 (mid-May–mid-Oct) and Mon–Fri 0800–1800 (mid-Oct–mid-May); www.NiagaraFallsTourism.com.

Inevitably, the weight of tourist traffic generates considerable commercial nastiness, particularly around the American town of Niagara Falls. If you do want to stay the night, the NFCVB can supply a list of bed and breakfasts. There is a budget hostel:

Hostelling International $ 1101 Ferry Ave; tel: (716) 282-3700. A Victorian house several miles from the Falls; closed 0930–1600.

On the Canadian side try the Niagara Parkway, lined with B&Bs as you enter the city. Rates drop as you move away from the river. The closest **campsite** to the Falls is Glen-View, 3950 Victoria Ave; tel: (905) 358-8689. It's on the people mover system and has a large swimming pool, but during the day helicopters land across the street.

Butterfly Manor $$–$$$ 4917 River Rd, L2E 3G5; tel/fax: (905) 358-8988.

Sheraton on the Falls $$$ 5875 Falls Ave, L2E 6W7; tel: (905) 374-4444 or (800) 325-3535.

Mist Fast Food Restaurant $ Maid of the Mist Plaza. Budget fast food with a view.

Capri Restaurant & Lounge $$ 5438 Ferry St; tel: (905) 354-7519. Local award winner, representing Niagara's large Italian population.

Skylon Tower $$–$$$ 5200 Robinson St; tel: (905) 356-2651. The dining room revolves once an hour 760 ft above the Falls.

WHERE NEXT?

Crossing the Rainbow Bridge takes you into Canada, either to Fort Erie and back across to Buffalo to the south or ***Toronto*** *to the north.* *See pp. 44–45 for visa requirements.*

Peter Ustinov said, 'Toronto is New York, run by the Swiss.' The largest city in Canada is truly everything a traveler could want. Toronto is a cosmopolitan mix of over a hundred ethnic groups, the financial centre of the country, completed with an extensive mix of museums, cafes and luxury stores.

Toronto is one of the few cities in North America where you can charter a boat, watch an Indy-car type race, go to the theatre, take in a film or jazz festival, see a hockey game or cheer for a baseball team, and top it all off with a ride to the top of the tallest free-standing structure in North America, the CN Tower.

And don't let winter deter you from visiting the city. An extensive series of underground malls, walkways and tunnels that interconnect the downtown, will keep you warm and dry. Canadians have a warm and welcoming nature, and the current dollar being slightly less than the US in value is an added bonus.

i Tourism Toronto, 207 West Queens Quay West, Suite 590, Toronto, Ontario, M5J 1A7; tel: (800) 363-1900 or www.tourismtoronto.com.

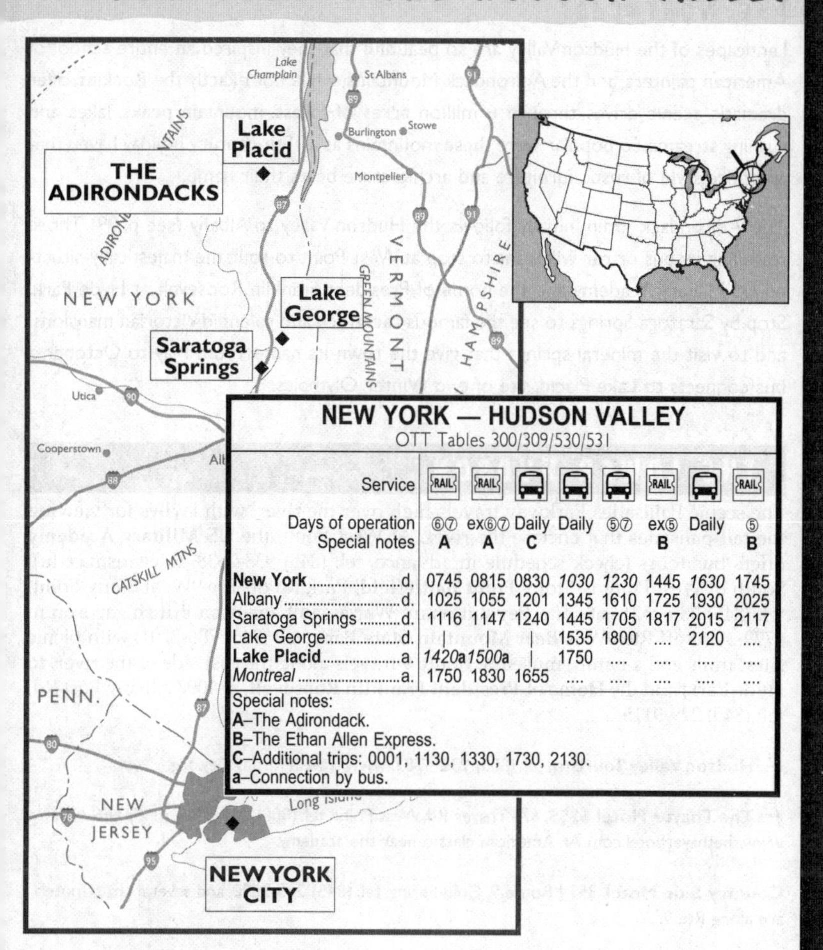

NEW YORK — HUDSON VALLEY
OTT Tables 300/309/530/531

Service	RAIL	RAIL	Bus	Bus	Bus	RAIL	Bus	RAIL
Days of operation	⑥⑦	ex⑥⑦	Daily	Daily	⑤⑦	ex⑤	Daily	⑤
Special notes	A	A	C			B		B
New York d.	0745	0815	0830	*1030*	*1230*	1445	*1630*	1745
Albany d.	1025	1055	1201	1345	1610	1725	1930	2025
Saratoga Springs d.	1116	1147	1240	1445	1705	1817	2015	2117
Lake George d.	|	|	|	1535	1800	....	2120	....
Lake Placid a.	*1420*a	*1500*a	|	1750	....	....	....	....
Montreal a.	1750	1830	1655	....	....	....	....	....

Special notes:
A–The Adirondack.
B–The Ethan Allen Express.
C–Additional trips: 0001, 1130, 1330, 1730, 2130.
a–Connection by bus.

Adirondack Trailways covers much of the same route by bus, and is an alternative way of seeing this beautiful corner of the States.

Notes

There are several extra Amtrak services to Albany and New London, also services to Stamford, Bridgeport, New Haven, Mystic, Hartford, Springfield, Burlington, St Albans and Utica.

Landcapes of the Hudson Valley are so beautiful that they inspired an entire school of American painters, and the Adirondack Mountains, while not exactly the Rockies, offer dramatic scenic drives through 6 million acres of forest, mountain peaks, lakes and rushing streams. So popular were these mountains as a 19th-century holiday haven that an entire style of rustic furniture and architecture bears their name.

The 'Adirondack' train initially follows the Hudson Valley to Albany (see p. 99). Those travelling by bus or car will want to stop at West Point to tour the majestically-situated US Military Academy and the home of President Franklin Roosevelt at Hyde Park. Stop by Saratoga Springs to see the famous racetrack and splendid Victorian mansions, and to visit the mineral springs that give the town its name. From May to October, a bus connects to Lake Placid, site of two Winter Olympics.

THE LOWER HUDSON

The scenic Pallisades Parkway travels high over the river, with laybys for viewing the tall palisades that enclose the river. At West Point, the **US Military Academy** offers bus tours (check schedule in advance, tel: (845) 938-2638, www.usma.edu). South of West Point is **Stony Point Battlefield**, Park Rd off Rte 9W, at Stony Point, tel: (845) 786-2521, site of a Revolutionary War assault against a British garrison in 1779. Also off Rte 9W is **Bear Mountain State Park**, tel: (845) 786-2701, with picnic sites, trails and a nature museum. Route 9 travels along the east side of the river, to Hyde Park, and the **Home of President Franklin Roosevelt**, at 4097 Albany Post Rd, tel: (845) 229-9115.

i **Hudson Valley Tourism**, tel: (800) 232-4782, www.travelhudsonvalley.org.

The Thayer Hotel $$$$, 674 Thayer Rd, West Point, tel: (800) 247-5047, (845) 446-4731, www.thethayerhotel.com. An American classic, near the academy.

Country Side Motel, 3524 Route 9, Cold Spring, tel: (845) 265-2090, and several chain motels are along Rte 9.

SARATOGA SPRINGS

Saratoga's history and society sprang from the presence of mineral waters bubbling up from the ground. It is also renowned for its racecourses and polo ground, which attract any visitors each year. It is an elegant town of Victorian architecture, neatly clipped gardens and a famous timetable of concerts and dance performances, as well as the prestigious Skidmore College.

Visit the Roosevelt or Lincoln bathhouses, in **Saratoga Spa State Park**, S Broadway, where you can soak in a tub of the mineral spring water. After your bath, an attendant wraps you in warm sheets and leaves you for quiet reflection. $$, call for appointments; tel: (518) 584-2535 or 587-3330. Or choose the more luxurious surroundings of Crystal Spa; tel: (518) 584-2556.

Saratoga Race Course presents thoroughbred horse-racing mid-July–Aug and may be the most civilised course in the USA: dresses, jackets and ties are 'appreciated' in the clubhouse. Breakfast is served at a trackside café 0700–0930. First race is 1300; closed Tues. For information, tel: (718) 641-4700 off season, (518) 584-6200 in season. **Saratoga Raceway**, Crescent Ave, tel: (518) 584-2110, offers a much longer season of harness racing, mid-Jan–late Nov, except for a break in April.

The **Saratoga Performing Arts Center**, in the park, is the summer home of the New York City Ballet, New York City Opera and the Philadelphia Orchestra. Popular music concerts are also staged here. Open June–Sept; tel: (518) 587-3330 (summer) or (518) 584-9330 (off-season).

Saratoga's other claim to fame is for a decisive battle of the American Revolution: Major-General John Burgoyne's campaign south from Canada was finally stopped when he surrendered on the heights here on 17 October 1777. The **Saratoga Battlefield** ($) is on Rtes 32 and 4, Stillwater; tel: (518) 664-9821.

i **Saratoga Springs Urban Cultural Park Visitor Center**, Drink Hall, 297 Broadway at Congress, Saratoga Springs; tel: (518) 587-3241. Gives a museum-quality overview of the city's history and society. Open daily 0900–1600; closed Sun Nov–Mar.

RAIL The Amtrak station is located at West Ave/Station Lane.

Many chain hotels can be found on Rtes 50 and 9 (see p. 578). Room rates tend to jump during racing season.

Cold Brook Campsites $$ 10 miles north of Saratoga in Gansevoort. Open May–early Oct.

Kimberly Guest House $ 158 S Broadway; tel: (518) 584-9006.

Brunswick House $$ 143 Union Ave; tel: (518) 584-6751.

Willow Walk $$$ 120 High Rock Ave; tel: (518) 584-4549.

Hattie's $$ 45 Phila St; tel: (518) 584-4790. New Orleans and Southern fare; home-made desserts.

9 Maple Avenue; tel: (518) 583-2582. Intimate bar that can get crowded Fri and Sat nights when live jazz can be heard.

Professor Moriarty's Dining and Drinking Saloon $$ 430 Broadway; tel: (518) 587-5981. Pub Atmosphere

WHERE NEXT?

The Amtrak Ethan Allen Express *runs from New York to Saratoga Springs, Glen Falls, Fair Haven and Rutland. It follows the western shore of Lake Champlain northwards into Canada, ending in Montreal.*

LAKE GEORGE

You'll know you've reached Lake George when your children spot the rollercoaster of **Great Escape and Splashwater Kingdom Fun Park**. North-east of the park, the town centre is a honky-tonk strip of shops, takeaway restaurants and fast-food stops. Further north along the lake you'll find more hotels and motels than homes. The life of the region is captured best at the **Adirondack Museum**, Blue Mountain Lake; tel: (518) 352-7311, open daily 0930–1730 (mid-June–mid-Oct).

Cannons still boom – just for show – and fife and drums are played at **Fort Ticonderoga**, strategically placed on the shores of nearby Lake Champlain. It was the site of several battles before and during the American Revolution. Built by the French in 1755, it was destroyed by the British in 1777, after its occupation by Ethan Allen and his Green Mountain Boys in May 1775. Restored to original condition, it is a military museum. Historical cruises on the lake are also on offer. $$, open daily 0900–1700 (May–June, Sept–Oct), 0900–1800 (July–Aug); tel: (518) 585-2821.

The **Hyde Collection**, 161 Warren St, Glens Falls, tel: (518) 792-1761, is for art lovers. Housed in a small Italian Renaissance-style mansion are small works by Van Dyck, Tintoretto and Botticelli. Open Tues–Sat 1000–1700, Thurs to 1900, Sun 1200–1700.

i **Lake George Regional Chamber of Commerce,**
PO Box 272, Lake George; tel: (518) 668-5755 or 1 (800) 705-0059. Operates a summer booth at Shepard Park, downtown on the waterfront, open daily 0900–1700 (July and Aug).
Adirondack Mountain Club, RR 3, Box 3055, Lake George, NY 12845; tel: (518) 668-4447, provides information on hiking, camping, canoeing and more in the region, with an information booth on Rte 9 (south of I-87 exit 21); open Mon–Sat 0830–1700 May–mid-Oct; Mon–Fri 0830–1630 rest of year.

The Blair House $$ Upper Canada St (Rte 9); tel: (518) 668-2871.
Amitolia-on-the-Lake $$ Rte 9L; tel: (518) 668-2269. Rooms and cottages with their own beach on the lake.
Lincoln Log Colony $$$ Rte 9/Canada St; tel: (518) 668-5326.

Lake George Village has plentiful dining options
Prospect Mountain Diner $ Canada St; tel: (518) 668-4381.
Rosie's Diner $$ Rte 9/9N junction; tel: (518) 668-2499.

LAKE PLACID

Lake Placid was the site of the 1932 and 1980 Winter Olympics, with New York state's highest mountain, Mount Marcy, looming in the background. US ski jumpers practise in summer on the 90 m Intervale Ski Jumps (Rte 73; tel: (518) 532-1655), $. The **Olympic Center ice rink**, Main St, tel: (518) 523-1655, is open in summer for public ice-skating Mon–Fri 1945–2115. Ride a bobsleigh, horse, or mountain bike, or go cross-country skiing at the **Olympic Sports Complex**, Mount Van Hoevenberg, Rte 73, tel: (518) 523-4436 or (800) 462-6236 ($$–$$$).

Ausable Chasm is a 1½ mile river gorge cut through sandstone, which you can explore on steps, steel bridges or in boats. $$, open daily 0900–1600 (late May–mid-Oct); tel: (518) 834-7454 or (800) 537-1211.

Tourist Information, The Olympic Center, 216 Main St, Lake Placid, tel: (518) 523-2445.

Lake Placid is a premier resort area, and the prices for accommodation are among the highest in the Adirondacks, rising sharply in season.
Whispering Pines Campground $ 6 miles south of the lake on Rte 73; tel: (518) 523-9322.
High Peaks Lodge $ Adirondack Lodge Rd, tel: (518) 523-3441, is a gold mine of information leaflets and provides lodging and breakfast at budget prices.
Irv-Inn $ 67 Parkside Ave; tel: (518) 523-4359. Simple but clean, and you can eat heartily at low prices.
Placid Bay Motor Inn $$ 140 Main St; tel: (518) 523-2001.
Mirror Lake Inn **$$–$$$** 5 Mirror Lake Drive, Mirror Lake; tel: (518) 523-2544. A palatial establishment with 120 rooms, a pool, health club and a good restaurant.

Montreal

Although it is the second largest French-speaking city in the world, Montreal is as decisively North American as it is francophone. Its early fortunes were made in furs and shipping as the furthest navigable port inland on the St Lawrence River, but today Montreal is a banking, manufacturing, software and world trade centre, and a polyglot city of great ethnic diversity. Perhaps no industry has so benefited from this immigration as the food service – it is hard to find a better place to eat in all of North America.

Vieux Montréal (the old town) has most of the historic buildings and colourful, narrow streets dating from the 17th and 18th centuries. Remnants of the 1642 town lie beneath the Point-à-Callière museum. **Vieux Port**, the waterfront area of Vieux Montréal, has been recently redeveloped to create a 2-mile promenade and entertainments on the old piers. Former warehouses and chandleries on the surrounding streets are blossoming as art galleries, restaurants and boutiques. Montreal is also a sociable city, and Montrealers consider entertainment to be incomplete without good conversation and drink – either alcohol or strong coffee – so you will never be short of a good bar or restaurant. Interest in jazz has blossomed in recent years, and there are good clubs to be found too: try the downtown area, near McGill and Concordia Universities, where shows featuring jazz and blues can be found most nights.

Infotouriste Centre, 1001 rue du square-Dorchester (Métro: Peel), tel: (514) 873-2015, is open daily 0830–1930 (June–early Sept), 0900–1800 (rest of year).

NEW YORK – BOSTON

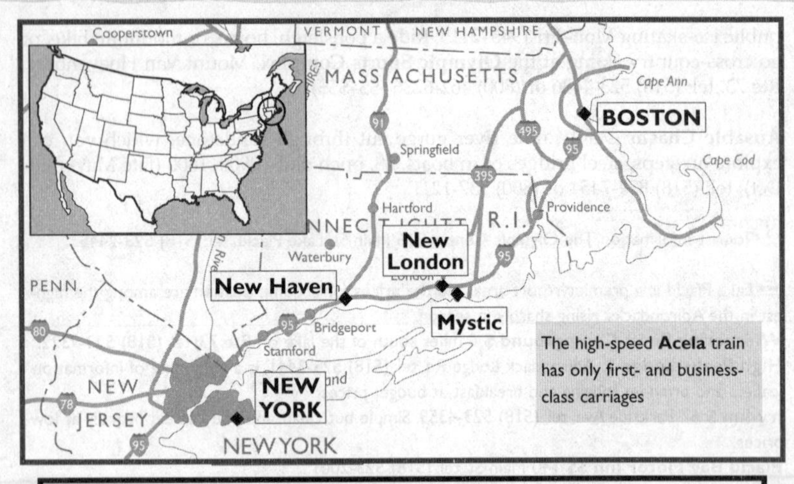

NEW YORK — BOSTON

OTT Tables 320/359/507/508

Service		RAIL		RAIL	RAIL		RAIL	RAIL	RAIL	RAIL		RAIL
Days of operation	Daily	Daily	Daily	Daily	ex⑥⑦	Daily	⑥⑦	ex⑥⑦	ex⑥⑦	⑥⑦	Daily	ex⑥⑦
Special notes	**C**				**A**	**D**		**B**	**F**			
Washington ....d.	....	2200	....	0300	0435	....	0525	0600	0700	0620	....	0730
New York ....d.	0030	0315	0445	0655	0800	0815	0900	0903	1003	1000	1030	1100
New Haven ....d.	|	0510	0745	0831	0935	1015	1038	|	1129	1138	1330	1238
New London ....d.	|	0600	0845	0919	1021	|	1123	|	|	1226	1430	1326
Mystic ....d.	|	|	|	0934**a**	|	|	|	|	|	1239	|	1339
Boston ....a.	0450	0815	1145	1059**b**	1159	1340	1259	1216	1327	1415	1835	1515

Service	RAIL	RAIL	RAIL		RAIL	RAIL	RAIL	RAIL	RAIL	RAIL	RAIL	RAIL
Days of operation	ex⑥⑦	⑥⑦	⑥	Daily	⑦	⑥	ex⑥⑦	⑥⑦	⑥⑦	ex⑥⑦	ex⑥⑦	⑦
Special notes				**E**								
Washington ....d.	0900	0925	1020	....	1125	1125	1205	1525	1325	1405	1605	1625
New York ....d.	1203	1300	1400	1400	1500	1500	1530	1900	1700	1740	1930	2000
New Haven ....d.	1329	1438	1538	1650	1638	1715	1730	2038	1835	1930	2108	2236
New London ....d.	|	1526	1623	1800	|	1815	1818	2126	1923	2019	2158	2220
Mystic ....d.	|	1539	|	|	|	1828	|	2139	|	|	2211	|
Boston ....a.	1527	1715	1805	2150	1859	2005	2000	2315	2105	2159	2350	2359

Special notes:

A–Additional trips (departure times from New York): 1300ex⑥⑦, 1400ex⑥⑦, 1503⑥⑦, 1803⑥⑦.
B–Acela Express. Additional trips (departure times from New York): 1503ex⑥⑦, 1800ex⑥⑦.
C–Additional trips: 0700 and hourly until 1900 then 2100, extra trips operate on the half hour on ⑤⑦.
D–Additional trips: 1700. **E**–Additional trips: 1030, 1615, 1915.
F–Acela Express. Additional trips (departure times from New York): 1203⑥⑦, 1403⑥⑦, 1600ex⑥⑦, 1603⑥⑦, 1700ex⑥⑦, 2000ex⑥⑦. **a**–⑥⑦ only. **b**–1105 ⑥⑦.

The short distances between station stops and the good supporting infrastructure – commuter-rail lines and intercity buses link numerous towns not on Amtrak's network – make train travel along this route a viable alternative to that ultimate symbol of American mobility: the car. The Connecticut–Rhode Island–Massachusetts segment of Amtrak's Northeast Corridor line is part of the railway's busiest route – understandably so, for this is a densely populated area, and New York and Boston are major 'anchor' destinations.

Much of this part of Amtrak's line follows the original course of the Boston Post Road, mile-posted in 1672 for mail delivery between New York City and Boston. Present-day contrasts are striking – a mixed bag of seascapes, beaches and boat harbours; pristine marshlands and nature sanctuaries; village greens; backyard-barbecue suburbia and New England academia; factories and power plants; woeful patches of urban blight; and the USA's per capita wealthiest county (Fairfield in Connecticut).

The total 205-mile journey runs along the coastal underbelly of Connecticut, curving through Rhode Island by way of Providence and finally zipping through a south-eastern stretch of Massachusetts to reach Boston. Coach passengers have access to no-frills food and beverage buffet service (smart travellers bring their own, more edible supplies on board). If you're carrying ponderous amounts of luggage, porterage is available at the larger stations. Be forewarned, however: there are no left-luggage facilities.

Travelling in Style

More convenient and comfortable than either train or bus, and at a price (about $75) competitive to the train, LimoLiner offers leather reclining seats (with ample legroom), large spotless restrooms, new-release movies, news channels, free and unlimited internet access at each seat, and snacks and beverages delivered to your seat. The service operates several times daily from the Hilton Hotel (near Boston's Prudential Center) to the New York Hilton in Midtown. Another benefit is that, unlike bus and train station, the hotels offer baggage checking for passengers who arrive early. Reservations (888) 546-5469, www.LimoLiner.com.

NEW HAVEN

The heart and soul of this mid-size city is **Yale**. This élite university in the eastern USA's so-called Ivy League has been a hugely prestigious and influential presence here since 1717, an influence most evident in the city's cultural institutions.

New Haven's Union Station is about a mile south from downtown, but walking is not recommended because of its location in a less-than-idyllic area. Take a taxi or use the Connecticut Transit bus service.

New Haven Green, bounded by Chapel, Church, College and Elm Sts, and divided by Temple St, is a textbook example of a New England town common, laid out in 1638. It is the site of three churches exemplifying Federal, Georgian and English Gothic design. In Chapel St are two notable art galleries. The **Yale Center for British Art**, 1080 Chapel St, tel: (203) 432-2800, has the biggest and broadest-ranging collection of British art outside the UK, a bequest from billionaire Yale alumnus Paul Mellon. Open Tues–Sat 1000–1700, Sun 1200–1700. At 1111 Chapel St is America's oldest academic art museum, **Yale University Art Gallery**, tel: (203) 432-0600. It was founded in 1832 and holds paintings, sculptures and decorative arts from ancient Egypt to French and American Impressionist periods. Open Tues–Sat 1000–1700, Sun 1300–1800 (Sept–July). The collection at another Yale institution, the **Beinecke Rare Book and Manuscript Gallery Library**, 121 Wall St, tel: (203) 432-2977, includes a Gutenberg Bible, Charles Dickens manuscripts and rare Audubon *Birds of America* prints; it also has a sunken sculpture garden. Open Mon–Fri 0830–1700, Sat 1000–1700.

The **Peabody Museum of Natural History** ($) at 170 Whitney Ave, tel: (203) 432-5050, was founded in 1866 and ranks among the world's best, with global 'finds' by university archaeologists. Open Mon–Sat 1000–1700, Sun 1200–1700.

SAFETY

Confine your sightseeing to Yale's immediate surroundings and areas adjoining the city-centre New Haven Green. This precaution becomes doubly applicable after nightfall.

i **Greater New Haven Convention and Visitors Bureau,** 59 Elm St, New Haven, CT 06510; tel: (800) 322-7829 or (203) 777-8550; www.newhavencvb.org.
Yale Visitor Information Center, 149 Elm St; tel: (203) 432-2300.

The best places to stay tend to be heavily booked during spring graduation time at Yale, and also in autumn when the football team does battle against a traditional Ivy League foe on the Yale Bowl gridiron. So plan accordingly.
Hotel Duncan $$ 1151 Chapel St; tel: (203) 787-1273. A long-time favourite of touring theatrical personalities; far from ritzy, just the basics – but clean, respectable, and centrally situated.
Colony Inn $$$ 1157 Chapel St; tel: (800) 458-8810 or (203) 776-1234; fax: (203) 772-3929. Handsome, low-rise downtown hotel with a restaurant and lounge.
New Haven Hotel $$$ 229 George St; tel: (800) 644-6835 or (203) 498-3100; fax: (203) 498-0911. Within the city's major hospital complex, a few blocks from Yale's campus; features two indoor pools.

Streets west and south of New Haven Green have plentiful choices of moderately priced and inexpensive restaurants.
Atticus Bookstore Café $ 1082 Chapel St. Professors and students linger over breakfast and lunch in this thoroughly collegiate bookstore.

EN ROUTE

Barnum Museum

The sole reason for a **Bridgeport** stopover is just a block away from the sizeable Amtrak station: the bizarre, neo-Byzantine-Romanesque museum recalling the career of the flamboyant circus impresario P T Barnum. $, 820 Main St; tel: (203) 331-1104. Open Tues–Sat 1000–1630, Sun 1200–1630; also Mon 1100–1630 (July–Aug).

Louis' Lunch $ 261 Crown St. A little cubbyhole where, in 1895, Louis Lassen made gastronomic history by cooking the first-ever American hamburgers.

Claire's Corner Copia $–$$ 1000 Chapel St. Mingle with the 'Yalies' in this non-smoking, vegetarian establishment serving soups, pastries and creative sandwich specials.

NEW LONDON

Wrapped around its deep-water harbour, New London prospered as a 19th-century whaling port. That nautical tradition endures with America's Coast Guard Academy and – across the Thames (rhymes with James) River in neighbouring Groton – evocative submarine lore.

The main nautical attractions are along the waterfront. At the **US Navy Submarine Base** you can clamber through the world's first nuclear-powered submarine, launched in 1954. There is also a museum, definitive as regards undersea warfare: 1 Crystal Lake Rd; tel: (800) 343-0079 or (860) 694-3174. Open Wed–Mon 0900–1700, Tues 1300–1700 (mid-Apr–mid-Oct), Wed–Mon 0900–1600 (mid-Oct–mid-Apr).

The **Lyman Allyn Art Museum** is strong on Colonial furniture, accessories and paintings – plus an outstanding collection of dolls, dolls' houses and antique toys. $, 625 Williams St; tel: (860) 443-2545. Open Tues–Sat 1000–1700, Sun 1300–1700. Eugene O'Neill grew up in **Monte Cristo Cottage**, which inspired his *Long Day's Journey Into Night* and *Ah! Wilderness*. $, 325 Pequot Ave; tel: (860) 443-0051. Open Tues–Sat 1000–1700, Sun 1300–1700 (May–early Sept).

Southeastern Connecticut Tourism District, 470 Bank St, New London, CT 06320; tel: (800) 863-6569 or (860) 444-2206; www.mysticmore.com. Information for Groton and Mystic as well as New London.

New London's railway station itself is small but significant, designed in rusticated neo-Romanesque style by celebrity architect H H Richardson in 1887. It's right downtown and well served by SEAT (Southeast Area Transit) buses taking passengers to outlying attractions.

Red Roof Inn $$$ 707 Colman St; tel: (800) 843-7663 or (860) 444-0001; fax: (860) 443-71541. A short taxi ride north from downtown gets you to this basic but satisfactory motel.

Queen Anne Inn B&B $$$$ 265 Williams St; tel: (800) 347-8818 or (860) 447-2600; fax: (860) 443-0857. For those wishing to splurge. A Victorian 'painted lady'; full breakfast and afternoon tea included.

Captain's $–$$ 8 Bank St. Directly across from Union Station: pasta, pizzas, chicken, seafood, high-calorie desserts. Outdoor terrace.

Dutch Tavern $$ 23 Green St. The oldest pub in town; have a

burger and a beer where Eugene O'Neill allegedly quaffed a few.
Whaler Grill $–$$ 247 State St. Locally popular breakfast and lunch hangout. Soups, sandwiches and 'heavenly hash'.

MYSTIC

Mystic Seaport is 19th-century maritime America recreated. Attractively (and profitably) situated at the mouth of the Mystic River, the seaport boasts the last surviving wooden whaling ship, a square-rigger and Gloucester fishing schooner, a coal-fired steamer (which takes passengers on river cruises), interactive demonstrations and craftspeople at work. It also has galleries of model ships, figureheads and seafaring paintings, and the largest nautical bookstore anywhere in the world. $$$, 75 Germanville Ave; tel: (860) 572-5315 or (888) 9-SEAPORT. Open daily, hours variable.

Mystic Seaport's stature as Connecticut's foremost tourism attraction seeps into the town in obvious ways: plenty of places to eat, sleep and shop. That could imply an overdose of touristy tackiness, but somehow Mystic retains its genuine old-time charm. See Beluga whales, sharks, penguins and bottle-nose dolphins among the 3500 aquatic creatures at the **Mystic Aquarium**, $$, 55 Coogan Blvd; tel: (860) 572-5955. Open daily 0900–1700, 0900–1800 in summer.

Mystic's tiny wooden train-station is about a mile from downtown, further from Mystic Seaport. Catch a cab or board the low-cost Mystic Trolley, which makes the rounds daily during summer high season.

While in town, consider a half-day or sunset cruise aboard the *Argia* schooner, or Long Island Sound day-tripping on a Mystic Whaler cruise.

i **Mystic Chamber of Commerce**, 16 Cottrell St, Mystic, CT 06355; tel: (860) 572-9578.

Whaler's Inn $$–$$$ 20 E Main St; tel: (800) 243-2588 or (860) 536-1506; fax: (860) 572-1250. A grouping of four 19th-century buildings in the bustling downtown district.
Old Mystic Motor Lodge $$$ 251 Germanville Ave; tel: (860) 536-9666; fax: (860) 536-2044. Advantageously close to Mystic Seaport; outdoor pool.

Christine's Heart and Soul Café $ 4 Pearl St. Ideal for light lunch or coffee break; save room for the choice of home-baked desserts. Downtown location.
Seamen's Inne $$–$$$ 105 Germanville Ave; tel: (860) 536-9649. Restaurant and pub, a few steps from Mystic Seaport's entrance.

New England's largest city by far is widely known as The Hub – a name bestowed by Oliver Wendell Holmes, who wrote about chauvinistic turn-of-the-century Bostonians who considered their city 'the Hub of the Universe'. The oldest major US city, founded in 1630, Boston still has a blue-blooded Yankee establishment, but it's matched by a feisty Irish one, and ethnic diversity is prevalent.

The city centre's compact size surprises visitors expecting Americanised urban sprawl, and then discovering that they can get nearly everywhere on foot. Walking the Freedom Trail (see p. 121) is a good introduction to historic Boston, and a trip out to Lexington and Concord (pp. 128–130) provides a vivid lesson in what sparked the American Revolution.

Learning and culture rank high in this 'Athens of America' (another often-used, lofty title), where the nation's first public elementary school was established in 1636. Today the metro area is energised by its student population, some 250,000 strong, attending more than 60 colleges and universities. Harvard and almost-as-famous Massachusetts Institute of Technology (MIT) are across the Charles River in Cambridge, part of Boston and yet separate, the city's 'Left Bank'.

MUST SEE/DO IN BOSTON

Wander through historic Fanueil Hall and the surrounding marketplace on a nice weekend afternoon

Walk the Freedom Trail for a look at Boston of the late 1700s; it also takes you through the Quincy Market area and the Italian North End

Devote a day to the Isabella Stewart Gardner Museum and the Museum of Fine Arts

Stroll through Harvard Yard, browse in Harvard Square's bookstores and visit the University Museums (from ancient civilizations to modern art)

Eat an ice cream in the city with America's highest per capita ice cream consumption

Tour the Public Garden lagoon in a Swan Boat; this may be the cheapest cruise you'll ever take

GETTING THERE

THE BIG DIG

Travelers entering the city from Logan Airport and South Station can't but wonder at the long, wide expanse of under-development open space that greets them. The Big Dig (officially the Central Artery Project) is the largest public-works endeavour in US history, costing billions of dollars of federal and state funds. This 7½-mile construction corridor has become a vehicle tunnel system and allows for the reconnection of the North End to downtown and Government Center by a beautified swathe of landscaping and public-works ornamentation. The surface road-and-tunnel network includes the stunning Leonard Zakim Bridge spanning the Charles River to link Boston and Charlestown.

Logan International Airport covers landfill in East Boston, directly across the Inner Harbor from downtown, 20–30 mins by public transport. A free shuttle connects the international terminal (E) to domestic terminals (A–D), and the Blue Line subway station. By bus or cab, downtown is 3 miles away via a toll tunnel. Hotel courtesy shuttles are available; for Concord Trailways bus service to coastal destinations in New Hampshire and Maine, tel: (603) 228-3300, fax: (603) 228-3524.

A free bus service runs froms the airport to Logan Wharves every 15 mins, from where you can take the Water Shuttle, which docks at Rowes Wharf downtown. For schedule and fares, tel: (617) 422-0392.

Amtrak operates frequent daily services to New York and Washington from South

NAVIGATING THE SUBWAY

(See colour map section, inside back cover)

Stops on the **Green Line** include Government Center (close to Faneuil Hall/Quincy Marketplace), Park St (Boston Common and main shopping district), Arlington (Boston Public Garden and Newbury St), Copley (Copley Sq., Boston Public Library, Back Bay) and Kenmore (Boston University, Fenway Park baseball stadium). Passengers using the Green Line's E branch reach the Museum of Fine Arts, Symphony Hall, Prudential Center and the Christian Science Center.

Take the **Red Line** northbound to Harvard and MIT, southbound to the John F Kennedy Library and Museum and historic sites in suburban Quincy. Also on the Red Line are the Old State House and South Station.

The **Blue Line** is the one to take for the New England Aquarium and Logan Airport, while the **Orange Line** (not recommended at night) has a Chinatown stop and goes to Arnold Arboretum. **Purple** designates MBTA commuter-rail service (see p. 115).

MONEY SAVERS

Visitor passes are available for one, three or seven consecutive days' unlimited travel on the 'T'.

Boston CityPass ticket books entitle users to half-price admittance at the Museum of Science, Museum of Fine Arts, New England Aquarium, JFK Library and Museum, John Hancock Observatory and Isabella Stewart Gardner Museum.

Both passes are available at visitor information centres.

Station, and a limited daily service to Portland from North Station which is also used by MBTA trains to Haverhill, Newburyport, Rockport, Lowell and Fitchburg.

Near South Station, the bus terminal accommodates Greyhound, tel: (800) 231-2222, Peter Pan Trailways, tel: (413) 781-2900, and other intercity motorcoach services.

GETTING AROUND

TRANSPORT MAP – inside back cover

OLDEST SUBWAY

One of numerous Bostonian 'firsts in America' is the underground's short initial stretch linking Park Street Station with Boylston Station, at opposite edges of Boston Common, inaugurated in 1897.

Public transport is essential in squeezed-together, traffic-congested Boston. The Massachusetts Bay Transportation Authority (MBTA or simply 'the T') operates streetcars, buses and subways in town, in across-the-river Cambridge and nearby suburbs. In addition, the T provides commuter ferryboat service between downtown landings and the Charlestown Navy Yard.

Subway tokens are sold at all T stations; bus drivers and streetcar conductors taketokens or exact change. MBTA Information Line: tel: (800) 392-6100 or (617) 222-3200; www.mbta.com.

INFORMATION

Greater Boston Convention and Visitors Bureau (GBCVB), 2 Copley Pl. (Suite 105), Boston, MA 02116-6510; tel: (888) 733-2678 or (617) 536-4100; www.bostonusa.com. The bureau operates visitor information centres on the Tremont St side of Boston Common and inside the Prudential Center.

Along the Freedom Trail (see p. 121), you'll find a **National Parks Service Visitors Center**, 15 State St; tel: (617) 242-5642; www.nps.gov.

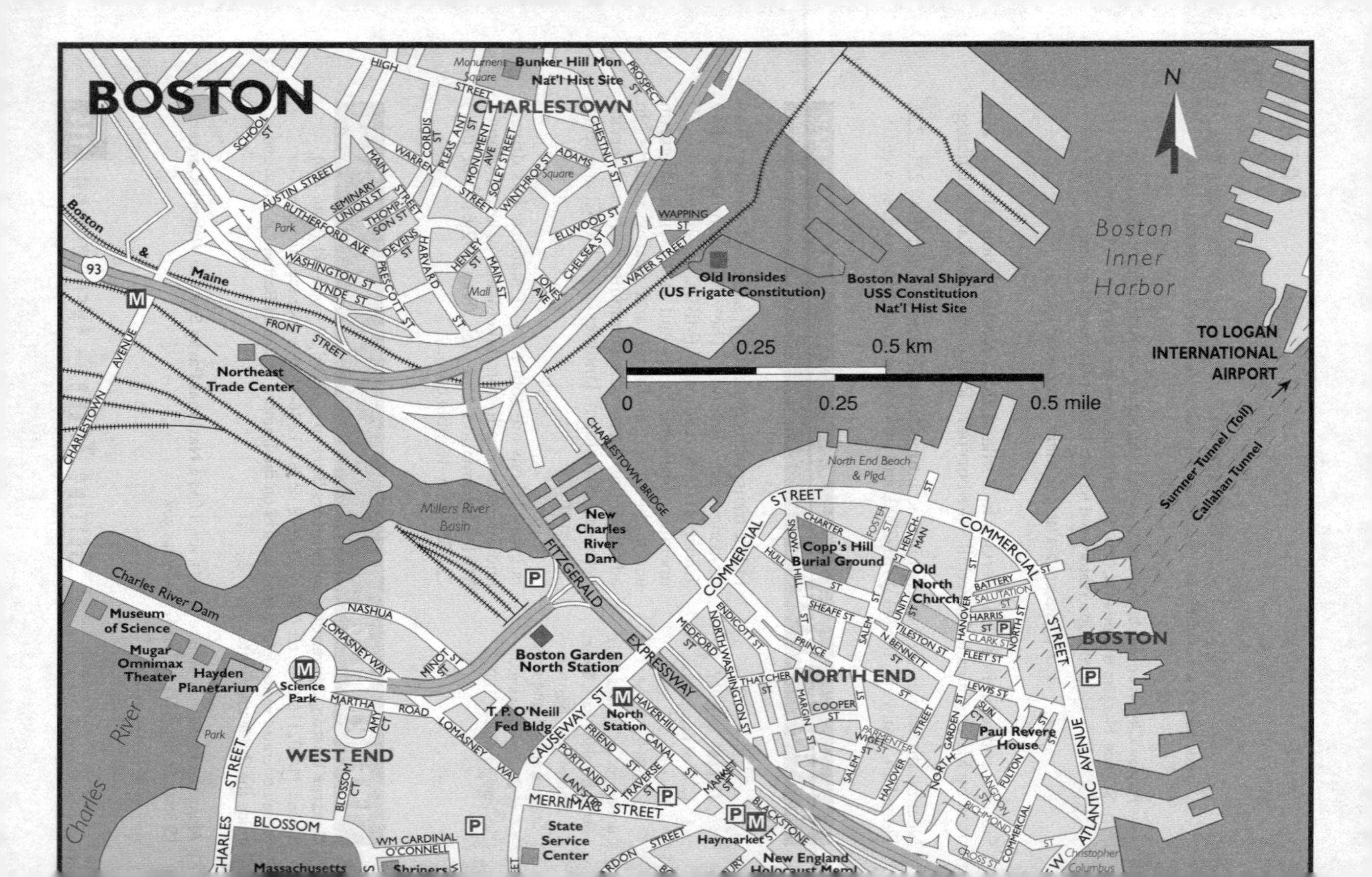
BOSTON
CHARLESTOWN
Bunker Hill Mon Nat'l Hist Site
Monument Square
Old Ironsides (US Frigate Constitution)
Boston Naval Shipyard USS Constitution Nat'l Hist Site
Boston Inner Harbor
N
0 0.25 0.5 km
0 0.25 0.5 mile
TO LOGAN INTERNATIONAL AIRPORT
Sumner Tunnel (Toll)
Callahan Tunnel
Northeast Trade Center
Millers River Basin
New Charles River Dam
Charles River Dam
Museum of Science
Mugar Omnimax Theater
Hayden Planetarium
Science Park
Boston Garden North Station
North Station
T. P. O'Neill Fed Bldg
WEST END
NORTH END
Copp's Hill Burial Ground
Old North Church
Paul Revere House
North End Beach & Plgd.
BOSTON
State Service Center
Haymarket
New England Holocaust Meml
Charles River
Boston & Maine
93
FITZGERALD EXPRESSWAY
CHARLESTOWN BRIDGE
COMMERCIAL STREET
ATLANTIC AVENUE
CAUSEWAY ST
MERRIMAC STREET
CHARLES STREET
BLOSSOM
BLOSSOM CT
WM CARDINAL O'CONNELL
Shriners
Massachusetts
Christopher Columbus
HIGH STREET
SCHOOL ST
AUSTIN STREET
RUTHERFORD AVE
WASHINGTON ST
LYNDE ST
FRONT STREET
CHARLESTOWN AVENUE
MAIN STREET
WARREN
CORDIS ST
PLEAS ANT ST
MONUMENT AVE
SOLEY STREET
WINTHROP ST
ADAMS
CHESTNUT ST
PROSPECT ST
WAPPING ST
WATER STREET
ELLWOOD ST
CHELSEA ST
JONES AVE
MAIN ST
HENLEY ST
HARVARD
PRESCOTT ST
DEVENS ST
THOMP-SON ST
UNION ST
SEMINARY
Park
Mall
Square
NASHUA
LOMASNEY WAY
MINOT ST
MARTHA ROAD
AMY CT
HAVERHILL
CANAL
FRIEND
PORTLAND ST
TRAVERSE ST
LANSTER
MARKET ST
BLACKSTONE
MEDFORD ST
NORTH WASHINGTON ST
ENDICOTT ST
THATCHER ST
MARGIN ST
COOPER ST
PRINCE
SHEAFE ST
SNOW-HILL ST
HULL
CHARTER
FOSTER ST
HENCH-MAN ST
UNITY ST
TILESTON ST
N BENNETT ST
SALEM ST
PARMENTER
WIGET ST
HANOVER
BATTERY
SALUTATION ST
HARRIS ST
NORTH ST
CLARK ST
FLEET ST
LEWIS ST
SUN CT
NORTH
GARDEN ST
FULTON
LANGDON
RICHMOND
COMMERCIAL
CROSS ST

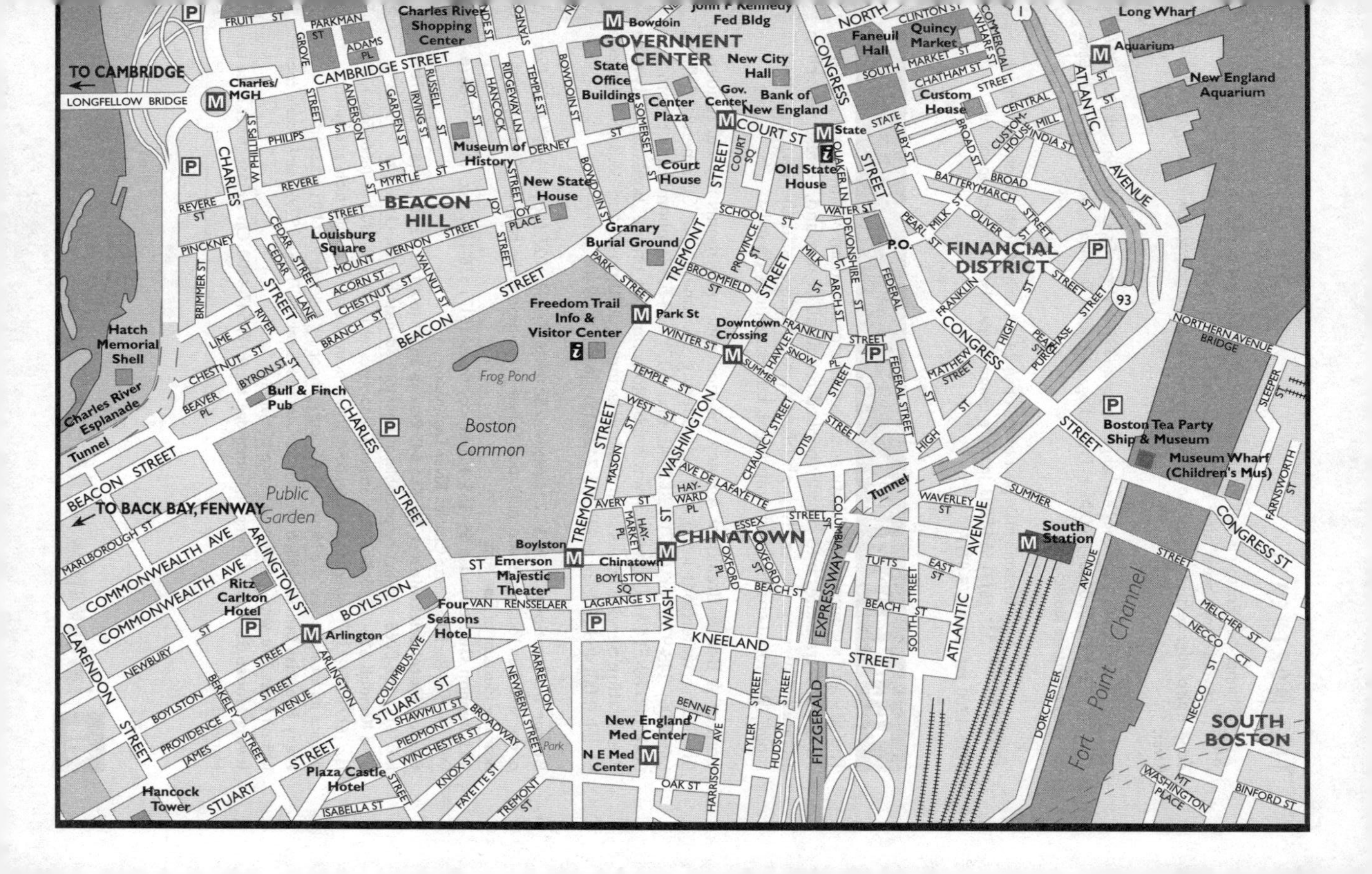

TO CAMBRIDGE
LONGFELLOW BRIDGE
Charles/MGH
Hatch Memorial Shell
Charles River Esplanade
Tunnel
TO BACK BAY, FENWAY
BEACON STREET
CHARLES STREET
Bull & Finch Pub
Public Garden
Boston Common
Frog Pond
Freedom Trail Info & Visitor Center
Park St
Granary Burial Ground
BEACON HILL
Louisburg Square
Museum of History
New State House
Charles River Shopping Center
CAMBRIDGE STREET
State Office Buildings
GOVERNMENT CENTER
Bowdoin
Center Plaza
Court House
Gov. Center
New City Hall
Bank of New England
Fed Bldg
Old State House
State
Faneuil Hall
Quincy Market
Custom House
Aquarium
Long Wharf
New England Aquarium
ATLANTIC AVENUE
FINANCIAL DISTRICT
P.O.
Downtown Crossing
TREMONT STREET
WASHINGTON
CHINATOWN
Chinatown
Boylston
Emerson Majestic Theater
Four Seasons Hotel
Arlington
Ritz Carlton Hotel
Plaza Castle Hotel
Hancock Tower
New England Med Center
N E Med Center
KNEELAND STREET
South Station
Fort Point Channel
Boston Tea Party Ship & Museum
Museum Wharf (Children's Mus)
NORTHERN AVENUE BRIDGE
CONGRESS STREET
SOUTH BOSTON
EXPRESSWAY
FITZGERALD
COMMONWEALTH AVE
MARLBOROUGH ST
NEWBURY STREET
BOYLSTON STREET
CLARENDON STREET
ARLINGTON ST
STUART STREET

SAFETY Inner-city Boston is well lit at night, full of people and therefore generally safe. Avoid 'fringe areas' after dark – especially the so-called, fast-shrinking Combat Zone – also edgy sections of the South End, as well as Esplanade walkways along the Charles River.

MONEY Travelex has a currency exchange facility at 399 Boylston St, Copley Sq.; tel: (800) 287-7362. Open 0900–1700 Mon–Fri. At Logan Airport's Terminal E, you'll find a Fleet Bank currency exchange kiosk.

POST AND PHONES Boston's main post office, open 24 hrs daily, is behind South Station; tel: (617) 654-5083. In more central Faneuil Hall, a branch opens daily 0930–1700; tel: (800) 275-8777.

ACCOMMODATION

The city and vicinity's popularity as a vacation, convention, business and academic destination translates into heavily booked rooms all year round, so reserve well in advance. Rates are generally high (the overall average is in the very pricey $175 range). National chains are omnipresent, but exceptions do exist.

Contact **A Bed & Breakfast Agency** for moderate-price rooms in local residences (including waterfront lofts) and self-catering apartments: 47 Commercial Wharf; tel: (800) 248-9262 or (617) 720-3540; fax: (617) 523-5761; phone direct from UK: 00-1 800-89-51-28. Or visit www.bnbboston.com for online booking. **Citywide Reservation Service** books rooms in hotels, inns, guesthouses and B&Bs: 839 Beacon St; tel: (800) 468-3593 or (617) 267-7424; fax: (617) 267-9408.

Boston International AYH $ 12 Hemenway St; tel: (617) 536-1027; fax: (617) 424-6558. Part of the American Youth Hostel organisation. Super-inexpensive; in the Fenway neighbourhood near the Museum of Fine Arts.

463 Beacon Guest House $$–$$$ 463 Beacon St; tel: (617) 536-1302; fax: (617) 247-8876. West end of Back Bay, near Charles River Esplanade.

Boston Hotel Buckminster $$–$$$ 645 Beacon St; tel: (800) 727-2825 or (617) 236-7050; fax: (617) 262-0068. Old but respectable; at Kenmore Sq. near Boston University.

The Kendall $$$–$$$$ 350 Main Street, Cambridge; tel: (617) 577-1300 or (866) 566-1300; fax: (617) 577-1377; www.kendallhotel.com. Stylish boutique hotel, comfortable and quiet, despite its location near the Museum of Science, shopping galleries and MIT museums.

Mary Prentiss Inn $$–$$$, 6 Prentiss St, Cambridge, tel: (617) 661-2929. Comfortable rooms just off Mass. Ave. within walking distance of Harvard Sq.

Irving House $$–$$$, 24 Irving St, Cambridge, tel: (617) 547-4600. On a quiet street close to Harvard Sq.

FOOD AND DRINK

Boston remains best known for fresh seafood. There's also no shortage of traditional Italian and Irish cooking, and such Yankee fare as pot roast, baked beans and Indian pudding. Added to that is a whole wider world of ethnic cuisine. Browse through the North End to take your pick of Italian eateries; do the same in Chinatown for big helpings of affordable Chinese and Vietnamese fare.

BEACON HILL AND DOWNTOWN

Faneuil Hall Marketplace has restaurants and food stalls cooking everything from pizza and hot dogs, soups and sandwiches to full-course lunches and dinners. The colonnaded middle building of this bustling complex contains the largest conglomeration of cheap eateries, with communal seating beneath the dome.

Black Rose $$–$$$ 160 State St; tel: (617) 742-2286. Irish pubs are plentiful in this most Irish of US cities. Food, drink, live Celtic entertainment, central location.

Durgin Park $$–$$$ 340 Faneuil Hall Marketplace; tel: (617) 227-2038. A no-nonsense taste of old Boston, with hearty New England fare.

Prezza $$ 24 Fleet St; tel (617) 227-1577. Upscale North End Italian with huge portions.

Union Oyster House $$$ 41 Union St; tel: (617) 227-2750. The US's oldest restaurant, in continuous existence since 1826. Enjoy oysters galore at the ancient mahogany raw bar.

New Golden Gate $–$$ 66 Beach St (Chinatown); tel: (617) 338-7721. Go between 1100 opening and 1500 for incredibly cheap luncheon specials, gigantic enough to carry back left-overs to the hotel for dinner.

WATERFRONT

The Wharf $$–$$$ 80 Atlantic Ave; tel: (617) 227-7280. Small, casual, chatty. On a dock poking into Boston harbour.

BACK BAY

Betty's Wok and Noodle Diner $$ 250 Huntington Ave; tel: (617) 424-1950. Retro-chic Asian-Latino diner offers noodle and rice dishes with do-it-yourself toppings. Near Symphony Hall, Huntington Theatre and New England Conservatory of Music.

Atlantic Fish Company $$$ 761 Boylston St; tel: (617) 267-4000. Boston's culinary essence: fresh-caught seafood.

Legal Sea Foods $$ 26 Park Plaza; tel: (617) 426-4444. Casual, noisy local chain with outlets in Copley Place, the Prudential Center and overlooking Boston Harbor at Long Wharf.

CAMBRIDGE

John Harvard's Brewhouse $$ 33 Dunster St; tel: (617) 868-3585. Inexpensive pub food attracts collegiate clientele.

Fire & Ice $$ 50 Church St; tel: (617) 547-9007; www.fire-ice.com. All-you-can-eat grill buffet, cooked to order while you watch. Great atmosphere and enthusiastic staff.

HIGHLIGHTS

BEACON HILL AND DOWNTOWN

Boston's earliest citizens lived on a tiny fist-shaped peninsula crowned with three prominent hills; atop the tallest during Colonial times stood a blazing signal beacon. Two hills were cut down and used as landfill, but this most Bostonian of old neighbourhoods remains 'the Hill', a British-looking warren of crooked streets and red-brick terraces. Among its photogenic highlights is **Louisburg Square**, a fenced-in, London-type crescent and a posh address. Beacon Hill is bordered by Boston Common and antiques-shop-lined Charles St. The neighbourhood's lower, 'flat' section borders Storrow Dr., with foot-bridges connected to the Charles River Esplanade.

THE BOSTON MASSACRE

The attempt by an impoverished British government to raise revenue by increased taxes and tighter trade regulations angered American Colonists, who had no representation in the parliament that was imposing the levies. Protests culminated on 5 March 1770 in the so-called Boston Massacre, in which five Colonists were shot by British soldiers facing a taunting mob. Many taxes (but not on tea) were repealed and a period of calm followed, to be broken by the Boston Tea Party (see p. 124).

'New' State House, in Beacon St, is Beacon Hill's oldest building (completed in 1798) and seat of Massachusetts' state government. Its dome is gilded with 23-carat gold leaf, and yellow Sienese marble adorns the Hall of Flags; a statue of John F Kennedy stands alongside the main entrance. Free tours Mon–Fri 1000–1530; tel: (617) 727-3676.

LAID TO REST

Three of Boston's cemeteries are historically significant. Granary Burying Ground (1660), Tremont St, is the last resting place of such notables as Paul Revere, John Hancock, Samuel Adams and Boston-born Benjamin Franklin's mom and dad. King's Chapel Burying Ground, Tremont St, is the city's oldest graveyard, predating 'Old Granary' by three decades. Interred here is John Winthrop, the Massachusetts colony's first governor. Slate headstones on the crest of Copp's Hill, Charter St, mark the graves of 17th-century Puritan settlers. For a pricey ($$$+), but fun and history-filled evening, reserve a place on the **Ghosts and Gravestones Tour**, a trolley/walking tour of Boston's historic cemeteries, with actors playing historic roles; tel: (617) 269-3626, www.ghostsandgravestones.com/boston.htm.

Now dwarfed by financial district high-rises, the **'Old' State House**, 206 Washington St, was the seat of British government from 1713 to 1776 (the building's eastern end still bears the royal lion and unicorn), and later that of the Massachusetts legislature. Inside is Boston's history museum ($; open daily 0900–1700), and outside is a cobblestone circle marking the site of the Boston Massacre.

TOURS

Old Town Trolley Tours, $$$; tel: (617) 269-7010. Hop aboard a trolley at any of 16 stops for a narrated ride. You can disembark and reboard as you please; the next trolley comes along every 15 mins. Full tour takes 100 mins. It's the same procedure for separate, shorter-length Cambridge touring.

Faneuil Hall, the 1742 meeting-house-atop-a-market-place in Dock Sq., was where such firebrand orators as Samuel Adams aired the ideas that led to the American Revolution, hence its 'Cradle of Liberty' title. Still an open-forum meeting hall upstairs, it now has a cluster of shops downstairs. Its grasshopper weathervane was inspired by the one above London's Royal Exchange. Open daily 0900–1700.

Between Congress and Union Sts stands the **New England Holocaust Memorial Carmen Park**. The six luminous glass towers etched with 6 million numbers, commemorating those who perished, make a haunting metaphor.

To the west of Beacon Hill, bordered by Tremont, Boylston, Charles, Beacon and Park Sts, is America's first public park, **Boston Common**. The 48-acre common was laid out in 1634 as a pasture for Colonists' cattle, and was also where that era's criminals were publicly hanged. Meandering walkways cross the open land and link monuments, memorials, fountains and the Frog Pond, frozen in winter for ice-skating.

Boston Public Garden abuts the common to the west. The nation's first botanical garden (1837), it is very Victorian in concept, with flowerbeds, weeping willows and a lagoon upon which the city's famous Swan Boats have taken passengers on lazy rides since 1877. (They operate Apr–mid-Sept.) Bronze ducks on the Beacon St side recall the Boston-based children's book *Make Way for Ducklings*.

BACK BAY

Originally a foul-smelling mudflat, this prestigious neighbourhood was created by an epic landfill project in the late 19th century. It is criss-crossed by a Boston rarity: streets laid in an orderly grid. A parallel row of them is alphabetically named (Arlington to Hereford) after English dukes. Commonwealth

THE FREEDOM TRAIL

In the most walkable of major US cities, it makes good sense to indulge in some self-guided sightseeing on foot – best accomplished by following this 2½-mile route connecting sites associated with the city's early history. The trail begins at the visitor centre near the Park St T station on Boston Common and, designated by a red line, slithers through downtown, the North End and over the water to Charlestown. You can pick up a map at the start-point, or halfway along at the National Park Service facility, where a better free map is available. (If you prefer knowledgeable guidance, Park Service Rangers lead 90-min tours, Mon–Fri 1100 and 1400, Sat–Sun 1000, 1300 and 1400.)

Ave is split down the middle by a graceful, wide promenade, tree-shaded and lined with statues. Many of Back Bay's town houses are occupied by schools, consulates and pricey condominiums.

For citywide panoramics, ride up to the **Skywalk Observatory** atop the Prudential Center skyscraper, one of New England's tallest. Enjoy spectacular day and night-time views from this 52nd-floor vantage point high above downtown's Back Bay neighbourhood. Souvenir shop and dining facilities. $, 800 Boylston St; open daily 1000-2200. Tel: (617) 859-0648.

The neo-Romanesque bulk of **Trinity Episcopal Church** is dramatically reflected in the John Hancock Tower's mirror-glass facade. Consecrated in 1877, it is considered by many to be H H Richardson's architectural masterpiece; the interiors were designed by John LaFarge. Open daily 0800–1800; free guided tours Sun 1215; organ concerts Fri 1215 (Sept–June).

Close by, in Dartmouth St, is **Boston Public Library**. Completed in 1895, it's regarded as one of the first outstanding examples of the Beaux Arts style in the US. The bronze doors were created by Daniel Chester French and a walk up the marble stairway is worthwhile to see murals by Puvis de Chavannes, Edwin Abbey and John Singer Sargent on second- and third-storey walls. You can also admire the courtyard garden and barrel-vaulted Bates Reading Room. Open Mon–Thur 0900–2100, Fri–Sat 0900–1700 all year; also Sun 1300–1700 (Oct–May).

The **Institute of Contemporary Art** is housed in a former Back Bay police station, with changing exhibitions of avant-garde paintings, sculptures and photographs. It's a venue, too, for concerts, lectures, films, videos and performance arts programmes: 995 Boyston St; open Wed–Sun 1200–1700 ($, free admittance Thur 1700–2100).

Taking up a whole block of Huntington Ave, the plaza and buildings of the **Christian Science Center** are dominated by the Mother Church of the Christian Science faith, founded locally by Mary Baker Eddy. Free tours Tues–Sat 1000–1600, Sun 1130.

Sightsee by day the multi-ethnic enclave of **South End** (not to be confused with South Boston) that spreads south of Back Bay, between Columbus Ave and Washington St. It encompasses the USA's largest concentration of Victorian terrace houses, some surrounding a pair of London lookalikes – Rutland Sq. and Union Park. There are innovative restaurants and chic cafés on the main thoroughfare, Tremont St. Its broad, pleasantly landscaped Southwest Corridor takes the place of a planned-for motorway extension, defeated by civic activists.

CHARLES RIVER ESPLANADE AND THE FENWAY

A lengthy green belt, the **Charles River Esplanade**, runs along Boston's side of the river. In summertime, the Hatch Shell hosts outdoor cinemas and concert series, including Boston Pops performances. Pedestrians, joggers and bicyclists can cross bridges to more parkway along Memorial Dr. on the Cambridge side.

The **Museum of Science** at the Science Park, downriver from the Esplanade, has more than 500 exhibits, and many hands-on activities covering all things scientific from anthropology to space exploration. Combination tickets or separate admittances ($$) to the **Hayden Planetarium** and **Mugar Omnimax Theater**. Museum open daily 0900–1700 (July–Sept), also Fri 1700–2100 rest of year.

Dropping south of the Esplanade is Boston's 'Emerald Necklace' of interconnected parklands, conceived a century ago by landscape maestro Frederick Law Olmsted. **Arnold Arboretum** (125 Arborway, Jamaica Plain) is part of the necklace, a 265-acre site with thousands of trees, shrubs and flowers, including 250 varieties of lilac. Open daily dawn–dusk.

A 1901 building (plus a modernistic wing) at 465 Huntington Ave houses the **Museum of Fine Arts** (MFA). The USA's second-largest public art collection spans all periods, but is particularly strong on Asian and Egyptian art, French Impressionism (43 Claude Monet paintings) and Early American works. $$, tel: (617) 267-9300; open Mon–Tues 1000–1645, Wed 1000–2145, Thur–Fri 1000–1700, Sat–Sun 1000–1745. West Wing stays open Thur–Fri until 2145. Free admittance Wed after 1600.

Works by Rembrandt, Botticelli, Titian and other old masters, along with tapestry and Greco-Roman statuary, form the eclectic collection of a 19th-century socialite. The **Isabella Stewart Gardner Museum** at 280 The Fenway is in her replicated 15th-century Italian *palazzo*, complete with lush, flowering courtyard; tel: (617) 566-1401. Open Tues–Sun 1100–1700.

HARBORFEST

The harbour, and indeed all of Boston, fills with visitors for the early-July Harborfest, an Independence Day celebration that features the city's rich history with re-enactments, walking tours, cruises, concerts, parties and a chowder cook-off. Most events are free. Tel: (617) 227-1528, www.bostonharborfest.com.

NORTH END AND THE WATERFRONT

The North End, Boston's 'Little Italy', overlooks the harbour and nearby downtown skyline. Centred around Hanover St, its narrow thoroughfares, especially Salem St, are chock-full of trattorias and cafés, and on summer weekends the streets are often alive with religious festivals.

Christ Church ('Old North'), built in 1723, is another stop on the history trail. In its steeple were hung the lanterns that signalled British troop movements ('one if by land, two if by sea'), and which in April 1775 started Paul Revere on his horseback ride through the night to warn patriot leaders at Lexington and Concord of the enemy's impending arrival (see p. 128): 193 Salem St; open daily 0900–1700. **Paul Revere**

THE BOSTON TEA PARTY

The arrival in Boston harbour in November 1773 of three British ships bearing cheap tea threatened to undermine the boycott on the taxed leaves. An angry mob, dressed as Mohawk Indians, swarmed aboard the ships and dumped the precious cargo into the harbour. An exhibition and re-enactments can be seen at Old South Meeting House ($, 310 Washington St; open daily 0930–1700), where angry citizens gathered to curse the Brits on the evening of the Tea Party; the Boston Tea Party Ship and Museum on the Congress St bridge has a replica of one of three vessels, *Beaver II*; $$, open daily 0900–1700 (Mar–Dec).

House is where the silversmith patriot lived for 30 years from 1770. It contains period furnishings and Revere memorabilia. $, 19 North Sq.; open daily 0930–1715 (Apr–mid-Oct), 0930–1615 (Nov–Dec).

Further along the waterfront, on Central Wharf, the **New England Aquarium** has sea-lion shows, penguin colonies and exhibits of exotic ocean life. The main feature is a four-storey tubular glass tank in which aquatic creatures – including turtles, sharks, moray eels and tropical fish – swim in and out of a coral reef. Café and gift shop in the silvery new West Wing. $$, open Mon–Tues and Fri 0900–1800, Wed–Thur 0900–2000, Sat–Sun 0900–1900 (July–Sept); Mon–Fri 0900–1700, Sat–Sun 0900–1800 (Sept–June).

At Museum Wharf there are three floors of hands-on exhibits, play areas and a kids' theatre at the **Children's Museum**, $$; open daily 1000–1700 (also Fri 1700–2100).

CHARLESTOWN

From downtown, take the commuter boat or cross the bridge to reach this blue-collar (but increasingly gentrified) section of Boston.Permanently docked at Pier One of Charlestown Navy Yard is **USS *Constitution*** ('Old Ironsides'), launched in 1797 and still part of the US Navy. The 52-gun frigate, the world's oldest commissioned warship, gained its nickname when its solid oak hull proved resistant to the enemy fleet's cannonballs during the war of 1812 with Britain. Open daily for free guided tours, 0930–1550. A museum telling the saga of 'Old Ironsides', with interactive exhibits, is open daily 1900–1800.

OUT OF TOWN

The John F Kennedy Library and Museum recalls the 'Camelot' era of the Boston-born 35th US president, in a stunning white harbourfront building out at Columbia Point (Morrissey Blvd, Dorchester), reached by free shuttle from the Red Line's JFK/UMass T Station. $$; tel: (617) 929-4500; open daily 0900–1700.

After the opening shots of the American Revolution had been fired at Lexington and Concord in 1775 (see p. 128), British redcoats tried to lift a rebel siege of Boston. The misnamed Battle of Bunker Hill (it actually took place on nearby Breed's Hill) on 17 June was a victory for Britain, though a costly one, for King George's troops evacuated Boston the following March. A 221-ft hilltop obelisk, the **Bunker Hill Monument**, marks the battleground; there are dioramas and exhibits in a building at the base, and you can climb the stairs to the top for panoramic views. Open daily 0900–1630.

Boston from the Water

Boston Duck Tours, $$$, tel: (617) 723-3825, provides 90-min narrated sightseeing jaunts aboard World War II amphibious vehicles, including splashdown in the Charles River for on-the-water views of Boston and Cambridge.

Boston Harbor Cruises, $$$, 1 Long Wharf; tel: (617) 227-4321, operates a daily variety of narrated excursions with the city skyline as a backdrop, including whale-watching cruises and stopover at George's Park (one of the Boston harbour islands), site of picnic grounds and a Civil War fort.

Spirit of Boston, $$$, tel: (617) 748-1450, offers a pricier way to cruise the harbour while enjoying lunch or dinner. Lunch cruise, 1130–1400; three-hour dinner cruises depart 1600, 1900, 2030 depending upon time of year.

Cambridge

Though tightly woven into the cultural and intellectual fabric of Boston, Cambridge is a separate, staunchly free-thinking, across-the-river municipality, home to Harvard University and the Massachusetts Institute of Technology.

i **Cambridge Office for Tourism**, 18 Brattle St; tel: (800) 862-5678 or (617) 441-2884; www.cambridge-usa.org.

Harvard Yard, the university's inner sanctum and the ultimate New England campus quadrangle, is surrounded by brick walls and reached through tall wrought-iron gates. The seated bronze figure memorialises the young English cleric John Harvard, who left half his money and all his books to the fledgling college when he died in 1638, two years after it was founded. Buildings in and around the yard span the history of US architecture.

The **Fogg Art Museum**, 32 Quincy St, features European and North American art from the Middle Ages to contemporary times. In Otto Werner Hall on the second floor the Busch-Reisinger Museum specialises in 19th–20th-century art of Germanic-speaking countries, notably the Vienna Secessionist and German Expressionist periods. $ (Sat free); open Mon–Sat 1000–1700, Sun 1300–1700.

Free student-led Harvard Yard tours courtesy of the Harvard Information Center, Holyoke Center, 1350 Massachusetts Ave; tel: (617) 495-1573. Tours Mon–Fri 1000 and 1400, Sat 1400 (Sept–May); Mon–Sat 1000, 1115, 1400 and 1515, Sun 1330 and 1500 (June–Aug).

A joint ticket gives admittance to the Fogg and the nearby **Arthur M Sackler Museum**. This striking post-modern building, designed by the British architect James Stirling, houses Harvard's collections of classical, Asian, Islamic and late Indian art. $, 485 Broadway; open Mon–Sat 1000–1700, Sun 1300–1700.

On an upper-class street north of Harvard Sq. once known as 'Tory Row' is the home of poet **Henry Wadsworth Longfellow** (1807–1882), who gave us *Hiawatha* and immortalised (and romanticised) Paul Revere's midnight ride. His 18th-century Georgian-style house depicts the Longfellow family's comfortable lifestyle. Earlier in history (1775–6), this was George Washington's headquarters. $, 105 Brattle St; guided tours Wed–Sun 1000–1630 (May–Oct).

Longfellow lies buried in **Mount Auburn Cemetery**, America's first 'garden cemetery', alongside such eminent personalities as the founder of Christian Science, Mary Baker Eddy (see p. 122), the writer Oliver Wendell Holmes and the social reformer and writer Julia Ward Howe, who wrote 'The Battle Hymn of the Republic': 580 Mt Auburn St; open daily 0800–1700 (till 1900 in summer).

MODERN ARCHITECTURE IN CAMBRIDGE

Le Corbusier's only US building (24 Quincy St) is used by the **Carpenter Center for the Visual Arts** for contemporary art exhibitions and nightly Harvard Film Archive cinema screenings. $, open Mon–Sat 0900–2300, Sun 1200–2200.

MIT's **List Visual Arts Center**, 20 Ames St, is a gridlike structure designed by I M Pei, with three galleries displaying contemporary art. Open Tues–Sun 1200–1800 (Fri until 2000). On MIT's **West Campus** there is more Cantabrigian architectural bravado, this one a cylindrical brick edifice desiged by Finland's Eero Saarinen, which is both a religious and concert venue. Open dawn–dusk.

SHOPPING

Boston's main shopping district is Downtown Crossing, a crowded car-free zone centred on Washington and Winter Sts, where both the big department stores (Filene's and Macy's) and a myriad of other stores are located. Bargain hunters delve into the frenzy of Filene's Basement, well known for 'automatic markdown' savings.

Back Bay's Newbury St is a people-watchers' paradise amid galleries, bookstores, indoor/outdoor cafés and boutiques ranging from stylish to offbeat. Across Boylston St from that trendiest of Boston thoroughfares is the Prudential Center's mall, an extensive galleria complex with eateries and 70 shops in various price ranges. That bazaar connects via covered walkway to Copley Pl. and its 100 stores with mostly higher price tags.

Near the harbourfront, wildly popular Faneuil Hall/Quincy Marketplace, packed with tourists and Bostonians day and night, consists of three renovated 1825 market buildings, supplemented by newer add-ons, that house 125 shops, restaurants, pubs and food stalls.

Over in Cambridge, Harvard Sq. and surroundings provide an additional splurge of shopping opportunities that include plenty of souvenirs displaying the Harvard emblem. This compact area boasts more bookshops per square foot than anywhere else on earth.

NIGHTLIFE

The Calendar section in each Thursday's *Boston Globe,* Scene in Friday's *Boston Herald* and listings in the weekly *Boston Phoenix* and *Improper Bostonian* tabloids contain updates of what's happening.

The theatre district around Tremont and Boylston Sts draws audiences to musicals and dramas at the cavernous Wang Center, the classy Colonial, the more intimate Wilbur and Emerson Majestic and the tiny Charles Playhouse. There's also a thriving small-theatre scene, and classical and contemporary drama are performed at the Lyric Stage (140 Clarendon St) and Boston University's Huntington Theater Company (264 Huntington Ave). More such doings in Cambridge, where Loeb Drama Center, 64 Brattle St, is home of the American Repertory Theater (ART). Boston area colleges and universities present reputable theatrical offerings, too. Half-price, same-day-performance tickets go on sale (cash only) at Bostix booths located alongside Faneuil Hall, and at Copley Sq.

New as of 2005, the Boston Center of the Arts' impressively designed **Calderwood Pavilion** presents new plays produced by the city's small theatrical companies. 527 Tremont St in the South End

The classical music scene is dominated by the Boston Symphony Orchestra (also the lighter-weight Boston Pops) at acoustically pitch-perfect **Symphony Hall**, 301 Massachusetts Ave; tel: (617) 266-2378 (information) or 266-1200 (tickets). For an ongoing school-year programme of (mostly) free concerts, Jordan Hall is at the nearby New England Conservatory, 290 Huntington Ave; tel: (617) 536-2412. Harvard-Radcliffe, Boston University, MIT, Tufts, Berklee Performance Center, Boston Conservatory and the Longy School also schedule high-calibre student performances. The Shubert Theater, 265 Tremont St, is home of the Boston Lyric Opera; tel: (617) 437-7122. For Boston Ballet performances, tel: (617) 695-6950.

Boston's historic, lavishly restored **Opera House** stages mega-big operatic and musical-theatre productions. 539 Washingston St; tel: (617) 931-2787.

THE FIRST SHOTS OF REVOLUTION

On 19 April 1775 British forces marched from Boston towards Concord for what they thought would be an easy task: to confiscate caches of arms owned by the increasingly restless Colonists. Instead they met with armed resistance from local militia – the Colonists had been forewarned of their imminent arrival by Paul Revere, riding through the night to warn the patriot leaders.

Unfair taxes (see the Boston Tea Party, p. 124) and a growing resistance to British rule meant it had been only a matter of time before a bid was made for independence, and the ensuing battles were the start of the American Revolution.

The **Minuteman National Historical Park** commemorates the events of the day the British regulars, the 'Redcoats' were driven back towards their Boston encampments. Most of the park follows Rte 2A along that retreat path, now called Battle Road. **Lexington Green**, site of the initial dawn skirmish, is surrounded by white-spired churches and the yellow clapboard Buckman Tavern, where the Colonial militiamen (called minutemen, for they could be ready in a minute) assembled the night before. The next major battle site was at **North Bridge** in Concord, and costumed re-enactments of both firefights are held in the early hours each April on the fateful date.

The **Museum of Our National Heritage** in Lexington, **Battle Road Visitors Center** (open mid-Apr–Oct only) and **North Bridge Visitor Center** in Concord all commemorate these historic times – the Battle Road Center presents an excellent video and a diorama tracing the first 4 miles of the British retreat.

Driven back to Boston, the British tried to lift a rebel siege, but despite their victory at the Battle of Bunker Hill were forced to withdraw from Boston the following March.

The area has a hyperactive pop, rock, jazz, blues, folk, country and cabaret scene at Kenmore Sq. and on nearby Lansdowne St, in the Faneuil Hall Marketplace vicinity, the student-populated Allston neighbourhood, in various parts of Cambridge and elsewhere. Abundant, too, are comedy clubs, among them Nick's Comedy Stop, 100 Warrenton St; tel: (617) 482-0930.

DAY TRIPS

There is much to see outside the central city area. MBTA's rapid-transit lines (the Purple Line) fan out from Boston's South and North Stations to such North Shore locales as Salem and Gloucester (covered on pp. 140–144), westbound to Concord and vicinity, and south to Plymouth.

PLYMOUTH P&B (Plymouth & Brockton) intercity buses connect Boston with Plymouth, where the Pilgrims aboard the *Mayflower* first settled (see p. 146). The Plymouth Line from South Station will take you to Plymouth's Cordage Park, a 19th-century rope mill transformed into a marketplace.

LEXINGTON AND CONCORD Just outside the city (Lexington is only 11 miles from Boston, and Concord a further 7), these were the villages that saw the very beginning of the American War of Independence (see p.128).

Concord was also the scene of an extraordinary blossoming of American letters in the mid-19th century, when writers seized on the philosophy of Ralph Waldo Emerson ('the Sage of Concord') by creating a self-consciously national literature. The **Emerson House** has been maintained largely as he left it, with books, furniture and personal belongings. Here, too is **Orchard House**, which Louisa May Alcott described in loving detail in *Little Women*. Both writers are among the Concord literati resting in peace on **'Author's Ridge'** in Sleepy Hollow Cemetery, alongwith Henry David Thoreau and Nathaniel Hawthorne. Thoreau's beloved Walden Pond, just south of Concord, is now popular for swimming and boating, and park rangers can provide directions to the site of his humble cabin, still marked by its crumbled chimney hearth.

Points of interest are widespread and rambling, so a car is the easiest option (beware of heavy traffic – this is a popular tourist trail). Alternatively, Concord Depot, half a mile from the town centre, is on the MBTA commuter-rail line from Boston's South Station; you could tour the outlying sites by taxicab – Colonial Livery, tel: (978) 369-3433, is a Concord-based company. Getting from Boston to Lexington is somewhat more complex. Take the Red Line T to Alewife Station; from there, take no. 62 or 76 MBTA bus to Lexington centre.

LINCOLN If you are interested in art and architecture, take a trip out to Lincoln, where you can visit **Gropius House**, the family home and first US building (1937) by architect Walter Gropius, founder of Germany's Bauhaus school of design. $, 68 Baker Bridge Rd; tel: (781) 259-8098. Open Fri–Sun 1200–1700 (June–mid-Oct).

For contemporary art and large-scale radical sculptures, try Lincoln's **DeCordova Museum and Sculpture Park**, housed in a turreted brick building set in 35 acres. $, 51 Sandy Pond Rd; tel: (781) 259-8355. Open Wed–Sun 1000–1700.

OLD STURBRIDGE VILLAGE See what daily life was like in New England in 1830. Spread over 200 acres, some 40 structures including a blacksmith's, water-powered saw mill, one-room school, general store, bank and printing office. 'Villagers' in authentic period garb demonstrate workaday activities with the seasons; special demonstrations include weaving and basket and broom-making. The Village's **Bullard Tavern** does lunches and snacks, or its restaurant offers a seasonal menu of New England fare.

Sturbridge Tourist Information Center, 380 Main St, Sturbridge; tel: (508) 347-7594 or (800) SEE-1830. $$$, village open daily 0900–1700 (Apr–end Oct); Tues–Sun 1000–1600 (Nov–Dec and Feb–Mar); www.osv.org.

OLD STURBRIDGE VILLAGE

This makes a very long one-day trip, and as tickets to the village are valid for two consecutive days, you may like to stay over. Apart from the omnipresent chain operations (see p. 52) there are a number of distinctive inns and B&Bs. Offering good value are **Colonel Ebenezer Crafts Inn**, a Federalist farmhouse on the common; **Old Sturbridge Village Lodges and Oliver Wight House** on Rte 20 W; and the **Sturbridge Country Inn** and **Sturbridge Host Hotel**, both on Main St.

Sturbridge is 60 miles west of Boston, 50 miles north of Providence; Peter Pan/Greyhound buses from South Station normally take 95 mins (buses continue to New York City via Hartford and New Haven).

WHERE NEXT?

Strike out north along the Massachusetts shore (see p. 139), perhaps travelling right up the coast of Maine (see p. 157); or head west via Concord along Rte 2 (the 'Mohawk Trail') into the Berkshire Hills, where Tanglewood is the esteemed Boston Symphony Orchestra's summer home (see p. 173). North of Concord lies Lake Winnipesaukee and the rugged scenery of the White Mountains (see pp. 166–171).

Southwards, there are Cape Cod and its islands to explore (see pp. 145 and 151). You can take the train down to New York via the old coastal towns of Connecticut (see p. 109); or detour to Providence and Newport in Rhode Island (see pp. 131–138).

RHODE ISLAND

Despite its name, the USA's smallest state is not actually an island, although numerous small islands, waterways, inlets and coves break up its scant 1214 square miles (about the same area as Cheshire or Nottinghamshire, UK). Its capital, Providence, offers plentiful attractions and visitor amenities, but is outshone by smaller Newport.

Rhode Island's 'founding father' was Roger Williams. Upon being kicked out of the Massachusetts Bay Colony by the Puritans for his 'new and dangerous opinions', he trekked south in 1636 to establish a plantation settlement dedicated to religious freedom. This little patch of New England is still officially named the State of Rhode Island and Providence Plantation.

Newport's exclusivity as an oceanfront resort began early in Colonial times, when southern plantation owners travelled north to escape oppressive humidity in favour of cool sea breezes. By the 1850s, wealthy New Yorkers were cruising to Newport via the Fall River Steamship Line. Thus began a seasonal influx of privileged families personifying America's Gilded Age. They commissioned 'summer cottages' of palatial scope and grandeur, and this small town on the southernmost tip of Aquidneck Island became high society's 'in' place to spend millions of dollars in a binge of conspicuous consumption. The town also became a summer colony for literary notables, including Henry Wadsworth Longfellow, Julia Ward Howe and Henry James.

For an insider's view of both cities, see *Secret Providence and Newport*, by Juliette Rogers (ECW Books), a spirited guide filled with places a tourist would never find.

GETTING THERE AND GETTING AROUND

Flights from, for instance, Boston and Cape Cod fly into T F Green Airport, 7 miles south of central Providence; tel: (401) 737-4000 or (888) 268-7222.

Providence is 45 miles south of Boston via Amtrak's Northeast Corridor rail service. From Boston travellers can also get to Providence by commuter rail and, from Boston's South Station Transportation Center, via Bonanza bus, tel: (401) 331-7500. The railway station in Providence is centrally located.

From central Kennedy Plaza, Providence RIPTA (Rhode Island Public Transit Authority) buses fan out for service throughout metropolitan Providence, and also to the airport, Newport, Bristol and smaller communities. For RIPTA fares and schedules, tel: (401) 781-9400.

PROVIDENCE

Providence's capital-city stature is augmented by the energising influence of upper-crust Brown University, plus a world-class school of design. Moreover, 'Little Rhody's' mini-metropolis is a top-notch restaurant town, partly because the design school has a culinary curriculum and Johnson & Wales University educates future chefs.

FOR FREE

There are free tours of the **Rhode Island State House**, an 1891–1904 hill-top whopper in white marble, crowned by one of the world's biggest self-supporting domes. Enter at 82 Smith St; tel: (401) 222-2357. Tours Mon–Fri 0830–1630.

Riverwalk and pedestrian bridges connect the handsome 4-acre **Waterplace Park** with city-centre attractions. It features an amphitheatre overlooking a lagoon, and a Venetian-type gondola takes passengers on waterway rides.

The third Thursday of each month is **Gallery Night**, when free ArTrolleys shuttle between galleries, museums, antiques shops, and art and performance events.

i **Providence Warwick Convention and Visitors Bureau**, 1 West Exchange St, Providence, RI 02903; tel: (800) 233-1636 or (401) 274-1636; www.providencecvb.com. A **Visitor Information Center** is located in the Rhode Island Convention Center.

POST The main post office is at 24 Corliss St; tel: (401) 276-6812.

Several of the US chain hotels are in town (see p. 52). Among more intimate alternatives are:

Old Court B&B $$$ 144 Benefit St; tel: (401) 751-2002; fax: (401) 272-4830. An Italianate-style Victorian mansion ideally situated for sightseeing the 'Mile of History'.

State House Inn B&B $$$ 43 Jewett St; tel: (401) 351-6111; fax: (401) 351-4261. Century-old house with ten guest-rooms in a West Side neighbourhood, close to the state capitol building.

There's no lack of elegant, pricey restaurants in Providence, and Italian trattorias pack the West Side's Federal Hill neighbourhood. Other options include:

Trinity Brewhouse $–$$ 186 Fountain St. Delectable barbecued sandwiches; house brands of ale and lager.

The Boathouse $–$$ 1 American Expressway. Dine downstairs or in the Admiral's loft on the upstairs balcony.

Meeting Street Café $$ 220 Meeting St. On College Hill, light fare including vegetarian offerings.

Barnsider's Mile and a Quarter $$$ 375 S Main St; tel: (401) 351-7300. Steak and seafood restaurant with popular salad bar.

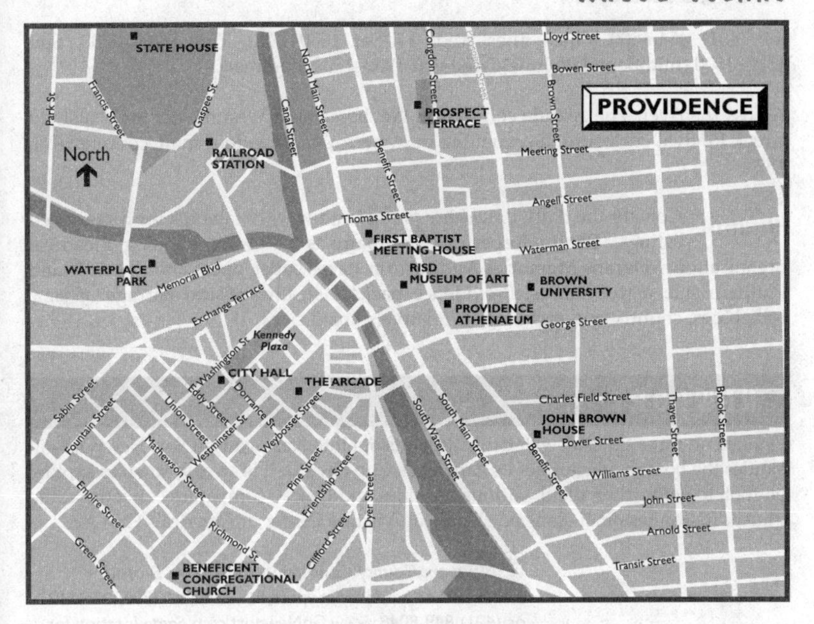

Café Nuovo **$$** 1 Citizen's Plaza. Enjoy indoor or outdoor seating overlooking the Riverwalk while dining on Caribbean, Asian or US Southwest cuisine.

HIGHLIGHTS Providence is compact and walkable. The Seekonk River, which meets up with the Providence River before emptying into Narragansett Bay, flows through the middle of the city, dividing the city into two.

Streets on the east side of town rise steeply to **College Hill**, where there's much in the way of fascinating history plus an artsy, academic atmosphere. For a great panorama of the city, climb up to the statue of Roger Williams that stands on Prospect Terrace, Congdon St.

Take a bus from Kennedy Plaza out to the excellent Roger Williams Park and Zoo. $, open daily 0900–1600 (Nov–Mar), Mon–Fri 0900–1700 (Apr–Oct).

Benefit Street, the east side's brick-paved 'Mile of History', encompasses the USA's most impressive concentration of domestic architecture from the Colonial through Victorian periods. The **RISD Museum of Art** is the Rhode Island School of Design's cultural treasure, with collections that range from French Impressionist paintings and 18th-century US furniture to ancient Greek bronzes and Roman mosaics. $ 224 Benefit St;

tel: (401) 454-6500. Open Tues–Wed, Fri–Sat 1030–1700, Thur 1200–2000, Sun 1300–1600 (mid-Sept–late June); Wed–Sat 1200–1700 (summer).

Across the river, **The Arcade** connecting Weybosset and Westminster Sts is a skylit Greek Revival enclosure that qualifies as America's first indoor mall, completed in 1828.

NIGHTLIFE Consult the daily *Providence Journal* and weekly tabloids for categorised listings. **Trinity Repertory Company** is an award-winning theatrical organisation. **Veterans Memorial Auditorium** stages ballet, opera and Rhode Island Philharmonic performances. Providence packs a steady musical barrage of jazz, folk, blues, country and rock into its relatively small size.

NEWPORT

Flanked on three sides by waterfront as it juts out into Narragansett Bay, Newport still exudes the boat-racing aura of its America's Cup heyday. It is an easy town to explore on foot; to get further afield, various bus lines and taxicab companies converge at the transportation terminal alongside Gateway Visitors Center in America's Cup Ave.

i Newport County Convention and Visitors Bureau, 23 America's Cup Ave, Newport, RI 02840; tel: (800) 976-5122 or (401) 849-8048; www.GoNewport.com. Same location for the Gateway Visitors Center, where services include accommodation bookings.

MONEY For foreign currency exchange, go to Citizens Bank, 8 Washington Sq.

POST AND PHONES Newport's main post office is at 320 Thames St; tel: (401) 847-2328.

Be mindful that room rates zoom steeply upwards during the summer. For a selection of B&Bs in various price ranges, there's no charge for bookings arranged by Taylor-Made Reservations, tel: (800) 848-8848 or (401) 848-0300; fax: (401) 849-8566; www.CityBytheSea.com.

Admiral Fitzroy Inn B&B $$$–$$$$ 398 Thames St; tel: (888) 848-8780 or (401) 848-8000; fax: (401) 848-8006. Seventeen nicely decorated guest-rooms in the Historic Hill neighbourhood.

Pineapple Inn $$–$$$ 372 Coddington Hwy (off Rt. 114); tel: (401) 847-2600 or (877) 847-2601; fax: (401) 847-5230. Modest, comfortable motel at the edge of town, good value for Newport.

Cycle rentals available at Ten Speed Spokes, 18 Elm St; tel: (401) 847-5609.

Hotel Viking $$$–$$$$ 1 Bellevue Ave; tel: (800) 556-7126 or (401) 847-3300; fax: (401) 849-8566. A vintage (1926) hotel in a quiet residential location three blocks from downtown.

Ocean Coffee Roasters $ 22 Washington Sq. Brews espresso, cappuccino and café au lait, and purveys an inexpensive array of sandwiches, scones, soups and chilli.
Gary's Handy Lunch $$ 462 Thames St. This hangout replicates a 1950s diner and – in that vein – dishes out soups, burgers, fries, meat loaf, American chop suey and daily specials.
Brick Alley Pub and Restaurant $$–$$$ 140 Thames St; tel: (401) 849-6334. Very popular, therefore very busy in all seasons. Steaks, ribs, chicken, pasta and a massive salad bar. Loaded with funky antiques.
Christie's $$$ Christie's Landing; tel: (401) 847-5400. Can't be beaten for harbour views. Ocean-fresh specialities include lobster, baked halibut and terrific Nantucket Bay scallops.
The Rhumbline $$$ 62 Bridge St; tel: (401) 849-6950. In a wooden Colonial-era house in Newport's bayfront Point district. Eclectic international menu ranges from Austrian Wiener schnitzel to Thai dishes.

SHOPPING Speciality stores cram Bannister's Wharf and Bowen's Wharf; the nearby Brick Market Place encompasses shops, galleries and clothing boutiques. Stores of all sorts line Thames St. Historic Hill's Spring St has a small-scale mercantile flavour with shops displaying antiques, pottery and ship models. The 1894 Armory, 365 Thames St, is occupied by antiques and fine-art dealers.

HIGHLIGHTS **Historic Hill**, one of New England's finest early American neighbourhoods, is reached by brick pavements sloping up from the harbour. Across town, facing Narragansett Bay, **the Point** neighbourhood is another showpiece of 18th- and 19th-century houses. The **Museum of Newport History**, housed in Brick Market Building (dating from 1762), has insightful displays and artefacts that focus on colourful local history. $, 127 Thames St; tel: (401) 841-8770. Open Mon and Wed–Sat 1000–1600, Sun 1300–1700. **Trinity Episcopal Church** in Queen Anne Sq. was modelled on English churches designed by Christopher Wren and has been in use since 1776 – look out for pew no. 81, where George Washington sat. Open Mon–Fri 1000–1600; Sun services 0800 and 1030.

Newport has several 'firsts' among its historic buildings, including the nation's oldest public library, in existence since 1747: **Redwood Library**, 50 Bellevue Ave, tel: (401) 847-0292, open Mon–Sat 0930–1730. It

TOURS

Request a map detailing the self-guided **Banner Trail**, marked by colour-coded flags at points of interest. In addition to State House, city centre and Benefit St vicinities, the route covers classy Brown University's campus and surroundings on College Hill and the hip Wickenden St historic district.
Take the RIPTA bus 4 miles north from downtown to tour the riverside **Slater Mill Historic Site**, 67 Roosevelt Ave; tel: (401) 725-8638. In 1793, Samuel Slater built the USA's first reliably operative textile plant, thereby launching the nation's industrial revolution.

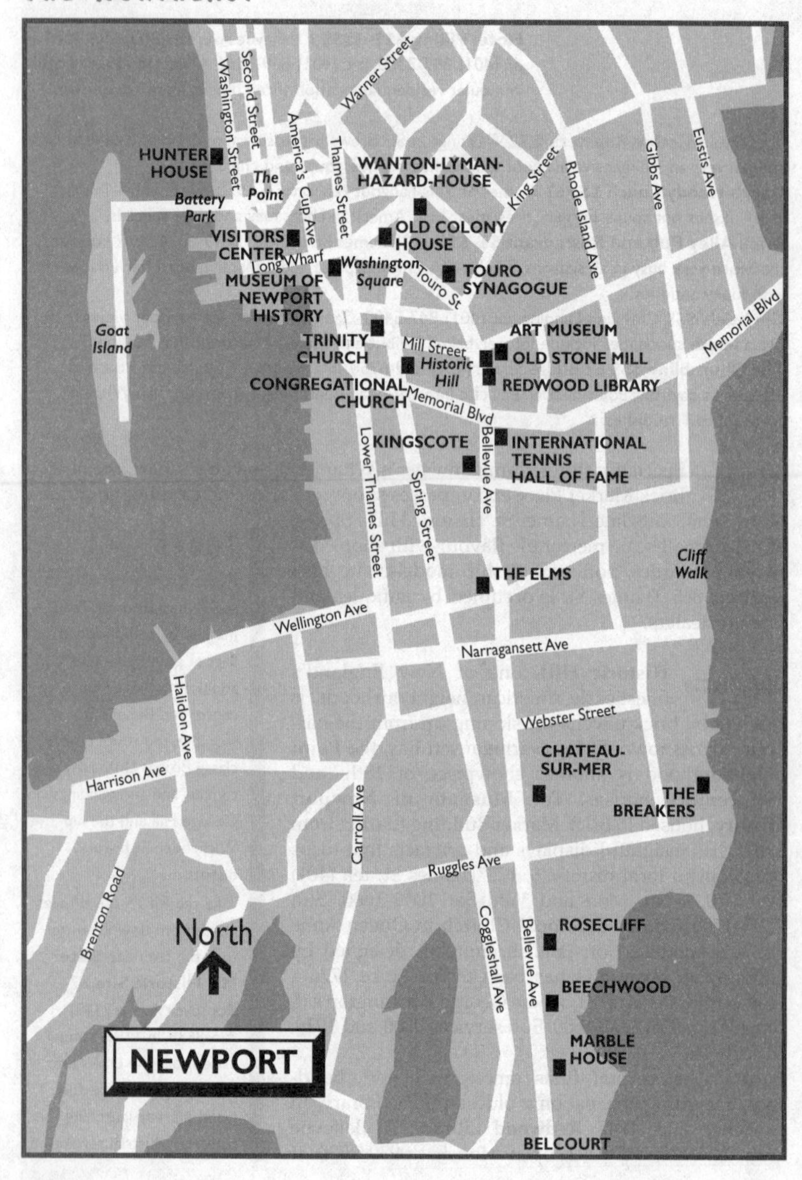
Warner Street
Second Street
Washington Street
America's Cup Ave
Thames Street
HUNTER HOUSE
The Point
Battery Park
WANTON-LYMAN-HAZARD-HOUSE
King Street
Rhode Island Ave
Gibbs Ave
Eustis Ave
OLD COLONY HOUSE
VISITORS CENTER
Long Wharf
Washington Square
Touro St
TOURO SYNAGOGUE
MUSEUM OF NEWPORT HISTORY
Goat Island
TRINITY CHURCH
Mill Street
Historic Hill
ART MUSEUM
OLD STONE MILL
REDWOOD LIBRARY
Memorial Blvd
CONGREGATIONAL CHURCH
Memorial Blvd
KINGSCOTE
Bellevue Ave
INTERNATIONAL TENNIS HALL OF FAME
Lower Thames Street
Spring Street
Cliff Walk
THE ELMS
Wellington Ave
Narragansett Ave
Halidon Ave
Webster Street
CHATEAU-SUR-MER
THE BREAKERS
Harrison Ave
Carroll Ave
Ruggles Ave
Brenton Road
North
Coggleshall Ave
Bellevue Ave
ROSECLIFF
BEECHWOOD
MARBLE HOUSE
NEWPORT
BELCOURT

also has North America's oldest Jewish house of worship (dedicated 1763), **Touro Synagogue**, 85 Touro St, tel: (401) 847-4794 (Fri services 1800 winter, 1900 summer; Sat services 0900); www.NewportMansions.org.

Covering history of a very different sort, the **International Tennis Hall of Fame** is the sport's Valhalla. Players still use the original 13 grass courts. $$, 194 Bellevue Ave, tel: (800) 457-1144 or (401) 849-3990. Open daily 1000–1700.

Newport's mansions, while not the only reason to go to this charming bayside city, are reason enough. The grandest of them are along Bellevue Avenue and the streets between it and Cliff Walk. Combination tickets ($$) are sold for all Preservation Society properties (the first five below), www.newportmansions.org, and for Beechwood, Belcourt Castle and the Tennis Hall of Fame. Beware that it is exhausting to visit more than two mansions in a day.

The Breakers, Ruggles Ave, $$, tel: (401) 847–1000. Only Vanderbilt fortunes could (or would) have built this Renaissance revival palace, Newport's most expensive and opulent. Decorative detail is lavished on almost every surface, and guided tours show the most spectacular rooms. Grounds include a Queen Anne playhouse.

Marble House, Bellevue Ave, $$, tel: (401) 847–1000. The most tastefully opulent, Newport's other Vanderbilt mansion has a ballroom inspired by the Hall of Mirrors at Versailles, almost entirely encrusted in gold and grander than its counterparts in European royal palaces. Visible from Cliff Walk is the Chinese Teahouse added in 1914.

Chateau-sur-Mer, Bellevue Ave, $$, tel: (401) 847–1000. Built in 1852, but 'modernised' by Richard Morris Hunt, Chateau is an American showcase of the British Charles Eastlake's geometric Arts and Crafts style. The library and dining room are ornately Italian.

Rosecliff, Belevue Ave, $$, tel: (401) 847-1000. Modelled, like Marble House, on the Grand Trianon at Versailles, this most livable of the mansions was designed by Stanford White, with Newport's largest ballroom and most gracefully elegant grand staircase. Open daily late Mar–Oct.

The Elms, Bellevue Ave, $$, tel: (401) 847-1000. Three grand doorways are spaced so that three carriages could unload

For Free

For views of mansion terraces and lawns – and great sea views – take the **Cliff Walk**, a pathway high above the ocean surf that extends from Memorial Blvd 3½ miles south to Bellevue Ave.

Tours

Viking Tours, tel: (401) 847-6921, offers a variety of narrated sightseeing excursions. Several other organisations operate boat cruises on Narragansett Bay; enquire at the visitor centre.

Day Trips

Bristol, 10 miles north of Newport, is an appealing waterfront town.

Blithewold Mansion and Gardens, the former summer estate of a coal baron, sprawls alongside Narragansett Bay. In Colt State Park, **Coggleshell Farm Museum** is a working farmstead relying solely on 18th-century agricultural methods. Pleasant restaurants and shops are on Hope St.

Information:

East Bay Chamber of Commerce, 654 Metacom Ave, Warren, RI 02885; tel: (888) 278-9948 or (401) 245-0750; www.eastbaychamberri.org.

passengers simultaneously. The interior details are all original, and the Venetian-inspired dining room has some of its original furnishings and Venetian paintings. The gardens are filled with exotic trees, fountains, statuary, teahouses and a formal sunken begonia garden. Open daily, May–Oct, weekends Jan–Apr and Nov.

The Astors' Beechwood, Bellevue Ave, $$, tel: (401) 846-3772. Mrs Astor's is the only mansion inhabited by a cast of performers who re-create in interactive theatre the social world of Newport's Gilded Age. Without the priceless furnishings and collections of other cottages, rooms are not roped-off and you can poke into the closets and see the maid's quarters. Open daily year-round.

Belcourt Castle, Bellevue Ave, $$, tel: (401) 846-0669. More than 300 stonemasons, woodcarvers and decorative artists from Europe built this castle-like 'cottage'. Explore with the help of a descriptive brochure to see medieval armour and America's finest collection of 13th-century stained glass, plus treasures dating from the 10th century. Open daily Feb–Dec.

Rough Point $$$, Bellevue Ave; tel: (401) 849-7300. Doris Duke inherited this palatial mansion in its spectacular cliff-top setting, when she was only 12 years old. A tour (by advance reservation online or through the Gateway Visitors Center, mid-Apr–Oct) includes a glimpse of her life, along with the mansion and the art she collected there, including works by Gainsborough, Van Dyck and Renoir.

FREE MANSIONS

You can get a free look inside several lesser but still impressive mansions. **Ochre Court**, at 100 Ochre Point Ave, is a late French gothic-style chateau with outstanding stained glass, now the Administration Building of Salve Regina University. **Edward King House**, off King St, is one of the earliest mansions, an 1846 Italianate villa restored and now a Senior Citizens Center. Both are open weekdays.

For an even greater choice of mansions to ogle, the looping 7-mile route of **Ocean Drive** passes some of America's costliest real estate, and is great for bicycling. Along the way look out for Brenton Point State Park, Fort Adams and **Hammersmith Farm**. This 50-acre bayfront estate of the Auchincloss family was where Jackie and John F Kennedy had their 1953 wedding reception. It is not open to the public, but visible from Ocean Drive.

NIGHTLIFE To sample Newport's resounding jazz and blues scene, head for the **Red Parrot**, 348 Thames St. Disco-dance at **The Candy Store**, Bannister's Wharf. For what's-going-on updates, dial the 24-hr Newport Activity Line: tel: (800) 976-5122.

WHERE NEXT?

For highlights of the Connecticut coastline west of Rhode Island, see pp. 108–112; eastwards you can explore the beautiful but hugely popular Cape Cod and the offshore islands of Nantucket and Martha's Vineyard (pp. 153–155). Beyond Boston (p. 113) the coast becomes increasingly rugged as you forge towards Maine and the Canadian border (see p. 157).

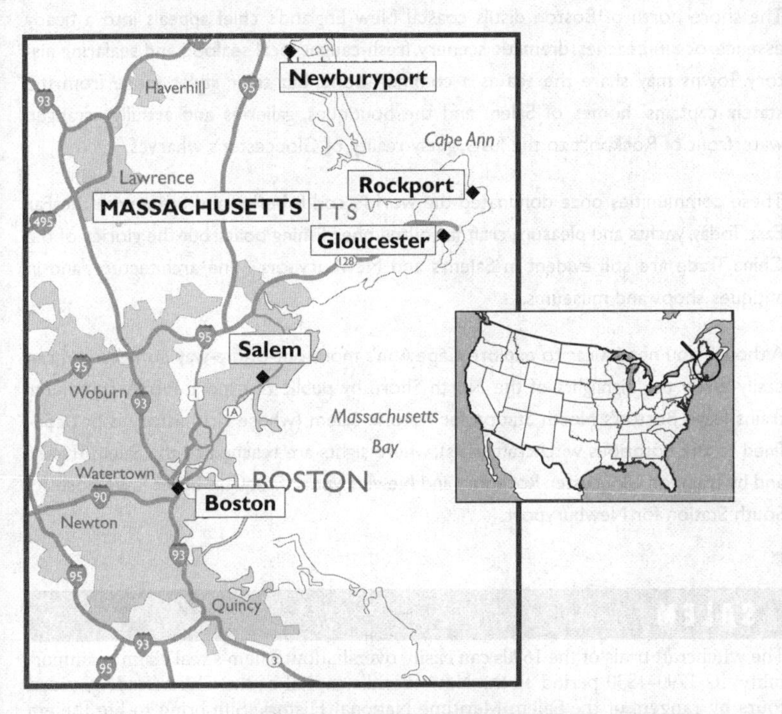

Notes:
Salem is the junction for the line to Gloucester and Rockport and the separate line for Newburyport. There is no railway link between Rockport and Newburyport.

BOSTON — NEWBURYPORT and ROCKPORT

OTT Table 381

Service	Bus	Bus	Rail	Rail	Rail	Bus	Rail	Bus
Days of operation	Daily	Daily	ex⑥⑦	ex⑥⑦	⑥⑦	Daily	⑥⑦	Daily
Special notes			A	B	C		D	E
Boston North .... d.	0540	0700	0735	0805	0830	0900	0930	1100
Salem .... d.	|	|	0809	0836	0859	|	0959	|
Newburyport .... a.	0650	0750	|	0909	|	0950	1031	1150
Gloucester .... d.	....	....	0841	....	0928	....	....	....
Rockport .... a.	....	....	0849	....	0937	....	....	....

Special notes:
A–Additional trips: 0830, 1015, 1215, 1415, 1600, 1700, 1725, 1810, 2240.
B–Additional trips: 0945, 1115, 1315, 1515, 1630, 1710, 1845, 1930, 2130.
C–Additional trips: 1015, 1215, 1415, 1730, 2030, 2330.
D–Additional trips: 1130, 1330, 1630, 1830, 2215.
E–Additional trips: 1300, 1500, 1600ex⑥⑦, 1630ex⑥⑦, 1700, 1720ex⑤⑥⑦, 1730⑤, 1740ex⑤⑥⑦, 1800ex⑥⑦, 1900, 2030, 2130, 2230, 2330.
Note buses leave from Boston South.

MASSACHUSETTS NORTH SHORE

The shore north of Boston distils coastal New England's chief appeals into a heady essence: ocean beaches, dramatic scenery, fresh-caught local seafood and seafaring history. Towns may share the sea as a common bond, but their styles range from the stately captains' homes of Salem and the boutiques, galleries and artfully arranged waterfront of Rockport to the lusty, gutsy reality of Gloucester's wharves.

These communities once dominated the world's cod fisheries and trade with the Far East. Today, yachts and pleasure craft far outnumber fishing boats, but the glories of the China Trade are still evident in Salem's and Newburyport's fine architecture, and in antiques shops and museums.

Although you need a car to explore Cape Ann's more out-of-the-way corners, you can easily enjoy the highlights of the North Shore by public transport. MBTA commuter trains leave Boston's North Station for historic Salem (whose rich history is not confined to the notorious witchcraft trials), where sights are reached by the Salem Trolley, and by train for Gloucester, Rockport and Newburyport. Frequent buses leave Boston's South Station for Newburyport.

SALEM

The witchcraft trials of the 1690s can easily overshadow Salem's real claim to immortality: its 1790–1830 period as the New World's capital of the China Trade. Guided tours by rangers of the Salem Maritime National Historic Site bring to life the era when the riches of the Orient spilled onto Salem's wharves.

The astonishing collections of the **Peabody Essex Museum** vividly capture life at sea and the lands the seafarers explored. Curios from their trips formed the basis of the Peabody's 100,000-object collection, including the world's most extensive in Asian export art. The Essex Institute branch complements this global view in galleries brimming with Salem's fine 17th- and 18th-century cabinetry. Three house museums in the grounds reflect Salem's expanding domestic wealth between 1684 and 1805. If you see nothing else in Salem, see this museum complex. $$, East India Sq., 132 and 162 Essex St; tel: (978) 745-9500. Open Mon–Sat 1000–1700, Sun 1200–1700 (Nov–late May closed Mon).

Stroll north to the 9-acre **Salem Common**, with bandstand, 19th-century cast-iron fence and leafy arcade. The houses at 74, 82 and 92 Washington St E are associated with Samuel McIntire, Salem's self-taught master architect of the early 19th century. Chestnut St is lined with merchants' and sea captains' mansions designed or inspired by McIntire. One of these, the **Stephen Phillips Trust House** at 34 Chestnut St, tel: (978) 744-0440, is now a museum, furnished in fine antiques and adorned with curios, collected from generations of family voyages. It is best known for its collections of Native American pottery and for its carriage house filled with vehicles from sleighs to vintage cars.

At the harbour stands the **House of Seven Gables**, inspiration for Nathaniel Hawthorne's third novel. The grounds include striking seaside gardens and the author's modest birthplace. $$, 54 Turner St; open daily 0930–1800 (July–Oct); 1000–1630 (Nov–June).

The witch trials, however shameful, are still a lucrative draw, 'inspiring' many made-for-tourist sites. The **Salem Witch Museum** features histrionic narration in darkness punctuated by suddenly lit dioramas: $, Washington Sq.; open daily 1000–1900 (July–Aug), 1000–1700 (Sept–June). The **Witch Dungeon Museum** dramatises transcripts from a trial and has recreated a dungeon: $, 16 Lynde St; open daily 1000–1700 (Apr–Nov). By contrast, the tasteful and reflective **Salem Witch Trial Memorial** stands on New Liberty St next to the old cemetery.

Boston's commuter rail system includes trains to Salem, but you can get there by boat and enjoy a cruise of Boston Harbor in the process with Boston Harbor Cruises. A boat leaves Boston's Long Wharf (Aquarium MBTA station) at 0900, 1200, 1500, 1800 May–Oct and 2100 May–Aug. Boats leave Salem Ferry Landing (near House of the Seven Gables) at similar intervals 0730–1900. Sat–Sun departures from Boston are 1000, 1330, 1630 May–Oct. Return fare is $16; tel: (617) 227-4321.

Salem Maritime National Historic Site Visitors Center, 193 Derby St; tel: (978) 740-1660; open daily 0900–1700. Guided tours $.

National Park Service Regional Visitors Center, 2 New Liberty St; tel: (978) 740-1650, open daily 0900–1700.

The Hawthorne Hotel $$–$$$ Salem Common; tel: (800) SAY-STAY or (978) 744-4080. Member of Historic Hotels of America, well located for touring.

Inn at Seven Winter Street $$$ 7 Winter St; tel: (978) 745-9520. An 1870s Empire-style B&B with period furnishings.

The Salem Inn $$$$ Chestnut St (Rte 114); tel: (978) 741-0680. A collection of beautifully restored old sea captains' homes.

Salem Waterfront Hotel $$$–$$$$ 225 Derby Street; tel: (888) 337-2536, or (978) 740-8788; fax: (978) 740-8722. Brand-new hotel with spacious rooms right on Salem's historic waterfront, close to all the attractions.

Bangkok Paradise $–$$ 90 Washington St; tel: (978) 825-9201. Well-prepared Thai dishes in an attractive setting.

Grapevine Restaurant $$$ 26 Congress St; tel: (978) 745-9335. Trattoria specialising in Mediterranean and New American foods.

Lyceum Bar and Grill $$ 43 Church St; tel: (978) 745-7665. Casual bar and more formal restaurant, serving stylish updates to classic dishes.

O'Neil's $–$$ Washington St is a friendly, authentic Irish pub, serving Salem's best burgers and chips.

BOAT TOURS

From Gloucester's busy fishing pier you can take a Harbour Water Shuttle to Rocky Neck or to island beaches, or just enjoy the ride, 1100–1700 (June–Sept). Whale Watch Cruises ($$$) carry naturalists on board and sometimes gather research data during cruises, Apr–Oct (reservations suggested). Yankee Fleet Whale Watch, 75 Essex St; tel: (978) 283-0313. Cape Ann Whale Watch, Rose's Wharf (near Rte 128); tel: (978) 283-5110. Captain Bill's Whale Watch, Harbor Loop (off Rogers St); tel: (978) 283-6995.

GLOUCESTER

Fishermen have gone to sea from the wharves here since 1623 and maritime painters have made the port their base for more than 150 years. The interplay of painting and fishing is captured at the **Cape Ann Historical Museum**, where exhibitions trace the fishing and boat-building heritage (Gloucester shipwrights invented the three-masted schooner). This is set against the magnificent paintings by native son Fitz Hugh Lane, America's premier maritime painter. $, 27 Pleasant St; open Tues–Sat 1000–1700; closed Feb. Lane's granite house and studio stand on a stone outcrop with a commanding view of the harbour.

Rocky Neck Art Colony, the oldest working artists' colony in the USA, sits directly across the harbour on a knob of land with a near 360-degree view of sky and water. The Neck retains a bohemian quality, and painters working on their decks or along narrow streets encourage curious visitors. Gloucester's dramatic seascape also attracted millionaires. Inspired by European journeys, inventor John Hays Hammond Jr built **Hammond Castle**, a medieval-style estate to house his collection of early Roman, medieval and Renaissance artefacts; $, 80 Hesperus Ave; open 1000–1700 (June–Oct). **Beauport**, also known as the Sleeper-McCann Mansion, is another fantasy house, where a theme from literature or history defines the decor in each of the 26 rooms. $, 75 Eastern Pt Blvd; open Mon–Fri 1000–1600 (mid May–mid Oct).

Because Gloucester lies just 15 miles from important whale feeding grounds, it is one of New England's best places for whale-watching cruises. Most operators guarantee whale sightings, usually of humpbacks and finbacks, but occasionally of northern right whales, of which only 300 remain.

FESTIVALS AND PAGEANTRY

The Gloucester Stage Company presents plays with local colour; 267 E Main St; tel: (978) 281-4099. Saint Peter's Fiesta takes place over four days in late June to honour the patron saint of fishermen: tel: (978) 283-1601. The Schooner Festival is a three-day regatta in early Sept: tel: (978) 283-1601.

i **North of Boston Convention & Visitors Bureau**, tel: (978) 977-7760, (800) 742-5306; fax: (978) 977-7758; www.northofboston.org.

Cape Ann Chamber of Commerce Information Center, 33 Commercial St; tel: (800) 321-0133 or (978) 283-1601; www.capeannvacations.com. Offers regional information and has menus from area restaurants.

Gloucester Visitors Welcoming Center, Stage Fort Park, Hough Ave; tel: (978) 281-8865.

Cape Ann Motor Inn $$ 33 Rockport Rd; tel: (978) 281-2900. Well-run motel with some self-catering units.

The Rudder $–$$ Rocky Neck; tel: (978) 283-7967. A little rowdy in high season, with good traditional seafood dishes.
McT's Lobster House and Tavern $$ 25 Rogers St; tel: (978) 282-0950. Set amid the fish docks, serves simple preparations of exceedingly fresh catch.

ROCKPORT

Every artist in town (and there are plenty of them) seems to have painted at least one canvas of the fishing shack on Bradley Wharf, aptly named Motif No. 1. The main activity in town is browsing in the galleries, boutiques and souvenir shops crammed onto Bearskin Neck, a rocky peninsula enclosing Rockport harbour. For the best, however, climb to the Rockport Art Association, 12 Main St, open Mon–Sat 1000–1700, Sun 1200–1700, and the surrounding Main St galleries.

BOAT TRIPS

Yankee Clipper Harbor Tours $$, Waterfront Park; tel: (888) 975-1842; 45-min tours 1100–1830 (May–Oct), sunset cruises 1830.

Capt. Lew Deepsea Fishing $$$, 54 Merrimac St; tel: (888) 234-3530 or (978) 465-3530; all-day trips Apr–Oct.

Newburyport Whale Watch $$$, 54 Merrimac St; tel: (978) 465-7165 or (800) 848-1111; daily 0830 and 1330 (July–Aug), Mon–Fri 1000 Sat–Sun 0830 and 1330 (June and Sept), shorter schedule May and Oct.

Rockport once supplied building granite for the entire Atlantic seaboard, and the quarries create a scenic foreground to sea views at **Halibut Point State Park**, a 54-acre reserve at the northern tip of Cape Ann. Picnic and walk trails border the ocean, one exploring a quarry: $, open dawn–2000 (Apr–Oct).

Rockport Chamber of Commerce, Upper Main St; tel: (978) 546-6575.

Bearskin Neck Motor Lodge $$–$$$ 74 South Rd; tel: (978) 546-6677. Modest eight-room motel near shops and restaurants with fine ocean views.
Inn on Cove Hill $$–$$$, 37 Mt Pleasant St; tel: (978) 546-2701. A 1791 house close to the beach and Bearskin Neck.

Rockport is a 'dry' town, so you may wish to bring beer or wine (available in Gloucester) when you dine out.
Peg Leg Restaurant $–$$ Beach St; tel: (978) 546-3038. Old favourite dishes with a creative touch; don't miss the chowders.
Harbor Grille $$ 8 Old Harbor Rd; tel: (978) 546-3030, Bearskin Neck seawall. Try a bucket of peel-and-eat shrimps followed by seafood stew or lobster roll.

NEWBURYPORT

The three-storey mansions crowned with cupolas in the **High St** attest to the wealth of Newburyport's 18th-century ship owners. Elegant cornices, doorways and windows carved by ships' carpenters place this district among the nation's finest examples of Federal architecture. Downtown Newburyport was built of red brick that came as ballast in ships from Asia. Cargo from later European trade was registered at the granite Custom House, now the **Maritime Museum**, where exhibitions evoke the town's overseas trade days. $, 25 Water St; tel: (978) 462-8681, open Mon–Sat 1000–1600 (closed Wed pm Nov–May), Sun 1300–1600.

Newburyport is the gateway to **Plum Island's Parker River National Wildlife Refuge**, 4662 acres of sand beach and dunes, bogs and tidal marshes, among North America's top ten bird-watching sanctuaries: $, Plum Island Turnpike; open daily sunrise–sunset.

On Merrimac, Water and State Sts are boutiques and antiques shops, and nearby Waterfront Park has summer concerts and fireworks. A boardwalk provides a vantage point to watch boats on the river, and you can also board a cruise here to whale watch or fish.

Beginning on the last Saturday in July is the Yankee Homecoming, nine days of parade, concerts, fireworks, craft exhibitions and food; tel: (978) 462-6680.

Greater Newburyport Chamber of Commerce, 29 State St; tel: (978) 462-6680.

Places to stay are scarce here, especially in budget range.

Clark Currier Inn $$$ 45 Green St; tel: (978) 465-8363. Antiques-filled rooms in a shipwright-built 1803 home.

The Windsor House $$$ 38 Federal St; tel: (888) TRELAWNY or (978) 462-3778. An 18th-century brick Federal mansion, with a British innkeeper.

The Bayou $–$$ 50 State St; tel: (978) 499-0428. Spicy Creole and southern cooking, local seafoods.

Glenn's Restaurant $$ 44 Merrimac St; tel: (978) 465-3811. Bistro with fresh fish and lively bar.

WHERE NEXT?

A daily bus service runs from Newburyport north to Portsmouth, New Hampshire, another fine Colonial seaport and gateway to the rugged Maine coast *(see p. 157)**.*

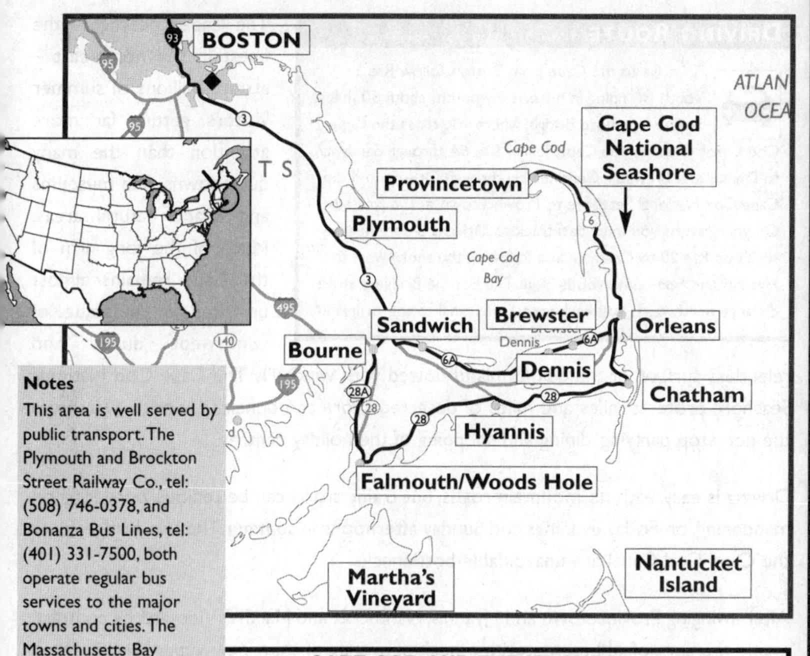

Notes

This area is well served by public transport. The Plymouth and Brockton Street Railway Co., tel: (508) 746-0378, and Bonanza Bus Lines, tel: (401) 331-7500, both operate regular bus services to the major towns and cities. The Massachusetts Bay Transportation Authority run trains to Plymouth.

CAPE COD AND THE ISLANDS

OTT Tables 381/451/455/522/522a

Service	Bus	Ferry	Bus	Bus	Bus	Bus	Bus	Ferry	Ferry	Bus		
Days of operation		Daily	Daily	Daily	Daily	Daily	Daily	Daily	Daily	Ⓐ		
Special notes	G	A		B	C	D		E	F	H		
New York ....d.	....	....	....	....	0730	0900	....	....	....	....	....	....
Boston Logan Airport ..d.	0645	....	0845	0915	|	|	1245	....	....	1445	....	....
Boston ....d.	0715	0800	0915	1000	|	|	1330	....	....	|	....	....
Woods Hole ....d.	|	|	|	1135	*1335*	|	|	E	....	|	....	....
Martha's Vineyard ....a.	|	|	|	....	|	|	|	E	....	|	....	....
Hyannis ....d.	0845	|	1100	....	1320	1720	1600	....	F	1600	....	....
Nantucket Island ....a.	....	|	|	....	....	....	|	....	F	....	....	....
Provincetown ....a.	....	0930	1220	....	....	....	1720	....	....	....	....	....

Special notes:

A–Additional trips: 1300, 1730. All services run mid May to mid October only.

B–Additional trips: 0730ex⑦, 1115, 1315, 1515, 1700, 1930

C–Additional trips: 0930, 1130, 1330, 1530.

D–Additional trip: 1400.

E–Minimum of 12 sailings daily, all of which take about 45 minutes. In high summer, there may be as many as 35 sailings per day.

F–At least 5 sailings daily. Departure times vary during the year. More frequent service available during high summer. High-speed ferries take 1 hour, normal ferries 2 hours.

G–Monday to Friday at 0745, hourly until 1345, then at 1845, 1945, 2045, 2145, 2315. Weekends at 0745 and hourly until 2145, 2315.

H–Mondays to Fridays at 1545, 1645, 1745.

DRIVING ROUTE

To drive to the Cape from Boston, follow Rte 3 south (stopping in historic Plymouth) about 50 miles to the Sagamore Bridge, where you cross the Cape Cod Canal. Once on the Cape, follow Rte 6A through Sandwich to Dennis and Brewster. Continue on through Orleans and the Cape Cod National Seashore to Provincetown, at the far end. On your return, you must backtrack to Orleans before heading south on Rte 28 to Chatham and following the shore west to Hyannis and Falmouth/Woods Hole. The Bourne Bridge, a short distance north, takes you back across the canal to the 'mainland'.

The Cape's beaches – the finest in the north-east – attract millions of summer visitors, getting far more attention than the many quiet towns, fine museums and inland natural areas. Much of the long arm of the Cape remains almost unvisited, a landscape of windswept dunes and relentless surf, or of tranquil farmland dotted with windmills. The Cape Cod National Seashore protects miles and miles of deserted shore and duneland, worlds away from the non-stop partying, dining and shopping of the holiday centres.

Driving is easy, with no mountain roads, but traffic snarls can be tedious, bordering on maddening, on Friday evenings and Sunday afternoons in summer. The two bridges over the Cape Cod Canal are unavoidable bottlenecks.

After swinging Provincetown and Hyannis, Nantucket and Martha's Vineyard, by contrast, exude the aura of old money, with a healthy overlay of shiny new yuppy wealth. Don't expect bargains on either island, but do expect a pleasant, genteel atmosphere where open space is prized and protected, and where a bicycle travels at just the right speed.

PLYMOUTH

In the American pantheon, the Pilgrims are right up there with George Washington. This grim lot of fervent religious dissidents crossed the Atlantic aboard the crowded *Mayflower* and established Plymouth – the first permanent English settlement between Newfoundland and Virginia.

Sites recalling Pilgrim endurance are close together in this handsome town. On Water St, a portico shelters **Plymouth Rock**, the supposed stepping stone where the newcomers clambered ashore. More accurate is *Mayflower II*, a faithful replica of the original three-masted barque, which actually followed its transatlantic course in 1954; State Pier, off Water St; tel: (508) 746-1622; open daily 0900–1900 (July–Aug); Thur–Sat 1000–1530 (June and Sept–mid-Oct). Pilgrim Hall Museum houses Pilgrim portraits, furniture, maps, humble clothing and personal goods; $, 75 Court St; tel: (508) 746-1620; open daily 0930–1630 Feb–Dec.

The Plymouth Rock Trolley Company runs narrated tours ($) that include south-of-town **Plimoth Plantation**; tel: (508) 747-3419. This is a recreated 1627 village where 'Pilgrims' cook, harvest, tend livestock, make candles and speak with visitors in Elizabethan dialect. A Wampanoag campsite demonstrates Native American life at the time. $$$, Rte 3A; tel: (508) 746-1622; open daily 0900–1700 Apr–Nov.

CAPE COD CHAMBER OF COMMERCE AND VISITOR BUREAU, junction of Rtes 6 and 132, Hyannis; tel: (888) 33CAPECOD or (508) 362-3225; www.capecodchamber.org, offers information for the entire Cape.

BASEBALL

Aficionados cite the semi-professional Cape Cod League as the purest surviving example of the all-American game. The schedule is posted in the *Cape Cod Times*; admission free.

Plymouth Visitor Information, 130 Water St; tel: (800) 872-1620 or (508) 747-7525.

Governor Bradford Motor Inn $$$ 98 Water St; tel: (800) 332-1620 or (508) 246-6200; fax: (508) 747-3032; www.governorbradfordinn.com. Overlooks Plymouth harbour, close to *Mayflower II*.

John Carver Inn $$$ 25 Summer St; tel: (800) 274-1620 or (508) 746-7100; fax: (508) 746-8299; www.johncarverinn.com. Central; indoor theme water park.

Best Western Cold Spring $$ 188 Court St.; tel: (800) 678-8667 or (508) 746-2222; fax: (508) 746-2744; www.bwcoldspring.com. A 10-min walk to harbour and *Mayflower II*. Outdoor heated pool; children 12 and under stay free.

Hearth 'n Kettle Restaurant $–$$ 25 Summer St, in John Carver Inn; tel: (508) 476-7100; www.hearthnkettle.com. Features same-day caught fish and generous proportions.

Weathervane $$–$$$ 6 Town Wharf; tel: (508) 746-4195.

Isaac's $$$ 114 Water St; tel: (508) 830-0001.

SANDWICH

The first in a row of placid communities strung along the Old King's Highway, Rte 6A, Sandwich overlooks Cape Cod Bay. Its historical streets are lined with 18th- and early 19th-century houses (many converted to B&Bs) and antiques shops. **The Sandwich Glass Museum** chronicles the pressed glass industry that flourished here 1828–88; $, 129 Main St; open daily 0930–1700 (Apr–Dec); Wed–Sun 0930–1600 (Feb–Mar). The **Thornton Burgess Museum** features a collection of the author's children's books and illustrations; $, 4 Water St; open Mon–Sat 1000–1600, Sun 1300–1600 (Apr–Oct).

ALMOST FREE

Cranberry World explains growing and harvesting the area's cash crop: 225 Water St; tel: (508) 747-2350; open daily 0930–1700 May–Nov. Samples are well worth the $1 charge.

Shady Nook Inn and Motel $$–$$$ 14 Old Kings Hwy (Rte 6A); tel: (508) 888-0409 or (800) 338-5208; www.shadynookinn.com. Set in terraced rock gardens; heated pool, free movies.

Belfry Inn and Bistro $$$ 8 Jarves St; tel: (508) 888-8550 or (800) 844-9542; www.belfryinn.com. The renovated Victorian church, with original stained glass, has state-of-the-art whirlpools. The Bistro serves contemporary versions of traditional dishes in the elegant dining room or patio.
Dan'l Webster Inn $$$ 149 Main St; tel: (508) 888-3622, www.danlwebsterinn.com. Very welcoming to families.

Spring Hill Motor Lodge $$–$$$ 351 Rte. 6A; tel: (508) 888-1486; www.springhillmotor-lodge.com. In a wooded setting, minutes from beaches, the motel offers single rooms, efficiency apartments and self-catering cottages, with tennis courts and pool.
Marshland Restaurant & Bakery $ 109 Rte. 6A; tel: (508) 888-9824. Friendly atmosphere, delicious baked goods, and the best value in Sandwich.
Dunbar House Tea Shop $$–$$$ 1 Water St.; tel: (508) 833-2485; www.dunbarteashop.com. Lunch and afternoon English-style tea, served in a c.1740 Carriage House.

DENNIS AND BREWSTER

Along with sea captains' homes, **Dennis** has the **Cape Museum of Fine Arts**, showing works by local artists; $, Main St; open Tues–Sat 1000–1700, Sun 1300–1700. **Cape Cod Playhouse**, in Main St, is the last of the summer stock venues; tel: (508) 385-3911 or (877) 385-3911 toll free; www.capeplayhouse.com.

Almost at the geographic centre of Cape Cod, **Brewster** makes good use of its sedate landscape with the **Cape Cod Museum of Natural History**. Activities target children, while the 82-acre site contains three self-guided nature trails. $, Rte 6A; open Mon–Sat 0930–1630, Sun 1100–1630. For more wide-ranging roaming, the 2000 acres of **Nickerson State Park** are dotted with glacial ponds and covered with trails.

Linnell Landing Beach, across Rte 6A from the park, is one of Brewster's best beaches, and has access for people with disabilities.

Nickerson State Park has the Cape's most popular tent and caravan (RV) pitches; tel: (508) 896-3491.
Michael's Cottages $$–$$$ 618 Main St, Brewster; tel: (508) 896-4025 or (800) 399-2967; www.sunsol.com/michaels. Rooms and self-catering cottages.
Pelham House Resort $$–$$$ 14 Sea St, Dennisport; tel: (508) 398-6076 or (800) 497-3542; www.pelhamhouseresort.com. Thirty-five ocean view rooms, continental breakfast, tennis court, outdoor pool.

Cobie's $ 3260 Main St, Brewster; tel: (508) 896-7021. Fried clams, lobster and crab rolls, ice cream at picnic tables or to take away, 1100–2100 daily, May–Aug.
Captain Frosty's Clam Shack $–$$ 210 Rte. 6A Dennis; tel: (508) 385-8548. A favourite with locals. Fried clams, clam cakes and lobster rolls, casual outdoor dining.
Red Pheasant Inn $$–$$$ 905 Rte. 6A Dennis; tel: (508) 385-2133 or (800) 480-2133; www.redpheasantinn.com. Local seafood, formal dining room, wine bar and bistro.

CAPE COD NATIONAL SEASHORE

Almost 45,000 acres of fragile dunes, fertile marshes, woodlands, pine barrens, cranberry bogs and long sandy beaches stretch between Chatham and Provincetown. Ranger-led programmes explore varied ecosystems, but no explanation is required to enjoy the beaches, which include Coast Guard Beach (excellent surfing), Nauset Light Beach (good surfing and surf-casting), Head of the Meadow Beach (views of dunelands), Race Point Beach (spectacular dunes and fine swimming) and Herring Cove Beach, which has the calmest waters and faces west into the sunset. Lifeguards are posted late June–early Sept. Watch for heavy surf and rip tides. Admission is free; beach parking lots $$.

The best way to explore the marsh near Nauset Beach is by canoe or kayak; both can be hired from Goose Hummock Shop, $$$, 15 Rte 6A, Orleans; tel: (508) 255-0455.

i **Cape Cod National Seashore Salt Pond Visitor Center**, Rte 6, Eastham; tel: (508) 255-3421; open 0900–1630, mid Mar–Dec.

Provincelands Visitor Center, Rte 6, Provincetown; tel: (508) 487-1256; open 0900–1700, late May–early Sept.

Hostelling International – Mid Cape $ 75 Goody Hallet Dr., Eastham; tel: (508) 255-2785; open mid-May–mid-Sept. Close to National Seashore Visitor Center and Cape Cod cycle path.

Whalewalk Inn $$$–$$$$ 220 Bridge Rd. Eastham; tel: (508) 240-0017 or (800) 440-1281; www.whalewalkinn.com. Elegant inn, ideal for couples, gourmet breakfast, onsite spa facilities.

PROVINCETOWN

Located at the very end of Cape Cod, Provincetown is the cape's most diverse town. Take a strong gay and lesbian community, a Portuguese fishing village and an art colony, mix well, and you have Provincetown. In high season (July–Aug) it's a good idea to walk or bicycle the crowded downtown area. Best time of year to visit is September to mid-October when crowds have thinned and shops, restaurants and galleries are still open.

Since the turn of the century Provincetown has been a mecca for artists of all genres. Two of the many stellar galleries are: **Provincetown Art Association & Musuem**; ($) 460 Commercial St; tel: (508) 487-1750; www.paam.org; open daily 1200–1700 and 2000–2200 pm (July–August); 1200–1600 (Oct–April); and **Gallery Voyeur**; 444 Commercial St; tel: (508) 487-3678; www.voy-art.com; open Wed–Sun 1100–1600 and 1900–2200 (May–Sept).

No matter how you arrive, getting to your lodgings will be easy: you can walk or take a shuttle bus. If you arrive after the bus season (July–Aug), a taxi, tel: (508) 487-2222, will take you the short distance.

Wellfleet Drive-In Flea Market, Rte 6A; tel: (508) 349-2520, is Cape Cod's largest flea market. Open Sat–Sun (mid-Apr–Sept); also Wed–Thur (July–Aug).

EXCURSIONS – BEST OF THE BEST

Art's Dune Tours tel: (508) 487-1950 or (800) 894-1951, Commercial & Standish. Narrated sunset tours.

Cape Cod Whale Watch tel: (508) 487-4079, MacMillan Wharf. Small, personal, environmentally involved.

Willy's Air Tour tel: (508) 487-1950, Provincetown Municipal Airport. 1930s Stinson Detroiter.

Beaches are what bring most people to P'town. **Race Point Beach** is the favourite, but within walking distance of town is more crowded **Herring Cove Beach**. Beachcombers and birdwatchers catch a water shuttle from Flyer's Boat Rental to Long Point Lighthouse or walk, following Commercial St and the stone breakwater. Nearby **Wellfleet Bay Wildlife Sanctuary** also draws birdwatchers; tel: (508) 349-2615; trails ($) open daily 0800–dusk; visitor centre open Tues–Sun 0830–1700. Self-guiding nature trails wind through Cape Cod National Seashore (see p. 149).

i **Provincetown Chamber of Commerce**, 307 Commercial St; tel: (508) 487-3424; fax: (508) 487-8966; www.ptownchamber.com; e-mail: info@ptownchamber.com.

Outermost Hostel $$ 28 Winslow St; tel: (508) 487-4378. A cottage colony with common kitchen, open May–Oct.
Lands End Inn $$–$$$ 22 Commercial St; tel: (508) 487-0706 or (800) 276-7088; www.landsendinn.com. Award-winning inn. Panoramic views from 16 antique-filled rooms.
Romeo's Holiday Guest House $$–$$$ 97 Bradford St; tel: (508) 487-3082 or (877) 697-6636; www.romeosholiday.com. Victorian bed and breakfast in the center of Provincetown. Shakespearean themed guest rooms.
Beaconlight Guesthouse $$$ 12 Winthrop St; tel: (800) 696-9603 or (508) 487-9603. Country-house atmosphere created by transplanted Brits.

Bubala's By The Bay $–$$ 183 Commercial St; tel: (508) 487-0773. Hip bistro with diversified menu; lobster salad, fajitas, calamari and pad Thai.
Commons Bistro $$–$$$ 386 Commercial St; tel: (508) 487-7800. Creative New American menu with chicken, meats, seafood, pizzas and vegetarian dishes.
Lobster Pot $$–$$$ 321 Commercial St; tel; (508) 487-0842; www.ptownlobsterpot.com. Legendary food and service, a must for anyone visiting outer Cape Cod. Dine in or takeaway.

PEDAL OR PADDLE

Provincetown Bikes at 42 Bradford St and 306 Commercial St; tel: (508) 487-8735, rents good broad-tyred bikes that work well in sand. Arnold's, 329 Commercial St, tel: (508) 487-0844, also rents bikes.

Flyer's Boat Rental, 131-A Commercial St, tel: (508) 487-0898 or (800) 750-0898, near the Coast Guard wharf, has watercraft for hire, including Sunfish, powered skiffs and plastic sea kayaks, perfect along the harbour, beaches and for exploring the shore.

Terra Luna $$–$$$ 104 Shore Rd. Rte. 6A North Truro; tel: (508) 487-1019. Chef owned, New American cuisine with an Italian flair, vegetarian choices.

NIGHTLIFE

Atlantic House 4 Masonic Place; tel: (508) 487-2400 for show reservations. One of the hottest places in town to see the famous drag shows of P'town. Full bar has a lively atmosphere and makes everyone feel comfortable.

Tropical Joe's 135 Bradford St; tel (508) 487-9941. Restaurant, bar and cabaret venue offering dinner and show packages. Reasonable cover charge for showgoers only. Also serves Sunday brunch.

CHATHAM

Retaining its quiet small-town air, Chatham blends old-money gentility with a working fishing industry. Art galleries and boutiques dominate the village, and its shell fishermen harvest some of the world's finest clams, oysters and mussels, which you can buy at the docks. The **Old Atwood House Museum** details local history and displays provocative murals by Alice Stallknecht depicting Christ as a modern fisherman; $, 347 Stage Harbor Rd; open Tues–Fri 1300–1600 (mid-June–Sept).

Sheltered Oyster Pond Beach, a block off Main St, is superb for small children, and the long strand of **Chatham Light Beach** is reached from the lighthouse parking lot. For birdwatchers, Massachusetts Audubon Society, tel: (508) 349-2615, and the Cape Cod Museum of Natural History, tel: (508) 896-3867, operate tours of **South Monomoy Island**, a barrier island bird sanctuary ($$$).

FOR FREE

During July and Aug, Fri evening band concerts are held in Kate Gould Park, tel: (508) 945-5199 – best enjoyed with chocolate-covered cranberries from Chatham Candies on Main St.

i **Chatham Chamber of Commerce Info Booth**, 533 Main St; tel: (800) 715-5567 and (508) 945-5199; www.chathaminfo.org.

Port Fortune Inn $$$ 201 Main St; tel: (800) 850-0792 or (508) 945-0792. Renovated B&B near Chatham Light.

Campers Haven $ 184 Old Wharf Rd, Dennisport; tel: (508) 398-2811; fax (508) 398-2811; www.campershaven.com. A 265-pitch campsite with private beach on Nantucket Sound.

Chatham Seafarer $$–$$$ Rte. 28 & Ridgevale Rd; tel: (508) 432-1739 or (800) 786-2772: www.chathamseafarer.com. Attractive rooms, caters to families, close to beaches and village.

Corsair and Crossrip Motel $$–$$$ 41 Chase Ave, Dennisport; tel: (508) 398-2278, www.corsaircrossrip.com. Well equipped twin oceanfront motels.

Red Nun $–$$ 746 Main St; tel: (508) 348-0469; www.rednun.com. Great local hangout, extensive beer menu, next door to where the Chatham A's play baseball.

Impudent Oyster $$ 15 Chatham Bars Ave; tel: (508) 945-3545. Fresh fish and draught beer.

HYANNIS

This sprawling commercial centre is haunted by memories of the Kennedys. The modest **John F Kennedy Hyannis Museum** include photographs taken at the nearby Kennedy compound. $, 397 Main St; open Mon–Sat 1000–1600, Sun 1300–1600 (mid-Apr–mid-Oct); shorter hours off-season. **Hyannisport Harbor Cruises**, Ocean St Dock; tel: (508) 778-2600, makes narrated hour-long tours ($$) past the Kennedy compound.

Lamb & Lion Inn $$–$$$ Rte. 6A Barnstable; (508) 362-6823 or (800) 909-6923; fax; (508) 362-0227; www.lambandlion.com. Extensively renovated inn, graciously appointed rooms offering wood burning fireplaces. Heated outdoor pool and hot tub.

Cape Codder Resort $$–$$$ Rte 132; tel: (508) 771-3000 or (888) 297-2200. Extensive renovations include theme pool and lavish suites.

Hearth 'n Kettle Restaurant $$ Rte 132; tel: (508) 771-3000. Traditional New England fare with same-day caught fish.

Alberto's Ristorante $$–$$$ 360 Main St. Hyannis; tel: (508) 778-1770; www.albertos.net. Chef-owned, Northern Italian cuisine served in an elegant setting

FALMOUTH/WOODS HOLE

The seaside town of Falmouth has a botanical garden, **Spohr Gardens**; tel: (508) 548-0623; free admission, 45 Fells Rd; open during daylight hours year round. On six acres 150 varieties of flora and fauna thrive amid a collection of antique church bells, lanterns and millstones. Best seen in early spring when thousands of daffodils are in bloom.

Falmouth's history is tied to the sea. The non-profit-making ***Ocean Quest***'s outgoing and well-informed staff teach curious visitors about the schooner and take samples from the bay, exploring marine life firsthand. Leaves from Wood Hole, tel: (508) 385-7656; call for times. The **Oceanographic Institute at Woods Hole** focuses on underwater research; $, 15 Market St; open Tues–Sat 1000–1630, Sun 1200–1630 (Apr–Oct), while the National **Marine Fisheries Service Aquarium** eschews high tech in favour of educational exhibits of local fish. Albatross St; open Mon–Fri 1000–1600 (daily mid June–mid Sept). You can watch seals in a pool even when the aquarium is closed.

SAILING ON NANTUCKET SOUND

Cruises and fishing trips leave from Falmouth's busy harbour, the most interesting of them the sailing schooner *Liberté*; tel: (508) 548-2626.

Falmouth Chamber of Commerce, 20 Academy Lane; tel: (800) 526-8532 or (508) 548-8500; www.falmouth-capecod.com. Provides an excellent brochure, *A Walk Through Falmouth History*.

Holiday Inn Falmouth $–$$ 291 Jones Rd, Falmouth; tel: (508) 540-2000, www.holiday-inn.com. Features on-site fitness and steakhouse along with other amenities.

Park Beach Ocean Front Motel $$–$$$ 241 Grand Ave S; tel: (800) 341-5700 or (508) 548-1010. Two-storey motel at Falmouth Heights beach.

Inn at West Falmouth $$$-$$$$ 6 Frazar Rd; tel: (508) 540-7696; www.innatwestfalmouth.com. Six elegant rooms; careful attention is paid to every detail at this romantic inn overlooking the ocean.

Betsy's Diner $–$$ 457 Main St; tel: (508) 540-0623. Casual atmosphere, eclectic menu.

Fishmonger Café $$ 56 Water St, Woods Hole; tel: (508) 548-9148. Creative, seafood meals three times daily except Mon.

NANTUCKET ISLAND

Nantucket keeps its 30-mile distance from the Cape's hubbub, and the spartan influences of Quaker whalers who made Nantucket's fortunes are still felt. The island is small enough to explore by bicycle, but dense with natural and historic sites, most in Nantucket Town. The former fishing village of Sconset is now an exclusive preserve on the east end of the island.

GETTING AROUND

The village clusters close to the ferry wharf, with most lodgings an easy walk. Nantucket Regional Transit Authority, tel: (508) 228-7025, operates buses between villages and a seasonal beach shuttle. Nantucket Regional Transit Authority; (508) 325-9571 or (508) 228-7025; www.nantucketshuttle.com. At the Wharf, Nantucket Bike Shop, tel: (508) 228-1999, and Young's Bicycle Shop, tel: (508) 228-1151, hire bicycles.

Spend at least a day wandering the streets of fine old homes and rose-entwined cottages. The **Nantucket Whaling Museum**, $, 13 Broad St; tel: (508) 228-1894; open daily 1000–1700; re-opened in June 2005 after being closed for a two-year, $11 million rehabilitation that included the addition of a new wing, Gosnold Hall. In the centre of the hall is the skeleton of a 46-ft bull sperm whale that died off a Nantucket beach in 1999. Surrounding it are original oil paintings of the sea captains that once hunted the behemoth's ancestors. Enquire at the museum for admission to historic houses, the oldest of which is the **Jethro Coffin House**, $, Sunset Hill, built in 1686. **Hichman House** is a museum of local flora and fauna, with a busy program of nature walks; $, 7 Milk St; tel: (508) 228-0898.

Great Point Natural History Tours, $$$, tel: (508) 228-6799, traverse the dunes and barrier beach at the northeast tip of the island in four-wheel-drive vehicles.

Nantucket Chamber of Commerce, 48 Main St; tel: (508) 228-1700.

All the following are in Nantucket Town. Camping is prohibited on the island.
Hostelling International $ 31 Western Ave; tel: (508) 228-0433. In a historic lifesaving station on a paved bike path opposite the beach. Open mid Apr–mid Oct, reservations essential.
Hawthorn House $$–$$$ 2 Chestnut St; tel: (508) 228-1468; www.hawthornhouse.com. Charming inn, hand-hooked rugs throughout, walk to ferry, shops, and downtown.
Beachside Inn $$–$$$ 30 North Beach St; tel: (508) 228-2251 or (800) 322-4433; www.thebeachside.com. Good value for Nantucket. Motel style rooms, heated outdoor pool, walk to beach and town, full continental breakfast included.

The Counter at Congdon's Pharmacy $–$$ 47 Main St; tel: (508) 228-4193. A favourite with locals, everything home-made. The best egg salad sandwiches on the island.
Company of the Cauldron $$$–$$$$ 5 India St; tel: (508) 228-4016; www.companyofthecauldron.com. This is the one splurge travellers should allow themselves. Award-winning, chef-owned bistro; New American cuisine.
Arno's $$ 41 Main St; tel: (508) 228-7001. Serves bountiful breakfasts as well as lunch and dinner in a casual atmosphere.

MARTHA'S VINEYARD

Smaller than Nantucket, Martha's Vineyard has more day-trippers who often don't get beyond the shops and ice cream parlours of Vineyard Haven, where the ferries dock. But the 100-square-mile island is worth exploring.

Methodists used to hold summer camps at **Oak Bluffs**, across the harbour, and more than 300 of the gingerbread-pretty cottages that superseded their original tents are lovely to stroll among. The Flying Horses Carousel ($) is one of America's oldest, and still working.

The majestic white-clapboard whaling captains' homes in **Edgartown** add historic charm to the town with the best beach access. Martha's Vineyard Preservation Trust offers tours of two houses and the 1843 Old Whaling Church daily in summer, less frequently in other seasons; $, 99 Main St; tel: (508) 627-8619.

Three-mile **Katama Beach** has good surfing and many shore birds; a ferry at Dock St crosses to **Chappaquiddick Island** (of Ted Kennedy fame), where the Cape Pogue Wildlife Refuge has 2 miles of stunning beach.

At the other end of the island, **Menemsha** is the Vineyard's last working fishing village and the brightly coloured Gay Head cliffs (owned by the Aquinnah Wampanoag tribe) capture 100 million years of geological history in layers of sand, gravel and clay.

GETTING AROUND

Martha's Vineyard Regional Transit Authority (VTA); tel: (508) 693-9440; www.vineyardtransit.com. Martha's Bike Rentals, 4 Lagoon Point Rd, Vineyard Haven, tel: (508) 693-6593, is next to the steamship docks.

NIGHTLIFE

Hot Tin Roof at Martha's Vineyard Airport is known for its live music.

i **Martha's Vineyard** Chamber of Commerce, Beach Rd, Vineyard Haven; tel: (508) 693-0085.

Like Nantucket, Martha's Vineyard has scarcely any budget places to stay. There is camping at **Webb's Camping Area** $ Barnes Rd; tel: (508) 693-0233, a wooded site 3 miles from either Vineyard Haven or Oak Bluffs.

Hostelling International $ West Tisbury; tel: (508) 693-2665; fax: (508) 693-2699.

Titticut Follies $–$$ 37 Narragansett Ave, Oak Bluffs; (508) 693-4986; www.titticutfollies.com. Quaint Victorian-style guesthouse; walk to town and beaches.

Hob Knob Inn $$–$$$ 128 Main St, Edgartown; tel: (508) 627-9510 or (800) 696-2723; www.hobknob.com. Elegant, suitable for couples, attention to detail in every aspect, full breakfast and afternoon refreshments.

Thorncroft Inn $$$–$$$$ 460 Main St, Vineyard Haven; (508) 693-3333; www.thorncroftinn.com. Romantic and secluded, with fireplaces and hot tubs, but near beaches and town.

Scottish Bakehouse $ 7 State Rd, Vineyard Haven. For breakfast, lunch and tea: scones, shortbread, meat pies and breads. Closed Wed.

Larsen's Fish Market $$ Menemsha Harbor. Steamers, lobsters and mussels to order, and always has chowder and crab cakes.

Linda Jean's Restaurant $–$$ 25 Circuit Ave, Oak Bluffs; (508) 693-4093. Friendly atmosphere, family style, terrific food at great prices.

Coach House at the Harbor View Hotel $$–$$$ 131 North Water St, Edgartown; (508) 627-3761. Chef-made cheeses and imaginative cuisine, in a bistro atmosphere overlooking Edgartown harbour.

WHERE NEXT?

By car from the Bourne Bridge you can head south along the shore to Providence and Newport, Rhode Island (see p. 131). Or take the ferry from Martha's Vineyard to New Bedford from where buses continue to Providence or, by changing at Fall River, to Newport.

MAINE COAST

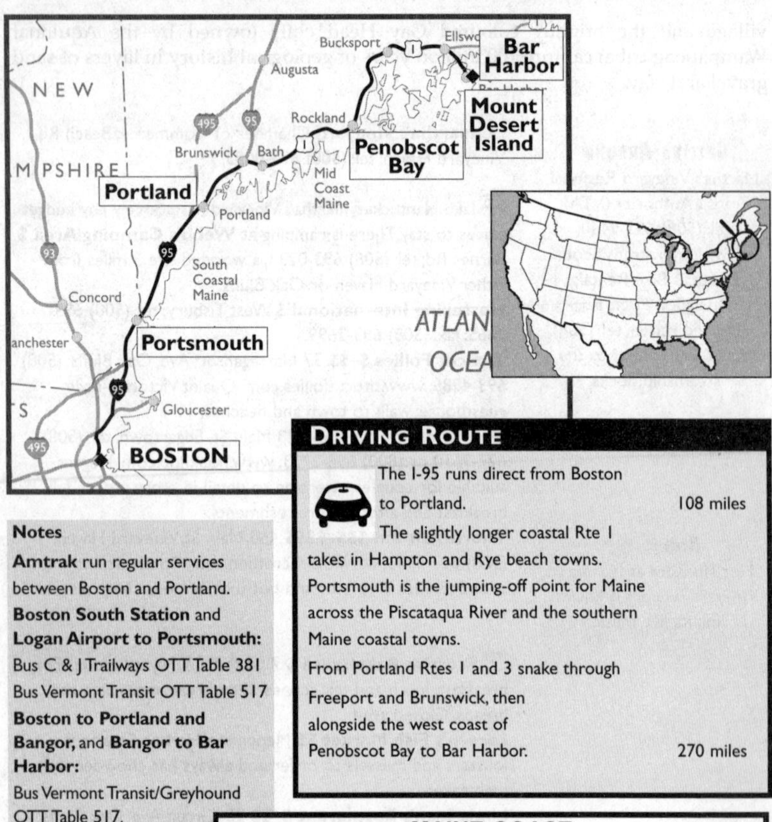

DRIVING ROUTE

The I-95 runs direct from Boston to Portland. 108 miles

The slightly longer coastal Rte 1 takes in Hampton and Rye beach towns. Portsmouth is the jumping-off point for Maine across the Piscataqua River and the southern Maine coastal towns.

From Portland Rtes 1 and 3 snake through Freeport and Brunswick, then alongside the west coast of Penobscot Bay to Bar Harbor. 270 miles

Notes

Amtrak run regular services between Boston and Portland.

Boston South Station and **Logan Airport to Portsmouth:**
Bus C & J Trailways OTT Table 381
Bus Vermont Transit OTT Table 517

Boston to Portland and Bangor, and **Bangor to Bar Harbor:**
Bus Vermont Transit/Greyhound OTT Table 517.

MAINE COAST

OTT Tables 322/381/517

Service	Bus	Bus	Rail	Rail	Bus	Bus	Bus	Bus
Days of operation	Daily	Daily	Daily	Daily	Daily	Daily	Daily	Daily
Special notes				A			B	
Boston d.	0600	0900	0945	1205	1201	1305	....	1600
Portsmouth d.	0705	1005	|	|	1325	|	....	|
Portland d.	0815	1115	1215	1435	1440	1505	....	1815
Bangor d.	1130	1355	....	....	1720	1735	1740	2110
Bar Harbour a.	....	....	....	....	....	....	1855	....

Special notes:
A–Additional trips: 1815ex⑥⑦, 1845⑥⑦, 2300.
B–Summer only.

This coastline is an unforgettable American composite: rocky shores with a lighthouse in the background, lobster traps stacked on a weatherbeaten dock in the foreground. To that tableau, add taciturn 'Mainers', acclimatised to whimsical weather, living in villages scarcely invaded by chainstore commercialism. Despite its splendours of oceanside nature and pockets of architectural opulence, this is the poorest New England state, off-set by admirable endurance and unspoiled simplicity.

Maine's coast measures 228 miles in linear distance, but tracing the myriad coves, inlets and bays adds up to 3478 miles of spectacular jagged shoreline. Towards the Canadian border, much of Mount Desert Island falls within Acadia National Park, with its hiking and wildlife trails, strange geological formations and dramatic scenery.

Give in to the temptation to follow the little roads leading to hamlets clustered around tiny coves. You'll find fishing boats, spectacular seascapes and real Mainers, in contrast to the yachting set that you're more likely to encounter in the big resort towns. Only a car will get you to the more remote places, but buses run from Boston to Portsmouth, on the New Hampshire–Maine border, and up to Portland; in summer, they continue on to Bar Harbor on Mount Desert Island.

PORTSMOUTH

Portsmouth's long history began with original settlement in 1623, and its fervour for preservation has saved its historic architecture. Craft shops, boutiques and restaurants enliven the old harbour, and a self-guided Harbour Trail (maps available at the information kiosk on Market Sq.) points out 18th-century houses from Portsmouth's merchant and seafaring past, many of them open for tours. **Strawbery Banke**, on Puddle Dock, is where Portsmouth began, and the 10-acre site recalls 300 years of domestic life in 40 buildings; $$, Marcy St; tel: (603) 433-1106. Open daily 1000–1700 (mid Apr–Oct).

Although history books treat slavery as peculiar to the south, it was not uncommon for New Englanders to hold slaves and Portsmouth was a northern point of the infamous 'Triangle Trade' of molasses, slaves and rum. The **Portsmouth Black Heritage Trail** recognizes this, through personal stories on attractive signs and in the self-guided walking tour brochure; www.seacoastNH.com/blackhistory.

i **Greater Portsmouth Chamber of Commerce**, 500 Market St, Portsmouth, NH 03802; tel: (603) 436-1118; fax: (603) 436-5118; www.portsmouthchamber.org. The bus drop-off point is in Market Sq.

Bow Street Inn $$$ 121 Bow St; tel: (603) 431-7760; fax: (603) 433-1680. Nine pleasant rooms in an ex-brewery overlooking the working harbour.

Inn at Strawbery Banke B&B $$$ 314 Court St; tel: (800) 428-3933 or (603) 436-7242. Spacious 19th-century inn with wraparound porch.

Seventy-five eateries are crammed into little Portsmouth.

Geno's Chowder Shop $ off Marcy St; tel: (603) 427-2070. Chowder, savoury soups and big, meaty lobster rolls to eat at picnic tables on the wharf.

Jumpin' Jay's Fish Café $$–$$$ 150 Congress Street; tel: (603) 766-3474; www.jumpinjays.com. The freshest of seafood; 'Catch of the Day' is always a good choice. Open from 1730 daily.

Portsmouth Brewery $$ 56 Market St. Varied daytime and evening menu; serves micro-lagers and ales.

The Stock Pot $–$$ Bow St; tel: (603) 431-1851. Harbour views from the deck, and excellent lobster rolls and chowder.

SOUTH COASTAL MAINE

Old seafaring ports, ticky-tacky beach towns and upmarket summer resorts are interwoven along this stretch of 'Downeast' Maine, where rocky outcrops dip into marshlands at the ocean's edge. The Yorks and the Kennebunks are photogenically historic; Ogunquit has a lively arts scene. Stay calm: summer traffic can be slow and heavy.

York was Maine's first permanent English settlement (1624). The Old York Historical Society preserves six 17th- and 18th-century buildings as a combined museum. $$, 207 York St; tel: (207) 363-4974; open Tues–Sat 1000–1700, Sun 1300–1700 (mid-June–Sept).

Nubble Light

Seeing (and photographing) this classic beacon atop the granite bulk of Cape Neddick is worth the slight detour off Rte 1 from York Village/York Beach.

Ogunquit, Maine's most gay-friendly resort, has clusters of galleries and boutiques downtown and at Perkins Cove. Marginal Way, a 1.2-mile clifftop footpath bordered by rose bushes, connects the cove with north-of-town beaches. The local art colony's eminence since 1900 is well represented at Ogunquit's **Museum of American Art**, $, Shore Rd; tel: (207) 646-4909. Open Mon–Sat 1030–1700, Sun 1400–1700 (July–Sept). The Oqunquit Playhouse ($$$) stages summer productions; Rte 1; tel: (207) 646-2402.

Kennebunk and its oceanfront adjunct grew wealthy from 19th-century shipbuilding, hence their showpiece Colonial, Federal, Greek Revival and Victorian homes. Kennebunk's **Brick Store Museum**, $, 117 Main St; tel: (207) 985-4802, focuses on maritime history and decorative arts. Open variable hours.

From Kennebunk, follow the signs along very coastal Rte 9 for less commercialised

Kennebunkport and **Old Orchard Beach**. Shops and eateries pack Kennebunkport's Dock Square area in the 'Port'. Beyond the yacht club ex-President George Bush Sr lives the good life on Walker's Point; continue north to Cape Porpoise and Goose Rock Beach.

i **Kennebunk-Kennebunkport Chamber of Commerce**, 17 Western Ave; tel: (207) 967-0857.

Beachmere Inn $$–$$$ 12 Beachmere Pl., Ogunquit; tel: (800) 336-3983 or (207) 646-2021; fax: (207) 646-2231. Victorian manse and modern motel with grand views; gate opens onto Marginal Way.
Fontenay Terrace Motel $$$ 128 Ocean Ave, Kennebunkport; tel: (207) 967-3556. Small motor hotel attractively situated on a tidal inlet.
York Harbor Inn $$$ Coastal Rte 1-A, York Harbor; tel: (207) 363-8903; fax: (207) 363-1130. Charmingly decorated rooms overlook the sea and the start of the coastal walking path. A cosy pub and bright dining room offer two good dining options.

Mabel's Lobster Claw $$ Kennebunkport; tel: (207) 967-2562. Nothing but real, ocean-fresh lobster tails and claws go into Mabel's lobster rolls.
Cape Pier Chowder House $$ Cape Porpoise; tel: (207) 967-4268, (800) 967-4268; www.capeporpoiselobster.com. The setting of this rustic lobster pound is perfect, with tables right on the pier at a rocky promontory.
The Goldenrod $$ Ocean Avenue, York Village. Immensely popular family restaurant with rustic decor and saltwater taffy (a chewy sweet) making demonstrations.
Barnacle Billy's $$–$$$ Perkins Cove, Ogunquit. Quintessential Maine: cracking boiled lobster while seated on a deck overlooking a boat-filled cove.

THE WEDDING CAKE HOUSE

Along Summer St (Rte 35) connecting Kennebunk and Kennebunkport, watch for a yellow and white confection, embellished with intricate wooden fretwork. The entire street is lined with masterpieces of Victorian architecture.

EN ROUTE

Rachel Carson National Wildlife Refuge, a haven for migratory birds, totals 4800 marshy acres overlooking barrier beaches, with a mile-long interpretive trail. It was created in memory of author Rachel Carson, whose 1962 *Silent Spring* made a strong case for ecological awareness.
Tel: (207) 646-9226. Open dawn–dusk.

PORTLAND

Through its history, Portland's docks have been lined in turn with boats – from sailing schooners to the fishing boats and modern cargo and cruise ships that decorate its waterfront today. Not that the harbour needs decorating – nature did that, with a rocky, tree-lined shore and a scattering of islands.

Rows of beautifully-restored old mercantile buildings hold restaurants, cafés, craftsmen's studios, galleries and shops make up the Old Port section, abusy area that becomes even livelier as evening falls. Within an easy walk, the daily **Portland Public Market** (Cumberland and Preble Sts; tel: (207) 228-2000) bustles with local food producers selling temptations from Maple syrup to fresh-baked bread. This is a good choice for breakfast or lunch: choose from a vendor and eat at the provided tables.

Both Vermont Transit and Amtrak connect the city to Boston, making it a popular weekend destination for city-dwellers, who relish Portland's brilliant dining scene. Along with having several outstanding upscale restaurants, the city offers good value and wide choices in all price and style ranges, from crystal-and-candlelight to lobster-in-the-rough at waterside picnic tables.

To take part in the entire lobster experience, join **Lucky Catch Cruises** ($$$ 170 Commercial Street, Portland 207-761-0941, www.luckycatch.com) on a genuine working lobster boat. Don oilskin overalls and gloves to haul traps, measure lobsters, bait the traps and toss them overboard. Pay 'boat price' (wholesale) for your lobster at the end of the cruise and go next door to **The Portland Lobster Co** ($) where they will cook it and provide the fixings at a table on their waterfront deck.

The **Portland Museum of Art**, $, 7 Congress Sq, tel: (207) 775-6148, has an outstanding collection of works by celebrated artists who lived in Maine, including Andrew and N C Wyeth, Winslow Homer, Edward Hopper and Rockwell Kent. Open Tues–Sat 1000–1700 (Thur until 2100), Sun 1200–1700. **Victoria Mansion** is over-the-top Victoriana in an 1858 Italianate villa; $, 109 Danforth St, tel: (207) 772-4841. Open Tues–Sat 1000–1600, Sun 1300–1700 (May–Oct). Danforth St leads to **Western Promenade**, a landscaped public walkway along the edge of a 175-ft high cliff in Portland's classiest neighbourhood.

South of the city (take Rte 77 across the harbour), on Cape Elizabeth rocky promontories, are Portland's much-pictured lighthouses: the 19th-century examples at **Two Lights State Park** inspired Edward Hopper paintings, and the **Portland Head Light** at Fort Williams State Park was commissioned by George Washington in 1791. There is a lighthouse museum ($) in the former keeper's quarters. Open daily 1000–1600 June–Oct.

Scattered over Casco Bay are the **Calendar Islands**; some are residential, others offer swimming and picnicking. Reach them from Casco Bay Lines' terminal, Commercial and Franklin St; tel: (207) 774-7871.

i **Convention and Visitors Bureau of Greater Portland**, 305 Commercial St, Portland, ME 04101; tel: (207) 772-5800; fax: (207) 874-9043; www.visitportland.com.

Portland Harbor Hotel **$$$** 468 Fore St; tel: (207) 523-2010, (888) 798-9090; fax: (207) 775-9990; www.portlandharborhotel.com. The warmth of a country inn, with classy hotel services and location – a few steps from the best dining, attractions and waterfront activities.
HI Hostel **$$** 645 Congress St; tel: (207) 874-3281. Open June–Aug, in college dorm.

Inn at St John B&B $$$ 939 Congress St; tel: (800) 636-9127 or (207) 773-6481; fax: (207) 756-7629. Within walking distance of downtown, near the Western Promenade.

Pomegranate Inn B&B $$–$$$ 49 Neal St; tel: (800) 356-0408 or (207) 772-1006; fax: (207) 773-4426. This 1884 Italianate home and carriage house has eight guest-rooms.

Becky's Diner $$ 390 Commercial St; tel: (207) 773-7070. Diner-style informality for lunch and dinner.

Mim's Brasserie $$$ 205 Commercial St; tel: (207) 347-7478. Seafood just off the boats you can see from the harbourside terrace and vegetables from nearby farms mean that ingredients are just as fresh as the chef's ideas for presenting them.

O'Naturals $–$$ 83 Exchange St; tel: (207) 321-2050. Fast-foods, but all organic, healthy and served on real plates. Internet access, play area with wooden toys, and special attention to any dietary restriction.

Gritty McDuff's $$ 396 Fore St; tel: (207) 772-2739. Portland's first brew pub serves English-inspired pub food.

The Lobster Shack $$ 225 Two Lights Rd, Cape Elizabeth; tel: (207) 799-1677. Lobster, clams, shrimp, burgers; eat 'em at ocean-view picnic tables.

MID-COAST MAINE

This oceanic expanse branches into hundreds of finger-like peninsulas fringed by villages where lobstering, clam-digging and scallop-dragging are primary sources of income. In **Bath** is the **Maine Maritime Museum** ($$, 243 Washington St; tel: (207) 443-1316, open daily 0930–1700). Located on the Kennebec River in what was once a wooden shipyard, the museum houses thousands of historic maritime artefacts. **Freeport** has 120 factory-outlet stores capped by L.L. Bean, the renowned outfitter, open non-stop. **Boothbay Harbor** still holds the charisma of the seafaring village that it was in the mid-eighteenth century. Also typical of that are **Wiscasset**, its town green ringed by Greek Revival-style sea captains' homes, and **Damariscotta** with lakes, ocean and state parks.

Popham, on a bluff overlooking where the Kennebec River meets the Atlantic, is the site of New England's first English colony (1607). The largest of these towns is **Brunswick**, surrounded by Bowdoin College, alma mater of Nathaniel Hawthorne and Portland-born Henry Wadsworth Longfellow. **Pejepscot Historical Society** (159 Park Row; tel: (207) 729-6606) maintains two house museums: **Skolfield-Whittier**

For Free in Brunswick

Bowdoin's Museum of Art, Walker Art Bldg, tel: (207) 725-3275, has an international spectrum of major works; and the Peary-MacMillan Arctic Museum commemorates two Bowdoin College graduates who became North Pole explorers. Hubbard Hall; tel: (207) 725-3416. Both free-admittance museums open Tues–Sat 1000–1700, Sun 1400–1700.

House ($) an 1850s Victorian house and the **Chamberlain Museum** ($), home of Joshua L. Chamberlain, who was hero of Little Round Top at Gettysburg during the American Civil War, Governor of Maine and President of Bowdoin College.

i **Southern Mid-Coast Maine Chamber of Commerce,** 59 Pleasant St, Brunswick; tel: (207) 725-8797 or (877) 725-8797; www.midcoastmaine.com. **Boothbay Harbor Regional Chamber of Commerce,** 192 Townsend Ave, Boothbay Harbor; tel: (800) 266-8422 or (207) 633-2353; www.boothbay-harbor.com.

Brunswick Bed & Breakfast $$–$$$ 165 Park Row, Brunswick; tel: (207) 729-4914 or (800) 299-4914; www.brunswickbnb.com. Delightful bed and breakfast with antique-filled rooms overlooking beautiful gardens; walk to Bowdoin College, museums, shops, restaurants.

Admiral's Quarters Inn $$$ 71 Commercial St, Boothbay Harbor; tel: (207) 633-2474 or (800) 644-1878; fax: (207) 633-5904; www.admiralsquartersinn.com. Guests staying in this renovated sea captain's house (1830) enjoy harbour-view decks.

Le Garage $$–$$$ Water St, Wiscasset; tel: (207) 882-5409. Dining room and glassed-in deck overlook the Sheepscot River.

Richard's German Cuisine $–$$ 115 Main St, Brunswick; tel: (207) 729-9673. A local favorite, authentic German dishes served in a lively family atmosphere; Wiener schnitzel, *Gemischter salat, Schlachtplatte*, impressive beer list..

PENOBSCOT BAY

Halfway along its length the Maine coast is split by the deep cleft of Penobscot Bay. It features some of Maine's most typical scenery. **Camden Hill State Park** has 30 miles of hiking trails, and boats sailing from pretty **Camden** allow you to experience the drama of the Maine coast from the sea.

Working-class **Rockland** features the Farnsworth Art Museum and Wyeth Center, with works by the Wyeths, Fitz Hugh Lane, Winslow Homer, Edward Hopper, Childe Hassam and Louise Nevelson. $, 356 Main St; tel: (207) 596-6457. Open daily 0900–1700 (late May–mid-Oct), Tues–Sat 1000–1700, Sun 1300–1700 (rest of year).

MAINE LOBSTER FESTIVAL

Rockland's annual bash, four days in early August, is a New England classic, with a parade, boat rides, lobster 'shore dinners' and the crowning of the Lobster Queen.

Drive or hike up Mount Battie for a stunning panorama of the town and its bowl-shaped harbour. You'll view it exactly as the poet Edna St Vincent Millay did in 1912.

A century ago, sea captains built their Federal and Greek Revival mansions in **Belfast**, at the head of the bay. On the eastern shore rural roads pass blueberry barrens and lead to yachting and lobstering harbours. **Castine**, established in the 17th century as a fur-trading centre, has many memorials to its chequered history. **Stonington**, on Deer Isle, is the departure point for ferries to **Ile au Haut**, inhabited by shore birds and harbour seals. Isle au Haut Boat Company, Seabreeze Ave; tel: (207) 367-5193.

A ROUTE AROUND PENOBSCOT'S EAST SHORE

Two miles beyond Bucksport, take Rte 175 which meets Rte 166 and leads to Castine. Leave Castine on Rte 166 northbound, turn right onto Rte 199, then right again on Rte 175 south. After 8 miles, Rte 15 crosses the Eggemoggin Reach to Deer Isle. Backtracking to the mainland, meet Rte 175 again for a 25-mile drive to Blue Hill.

i **Camden-Rockport-Linconville Chamber of Commerce** Public Landing, Camden; tel: (800) 223-5459 or (207) 236-4404; fax: (207) 236-4315; www.visitcamden.com.
Rockland-Thomaston Area Chamber of Commerce, Harbor Park, Rockland; tel: (800) 562-2529 or (207) 596-0376.

Tidewater Motel $$–$$$, P.O. Box 546, Vinalhaven; tel: (207) 863-4618; www.tidewater-motel.com. Motel is built on a bridge, so all rooms have water view, either harbour or pond. Leave your vehicle on the mainland and experience one of Maine's premier outer islands and artists colonies, Vinalhaven, on foot or bicycle. Daily ferry service from Rockland.
Castine Inn $$$ 33 Main St, Castine; tel: (207) 326-4365; fax: (207) 326-4365. Choicest rooms in this old inn feature harbour views.

Cappy's Chowder House $$ 1 Main St, Camden. The New Englandy name says it all; moosehead on the wall.
Capt'n Andy's $$ 156 Washington St, Camden. Lobster fresh off the boat, then cooked to order for a sit-down meal or takeaway.
Rockport Corner Shop $ Central St, Rockport. Family atmosphere for breakfast and lunch overlooking Rockport's fishing boat harbour.

MOUNT DESERT ISLAND Pronounced 'dessert' by Mainers, Mount Desert has a landscape consisting of deep glacial valleys and granite mountains rising straight up from the Atlantic. **Bar Harbor** is the principal town to shop, stay and dine in, a counterpoint to the park's serenity. Enquire about whale-watch cruises. Southwest Harbor and Bass Harbor, on the opposite shore, are less inundated with 'summer people'.

Offshore from Southwest Harbor are a scattering of pristine islands, the Cranberries. Cranberry Cove Boating operates ferries to three of them; $$, Town Dock; tel: (207) 244-5882.

Acadia National Park ($, day use) covers nearly half the island. It has more than 120 miles of hiking trails that ascend every summit and traverse every valley. The 27-mile Park Loop Rd passes all of Acadia's better-known highlights; from it, a 3.5-mile road twists to Cadillac Mountain's 1530-ft summit for sweeping views. At Thunder Hole, tidal wave motion creates thunderclaps inside hollow rocks. An astonishing variety of life forms thrive in Otter Point's tide pools, with peregrine falcons soaring overhead.

i **Acadia National Park Visitor Center**, Park Loop Rd, Hulls Cove; tel: (207) 288-3338.
Bar Harbor Chamber of Commerce, 93 Cottage St; tel: (207) 288-5103; www.barharborinfo.com.

Bar Harbor is stuffed with some four-dozen lodgings in every price niche and style. Summertime reservations are essential. The park has two tent-pitch campsites ($), Blackwoods and Sewall. Reservations required at Blackwoods; tel: (800) 365-2267.

Island Chowder House $$–$$$ 38 Cottage St. Informal, centrally located.
Jordan Pond House $$–$$$ Park Loop Dr. In the park: lunch, afternoon tea and dinner.
Maggie's Classic Scales $$–$$$ 6 Summer St. Fresh seafood; sun porch dining.
West Street Café $$$ 176 West St. Old-fashioned restaurant offering the traditional Downeast meal of fish chowder, steamed lobster and blueberry pie.

MOOSEHEAD LAKE

For a taste of the real wilderness that makes up most of northern Maine, head inland to **Moosehead Lake**. This sprawling stretch of water is surrounded by round-topped, forested mountains, through which hikers travel via the **Appalachian Trail**. Activities around Moosehead Lake centre in the little town of **Greenville**, at its southern end, and include scenic flights in a vintage float-plane, cruises on a restored paddle-wheeler, wildlife-watching by boat or canoe and fishing. Guests at **The Birches** (below) can enjoy all of these, as well as white-water rafting trips, for a full Maine experience.

i **Moosehead Lake Chamber of Commerce,** tel: (207) 695-2702; www.mooseheadlake.org.

The Birches Resort $$-$$$ Rockwood; tel: (207) 534-2242, (800) 825-9453; fax: (207) 534-8835, www.birches.com. Low key, rustic cabins on the lake, with dining and a full range of outdoor experiences on offer.
Little Lyford Pond Camps $$, Greenville; tel: (207) 280-0708; www.outdoors.org/lodging/lyford/index.cfm. Cabins, operated by the Appalachian Mountain Club, are perfect for outdoor enthusiasts and hikers, with access to the Appalachian Trail and other day hikes. Hearty home-style dinners and trail lunches.

THE QUODDY LOOP

North of Mt Desert Island, Maine's coast heads almost due east, reaching the country's easternmost point at Eastport. The waters of the giant Bay of Fundy, where the world's highest tides are recorded, are forced in and out of Passamaquoddy Bay twice a day, creating whirlpools, reversing rapids and picturesque wave-sculpted headlands.

Using the Deer Island ferries and the Lubec Bridge, you can explore the area by car, making a circle in either direction. Begin at Machias, Maine, following Rte 1 north to the border at St Stephen. After crossing into Canada, follow Rte 1 to St George, then Rte 772 to Letete, where a free ferry takes cars daily every half hour 0700–2200 July–Aug and 0700–2100 Sept–June, to **Deer Island.** There another ferry ($$) continues to Campobello Island. The first is government-run, the second is operated by East Coast Ferries; tel: (506) 747-2159, daily June–Sept. From Campobello, a bridge crosses to **Lubec, Maine**, and connects via Rte 189 to US Rte 1. Worthwhile stops en route are the short loop to visit the lovely seaside town of **St Andrews** and Franklin Roosevelt's summer home on Campobello Island, the **Roosevelt Campobello International Park**, tel: (506) 752-2922. In St George, an **Adventure Center,** 13 Adventure Lane, tel: (506) 755-1023, can arrange for boat trips, kayaking, cycling, and many other activities.

i **Tourism New Brunswick**, PO Box 12345, Fredericton, NB E3B 5C3; tel: (506) 453-3984, (800) 561-0123.

Quoddy Coastal Tourism Association, PO Box 446, St Andrews, NB E0G 2X0; tel: (506) 529-4677.

Provincial Information Centre, Rte 1, St Stephen, NB E3L 2W9; tel: (506) 466-7390, open daily 0800–2100 May–Aug, shorter hours through Oct.

WHERE NEXT?

The famously rocky coast continues north, past the lighthouse at West Quoddy Head to land's end at Eastport – the easternmost US town. You can cross the Canadian border into New Brunswick province at Calais (pronounced 'callus'). A summer-only car ferry connects Bar Harbor with Yarmouth, Nova Scotia; Bay Ferries; tel: 888 249-7245.

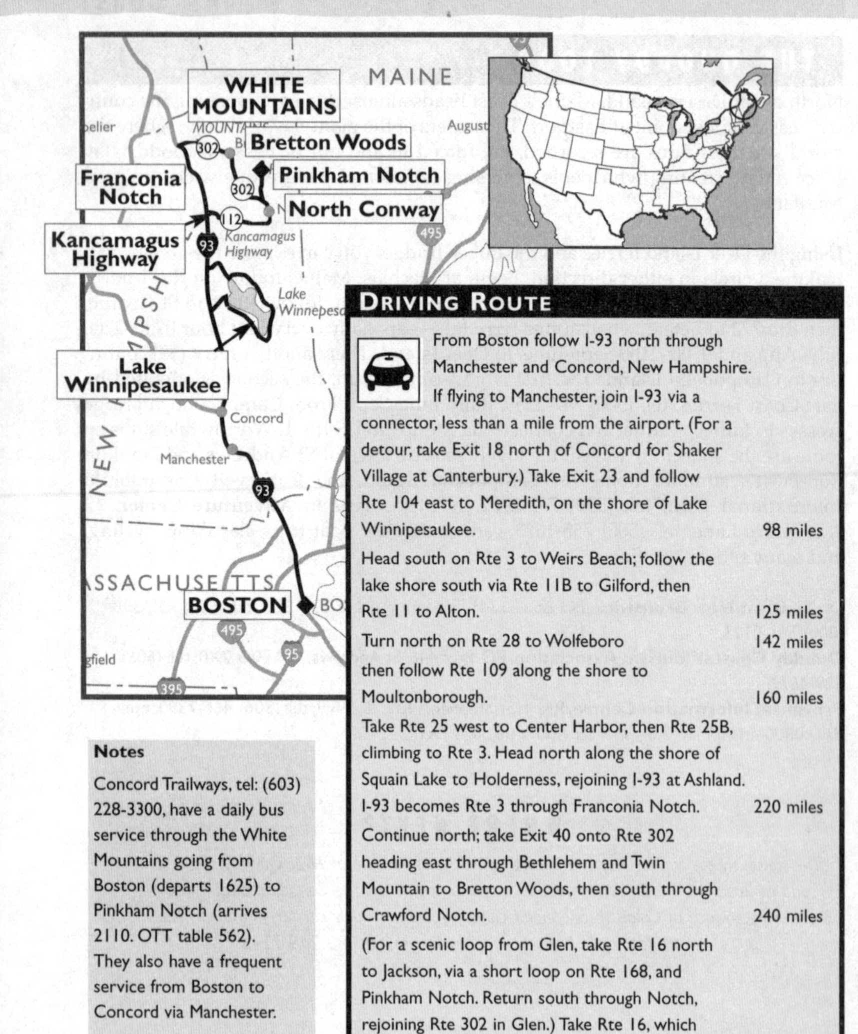

Driving Route

From Boston follow I-93 north through Manchester and Concord, New Hampshire. If flying to Manchester, join I-93 via a connector, less than a mile from the airport. (For a detour, take Exit 18 north of Concord for Shaker Village at Canterbury.) Take Exit 23 and follow Rte 104 east to Meredith, on the shore of Lake Winnipesaukee. — 98 miles

Head south on Rte 3 to Weirs Beach; follow the lake shore south via Rte 11B to Gilford, then Rte 11 to Alton. — 125 miles

Turn north on Rte 28 to Wolfeboro — 142 miles

then follow Rte 109 along the shore to Moultonborough. — 160 miles

Take Rte 25 west to Center Harbor, then Rte 25B, climbing to Rte 3. Head north along the shore of Squain Lake to Holderness, rejoining I-93 at Ashland. I-93 becomes Rte 3 through Franconia Notch. — 220 miles

Continue north; take Exit 40 onto Rte 302 heading east through Bethlehem and Twin Mountain to Bretton Woods, then south through Crawford Notch. — 240 miles

(For a scenic loop from Glen, take Rte 16 north to Jackson, via a short loop on Rte 168, and Pinkham Notch. Return south through Notch, rejoining Rte 302 in Glen.) Take Rte 16, which blends with Rte 302, south through North Conway, continuing through to Conway. — 286 miles

Take Kancamagus Highway, Rte 112 west, returning to I-93 in North Woodstock. — 324 miles

Notes

Concord Trailways, tel: (603) 228-3300, have a daily bus service through the White Mountains going from Boston (departs 1625) to Pinkham Notch (arrives 2110. OTT table 562). They also have a frequent service from Boston to Concord via Manchester.

The White Mountains are the quintessence of the rugged Appalachians, reaching their highest northern elevation at Mount Washington. Grand hotels once refreshed the wealthy from the cities' summer heat, and a rare few still cater for holiday-makers, who view the mountains from their wide verandahs. On the way north, stop at a Shaker village and make a scenic detour around Lake Winnipesaukee before continuing into the heart of the White Mountains.

Take a break from driving by taking a cog railway, aerial tramway or gondola to a mountain top for even grander views. Stop also to enjoy the outdoor pleasures of streams to fish in, rivers and lakes to canoe, waterfalls and miles of hiking trails.

Views spread before you as you drive: row upon row of mountains, with tiny villages clustered around a white church. Expect some steep winding roads, and heavy traffic at summer weekends, especially around the shopping mecca of North Conway. Travelling in the evening or night, be wary of moose – huge creatures which have no fear of cars. In a head-on confrontation, the moose will win, so drive slowly and scan the roadsides.

LAKE WINNIPESAUKEE

Meredith borders a dock-lined lakefront with hotels, shops and eateries. At its centre, Mills Falls Marketplace, tel: (603) 279-7006, is a multi-storey complex of 18 shops, selling everything from local books to ice cream and fashionwear.

Boat Tours

Board the 65-foot MV *Judge Sewall*, tel: (603) 569-3016, at the Town Dock, for a narrated cruise past a loon refuge, old boatyards and several islands. MV *Sophie C* sails among Winnipesaukee's 365 islands and into secluded coves, all in a day's work for a genuine working mailboat. Day or sunset cruises are 2–3 hours; $, tel: (603) 366-5531; operates Sat–Sun (May–early June); (Sept–mid-Oct); daily (mid-June–Aug). The larger, pricier MS *Mount Washington* departs Weirs Beach for Wolfeboro, Center Harbor and Alton Bay. Evening cruises include dinner and dancing to live music; $$, tel: (603) 366-BOAT; daily, 1000 and 1230 (May–Oct); 1500 (July–Aug). Board either tour at Lakeside Ave, Weirs Beach.

Just south is **Weirs Beach**, a touristy town popular with families who flock to the water slides, wave tanks, miniature golf, bowling, kiddy rides and game arcades that seem to fill its every inch. It is port for several boat tours of the lake, for many its only redeeming feature.

Wolfeboro, on the lake's 'quiet side', is a pleasant place to stroll, with a

EN ROUTE
CANTERBURY SHAKER VILLAGE

From Canterbury Center (at Exit 18), follow brown signs east to a perfectly preserved set of 24 housing, farm and workshop buildings, now a museum perpetuating the art and ideals of the 19th-century religious sect, the Shakers. Tours not only show the buildings, but explain Shaker philosophy and daily life. $$, tel: (603) 783-9511. Open 1000–1700 daily (May–Oct); Fri–Sun (Apr, Nov–Dec). The Creamery Restaurant recreates authentic Shaker meals ($$–$$$); open daily for lunch (May–Oct); Fri–Sun (Apr, Nov–Dec); Fri–Sat 1845. Candlelight dinner ($$$) by reservation only. The Summer Kitchen ($) sells snacks.

quaint museum complex (free) of vintage buildings open on a limited schedule, and the Libby Museum, focusing on the area's natural history (native birds and animals) and a collection of local Indian artefacts; $, Main St; open Tues–Sun 1000–1600 (June–Sept).

Instead of driving around the lake, you can see its port towns and surrounding mountain scenery during a narrated boat ride.

i **Information Center**, Dockside, Meredith; tel: (603) 279-6121; open daily May–Oct.
Wolfeboro Chamber of Commerce, 32 Central Ave; tel: (603) 569-2200 or (800) 516-5324.

Lakehurst Housekeeping Cottages $$ Rte 11-D, Alton Bay; tel: (603) 875-2492; May–June nightly, July–Sept weekly only. Well-kept lakefront cottages.
Lin-Joy Cabins $$ Robert's Cove Rd, Alton; tel: (603) 569-4973. Rustic self-catering cabins with a swimming pool.
Tuc-Me-Inn B&B $$ 118 North Main St, Wolfeboro; tel: (603) 569-5702. Comfortable, unpretentious and downtown.

Gunstock Inn $$ Guilford; tel: (800) 654-0180; www.gunstockinn.com. Overlooking the lake, near Gunstock Recreation Area, with a dining room where children have their own menu.

FRANCONIA NOTCH

Between the towns of North Woodstock and Franconia, I-93 and Rte 3 join to become the Franconia Notch Parkway, a dual carriageway through one of the White Mountains' scenic notches. The first exit leads to the **Flume**, a natural chasm with vertical walls. A boardwalk runs through it close to river level; $$, open daily 0900–1700 (mid-May–late Oct).

The Basin is a 20-foot natural pothole at the base of a small waterfall, where melting glaciers wore away the granite with their swirling force. A short walk beyond are the sloping ledges of Kinsman Falls, a lovely series of cascades.

Notches are glacially carved passes through the mountain ranges. Low points over which roads can pass, they are characterised by their bowl-like shape, a result of the circular glacial scouring that formed them.

Until May 2003 Franconia Notch's highlight was the 40-ft group of granite ledges forming the **Old Man of**

the Mountain. The giant profile fell, leaving only a ledge and the Old Man of the Mountain Museum, which explains the geology of the profile and attempts at its preservation; tel: (603) 823-5563; open daily 1000–1730 (June–mid-Oct).

The Aerial Tramway, one of New Hampshire's several summit lifts, begins at the northern end of the notch, carrying passengers to the 4200-ft summit of Cannon Mountain. Views extend to Canada on clear days, and trails circle the summit. $$, tel: (603) 823-5563; open daily mid-May–Oct.

White Mountain Attractions Association, Rte 112 at Exit 32 off I-93, North Woodstock; tel: (603) 645-9889 or (800) 346-3687; www.VisitWhiteMountains.com.

Apart from camping, accommodation can be found only at either end of the State Reservation, in Thornton and North Woodstock (south) or Franconia and Sugar Hill (north).

Lafayette Campground $ Rte 3; tel: (603) 823-9513. Well-spaced tent pitches and a campers' store.

Hilltop Inn $$–$$$ Main St, Sugar Hill; tel: (603) 823-5695. B&B with well-decorated, very comfortable rooms and lively hosts. Children (even babies) are welcome.

Like lodgings, dining is available outside the state reservation. Basic picnic supplies are available at Lafayette Campground.

Frannie's $–$$ Rte 3 (just south of Exit 30, I-93), Thornton; tel: (603) 745-3868. Plain decor, friendly atmosphere, very good food.

Polly's Pancake Parlor $$ Rte 117, Sugar Hill; tel: (603) 823-5575; open Mon–Fri 0700–1500, Sat–Sun 1700–1900. Serves fresh-made pancakes with real maple syrup.

Woodstock Station and Brewpub $$ 80 Main St, North Woodstock; tel: (603) 745-3951. Three meals daily, good ales.

BRETTON WOODS

The imposing **Mount Washington Hotel** is the centrepiece of this mountain valley, a last reminder of an opulent era, gleaming in meticulous restoration. Free daily tours show its historic interior, often also a water-powered print shop and Stickney Chapel, with Tiffany windows.

The **Mount Washington Cog Railway** has puffed its way up the steep mountainside to the summit since the 1860s. The pricey 3-hr return trip allows time to explore New England's highest peak or you can take an early train to spend the day hiking above the tree line; $$$, tel: (603) 846-5406 or (800) 922-8825; operates Sat–Sun (May, daily June–late Oct); reservations suggested.

On a clear day the views from the summit of Mount Washington seem endless. The Mount Washington Observatory at the summit has clocked winds to 231 miles per hour, so hold onto your hat. To climb the mountain, wait for good weather, begin early, and take layers of warm clothing. The **Ammonoosuc Ravine Trail** begins at the Cog Railway's base station, passing a waterfall and Lake of the Clouds en route. A shorter, easier climb with a view is nearby Mount Willard, overlooking Crawford Notch's steep walls.

The Bretton Arms $$$–$$$$ Rte 302; tel: (603) 278-1000 or (800) 258-0330. In the grounds of the Mount Washington Hotel.
Sugarloaf National Forest Campground, off Rte 302, between Twin Mt and Bretton Woods. No tel. Nicely separated tent pitches without the touristy development of commercial campgrounds.

Fabyan's Station $–$$ Rte 302; tel: (603) 278-2222. Hamburgers and hearty dishes in Victorian rail station.

PINKHAM NOTCH

Rte 16 climbs from the picturesque village of Jackson, with fine views of Mount Washington, which forms its western slopes. Take the short walk to **Glen Ellis Falls**, which drop 65 ft through a granite cleft.

The **Pinkham Notch Visitors Center** is the headquarters of the Appalachian Mountain Club, with books, maps and information about trails, wildlife and nature, and a giant relief map of Mount Washington. Year-round programmes include nature hikes, botany, photography and travelogues, some free.

The **Mount Washington Auto Road** ($$$) is an 8-mile 12 per cent climb with breathtaking views. Drive or ride in a van. At the base are Glen House Carriage Barns (free), with vehicles that have carried passengers up the mountain since the first horse-drawn coach.

White Mountain National Forest charges $5 per vehicle for a one-week pass, currently available only in Lincoln, Conway or Pinkham Notch; tel: (603) 528-8721.

The notch is within the National Forest, without commercial ventures, so look for places to stay in Jackson (south) or Gorham (north).
Dolly Copp Campground Rte 16, Gorham; tel: (603) 466-2713.
Appalachian Mountain Club $ Rte 16, Gorham; tel: (603) 466-2727. Rustic lodging and three daily meals.
Carter Notch Inn $–$$ Carter Notch Rd, Jackson; tel: (603) 383-9630 or (800) 794-9434. Bed and great breakfasts.
Town and Country Motor Inn $$ Route 2, Gorham; (603) 466-3315. Well-kept motel with swimming pool.
Gorham House B&B $$ 55 Main St; tel: (603) 466-2271. Victorian inside and out.

Yokohama Restaurant $–$$ 288 Main St, Gorham; tel: (603) 466-2501. Asian menu, with emphasis on Japanese.
Wilfred's Turkey Dinners $$ Main St, Gorham; tel: (603) 466-2380. Turkey and other country foods.

NORTH CONWAY

Shoppers' heaven, this historic resort town is also a drivers' hell on summer weekends when traffic nearly stops on Rte 16. The largest concentration of cut-price retail outlets in the north-east sells 'blems' (seconds) and overstocks, often at drastically reduced prices, even better since New Hampshire has no sales tax.

But there's more to North Conway than retail outlets and traffic. **Cathedral Ledge** rises from Echo Lake State Park, and a road leads to the top for views of the valley. The lake has a fine – although often crowded – swimming beach ($) and picnic area. **Conway Scenic Railway** ($$), tel: (603) 356-5251, travels along the wide valley from the Victorian Railway Station, a free museum of vintage trains.

EN ROUTE

Explore New England history at **Heritage New Hampshire**, beginning on the realistic pitching ship that brought the first settlers. Although it is designed for children, adults will enjoy the engineering of interactive displays detailing 'King's Pines', royal grants and Native Americans. $$, Rte 16, Glen; tel: (603) 383-4186; open daily 0900–1700 (mid-May–mid-Oct).

Mount Washington Valley Chamber of Commerce, Rte 16; tel: (603) 356-3171 or (800) 367-3364; www.mountwashingtonvalley.org.

Fox Ridge $$ Rte 16; tel: (603) 356-3151 or (800) 343-1804. Well-decorated motel with balconies and sports facilities.
Green Granite Resort $$–$$$ Rte 16; tel: (603) 356-6901 or (800) 468-3666. Family-friendly modern hotel with pools, sauna. Breakfast buffet is included.

KANCAMAGUS HIGHWAY

Stretching 35 miles through National Forest from Conway to Lincoln, the road is sometimes steep and winding, but a number of lay-bys offer vistas not seen from the road. At the Conway end, Rocky Gorge and Lower Falls are popular for swimming and picnics. Shortly after a covered bridge is the trail to Sabbaday Falls, a gorge with 40-ft walls and glacial potholes.

WHERE NEXT?

To explore the Maine Coast (see pp. 156–165), remain on Rte 302 south of North Conway, following it eastward along Maine's Sebago Lake to Portland.

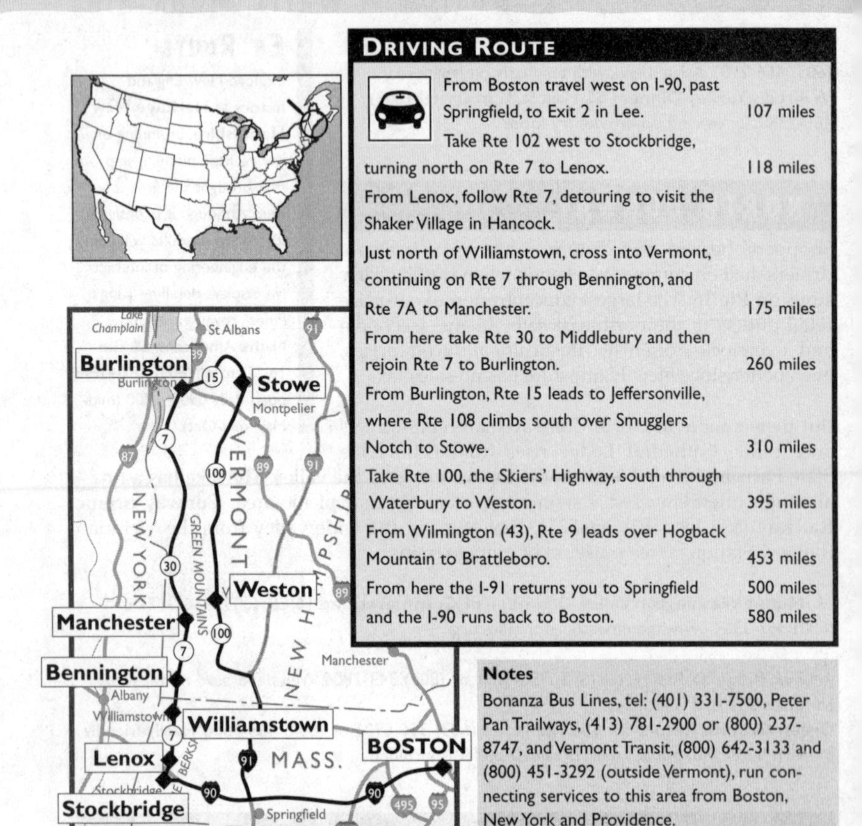

Driving Route

From Boston travel west on I-90, past Springfield, to Exit 2 in Lee.	107 miles
Take Rte 102 west to Stockbridge, turning north on Rte 7 to Lenox.	118 miles
From Lenox, follow Rte 7, detouring to visit the Shaker Village in Hancock. Just north of Williamstown, cross into Vermont, continuing on Rte 7 through Bennington, and Rte 7A to Manchester.	175 miles
From here take Rte 30 to Middlebury and then rejoin Rte 7 to Burlington.	260 miles
From Burlington, Rte 15 leads to Jeffersonville, where Rte 108 climbs south over Smugglers Notch to Stowe.	310 miles
Take Rte 100, the Skiers' Highway, south through Waterbury to Weston.	395 miles
From Wilmington (43), Rte 9 leads over Hogback Mountain to Brattleboro.	453 miles
From here the I-91 returns you to Springfield	500 miles
and the I-90 runs back to Boston.	580 miles

Notes

Bonanza Bus Lines, tel: (401) 331-7500, Peter Pan Trailways, (413) 781-2900 or (800) 237-8747, and Vermont Transit, (800) 642-3133 and (800) 451-3292 (outside Vermont), run connecting services to this area from Boston, New York and Providence.

From the manicured, gentrified Berkshire Hills in western Massachusetts to the more rustic and higher Green Mountains of Vermont, this route covers much of western New England. Wealthy New Yorkers and Bostonians 'found' the Berkshires at the end of the 19th century, building lavish summer retreats and bringing music events that still thrive more than a century later.

Some of Vermont's most idyllic towns lie nestled in the rolling Green Mountains, where stylish Manchester was once the darling of New York socialites. Despite these citified incursions, the Green Mountains are still filled with the elements that personify Vermont: green-clad mountains, skiing, white churches, country stores and craft studios.

Caught between the Green Mountains and huge Lake Champlain, Burlington rises from its marina to a lively downtown. Expect a steep, winding road over Smugglers Notch, but otherwise gentle gradients as you explore these hills and mountains, for which you should allow at least four days.

STOCKBRIDGE AND LENOX

A far cry from its Puritan origins, Stockbridge reeks of old money, its impressive Main Street homes only a hint of the sumptuous 'cottages' on its fringes. The illustrator Norman Rockwell set many of his small-town American scenes here; many are in the **Norman Rockwell Museum**, $$, Rte 183; open daily 1000–1700 (May–Oct), Mon–Fri 1100–1600 (Nov–Apr).

Chesterwood was the summer estate of sculptor Daniel Chester French, best known for his Lincoln Memorial in Washington. Tours feature his house, gardens and studio, filled with drawings, casts and bronze models. $$, Williamsville Rd; open daily 1000–1700 (May–Oct).

To see how the rich summered here, visit **Naumkeag**, residence of America's ambassador to Great Britain from 1899 to 1905; it has 26 rooms filled with antiques and Chinese decorative arts. $$, Prospect Hill Rd; open daily 1000–1700 (late May–mid-Oct).

Lenox is the real centre of Berkshire's society, which revolves around music, theatre and dance. You'll find boutiques, restaurants and upmarket lodgings, along with more 'cottages'. Most interesting is **The Mount**, completed in 1902 for novelist Edith Wharton, who designed this estate after a Lincolnshire manor house, adding French and Italian accents. $, Plunkett St and Rte 7; tel: (413) 637-1899; open daily 0900–1500, last tour 1400 (late May–Oct).

Summer Theatre and Music

The Mount's bosky grounds are the stage for Shakespeare & Company, enjoyed while picnicking on the lawn; tel: (413) 637-3353 for performance details.

Tanglewood is summer home to the Boston Symphony Orchestra, chamber music and jazz. Priciest tickets are for 'the Shed', a roofed open auditorium, but lawn tickets are more fun; bring a picnic. Tel: (413) 637-5165; performances late June–early Sept.

Berkshire Theater Festival, on Main St in Lenox, tel: (413) 298-5536, is set in a Gilded Age playhouse.

i **Stockbridge Information**, Main St, where they would as soon look straight through you as answer your question. The **Lenox Chamber of Commerce**, 75 Main St; tel: (800) 255-

EN ROUTE

Hancock Shaker Village

A short detour off Rte 7 south of Williamstown leads to the 'City of Peace', inhabited 1790–1959 by the communal Shakers. Twenty artefact-filled buildings illustrate their ways. In the five-storey 1830 Brick Dwelling, pegs for hanging clothes, tools, chairs and brooms speak of the Shaker penchant for order. The highlight is the 1826 Round Stone Barn. $$$, Rtes 20 and 41; tel: (413) 443-0188. Open daily 0930–1700 (late May–Oct), 1000–1500 (Apr–May and Nov).

3669 or (413) 637-3646, is much more hospitable.

For further information on the Berkshires, call the Berkshire Visitors Bureau: (413) 443-9186 or (800) 237-5747.

Monument Mountain Motel $$ 249 Stockbridge Rd (Rte 7), Great Barrington; tel: (413) 528-3272. Not fancy, but the in-room movies are free.

Red Lion Inn $$$–$$$$ 30 Main St; tel: (413) 298-5545. A local landmark since the 18th century. Semi-formal dining room serves traditional fare.

Cactus Café $ 54 Main St, Lee; tel: (413) 243-4300. Mexican decor and food, informal in atmosphere and service.

Theresa's Stockbridge Café $$ Main St; tel: (413) 298-5465. Refreshingly un-snooty oasis, with many vegetarian choices.

Martin's $ 49 Railroad St, Great Barrington; tel: (413) 528-5455. Breakfast and lunch only; omelets are a specialty.

La Bruschetta $$$ 1 Harris St, West Stockbridge; tel: (413) 232-7141. Stylish and pricey, but brilliant use of local produce, cheeses and meats.

WILLIAMSTOWN

The **Sterling and Francine Clark Art Institute** puts this tidy college town on the art map with impressive collections of Renoir, Monet, Turner and Winslow Homer. $, 225 South St; tel: (413) 458-2303, open Tues–Sun 1000–1700 (Sept–June), daily 1000–1700 (July and Aug). On Main St, the **Williams College Museum of Art** complements it with modern, contemporary and non-Western art; tel: (413) 597-2429, open Tues–Sat 1000–1700, Sun 1300–1700. The annual **Theater Festival**, June–Aug, includes classics, premières and cabaret; 1000 Main St; tel: (413) 597-2429.

In the 12,500-acre **Mount Greylock State Reservation**, off Notch Rd, the mountain is laced with 45 miles of marked trails. Loops near the summit can be traversed in under an hour to see rare alpine flora and birds.

Williamstown Chamber of Commerce, Rtes 2 and 7; tel: (413) 458-9077 or (800) 214-3799.

Bascom Lodge $ Mount Greylock summit; tel: (413) 743-1591. Rustic lodge has mixed-sex bunkrooms and four private rooms. Hearty meals are served family style.

Northside Motel $–$$ 45 North St; tel: (413) 458-8107. Convenient downtown location.

Field Farm Guest House $$–$$$ 554 Sloan Rd; tel: (413) 458-3135. Modern lodging, with wild flowers and 4 miles of hiking trails.

101 North Restaurant and Lounge $$ 101 North St; tel: (413) 458-4000. Contemporary food, plus cabaret by the performers at Williamstown Theater Festival.
The Orchards $ (tea), Rte 2; tel: (413) 458-9611 or (800) 225-1517. Serves afternoon tea daily. The dining room is pricey, but superb; actor Paul Newman is often a guest here in the summer.

BENNINGTON

The 306-ft **Bennington Battle Monument** marks the turning point of the American Revolution, where the British General Burgoyne rethought his northward thrust. A lift to the top yields views of three states. Old Bennington is worth seeing for its fine colonial-era homes and for the **Bennington Museum**, with early American glass, pottery, quilts and primitive paintings. $, Rte 9; tel: (802) 447-1571; open daily 0900–1700 (Mar–Nov).

In North Bennington, **Park-McCullough House** is among America's earliest Second Empire homes, with a carriage barn, flower gardens and a playhouse. $, off Rte 67A, North Bennington; tel: (802) 442-5441; open Thur–Mon (June–Oct).

i **Bennington Chamber of Commerce**, Rte 7A; tel: (802) 447-3311.

Greenwood Lodge $ Rte 9; (802) 442-2547; open mid-May–mid-Oct. Mountainside hostel close to hiking trails.
Molly Stark Inn $ 1067 East Main St; tel: (802) 442-9631. Victorian inn with a homey country feel and handmade quilts.

Alldays and Onions $ 519 East Main St; open 0800–2100 Mon–Sat. Serves healthy whole-grain sandwiches and delectable pastries.
Blue Benn Diner $ Rte 7. Old-fashioned diner atmosphere, but with a modern twist to the menu.

MANCHESTER

Manchester Village's genteel gathering of impeccable large homes surrounds the pillared façade of the Equinox, a vintage grand hotel. Wealthy New Yorkers once summered in the mansions, including Robert Todd Lincoln's **Hildene**, $, built in

1902 by Abraham Lincoln's son. Restored gardens are at their height in June and July; tel: (802) 362-1788; open daily (mid-May–Oct).

The **Vermont State Craft Center**, opposite the Equinox, features works by top craftsmen in all media, from pottery and wood to weaving and art glass. Behind the hotel rises Mount Equinox, reached via the 5-mile **Mount Equinox Skyline Drive**. $$, tel: (802) 362-1113; open May–Oct.

EN ROUTE
Vermont Marble Exhibit

Top American landmarks such as the Jefferson Memorial are made of Vermont marble. This stunning presentation ($) shows how to turn a mountain into a magnificent building. Detour 7 miles from Rutland to Proctor's Main St; tel: (802) 459-2300 or (800) 427-1396; www.vermont-marble.com. Open daily 0900–1730 (mid-May–Oct).

Just north is **Manchester Center**, a succession of factory outlet malls selling cut-price brand-name clothing and home decorations.

i **Manchester and the Mountains Chamber of Commerce**, 2 Main St, Manchester Center; tel: (802) 362-2100; www.manchestervermont.com.

Barnstead Instead $$ Rte 7A, Manchester Center; tel: (802) 362-1619, fax: (802) 362-1619. In a converted barn, a short walk from shops and restaurants.

Hapgood Pond Recreation Area Peru; tel: (802) 362-2307. National Forest campground with swimming beach.

Garlic John's $–$$ Rtes 11 and 30, Manchester Center; tel: (802) 362-9843. Casual setting where families are welcome.

BURLINGTON

Lake Champlain is part of downtown Burlington, bordered by parks, cycling/footpaths, beaches and playgrounds. **Church Street Marketplace** is alive with activity, especially in good weather, filled with sidewalk cafés, vendors and music. A free shuttle trolley connects the two.

Ten miles south, the **Shelburne Museum** features folk arts: early New England quilts, roundabout horses, horse-drawn sleighs, carriages, a covered bridge and the SS *Ticonderoga* are among the 80,000 artefacts. $$, Rte 7; tel: (802) 985-3346; open daily late May–mid-Oct 1000–1700, shorter winter hours.

Shelburne Farms is a 1400-acre working 'gentleman's farm' with wagon tours of gardens, historic barns, a children's farmyard where you can try milking a cow, and a dairy where cheese is made. $, Harbor Rd; tel: (802) 985-8686; tours daily 0930–1330 (June–mid-Oct).

i **Lake Champlain Regional Chamber of Commerce**, 60 Main St; tel: (802) 863-3489.

BOAT TOUR
The *Spirit of Ethan Allen II* takes passengers on narrated dinner and sunset cruises $, tel: (802) 862-8300.

Look for 'Motel Row' on Rte 7 south of the city.
Mrs Farrell's Home Hostel $ (directions with reservation); tel: (802) 865-3730. Curfew 2200.
Anchorage Inn $$ 108 South Dorset St, South Burlington; tel: (802) 863-7000 or (800) 336-1869; fax: (802) 658-3351. Modern hotel with pool, sauna, breakfast included.
Burlington Redstone B&B $$ 497 S Willard St (Rte 7); tel: (802) 862-0508. Historic home within easy walking distance of downtown.

Penny Cluse Café $$ 169 Cherry St; tel: (802) 651-8834. Serves breakfast and lunch daily, with dinners at weekends, with pancakes always on the menu.
Trattoria Delia $$–$$$ 152 St Paul St (City Hall Park); tel: (802) 864-5253. Unforgettable Mediterranean dining with wild game specialities.

STOWE AND SMUGGLERS NOTCH

The road over Smugglers Notch, Rte 108, is so narrow that caravans are unable to manoeuvre the sharp turns between giant boulders that line its sides. Park between them and climb a short distance for a panoramic view of Vermont, New York State and Canada. When the road closes for the winter, you can ski over the top, Alpine-style, from Smugglers Notch Ski Resort; tel: (802) 644-8851 or (800) 451-8752; www.smuggs.com.

On the Stowe side, a short trail leads to **Bingham Falls**, one of the state's most beautiful, with potholes carved by swirling waters.

Stowe is popular year-round for shopping, restaurants and lodgings. Crafts and hand-made goods shops predominate in upmarket Main Street, where you can rent bicycles at Stowe Hardware Store, tel: (802) 253-7205, to cycle the paved 5.3-mile Stowe Recreation Path.

TO THE TOP
The Gondola Skyride, $, tel: (802) 253-3000, scales Mount Mansfield for sweeping views and access to hiking trails, or a 4.5-mile Auto Road ($$) leads to the summit.

i **Stowe Area Association**, Main St; tel: (877) GOSTOWE; www.gostowe.com.

The Gables $$–$$$ 1457 Mountain Rd; tel: (802) 253-7730 or (800) GABLES-1; www.stoweinfo.com/saa/gables or www.gablesinn.com. Warm and family-owned inn with fire-places, whirlpool tubs and mega-breakfasts.
Green Mountain Inn $$–$$$ Main St; tel: (802) 253-7301 or (800) 253-7302; fax: (802) 253-5096;

STOWE EVENTS

At the Trapp Family Lodge the hills *are* alive with the sound of music, all summer long, when the von Trapps host Meadow Concerts (bring a picnic and watch the sunset to music). $$; performances late June–Aug. The Vermont Mozart Festival ($$) takes place in late July. Tel: (877) GOSTOWE.

The Smugglers Notch Area Winter Carnival, in early February, has Nordic races, snow sculptures, food, snowshoe hikes and social events; tel: (802) 644-8851.

www.greenmountaininn.com. Canopy beds, whirlpool baths, afternoon cider and fresh-baked biscuits.

The restaurants at The Gables and Green Mountain Inn are both open to the public ($–$$).

Gracie's $ Main St; tel: (802) 253-8741. Big burgers, sandwiches and generous dinners until 2400 daily.

WESTON

Clustered around its village green and bandstand, Weston is home to the **Vermont Country Store**, a real original, complete with high button shoes, pot-bellied stove, and rows of penny candy jars. More than a museum, it's an emporium of carefully chosen country clothing, housewares and foods; open Mon–Sat 0900–1700. The **Weston Bowl Mill** has made wooden wares since 1902; open Mon–Sat 0900–1500, Sun 1000–1500. **Weston Playhouse** presents Broadway musicals late June–early Sept, with pre-theatre dinner and cabaret; tel: (802) 824-5288.

Colonial House Inn and Motel $ Rte 100; tel: (802) 824-6286. A homey B&B motel, with home-cooked meals and a bakery famed for peach pie.

Village Sandwich Shop $; open daily 1000–1730. Sandwiches, light meals and pastries.

EN ROUTE

Vermont's favourite ice creams are made at **Ben and Jerry's Ice Cream Factory**, where you can sample this stuff everyone raves about and see it made. Tours include samples. $, Rte 100; tel: (802) 244-5641; open daily year round.

WHERE NEXT?

From Brattleboro you can follow Rte 9 east, which becomes Rte 101 in Keene, NH, continuing to Manchester for the start of the White Mountains Route (see p. 166). Or you can continue on Rte 101 to the coast to join the Maine Coast Route (p. 156). Lake Champlain straddles the border with Canada and from Burlington it is just under 100 miles to Montreal.

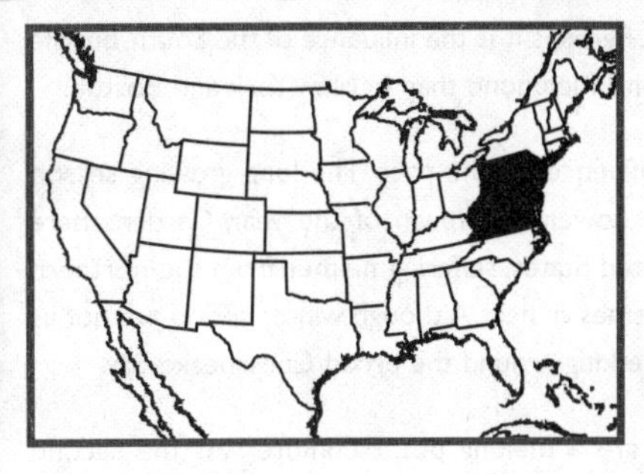

Along with the Northeast, the Middle Atlantic – Pennsylvania, Delaware, New Jersey, Maryland, Virginia, West Virginia and the nation's capital city of Washington DC – has the highest concentration of historic sites in America. The Revolutionary War was fought and ended here, and the document that sealed the separation of Britain's 13 American colonies was written and signed in Philadelphia. Much of the Civil War was also fought in these borderlands between the North and the South, as the Confederate Army tried repeatedly to surround and take the nation's capital.

The area's history is not defined by wars, however. Gracious tidewater plantations date from the earliest settlements, and historic restorations such as Colonial Williamsburg and St Mary's City in Maryland show today's visitors what life was like in colonial America. Entire blocks of Annapolis look much as they did when George Washington resigned his commission as general at its state house. Virginia was home to both Thomas Jefferson and George Washington, and their homes at Monticello and Mount Vernon are two of the loveliest plantations in America.

The region that spawned so many leaders in America's early history continued to be important as the nation grew up. Coal from the mountains of West Virginia and western Maryland moved by ships from Baltimore to fire the furnaces of the Industrial Revolution's mills in New England. Wagon trains moved westwards across those same mountains to settle the west.

Travellers who love New England will also be at home in the Middle Atlantic, with its small villages, short distances and colonial ambience. Historic homes and buildings abound, and entire streets seem to have dropped in from another century. But these states have an entirely different flavour of their own, quite distinct from their northern neighbours. Perhaps it is the influence of the South, but life moves just a little slower in Baltimore and Richmond than in New York and Boston.

The milder climate may also have an influence on the pace. The long growing season keeps landscapes green and filled with flowers for much of the year. Gardens here include some of the loveliest in the United States, suffering neither from the northern extremes of cold nor the southern extremes of heat. Although winter sports are not as big in the middle states, water sports are king around the broad Chesapeake Bay.

Like the Northeast, the central states are a melting pot. Baltimore was the second largest port of entry for the great immigration waves in the 19th and early 20th centuries. Many of these newcomers never went any further. Today the city, and the area around it, reflects the multiple cultures of these various ethnic groups, and has retained its distinct Italian, Greek, Polish and other neighbourhoods.

But the cities are not alone in their ethnic character. An entire region of Pennsylvania, near Lancaster, is known as 'Pennsylvania Dutch Country', not for any connection with the Netherlands but for its many German families ('Dutch' comes from *Deutsch*), many descendants of Hessian soldiers who fought in the Revolution. Mennonite and Amish communities still maintain old ways of dress and transportation by buggy.

Travellers today enjoy sharing for a time in this old-fashioned way of life, and especially in the home-cooked foods that are traditional here. Look for shoo-fly pie, made with treacle, and for hearty soups with thick dumplings. Cured meats, farm cheeses and beautiful fresh fruits and vegetables are plentiful, along with delicious baked goods and sweets.

The Pennsylvania Dutch do not have a monopoly on interesting and delicious foods in the Middle Atlantic, of course. Baltimore's Little Italy and Greek quarter and Washington's Chinese and Caribbean neighbourhoods provide plenty of other exotic flavours. But the crowning glory of the entire Chesapeake Bay region is the blue crab and its fellow shellfish.

In Baltimore and in waterside restaurants all around the bay you can join natives around long tables piled high with boiled Chesapeake crabs. A quick lesson in handling the wooden mallet and you'll be an expert 'crab-picker'. Or you can let someone else do the work and enjoy them in crabcakes, which may be sautéed, deep fried or grilled, but should always be filled with big chunks of backfin crabmeat.

In the cities of Baltimore, Washington and Philadelphia expect to find some restaurants with up-to-date menus of sophisticated 'New American' dishes, along with the ethnic favourites and traditional American cooking. Baltimore is known for its smoked beef and Philadelphia is home of the cheesesteak sandwich, both of which you will want to try.

Outside the cities, dining is more traditional here than in some stylish New England restaurants, although you will find some notable exceptions. Seafood is often deep fried, which can get a little tiresome after several days of restaurant meals, but you will find an increasing number of chefs offering sautéed (called 'pan-fried' here) or grilled alternatives. Don't be surprised to see shellfish identified on menus by their waters of origin: Chincoteague oysters are known nationwide for their high quality.

However strong the influence of the sea is around the Chesapeake Bay, it would be a mistake to envision this entire region as coastal. As you move west from the Atlantic shore, the land begins to rise in rolling hills, which roll higher until they reach the Blue Ridge and Great Smokey Mountains of the Appalachian chain. One of America's most scenic motor trips is along the 'Skyline Drive' which follows the crest of Virginia's mountains.

Can you claim to know what the United States is really like after visiting just this heartland of its colonial era and its present-day capital? Yes and no. You can see a wide sampling here. Along with the scenes of its birth and the political centre of its history as a nation (and hence many of its most sacred sites of patriotic pilgrimage), you will see the only area where the traditional North and South come together, blend, clash, mix and create cultural patterns of their own. Here you will find the history of two ways of life even in one state (Maryland was a slave state, but cast its lot with the North in the Civil War), and some of the most appealing traditions of both North and South.

Visitors here will see one of America's most important cities: Washington DC. While not its largest, nor its most important economically, Washington is where the decisions are made that affect nearly every phase of American life, and the lives of many others all over the world. The sights of Washington alone could easily fill a week or even a fortnight. Indeed, many Americans do spend a week here at least once in their life. It is the traditional 'class trip' for graduating students from all over the United States.

Washington's imposing and art-filled government buildings, its monuments, historic sites and museums reflect the multiplicity of American life and interests. Many of the most interesting of these places are free, which helps makes up for the higher cost of lodging and food in a city.

In this area you will also get a feel for the small-town life, which many consider to be the cornerstone of America. Sleepy tidewater fishing villages and rural farming towns reflect the small-town values and traditions so close to America's heart, as do others tucked deep into the wooded hollows of Virginia's and Maryland's mountains. Some of the country's most appealing small cities – Annapolis, Charlottesville, Frederick, Lancaster and Wilmington – offer yet another view of American life.

Transport here is the easiest anywhere in the country. Train, plane, bus, bike, boat and foot travel are all easy options, which is not true everywhere else. It's the one part of America you can see – at least most of it – without a car. Of course, to see the more remote and rural areas, four wheels of your own would be handy, but public transport will serve you well here. In the summer you can even cross the Chesapeake Bay by boat to visit the Eastern Shore on a day trip. Much of the land is flat and invites cycling; nearly 200 miles of wide flat trail follow the towpath of a canal built in the early 1800s, and nearby inns can arrange to have your baggage transferred each day.

While the warmer climate makes travel pleasant in the early spring and late autumn, and often brings mild days even in the winter, it also brings wilting midsummer heat and humidity. In July and August the best places to be in the cities are inside air-conditioned buildings. The good news is that almost everywhere is air-conditioned – hotels, restaurants, museums and public buildings. For the best garden displays, travel in May and June. To see Washington's famous cherry blossoms, or at least the best displays of azaleas and other spring-blooming shrubs and trees, aim for April. And remember that the western mountains of Maryland and Virginia are ablaze with coloured foliage in autumn.

OUR CHOICE

The Capitol Building

Smithsonian museums

The National Mall's monuments

Colonial Williamsburg

Monticello

Mount Vernon

The Skyline Drive

Historic Annapolis

Baltimore's Inner Harbor

Pennsylvania Dutch Country

HOW MUCH YOU CAN SEE IN A ...

WEEK (7 DAYS)

Washington and Annapolis, with a stop in Baltimore

Washington, Tidewater Virginia and Williamsburg

Washington, Baltimore and Pennsylvania Dutch Country

Washington, Philadelphia and Pennsylvania Dutch Country

The Eastern Shore and Tidewater Virginia with Williamsburg

Annapolis and the Eastern Shore

FORTNIGHT (14 DAYS)

Washington, Annapolis, the Eastern Shore, Tidewater Virginia and Williamsburg

Washington, Richmond, Tidewater Virginia, Williamsburg and the Shenandoah

Philadelphia, Pennsylvania Dutch Country, Baltimore, Annapolis and Washington

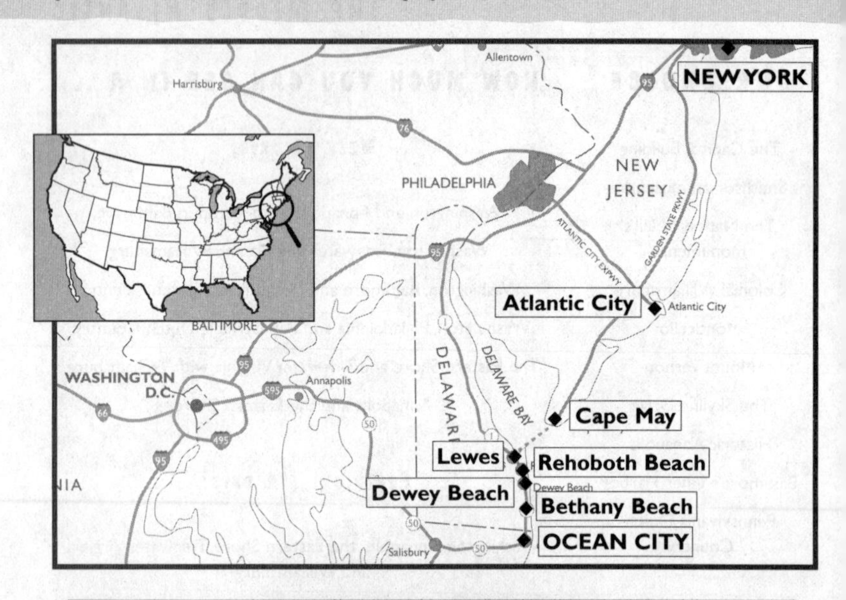

NEW YORK — OCEAN CITY

OTT Tables 320/380n/385/472/502/580/682

Service	RAIL	Bus	RAIL	Bus	Bus	Bus	Bus	Ferry		Bus	Bus	
Days of operation	Daily	Daily	Daily	Daily	Daily	Daily	Daily	Daily		Daily	Daily	
Special notes	A	B	C	D	E	F	G	H				
New York ....d.	A	B	....	....	....	0730	....	....	....	....	....	....
Philadelphia ....d.	A	B	0544	....	0820	|	0935	....	....	1800	....	....
Washington ....d.	....	....	|	....	|	|	|	....	....	|	2305	....
Atlantic City ....d.	....	....	0719	0850	0950	1035	|	....	....	|	|	....
Cape May ....d.	....	....	....	1056	....	....	1249	1430	....	|	|	....
Lewes ....d.	....	....	....	....	....	....	....	1540	....	2135	|	....
Rehoboth Beach ....d.	....	....	....	....	....	....	....	....	....	2145	|	....
Bethany Beach ....d.	....	....	....	....	....	....	....	....	....	2205	|	....
Ocean City ....a.	....	....	....	....	....	....	....	....	....	2230	0335	....

Special notes:

A–Frequent daily service. Journey time 80 minutes.
B–Frequent services 0230, 0700 and at least hourly till 2330. Journey time 2 - 3 hours.
C–Additional trips: 0050, 0626, 0752, 0930, 1148, 1347, 1517, 1649, 1738, 1914, 2030, 2150, 2242.
D–Additional trips: 0230, 0430, 0640, 1050 and hourly until 1650, then 1740 and hourly until 0040.
E–Additional trips: 0120, 0235, 0350, 0450, 0550, 0620, 0650 and at 20 and 50 minuets past each hour till 2350.
F–Additional trips: 0700⑥⑦, 0900, 1030, 1130⑥⑦, 1230, 1430⑥⑦, 1630⑥⑦, 1645ex⑥⑦, 1730⑥⑦, 1745ex⑥⑦, 1845ex⑥⑦, 1850⑥⑦, 1945⑥⑦, 2045, 2315.
G–Additional trips: 0630, 1035, 1335, 1735, 2035.
H–Additional trips: 0730, 1100, 1800. Additional sailings operate during weekends, summer and at other holiday times.

The Shores of New Jersey and Maryland

The eastern seaboard may not be as well known as the California coast, but the Jersey shore is summer holiday home to untold numbers of New Yorkers and Philadelphians. There are lots of good beaches, and the attractions range from the outlandish gambling haven of Atlantic City to the Victorian-era refinement of Cape May. A ferry ride across the Delaware Bay takes you to Lewes, from which a string of beaches and offshore islands runs south through Delaware and Maryland. Lewes and the adjacent Cape Henlopen State Park are quiet and peaceful places, while nearby Rehoboth Beach is much more vigorous. On southward, Dewey and Bethany beaches are again more reserved, but summer sun-and-fun reaches its zenith in raucous Ocean City. At the end of this road is Assateague Island, a wildlife preserve and a wonderful space to unwind.

Public transport will get you to Atlantic City and Cape May from Philadelphia and New York. Trailways buses run from Washington DC to Rehoboth Beach and to Ocean City once a day, but there is no public transport along the Delaware–Maryland coast.

ATLANTIC CITY

Atlantic City today would like to be an East Coast version of Las Vegas, with its 24-hr casino action and glittery shows featuring big-name entertainers. This identity only dates back to 1976, though, when the run-down, has-been resort introduced the casinos as a means of financial rescue. Absecon Island, on which Atlantic City sits, has been a seaside resort since the 1850s, when a newly built railway helped the masses to escape the steamy summers of Philadelphia and New York City. Atlantic City has had a hand in creating much of America's pop culture: in 1870 its famous Boardwalk appeared, and in 1921 it launched the Miss America Beauty Pageant. The city's street names (such as Baltic Ave and Park Place) have been immortalised in the American version of the board game 'Monopoly'.

Arrival Points

The **bus terminal** is downtown at Arctic and Arkansas Aves; the train station is a few blocks over at the end of the Atlantic City Expressway. If you're driving, the Atlantic City Expressway runs you right into town.

The 4½-mile **Boardwalk** is the place for strolling, bicycling and people-watching – or let an attendant push you in a three-wheeled, wicker 'rolling chair' (price depending on distance). The usual (albeit tacky) fun-fair entertainment – mini-rides and games – is available at the Central Pier, and the sandy beaches offer good swimming and boating.

Gamblers can try their luck at any time of day or night at the casinos. You must be 21 to enter, and you're expected to be presentably dressed – don't just wander in from the beach. The 'oldest' casino is **Sands**, at the Boardwalk and Indiana Ave, a boisterous place which also features occasional boxing matches. **Caesars**, at the Boardwalk and Arkansas Ave, is loaded down with bogus statues and images from the ancient Mediterranean, while the **Taj Mahal**, at the Boardwalk and Virginia Ave, is an outrageous mega-palace of Eastern-themed plastic.

SAFETY
Beyond all the pseudo-glitz and crowds of the Boardwalk, the back streets can be dangerous.

The Atlantic City Convention and Visitors Authority, 2314 Pacific Ave; tel: (800) 262-7395 for information by post or (888) 228-4748; www.atlanticcitynj.com. Open 0900–1700. They have a helpful information booth in the old Convention Hall at Boardwalk and Mississippi Ave.

Many hotels offer package rates (especially midweek) that include casino coins and free or discounted show tickets, meals and parking; ask at the visitor centre. The casinos on the Boardwalk casinos all have pricey rooms, but cheaper chain motels line the streets behind the Boardwalk. The streets are dangerous, however. Campsites are available nearby in Pleasantville and Mays Landing.

Ascot Motor Inn $$$ 101 South Iowa and Pacific Aves; tel: (609) 344-5163 or (800) 225-1476. Good enough location and decent rooms.

Quality Inn $$$$ South Carolina and Pacific; tel: (609) 345-7070 or (800) 874-5856. A mid-range chain hotel that is more expensive in the summer. Reserve in advance.

Trump's Taj Mahal Casino and Resort $$$$ Boardwalk and Virginia Ave; tel: (800) 677-7378 or (609) 449-1000. Since you're here, you might as well go all the way.

Gamblers often don't bother to leave the casino at mealtime, relying instead on casino-hotel restaurants. There's no shortage of fast-food joints along the Boardwalk for your beach snacks.

White House Sub Shop $$ 2301 Arctic Ave; tel: (609) 345-1564. Great submarine sandwiches: the photo-covered walls advertise 75 years' worth of famous patrons.

Dock's Oyster House $$$ 2405 Atlantic Ave; tel: (609) 345-0092. Good local seafood.

CAPE MAY

Cape May, 50 miles away at the southernmost tip of New Jersey, is a far cry from Atlantic City's crassness, offering a glimpse of the architecture and ambience of America's Victorian era. It was founded in 1620 and became a resort in the mid-19th century, when exuberant, colourful homes were put up by wealthy Philadelphians and Southerners. Many of these are today on the register of national historic buildings, and although the resort has spread in all directions, it maintains its serenity. The beaches are excellent, and among the highlights in warm weather is the opportunity to go whale-watching.

Information on whale- and dolphin-watching cruises and on bike rental is available at the information centres, or pick up any of the free visitor guides available from shops and restaurants.

The Victorian homes on and around Jackson St are great fun to stroll past; most are now B&Bs. The beach itself is, of course, Cape May's *raison d'être*, and the waves here can be particularly exhilarating. To use the beaches, though, you must purchase a pass ($). A few miles south of the central beach area, **Cape May Point State Park** is a preserved wetland. Its lighthouse is visible for miles around, and a boardwalk leads through the marshes. The beach here is less crowded than in Cape May.

CAPE MAY SEASHORE LINES

Trains run the 13 miles from Cape May City to Cape May Courthouse at weekends from the end of May and daily from the end of June until the beginning of September. The railway hopes to eventually connect to New Jersey Transit's Atlantic City line. Tel: (609) 884 2675; www.seashorelines.com; OTT table 368.

An off-season package tour takes visitors from Cape May to Lewes and Rehoboth on the ferry, including transport to the outlet stores and discount shopping coupons. Enquire at information centres.

The Welcome Center, 405 Lafayette St; tel: (609) 884-9562; open daily 0900–1600 (Apr–Oct), can help with accommodation. **The Mid-Atlantic Center for the Arts**, 1048 Washington St, gives guided tours of the town. A good website to peruse is www.capemaymac.org; tel: (800) 275-4278 or (609) 804-5404.

New Jersey Transit buses use a tiny station just west of centre on Lafayette St.

B&Bs abound in the city's Victorian homes, but they don't come cheap and you'll have to book well in advance. Weekday rates can be significantly lower than weekends. There are several campsites around the town and a cluster of lesser-priced motels at the southern end of the beach – though these too are more expensive than usual.

Surf Motel & Apartments $$–$$$ 211 Beach Dr.; tel: (609) 884-4132. Quiet location near the southern end of the beach.

The Chalfonte $$$–$$$$ 301 Howard St; tel: (609) 884-8409. Pleasant, Victorian-looking hotel, a tad less pricey than others.

Windward House $$$$ 24 Jackson St; tel: (609) 884-3368. Cosy antique-laden rooms right in the Victorian centre.

The seafood is excellent here, but at a price. Cheap sandwiches are available on the waterfront, and a number of good cafés and pubs line the pedestrian Washington St mall.

Ugly Mug $$–$$$ Washington Mall at Decatur St; tel: (609) 884-3459. Local pub with relatively inexpensive sandwiches and seafood platters.

Ebbitt Room $$$$ 25 Jackson St; tel: (609) 884-5700. Fine place for dinner right on Cape May's most Victorian street.

LEWES AND CAPE HENLOPEN STATE PARK

Delaware's oldest settlement dates from 1631, when a Dutch colony was established here. The **Zwaanendael Museum**, at Savannah Rd and Kings Hwy, has artefacts relating to the original settlement and other aspects of the town's history. Open

Tues–Sat 1000–1630, Sun 1330–1630; donations accepted. Many old buildings in town date from as far back as 1730, and form the **Lewes Historical Society Complex** on and around Shipcarpenter Sq. and Front St. Most of these were actually moved here from neighbouring villages; they include an early 18th-century farmhouse, a turn-of-the-century doctor's office and country store, and a log cabin of unknown origin. Open Tues–Fri 1100–1600, Sat 1000–1230 (mid-June–early Sept). Also along here, the Lewes–Rehoboth Canal sports the Lightship *Overfalls*, a sea-going lightship that patrolled the entrance to Delaware Bay from 1892 to 1961.

One mile east of Lewes, **Cape Henlopen State Park** is a lovely area of shady trees and sandy beaches, and the highest dunes in the mid-Atlantic. It also has a nice campsite.

The **Visitor Centre**, 120 Kings Hwy, Lewes; tel: (302) 645-8073 or (877) 465-3937, is a useful source of information on sites and accommodation in the region.

Accommodation should not be the problem that it is in Cape May or Rehoboth Beach.

Cape Henlopen Motel $$$ Savannah and Anglers Rds; tel: (302) 645-2828 or (800) 447-3158. Centrally located and convenient for Delaware Bay and the historic district.

Wild Swan Inn $$$ 525 Kings Hwy, Lewes; tel: (302) 645-8550. A B&B in a Queen Anne-style house.

Lewes Crab House $$–$$$ corner of Bay and Henlopen Sts. Serves up piles of steamed crabs.

Gilligan's Harborside Restaurant and Bar $$$ Front and Market Sts; tel: (302) 645-7866. Waterfront dining and a canalside bar.

REHOBOTH BEACH

Of the beach communities along the 24 miles of Delaware coast, Rehoboth Beach has the most video games, mini-carnival rides and nightlife. The name sounds biblical – and it is: Rehoboth appropriately means 'room enough'. Permanent residents number fewer than 1300, but people swarm in from Washington DC at the first sign of spring and throughout the hot weather, giving the resort its 'Nation's Summer Capital' tag. The thing to do is just laze on the beach and stroll the boardwalk, eat salt-water taffy (a chewy sweet) and dine in one of the many seafood restaurants.

Rehoboth Beach/Dewey Beach Chamber of Commerce, 501 Rehoboth Ave; tel: (302) 227-2233 or (800) 441-1329; www.beach-fun.com. Ask here too about local outdoor activities like crabbing or para-sailing.

Rooms are heavily booked in July and Aug.

The Sandcastle Motel $$–$$$ 123 2nd St; tel: (302) 227-0400 or (800) 372-2112. Just off the Boardwalk.

Delaware Inn $$$–$$$$ 55 Delaware Ave; tel: (302) 227-6031 or (800) 246-5244. A very pleasant B&B, one of several that line Delaware and Baltimore Aves.

The usual beach junk food is available on the Boardwalk, with **Grotto Pizza** (36 Rehoboth Ave; tel: (302) 227-3278) a local favourite. Try the seafood, though. **Jakes Seafood House Restaurant** (1st St and Baltimore Ave; tel: (302) 227-6237) is good, as is **Dogfish Head Brewings and Eats** (320 Rehoboth Ave; tel: (302) 226-2739; closed Tues–Wed). Both $$$.

DEWEY BEACH AND BETHANY BEACH

If the crowds are a bit much in Rehoboth, there's less hoopla in Dewey Beach, connected to its southern edge, and Bethany Beach, some 10 miles down the shore. The long and narrow **Delaware Seashore State Park** has a campsite and beach.

Journey's End $$ Atlantic Ave, Bethany; tel: (302) 539-9502. Gracious, simple and central.

OCEAN CITY

ASSATEAGUE ISLAND

A greater contrast to Ocean City could not be imagined. Assateague Island National Seashore, just a few miles south of the stampede, is an utterly tranquil stretch of pine forest and empty beaches. It is maintained as a wildlife preserve, and wild horses roam free from here all the way down to Chincoteague, 30 miles south (see p. 240). Several campsites dot the island: tel: (410) 641-2120 for information, and there are three nature trails taking in this special ecosystem.

The last of this string of beaches is Ocean City, Maryland, and it's the gaudiest of them all. Drunken college students, redneck bars and a general sense of sun-blinded fun prevail on this long strip of land just off the coast. If this is your scene, then find a place to stay and jump right in.

Don't expect seclusion, especially when summer sun warms its 10-mile beach – four million visitors annually tread Ocean City's 3-mile boardwalk, alive with shops, restaurants, music and entertainment. The beach and sundry seaside amusements are the draw, although **Ocean City Life-Saving Museum** (410) 289-4991 takes an enlightening look at everything from wrecks and storms to marine life and mermaids. $ Boardwalk at the Inlet; open daily 1100–2200 (June–Sept); 1100–1600 (May and Oct); winter weekends 1200–1600.

Stop at **Trimper's Rides** (410) 289-8617, opened in 1890, to ride the 1902 Herschel Spellman carousel with hand-carved and painted animals; $ Boardwalk; open 1300–2400.

Chamber of Commerce, 40th St and Hwy 1; tei: (410) 289-8181 or (800) 62-OCEAN62326; www.ococean.com. They can also assist with rooms.
Ocean City Visitors and Convention Bureau, PO Box 116, 4001 Coastal Hwy, Ocean City; tel: (410) 289-8181; or 40th St, Ocean City; tel: (800) OC-OCEAN626-2326.

Along with 9500 rooms, Ocean City has 25,000 condominium units, apartments and beach houses, and several B&Bs, so beds aren't scarce. But expect a room that costs $55 in the winter to approach $200 in summer.
Commander Hotel $$–$$$ 1404 Baltimore Ave; tel: (410) 289-6166 or (888) 289-6166. Newly restored with spacious rooms overlooking the beach..
Ocean City Weekly Rentals, 7th St, 54th St and 87th St, Oceanside; tel: (800) 851-8909 or (410) 524-7486. Apartments sleeping 4–10, with fully equipped kitchens, from $500 a week in season.

Ocean City Princess runs deep-sea fishing and nature cruises with an expert on hand to interpret the dolphins, whales, sea turtles and marine life which you see. Cruises run May–Sept; tel: (410) 213-0926.

Sun 'n' Fun Motel $$–$$$ 29th St and Baltimore Ave; tel: (410) 289-6060. Rooms with refrigerator and microwave.

Eateries line the streets and boardwalk; seek local advice to navigate this changing scene.
Finnegan's Pub & Eatery $$ 4801 Coastal Hwy; tel: (410) 723-3150. Tex-Mex all-you-can-eat buffet Mar–Oct.

WHERE NEXT?

Hwy 50 heads inland across the Peninsula to Washington (see p. 204), 145 miles away. Many of the small towns along the way are worth a stop for a taste of Chesapeake Bay backwater life; Annapolis is also en route (see p. 227). Or continue south to the Chesapeake Bay Bridge-Tunnel and the heart of American Revolution country (pp. 232–242 in reverse).

Anyone returning to Philadelphia after a gap of several years will be gratified to find the city has done much to turn around its bad reputation, which was only partly deserved. Its selling points – a rich colonial history, excellent museums, and good dining and nightlife – are worth the trip.

Philadelphia is the birthplace of the nation. William Penn founded the City of Brotherly Love in 1682, and it quickly became the centre of Colonial America. The Declaration of Independence was signed here, the US Constitution was written here, and the city served as the nation's first capital from 1791 to 1800. But as Washington and New York became major political and commercial centres, Philadelphia was elbowed out and went into a long, slow period of urban decline. In the early 20th century it was an industrial powerhouse and one of the largest cities in the world, but heavy industry bottomed out by the 1950s, and comments such Philadelphia-born comedian W C Fields's wisecrack, 'On the whole, I'd rather be in Philadelphia', took a lot of living down. In the 1990s, though, the city pulled itself up by the bootlaces, invested in its future and put itself back on the tourist map.

The Independence National Historical Park and the Philadelphia Museum of Art, one of the finest in the world, are complemented by a whole host of other museums and galleries. Don't visit the city without exploring one of its many intriguing neighbourhoods: Philadelphia's working-class soul opens its heart in the gritty, exuberant Italian Market, while other areas worth exploring include Society Hill, Old City and arty, historic Manayunk.

MUST SEE/DO IN PHILADELPHIA

See where the United States was born, at Independence National Historic Park

Stroll down Elfreth's Alley to see the old homes

Have a cheesesteak sandwich in South Philly, and wander through the Italian market on a Friday or Saturday morning

View the city from a gargoyle's perspective, on the City Hall's observation deck

Enjoy a free concert on Rittenhouse Square

Visit the medieval cloister in the Philadelphia Museum of Art on a Sunday morning

GETTING THERE AND GETTING AROUND

PARKING
Parking is not easy downtown on the street, but there is no shortage of parking lots in the centre. Try around Penn's Landing (for Old City, Society Hill and South Street) or Locust or Walnut Sts downtown.

AIR Philadelphia airport was recently voted best airport in America in terms of convenience, appearance and safety. It is in fact very handy – easy and cheap by public transport to the centre, clean, manageable (not too big), but with lots of flights, including a growing number to Europe.

TRAIN/BUS The reasonably priced Airport Rail Line operates between Philadelphia International Airport and Center City daily every half-hour from about 0430–2330.

Trains and buses connect New York and Washington via Philadelphia almost every hour. The suburban sprawl between New York and Washington, in effect one megalopolis, has precious little appeal, but the fast track can be fast indeed: Amtrak's Metroliner and Acela Express trains reach Philadelphia from New York in just 1¼ hrs, while Regional trains take a few more minutes. Amtrak trains from New York, Washington, Chicago and Lancaster use the beautiful 30th St Station, just across the Schuylkill River from Center City at 30th and Market Sts (take the subway into the centre).

Greyhound run an hourly bus service between New York and Philadelphia and from Philadelphia to Washington. Other operators run from Chinatown and offer services on comfortable modern buses, often at a lower price than Greyhound.

CAR Signs to the I-95 spur via either I-195 or I-295 will take you into Philadelphia from the New York–Washington I-95. If you want more scenery from Washington, Hwy 301 traverses rural eastern Maryland before crossing the dramatic Chesapeake Bay Bridge; it joins I-95 just south of Wilmington.

SEPTA (Southeastern Pennsylvania Transportation Authority) runs a subway system, buses and an extensive commuter rail network. Buy tokens in advance from a station if you plan to take more than one trip – packs of two or more tokens work out cheaper.

INFORMATION

The Independence Visitors Center is at 6th St and Market St; tel: (215) 965-7676 or (800) 537-7676; open daily 0900–1700 (1800 in summer); www.gophila.com. A separate visitor centre handles the monuments of Independence National Historical Park at 3rd and Chestnut Sts; tel: (215) 597-8974; open daily 0900–1700.

SAFETY At night, the main, well-lit streets are generally safe – just don't stray away from these after hours. South St develops a hard edge at night, and the subway can be a little intimidating as well.

MONEY Travelex is central at 1800 John F Kennedy Blvd; open Mon–Fri 0900–1700. Banks all over town have automatic cash dispensers.

POST AND PHONES The main post office at 30th and Market Sts is open 24 hrs (use zip code PA 19104 for poste restante), but more convenient post offices are located at 3rd and Market Sts and at Sansom and S Broad Sts.

ACCOMMODATION

Philadelphia's primary role as a business centre means there is no shortage of chain hotels, and some have good weekend rates. The central area is also blessed with several good value B&Bs, though you'll have to book in advance. **Bed and Breakfast of Philadelphia**, tel: (215) 735-1917 or (800) 448-3619, fax: (610) 995-9524, www.bnbphiladelphia.com, can set you up in fun neighbourhoods such as Society Hill, Rittenhouse Sq., the Art Museum area or University City for $50–150.

The city's annoying liquor laws mean many restaurants don't serve alcohol, but are happy to pour wine or beer that you bring yourself (BYOB means 'bring your own bottle').

Bank Street Hostel $ 32 S Bank St; tel: (215) 922-0222 or (800) 392-4678. HI hostel in central, atmospheric location.

HI – Chamounix Carriage House $ Chamounix Dr., W Fairmount Park; tel: (215) 878-3676 or (800) 379-0017. An alternative if Bank Street is full, situated in a lovely mansion in sprawling Fairmount Park, but a little awkward to get to. Take bus 38 from Market St downtown to the corner of Ford and Cranston Sts, then walk along Ford St to Chamounix Dr.

Antique Row B&B $$ 341 S 12th St; tel: (215) 592-7802; fax: (215) 592-9692. Good value and a full breakfast in 180-year-old town house.

International House $$ 3701 Chestnut St; tel: (215) 387-5125. Part of a dormitory complex of the University of Pennsylvania; call ahead for availability.

The Gables Bed & Breakfast $$$ 4520 Chester Ave; tel: (215) 662-1918. Lovely Victorian home with period furnishings in West Philadelphia, just beyond the University of Pennsylvania campus. Take subway-surface trolley 13 (the Green Line) from Market St downtown to 46th and Chester.

Center City B&B La Reserve $$$ 1804 Pine St; tel: (215) 735-1137; fax (215) 735-0582. A well-preserved town house on a pretty street near Rittenhouse Sq.

Best Western Center City Hotel $$$–$$$$ 501 N 22nd St; tel: (215) 568-8300 or (800) 528-1234; fax: (215) 557-0259.

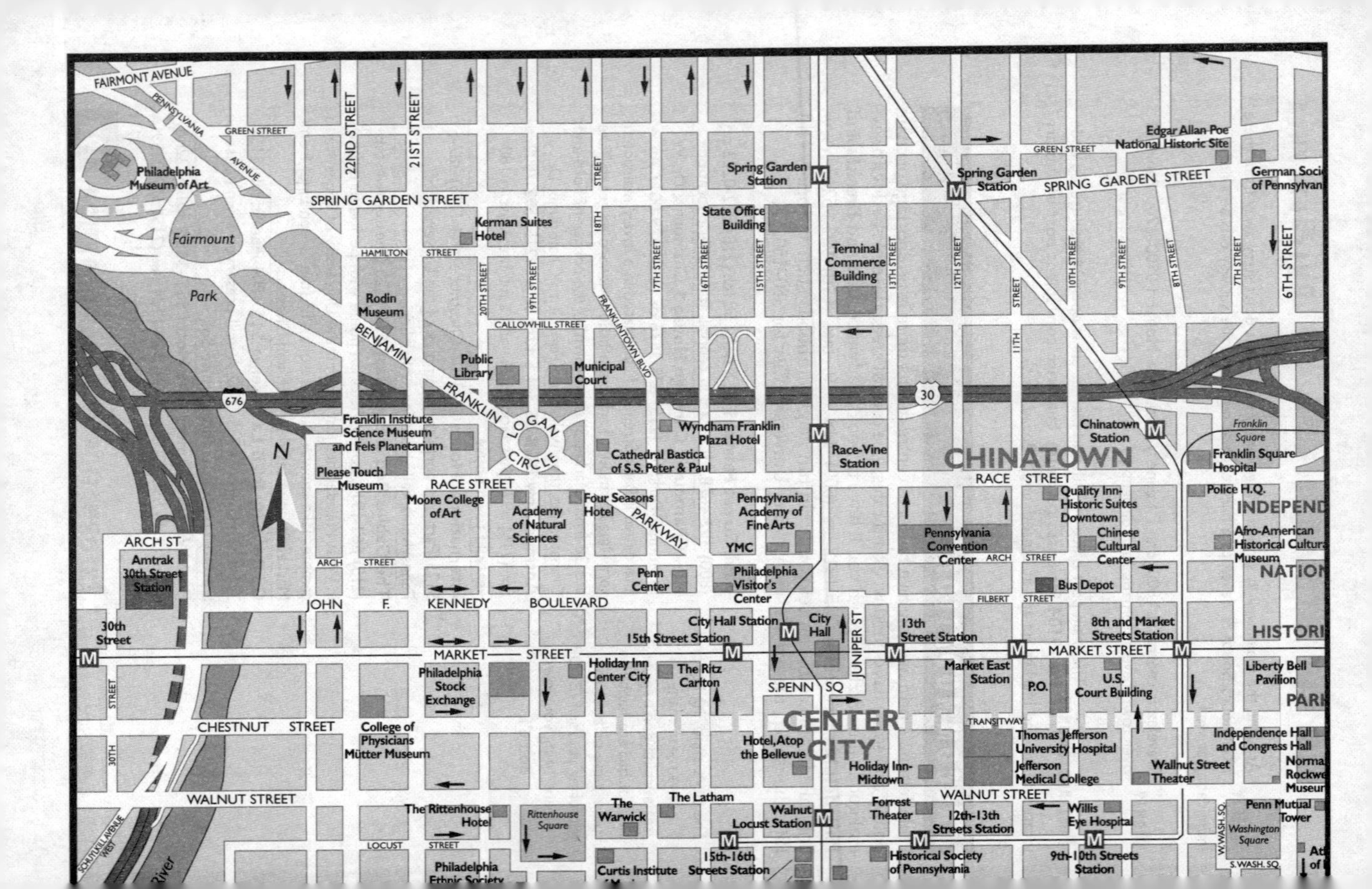
FAIRMONT AVENUE
PENNSYLVANIA AVENUE
GREEN STREET
22ND STREET
21ST STREET
18TH STREET
17TH STREET
16TH STREET
15TH STREET
13TH STREET
12TH STREET
11TH STREET
10TH STREET
9TH STREET
8TH STREET
7TH STREET
6TH STREET
20TH STREET
19TH STREET
Philadelphia Museum of Art
Fairmount
Park
SPRING GARDEN STREET
Spring Garden Station
Edgar Allan Poe National Historic Site
German Society of Pennsylvania
Kerman Suites Hotel
HAMILTON STREET
State Office Building
Terminal Commerce Building
Rodin Museum
CALLOWHILL STREET
FRANKLINTOWN BLVD
BENJAMIN FRANKLIN PARKWAY
Public Library
Municipal Court
676
30
LOGAN CIRCLE
Franklin Institute Science Museum and Fels Planetarium
Please Touch Museum
Wyndham Franklin Plaza Hotel
Cathedral Bastica of S.S. Peter & Paul
Race-Vine Station
Chinatown Station
Franklin Square
Franklin Square Hospital
CHINATOWN
N
RACE STREET
Moore College of Art
Academy of Natural Sciences
Four Seasons Hotel
Pennsylvania Academy of Fine Arts
YMC
Pennsylvania Convention Center
Quality Inn-Historic Suites Downtown
Chinese Cultural Center
Police H.Q.
INDEPEND
Afro-American Historical Cultural Museum
NATION
ARCH ST
Amtrak 30th Street Station
ARCH STREET
Penn Center
Philadelphia Visitor's Center
Bus Depot
FILBERT STREET
JOHN F. KENNEDY BOULEVARD
30th Street
City Hall Station
15th Street Station
City Hall
JUNIPER ST
13th Street Station
8th and Market Streets Station
HISTORI
MARKET STREET
Philadelphia Stock Exchange
Holiday Inn Center City
The Ritz Carlton
S.PENN SQ
Market East Station
P.O.
U.S. Court Building
Liberty Bell Pavilion
PARK
30TH STREET
CHESTNUT STREET
College of Physicians Mütter Museum
CENTER CITY
Hotel, Atop the Bellevue
TRANSITWAY
Thomas Jefferson University Hospital
Jefferson Medical College
Independence Hall and Congress Hall
Holiday Inn-Midtown
Wallnut Street Theater
Norman Rockwell Museum
WALNUT STREET
The Latham
Forrest Theater
The Rittenhouse Hotel
Rittenhouse Square
The Warwick
Walnut Locust Station
12th-13th Streets Station
Willis Eye Hospital
Penn Mutual Tower
W.WASH. SQ.
Washington Square
SCHUYLKILL AVENUE WEST
River
LOCUST STREET
Philadelphia Ethnic Society
Curtis Institute
15th-16th Streets Station
Historical Society of Pennsylvania
9th-10th Streets Station
S.WASH. SQ.

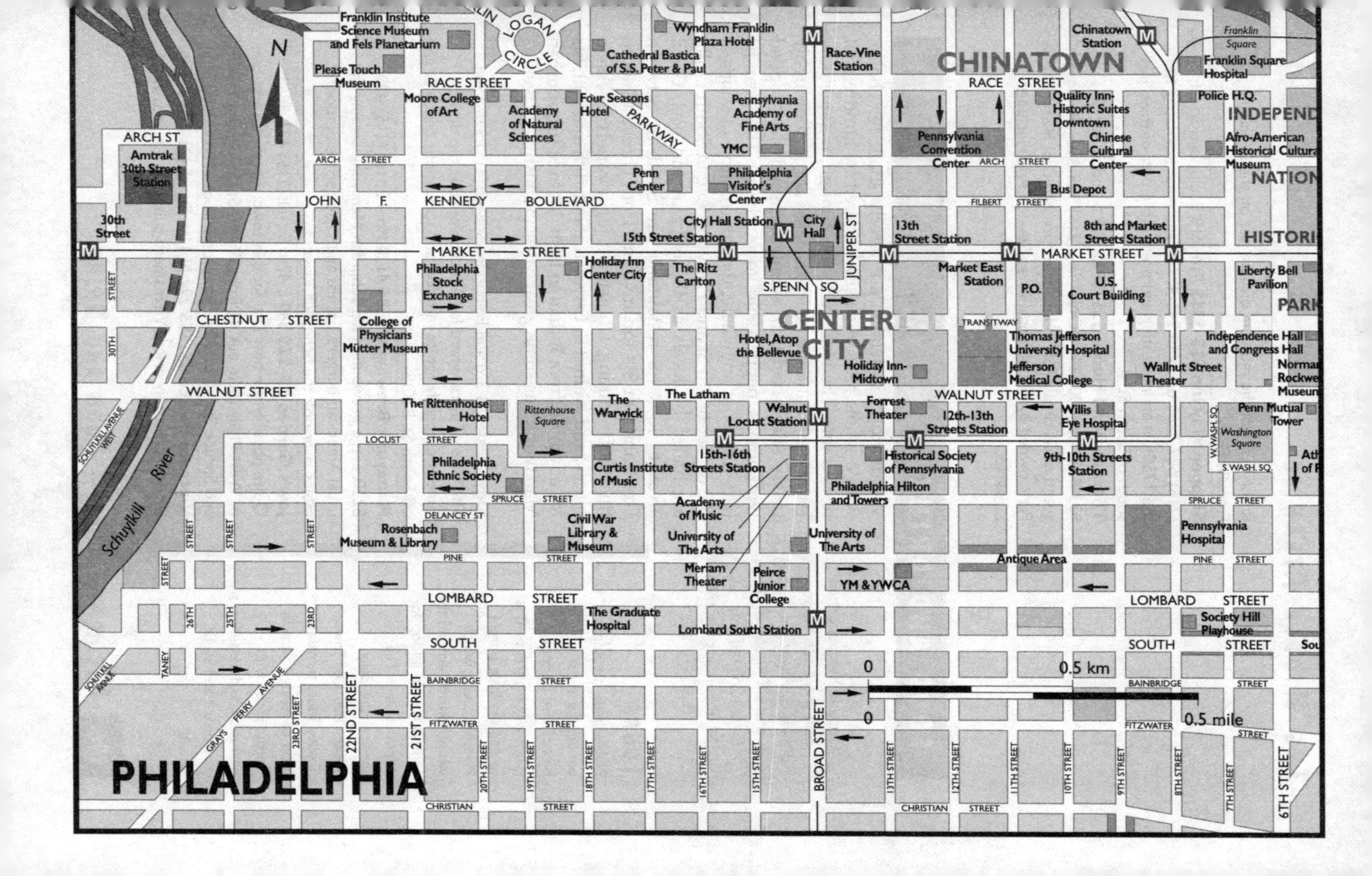

PHILADELPHIA
N
CHINATOWN
CENTER CITY
LOGAN CIRCLE
Franklin Square
Washington Square
Rittenhouse Square
Franklin Institute Science Museum and Fels Planetarium
Please Touch Museum
Moore College of Art
Academy of Natural Sciences
Four Seasons Hotel
Cathedral Bastica of S.S. Peter & Paul
Wyndham Franklin Plaza Hotel
Race-Vine Station
Pennsylvania Academy of Fine Arts
YMC
Pennsylvania Convention Center
Chinatown Station
Franklin Square Hospital
Police H.Q.
Quality Inn-Historic Suites Downtown
Chinese Cultural Center
Afro-American Historical Cultura Museum
Bus Depot
Amtrak 30th Street Station
Penn Center
Philadelphia Visitor's Center
30th Street
City Hall Station
15th Street Station
City Hall
13th Street Station
8th and Market Streets Station
Philadelphia Stock Exchange
Holiday Inn Center City
The Ritz Carlton
Market East Station
P.O.
U.S. Court Building
Liberty Bell Pavilion
College of Physicians Mütter Museum
Hotel, Atop the Bellevue
Holiday Inn-Midtown
Thomas Jefferson University Hospital
Jefferson Medical College
Independence Hall and Congress Hall
Walnut Street Theater
The Rittenhouse Hotel
The Warwick
The Latham
Walnut Locust Station
Forrest Theater
12th-13th Streets Station
Willis Eye Hospital
Penn Mutual Tower
Philadelphia Ethnic Society
Curtis Institute of Music
15th-16th Streets Station
Historical Society of Pennsylvania
Philadelphia Hilton and Towers
9th-10th Streets Station
Rosenbach Museum & Library
Civil War Library & Museum
Academy of Music
University of The Arts
Meriam Theater
University of The Arts
Peirce Junior College
YM & YWCA
Antique Area
Pennsylvania Hospital
The Graduate Hospital
Lombard South Station
Society Hill Playhouse
Schuylkill River
RACE STREET
ARCH ST
ARCH STREET
JOHN F. KENNEDY BOULEVARD
PARKWAY
FILBERT STREET
MARKET STREET
JUNIPER ST
S.PENN SQ
CHESTNUT STREET
TRANSITWAY
WALNUT STREET
LOCUST STREET
SPRUCE STREET
DELANCEY ST
PINE STREET
LOMBARD STREET
SOUTH STREET
BAINBRIDGE STREET
FITZWATER STREET
CHRISTIAN STREET
W.WASH. SQ.
S.WASH. SQ.
SCHUYLKILL AVENUE WEST
SCHUYLKILL AVENUE
GRAYS FERRY AVENUE
TANEY
30TH STREET
26TH
25TH
23RD
23RD STREET
22ND STREET
21ST STREET
20TH STREET
19TH STREET
18TH STREET
17TH STREET
16TH STREET
15TH STREET
BROAD STREET
13TH STREET
12TH STREET
11TH STREET
10TH STREET
9TH STREET
8TH STREET
7TH STREET
6TH STREET
0
0.5 km
0
0.5 mile

In the heart of the museum district, just off the Benjamin Franklin Pkwy.

Shippen Way Inn $$$–$$$$ 416–418 Bainbridge St; tel: (215) 627-7266 or (800) 245-4873. Family-run inn dating from the 1750s, in an interesting and pretty little part of town just south of South St.

Thomas Bond House $$$–$$$$ 129 S 2nd St; tel: (215) 923-8523 or (800) 845-BOND; fax: (215) 923-8504. Restored guesthouse, circa 1769, in Independence National Historical Park; owned by the National Parks Service. Price includes breakfast.

FOOD AND DRINK

Outside Independence Hall you'll see horse-drawn carriages lined; you can trot off in one of these for a narrated tour of INHP and Society Hill.

Visitors to Philadelphia are utterly spoilt for choice, with a whole atlas of cuisines offered by hundreds of restaurants. The local favourite, though, is something far more mundane: cheesesteaks are a thoroughly messy sliced-beefsteak submarine sandwich, topped with onions, peppers and gooey cheese. These can be had just about anywhere, though a couple of shops at the corner of 9th St and Passyunk Ave in South Philly are hailed by locals as the original and best. Good areas to look for restaurants are South St between Front and 8th Sts for anything from cheesesteaks to fine Italian dining, Chinatown for a variety of Asian places, and Walnut St between about 10th and 20th Sts for anything from Indian to Irish. Main St in suburban Manayunk has some great cafés and bistros as well.

TOURS

Philadelphia is compact enough for most of it to be covered on foot. A quick way from A to B is to use the little purple Phlash trolleys, which whisk tourists around the central area in a loop for a modest fare. The service runs daily 1000–1800. Old Town Trolley Tours move in a loop covering 15 major tourist stops with narration, and passengers may board and alight at will.

Judy's Café $$ 3rd and Bainbridge Sts; tel: (215) 928-1968. The type of place where locals queue outside the door; famous especially for its meatloaf and its luscious desserts. Just off South St; BYOB.

Manayunk Brewing Co. $$ 4120 Main St; tel: (215) 482-8220. Large brewpub in hip suburban Manayunk serving the usual American burgers, nachos and salads; some outdoor tables overlook the Schuylkill River.

Jow's Garden $$–$$$ 349 S 47th St; tel: (215) 471-3663. Quite possibly the best Thai food in town; worth the trip out to West Philly (take bus 42 from Walnut St downtown to 47th and Spruce Sts). Open for dinner only from 1700; closed Mon.

Vietnam Palace $$–$$$ 222 N 11th St; tel: (215) 592-9596. Good, reasonably priced Vietnamese cuisine in Chinatown.

Brigid's $$$ 726 N 24th St; tel: (215) 232-3232. The menu includes duck chambord, bouillabaisse ostendaise and a splendid collection of Belgian beers.

Philadelphia Fish & Co. $$$ 207 Chestnut St; tel: (215) 625-8605. Excellent grilled fish, plus nightly specials and good beer. Try to get an outdoor table.

Buddakan $$$–$$$$ 325 Chestnut St; tel: (215) 574-9440. Ultra-hip pan-Asian establishment.

Ristorante Primavera $$$–$$$$ 146 South St; tel: (215) 925-7832. In a city loaded with Italian restaurants, this is one of the best, and not too dear.

HIGHLIGHTS

Old City and Society Hill

Independence National Historical Park (INHP) covers the area between Market St and Walnut St, from 2nd St to 6th St, and encompasses some of the most hallowed historical shrines in the USA. Buildings within the park are open daily 0900–1700 year round and admission is free. The real highlight of the park is **Independence Hall**, the 'birthplace of the nation'. This solemn, pretty, Georgian hall and tower was host to the signing of the Declaration of Independence on 4 July 1776, and the writing of the US Constitution in 1787. It is close to **Carpenters' Hall**, where the First Continental Congress met in 1774, and **Congress Hall**, where the US Senate and the House of Representatives met in the early days of the young nation. These are all somewhat overshadowed by neighbouring office buildings. Equally renowned in American lore is the **Liberty Bell**, the bell with the famous crack, which used to hang from Independence Hall's tower. It now sits low down in an unseemly modern pavilion opposite, the better to gaze upon it.

Resounding in colonial glory just off 2nd and Market Sts, the red-brick and creamy-white **Christ Church** dates from 1727, and is where the American Episcopal Church was created in 1789. The interior is a testament to Georgian-era values of solemnity, simplicity and grace.

The streets around here, particularly 2nd and 3rd Sts north of Market St, are packed with galleries and bars. On the first Friday of each month, all open their doors to the eclectic crowds who descend on the area, creating a sort of open block party.

Little Italy

A world unto itself, South Philadelphia was populated in the late 19th century by Italian immigrant labourers, who settled into block after block of low terraces, and whose descendants manage to keep the Old World alive today in a unique east coast urban setting. Along with the Italian Market, Passyunk Ave is its unofficial main street – a fun place simply to wander and enjoy a pocket of a different America; you'll probably even hear Italian spoken.

Elfreth's Alley, off 2nd St between Arch and Race Sts, is a quaint cobblestoned passage of homes continuously inhabited since 1727, said to be America's oldest continually residential street.

Abutting the southern edge of the INHP, **Society Hill** – really no more than a swell – is one of Philadelphia's most exclusive districts, though the name comes from the Free Society of Traders, a colonial merchants' social organisation. Strolling the brick and cobblestone streets here is a joy more for the colonial atmosphere than any particular sites. While wandering, take note of Head House Sq., Philadelphia's original covered market, which has been preserved as a graceful public space. Wander down Pine St to 3rd St and St Peter's Episcopal Church and Cemetery, where George Washington worshipped. The building and grounds are almost bucolic. Further on down Pine St at 8th St, the Pennsylvania Hospital was America's first, founded by Benjamin Franklin. The gorgeous domed edifice includes an authentic surgery theatre, open to the public.

> The historical suburb of Manayunk has spruced itself up to become a super-hip shopping and dining centre. To reach it, take SEPTA's commuter rail R6 line from 30th St Station, Suburban Station (15th and Market Sts) or Market East Station (11th and Market Sts).

SOUTH PHILADELPHIA

A quick dip south from here takes you to lively South St. Push on a few more blocks to the marvellous **Italian Market**, a real Philadelphia institution and the heart and soul of working-class South Philly. This festive, open-air street market stretches several blocks down 9th St, concentrated particularly between Christian St and Washington Ave. This is the place to come for fresh fruit and vegetables, fresh-cut pasta, meats, cheeses and spices and, most of all, the atmosphere itself. On Fri and Sat mornings especially, the market is frenetic with activity, and it's impossible not to get caught up in the energy. Connoisseurs of the bizarre will get a kick out of butchers' shops selling ostrich and rattlesnake meat, and spice shops selling things you may never have seen before.

CENTER CITY

Philadelphia's so-called Center City is its financial and commercial focus. After having been fairly run-down, it's come back with flashy new skyscrapers and some good shops and restaurants.

City Hall – some love it; most hate it. This colossus was the largest municipal building in the USA when it was built in 1901. Its only noteworthy feature today is its tower's observation deck, which offers fine, if quite unflattering, views of the city alongside fabulous gargoyles.

A few streets north and east of here the elaborate Chinese Arch at 10th and Arch Sts announces the presence of lively, bustling **Chinatown**, one of America's largest such neighbourhoods. Streets on all sides are lined with restaurants, herb and spice shops, and busy electronics shops. **Reading Terminal Market** (tel: (215) 922-2317), nearby at 12th and Arch Sts, is in the former main railway station. This is a favourite lunchtime rendezvous, with plenty of ethnic eateries, speciality food and craft stalls with more than 80 vendors. Open Mon–Sat 0800–1800.

For a piece of urban calm after the rush of Center City, make for **Rittenhouse Square**, at 18th and Walnut Sts. One of the original four squares planned for William Penn's 'green countrie towne', this is a fine place to bring a picnic or catch a free summer evening concert. One of the city's more bizarre attractions is nearby at 22nd and Chestnut Sts. The **Mütter Museum** in the Philadelphia College of Physicians is crammed with medical oddities, such as the preserved bodies of Siamese twins, the 'Elephant Man' and the 'Soap Woman'. $, open Mon–Sat 1000–1600, Sun 1200–1600.

MUSEUM ROW Philadelphia's greatest cultural treasures are clustered in the north-west corner of the centre, along the broad, green, flag-decked Benjamin Franklin Parkway.

> Admission to the Museum of Art is free Sun before 1300, and on Wed nights it stays open until 2100 for talks, films and special dinners all focused around a theme.

Though not quite as large as New York's Met or Paris's Louvre, the **Philadelphia Museum of Art** is often mentioned in the same breath. Its top-flight collection of art spans virtually all eras in European, American and Asian history. The gallery's particular strengths include sections on Impressionism and 20th-century art – with an entire room full of Marcel Duchamp. Other enticements include glorious reconstructions of a Gothic cloister, a Buddhist temple and a Japanese tea garden, and a lively collection of Shaker furniture. $$, open Tues–Sun 1000–1700 (Wed and Fri to 2045).

The elegant **Rodin Museum** contains the largest collection of Rodin statues outside Paris, including several casts of *The Thinker* as well as *The Gates of Hell*. Open Tues–Sun 1000–1700; donation requested.

> **FOR FREE**
> All of the INHP sites are free, and much of Old City and Society Hill's charm is the streets themselves. Similarly, the Italian Market and South Philly are all about strolling – and the Museum of Art is free on Sun mornings.

Up 22nd St a few blocks, at 2124 Fairmount Ave, the **Eastern State Penitentiary** is one of Philadelphia's more enticing off-beat attractions. This enormous crumbling structure looks like a medieval fortress, and functioned as a prison until 1971. It was originally inspired by Quaker ideals of rehabilitation, which meant solitary confinement in vaulted cells supposed to resemble mini-chapels, with a Bible as the only decoration. $$, open Wed–Sun 1000–1700 Apr–Nov)

Fairmount Park, starting behind the Art Museum, is acclaimed as the world's largest landscaped city park – 8900 acres of meadows, woodland, creeks and trails on both sides of the Schuylkill River, and several intriguing early American mansions. Kelly Dr., behind the Art Museum, contains a series of pretty boathouses, and you can rent bicycles and in-line skates here to explore the park.

WEST PHILADELPHIA Across the Schuylkill River, the university campus dominates the scene. The **University of Pennsylvania Museum of Archaeology and Anthropology** at 33rd and Spruce Sts is a marvellous collection of antiquities and artefacts from cultures as diverse as the Canadian Inuits, Ancient Egyptians and Javanese monks. Much of the material comes from the university's own work around the world, and highlights include some scarily preserved mummies. $, open Tues–Sat 1000–1630, Sun 1300–1700.

Across campus at 36th and Sansom Sts, the **Institute of Contemporary Art** is a hotbed of current trends in the art world: Andy Warhol and Roy Liechtenstein had early-career exhibitions here. $, open Wed–Fri 1200–2000, Sat–Sun 1100–1700 (free Sun 1100–1300).

SHOPPING

Philadelphia's many neighbourhoods make it a good city to window-shop. South St is trendy with New Age bookshops, antique shops and random off-beat places appealing to anyone with an eye for the unusual. Nearby Pine St, between about 8th and 13th Sts, has been designated Antique Row for its series of small antique shops. Some of the city's finest upmarket shops are located near Rittenhouse Sq.

NIGHTLIFE

Philadelphia is something of an unheralded mecca for the fine and performing arts. The Philadelphia Orchestra has long been regarded as one of the best in the world, and it performs most Tues, Thur, Fri and Sat nights at the **Kimmel Center** for Performing Arts. The Opera Company of Philadelphia and the Pennsylvania Ballet also perform here.

Theatres include the **Walnut Street Theater**, 9th and Walnut Sts (which claims to be the longest continually running theatre in the English-speaking world); the **Forrest Theater**, 1114 Walnut St; the **Merriam Theater**, 250 S Broad St; and the **Wilma Theater** across the street. All of these feature Broadway-type shows, and the Wilma also does modern dance and avant-garde film.

Center City in the Rittenhouse Square area and Old City are the hottest for nightlife.

Pick up the free weekly *Philadelphia City Paper* or the *Philadelphia Weekly* at just about any street corner or bar for information on entertainment and nightlife.

Monk's Café, 264 S 16th St; tel: (215) 545-7005. Fabulous place for Belgian beers – close to 100 different kinds. Excellent dinner menu too, with steamed mussels.

Dickens Inn, 421 S 2nd St; tel: (215) 928-9307. Atmospheric English-style pub, renowned for its array of whiskies.

Khyber Pass, 56 S 2nd St; tel: (215) 440-9683. One of Philly's most established bars, with a long beer list and good local bands.

Warmdaddy's, Front and Market Sts; tel: (215) 627-2500, is the city's top jazz club, drawing big names and charging a high cover.

Egypt, 520 N Delaware Ave; tel: (215) 922-6500. Raunchy dance club with a different theme on each of its three floors.

Katmandu, 417 N Delaware Ave; tel: (215) 629-7400. Pumps out world music until all hours.

Trocadero, 10th and Arch Sts; tel: (215) 922-5483. Converted art deco theatre, with good live rock and alternative bands most nights.

Woody's Bar, 202 S 13th St; tel: (215) 545-1893. Popular gay bar and nightclub, friendly to all.

WHERE NEXT?

As well as New York (see p. 75) and Washington (see p. 204), Philadelphia is well connected with Atlantic City (see p. 185). Or experience the other side of Pennsylvania in the rural communities of the Pennsylvania Dutch (see p. 202).

PENNSYLVANIA DUTCH COUNTRY

A side track west from Philadelphia takes you into beautiful Lancaster County, also known as Pennsylvania Dutch country, where you get a chance to explore a totally unique culture, that of the fundamentalist but friendly Amish and Mennonites.

The countryside here is rolling, pretty and utterly pastoral, particularly with the unusual absence of electrical and telephone wires, and the presence of so many horse-and-buggies on the roads. Lancaster County is home to some 80,000 Amish and Mennonite farmers, who continue to thrive without electricity, telecommunications or cars. The town of Lancaster is the focus, but you may find yourself in or around Strasburg (7 miles south-east) or in numerous villages dotted about – many of which have great names like Intercourse, Paradise and Bird in Hand.

GETTING THERE AND GETTING AROUND

Amtrak runs from Philadelphia to Lancaster eleven times daily on weekdays and six times daily at weekends (1½ hours), but you really need a car or bicycle to get out into the countryside. By car from central Philadelphia, take I-76 west to King of Prussia (20 miles), then Hwy 202 approximately 12 miles to the Hwy 30 interchange. Hwy 30 goes all the way to Lancaster, some 40 miles further on.

Most of the things to see are not really 'sights' themselves, but simply the countryside and the people, so forget the tourist brochures and explore the back roads. Cycling is by far the best way to get out and see things, and bikes can be rented at the Strasburg Historic Railroad, on Rte 741 just east of Strasburg. And remember: you are likely to see more horses than cars on the road, so drive carefully.

THE AMISH AND MENNONITES

The term Pennsylvania Dutch is a misnomer, 'Dutch' deriving from the 'Deutsch' or German that the Amish and Mennonites spoke (and on occasion still do speak). They came from Switzerland at the invitation of William Penn in the early 18th century, and are descendants of strict Anabaptists. The Amish adhere rigorously to the Bible, which they believe forbids them from using machinery that may link them with the outside world. Their dress is strictly conservative: men wear black trousers, braces, a straw hat and beard, and women wear simple dresses just above the ankle, and lace bonnets. They also consider photography in the same light as phones and cars, so no matter how tempting it may be, don't point a camera at them – buy postcards instead. The Mennonites, similar in appearance and belief, are more integrated into the modern world.

INFORMATION

In Lancaster, the **Pennsylvania Dutch Convention and Visitors Bureau**, 501 Greenfield Rd, off Hwy 30, tel: (717) 299-8901 or (800) 723-8824, is open daily 0900–1700. The **Mennonite Information Center**, 2209 Millstream Rd, tel: (717) 299-0954, is mainly about the Mennonite Church, but also has information on inns and Mennonite guest houses. Open Mon–Sat 0800–1700. For more information, visit www.padutchcountry.com.

ACCOMMODATION AND FOOD AND DRINK

There are many motels and campsites just outside Lancaster around Hwy 30 E. Food is central European with a dose of Americana, meaning meat-and-potato dishes in huge portions. A local dessert is shoo-fly pie, made chiefly from eggs and treacle. Many restaurants are alcohol-free, but Lancaster has several downtown pubs.

Garden Spot Motel $$ 2291 Hwy 30 E; tel: (717) 394-4736. Decent motel 3 miles east of Lancaster.

Hotel Brunswick $$–$$$ Chestnut and Queen Sts; tel: (717) 397-4801 or (800) 821-9258. Comfortable, central accommodation in Lancaster.

Historic Strasburg Inn $$$ Rte 896, Strasburg (8 miles south-east of Lancaster, off Hwy 30); tel: (717) 687-7691 or (800) 872-0201. Colonial-style inn overlooking Amish country.

Good'n'Plenty $$–$$$ Eastbrook Rd (Rte 896); tel: (717) 894-7111, just north of Strasburg. Amish food place where you don't even order, they just serve piles of meats and vegetables.

Hershey Farm Restaurant $$$ 240 Hartman Bridge Rd off US Rte 30 on PA Rte 896, Ronks; tel: (800) 827-8635 or (717) 687-8635. All-you-can-eat buffet of hearty, Amish-style cooking: pot pie, fried chicken. Reserve ahead at weekends.

HIGHLIGHTS

Interesting independent touring can be done either side of Hwy 30, east of Lancaster city. Visit the **Amish Village**, Rte 896, 2 miles north of Strasburg, for tours of an Amish house, blacksmith's shop, schoolhouse, smokehouse and waterwheel. $$, open daily 0900–1700 (spring and autumn); 0900–1800 (summer). A few miles north, in **Intercourse**, the People's Place interprets the lifestyle of local Mennonites and Amish. $, open Mon–Sat 0930–1700 (until 2000 end May–early Sept). Lancaster, a pleasant college town, has examples of local crafts in the **Heritage Center Museum**, Penn Sq.; open Tues–Sat 1000–1700; donation requested. A few miles south, off Hwy 222, the **Hans Herr House** is considered the finest example of medieval-style German architecture in North America, dating from 1719. $, open Mon–Sat 0900–1600 (Apr–Nov).

The nation's capital happens to be one of its most unusual and appealing cities. Power is, of course, Washington's defining feature, but many visitors are surprised both by its seemingly small size and by its wealth of cultural attractions. The city feels different from most other American cities, mainly because it has no skyscrapers (no commercial building in the city may stand taller than the Capitol). And when the skies are clear (as they usually are), the marble of its classical architecture is dazzling. The downside to this is that Washington does have a certain sterility: the glamour of so many impressive – and similar – monuments can wear off, and given the city's high residency turnover rate (due to the frequent change in governments) it's difficult to pin down the city's actual character. Yet locals and visitors alike have revelled in the recent dining and nightlife resurgence.

Since the 1960s, Washington has transformed from a slightly sleepy, southern town to one of the country's most ethnically diverse metropolitan areas. With a broad-based economy – much of which is set in affluent suburbs – and with embassies and cultural centres fueling urban renewal, Washington is at last realizing its full cosmopolitan potential.

Most of what you'll see is in the centre of town,

MUST SEE/DO IN WASHINGTON DC

Take a tour of the Capitol building

Stroll down the National Mall, the green heart of the city

Drop in on any, or all, of the Smithsonian Institution's magnificent facilities, particularly the National Air and Space Museum

Walk from the Washington Monument to the National World War II Memorial, then along the Reflecting Pool past the Vietnam War Veterans Memorial to the Lincoln Memorial

Stop and spend some time at the Vietnam War Veterans Memorial

Saunter along the Tidal Basin, particularly at Cherry Blossom Time, including the Jefferson Memorial

See some famous examples of modern art in the Phillips Collection, Dupont Circle

Visit Georgetown, with its historic architecture, fine restaurants and shops and great nightlife

Cross the Potomac River to visit Arlington National Cemetery, with its civil war memorials, grave of John F Kennedy and Changing of the Guard at the Tomb of the Unknown Soldier

Escape the city to visit Mount Vernon, 18th-century home of George Washington

although this is quite spread out. The main monuments are located on or near the National Mall, and one of Washington's greatest features is that admission to virtually all buildings, museums and galleries is free. For dining and nightlife, however, you'll want to get just out of downtown and the Mall to the Georgetown and Adams-Morgan districts.

DISTRICT OF COLUMBIA

To its residents Washington DC is just DC. Uniquely, it is a federal district ('Columbia' is a reference to Christopher Columbus), not a state – and not to be confused with Washington State, on the west coast. The city was founded in 1791 specifically to be the nation's seat of government, and the location was chosen for its nearness to the Mason–Dixon line dividing North and South.

GETTING THERE

AIR DC is served by three airports: Washington Dulles International, Reagan National and Baltimore/Washington International (BWI). Dulles, the largest, is about 26 miles west of downtown, with direct flights to and from many European and North American cities, as well as a full complement of low-cost carriers serving domestic routes. Washington Flyer buses run every half hour to the West Falls Church metro station ($8). Taxis to the centre cost about $50.

BWI, also served by international carriers, is on the southern fringes of Baltimore, a 45-min drive from DC. Buses run every hour (0700–2200) to central Washington and BWI also has its own railway station (catch a shuttle bus from the arrivals terminal) with regular MARC (commuter rail) and Amtrak connections to Baltimore and to Washington's Union Station. A 24-hr reservable shuttle van network is also available.

Reagan National Airport is almost in the centre of town, and handles shorter domestic routes. Security here is no tighter than at the other airports servicing the area, with the exception of the 30-minute rule. Passengers are required to remain in their plane seats for the last 30 minutes of the flight before arrival, or the first 30 minutes after departure (while over Washington DC airspace). Taxis charge $12–15 but the easiest and cheapest trip is from the airport's own metro station at terminals B & C, connecting shuttle bus from other terminals.

RAIL/BUS Amtrak's Union Station has been gloriously reconstructed, and serves routes north to New York and Boston, south to Miami, and to various points west. It is located at 1st St and Massachusetts Ave NE, just a few blocks from the Capitol, and is connected to the city by metro. Greyhound and Peter Pan buses run from a fairly small station a few blocks north, at 1st and L Sts NE.

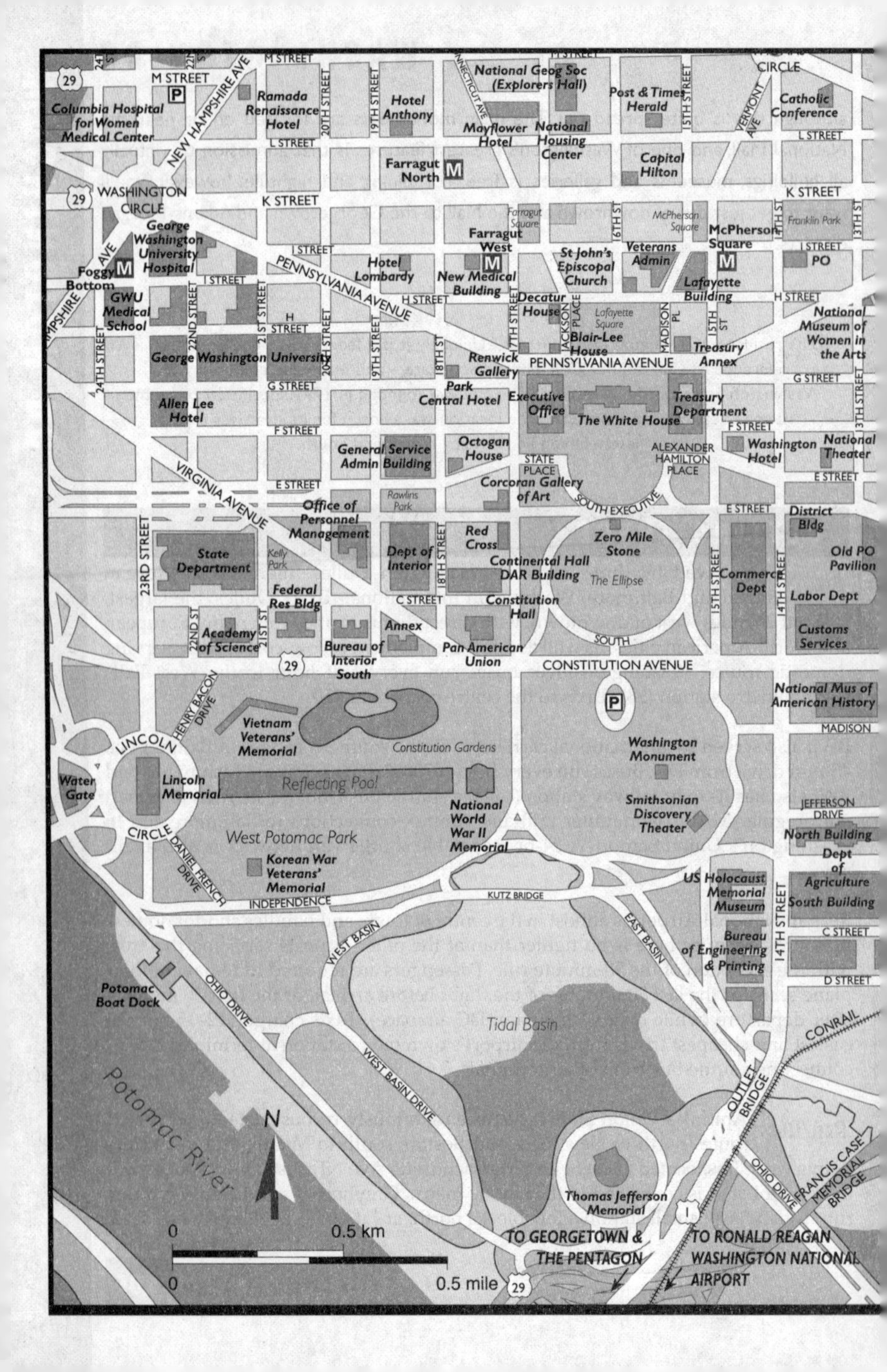

M STREET
Columbia Hospital for Women Medical Center
NEW HAMPSHIRE AVE
Ramada Renaissance Hotel
20TH STREET
19TH STREET
Hotel Anthony
National Geog Soc (Explorers Hall)
Mayflower Hotel
National Housing Center
Post & Times Herald
15TH STREET
VERMONT AVE
Catholic Conference
L STREET
Farragut North
Capital Hilton
WASHINGTON CIRCLE
K STREET
George Washington University Hospital
Farragut Square
Farragut West
McPherson Square
16TH ST
14TH ST
13TH ST
Franklin Park
I STREET
Foggy Bottom
Hotel Lombardy
New Medical Building
St John's Episcopal Church
Veterans Admin
PO
PENNSYLVANIA AVENUE
GWU Medical School
22ND STREET
21ST STREET
H STREET
Decatur House
JACKSON PLACE
Lafayette Square
MADISON PL
Lafayette Building
National Museum of Women in the Arts
24TH STREET
George Washington University
18TH ST
17TH STREET
Renwick Gallery
Blair-Lee House
Treasury Annex
G STREET
Allen Lee Hotel
Park Central Hotel
Executive Office
The White House
Treasury Department
13TH STREET
F STREET
General Service Admin Building
Octogan House
STATE PLACE
ALEXANDER HAMILTON PLACE
Washington Hotel
National Theater
VIRGINIA AVENUE
E STREET
Corcoran Gallery of Art
Rawlins Park
SOUTH EXECUTIVE
Office of Personnel Management
District Bldg
23RD STREET
State Department
Kelly Park
Dept of Interior
18TH STREET
Red Cross
Zero Mile Stone
Continental Hall DAR Building
The Ellipse
15TH STREET
Commerce Dept
14TH STREET
Old PO Pavilion
Federal Res Bldg
C STREET
Constitution Hall
Labor Dept
22ND ST
21ST ST
Academy of Science
Annex
Bureau of Interior South
Pan American Union
SOUTH
Customs Services
29
CONSTITUTION AVENUE
HENRY BACON DRIVE
Vietnam Veterans' Memorial
National Mus of American History
MADISON
LINCOLN
Constitution Gardens
Washington Monument
Water Gate
Lincoln Memorial
Reflecting Pool
National World War II Memorial
Smithsonian Discovery Theater
JEFFERSON DRIVE
North Building
CIRCLE
West Potomac Park
DANIEL FRENCH DRIVE
Korean War Veterans' Memorial
Dept of Agriculture South Building
US Holocaust Memorial Museum
INDEPENDENCE
KUTZ BRIDGE
WEST BASIN
EAST BASIN
Bureau of Engineering & Printing
D STREET
Potomac Boat Dock
OHIO DRIVE
Tidal Basin
CONRAIL
WEST BASIN DRIVE
OUTLET BRIDGE
Potomac River
N
FRANCIS CASE MEMORIAL BRIDGE
Thomas Jefferson Memorial
1
0
0.5 km
0.5 mile
TO GEORGETOWN & THE PENTAGON
TO RONALD REAGAN WASHINGTON NATIONAL AIRPORT

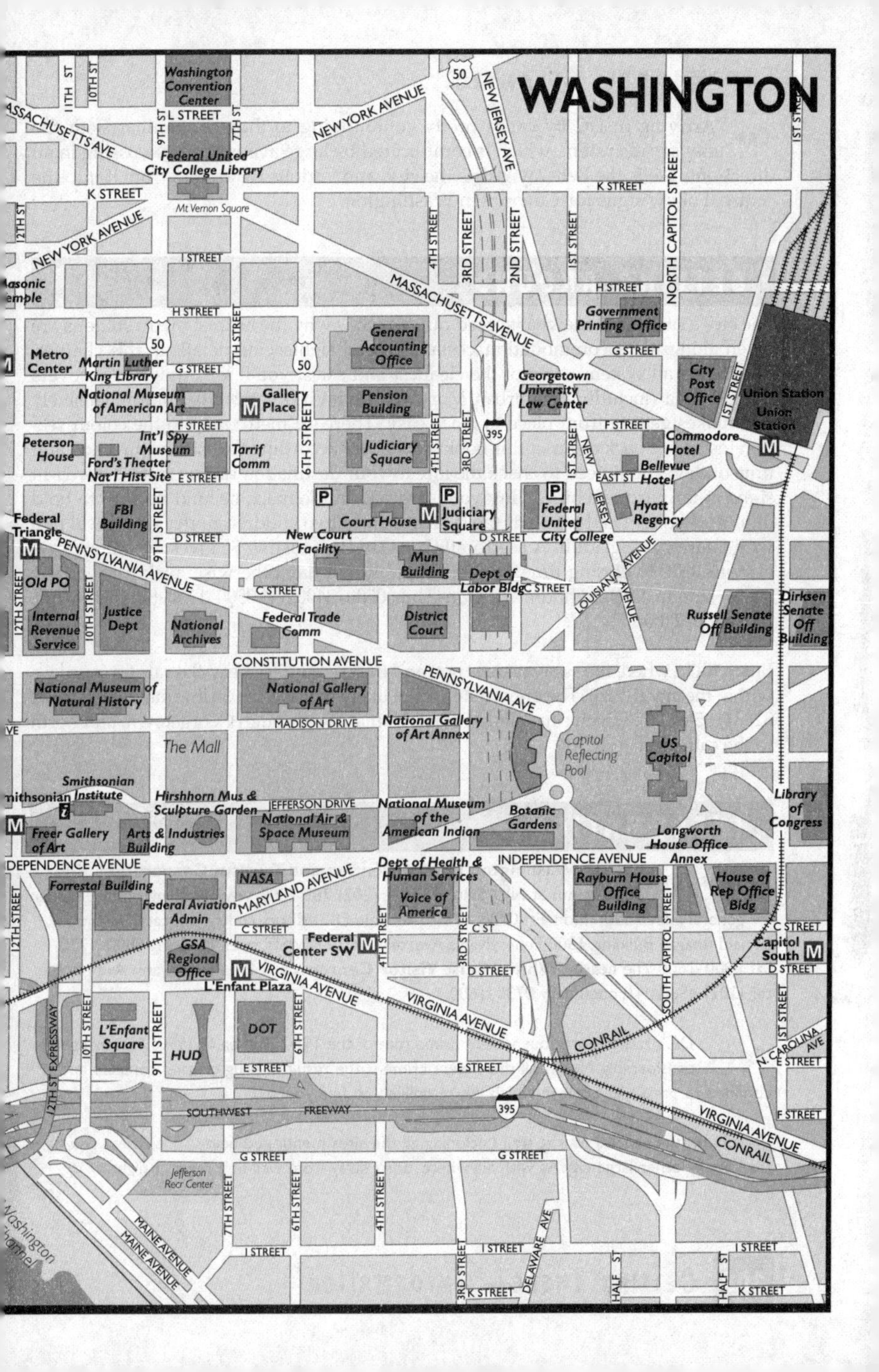
WASHINGTON
Washington Convention Center
Federal United City College Library
Mt Vernon Square
Masonic Temple
Metro Center
Martin Luther King Library
National Museum of American Art
Gallery Place
General Accounting Office
Pension Building
Georgetown University Law Center
Government Printing Office
City Post Office
Union Station
Peterson House
Int'l Spy Museum
Ford's Theater Nat'l Hist Site
Tarrif Comm
Judiciary Square
Commodore Hotel
Bellevue Hotel
Hyatt Regency
Federal United City College
FBI Building
Federal Triangle
Court House
New Court Facility
Mun Building
Dept of Labor Bldg
Old PO
Internal Revenue Service
Justice Dept
National Archives
Federal Trade Comm
District Court
Russell Senate Off Building
Dirksen Senate Off Building
National Museum of Natural History
National Gallery of Art
National Gallery of Art Annex
The Mall
Capitol Reflecting Pool
US Capitol
Smithsonian Institute
Hirshhorn Mus & Sculpture Garden
Freer Gallery of Art
Arts & Industries Building
National Air & Space Museum
National Museum of the American Indian
Botanic Gardens
Library of Congress
Longworth House Office Annex
Forrestal Building
NASA
Federal Aviation Admin
Dept of Health & Human Services
Voice of America
Rayburn House Office Building
House of Rep Office Bldg
GSA Regional Office
Federal Center SW
Capitol South
L'Enfant Plaza
L'Enfant Square
HUD
DOT
Jefferson Recr Center
Washington Channel
MASSACHUSETTS AVE
NEW YORK AVENUE
NEW JERSEY AVE
K STREET
I STREET
H STREET
G STREET
F STREET
E STREET
EAST ST
D STREET
C STREET
PENNSYLVANIA AVENUE
CONSTITUTION AVENUE
MADISON DRIVE
JEFFERSON DRIVE
INDEPENDENCE AVENUE
MARYLAND AVENUE
LOUISIANA AVENUE
VIRGINIA AVENUE
NORTH CAPITOL STREET
SOUTH CAPITOL STREET
12TH ST EXPRESSWAY
SOUTHWEST FREEWAY
CONRAIL
MAINE AVENUE
DELAWARE AVE
N. CAROLINA AVE
HALF ST
1ST STREET
2ND STREET
3RD STREET
4TH STREET
6TH STREET
7TH STREET
9TH STREET
10TH STREET
11TH ST
12TH STREET
50
395

CAR Arriving in DC by car is pretty confounding to those unfamiliar with the city's grid system, which is complicated by large avenues criss-crossing in all directions. I-495, the Beltway, skirts the city, and various roads lead from it into the centre. Follow signs for Downtown Washington.

GETTING AROUND

The city's sites are somewhat spread out, which is why the nearest metro stations are given alongside accommodation, restaurant and sightseeing details in this chapter. The Metrorail system – one of the cleanest and safest you'll see anywhere – covers the DC area (including suburban Maryland and Virginia) pretty comprehensively and makes getting from place to place easy. There's a metro map in the colour section inside the back cover of this book. Fares vary according to distance travelled and time of day; you'll need to check the fare to your destination station from the well-lit signs at farecard machines. Buy your farecard in the machine, and be sure to hold onto it as you'll need it to exit the system. Up to two children under five travel free with a fare-paying adult. A Metrorail One Day Pass costing $6 gives unlimited travel from 0930 to closing time on weekdays and all day otherwise; pick it up at any Metro station. System hours are Mon–Thur 0500–2400, Fri 0500–1300, Sat 0700–0300, Sun 0700–2400.

Buses fill in where the subway does not, and there is a quite cheap flat rate for journeys within the city ($1.25). The only route you're likely to use is the 30 line (any of buses 30, 32, 34, 35 or 36), which runs along Pennsylvania Ave through Georgetown, and north to the cathedral.

INFORMATION

TRANSPORT MAP – inside back cover

TOURIST OFFICES The **Washington DC Convention and Tourism Corporation**, 901 Seventh St NW, Suite 400, tel: (202) 789-7000, www.washington.org, is open for general information Mon–Fri 0900–1700. The main DC visitors centre is located in the Ronald Reagan Building, 1300 Pennsylvania Ave, tel: (202)-DCVISIT, open Mon–Fri 0800–1730, Sat 0900–1600. The nearby **White House Visitor Center** is at 1450 Pennsylvania Ave NW; tel: (202) 456-7041, open daily 0730–1600.

SAFETY DC's rather notorious violent crime rate of the 1980s and early 1990s has dropped considerably. Nearly all the violent crime is the result of drug or gang conflicts, and is confined to particular areas in which you're unlikely to find yourself.

Visitors on the general tourist trail (including all the sites mentioned below) are at less risk here than in any other large city. As with anywhere, don't stray from well-lit streets at night.

MONEY A central Travelex exchange office is at 1800 K St NW; tel: (800) CURRENCY or (202) 872-1427 (metro: Farragut North or Farragut West). Open Mon–Fri 0900–1700. There are also offices at all airports and one at Union Station, tel: (202) 371-9219, which is open late and at weekends.

POST AND PHONES The main post office is next to Union Station at 2 Massachusetts Ave NE. A handy post office near the Mall is in the Post Office Pavilion at 11th St and Pennsylvania Ave NW.

ACCOMMODATION

Central hotels are expensive during the week, but rates drop at weekends and in July–Aug and Dec–Jan, when Congress is in recess and business and convention travel slows down. In addition, many hotels extend their lower weekend rates to cover a seven-day stay, and similar low-priced packages are available during holiday periods. Always call ahead for reservations – up to a month in advance is recommended – as the city is a hugely popular tourist destination.

No district of the city is favoured with inexpensive housing. Recent developments have made Downtown a much more interesting place to stay than before, but prices may be lower in other areas. Dupont Circle and Georgetown are well known for lively night life, but the newest up-and-coming areas such as Adams-Morgan and U St/Logan Circle are good alternative locations. Motels outside the District (of Columbia) can offer better parking facilities.

Reservations services include **Capitol Reservations**, tel: (800) VISIT-DC or (202) 452-1270; **Washington DC Accommodation**, tel: (800) 554-2220 or (202) 289-2220; and **Bed and Breakfast Accommodations**, tel: (202) 328-3510; www.washington.org and www.dchousing.net.

DOWNTOWN

HI – Washington International Hostel $ 1009 11th St NW; tel: (202) 737-2333; www.hiwashingtondc.org (metro: Metro Center). Huge hostel with kitchen, laundry, information desk and tours. Quite central, though nondescript area.

Harrington Hotel $$$ 1100 E St NW; tel: (202) 628-8140 or (800) 424-8532; www.hotel-harrington.com (metro: Metro Center). Decent old hotel near the White House and the Mall.

DUPONT CIRCLE/ ADAMS-MORGAN

Simpkins' B&B $$ 1601 19th St NW; tel: (202) 387-1328 (metro: Dupont Circle). No-frills guesthouse near Dupont Circle. Show a passport (US or foreign) for entry.

Kalorama Guest House $$–$$$ 1854 Mintwood Place NW; tel: (202) 667-6369; and 2700 Cathedral Ave NW, tel: (202) 328-0860 (metro: Woodley Park–Zoo). Long-time favourite B&B in several fine town houses in Adams-Morgan and Woodley Park.

Tabard Inn $$$ 1739 N St NW; tel: (202) 785-1277; www.tabardinn.com (metro: Dupont Circle). Homey guesthouse on the cusp of Dupont Circle and downtown.

Topaz Hotel $$$$ 1733 N St NW; tel: (202) 393-3000 or 1(800) 424-2950, www.topazhotel (metro: Dupont Circle). Stylish, elegant and quirky (suites available with meditation stones and in-room exercise bikes). Conveniently located for central Washington.

Windsor Inn $$$–$$$$ 1842 16th St NW; tel: (202) 667-0300 (metro: Dupont Circle). B&B-style hotel in the active Dupont Circle area.

Adam's Inn $$–$$$ 1744 Lanier Pl. NW; tel (202) 745 3600, www.adamsinn.com. Simple guesthouse close to the action in Adam's Morgan.

Allen Lee Hotel $–$$ 2224 F St NW; tel: (202) 331-1224 or (800) 462-0186, www.allenlee hotel.com (metro: Foggy Bottom-GWU). Basic but cheap and convenient.

Woodley Park Guesthouse $$–$$$ 2647 Woodley Rd NW; tel: (202) 667-0218, www.woodleyparkguesthouse.com (metro: Woodley Park-Zoo). Nice B&B in a quieter neighbourhood but with good restaurants/nightlife nearby and easy metro access to the centre.

FOOD AND DRINK

As might be expected of the world's most powerful capital city, Washington offers a culinary choice that sweeps across the international spectrum. Adams-Morgan (around 18th St and Columbia Rd NW) is the ethnic hotspot in town, with a rich selection of Ethiopian, Mexican and French restaurants, and lots of great bars and clubs. The nearby area surrounding U St NW, between 13th and 18th Sts, is rough around the edges, but is becoming a happening restaurant and nightlife centre. Georgetown (around Wisconsin Ave and M St NW) is a long-established part of social life in DC, with everything from cheap diners and Irish pubs to fine Italian restaurants, and lively nightlife. Old Town Alexandria in suburban Virginia (along King St) is another historical and spirited part of town, with several good seafood places. Most of the Smithsonian museums have café/restaurants, which are good for a cheap lunch or snack. For a quick lunchtime bite, wander down 7th St into Chinatown with its huge variety of excellent eateries.

DOWNTOWN

Old Ebbitt Grill $$–$$$ 675 15th St NW (metro: Metro Center). Favourite White House location good for steaks, oysters, lunchtime burgers and Washington hob-nobbing.

Jaleo $$ 480 7th St. NW (corner of E St, metro: Gallery Place). Spanish tapas and mains right by MCI Center in the newly hopping downtown.

DUPONT CIRCLE/ ADAMS-MORGAN

Firefly $$–$$$ 1310 New Hampshire Ave NW (metro: Dupont Circle). Friendly local restaurant serving innovative American cuisine.

Kramerbooks and Afterwords Café $$ 1517 Connecticut Ave NW (metro: Dupont Circle). Satisfy mind and body in this bookstore and café, which serves salads, sandwiches, vegetarian dishes and weekend brunch.

Lauriol Plaza $$–$$$ 1835 18th St NW (metro: Dupont Circle). Very hip, with exquisite Mexican cuisine and a nice outdoor roofdeck.

Meskerem $$–$$$ 2434 18th St NW (metro: Woodley Park–Zoo or Dupont Circle). The best of many Ethiopian restaurants in Adams-Morgan; don't miss the honey wine.

GEORGETOWN

Bangkok Bistro $–$$ 3251 Prospect St NW. Divine Thai cuisine at equally pleasing prices; try the cheap lunch specials.

Clyde's $$ 3236 M St. Good Georgetown place serving 'American saloon food' – burgers, seafood, fajitas, soups and salads, plus excellent home-brewed lager.

Bistro Français $$$–$$$$ 3128 M St. Excellent and reasonably priced French cuisine in a romantic setting. Arrive before 1900 for dinner specials.

ALEXANDRIA

The Fish Market $$–$$$ 105 King St (metro: King St). Characterful place with excellent fish dishes, and not too dear.

HIGHLIGHTS

THE MALL AND AROUND

The **National Mall** is the city's centrepiece, a long rectangular swathe of open green, book-ended by the US Capitol and the Washington Monument, and lined by grandiose Smithsonian museums. The Mall is often the scene of marches and demonstrations. Just past the Washington Monument is the new National World War II Memorial, beyond which stretches the Reflecting Pool, leading to the Lincoln Memorial, from where Martin Luther King Jr delivered his electrifying 'I Have A Dream' speech in 1963.

The **Smithsonian Institution** is one of the finest museum complexes in the world, with 18 separate institutes plus the National Zoo – all begun with a bequest from an English chemist who had never been to the USA. All are open daily 1000–1730; many extend their hours in the summer (check locally). All are free, and you could easily spend a solid week in the museums on the Mall alone. For general information, tel: (202) 357-2700. All sites on the Mall are served by the Smithsonian metro station.

The most popular Smithsonian museum is the fantastic **National Air and Space Museum**, at the south-eastern corner of the Mall near the Capitol. A big hit with kids, it can't fail to impress visitors of all ages with its array of real air- and spacecraft. Notable exhibits include the Wright Brothers' first plane ever flown, Charles Lindbergh's *Spirit of St Louis*, in which he made his solo transatlantic flight, an original Saturn V rocket and several (decommissioned) American and Soviet nuclear warheads. **The Stephen Udvar-Hazy Museum**, located at Dulles Airport about an hour away, is a new extension of the museum with air- and spacecraft on display in an enormous hangar, including the WWII *Enola Gay* and the shuttle *Enterprise*. Entrance to both

TOURS

Tourmobile Sightseeing, tel: (202) 554-5100, offers a narrated shuttlebus service ($$), with unlimited reboarding at 18 major sites all day. The service runs daily every 15 mins 0930–1630. **Old Town Trolley Tours**, tel: (202) 872-1765, runs 2-hr narrated tours ($$$) every half-hour, daily 0900–1600; free reboarding at 17 sites. (See also p. 217 for some suggested independent walking tours.)

museums is free, with a shuttle ($7) running between the two sites. Each has an IMAX® cinema.

Right next to the National Air and Space Museum is the new **National Museum of the American Indian (NMAI)**. As well as being an exhibition space for Indians of the Americas, both North and South, the facility is also a centre for performance and ceremonies. Much of the focus is on current life.

Further down the Mall, the **Freer Gallery** is a smaller collection of works donated by the 1920s industrialist James Freer: his personal favourites were James McNeill Whistler, as well as pieces from ancient China and Byzantium. Beneath the Freer, in a three-level underground gallery, are the **Sackler Gallery** featuring precious manuscripts and objects from ancient China and the Middle East, and the **National Museum of African Art**. This covers a broad range of sculptures, paintings and crafts from the African continent, including beautiful ivory carvings.

Along the north side of the Mall, the first building west of the Capitol is the **National Gallery of Art** founded by industrialist Andrew Mellon. There are in fact two galleries, the original, gold-domed West Wing, and the super-modern (even now, over a quarter of a century later) East Wing; the two are connected by an underground walkway. The original gallery houses the likes of Rembrandt, Rubens, Botticelli, Monet, Gauguin and Van Gogh. The East Wing focuses on contemporary art, and has a steady stream of visiting exhibitions. Its permanent collection includes works by Picasso, Liechtenstein and Warhol, and the building itself is worth seeing.

The **National Museum of Natural History** next door is a wonderful collection of the planet's physical being. Highlights include reconstructed skeletons of dinosaurs such as a brontosaurus and a pterodactyl; an extensive collection of precious gems,

HEIGHTENED SECURITY

Despite the horrific attacks of 11 September 2001, the nation's capital is slowly, if warily, returning to normal. Security remains a priority, with entry to many offices and tourist sites contingent upon going through a thorough bag search and X-ray screening, leading to long queues at the most popular ones. There are armed military at high-visibility icon sites, as well as surprisingly reassuring guards stationed at locations throughout the city.

Some of the attractions that were closed after the attacks are open again, while the doors of others remain shut.

including the notorious Hope Diamond (the largest in the world); displays on the lives of Native American peoples and a creepy crawly insect zoo, which includes live tarantulas and scorpions.

The **National Museum of American History** has constantly changing exhibits of important events in America's history. Its greatest strength is that it doesn't try to glamorise: exhibits include rich displays on, for example, the so-called Great Migration of African Americans northwards after the Civil War, and the altered lives of Navajo and Zuni Indians in New Mexico today. Other sections are pure fun, such as turn-of-the-century locomotives and the collection of inauguration ball gowns worn by First Ladies.

The **Washington Monument**, on the Mall at 15th St NW, is one of the city's most recognisable symbols, a 555 ft obelisk. Views from the top on clear days spread all the way to the Blue Ridge Mountains. Arrive early for free timed tickets; the monument is open daily 0900–1645. At the eastern bank of the Reflecting Pool, stretching nearly 600 yards to the Lincoln Memorial, is the new **National World War II Memorial**. With 56 pillars representing the states, territories and District of Columbia that were part of the USA at the time, this dramatic monument stands for the unity that existed during World War II. As well as in the central Rainbow Pool, water flows through fountains at the Atlantic and Pacific pavilions and waterfalls along the Freedom Wall. The **Lincoln Memorial** (metro: Foggy Bottom–GWU) at the other end houses a statue of a seated Abraham Lincoln inside a Grecian-style memorial temple.

Lincoln's gaze falls kindly on the **Vietnam Veterans' Memorial**, just north of the Reflecting Pool. More than 58,000 names of those who died or remain missing in the Vietnam War are inscribed on the black granite V-shaped memorial, and the site is particularly moving as it's well visited by relatives of the dead. Across the pool, the **Korean War Veterans' Memorial** is composed of stainless steel sculptures of 19 ground troops.

More tragedy is on hand in the **US Holocaust Memorial Museum**, on 15th St just south of the Washington Monument (metro: Smithsonian). The harrowing story of the Nazi genocide is told here through photographs, artefacts, film, videotaped histories and other exhibits. Particularly moving is the Tower of Faces, an actual barrack building from Auschwitz. Open daily 1000–1730; free, but timed tickets are required, and you may well have to arrive early to get tickets for later in the day.

THE WHITE HOUSE

The **White House**, 1600 Pennsylvania Ave NW (metro: Metro Center or McPherson Sq.), remains high on most visitors' lists of things to see. Public visits have been severely curtailed, although it is possible to arrange tours several months in advance for groups of ten or more. US citizens must contact their member of congress while foreign visitors should get in touch with their relevant embassy Office of Procedure and Protocol. As a consolation, the White

House Visitor Center at 1450 Pennsylvania Ave is worth seeing in its own right, with historical exhibits and displays of photographs showing life and special functions at the White House down the years. If tours resume, this is where you come to pick up free tickets, which disappear fast: arrive as early as possible. The visitor centre is open daily 0730–1600; tel: (202) 456-7041.

Leafy **Lafayette Square**, the traditional gathering point in front of the White House for low-key protestors of all ilks, is currently undergoing significant building works. **St John's Episcopal Church**, on the northern edge of the park at 1525 H St NW, is the church of the presidents – since the time of James Madison they have worshipped here in pew 54. The pretty landmark dates from 1816.

THE GOVERNMENT AT WORK

To get a Congressional pass and watch the proceedings, Americans apply to their senator or representative, but foreign visitors may be able to obtain House passes at the gallery check-in desk on the third floor and Senate passes at the Senate appointment desk on the first floor, all subject to availability. *The Washington Post* records when Senators and Representatives are sitting.

CAPITOL HILL

The **US Capitol**, the seat of the US government, is the nerve centre of all that is Washington. All four city districts converge on this point, and the building has obvious appeal for its physical beauty (its white dome is particularly striking at night) as well as the fact that you can witness Congress in session. Capitol South metro station is convenient to all sites in this area. The Capitol building is open 0900–1630 Mon–Sat, with free guided tours offered every 15 minutes 0900–1545. Tickets for same-day free guided tours are distributed at 0900 from the visitors' kiosk. Lines form early; tel: (202) 225-6827; www.house.gov. The buildings lining Constitution Ave to the north house Senate offices, and those lining Independence Ave to the south are used by members of the House of Representatives.

Behind the Capitol are a number of other buildings important to America. The **Library of Congress**, at 1st St and Independence Ave SE, is a research library created in 1800 to serve Congress, and now holds close to 100 million books and documents. A room in the James Madison building (there are three library buildings in the complex) contains a Gutenberg Bible and Martin Luther King's 'I Have a Dream' speech. Open Mon–Sat 1000–1730.

The **US Supreme Court** building, a block up at 1st St and Maryland Ave NE, has displays and a film outlining procedures in the nation's highest court. Lectures are given every hour on the half-hour Mon–Fri 0930–1530 when not in session. Court hearings may be watched on a first-come, first-served basis, but public seating is limited. For a brief look, join the 3-min queue; to attend an entire case, join the regular queue. The court sits weekdays 0900–1630.

Also in the area is the surprisingly good **Folger Shakespeare Library**, 201 E Capitol

St SE, a recreation of Shakespeare's original Elizabethan theatre and one of the world's greatest collections of Shakespearean and Renaissance material. Open Mon–Sat 1000–1600.

DOWNTOWN The central business district is beginning to develop real character, with restaurants, attractions and events competing with the draw of the more solid memorials and museums that pepper the area. Near the Mall, the **National Archives** building, 8th St and Pennsylvania Ave NW (metro: Archives-Navy Memorial), has been renovated to better present its permanent display of the original US Constitution, the Declaration of Independence and the Bill of Rights. Open daily 1000–1730, except Christmas.

While the FBI building remains closed for renovation, a more entertaining alternative to visit is the new **International Spy Museum**, 800 F St NW, $$, open daily 1000–1900, 1000–1700 Nov–Mar (metro: Gallery Place/Chinatown). Exhibits range from analysis of what it takes to be an international spy and gadgets used to aid espionage to learning about the history and future of the intelligence game. The museum is fun and extremely popular, so the advance purchase of timed tickets is essential.

A block up, at 511 10th St NW, the pretty restored **Ford's Theatre** is where Abraham Lincoln was shot on 14 April 1865. The president's box, above the stage, was a fairly easy target for his assassin, John Wilkes Booth. Lincoln died hours later in **Petersen House** across the street, also open to the public. A museum underneath Ford's Theatre has more information on the assassination. Open daily 0900–1700.

There are several more art galleries of note downtown as well. The **National Museum of Women in the Arts**, 1250 New York Ave NW (metro: Metro Center), contains more than 1500 works by 400 women from 28 countries. Open Mon–Sat 1000–1700, Sun 1200–1700; donation requested. Near the White House, the **Corcoran Gallery of Art** at 17th St and New York Ave NW (metro: Farragut West) is a fine collection of romantic and contemporary American art. Open Mon, Sat, Sun 1000–1700, Wed, Thur, Fri 1000–2100; donation suggested. Fanning out a little to the north, the **Phillips Collection**, 1600 21st St NW (metro: Dupont Circle) is an excellent private collection of 19th- and 20th-century paintings, including works by Renoir, Georgia O'Keeffe, Paul Klee and Jacob Lawrence. $$, open Tues–Sat 1000–1700 (Thur till 2030), Sun 1200–1900.

For something a little different, the **National Geographic Society** headquarters at 1600 M St NW (metro: Farragut North) has exhibits covering early humans, the earth, its geography, and the fragile balance between its inhabitants. Open Mon–Sat 0900–1700, Sun 1000–1700.

BEYOND CENTRAL WASHINGTON **Georgetown** is a wonderful place just to wander around, window-shop and stop for a meal. This was founded as a port before the city of Washington was built, just west of centre on the

Potomac River (the intersection of Wisconsin Ave and M St is its centre) and today its mostly 19th-century buildings, including several private mansions, are gorgeous to stroll by. The Chesapeake and Ohio Canal, built for trade between the Georgetown docks and rural Maryland in the mid-19th century (see Great Falls Park, p. 220), runs parallel to M St and the river, and is a pleasing little stretch to walk along.

A few miles up Wisconsin Ave at Massachusetts Ave, the **Washington National Cathedral** bears stunning similarity to many of Europe's finest cathedrals. Craftsmen used 14th- and 15th-century skills to build and adorn this Gothic house of worship for the Episcopal Church. It was completed in 1990 and is the world's sixth largest cathedral. The Cathedral is a gathering point for moments of national importance. The gardens make a soothing respite from the summer heat. Take Metrobus nos. 30, 32, 34, 35 or 36 from Foggy Bottom–GWU or Tenleytown metro stations, or walk the 1½ miles from Tenleytown. Open daily 1000–1630. Guided tours Mon–Sat 1000–1515, Sun 1230–1445; donations appreciated.

Rock Creek Park is a quite remarkable phenomenon, a forest right in the city, extending from the river right out into suburban Maryland. From Woodley Park–Zoo metro follow through to the bottom of the zoo, and from here you can walk in either direction along the creek. If you follow the creek northwards, you reach the 18th-century Pierce Mill after a mile or so, and from here, Tilden St runs back up to Connecticut Ave and Van Ness–UDC metro – a 2-hr circular walk. You can also access the park from M St or P St in Georgetown.

Arlington National Cemetery, across the river from the Lincoln Memorial (metro: Arlington Cemetery), is the final resting place of hundreds of thousands of US servicemen and women, and of President John F Kennedy. One of the cemetery's most serene sites is the Tomb of the Unknown Soldier. Open daily 0800–1900 (summer); 0800–1700 (winter).

Not far away is the **Pentagon** (metro: Pentagon), home of the US Department of Defense – which rendered it a terrorist target on 11 September 2001. The hijacked plane slammed into one of the western edges of the massive five-sided structure, destroying a good chunk of the outer wall and two inner rings, and killing nearly 250 people, both in the plane and in the building. Its reconstruction began almost immediately, and continued at a breakneck pace as crews aimed at finishing the job by the one-year anniversary of the tragedy. There's not a lot to see now, but to view the point of impact exit the metro station and walk around the southern edge of the Pentagon towards the highway that passes alongside the western portion of the building.

The Pentagon is now closed to tours. Phone (703) 697-1776 for further details. The building is a foreboding Cold War testament to grandeur and bureaucracy, and is the largest office building in the world (space is held in its girth rather than its height) and one of the true nerve centres of the US government.

One site off the beaten track but worth the trip into south-east Washington is the **Frederick Douglass home**, 1411 W St SE (metro: Anacostia, then bus B2). Douglass, a self-educated African-American who was one of the great figures in the emancipation of slavery, became a successful businessman, and his home has been restored to its mid-19th-century appearance. Open daily 0900–1700 (spring–summer); 0900–1600 (autumn–winter). This area can be dangerous, so travel in a group.

In upper north-east Washington are two religious centres worth visiting if you have time. The **National Shrine of the Immaculate Conception**, on the campus of the Catholic University of America at 4th St and Michigan Ave NE (metro: Brookland-CUA), is the largest Catholic church in the USA, with more than 50 chapels and a wealth of stained glass. The enormous dome is nearly 240 ft high, and the beautiful 329 ft Knights' Tower has a carillon of 56 bells. Open 0700–1800 daily (until 1900 Apr–Oct). Not far away, the **Franciscan Monastery**, 1400 Quincy St NE (metro: Brookland-CUA), is a retreat in the Byzantine style, with replicas of Holy Land shrines. A statue of St Francis stands in the enclosed garden. Open daily 0900–1700.

WALKING TOURS

DC is a good city for exploring on foot. Organised walking tours are offered by several companies, including Georgetown & Dupont Circle Walking Tours, tel: (301) 588-8999, and Washington Walks, tel: (202) 484-1565. Here are a few more suggestions for independent walkers.

Potomac River: Georgetown to the Mall. This is a pleasant way to see the river and several interesting buildings along the way. From K St in Georgetown walk through Washington Harbor (an office, apartment and restaurant complex) along the banks of the Potomac past the **Watergate** and **Kennedy Center**. Cross the street at the Lincoln Memorial and continue on to the Mall. Time: 1 hr to the Lincoln Memorial; another 1 hr across the Mall to the Capitol without stops.

Embassy Row: Massachusetts Ave north-west of Dupont Circle has the highest concentration of embassies in the city, hence its nickname. Many of these are in fine mansions. Along the way you will also see the beautiful **Islamic Mosque and Cultural Center** (2551 Massachusetts Ave), which is open daily 1000–1700 – women must be modestly clothed and everyone must remove their shoes – and the **Vice President's Mansion**, 34th St and Massachusetts Ave (not open). Time: 1 hr without stops, all uphill.

Old Town Alexandria: the town of Alexandria, a few miles south of central DC, was established in 1749 by Scottish tobacco merchants, and its prominent citizens have included George Washington and Robert E Lee. Many historical structures have been preserved. King St metro is an easy access point to Old Town, and King St itself is the main street leading straight toward the river. Stop off at **Christ Church** (118 N Washington St), **Carlyle House** (121 N Fairfax St) and **Ramsey House** (221 King St), all dating from the early to mid-18th century. Time: 30 mins from King St metro to the river without stops.

SHOPPING

The Smithsonian museums' gift shops are excellent places to pick up anything from souvenirs to fine quality art posters and books. Political memorabilia is a hot item. Washington's busiest shopping area is probably along Wisconsin Ave and M St NW in Georgetown, which has many good speciality boutiques. Alexandria Dupont Circle and Adams-Morgan are also great places for everything from funky to fine.

NIGHTLIFE

Washington has a buzzing concert and theatre scene. Listings of current shows, plays and concerts are given in *Where Washington*, *Washington City Paper* and the *Washington Post*.

John F Kennedy Center for the Performing Arts, Virginia and New Hampshire Aves NW, tel: (202) 467-4600 (metro: Foggy Bottom–GWU). World-class orchestral, opera and dance performances. The **National Symphony Orchestra**'s season runs Sept–May.

National Theater, 1321 Pennsylvania Ave NW; tel: (202) 628-6161 (metro: Metro Center). Broadway shows.

Warner Theater, 1299 Pennsylvania Ave NW; tel: (202) 783-4000 (metro: Metro Center). Beautifully remodelled theatre.

Ford's Theater, 511 10th St NW; tel: (202) 347-4833 (metro: Metro Center).

Folger Shakespeare Library, 201 E Capital St SE; tel: (202) 544-7077 (metro: Capitol South). See p. 215.

Arena Stage, 1101 6th St SW; tel: (202) 554-9066. Acclaimed theatrical venue, mainstream to avante-garde productions.

DC has rediscovered professional sports in recent years, with the return of baseball and the opening of MCI Center. The city finally regained a baseball team in 2005 after 34 years – the Nationals play home games at **RFK Stadium** (metro: Stadium Armory) until a new stadium is built. For tickets call tel: (202) 675-NATS. RFK is also home to the DC United soccer team. Since MCI Center (metro: Gallery Place) was built in an abandoned part of downtown DC in 1997, crowds have flocked to see the Wizards (basketball) and Capitals (hockey) – and stayed to enjoy the burgeoning restaurant and bar scene. For tickets to all sporting events, call Ticket Master at tel: (202) 397 SEAT.

DC nightlife has really picked up in the last few years, and Georgetown (particularly Wisconsin and M Sts) and Adams-Morgan (around 18th St and Columbia Rd) are happening neighbourhoods with plenty of bars and clubs. DC has an unusually good collection of jazz and blues spots, and many bars and clubs take up politically inspired themes. Most clubs have a fairly nominal cover charge ($5–10), but in some it can be much more.

DUPONT CIRCLE/ ADAMS-MORGAN

Brickseller Inn, 1523 22nd St NW; tel: (202) 293-1885 (metro: Dupont Circle). Large but cosy pub with an amazing menu of more than 800 beers.

Madam's Organ, 2461 18th St NW (metro: Woodley Park–Zoo). Playing on the name of its Adams-Morgan location, this bar/club offers a variety of music from world to bluegrass.

GEORGETOWN/FOGGY BOTTOM

Blues Alley, rear of 1073 Wisconsin Ave NW (metro: Foggy Bottom–GWU 20 mins walk or bus 30/32/34/35/36). Long-established, upmarket, intimate jazz club in Georgetown, presenting the top names. Shows are twice nightly Sun–Thur, thrice Fri and Sat. Hefty cover charge for top national and international acts.

One Step Down, 2517 Pennsylvania Avenue NW (metro: Foggy Bottom–GWU). This Foggy Bottom/Georgetown jazz and blues club is less showy than Blues Alley, but still authentic.

Saloun, 3239 M St (metro: Foggy Bottom–GWU 20 mins, bus 30/32/34/35/36). Usually a fine place to catch local jazz and blues bands, and a good beer list.

DOWNTOWN/ 14TH AND U STS

The Black Cat, 1811 14th St NW (metro: U Street–Cardoza). Good barand connected hall featuring good alternative local and national bands.

9:30 Club, 815 V St NW (metro: U Street–Cardoza). DC's long-time best venue for rock and pop acts.

Polly Esther's, 605 12th St NW (metro: Metro Center). Huge dance club with separate floors for the 1960s, 70s, 80s and 90s.

FESTIVAL TIME

DC puts on a number of colourful events throughout the year. Here are a few of the very best.

National Cherry Blossom Festival (usually early April). A week-long exultation of more than 6000 Japanese cherry trees in bloom along the Tidal Basin and Washington Monument. The bright pink flowers are stunning, but it's hard to predict when the trees will be at full bloom, and it only lasts a few days.

Festival of American Folklife (late June/early July). Music, arts, crafts and cuisine with different geographical themes, each year on the Mall.

Independence Day Washington celebrates 4 July with activities on the Mall all day, a free concert by the National Symphony Orchestra on the west steps of the Capitol in the evening, and a glorious fireworks display at night.

DAY TRIPS

MOUNT VERNON

A must-see for American history fans, and an enjoyable day trip from DC, is Mount Vernon, the home of George Washington. Set in 500 acres of riverfront Virginia countryside, 16 miles from Washington DC, the former plantation and seat of the great Revolutionary general and first president of the United States is simple and gracious. The grounds include slave quarters – an irony of many founding fathers was their ownership of slaves, despite proclamations that 'all men are created equal' – and George and Martha Washington's tombs, plus an innovative 16-sided threshing barn, built using hand-made bricks and hand-forged nails. The almost circular design served as an indoor arena for a horse to trample the straw, causing the grain to sift through to the floor below.

TASTE OF DC

Over the weekend closest to Columbus Day (12 October), more than 40 restaurants present samples of their wares, accompanied by entertainment.

Mount Vernon is open daily 0900–1700 (Mar and Sept–Oct); 0800–1700 (Apr–Aug); 0900–1600 (Nov–Feb); $$; www.mountvernon.org. The house is best seen on an organized tour, approached either by water, via the Potomac River boat trips of companies such as Spirit Cruises, tel: (202) 554-8000, or land, with Grayline, tel: (202) 289-1995. Fairfax Connector bus 101 runs every 30 mins (rush hour) or every hour (non-rush hour and weekends) from Huntington metro station to the house. By car, take the George Washington Memorial Pkwy, which runs along the west bank of the river through Arlington and Alexandria.

GREAT FALLS PARK The fall line of the Potomac River is about 15 miles upstream from Georgetown, a dramatic, rocky narrowing through which the river shoots with extraordinary velocity – the kind of wild river scenery you would expect to find in the West. The falls are part of the Chesapeake and Ohio Canal National Historical Park, straddling both the Maryland and Virginia sides of the river. Both sides have good views, but the Maryland side is by far the more interesting, as the C&O Canal passes alongside the northern bank. The canal offers a glimpse into an intriguing part of America's 19th-century industrial history – the building of an inland waterways system to transport goods from rural Maryland and Ohio to Washington, DC. Soon after construction of the canal began, however, the railway began its romp across the country, and the romantic endeavour of the canal was overwhelmed. You can gain a perspective on the canal at the Great Falls Tavern Visitor Center.

To see the falls, cross the bridge onto Olmsted Island for superb views. You can also stroll along the canal bank for miles in either direction, and slip down to the river for a little peace and quiet: this is a popular weekend destination for Washingtonians. Great Falls Park is open daily from dawn to dusk; $. There is no public transport – to reach the Maryland side by car take Macarthur Blvd from Georgetown (an extension of M St).

WHERE NEXT?

The District of Columbia is an enclave of Maryland and Virginia, both of which have stunning scenery and many attractions: historic Jamestown, Richmond and Williamsburg and the shores of Chesapeake Bay (see pp. 232–242) lie to the south-east, and the dramatic sweep of the Blue Ridge Mountains and Shenandoah National Park to the south-west (see p. 244). Baltimore and Annapolis (see pp. 221–231) are just an hour or so away by road or rail, and Philadelphia (see p. 191) is 2–3 hours away. For the route to Chicago see p. 362.

BALTIMORE

Developed beside a natural harbour in Chesapeake Bay, Baltimore began as a distribution port for 18th-century grain farmers and tobacco growers. The city grew quickly, as shipwrights and merchants anxious to carry flour to distant reaches of the British Empire settled round the harbour fringes. Today, Baltimore is the thirteenth largest city in the USA and the fifth busiest port, filled with evidence of its rich Colonial and maritime history. It is a gutsy 'blue collar' city, a high-spirited place, with its busy Inner Harbor, restaurants, entertainment and activities along its hilly streets.

MUST SEE/DO IN BALTIMORE

Find Edgar Allan Poe's grave at Westminster Hall Burying Ground, Fayette and Greene Sts

Step back into the big-hair and cat-glasses era with a walk down on 34th St in Hampden with lunch at Café Hon

Take a water taxi or a cruise from Inner Harbor

Sample crabcakes in any of the city's covered market buildings

Spend half a day with sea creatures in the Baltimore Aquarium

Tour the museum ships in Inner Harbor, especially USS *Constellation*

GETTING THERE AND GETTING AROUND

AIR Baltimore/Washington International Airport (BWI), tel: (410) 859-7100, is a major gateway for passengers arriving from Europe.

A free shuttle runs between the main terminal and the airport station, and Amtrak and MARC (Maryland Area Rail Commuter), tel: (800) 325-RAIL, connect the airport and Baltimore, a 20-min journey which MARC makes only Mon–Fri. Bus no. 17, operated by MTA (Mass Transit Administration), tel: (410) 539-5000, connects the airport with the city centre, and the BWI Airport Shuttle, tel: (800) 776-0323, serves Inner Harbor hotels.

RAIL/BUS Amtrak, tel: (800) USA RAIL or (800) 872-7245, connects Baltimore to New York and Washington, DC. The Amtrak station is nearly 2 miles from the harbour, accessed by bus nos. 3 or 11 North. MARC connects Baltimore and Washington, a 1-hr trip.

ROAD Baltimore is reached by I-95, the major east coast route, and from the north by I-83. The city is surrounded by I-695, the Baltimore Beltway, from which roads lead in to the city centre.

GETTING AROUND Most major attractions are within walking distance of the Inner Harbor; sights further out are reached by tourist trolley or MTA bus and rail services. Intended to serve commuters, not tourists, buses may involve a number of transfers. None of the Metro's half-dozen downtown stations is closer than three blocks from Inner Harbor.

More fun, and cheaper, is the Water Taxi, tel: (410) 563-3901 or (800) 658-8947, a year-round service with 15 stops near sights around the Inner and Outer Harbors. Passengers are given a useful *Waterfront Guide* with maps and information on attractions and restaurants. It operates Wed–Sun Nov–Mar, daily the rest of the year. Buy an all-day pass on board.

A nicely done brochure (free at the TIC) will lead you on a tour of the Historic Mount Vernon neighbourhood.

INFORMATION

CITY MAP – inside back cover

TOURIST OFFICES **Baltimore Area Visitors Center**, next to the Light Street Pavillion at Harbor Place; tel: (877) 225-8466, www.baltimore.org. Well located among the major waterfront attractions but crowded during busy periods.

Maryland Office of Tourism Development, Department of Business and Economic Development, 217 E Redwood St, Baltimore, MD 21201; tel: (410) 767-6270; www.mdisfun.org.

SAFETY The usual commonsense precautions apply. Don't walk around alone late at night, and stick to well-lit streets.

MONEY Cash machines in Baltimore-Washington International Airport are located at the Main Terminal, Pier C; also at nearly all downtown banks.

POST AND PHONES The main post office is at 900 E Fayette St; tel: (410) 655-9832. When using the phone you must dial the area code even for local calls.

You can buy tickets, often discounted, for museums, concerts, tours and cruises at the City Life Tickets kiosk, Inner Harbor Promenade, West Shore (between Harborplace and Maryland Science Center); tel: (410) 396-8342.

ACCOMMODATION

As in most major cities, budget accommodation is scarce, but you can save by staying 3–4 miles from the Inner Harbor; and there are offers in the current issue of the

Baltimore Quick Guide and Baltimore Street Map and Visitor Guide, both available at the TIC.

A useful reservation service is at http://baltimore.lodging.com.

Comfort Inn $$ 6700 Security Blvd, West Baltimore; tel: (410) 281-1800. Ten miles from the Inner Harbor; offers airport shuttle and free breakfast.
Holiday Inn Express $$$ 1401 Bloomfield Ave; tel: (410) 646-1700. Four miles from the Inner Harbor, with generous continental breakfast.
Mr Mole Bed and Breakfast $$$ 1601 Bolton St; tel: (410) 728-1179. Highly regarded non-smoking accommodation in an 1870 renovated terraced house furnished with antiques. Complimentary Dutch-style breakfast.
Days Inn Baltimore/Inner Harbor $$$$ 100 Hopkins Pl.; tel: (410) 576-1000. Children under 17 stay free.

FOOD AND DRINK

You could spend two weeks dining in a different Baltimore restaurant every night and still not sample all the ethnic cuisines served in the downtown area and central communities like Fells Point and Little Italy. Seafood is abundant, with crab cakes a local speciality. Buy food for picnics at Lexington Market, 400 W Lexington St; open Mon–Sat 0800–1800 or Broadway Market in Fells Point; open Mon–Sat 0700–1800.

Bertha's $ 734 S Broadway, Fells Point; tel: (410) 327-5795. *The* place to go for mussels, chowder and afternoon tea with scones.
Germano's Trattoria $$300 S High St, Little Italy; tel: (410) 752-4515. Busy place specialising in good Tuscan fare.
Henninger's Tavern $$–$$$ 1812 Bank St, Fells Point; tel: (410) 342-2172; dinner Tues–Sat. American dishes served in a century-old tavern.
Peter's Inn $–$$ 504 South Ann St; tel: (410) 675-7313. Half a dozen tables in a bar-like surrounding; great creative food, with an eastern Mediterranean accent.
Ze Mean Bean Café $–$$$ 1739 Fleet St; tel: (410) 675-5999. Eastern European dishes (pierogi, blinchika filled with ricotta and wild mushrooms, kielbasa with sauerkraut) and Mediterranean specialities. Live music, BYOB.

HIGHLIGHTS

From the Harbour head north to Mount Vernon Place, to the **Washington Monument** ($). This was the first in the nation honouring George Washington, and the 228-step climb rewards you with a bird's-eye view of the city.

Just to the south, the **Basilica of the National Shrine of the Assumption of the Blessed Virgin Mary**, at Cathedral and Mulberry Sts, was the first Roman Catholic cathedral in the USA. Designed by Benjamin Latrobe, architect of the White House, it is one of the world's best examples of neo-classical architecture. Tours after 1045 Sun mass or by appointment.

Just west of the monument, the **Maryland Historical Society Museum and Library** ($) includes the Radcliffe Maritime Museum, the Darnall's Children's Gallery, Enoch Pratt House and Civil War and War of 1812 galleries. The original manuscript of 'The Star-Spangled Banner' is here, along with important collections of American silver, decorative arts and paintings: 201 W Monument St; open Tues–Fri 1000–1700, Sat 0900–1700.

A block away, the **Walters Art Gallery**, $$, 600 N Charles St, represents 5000 years of art from four continents, from medieval armour and Fabergé eggs to Ancient Egyptian and art nouveau. Asian arts are at **Hackerman House**, 1 Mount Vernon Pl.; open Tues–Sun 1100–1700, free Sat 1100–1200.

A little out of the way, but a sampling of Americana you won't find anywhere else, is the **Dime Museum**, at 1808 Maryland Ave, near North St; tel: (410) 230-0263, www.dimemuseum.com. This bizarre and often hilarious collection of curios represents an early type of 'museum' that evolved into the travelling carnival sideshow. The 9-foot mummified 'Amazon' and the unicorn are highlights. Open Wed–Fri 1200–1500, Sat–Sun 1100–1600; $.

Another offbeat but surprisingly interesting attraction is the **National Museum of Dentistry**, at 31 S Greene St; tel: (410) 706-0600, www.dentalmuseum.umaryland.edu. The lively collection, beautifully displayed, features Queen Victoria's private dental tools and George Washington's legendary dentures, which are not made of wood, as commonly believed. Open Wed–Sat 1000–1600, Sun 1300–1600, $.

Inner Harbor: the highlight of the waterfront is the restored USS *Constellation* ($), launched in Baltimore as a sloop of war in 1854. Her missions included blocking slave ships off Africa. The *Pride of Baltimore II* is a replica of the famous Baltimore clipper, many of which were built between the Revolutionary War and the mid-19th century.

HARBOUR CRUISES

The topsail schooner *Clipper City*, tel: (410) 539-6277, www.sailingship.com, makes two-hour sailing tours from Harborplace, departing from the pier next to the Science Center Mon–Sat 1200 and 1500, Sun 1500 and 1800, **$$$**. At Fells Point, the tall ship *Nighthawk*, tel: (410) 276-7447, cruises daily from the Thames St Pier, and the replica paddle-wheeler steamboat *Harbor Belle*, tel: (410) 764-3928, departs Fri 1730 for a cocktail cruise and Sat 1915 for a buffet dinner sunset cruise.
Baltimore Harbor Tours, tel: (410) 783-4660, docks its boats opposite the TIC at Inner Harbor, offering hour-long narrated cruises.

> **A Baseball Legend**
>
> The new, updated home of the Baltimore Orioles, Oriole Park at Camden Yards, seats 48,000 fans. Daily tours (Mar–Dec) include the scoreboard control room and press box, and interactive computer and laser technology enable you to stand in the batter's box and slam at the ball; tel: (410) 547-6234. The birthplace of one of baseball's greats, Babe Ruth, is nearby in Pratt St and can also be visited.

The 160-ft topsail schooner sails as Maryland's goodwill ambassador, but you can board if it's in port; tel: (410) 539-115.

Three more ships are part of **Baltimore Maritime Museum**: the coastguard cutter *Taney* is the only ship still afloat that survived the attack on Pearl Harbor; the US submarine *Torsk* sank the last Japanese combatant ship of World War II; and the *Chesapeake* is a 1930s floating lighthouse. $, tel: (410) 396-3453; open Mon–Fri 0930–1700, Sat–Sun 0930–2000; Fri–Sun 0930–1700 (Dec–Feb).

Next door is the **National Aquarium**, a world-class aquatic museum, where 7000 creatures, representing at least 500 species of fish, birds, reptiles, amphibians and marine mammals, live in recreated habitats. Highlights are a giant octopus, an Atlantic coral reef, an Open Ocean exhibit that brings visitors face to face with sharks, and a reproduced South American rain forest. Dolphins perform daily in 25-min shows. $$, open daily 1000–1800 (Fri–Sat until 2000); opens 0900 July–Aug.

Across the harbour is the **Maryland Science Center**, covering space exploration, television, energy and Chesapeake Bay through hands-on exhibits. The IMAX® theatre has a screen five storeys high, and the Davis Planetarium has excellent shows. $$, 601 Light St; open daily 1000–1800 (1000–2000 Fri–Sun in summer).

Away from the Center: the star-shaped brick fort at the end of E Fort Ave is **Fort McHenry National Monument**, sacred to Americans. It was built in 1790, and successfully thwarted the British attack on Baltimore in 1814. (The battle inspired Francis Scott Key to compose 'The Star-Spangled Banner', the national anthem.) You'll see officers' quarters, guardrooms, and powder magazine; re-enactments of life in the garrison are presented by guardsmen in period uniform on weekend afternoons mid-June–Aug. $, open daily 0800–1700 (0800–2000 June–Aug).

Also a little way out of the city centre is **Mount Clare Museum House** in Carroll Park, Baltimore's only pre-revolutionary war mansion. Built in 1760, it is considered one of the finest examples of Georgian architecture in the USA. The 18th- and 19th-century furniture is original to the house. $, tel: (410) 837-3262; tours hourly Tues–Fri 1000–1500, Sat–Sun 1300, 1400, 1500.

A bit out of the centre in the opposite direction is the outstanding **Baltimore Museum of Art**, whose post-Impressionist and modern art collection includes upwards of 500 works by Henri Matisse. While the Old Masters are well represented, along with ed, along with African, Asian and other arts, the museum's American decorative arts are particularly noteworthy, displayed chronologically to show the changes in styles and tastes through the country's history. $, open Wed–Fri 1100–1700, Sat–Sun 1100–1800; tel: (410) 396-7100. Take MTA bus no. 3 or 11.

NIGHTLIFE

Along with top-class music and theatre, Baltimore has a busy club and pub scene, with comedy and dance clubs and live bands in bars and taverns.

The Vagabond Players, 806 S Broadway, Fells Point; tel: (410) 563-9135. Affordable, quality theatre year-round Fri–Sun.

Fells Point Corner Theater, 251 S Ann St; tel: (410) 276-7837 or 466-8341. Premières of off-Broadway plays Fri–Sun.

Baltimore Opera Company, Lyric Opera House, 140 W Mount Royal Ave; tel: (410) 727-6000. Resident company for grand opera with international artists and full orchestra.

Baltimore Symphony Orchestra, Joseph Meyerhoff Symphony Hall, 12121 Cathedral St; tel: (410) 783-8000. High-profile programmes with guest performers.

Peabody Conservatory of Music, 1 E Mount Vernon Pl.; tel: (410) 659-8124. Student and guest artist recitals, symphony and opera.

Fat Lulu's, 1818 Maryland Ave; tel: (410) 685-4665. Jazz and blues with your Cajun and Creole meal.

Annapolis, just 25 miles to the south, is one of America's most charming small cities. It rises from a boat-filled harbour to a gracious brick-clad hill top crowned by a State House built at the time of the American Revolution. It was, briefly, the nation's capital in 1783–4. Founded in 1649, the entire city is today a National Historic Landmark, with many houses and public buildings more than 200 years old. It has more surviving Colonial buildings than anywhere else in the USA. The nautical character remains, bolstered by the US Naval Academy, whose buildings fill the eastern end of town and whose cadets are a vibrant part of the community.

GETTING THERE AND GETTING AROUND

RAIL/BUS MTA buses link Baltimore and Annapolis, also an hour apart. Greyhound/Trailways buses connect Annapolis to Washington, DC, 45 mins away.

ROAD Rte 301/50 runs east–west across the north of Annapolis. Follow Rte 70 south to the city centre. Rte 2 leads from the south to Rte 450 W, which ends near the State House.

GETTING AROUND Narrow streets, while lovely for strolling, leave few parking places. It's best to park all day (at a reasonable rate) at the Navy-Marine Corps Memorial Stadium, north of College Creek, and take the Annapolis Trolley Express Shuttle downtown. It stops at the visitor centre, Maryland Ave, the Naval Academy and Main St.

Most attractions are an easy walk apart in the central area. Other places – especially the restaurants along Spa and Back Creeks – are reached by Jiffy Water Taxi, Slip 20, City Dock. In summer (mid-May–early Sept) boats depart hourly: Mon–Thur 0930–2400, Fri 0930–0100, Sat 0900–0100, Sun 0900–2400; shorter hours during spring and autumn.

INFORMATION

TOURIST OFFICES **Annapolis and Anne Arundel County Visitors Bureau,** 26 W St, Annapolis, MD 21401; tel: (410) 280-0445. A tourist information booth is located on the City Dock. Free parking is available at the West St office.

ACCOMMODATION

Annapolis has 20 B&Bs in the historic district alone, with budget motels along Rte 301/50. During late May and all of October, accommodation is almost impossible to find.

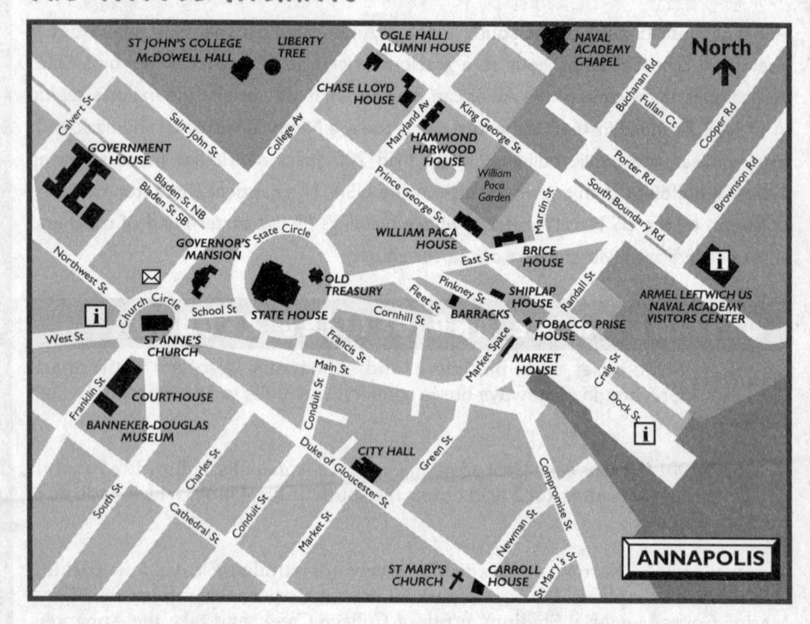

Annapolis Accommodations, 66 Maryland Ave, Annapolis, MD 21401, tel: (410) 280-0900 or (800) 715-1000, is a useful reservation service.

MainStay Suites $$–$$$ 120 Admiral Cochrane Dr.; tel: (800) 660-MAIN. A bargain for those with a car, offering full kitchens, pool and weekday breakfast.

Historic Inns of Annapolis $$$–$$$$ 16 Church Circle; tel: (410) 263-2641. Three inns from the 18th and early 19th centuries – the Maryland Inn, Governor Calvert House and Robert Johnson House – are clustered around the two circles at the heart of Annapolis.

Gibson's Lodgings $$$–$$$$ 110 Prince George St; tel: (410) 268-5555. Near the City Dock in the historic district, with courtyard parking, complimentary sherry and continental breakfast.

FOOD AND DRINK

Downtown, the greatest concentration of eateries is along West St, Main St and around the City Dock. Eastport/Annapolis Neck south of Spa Creek, at the end of Duke of Gloucester St, has an eclectic mix.

City Dock Café $ 18 Market Space. Small, casual and friendly coffee house with freshly baked confections. A good place for people-watching.

Acme Bar and Grill $–$$ 163 Main St; tel: (410) 280-6486. Serves American cuisine – chicken wings, crab cakes and pastas – in a classic saloon setting, daily 1130–0200.

Ram's Head Tavern $–$$ 33 W St; tel: (410) 268-4545. Restaurant and home of the Fordham Brewing Co., a traditional tavern featuring 26 beers on draught, and lunch and dinner daily. Frequent live music.

Carrol's Creek $$–$$$ 410 Severn Ave, Eastport; tel: (410) 269-1406. Overlooking the marina and a superb view of Annapolis, serving inspired versions of regional seafood and more.

Middleton Tavern Oyster Bar and Restaurant $$–$$$ 2 Market Space; tel: (410) 263-3323. Traditional Maryland fare served in a restored 1750 building overlooking the harbour.

HIGHLIGHTS

TOURS

Knowledgeable guides in Colonial costume lead 2-hr tours daily of the historic district ($$). Contact **Three Centuries Tours of Annapolis**, 48 Maryland Ave; tel: (410) 263-5401. Self-guided audio-cassette tours may be purchased at the **Historic Annapolis Foundation Museum Store**, 77 Main St, open daily; tel: (410) 268-5576. Or be guided by an architectural historian ($$) from **Annapolis Walkabout**, 223 S Cherry Grove Ave; tel: (410) 263-8253.

Annapolis is a joy for budget travellers, rich in free sights. The streets themselves, and the houses that line them, are an open-air architectural museum with more than 1000 buildings of 15 different styles predating 1900.

Begin at the top of the hill, with the **Maryland State House**, on State Circle. The focal point of Annapolis and the country's oldest state house in continuous use, this was once the capitol of the USA and was the setting for George Washington's resignation as commander-in-chief and the ratification of the Treaty of Paris, which officially ended the American Revolution. Tours daily 1100 and 1500.

Government House, also on State Circle, was built during the Victorian period, to be the official residence of the Governor of Maryland. Open Tues–Thur 1000–1400 (closed Wed Jan–Mar). Tours of its collection of art and antiques are by reservation; tel: (410) 974-3531.

Church Circle adjoins State Circle via School St, and in its centre is the graceful **St Anne's Church**, rebuilt in 1859, more than 150 years after its founding. Its Tiffany window won first prize at the Chicago World's Fair in 1893; open daily 0800–1800.

Just off Church Circle, **Banneker-Douglass Museum**, at 84 Franklin St, is the state repository of African-American cultural material. Collections include artefacts and photographs of black life in Maryland, as well as African and African-American art and rare books; tel: (410) 974-2893. Open Tues–Fri 1000–1500, Sat 1200–1600.

All in the same area, between State Circle and the Naval Academy, are three outstanding historic homes to visit. **Chase-Lloyd House**, $, 22 Maryland Ave, was built in 1769 by a signatory to the Declaration of Independence. The Georgian town house, noted for fine interior detail, is open Tues–Sat 1400–1600 (Tues, Fri and Sat only, Jan–Feb); tel: (410) 263-2723.

Hammond-Harwood House, at 19 Maryland Ave, was built in 1774 for Matthias Hammond, a Revolutionary patriot. Considered one of the most beautiful examples of late Colonial architecture, the house stands in a charming garden and features late 18th- and early 19th-century Maryland furniture and paintings. $, tel: (410) 269-1714; open Mon–Sat 1000– 1600, Sun 1200–1600.

William Paca House and Garden, 186 Prince George St, home of another signatory, was built between 1763 and 1765 in a 2-acre garden featuring five terraces of formal parterres. $, tel: (410) 263-5553; open Mon–Sat 1000–1600, Sun 1200–1600 (Fri–Sun only Jan–Feb).

South of the Circle, towards the bridge to Eastport, is **Charles Carroll House**, 107 Duke of Gloucester St. The restored birthplace of Charles Carroll, one of the wealthiest men in Colonial America and the only Catholic to sign the Declaration of Independence, has terraced gardens. $, tel: (410) 269-1737; open Fri and Sun 1200–1600, Sat 1000–1400.

In Eastport itself, the **Barge House Museum**, on Bay Shore Dr. (end of Second St), features boat building, historic and maritime artefacts, maps and photographs, Sat 1100–1600 and by appointment; tel: (410) 268-1802.

THE NAVAL ACADEMY

Annapolis is synonymous with the US Navy, and the Naval Academy has several interesting sights, all of which are free. The Visitor Center, inside Gate 1, off King George St, is the starting point for guided tours; $, tel: (410) 263-6933; open daily 0900–1700 (until 1600 Dec–Feb).

Bancroft Hall is home to the entire brigade of midshipmen, with 1873 rooms along 5 miles of corridors; you can visit a sample midshipman's quarters.

The Chapel, often called the Cathedral of the Navy, contains Tiffany windows and the Crypt of John Paul Jones, naval hero of the American Revolution, whose remains were returned in 1905 after more than a century of obscurity in a Paris cemetery. Gallery of Ships is an exhibition of model ships dating from the 17th century, some made of bone and wood, in The Naval Academy Museum, which contains 50,000 items, including arms, uniforms, wartime exhibits, paintings and prints; open Mon–Sat 0900–1700, Sun 1100–1700.

SHOPPING

In spite of its popularity with visitors, Annapolis manages to maintain a small-town ambience, where shopkeepers welcome browsers along Main and West Sts and around the City Dock.

Watch potters work at Annapolis Pottery, 40 State Circle, and visit Historic Annapolis Foundation Museum Store, 77 Main St, for souvenirs that reflect the heritage of Annapolis, including reproductions of 18th-century artefacts and books. Save the Bay Shop, 188 Main St, sells books, clothing and gifts to support the Chesapeake Bay environment.

NIGHTLIFE

Annapolis is a lively, busy place, with around a dozen organisations involved in the performing arts. Major performances are staged at the **Maryland Hall for the Creative Arts**, 801 Chase St; tel: (410) 263-5544. Calendars for all events are published in *The Capital* daily, and *The Publick Enterprise*.

Annapolis Opera, tel: (410) 263-2710 or 267-8135. Performs opera, operettas and musicals year-round.
Annapolis Chorale, tel: (410) 263-1906. 150-voice chorus and chamber orchestra.
Annapolis Summer Garden Theatre, 143 Compromise St; tel: (410) 268-9212. Presents Broadway musicals nightly late May–early Sept.
Annapolis Symphony Orchestra, tel: (410) 269-1132. Performs a classical repertoire.
Ballet Theatre of Annapolis, tel: (410) 263-8289. Classical and modern ballet.
Colonial Players, 108 East St; tel: (410) 268-7373. Presents plays in a 180-seat theatre-in-the-round.

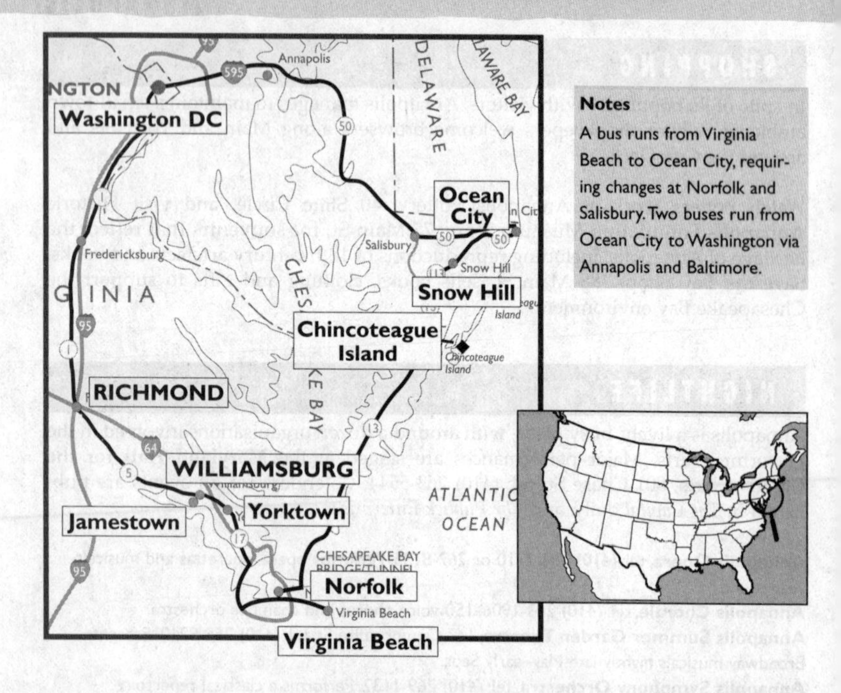

Notes

A bus runs from Virginia Beach to Ocean City, requiring changes at Norfolk and Salisbury. Two buses run from Ocean City to Washington via Annapolis and Baltimore.

DRIVING ROUTE

Leave Washington on I-395, taking exit 11 to Washington St through historic Alexandria, then the Mount Vernon Memorial Hwy to Mount Vernon (16 miles). Rte 235 joins Rte 1 south to Fredericksburg and, 60 miles further on, Richmond. Beside it is the faster I-95 (124 miles). From Richmond Rte 5 meanders to Williamsburg (179 miles). Colonial Parkway leads west to Jamestown and on to Yorktown (201 miles). Go south on Rte 17 to I-64, which leads through Newport News and Norfolk. For downtown Norfolk take exit 276, heading south on Rte 460 (Granby St) (227 miles). (For Virginia Beach, 13 miles further on, continue on I-64 to exit 284 and take Rte 44 east.) Atlantic Ave heads north, becoming Rte 60; turn right on Rte 13, signposted Chesapeake Bay Bridge-Tunnel. Leaving the bridge-tunnel, Rte 13 travels north up the narrow peninsula; sidetrack onto Rte 175 to Chincoteague Island (325 miles). From Pocomoke City, follow Rte 113 north through Snow Hill to Berlin then Rte 50 east to Ocean City (362 miles). From Ocean City, head north on Rte 528 and turn left on to Rte 90 to join Rte 50 for Salisbury (395 miles). Continuing north-west, Hwy 50 passes through Cambridge, then Easton (444 miles). Join Rte 301 and cross Chesapeake Bay to Annapolis (488 miles) (exit 24 leads into town on Rte 70 south). Rte 50 returns you to Washington (total 523 miles).

TIDEWATER DRIVING TOUR

Not quite in the Deep South, though filled with gracious plantations, Maryland and Virginia's tidewater country is a beautiful land all its own. From the gently rolling hills and well-groomed estates of the mainland to the flat farmlands and rough-and-ready watermen of the Eastern Shore peninsula, the region is diverse, interesting and beautiful.

Set like gems in this fine setting are such diverse places as the entire restored Colonial city of Williamsburg and the wild, barrier island of Chincoteague, where wild ponies roam. Spring comes early in a profusion of blooming trees and flowers; miles of beaches beckon in the summer; autumn paints the land in glorious colour, and winter is filled with holiday festivities and cultural events. Hospitality is the way of life all year round.

WASHINGTON — VIRGINIA BEACH

OTT Tables 320/564

Service	Bus	Bus	Rail	Bus	Bus	Rail	Bus	Bus	Rail	Bus	Rail	Bus
Days of operation	Daily	Daily	Daily	Daily	Daily	ex⑥⑦	ex⑥⑦	Daily	⑥⑦	⑥⑦	⑤	⑤
Special notes	**B**				**B**							
Washington A d.	0150	0705	0730	....	1245	1430	....	1455	1700	....	1750	....
Richmond **A** d.	0700	1030	0945	....	1530	1645	....	1845	1910	....	2010	....
Williamsburg d.	0800	1130	1104**s**	....	1630	1801	....	1945	2028	....	2128	....
Newport News d.	|	|	1150	1205	|	1850	1905	|	2115	2130	2215	2225
Norfolk d.	0945	1320	....	1250**s**	1815	....	1950	2115	....	2200	....	2255
Virginia Beach a.	1035	1355	....	1330	1850	....	2030	....	....	2230	....	2325

Special notes:
A–Additional trains run from Washington to Richmond at 0955, 1055, 1500⑥⑦, 1750①②③④, 1900ex⑥.
B–Change buses at Richmond. Additional service at 0040.
s–Calls to set down only.

RICHMOND

The state capital of Virginia and capital of the Confederacy between 1861 and 1865, Richmond offers historic sites, gardens, and pleasant diversions. Close by are Civil War battlefields and riverside plantation homes. Monument Ave, with its statues of Civil War generals and others, is considered one of America's most beautiful streets. The Fan District, with streets fanning out westwards from Monroe Park, is one of the largest intact Victorian neighbourhoods in the USA.

i **Richmond Metropolitan Convention and Visitors Bureau**, 401 North Third St, tel: (888) RICHMOND, (804) 782-2777, can assist with lodging reservations and provide a wide range of information. **Richmond Region Visitor Center**, 405 North Third St, tel: (804) 783-7450, is open daily 0900–1700 (until 1800 June–Aug). There are also Visitor Centers at Richmond International Airport, the Tredegar Iron Works, 470 Tredegar St, and at Ashland Hanover, 112 N Railroad Ave.

For reservations throughout the Richmond area, tel: (888) RICHMOND. **Americamps $** 11322 Air Park Rd, Ashland (20 miles north on Hwy 1), tel: (804) 798-5298, has camping.
William Catlin House B&B $$$ 2304 E Broad St; tel: (804) 780-3746. Circa-1845 B&B conveniently located in the historic Church Hill neighbourhood.
Linden Row Inn $$$ 100 E Franklin St; tel: (804) 783-7000. This row of Greek revival town houses comprises 70 upscale rooms. Daily wine-and-cheese socials.

Browse in the Fan District or in Shockoe Slip, bounded by 15th, 21st, Dock and Broad Sts, where many former ware-houses are now restaurants and bistros.
Dogwood Grille $$$ 1731 W Main St; tel: (804) 340-1984. Popular venue serving American and European cuisine.
O'Toole's $–$$ 4800 Forest Hill Ave; tel: (804) 233-1781. Family-owned place offering barbecued dishes.
Southern Culture $–$$$ 2229 West Main, in the Fan District; tel (804) 355-6939. Lively and casual, serving generous updated Southern dishes.
Strawberry Street Café $$–$$$ 421 N Strawberry St, in the Fan District; tel: (804) 353-6860. Famous for its salad bar and diverse menu.

HIGHLIGHTS

Richmond is going through major urban reconstruction in preparation for the 400-year anniversary celebrations of the state of Virginia, in the year 2007. Therefore, many of the city's favourite attractions are closed, or may be so in the near future. For the moment, at least, some landmarks remain accessible. **Virginia's State Capitol**, designed by Thomas Jefferson in 1785 as the first neo-classical building in the New World, is open Mon–Fri 0900–1700, Sat 1000–1600, Sun 1300–1600. Nearby, the **White House of the Confederacy** was the Civil War home of Confederate President Jefferson Davis. The adjacent museum claims the world's largest collection of Confederate artefacts. $, 1201 E Clay St; tel: (804) 649-1861; www.moc.org. Open Mon–Sat 1000–1700, Sun 1200–1700.

South of Washington, stop off at **Mount Vernon**. George and Martha Washington's beautifully maintained former home and gardens (see p.219).

A block west is the **Valentine Richmond History Center**, $, 1015 E Clay St, illustrating social history, decorative arts, costumes and architecture, and adjoining 1812 **Wickham House**, with outstanding neo-classical wall painting; tel: (804) 649-0711. Open Tues–Sat 1000–1700, Sun 1200–1700.

BARKSDALE THEATER

This well-known theatre company presents professional dramas, comedies and Broadway musicals year-round; 1601 Willow Lawn Dr., Richmond; tel: (804) 282-2620.

Church Hill is a historic neighbourhood, bounded by Broad, 29th, Main and 21st Sts. Here are some 70 (pre-Civil War) homes, many with cast-iron ornamentation. The new **Richmond National Battlefield Park Visitor Center,** located at the Tredegar Ironworks which supplied armaments for the Confederate army, can supply you with a detailed 97-mile self-guided motoring tour of battlefields and sites around Richmond: 500 Tredegar St; tel: (804) 226-1981; open daily 0900–1700.

SHIRLEY AND BERKELEY

Two particularly fine plantations border the James River, on Rte 5 between Richmond and Williamsburg. **Shirley**, Virginia's oldest plantation, has a unique flying staircase and fine antiques: $$, tel: (804) 829-5121; open daily 0900–1700. Just beyond is **Berkeley**, $$, open daily 0800–1700. Coach House Tavern, on the plantation, serves lunch and traditional dinners by candlelight: $$$, tel: (804) 829-6018.

The 1753 **Wilton House** typifies the opulent homes of wealthy planters, with noted interior panelling and antiques: $, 215 S Wilton Rd; tel: (804) 282-5936; open Tues–Sat 1000–1630, Sun 1330–1630. **Lewis Ginter Botanical Garden** has an extensive display of flowers, a magnificent glass-domed conservatory and a teahouse: $, 1800 Lakeside Ave; tel: (804) 262-9887; open daily 0900–1700.

WILLIAMSBURG

Don't confuse touristy Williamsburg, the town, with Colonial Williamsburg, a 173-acre museum town of houses, shops, taverns and public buildings peopled with costumed shopkeepers, craftsmen, soldiers, slaves, housewives and public officials – all vividly recalling Virginia's pre-Revolutionary capital in 1774. It provides a rare chance to step into another era, one very important to America's history.

i **Williamsburg Area Convention and Visitors Bureau**, 421 North Boundary St, Williamsburg, VA 23187; tel: (757) 253-0192 or (800) 368-6511; www.visitwilliamsburg.com, for information on the entire area.
Colonial Williamsburg Foundation, PO Box 1776, Williamsburg, VA 23187-1776; tel: (757) 220-7645 or (800) HIS-TORY (447-8679), arranges accommodation and dining reservations in the Historic Area. Purchase tickets at the **Visitor Center** on Colonial Parkway at Rte 60, tel: (757) 220-7645, see an introductory film, and pick up the *Visitor's Companion* for details and to help plan your time. Open Mon–Fri 0900–1700, Sat–Sun 0830–1800.

To reach the Historic Area use the shuttle buses (included in admission) or walk over the bridge from the visitor centre. There is a large free parking area here. Alternatively, park near Merchant's Square (there is a charge), and enter the complex at Duke of Gloucester St, the restored town's main thoroughfare.

Williamsburg is busiest Apr, May and Oct; cheapest in Jan and Feb. **Williamsburg Hotel and Motel Association**, tel: (800) 899-9462, runs a free reservations service. Private guest homes $–$$ are listed in the *Visitors' Guide*, which is available in advance. Guests in Colonial Williamsburg-owned hotels get discounted admission, free tours and preferential reservations in taverns (see p.236). The least expensive of these is:

Governor's Inn $$$ 506 N Henry St; tel: (757) 253-2277 or (800) HISTORY (447-8679). A modern motel three blocks from the Historic Area.
Colonial Gardens B&B $$–$$$ 1109 Jamestown Rd; tel: (757) 220-8087 or (800) 886-9715. In woodland 5 mins by car from Colonial Williamsburg, furnished with antiques.
There are excellent campsite facilities at KOA's twin sites: **Williamsburg KOA**, 5210 Newman Rd, tel: (757) 565-2907 or (800) KOA-1733, and **Colonial Central KOA**, 4000 Newman Rd, tel: (757) 565-2734 or (800) KOA-7609. Both have cabins.

Four Colonial taverns ($$–$$$) in the Historic Area serve dishes that would have been familiar to Redcoats and Patriots, in an atmosphere of minstrels and serving wenches:
Chowning's Tavern, tel: (757) 229-1000, recalls an English alehouse. Open daily 1100–2100.
Christiana Campbell's Tavern, tel: (757) 229-1000, was George Washington's favourite. Open Tues–Sat 0930–1430, 1700–2100.
The King's Arms Tavern, tel: (757) 229-1000, as posh as in Colonial times. Open daily 1130–1430, 1700–2130.
Shields Tavern, tel: (757) 229-1000, has a tasting sampler of 18th-century dishes. Open daily 1130–1500, 1700–2130.
Outside the restorations try **Chez Trinh** $–$$ 157 Monticello Ave; tel: (757) 253-1888. Vietnamese food in a casual atmosphere or to take away.
Old Chickahominy House $$ 1211 Jamestown Rd; tel: (757) 229-4689. A local favourite for plantation cooking in a non-touristy 18th-century setting. Open daily 0830–1015, 1130–1415.

Colonial Williamsburg ($$$) takes more than a full day to see. Begin with an Orientation Walk (daily 1000–1500). Along with the primary sites, visit the 20 shops – apothecary, blacksmith, carpenter, gunsmith, shoemaker, silversmith, wigmaker, etc. – where interesting demonstrations are always in progress.

HIGHLIGHTS The imposing **Governor's Palace** is a reconstruction of the 1722 residence of seven royal governors, furnished in 1770s style. The **Capitol** reconstructs the seat of colonial government from 1701. It was here that a resolution declaring independence from Britain was unanimously adopted in May 1776, nearly two months before the Declaration of Independence was adopted in Philadelphia. **Raleigh Tavern** reconstructs the 1717 tavern where patriots plotted these events.

Bruton Parish Church, in continuous use since 1715, may be toured Mon–Sat 0900–1700, Sun 1200–1700. The **Public Gaol** is where wrongdoers – including the pirate Blackbeard – were incarcerated. **Brush-Everard House** is another original building, showing slave life in Williamsburg.

Adjoining the restored area, the **Abby Aldrich Rockefeller Folk Art Center** preserves American folk art in 18 galleries, with a collection of primitives, weathervanes, toys, needlework and other folk arts. The **DeWitt Wallace Decorative Arts Gallery** on Francis St houses an exceptional collection of English and American decorative arts to 1830, including Virginia-made furniture; tel: (757) 220-7724. Both $, open daily 1000–1800.

Carter's Grove, Rte 60, east of Williamsburg, is an 18th-century James River plantation, with a colonial mansion once described as America's most beautiful house, slave quarters and the Winthrop Rockefeller Archaeology Museum, interpreting the partly reconstructed site of an early English settlement here. Tel: (757) 220-7645; open Tues–Sun 0900–1800 (1000–1600 Nov–Dec). $$, open daily 0900–1700 mid-June–Aug, 0900–1600 rest of year.

In contrast to tasteful Colonial Williamsburg's historic ambience, **Busch Gardens**, 3 miles south on Rte 60, is a theme-park version of 17th-century Europe, with thrill rides, live shows, eateries and shops. $$$$+ plus parking; tel: (757) 253-3350; open Fri–Sun (mid-Apr–mid-May); daily (mid-May–Aug); Fri–Tues (Sept–Oct); closed winter.

EVENTS DIARY

Happenings at Williamsburg tie in with the time of year, whether re-enacting political speeches of the day or recreating an 18th-century Christmas celebration. Check with Colonial Williamsburg, (800) HISTORY (447-8679), for seasonal festivities.

JAMESTOWN AND YORKTOWN

Tree-lined Colonial Parkway connects these two major sites in American history, on either side of Williamsburg. **Jamestown** was the first permanent English settlement in North America. A temporary structure acts as the Visitor Center (the more permanent one having been severely damaged by Hurricane Isabel in September 2003), but on-site guides are available to answer questions. You can tour excavated ruins of early homes, see the remains of the first industries established here and get some idea of how the first Anglo settlers set up their colony. $, open daily 0830–1630.

Jamestown Settlement, along Rte 31, depicts life for the first settlers in full-sized replicas of ships, a recreated fort and Powhatan Indian village; $$, tel: (757) 253-4838 or (888) 593-4682; open daily 0900–1700.

Yorktown Battlefield is where the British army under Lord Cornwallis surrendered to Washington's allied French and American forces in 1781, events which are described in a film and exhibits. You can see tents used by Washington and parts of a reconstructed British frigate; pick up a brochure and audiotape for self-guided driving tours. Highlights are Moore House, where the Articles of Capitulation were drafted, and Nelson House, home of patriot Thomas Nelson, open daily 0830–1730.

Yorktown Victory Center describes the American Revolution through a timeline walkway, galleries, a film, a recreated continental camp and 18th-century farm where costumed interpreters demonstrate cooking, military and rural skills. $, tel: (757) 253-4838 or (888) 593-4682; open daily 0900–1700.

The **Watermen's Museum** at 309 Water St, tel: (757) 887-2641, tells the story of those who sailed Chesapeake wooden craft. Open Tues–Sat 1000–1600, Sun 1300–1600.

Colonial National Historic Park, Colonial Parkway, Yorktown; tel: (757) 898-2410.

Nick's Seafood Pavilion $–$$$ Water St (near bridge); tel: (757) 887-5269. Local favourite for seafood.

Duke of York Motor Hotel $$–$$$ 508 Water St; tel: (757) 898-3232. Has a pool and restaurant.

NORFOLK AND VIRGINIA BEACH

Side-by-side cities, one dominated by the navy, the other by beaches, guard the entrance to Chesapeake Bay. Travellers with a passion for things nautical will explore the former, while those who enjoy fun-filled beach resorts will head east to Virginia Beach, where a 3-mile boardwalk borders part of its 35 miles of ocean and bayfront beaches.

Norfolk Convention and Visitors Bureau, 232 E Main St, tel: (757) 664-6620 or (800) 368-3097, can help find accommodation. Open daily 0830–1700.

Virginia Beach Information Center, 2101 Parks Ave, Suite 500; tel: (757) 436-4700; www.vbfun.com.

Comfort Inn Naval Base $$ 8051 Hampton Blvd; tel: (757) 451-0000. Inexpensive member of the familiar chain, with indoor heated pool.

Tides Inn $$ 7950 Shore Dr., Norfolk; tel: (757) 587-8781 or (800) 284-3035. Motel with outdoor pool, close to restaurants and shops.

In Virginia Beach, contact **City of Virginia Beach Reservations**, tel: (800) VA-BEACH (800) 822-3224) or to rent furnished cottages, Sandbridge Realty, 581 Sandbridge Rd, tel: (757) 426-6262 or (800) 933-4800.

Angie's Guest Cottage Hostel $ 302 24th St; tel: (357) 428-4690, www.angiescottage.com. B&B, hostel and duplex rooms a block from the beach and no curfew. Although hostel is open only Apr–Sept, nearby Ocean Cove Motel will accommodate out-of-season visitors.

Colonial Inn $$ 2809 Atlantic Ave; tel: (757) 428-5370. Clean, 'no-frills' accommodation with friendly staff. Indoor and outdoor pools and nature packages.

Comfort Inn Virginia Beach $$ 2800 Pacific Ave; tel: (757) 428-2203. Has a pool and includes continental breakfast.

THE CHESAPEAKE BAY BRIDGE-TUNNEL

Opened in 1964, this is nearly 18 miles long and an extraordinary feat of engineering that serpentines above and below the water. If you want to pause before going under the waves, there is a viewing point with café on the southernmost of the four man-made islands. Keep to the right of the entrance as you go through the toll, and make sure you do a U-turn to get back to the tunnel entrance afterwards – otherwise you will have to pay the toll again.

WATER TOURS

American Rover, a three-masted schooner modelled on the 19th-century Chesapeake Bay craft, takes narrated cruises under sail Apr–Oct: $$$, tel: (757) 627-SAIL; www.americanrover.com.

The world's largest naval base is best viewed by boat. Try the *Spirit of Norfolk*, $$$, tel: (757) 625-FUNN (3866), www.spiritofnorfolk.com, or Victory Rover Naval Base Cruises, $$, tel: (757) 627-7406.

For a nominal fare you can also ride on the *Waterside*, the charming little sternwheeler that acts as a ferry across the Elizabeth River to Portsmouth.

OTHER WATER TOURS

Virginia Aquarium and Marine Science Center offers seasonal boat trips, tel: (757) 425-3474, www.vmsm.com. Guided kayak tours by Kayak Nature Tours Ltd, tel: (757) 480-1999 or (888) 669-8368, www.TidewaterAdventures.com.

First Landings State Park and Natural Area Campground, 2500 Shore Dr.; tel: (757) 412-2300 for information, (800) 933-7275 for reservations. Also has housekeeping cabins. Open Mar–Dec.

Browse around Norfolk's waterfront and in the Ghent neighbourhood's turn-of-the-century streets. Try the **Baker's Crust Bread Market $–$$,** 330 W 21st St, tel: (757) 625-3600, for sandwiches, soups and salads – and a creperie in the back. Among Virginia Beach's hundreds of eateries, **Taste Unlimited $–$$** has three locations for sandwiches and picnics: 36th St and Pacific Ave, 4097 Shore Dr., and Hilltop West Shopping Center.

Mahi-Mah's $–$$ 615 Atlantic Ave; tel: (757) 437-8030. Panoramic views of the ocean and beaches over sushi and seafood. Winner of service awards.

Famous Uncle Al's at the Beach $ 300 28th St. Sells hot dogs – satisfying and cheap.

Mary's Restaurant $ 616 Virginia Beach Blvd; tel: (757) 428-1355. Popular 'all-American' diner.

HIGHLIGHTS Norfolk's **Nauticus** interprets the whole maritime world, from sciences and exploration to shipbuilding, international trade and warfare. High-tech exhibits let you navigate, chase submarines and design ships. You can also tour US Navy and foreign vessels in port. $$, 1 Waterside Dr.; tel: (757) 664-1000 or (800) 664-1080; open daily 1000–1800 (June–Aug); Tues–Sat 1000–1700, Sun 1200–1700, Sept–May.

Naval Station Norfolk, 9079 Hampton Blvd, is the world's largest naval installation. Forty-five minute guided bus tours ($) are offered throughout the year. Tel: (757) 444-7955 for current schedule.

MacArthur Memorial, $, MacArthur Sq; tel: (757) 441-2965; open Mon–Sat 1000–1700, Sun 1100–1700.

ENTERTAINMENT

The Waterside Festival Marketplace on Waterside Dr. has live entertainment and concerts. A brick promenade leads to Towne Point Park, venue for free outdoor concerts and festivals. Summertime begins enthusiastically in Virginia Beach with live entertainment along Beach St USA and a bevy of oceanfront festivals and events.

An artefact-filled museum devoted to the epochal life and times of the five-star general. Includes newsreel footage, photographs, uniforms, medals and the general's 1950 Chrysler Imperial limousine. MacArthur and his wife are interred beneath the rotunda of this 19th-century building, Norfolk's former city hall.

For a panorama, climb **Old Cape Henry Lighthouse** in Virginia Beach, the oldest government-built lighthouse in the US. Built in 1791 to warn mariners entering Chesapeake Bay, it is located near the site where America's first English settlers touched shore in the New World in 1607 before heading to Jamestown. $, open daily 1000–1700 (Jan–Nov).

NORFOLK TROLLEY TOUR departs from Norfolk's Waterside Festival Marketplace for hop-on hop-off tours through historic downtown and neighbourhoods. $, Waterside Dr.; tel: (757) 640-6300; tours daily 1200–1600 (May–Sept).

Birdwatchers should visit **Back Bay National Wildlife Refuge**, 7700 acres of beach, dunes, woodland and marsh filled with migratory waterfowl. Dec–Jan is best for peregrine falcons and bald eagles. The 10 miles of hiking and biking trails are open daily dawn–dusk. $, 4005 Sandpiper Rd; tel: (757) 721-2412; visitor centre open Mon–Fri 0800–1600, Sat–Sun 0900–1600.

CHINCOTEAGUE ISLAND

Chincoteague is famous for the wild ponies that roam it, frequently spotted along the roadsides. The island is also famous for oysters, shown at the **Oyster and Maritime Museum** in displays of live sea creatures. $, 7125 Maddox Blvd, Chincoteague; open 1100–1700 daily (May–mid-Sept); Sat–Sun (mid-Sept–Nov).

On the way to Chincoteague, on Rte 175, is the **NASA Visitor Center**, open Thur–Mon 1000–1600 (Mar–Nov); daily (July–Aug). Get maps of biking and hiking trails at the **National Seashore Visitors Center**, tel: (757) 336-6577; open 0800–1800 (mid-June–Aug), 0900–1600 (spring and autumn).

i **Eastern Shore Tourism Commission**, PO Box 460, Melfa, VA 23410; tel: (757) 786-2460.

Cape Charles House B&B **$$** 645 Tazewell Ave; tel: (757) 331-4920. Near the beach, with bicycles available.
There are also tent pitches and caravan sites at **Kiptopeke State Park**, Cape Charles; $, tel: (757) 331-2267.
Places to stay are more plentiful at Chincoteague than further south, but also pricier.

Colour Section
(i) Maine (pp. 157–165), Bar Harbor; Portland Indoor Market
(ii) Washington (pp. 204–220), Jefferson Memorial; National Air and Space Museum
(iii) The Inner Harbor at Baltimore (pp. 221–226); on parade in Williamsburg (p. 235)
(iv) Chicago skyline at night (pp. 325–339); inset: *antebellum* house in Charleston (pp. 262–268)

SHERMAN'S
BOOK
SHERMAN'S BOOK STORE
A.J. KENNEDY'S
Fruit & Vegetables
BOREALIS

NASA
66670
U.S. AIR FORCE
USAF
FUEL VENT

Miss Molly's $$$–$$$$ 4141 Main St; tel: (757) 336-6686. Serves full breakfast and afternoon tea; open Mar–Dec.
Duck Haven Cottages $$$ 6582 Church St; tel: (757) 336-6290. Minutes from the beach.

EN ROUTE

From the cheery harbour at Crisfield, summer passenger boats go to **Tangier Island**, 12 miles out in Chesapeake Bay. Its residents (fewer than 1000 of them) trace their ancestry back to 1686 and speak with an accent that even many Americans have difficulty in understanding. Tangier Island Cruises, 1001 W.Main St, Crisfield; tel: (800) 863-2338.

WHERE NEXT?

From the tranquillity of Chincoteague, the route continues north to the contrasting non-stop summer party that is **Ocean City**, *included in the New York to Ocean City route* *(see p. 189).*

SNOW HILL

The peninsula widens as you cross into Maryland, and the land is deeply cut by tidal estuaries lined by wildlands and cypress trees. Paddle among them from Snow Hill, renting a canoe from Pokomoke River Canoe: $$, tel: (410) 632-1700. Alternatively walk the self-guided tour of the town's 100-plus century-old homes. Nearby **Furnace Town** is a recreation of the 1840s village surrounding the enormous brick iron furnace, featuring broom and blacksmith shops, a smokehouse and a print shop. $, tel: (410) 632-2032; open daily 1100–1700 (Apr–Oct).

i **Worcester County Tourism Office**, PO Box 208, 105 Pearl St, Snow Hill; tel: (410) 632-3617.

River House Inn, 201 E Market St; tel: (410) 632-2722. A gracious mansion with warm hosts.

MARYLAND'S EASTERN SHORE

Some of the loveliest villages and towns are in this part of Maryland, separated from the rest of the state by Chesapeake Bay. Close to Rte 50 are Salisbury, Cambridge, Easton, Oxford and St Michaels, each with streets lined by gracious historic homes. It would be a shame to miss any of them.

Salisbury's reconstruction following a fire in 1886 created the Newtown neighbourhood, street after street of fine Victorian architecture. The Ward Museum of Wildfowl Art shows decoy carving as a fine art, with the world's most comprehensive collection of wildfowl carving. $, 909 Schumaker Dr.; open Mon–Sat 1000–1700, Sun 1200–1700.

Ocean City's municipal bus service runs round the clock and costs $1 for all day travel.

FOR FREE

Salisbury Zoo, on the banks of a stream, has some 400 mammals, birds and reptiles, including spectacled bears, spider monkeys, jaguars, bison and exotic birds in naturalistic habitats. It is open daily 0800–1630 (until 1930 in summer).

Settled in 1682, **Easton** is an attractive community of quaint, tree-lined streets, voted one of America's top 100 small towns. **St Michaels**'s postcard-perfect lighthouse is now a museum.

i **Wicomico County Convention and Visitors Bureau**, Rte 13, Salisbury, MD 21801; tel: (410) 548-4914 or (800) 332-TOUR.

Dorchester County Tourism, 203 Sunburst Hwy, Cambridge, MD 21613; tel: (410) 228-1000.

Talbot County Conference and Visitors Bureau, PO Box 1366, Talbot Chamber Building, Tred Avon Sq., Easton, MD 21601; tel: (410) 822-4606.

The Bishop's House $$–$$$ 214 Goldsborough St, Easton; tel: (410) 820-7290 or (800) 223-7290. B&B in a restored Victorian villa furnished in period style.

Legal Spirits $$–$$$ 42 E Dover St, Easton; tel: (410) 820-0033. Maryland crab cakes and massive salads in a former 1922 music hall decorated in Prohibition speakeasy style.

OCEAN CITY

Ocean City and Assateague Island are covered on pages 189–190.

WHERE NEXT?

From Ocean City, the route described on pp. 184–190 continues up the coast all the way to New York. Annapolis and Baltimore (pp. 221–231) are alternative destinations to returning to Washington DC.

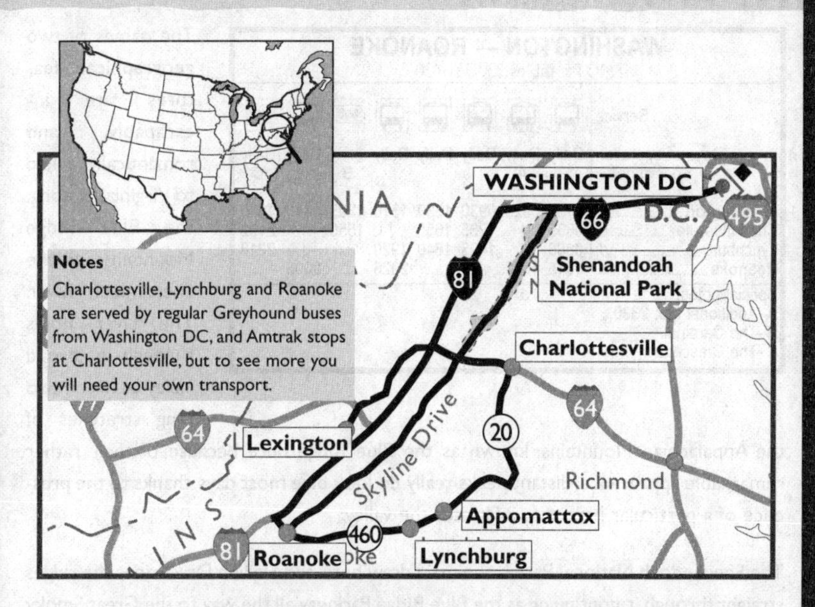

Notes

Charlottesville, Lynchburg and Roanoke are served by regular Greyhound buses from Washington DC, and Amtrak stops at Charlottesville, but to see more you will need your own transport.

Driving Route

By car from Washington, the quickest way to Shenandoah National Park is along I-66 to Front Royal, the northern entrance to Skyline Drive (78 miles). Just over 100 miles south, this becomes the Blue Ridge Parkway, which continues to Roanoke (268 miles).

If you break the journey at Waynesboro (210 miles from Washington), Hwy 340 cuts across a few miles to Rte 11 south, which then takes you to Lexington (240 miles), and on to Natural Bridge (252 miles). From here, I-81 runs down to Roanoke (about 292 miles). From Roanoke Hwy 460 heads east to Lynchburg (347 miles) and then Appomattox (372 miles). From Appomattox to Charlottesville it's an enjoyable drive along a few back roads: take Rte 24 east to Hwy 60 east (392 miles). Turn right, and at Sprouse's Corner (399 miles), turn left onto Hwy 15 north. After ! mile turn left onto Rte 20 north, which takes you into Charlottesville (436 miles).

Charlottesville can also be reached from the southern end of Skyline Drive via I-64 or the prettier Hwy 250, and directly from Washington by Hwy 29 off I-66 (95 miles).

WASHINGTON — ROANOKE
OTT Tables 330/331/630

Service	Bus	Bus	Bus	Bus	Bus	Rail	Bus	Rail
Days of operation	Daily	Daily	Daily	Daily	Daily	③⑤⑦	Daily	Daily
Special notes		A				B		C
Washington d.	0150	0925	0930	1330	1310	1305	1740	1840
Charlottesville d.	0655	|	1235	1650	|	1550	|	2102
Lynchburg d.	0900	|	1425	1840	1920	....	|	2218
Roanoke a.	1015	1600	....	....	2025	....	0005	....

Special notes:
A–Additional trip: 2330.
B–The Cardinal.
C–The Crescent.

The names of two geographical features are inescapably and romantically linked to Virginia by song: the Blue Ridge Mountains and the Shenandoah River. The river flows through a broad valley between two long stretches of the Appalachian Mountains, known as the Blue Ridge here because of their rather remarkable appearance: distant peaks really do look blue most days, thanks to the presence of a particular haze that infiltrates the valley.

The Shenandoah National Park is the main draw here, and Skyline Drive rides the ridges straight through it, continuing as the Blue Ridge Parkway all the way to the Great Smoky Mountains of North Carolina. Further south in the Shenandoah Valley, the towns of Lexington and Roanoke have interesting cores and merit a brief stop.

East of the mountains lie several sites of historical importance. Appomattox is a fascinating little village and site of the signing of papers that ended the Civil War. Lynchburg and Charlottesville are attractive small cities, and the area around Charlottesville is Virginia's wine country: several dozen wineries here give free tours and tastings. Nearby is Thomas Jefferson's wonderful mansion of Monticello.

SHENANDOAH NATIONAL PARK

ENTRANCES TO THE PARK

There are four road entrances: **Front Royal** (via I-66), **Thornton Gap** (via Hwy 211), **Swift Run Gap** (via Hwy 33), and **Rockfish Gap** (via Hwy 250 and I-64).

Straddling the eastern ridge of the Blue Ridge Mountains, Shenandoah National Park extends for about 80 miles north-east to south-west. You can traverse it along **Skyline Drive** in less than 3 hours – but only those with a soul of stone could fail to stop and take in the many stunning views, or embark on a short hike. The park is open year-round ($), though Skyline Drive may be closed at times because of bad weather conditions. There is no public transport to or through the park.

WILDLIFE IN THE PARK

The mountains are home to an estimated 500 black bears. There are two species of poisonous snake: the copperhead and rattlesnake. Less fearsome creatures include Virginia white-tail deer, red and grey foxes, skunks, bobcats, raccoons, groundhogs and chipmunks. More than 1000 species of plantlife are found in the park, including 18 types of orchid (picking flowers is forbidden). Most of the park's trees are deciduous, with oaks and hickories predominating.

Skyline Drive affords drivers the luxury of enjoying the scenery with no physical exertion – viewpoints grace both sides of the road, so you *could* just wheel on down the road without even getting out, but this defeats the purpose of being in the mountains. There are some 300 miles of trails here, and the brochure given out at the park entrances gives some tips on hikes – everything from quick jaunts to take in a view or a waterfall, to longer circuits that can take several hours or even days. The Appalachian Trail, which extends over 2200 miles from Maine to Georgia, winds through the park, marked with a white blaze. To plan longer hikes, including overnight camping, pick up a map at any visitor centre.

BIRD-SPOTTING

Most commonly seen, especially from Skyline Drive, are the turkey vulture and black vulture. The turkey vulture, also known as a buzzard, has a wingspan up to 6 ft and a red head; the smaller black vulture has a pale patch on the underside of each wing. Wild turkeys, the largest of the park's bird species, are frequently seen too, especially in the northern section.

Skyline Drive continues south some 350 miles as the **Blue Ridge Parkway**, linking up with the Great Smoky Mountains National Park in North Carolina. While less 'developed' than Shenandoah National Park, the Parkway has much to offer. Virginia's **Explore Park**, at milepost 115, is a living history museum on 1300 acres, featuring a settlement from the 19th century, with costumed interpreters, a Native American village and bluegrass musicians. $, open Sat–Mon, 0900–1700 (Apr–Oct).

TWO MINI-WALKS

Just north of Skyland is a 1.5-mile walk up to **Stony Man Mountain**, or take the 0.7-mile stroll down to **Dark Hollow Falls** from just south of Big Meadows.

ON THE HOOF

An exhilarating way of exploring the area is on horseback. There are stables with horses for hire at Skyland, and a guide accompanies all trips. Tel: (540) 999-2210.

i All entrances to Shenandoah National Park are staffed with helpful rangers, who give out maps and information. There are regular visitor centres at Dickey Ridge (Mile 4.6) and Big Meadows (Mile 51), both open daily 0900–1700. For general park information, tel: (540) 999-3500.

Two lodges – at Skyland (Mile 41.7) and Big Meadows (Mile 51.2) – offer motel-type accommodation and rustic cabins for rent, $$$. A few cabins are also available at Lewis Mountain (Mile 57.5). The lodges are usually open early April–Nov and Lewis Mountain cabins May–late Oct; it is imperative to book well in advance: tel: 1 (800) 999-4714. There are four camp sites, at Big Meadows, Mathews Arm (Mile 22.2), Lewis Mountain and Loft Mountain (Mile 79.5). Reserve in advance for Big Meadows, and arrive early to get a spot at the others.

There are dining facilities every 20 miles or so along Skyline Drive, and you can pick up groceries at Skyland, Big Meadows and Loft Mountain (all Apr–Oct only).

LEXINGTON

Home to two universities and several historic buildings, Lexington is a pleasant place to break the journey and soak up small-town Virginia. The presence of the **Virginia Military Institute** (VMI) has much to do with the town's identity: it supplied the Confederacy with soldiers throughout the Civil War, and two of its most famous sons have museums here in their honour. Stonewall Jackson, a celebrated commander of the Confederate army, taught at VMI and owned a house in the centre of town which has been restored. George C Marshall, author of the Marshall Plan to rebuild countries destroyed in World War II, graduated with the institute's class of 1901. Main St and Nelson St have some quaint boutiques and antique shops.

i A visitor centre is located at 106 E Washington St, tel: (540) 463-3777.

Of the many motels on the northern edge of town, **EconoLodge** $, tel: (540) 463-7371, is the cheapest.
Tourist Home $ 216 W Washington St; tel: (540) 463-3075. No real name but remarkably cheap, $10 a bed.
The Southern Inn Restaurant, 37 S Main St. Features tasty main dishes and local wines, with live music Fri and Sat nights.

EN ROUTE

NATURAL BRIDGE

The 90-ft span of this natural stone bridge is part of Rte 11, but you may scarcely be aware of it until you marvel at it from the bank of Cedar Creek 215 ft below. The setting is beautifully rural, but the lure of tourist dollars means an extravagant hotel, a silly wax museum, and an admission fee ($$) to see the archway. Despite these annoyances, the bridge is quite spectacular, and a path beneath it leads along the creek to some deep-pocket caverns.

ROANOKE

Roanoke is a surprisingly urbane city with enough attractions to keep you busy for a few hours at least. It was settled by German, Welsh and Scottish immigrants in the mid-18th century, but didn't come into its own until over a hundred years later. A slight European tinge pervades, from an ochre-coloured neo-classical church to the very German-looking Hotel Roanoke. Greyhound

In operation since 1882, the open-air farmers' market sets up daily at the intersection of Market St and Campbell St.

buses pull in to 26 Salem Ave, right in the centre.

The central area has the feel of the important industrial centre it once was, and the nearby railway tracks seem to assert its continued sense of purpose. Campbell St is a trendy stretch of arty shops and international restaurants – good for a stroll.

Roanoke has made it easy for visitors to wallow in culture for hours at a time without flagging. Three independent museums and a theatre are housed under one roof at the Center in the Square, 1 Market St, a restored and converted warehouse. All are open Tues–Sat 1000–1700, Sun 1300–1700. The **Science Museum of Western Virginia** ($) is a big hit with kids, while the **Art Museum of Western Virginia** (free) displays nationally important American art of the 19th and 20th centuries, as well as folk art of the region. On the top floor, the very good **Roanoke Valley History Museum** ($) gives an insight into the development of the area from the days before Colonial settlement, through the Civil War and the arrival of the railway, which brought prosperity and expansion.

i The **Visitor Centre** is at 114 Market Place; tel: (540) 342-6025 or (800) 635-5535; open daily 0900–1700.

The nearest campsite is in neighbouring Salem, or you could head on to the Blue Ridge Parkway for the **Peaks of Otter Campground** at milepost 86.
Jefferson Lodge $$ 616 S Jefferson St; tel: (540) 342-2951. Central and reasonably priced.
Mary Bladon House $$$ 381 Washington Ave; tel: (540) 344-5361. More atmospheric.

Stroll down Campbell St and Market St for a surprising range of restaurants that includes Vietnamese, Indian, Brazilian and Chesapeake Bay seafood.
Star City Diner $–$$ 118 Campbell Ave. Fun, family-oriented place, open late.
Awful Arthur's $$–$$$ 108 Campbell Ave. Extensive raw bar and fresh seafood, and live entertainment Wed and Thur evenings.
Carlos Brazilian International Cuisine $$$ 312 Market St. Popular restaurant representing a range of cuisines.

LYNCHBURG

Settled in 1727, Lynchburg sprawls across seven steep hills above the James River. The city began as a ferry crossing and developed as a tobacco town; for more than a century tobacco was processed, auctioned and made into cigarettes and plugs for chewing. During the Civil War, the city was a major Confederate storage depot and a burial place for the war dead.

For Free

The riverside **Miller-Claytor House** on Rivermont Ave dates from 1791 and is now a free-admission 'living history' museum, with demonstrations of early crafts. Open Thur–Mon 1300–1600 (May–Sept).

Several streets are designated historic districts. Start by walking around the central area, around Main St, Church St and Court St between 5th and 12th Sts. The **Old Court House**, at 901 Court St, dates from 1855 and contains a decent museum on the city's history; $, open daily 1300–1600. On the corner of 12th and Main Sts, the **Community Market** was a favourite of Thomas Jefferson, and is still the place to come for fresh produce and home-made crafts. Across town, the **City Cemetery** at 4th and Taylor Sts contains the graves of men who fought in the Revolutionary War; most poignant is the Confederate section with the graves of 2701 soldiers from 14 states who died in the Civil War.

i **Lynchburg Visitors Center**, 216 12th St; tel: (804) 847-1811, is very helpful, particularly with local accommodation.

The usual budget motels are located just off Rte 29 south of centre, or for more comfort in town, there are several B&Bs to choose from.

Lynchburg Mansion Inn $$$$ 405 Madison St; tel: (804) 528-5400 or 1 (800) 352-1199. A comfortable inn in the Garland Hill historic district.

Madison Bed and Breakfast $$$–$$$$ 413 Madison St; tel: (804) 528-1503. Just down the street from Lynchburg Mansion and equally atmospheric and cosy.

Percival's Isle Java Tavern $ 1208 Main St; tel: (804) 447 3059. Central café/restaurant with pizzas, sandwiches, and a few dinner entrées.

APPOMATTOX

This quiet little community was the scene of one of the most significant events in the history of the USA – the ending of the Civil War. Here, on 9 April 1865, General Robert E Lee surrendered the Confederate army of Northern Virginia to General Ulysses S Grant, commander of the Union forces. Though skirmishes flared up in a few southern states for another two months, the agreement between Lee and Grant effectively began the long period of reconciliation.

The **Appomattox Court House National Historical Park**, $, 3 miles from the modern town (open daily 0900–1730), encompasses the original village, restored to its 1865 appearance after falling into disrepair. This was only a tiny village at the time, with a courthouse, jail, tavern, store, law office, and a few homes; many still stand or have

WAR'S END

The Civil War ended miserably for the 28,000 Confederate soldiers. They had made slow and rain-sodden progress westward across Virginia and on 6 April fought what proved to be their last major battle. Their dawn attack on the Union army at Appomattox three days later was short-lived – by 10 am it was clear that further fighting was useless, and General Lee signed the surrender document the same day.

been rebuilt, and can be visited on a self-guided tour. The courthouse contains the visitor centre and museum, but the momentous document-signing actually took place in a private home, the McLean House, which has been reconstructed. Appomattox is really very small, but there is something haunting about the village and the gently rolling countryside around that makes it a must-see.

CHARLOTTESVILLE

An elegant yet lively city dating from colonial times, Charlottesville is dominated by its beautiful university. The compact residential downtown area is worth investigating, and the countryside around is not to be missed, especially Thomas Jefferson's Monticello and the local wineries.

The **University of Virginia** campus is a stately collection of dignified red-brick buildings, smooth green lawns and carefully placed trees, and has been designated an important architectural site. Much of it was designed by Thomas Jefferson himself, who founded the university. The centrepiece is the Rotunda, from which you can join a free guided tour of many university buildings.

Central Charlottesville has a pedestrianised main street known as the Downtown Mall, with several buildings from the 19th century – a pleasant place to stroll and stop for ice cream or browse in antique shops. Two blocks north at 5th and Jefferson Sts, the **Albemarle County Court House** includes an 1820s chapel that was shared by Baptists, Episcopalians, Methodists and Presbyterians; worshippers included Presidents Jefferson, Monroe and Madison.

MONTICELLO Charlottesville's *pièce de résistance* is the stately, though eccentric home designed by Thomas Jefferson, the third president of the United States. Preserved as a national monument to Jefferson, Monticello is located on a hill top just south of Charlottesville off Rte 20, and allows an insight into the mind of the squire revered as one of the founding fathers of the United States. Inside are many of the original furnishings, and the grounds – which include an orchard, vineyard and 1000-ft-long kitchen garden – are well worth a visit. $$, open daily 0800–1700 (Mar–Oct), 0900–1630 (Nov–Feb).

ARRIVING

The Amtrak and Greyhound stations are near each other on W Main St, which links downtown Charlottesville with the university campus.

i **Charlottesville/Albemarle Convention and Visitors Bureau**, tel: (804) 977-1783, shares a building with the **Monticello Visitor Center**, tel: (804) 984-9822, on Rte 20 south of town; both open daily 0900–1700.

There is a KOA campsite on Rte 1 about 10 miles south of Charlottesville. The usual cheap motels are clustered on Emmett St (Business Rte 29) west of centre.

Budget Inn $$ 140 Emmett St; tel: (804) 293-5141 or 1 (800) 293-5144. Reasonable motel within walking distance of campus.
1817 Historic Bed and Breakfast $$$$ 1211 W Main St; tel: (804) 979-7353 or 1 (800) 730-7443. Pretty interior, and right near the UVA campus.
200 South Street $$$$ 200 South St; tel: (804) 979-0200. Gracious Southern home right in the centre.

The **Downtown Mall** has several dining options; follow it west towards campus for more student-oriented establishments.
Hardware Store Restaurant $$–$$$ 316 E Main St. A century ago this really was a hardware store, and some of the old ironmongery and advertising signs are on display. Specialities include seafood, chicken and huge deli sandwiches.
Tastings $$$ 5th and Market Sts. Classy but casual Virginia fare and local wines.

WINERIES

Jefferson Vineyards, between Ash Lawn and Monticello on Rte 53, stands on the site where Jefferson planted the colony's first vines. Open daily 1100–1700.

Oakencroft Winery, Barracks Rd, west of Emmet St (Rte 29 north). Charlottesville's nearest vineyard is said to be one of Virginia's most picturesque. Tours and tastings offered daily 1100–1700 (Apr–Dec); 1100–1700 weekends in Mar; Jan–Feb by appointment only.

Barboursville Vineyards, Rte 777, Barboursville, 17 miles north-east of Charlottesville off Rte 20. Open Mon–Sat 1000–1700, Sun 1100–1700.

Horton Cellars, 6399 Spotswood Trail, Gordonsville, off Hwy 33 west. Tastings are held daily in a magnificent stone winery. Open daily 1100–1700 (weekends only during Mar).

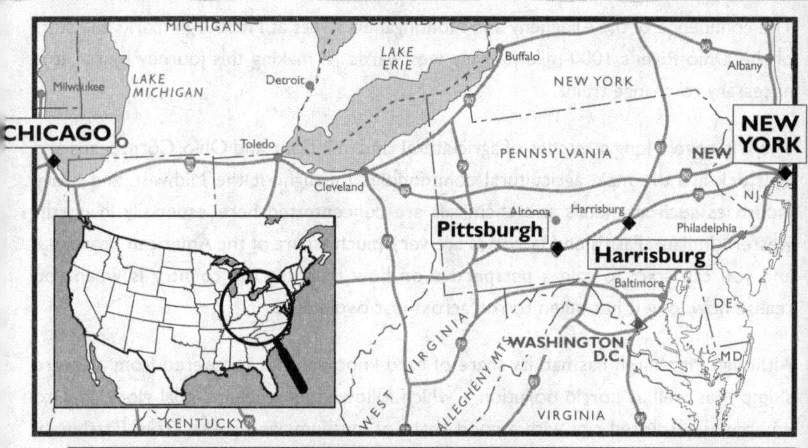

CHICAGO — NEW YORK

OTT Tables 324/333/501/502/503

Service	RAIL	RAIL	RAIL	RAIL	RAIL	RAIL	RAIL	RAIL	RAIL	RAIL	RAIL	RAIL
Days of operation	Daily	⑥⑦	ex⑥⑦	ex⑥⑦	⑥⑦	ex⑥⑦	⑦	ex⑦	ex⑥⑦	⑥⑦	⑥⑦	⑦
Special notes	A							B		C	D	B
Chicago .... d.	1735	....	....	....	....	....	....	....	....	....	....	....
Cleveland .... d.	|	....	....	....	....	....	....	....	....	....	....	....
Youngstown .... d.	|	....	....	....	....	....	....	....	....	....	....	....
Pittsburgh .... d.	0405	....	....	....	....	....	....	0720	....	....	....	1320
Harrisburg .... d.	....	0700	0720	0830	0850	1100	1255	1255	1450	1535	1730	1855
Philadelphia **X** .... d.	....	0930	1005	1046	1110	1316	1510	1510	1728	1810	1925	2125
New York X .... a.	....	1056	1131	1202	1230	1443	1635	1635	1858	1935	....	2250
Service	Bus	Bus	Bus	Bus	Bus	Bus	Bus	Bus	Bus	Bus	Bus	
Days of operation	Daily	Daily	Daily	Daily	Daily	Daily	Daily	Daily	Daily	Daily	Daily	
Special notes	E	E		E	E	E	E		E	E		
Chicago .... d.	....	....	2330	....	....	....	....	1145	....	....	1700	....
Cleveland .... d.	*2145*	*0215*	0850	*0600*	*0600*	*0825*	*1130*	2145	*1535*	*0645*	0230	....
Youngstown .... d.	|	|	1030	|	|	*1030*	*1400*	|	|	*2120*	|	....
Pittsburgh .... d.	0200	0530	|	0930	0915	1230	1620	|	1850	0001	|	....
Harrisburg .... d.	0620	1025	|	1425	1725	1740	2105	|	2315	|	|	....
Philadelphia **X** .... d.	0930	1315	|	1735	2010	|	0001	|	0135	0645	|	....
New York X .... a.	1205	1535	1855	2030	2245	2205	0210	0620	0355	0905	1105	....

Special notes:

A–The Capitol Limited. This train has sleepers and a dining car available, and all journeys should be reserved in advance.
B–The Pennsylvanian.
C–Additional trips: 0500ex⑥⑦, 0625⑥⑦, 1635.
D–Additional trips: 0925ex⑥⑦, 1855⑥, 2015ex⑥⑦.
E–Change buses at Pittsburg.
X–Frequent daily services operate between Philadelphia and New York.

The confluence of the Allegheny and Monongahela rivers at Pittsburgh marks the start of the Ohio River's 1000-mile journey westwards. If making this journey by rail, it is necessary to change trains.

The trip covers long stretches of agricultural land in Indiana and Ohio. Corn, beans and livestock are the main agricultural commodities throughout the Midwest, and heavy industries such as metals and chemicals are concentrated here, especially in north-western Indiana. Farms and factories are very much a part of the American heartland, and you can start to gain a perspective on how truly big the country is when you realise how long it has taken to roll across just two states.

Although Pittsburgh has had its share of hard knocks, it has recovered from a severe slump – as well as horrid pollution – which followed its steel-and-coal glory days, to emerge as a spirited city with a good share of museums and parks. From Pittsburgh, the train whistles through the Allegheny Mountains, on its way to Harrisburg and the chocolate fantasyland of Hershey Park, then speeds through the wonderfully picturesque landscape of Lancaster County before being caught by the dense grasp of the east coast.

PITTSBURGH

Once the world's largest steel producer and a major coal centre, Pittsburgh has re-invented itself after a long depression. Home of the first professional football game in 1892 and the first modern World Series in 1903, Pittsburgh is a city where sports matter. Its football team, the Steelers, once won four Super Bowl championships in six years. Two new stadiums keep facilities state-of-the-art; the hometown Pittsburgh Pirates will now play baseball with a dramatic skyline view (for tickets tel: (412) 321-BUCS or (800) BUY-BUCKS).

The newly dubbed 'Golden Triangle', wedged between the rivers, retains elements of its former industrial might in the form of restored warehouses and other turn-of-the-century buildings, while the shiny new skyline juts upwards in a profusion of steel and glass. Much of this is concentrated around the very central **Market Square**, and along Penn Ave to the north.

Pittsburgh started off as a frontier post, guarded by **Fort Pitt** at the rivers' convergence. Set in the midst of **Point State Park**, and fronted by an impressive fountain, the fort provides a good viewpoint over the city skyline. The **Fort Pitt Museum** within has displays on its frontier days. $, open Wed–Sat 1000–1630, Sun 1200–1630. From here, it's not hard to imagine the rows of steel mills which once lined the rivers. A relic of those days now carries sightseers up **Duquesne Incline** for views of the city and a museum demonstrating Pittsburgh's industrial age.

A two-tier **Allegheny Riverfront Park** overlooks the river, and in the Oakland neighbourhood the outstanding quartet of Carnegie Museums includes the **Museum of Art**, **Museum of Natural History** (with one of the finest dinosaur collections in the world), **Science Center** and the **Andy Warhol Museum** at 117 Sandusky St, a rich collection of works by Pittsburgh's favourite pop-artist son, born here in 1928, who defined the pop era through his paintings and films of personalities and objects of the 1950s, 1960s and 1970s. $$, open Tues–Sun 0010–1700, Fri until 2000.

While there, see the stunning stained-glass windows of nearby **Heinz Chapel** and the perpetual springtime of the **Phipps Conservatory & Botanical Gardens**, a century-old glasshouse with flowers, bonsai and butterflies. Open Tues–Sun 0900–1700.

En Route

Between Pittsburgh and Harrisburg the train pulls in at **Johnstown**, renowned for its tragic floods; raging waters drowned 2000 residents in 1889. The main reason is the town's position at the meeting of three rivers. Johnstown today is pretty enough, but there is little to see other than its flood memorial.

As though the artistic riches of the Carnegie complex were not enough, the free **Frick Art and Historical Center** has even more, and also Clayton, $$, the mansion of the wealthy industrialist who began the collection. Open year-round Tues–Sat 1000–1700, Sun 1200–1800.

i The visitor centre is downtown at Liberty Ave near Point State Park; tel: (800) 366-0093; www.visitpittsburgh.com.

Amtrak is located at Liberty Ave and Grant St, at the north-east corner of downtown.

Central hotel prices are lower at weekends, arranged through the **Weekend Package** hotline, tel: (800) 927-8376.
HI Youth Hostel $ 830 E Warrington Ave; tel: (412) 431-1267 or (800) 909-4776. The cheapest option.
The Priory $$$$ A City Inn, 614 Pressley St; tel: (412) 231-3338; fax: (412) 231-4838. Exceptionally comfortable, a converted monastery on the north side of the Allegheny River.

The Strip District, just north-east of centre, is a lively area of markets, bars and various eateries.
Southwest Bistro $$ 129 6th St. Well-balanced combination of South-west and European cuisines.
Valhalla $$ 12th and Smallman St; tel: (412) 434-1440. Restored warehouse with home-brewed beer and an outdoor deck. Half-price ales Mon–Thur 1700–1900.

Other Attractions

Enjoy the **Pittsburgh Zoo & Aquarium** in Highland Park, with its special **Kids Kingdom**.

Gateway Clippers cruise the river in replica paddle-wheelers, for sightseeing, dancing and dinner cruises; tel: (412) 355-7980.

HARRISBURG

Pennsylvania's state capital, while certainly lacking the verve and grit of Philadelphia or Pittsburgh, nevertheless maintains a pretty atmosphere, with numerous old homes and interesting buildings. Predominant among these are the **State Capitol**, with a dome modelled on St Peter's in Rome. Nearby **River Park** is a luxuriant stretch of landscaped gardens.

America's fascination with the big and the tacky is put on display in Hershey, 10 miles east of Harrisburg. The town was established as a planned community for workers at the Hershey chocolate-factory, one of the country's largest. Chocolate is still churned out here en masse, and in addition to the pseudo-chocolate-factory tour at **Hershey Chocolate World**, you can spend the day whirling on the roller-coaster rides at adjacent Hershey Park or treating your body to a chocolate wrap (we're serious) at Hershey's spa.

EN ROUTE

Philadelphia, the last major stop before New York, is a city that is at long last shaking off a bad reputation and industrial slump to enjoy its ethnic diversity and status as birthplace of the nation (see p. 191).

ALTOONA

One of America's favourite thrills for railway enthusiasts is the great hairpin turn the tracks take near Altoona.

PENNSYLVANIA DUTCH COUNTRY

The farmland of Lancaster County has been shaped by the European religious communities that settled here. The Mennonite and Amish rejection of the technological trappings of modern life mean a pleasing lack of billboards, telephone wires and agricultural machinery, with quaint pastoral scenes from a bygone era. See p. 202.

i **Harrisburg-Hershey-Carlisle Tourism and Convention Bureau**, 25 N Front St; tel: (717) 231-7788 or (800) 995-0969; www.visithhc.com. **Historic Harrisburg Resource Center**, 1230 North Third St; tel: (717) 233-4646, has an array of brochures and information, and organises bus and walking tours.

The Harrisburg and Hershey area has plenty of accommodation options and is well represented by the familiar hotel and motel chains (see p. 52).

The nearest KOA campsite is 6 miles south of Hershey on Rte 743.

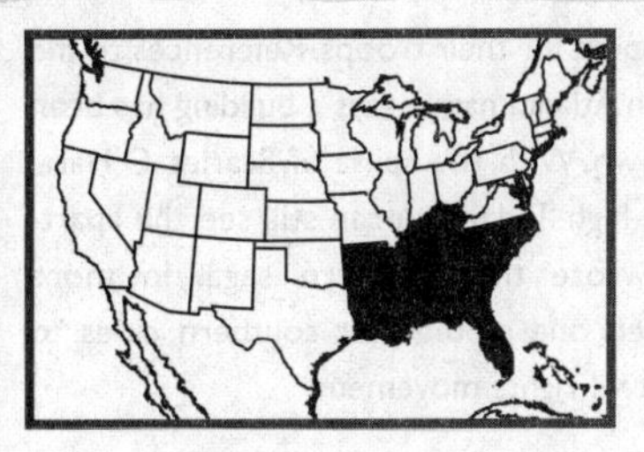

Thanks to Margaret Mitchell's *Gone With The Wind*, the South is often envisioned as a delicate landscape of drawling débutantes and heroic men. This romantic image of the South has captured the hearts of many a hopeful visitor. And although you will find this picture in plenty of sprawling plantations and fine *antebellum* (pre-Civil War) houses, the modern cities that have sprung up throughout the Old South are as in tune with today as any in America. The South's Civil War sights and rich political past will be sure to satisfy travellers with a love of history. Cotton may no longer be king, but the southern way of life is alive and well.

You will find that southerners' attitudes match their speech. Just as they never hurry their words, a 'New York Minute' is the antithesis of southern living. Don't expect anything to move too fast, including service, but this is out of a casual attitude, not laziness. This unhurried manner is more than apparent in the warmth of typical southern hospitality. People here seem to have time for friends and strangers alike. Few southerners will challenge this stereotype; they are by far some of the friendliest and most accommodating of hosts.

The red clay earth of Georgia just accents the lush greens of the state's beautiful rolling landscape and miles of farmland. Atlanta, in its centre, is hard to miss if you're travelling the region by car, plane or train. Three major interstate motorways converge here, it is a rail hub and the city houses one of the country's largest international airports. Atlanta has been referred to for many years as the 'crossroads of the South'.

Atlanta's fate in the history of the Civil War was tragic, as nearly all its grand old homes were destroyed as the northern army swept through in an attempt to crush southern supply lines and support for their troops. References to the Civil War still linger in Georgia speech: when an Atlanta native says a building has been 'sold to the Yankees' they mean it burned down. With the spirit of Scarlet O'Hara, however, Atlanta has carried on, with its pride high. Today you can still see the apartment building where Margaret Mitchell wrote the southern saga. In more modern history, Atlanta is proud to have been one of the first southern cities to voluntarily desegregate its schools during the civil rights movement.

If fires of war left Atlanta few examples of the Old South's architecture, Savannah was luckier. Some say that General William Sherman could not bring himself to burn it down because of its grandeur. Others say that the people of Savannah instantly surrendered to Sherman in order to save their city during the Civil War, but the common theme in both stories is that it was just too beautiful to be sacrificed to politics.

The graceful shaded parks, their trees adorned with the delicate Spanish moss, provide a romantic backdrop for travellers following the trail of *Midnight in the Garden of Good and Evil.* Spring is the best time to see the city and its bright gardens at their best, especially if you want to enjoy the stunning *antebellum* architecture in a walking tour without being overwhelmed by midsummer heat.

Georgia's 'Golden Isles' are a naturalist's wonderland of dunes, marshes, estuaries, beaches, lakes and ponds, filled with wildlife. Snowy egrets and wood storks are among more than 300 bird species that may be seen in the air here, while armadillos, alligators and wild horses live closer to the ground.

Alabama's landscape is filled with incredible scenery and surprising variety. In perfect southern style, the wide rivers of Alabama meander unhurriedly through the landscape. Hills filled with caves spark the interest of spelunkers, and everyone will admire the large, quiet lakes. The southern coast offers the bonus of soft sandy beaches.

Mobile's southern charm, its broad streets shaded by ancient oak trees, is perhaps epitomized by the 50-plus varieties of azaleas, which earn it the nickname of 'The Azalea City'. The time to see these is in the spring, when different varieties provide a succession of bloom for several weeks. This typically southern city also has strong French influence and celebrates its own Mardi Gras each year, a nice alternative for those who wish to avoid the frenetic beat of the carnival season in New Orleans.

That city on the Mississippi Delta has a mystique all its own, and is like no other place in America – or the world. The thick Cajun influence has seeped into New Orleans language and culture, but most importantly, into the food. The spicy seafood creations of Cajun cooking – crayfish, thick gumbos and exuberant jambalayas – can only truly be experienced here, where they were born. It is a cooking style quite distinct from that of its southern neighbours.

The other major ingredient in the spicy cultural jambalaya of New Orleans is the early and heavy influence of its African descendants. The mysterious practice of voodoo is just one of the many unique features they brought that still characterize New Orleans. Also born in the black society was a phenomenon that captured America's heart and set its feet tapping well over a century ago. New Orleans was one of the birthplaces of jazz, a hallowed spot in history that it shares, in part, with Memphis.

But Memphis shares none of the glory as the home of rock 'n' roll, the music phenomenon of the mid-20th-century. No popular music fan should miss visiting Graceland, Elvis Presley's legendary home. Memphis is also one of the best places to take a steamboat ride on the Mississippi.

While Florida shares much of the grace of the Old South, its gentle chords are enlivened by a calypso and reggae beat brought by the large Hispanic community that has settled there from the Caribbean islands. Much of Florida's aura of southern charm is overshadowed in the traveller's vision by the world-famous Walt Disney World and the multitude of tourist attractions that have grown up around it as a result of its popularity. Along with Disney's own theme parks – The Magic Kingdom, Disney-MGM Studios, Epcot Center, Animal Kingdom plus three water theme parks – visitors can tour the mind-boggling Universal Studios Florida to get behind the scenes of some of their favourite Hollywood hits.

Traditional southern cooking is relatively bland and, to many northern tastes, overly sweetened. Treacle, called molasses here, is the sweetener of choice, and you'll recognize its flavour in the great southern dessert, pecan pie. Fried chicken, biscuits and gravy (remember that in America biscuits are a breadroll served with meals, not a tea-time treat), cornbread, sweet potatoes (a bright orange tuber served everywhere) and barbecued pork are favourites. You'll also be served hush puppies, which are a deep-fried bread, and grits. This porridge of white corn is a breakfast staple, but may appear with any meal as a side dish.

HURRICANE KATRINA

On 29 August 2005, the deadliest hurricane the United States has ever known hit **New Orleans**. Within hours, the levees – huge dykes that hold back Lake Ponchartrain – had been breached and 80 percent of the city was flooded, under as much as 20 feet of water in some places. High winds and rain also damaged coastal regions of **Mississippi**, **Alabama** and **Louisiana**, displacing more than a million people and leaving entire areas uninhabitable. Severe damage covered 90,000 square miles, an area almost the size of the UK.

As this book goes to press, it is too soon to fully assess the damage, but it will be years before New Orleans (see pp. 314–315) will be rebuilt, and many months before it can welcome tourists to its Big Easy ambience again. The good news is that the French Quarter was largely spared the storm surge, so was not flooded. Long before the rest of the city is back to normal, it will be possible to visit this historic centre. The city's website, www.neworleanscvb.com, has continuing detailed updates on what is open, including hotels.

The **North Shore** (p. 314), while hard hit, did not suffer the wholesale destruction that struck the city. Flooding, fallen trees and wind caused extensive damage, but facilities for tourists should be operational long before those in the city itself. For updates, visit www.NewOrleansNorthShore.com (where you can ask specific questions by email) or call (985) 892-0520 or (800) 634-9443.

Lafayette and the surrounding **Cajun Country** (page 315) was not in the hurricane's path. It came through the storm unscathed and still welcomes travellers with its usual hospitality. **Mobile**, Alabama (pp. 316–319) suffered some damage, but tourist sites, hotels and restaurants are open.

Summer in the Deep South can be brutally hot for those not used to the climate. But there are many who feel that the heat is part of the South, and only in its summer can you sense its real heart and soul. That said, you will enjoy it a lot more in another season, when you can spend time outdoors strolling its pleasant streets. Spring, which begins here in early February, is the best time to visit if you want to see the southland dressed in its floral finery. Autumn's pleasant weather lasts through Christmas, and Yankees escape snow by the droves to enjoy the mild winters here.

To get a feel for the Deep South, which even many Americans still find puzzling, try to see the films *Steel Magnolias* and *Fried Green Tomatoes*.

OUR CHOICE

Savannah's streets and garden squares

Charleston's Historic District and Old City Market

Patriot's Point Naval and Maritime Museum

Universal Studios Florida

The Magic Kingdom

Epcot Center

John F Kennedy Space Center

Everglades National Park

St Augustine

Graceland (for Elvis fans)

Mississippi steamboat ride

New Orleans' French Quarter and Garden District

Cajun Country

At least one plantation house

HOW MUCH YOU CAN SEE IN A ...

WEEK (7 DAYS)

The Disney parks and Universal Studios Florida

The Kennedy Space Center, Florida Keys and the Everglades

New Orleans, the bayou country and Mobile

New Orleans and some of the Disney attractions

Savannah, Charleston and St Augustine

Chicago, Memphis and New Orleans, via the Blues Train

FORTNIGHT (14 DAYS)

The Disney parks, Universal Studios Florida, St Augustine, Kennedy Space Center, Florida Keys

The Disney parks, St Augustine, Kennedy Space Center, Florida Keys and the Everglades

The Disney parks, St Augustine, Savannah and Charleston

New Orleans, the bayou country, Mobile, the Disney attractions and Universal Studios Florida

New Orleans, the bayou country, Mobile, St Augustine, Savannah and Charleston

Richmond, Tidewater Virginia, Williamsburg, Savannah and Charleston, possibly returning via the Shenandoah

New Orleans, bayou country, Memphis, Charleston and Savannah, possibly with St Augustine

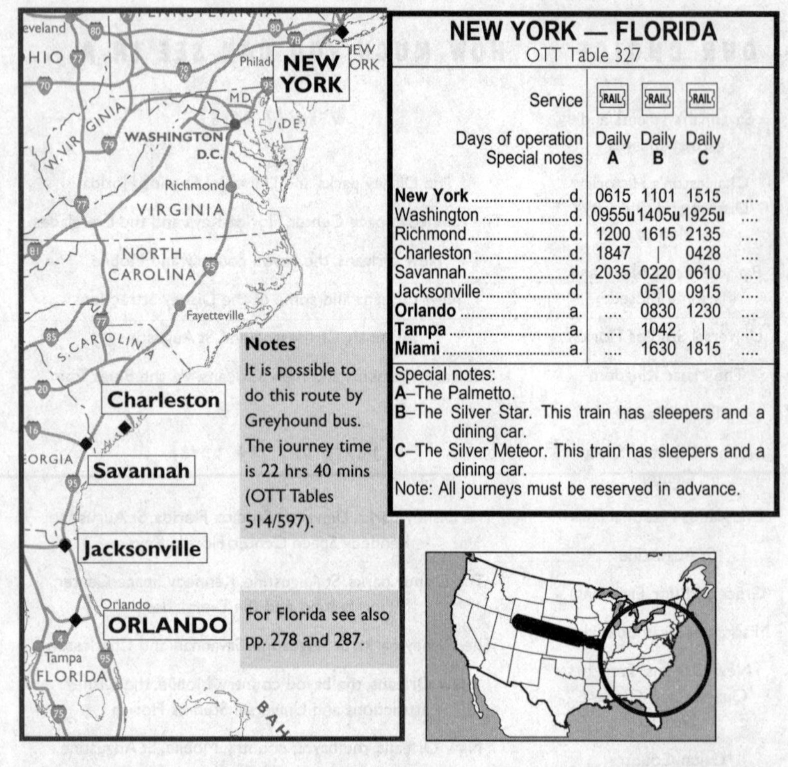

NEW YORK — FLORIDA
OTT Table 327

Service	RAIL	RAIL	RAIL	
Days of operation	Daily	Daily	Daily	
Special notes	A	B	C	
New York .... d.	0615	1101	1515	....
Washington .... d.	0955u	1405u	1925u	....
Richmond .... d.	1200	1615	2135	....
Charleston .... d.	1847	|	0428	....
Savannah .... d.	2035	0220	0610	....
Jacksonville .... d.	....	0510	0915	....
Orlando .... a.	....	0830	1230	....
Tampa .... a.	....	1042	|	....
Miami .... a.	....	1630	1815	....

Special notes:
A–The Palmetto.
B–The Silver Star. This train has sleepers and a dining car.
C–The Silver Meteor. This train has sleepers and a dining car.
Note: All journeys must be reserved in advance.

Notes
It is possible to do this route by Greyhound bus. The journey time is 22 hrs 40 mins (OTT Tables 514/597).

For Florida see also pp. 278 and 287.

Amtrak runs trains daily from New York down the Atlantic coast: 'Palmetto' as far as Savannah and 'Silver Star' and 'Silver Meteor' right down to Miami. The 'Silver Star' offers the more scenic opportunities during daylight hours. From New York your morning journey takes you through the industrialised 'north-east corridor' connecting New York, Philadelphia and Washington DC. Leaving Washington in the afternoon, you continue through the rolling hills of Virginia. Night-time robs you of the sight of the Appalachian mountains and of Carolina's Lowcountry. From Jacksonville, your introduction to Florida, you can access the beaches of Amelia Island, quaint St Augustine and Daytona. By mid-morning you will have left the scrubby landscape of Florida's east coast, and be headed for the tourist havens of central Florida. If you plan to stop in Savannah, note that the southbound 'Silver Star' arrives at an awkward 0220. The 'Silver Meteor' arrives at 0610, easier for hotel check-in.

JACKSONVILLE

Jacksonville sprawls in many directions. To see the city at its best, stroll along the **Southbank Riverwalk**, a 1-mile boardwalk that runs from just east of Acosta Bridge to about ½ mile east of the Main St Bridge; or take a cruise on the river. The 12-mile bus ride to the beaches can take up to an hour, but the wide and wild expanses of sand are worth the trip. **Jacksonville Landing**, downtown on the St Johns River, is an attraction in its own right, a busy marketplace and entertainment venue of 36 shops and 15 restaurants, open Mon–Thur 1000–2000, Fri–Sat 1000–2100, Sun 1200–1730. **The Beaches** are a string of coastal resorts: Atlantic Beach, Jacksonville Beach, Neptune Beach, Ponte Vedra Beach, South Ponte Vedra Beach, North Beach and Vilano Beach.

Parks and Beaches

Little Talbot State Park, $, 12157 Heckscher Dr., tel: (904) 251-2320, has 51/2 miles of swimming beach, low-level dunes, bike and canoe hire, camp sites, nature trails and picnic areas. Open daily 0800–dusk. **Big Talbot Island**, $, 12157 Heckscher Dr., tel: (904) 251-2320, is an undeveloped rocky shoreline area popular with fishermen and watersports enthusiasts. Open daily 0800–dusk. **Huguenot Memorial Park**, $, 10980 Heckscher Dr., tel: (904) 251-3335, is another popular beach area offering surfing, windsurfing, fishing and swimming. Open daily 0600–dusk. **Fort Caroline National Memorial**, 12713 Fort Caroline Rd, Arlington, tel: (904) 641-7155, open daily 0900–1700, was where French Huguenots landed in 1564, establishing North America's first Protestant colony. Its 680 acres contain a replica of the Huguenots' fort, a museum of French and Native American artefacts and a nature trail.

The Amtrak station is 6 miles north-west of downtown. Bus no. K2 connects the Amtrak station with the downtown FCCJ station. It runs every 30 mins from 0527 until 1927, 2027, 2127 on weekdays, hourly from 0642 until 2042 on Saturdays, and at 0823 and every 90 mins until 1853 on Sundays. Tel: (904) 743-3582; www.jtaonthemove.com.

i **Jacksonville and the Beaches Convention and Visitors Bureau**, 3 Independent Dr.; tel: (904) 798-9111 or (800) 733-2668; www.jaxcvb.com. Open Mon–Fri 0800–1700.
Amelia Island Chamber of Commerce, tel: (904) 261-3248.

Sea Turtle Inn $$$ 1 Ocean Blvd, Atlantic Beach, tel: (904) 249-7402, has nearly 200 rooms, sea views and seafood.
Holiday Inn Sunspree Resort $$$ Jacksonville Beach; tel: (904) 249-9071 or (800) 590-4767.
Sea Horse Oceanfront Inn $$–$$$ 120 Atlantic Blvd, Neptune Beach; tel: (800) 881-2330.

River City Brewing Company $$ 835 Museum Circle, tel: (904) 398-2299, offers good food with music and home-brew.
Sterling's Café $$ 3551 St Johns Ave, tel: (904) 387-0700, has an enticing menu of out-of-the-ordinary dishes.
Coney Island Joe's International Deli $ 420D Wharfside Way, tel: (904) 399-5736, is the place to pick up a burger or sausage sandwich and home-made lemonade.

Enduring elegance is the hallmark of Charleston, a city that has survived and thrived in spite of three turbulent centuries of epidemics, fires, earthquakes, hurricanes and revolution. This genteel lady of a city has a spine of steel and a soul of velvet.

Charleston is not all magnolias and moonlight. One of the most charming aspects of its personality is that it has managed to escape the contemporary architectural homogenisation that has overtaken most American cities. Generations of Charlestonians have toiled tirelessly to rescue and renovate the old downtown homes and commercial buildings, and their efforts have created one of the South's best-preserved cities. Not even Hurricane Hugo, which caused extensive damage in 1989, could significantly alter the cityscape.

The Spanish were the first Europeans to arrive in 1521, soon followed by French Huguenots, but it was the arrival of English settlers in 1670, in pursuit of land to farm, which laid the groundwork for today's city. In part, the British colony's economic success led to its participation in the first significant victory of the American Revolution, fought off the coast at Charleston, at Fort Moultrie on Sullivan's Island.

No group contributed more to the colony's character than the slaves from Africa and Barbados, and 'Gullah' culture is still dominant in the cuisine, crafts and lifestyle of Charleston.

MUST SEE/DO IN CHARLESTON

Explore the Historic District filled with *antebellum* houses and historic sites

Sample Low Country cuisine at Poogan's Porch

Watch the 'basket ladies' at the Old City Market weave their craft

Relive the first siege of the Civil War at Fort Sumter National Monument

Immerse yourself in a 17th-century village at Charles Towne Landing

Take a tour of Magnolia Plantation and Gardens, home to over 250 varieties of azalea

GETTING THERE AND GETTING AROUND

Charleston International Airport, 12 miles west of the city centre on I-26, is served by several major carriers. The Amtrak station, at 4565 Gaynor Avenue, North Charleston, is 8 miles north of the centre in a rundown neighbourhood. The Greyhound terminus is also in North Charleston, at 3610 Dorchester Rd. CARTA (Charleston Area Regional Transit Authority) buses run from both these arrival points to the city centre every 30 mins.

By car, Charleston is reached from north or south by I-26, a turning east off I-95. US 17, a north–south coastal route, passes through the city.

CARTA, tel: (843) 724-7420, (800) 774-0006, operates bus services within the city and to North Charleston and the beaches. Fares are cheap and the service operates 0500–0100 daily. DASH (Downtown Area Shuttles), run by CARTA, operates an extensive network of routes through downtown and the historic district at a reasonable fare (children under six travel free). Services operate every 15 mins, Mon–Fri, from 0800 (last bus times vary). Charleston is easily walkable.

FLOWER TIME

Spring is the prime time to visit Charleston, when the city is ablaze with azaleas, magnolias, dogwood and flowering jasmine. But the city blooms year round – in summer you'll find day lilies, magnolias and hydrangea, while autumn blooms with crape myrtles and gerberas, and in winter camellias and pansies abound.

INFORMATION

Charleston Visitors Center, 375 Meeting St; tel: (843) 853-9000 or (800) 868-8118; www.charlestoncvb.com. Housed in a renovated freight depot and open daily 0830–1700; closed on Thanksgiving, Christmas and New Year's holidays.

SAFETY Lone travellers should avoid the area around the Amtrak station at night.

MONEY Currency can be exchanged at larger banks; ATMs are common.

POST AND PHONES The central post office is at 83 Broad St; open Mon–Fri 0830–1735; Sat 0930-1400.

ACCOMMODATION

Cheaper lodgings can be found in Mt Pleasant, 3 miles from the centre.

Maison Du Pré $$$ 317 E Bay St; tel: (843) 723-8691 or (800) 844-4667; www.maisondupre.com. This B&B manages to be both elegant and cosy at the same time. Continental breakfast and afternoon tea are included.

1837 Bed and Breakfast and Tea Room $$ 126 Wentworth St; tel: (843) 723-7166. Not as fancy as the Maison Du Pré but comfortable and cosy, with canopied beds. Rate includes generous breakfast and afternoon tea.

King Charles Inn $$ 237 Meeting St; tel: (843) 723-7451 or (866) 546-4700. Clean and convenient; some rooms have balconies.

The Ashley and Cannonboro Inn Bed & Breakfast $$–$$$$ 184 Ashley Ave; tel: (843) 723-8572; www.charleston-sc-inns.com. A downtown architectural treasure, full of warmth and charm; full Southern breakfast.

FOOD AND DRINK

Lowcountry food is simply sensational. Dominating the menu are shrimp, crab and oysters, combined with rice (or that creamy maize porridge of the South – grits) and an array of vegetables. Try the roasted oysters, okra gumbo and palmetto heart pickle for an authentic taste of the area.

Gaulart and Maliclet French Café $ 98 Broad St; tel: (843) 577-9797. Casual café with counter service, specialising in sandwiches, soups, quiches and omelettes.

Magnolias Uptown/Down South $ 185 E Bay St; tel: (843) 577-7771. Popular with locals. Seafood and innovative appetisers.

82 Queen $$$ 82 Queen St; tel: (843) 722-4428. Famed for its she-crab soup and other Lowcountry specialities. Reservations recommended.

Poogan's Porch $$ 72 Queen Street, tel: (843) 577-2337. Downtown local favourite serves up fresh seafood and Low Country cuisine in an amiable atmosphere.

HIGHLIGHTS

If you only have a short time to spend in Charleston, concentrate on the compact historic district in the city's heart, where historic sites, graceful *antebellum* (pre-Civil War) houses and captivating cafés are footsteps apart. The mostly residential area is bounded by Calhoun St on the north and King St on the west, and the best way to see it is on foot. Less taxing, particularly in the summer heat, is to take a carriage or trolley tour from the Market area. The visitor centre in Meeting St is a good place to start, and it's worth taking time to see *Forever Charleston*, a great film that explains the city's history.

Across the street from the visitor centre is the **Charleston Museum**, the oldest city museum in the United States, founded in 1773. An architecturally nondescript building, it houses an extensive collection of South Carolina decorative arts and objects focusing on Charleston and its history, ranging from silversmithing, fashion, plantation life, slavery and Native American life to the region's flora and fauna. $$, 360 Meeting St; open Mon–Sat 0900–1700, Sun 1300–1700 (combination ticket for museum and houses – the Heritage Pass is available from the Visitors Centre, $32, or from the attractions it covers); www.charlestonmuseum.com.

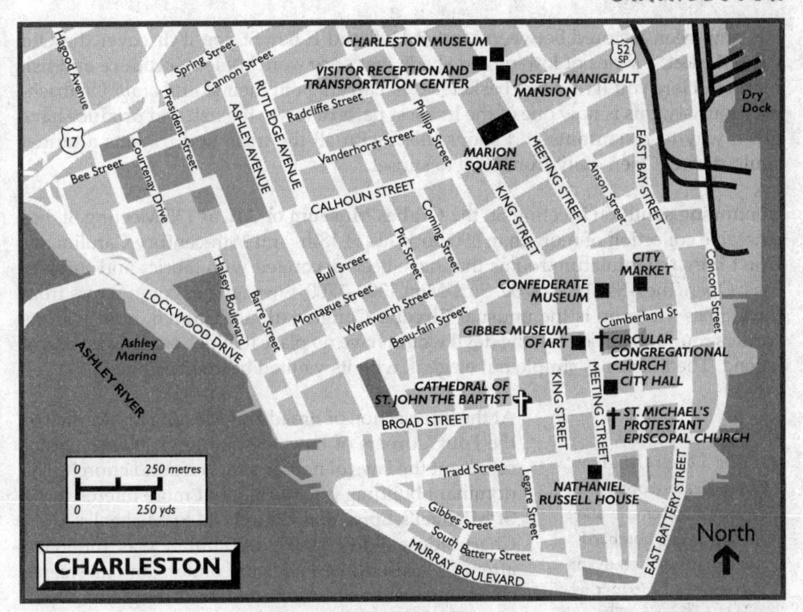

Many of the historic homes are open to the public, but plan carefully, as individual admissions can add up quickly. The **Joseph Manigault House** is an outstanding example of Adamesque architecture; the stunning front hall boasts a beautiful curving staircase. Furnishings include rare tricolor Wedgwood pieces. A fascinating feature is the secret stairway between the second and third floors. $$, 350 Meeting St; open Mon–Sat 1000–1700, Sun 1300–1700 (visit with combination ticket from the Charleston Museum).

> **THE HOLY CITY**
>
> The immigration of French Huguenots in the 1560s established Charleston's reputation for religious freedom. Today, Charleston boasts more than 185 churches of 25 denominations and is still referred to as the 'Holy City'.

To untrained eyes, many of Charleston's historic homes appear simple and unassuming when viewed head-on – the first impression is just of an unadorned façade broken by windows and a doorway to one side. But glance to the side and you'll find the door actually opens onto a porch or piazza that runs front to back along the side, transforming the house into a stately, elegant home.

Walk south along Meeting St to Market Hall, modelled after the Temple of Nike in Athens. Inside you'll find the **Confederate Museum** with uniforms, swords and Civil War memorabilia. Badly damaged by Hurricane Hugo in 1989, the museum has now been restored.Between Market Hall and E Bay St you'll discover the **Old City Market**, a series of low-roofed sheds that once were home to produce and fish markets. Here you'll find the 'basket ladies' carrying out their skilful craft. Unabashedly touristy, this is now one of the liveliest parts of town: the fish and produce have given way to restaurants and shops filled with all the trash and trinkets a tourist could desire. Open daily from 0900 to sunset.

Continuing south on Meeting St, the **Gibbes Museum of Art**, at 135 Meeting St, has a notable collection of more than 400 portraits of 18th- and 19th-century Carolinians. Don't miss the miniature rooms that have been decorated with fabrics and furnishings. Open Tues–Sat 1000–1700, Sun–Mon 1300–1700; www.gibbes.com. Across from the Gibbes Museum is the unusual **Circular Congregational Church**, built with its corners rounded off so that 'the devil would have no place to hide', according to local legend. The interior is simple but elegant, with its vaulted beamed ceiling.

Fort Sumter

On 12 April 1861, Confederate troops fired on Fort Sumter, the start of a two-day bombardment that resulted in the surrender of the fort by Union troops. The Confederacy held the fort until it was evacuated on 17 February 1865. During that time, the fort experienced one of the longest sieges in history – almost two years – during which 46,000 shells were fired at it. When the Confederate forces finally evacuated the fort it was little more than a pile of rubble.

At the intersection of Broad and Meeting Sts, known as the Four Corners of Law, the buildings at each corner represent the laws of nation, state, city and church. The dominant building is City Hall, but more interesting is **St Michael's Episcopal Church**, 14 St Michael's Alley. Charleston's oldest surviving church was modelled after St Martin-in-the-Fields in London, and its steeple clock and bells were imported from England. Open Mon–Fri 0900–1700, Sat 0900–noon.

Towards the southern end of Meeting St, graceful Nathaniel Russell House (no. 51) represents the epitome of the Federal style, with its daring flying staircase that rises, apparently unsupported, for three floors. $$, open Mon–Sat 1000–1700.

On the Waterfront Not all of Charleston's treasures are indoors. **Waterfront Park**, located just off East Bay and Concord Sts, is a magnificent park on the harbour. Once a seedy neighbourhood of derelict warehouses, this stretch of riverfront along the Cooper River has been transformed with grassy areas, flower-filled planters and fountains.

Across the river, **Patriot's Point Naval and Maritime Museum** at Mount Pleasant (reached along Hwy 17) is the world's largest naval and maritime museum. It is the home of the submarine *Clamagore*, the World War II aircraft carrier *Yorktown* and the destroyer *Laffey*. The Medal of Honor Museum here features displays of vintage weapons and military aircraft. This living and working area for ships is open daily for touring, 0900–1700; tel: (843) 881-5930. $$; www.patriotspoint.org.

From Patriot's Point you can board a ferry boat to tour the **Fort Sumter National Monument**, where the Civil War began. Located on a small man-made island at the entrance to Charleston harbour, it is accessible only by boat. Fort Sumter Tours, 360 Concord St; tel: (843) 881-7337, organise daily tours at 1330, more frequently during holidays. $$; www.nps.gov.

South Carolina Aquarium $, 100 Aquarium Wharf, tel: (843) 720-1990, (800) 343-9899 or www.scaquarium.org. On the historic waterfront, the aquarium is home to thousands of fish and live plants and animals that highlight South Carolina's various aquatic habitats, both sea and inland.

DAY TRIPS

Magnolia Plantation and Gardens, 10 miles north of the city along Hwy 61, has over 250 varieties of *Azalea indica* and 900 varieties of *Camellia japonica*. There are cycling and walking paths, a pet zoo, a canoe trail and picnic areas. $$, open daily 0800–1730; admission to the house is extra ($); www.magnoliaplantation.com.

The early years of Charleston have been brought to life at **Charles Towne Landing**. This 80-acre park is an outdoor interpretative centre of the Lowcountry's earliest European settlers. There is a 'settler village'; a 17th-century replica of a coastal trading vessel; and the Animal Forest 'wilderness', complete with wildlife. You can take a tram tour or explore on your own – bikes can be rented by the hour. The park is 6 miles from the city, along Hwy 171 between I-26 and Hwy 17, $, open daily 0830–1700; www.southcarolinaparks.com.

Public beaches close to the city and easily accessed by public transport include Sullivan's Island, Isles of Palms, James Island, Folly Beach and Beachwalker Park on the west end of Kiawah Island.

The **Spoleto Festival** begins in late May and lasts for about 18 days, bringing the best of international theatre, music, art and dance to Charleston. It's a magical time to be in the city. This popular festival fills Charleston's hotels, so book early. Tel: (843) 579-3100 for information; www.spoletousa.org.

NIGHTLIFE

Charleston has several theatres, including the historic **Dock Street Theater**, with its intimate box seats and terrific acoustics. The **Charleston Stage Company**, 133 Church St, tel: (843) 577-5967 or (800) 454-7093, performs original works as well as more family-oriented productions, and the **Footlight Players**, 20 Queen St, tel: (843) 722-4487, are an old-established community theatre company. Try out the following for relaxed entertainment.

DANCING THE CHARLESTON

The dance craze of society flappers in the 1920s originated with black children, dancing for pennies on the city's streets.

Mills House, 115 Meeting St; tel: (843) 577-2400. Good place to gather for an after-dinner drink while listening to big band tunes or jazz guitar.

Indigo Lounge, 5 Faber St, tel: (843) 577-7383. Live Motown entertainment every weekend in one of Charleston's most upscale nightclubs.

The Have Nots, Theater 99, Cumberland St, tel: (843) 853-6687. Charleston's local improv comedy group delights audiences with its wacky and hilarious shows.

Roof Top Terrace at the Vendue Inn, 19 Vendue Range, tel: (843) 577-7970. This open-air bar is one of the best places to watch the sun go down over Charleston Harbor.

THE DOCK STREET THEATER

The theatre combines the early playhouse (one of the nation's first) that originally stood on this site and the preserved Planter's Hotel. Visitors can partake of a backstage tour, except on those days that technical work for a production is taking place. 135 Church St; tel: (803) 720-3968. Open Mon–Fri 1000–1600.

PORGY AND BESS

In 1925, Du Bose Heyward immortalised one of the traditional stories of the Low Country when he created *Porgy*, the tale of a lame Charleston street vendor and his love for Bess. Gershwin brought *Porgy and Bess* to Broadway in 1935, but it was not until 1970, when Charleston was finally desegregated, that it played in Charleston's Gaillard Auditorium.

Atlanta. The name once evoked images of Scarlett O'Hara bravely defending Tara from marauding Yankees. Her valiant efforts paid off. Atlanta with its bustling and cosmopolitan energy represents the 'new South'. Trend-setting restaurants, skyscrapers and ultra-modern sports facilities blend seamlessly with traditional architecture and down home eateries. Whatever you eat don't forget to wash it down with a Coca-Cola ('co-cola'), the house wine of the South and headquartered here. Atlanta loves to be big. It has the world's largest diorama (Cyclorama), the tallest escalator in the South and is physically one of the largest cities in the world. The geography of this sprawling metropolis of over 136 square miles represents a challenge for seeing all the sites. The best bet is to use the local transport system (MARTA).

GETTING THERE AND GETTING AROUND

Hartsfield International Airport, the South's busiest, is 10 miles south of the city. The easiest and least expensive route to the centre is via the MARTA light rail system, with a station inside the airport, steps from the baggage retrieval area. Plenty of taxis and shuttle bus service are available. A taxi ride is approximately $20.

The Amtrak Passenger Rail station is located at 1688 Peachtree Street. A MARTA bus, No. 23 southbound, will connect you to the light rail system at Arts Center Station. If you are arriving by bus, the Greyhound Terminal is located on 232 Forsyth Street in the downtown area. Be cautious in this area at night.

Airport Alert

Arriving from overseas, after you clear customs and immigration in Terminal E, you must then recheck your baggage and reclaim it in the main terminal building. Baggage is not allowed on the airport's subway system.

Three interstate highways converge in Atlanta: I-75, I-85 and I-20, all linked by a 63-mile perimeter road, I-285. Avoid driving during morning and evening 'rush hours'.

MARTA, tel: (404) 848-5000 or 4711, includes both light rail and bus services. The rail service operates 0500–0030 daily.

INFORMATION

Atlanta Convention and Visitors Bureau, 233 Peachtree St, tel: (404) 521-6600 or (800) ATLANTA, is open daily 0830–1730; www.atlanta.net.

Money Travelex foreign exchange is located in the 'E' Concourse (international departures and arrivals), tel: (404)761-6332. Within the city most local banks can handle currency exchange for a fee. You will also find numerous ATMs.

RING-A-DING-DING!

In Atlanta you must use the area code (404, 770 or 678) for all local calls, including those with the same area code.

SAFETY

Be particularly cautious at night in the downtown area. Atlanta's Ambassadors, brightly clad in teal and red uniforms topped with white pith helmets, patrol the downtown area to assist tourists with questions, directions and concerns. If you are on foot be especially aware that Atlanta drivers possess little, if any, respect for pedestrians so cross streets carefully.

UNDERGROUND ATLANTA

Peachtree at Alabama St is built on the underpinnings of early Atlanta, an urban marketplace of restaurants, shops and entertainment perfect for a rainy day.

ACCOMMODATION

Atlanta is a major city for conventions, and hotels in all price ranges are abundant. The safest place to stay is north of the city and unless you stay in high-end hotels, avoid the airport locations. Best prices are weekends, when the business travellers have fled.

HI Hostel $–$$ 223 Ponce de Leon Ave; tel: (404) 872-1042. Mid-town location, free morning coffee and donuts.

Howard Johnson Plaza Suites@Underground $$–$$$ 54 Peachtree St; tel: (404) 223-5555. This unassuming little hotel overlooking Underground Atlanta features small suites.

Sheraton Colony Square $$–$$$ 188 14th St NE; tel: (404) 892-6000 or 1 (800) 325-3535. An excellent location for symphony, theatre, restaurants and the High Museum.

FOOD AND DRINK

Don't expect a steady diet of traditional black-eyed peas and grits; Atlanta's restaurants accommodate almost every taste and pocket. But do try the barbecue.

Pittypat's Porch $$–$$$ 25 International Blvd; tel: (404) 525-8228. Local favourite serving barbecue, sweet potato pie and Southern hospitality.

Vortex Bar and Grill $–$$ 438 Moreland Ave; tel: (404) 688-1828. Order breakfast all day long, indulge in burgers to die for and be sure to read the back of the menu which advises 'everything you need to know is printed somewhere on this menu'.

HIGHLIGHTS

Atlanta is a city with one foot in its history and the other in the future. Downtown, tour **One CNN Center**, $, global headquarters of the news channel. On the insider tour, slightly pricier, you can don an anchor's jacket and 'deliver the news'. Open daily 0900–1800; tel: (404) 827-2300. **Margaret Mitchell House and Museum**, $$, 999 Peachtree St, tel: (404) 249-7012, is the apartment where author Margaret Mitchell created the bulk of her epic novel, *Gone With the Wind*. Open daily 0900–1600. **Martin Luther King, Jr. National Historic Site**, 450 Auburn Ave NE, is free, but you must obtain a ticket from the Parks Services office.

From its early days Savannah has been a beautiful city. So beautiful, in fact, that Union General William Tecumseh Sherman could not bring himself to burn it down in his famous March to the Sea during the Civil War. The English General James Oglethorpe designed the city in the 1730s on a defensible grid pattern of 24 tree-filled squares. Savannah today, with its trees draped romantically in Spanish moss, has a pervasive spirit of fun.

A major port for the growing cotton industry, Savannah bounced back from the Civil War much faster than its neighbours and remained prominent until the collapse of the cotton market at the beginning of the 20th century. Seeing their city's fine architectural heritage in decay, a group of Savannah women established the Historic Savannah Foundation in 1955, the country's first restoration attempt.

March and early April are good times to visit, before the summer's scorching heat and while the city's many gardens are in their full glory. December is another good time, with pleasant weather and a round of Christmas activities, including festivals, parades and tours of private homes decked for the holidays. Tourism has soared in Savannah since John Berendt's best-selling *Midnight in the Garden of Good and Evil*; everyone wants to see the places mentioned in the book and shown in the film, which was shot here.

MUST SEE/DO IN SAVANNAH

Visit in April when gardens are in full bloom and the air is filled with fragrance

Follow the sights from *Midnight in the Garden of Good and Evil*

Wander through the historic squares, attend a free Dixieland jazz concert in one of them

Remember the city for years to come, with a sweetgrass basket

GETTING THERE AND GETTING AROUND

Trains and buses connect Savannah to Charleston, Jacksonville and Washington DC. The Greyhound bus station is the more accessible to downtown, at 610 W. Oglethorpe Ave; tel: (912) 232-2135. The Amtrak station is about 4 miles out of the city, a short cab ride away, at 2611 Seaboard Coastline Dr.; tel: (800) 872-7245.

If you arrive by car, follow I-95 from either direction to I-16 East, which leads directly into the city. US 17 also runs north–south through the centre of the city.

Chatham Area Transit (CAT), tel: (912) 233-5767, runs city buses daily 0600–2400. C&H Bus, 530 Montgomery St, tel: (912) 964-7332, offers the only public transport to Tybee Beach. Buses leave from the Civic Center three times a day in summer.

INFORMATION

Savannah Area Convention and Visitors Bureau, PO Box 1628 Savannah, GA 31402-1628, responds to written information requests, or check their website at www.savannahvisit.com.

The Savannah Visitors Center, housed in a restored 1860s railway station at 301 Martin Luther King Jr Blvd, tel: (877) 728-2662 or (912) 944-0456, is open Mon–Sat 0900–1700, Sun 1100–1700. It has free maps and leaflets on attractions, dining, accommodation and tours. It offers four walking tour maps of the city and recorded cassette tapes for walking and driving tours, along with cassette players. Ample parking and free reservations for accommodation.

SAFETY The railway station is an area that turns grim after dark. Avoid low-cost hotels and boarding houses in outlying districts, sticking to the area known as the Historic District. This coincides with the downtown area, a square bordered by Martin Luther King Jr Blvd, Gwinnet St, East Broad and the river.

The midsummer heat can be oppressive and even dangerous. Stop often for non-alcoholic drinks and seek shade in the leafy squares at every opportunity.

MONEY Most banks have automated cash access from credit cards, but cashing traveller's cheques in anything but dollars is unlikely here.

POST AND PHONES Savannah's main post office, 2 N Fahm St, tel: (912) 235-4646, is open Mon–Fri 0830–1700. Use the zip code 31402 for poste restante.

ACCOMMODATION

Savannah has a wealth of major hotels and some 45 historic inns and B&Bs. The TIC has a complimentary reservations system for accommodation; tel: (800) 444-2427. **RSVP Bed and Breakfast Reservation Service of Savannah**, 219 W Bryan St, tel: (800) 729-7787 or (912) 232-7787 (Mon–Tues, Thur–Fri 0930–1730), represents 32 inns and guesthouses in the city. Try also Historic Reservations, tel: (800) 791-9393.

Savannah International Youth Hotel $ 304 E Hall St; tel: (912) 236-7744. Office hours 0700–1000 and 1700–2300; closed Feb. Close to the Riverfront Plaza and many other attractions, the hostel is in an 1884 home. No curfew.

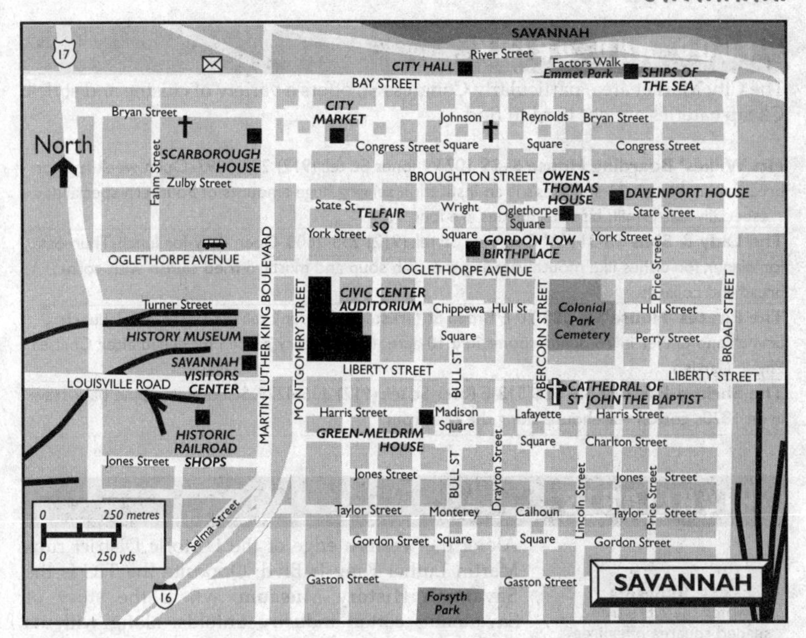

Azalea Inn $$–$$$ 217 E Huntington St; tel: (800) 582-3823. Historic inn in 1889 home.

Best Western Savannah Historic District $$–$$$ 412 W Bay St; tel: (912) 233-1011; fax: (912) 234-3963. Attractive locally owned hotel in good neighbourhood.

Eliza Thompson House $$–$$$ 5 West Jones St; tel: (912) 238-1920 or (800) 348-9378. An 1847 mansion with a stunning fountain in its courtyard.

Quality Inn Heart of Savannah $$–$$$ 300 W Bay St; tel: (912) 236-6321. Adjacent to River St, half a block from the city market. In the heart of the historic district, probably the best buy in Savannah.

Savannah's Bed and Breakfast Inn $$$ 117 W Gordon St; tel: (912) 238-0518. 1853 house with home-cooked breakfasts.

Foley House Inn $$$$ 14 W Hull St (Chippewa Sq.); tel: (800) 647-3708 or (912) 232-6622. One of 25 historic inns that sit around the city's squares.

Hampton Inn Historic District $$$$ 201 E Bay St; tel: (800) 576-4945 or (912) 231-9700. Across from the river.

KING COTTON

In 1793 on a plantation near Savannah, Eli Whitney invented the cotton gin. This machine to separate the seeds from the cotton revolutionised the industry. Soon traders were referring to the bountiful product as 'white gold', and the industry itself gained the title 'King Cotton'.

FOOD AND DRINK

The City Market area, particularly Congress St, offers a variety of cuisine and styles. Cheap eateries are not hard to find.

Mrs Wilkes' Boarding House $–$$ 107 W Jones St; tel: (912) 232-5997. Open weekdays for breakfast and lunch, Mrs Wilkes's is an institution serving huge amounts of Southern specialities – especially buttermilk biscuits; queues are long.

The Lady & Sons $$ 311 W Congress St; tel: (912) 233-2600. Open daily for lunch, Thur–Sat for dinner, for dishes like mouthwatering she-crab soup and mustard-fried catfish with cornbread and collards.

The Pirates' House $$–$$$ 20 E Broad St (Trustees' Garden); tel: (912) 233-5757. Lunch, brunch and dinner in 16 dining rooms in a 10-acre, 18th-century garden modelled after Chelsea Physic Garden.

The Shrimp Factory $$–$$$ 313 E River St; tel: (912) 236-4229. Seafood and pine bark stew in an 1820s cotton warehouse along the riverfront.

HIGHLIGHTS

FREE CONCERTS

Two of the city's tree-shaded squares offer free live concerts Fri and Wed 1130–1330 during summer months. Bring a picnic lunch and listen to blues, jazz or real Dixieland. Concerts alternate between Franklin and Johnson Squares.

Along the western edge of the Historic District runs Martin Luther King Jr Blvd. Opposite the TIC is the **Savannah History Museum**, where the story of Savannah's cotton industry unfolds, along with its part in the Civil War and its railway glory days; $, tel: (912) 238-1779; open daily 0900–1700.

The Historic Railroad Shops continue the story, and are acclaimed as the USA's oldest and most complete pre-Civil War railway manufacturing and repair facilities. The 13 original structures (including roundhouse and turntable) are filled with rail memorabilia, machinery and restored locomotives. $, 601 W Harris St; tel: (912) 651-6823; open daily 1000–1600.

Ralph Mark Gilbert Civil Rights Museum covers Savannah's African-American history, too easy to neglect in the opulence of the grand *antebellum* homes to follow. $ 460 Martin Luther King Jr Blvd; tel: (912) 231-8900; open Mon–Sat 0900–1700.

Continuing north almost to the river, **Ships of the Sea Maritime Museum** has over 50 model ships, including Viking warships and the SS *Savannah*, the first steamship to cross the Atlantic, plus a ship-in-the-bottle collection. $, 41 Martin Luther King Jr Blvd (Scarborough House); tel: (912) 232-1511; open Tues–Sun 1000–1700.

The **historic squares** are Savannah's heart. Romantic history oozes from Savannah's pores; secret gardens hint of indiscreet liaisons; fancy grillework conjures actual or imagined murders. Historic markers, many relating to Civil War personalities, plaster the historic districts. In Thunderbolt, east of the city centre, is Bonaventure Cemetery, where many generations of old families are buried, and where Berendt heard true tales of murder and intrigue, later retold in his book. The best place to begin touring these gracious squares is at the riverfront, where the recently restored Factor's Walk, once the thriving centre of the city's shipping, runs between Bay St and the riverbank bluff. The street is cobbled with stone brought from Europe as ballast for ships returning full of cotton. Bay St marks the northern boundary of Oglethorpe's original grid, now the Historic District.

THE NEGRO HERITAGE TRAIL

Daily tours from the King-Tisdell Cottage, a museum of Afro-American history at 514 E Huntington St, highlight the city's black heritage; $, tel: (912) 234-8000.

Two blocks west of Bull St, at Telfair Sq., is the **Telfair Museum of Art**, designed in 1819 by English architect William Jay. Many of the rooms are furnished with period furniture, including the fine Octagon Room. The mansion also displays several Impressionist paintings by European and American artists. $ 121 Barnard St; tel: (912) 232-1177; open Tues–Sat 1000–1700, Sun 1300–1700, Mon 1200–1700.

The **Juliette Gordon Low Birthplace**, at 142 Bull St, honours the woman who founded the Girl Guide movement in the USA in 1912. Her birthplace, a National Historic Landmark, has been restored in late 19th-century style with many of the family furnishings and a Victorian garden surrounded by the original outbuildings. $, tel: (912) 233-4501; open Mon, Tues, Thur–Sat 1000–1600, Sun 1230–1630.

Two blocks east, at Lafayette Sq., is **Andrew Low House**, built in 1848 and home of Juliette Gordon Low (see above). Its rooms, embellished with crystal

TOURS

It is easy and enjoyable to get around the 2.2 sq. mile Historic District on foot. To see the highlights, begin at the City Hall, near the river, and walk south on Bull St through five of the historic squares to Forsyth Park. Walk east two blocks to Abercorn St, turning left (north) to return through four more squares and along the edge of Colonial Park Cemetery. Though there is plenty to see on the route itself, many of the other highlights described here are within a block or two.

In the heat of summer you may prefer a narrated bus or trolley tour. **Old Town Trolley Tours**, $$$, 601 Cohen St, tel: (912) 233-0083 or (800) TOURHTA, leave from the Visitor Center daily, every half-hour 0900–1630 reboard at designated stops. **Gray Line** offers both on/off Trolley Tours and special interest tours, including the Evening Haunted Tour and a Low Country Tour, tel: (912) 234-8687, www.graylineofsavannah.com.

Walking tours ($$) offer closer glimpses inside the heart of Savannah, exploring architecture, gardens, ghosts and the sites associated with *Midnight in the Garden of Good and Evil.* Ask the Visitors Center or visit www.savannahvisit.com.

Savannah Riverboat Cruises, $$$, 9 E River St, tel: (912) 232-6404 or (800) 786-6404, offers a selection from 1-hr sightseeing tours to brunch and dinner cruises. Reservations needed for all meals.

chandeliers and intricate woodwork, once housed General Robert E Lee, the commander of the Confederate (southern) forces in the Civil War. $, 329 Abercorn St; tel: (912) 233-6854. Tours every half hour Mon–Wed and Fri–Sat 1030–1600, Sun 1200–1600.

The **Owens-Thomas House and Museum**, designed by William Jay in 1816, and facing Oglethorpe Sq., is an interesting example of an American home modelled on an English villa, with rare antiques, a restored carriage house, slave quarters and an English parterre garden. $$, 124 Abercorn St; tel: (912) 233-9743; open Tues–Sat 1000–1700, Sun 1400–1700, Mon 1200–1700.

On Columbia Sq. stands the 1815 **Isaiah Davenport House Museum**, with period furnishings, delicate ironwork and plasterwork, and an unusually elegant elliptical staircase that combine to make this one of the best houses to visit. $, 324 E State St; tel: (912) 236-8097. Tours every 30 mins Mon–Sat 1000–1600, Sun 1300–1600.

Out of town a little, but of special interest to World War II aficionados is the **Mighty Eighth Air Force Heritage Museum**, celebrating a unit formed in Savannah which served in World War II and was later moved to the UK. $$, 175 Bourne Ave (from I-95 take exit 18); tel: (912) 748-8888; open daily 0900–1800.

FOR FREE

Forsyth Park, at the southern end of the historic district, has 75 acres of landscaped green space with playgrounds, a beautiful fountain, and fragrant gardens for the blind. The park is particularly beautiful in the early spring when filled with blooming azaleas.

The **Cathedral of St John the Baptist** is one of the largest in the south. Just wander and marvel at the extensive marble work, stained glass and impressive woodcarvings, or join a free tour (available Mon–Fri 0900–1700, Sun 0800–1700 unless a service is in progress). 222 E Harris St; tel: (912) 233-4709.

Just out from the centre, on the banks of the Savannah River, **Old Fort Jackson** was started in the early 19th century and includes exhibits depicting the American Revolution, the War of 1812 and the Civil War, in each of which it played an active role. Entrance is free, but in spring and summer there are frequent special 'living history' exhibitions ($); tel: (912) 232-3945.

SHOPPING

The local speciality is sweetgrass baskets, woven of sweet-scented grass, which you will find at The Basket Place, 305 E River St; tel: (912) 232-4546. The **City Market** is a renovated four-block sector of the Historic District. Among the cafés, shops, clubs and restaurants many artists work and exhibit their works for sale – fun to browse even if you're not buying. Specialist shops of the **De Soto Historic District** and the galleries and boutiques of **River St**'s nine blocks provide gifts and mementoes. River Street Gallery, 207 E River St, has paintings and prints from the Southern states, hand-made jewellery and other crafts. River Street Zoo, 215 W River St, specialises in childrenswear and toys. Renowned Shaver's Bookshop, 326 Bull St, tel: (912) 234-7257, has 12 rooms of books. Très-cool vintage clothing and bibelots are at Once Possessed, 141 E Bull St (corner of York Lane).

SPECIAL EVENTS

First Saturday is a monthly festival at Riverfront Plaza, with arts, crafts, entertainment and street buskers.

River St goes unexpectedly Irish on 17 Mar with a wild **St Patrick's Parade**. **Savannah's Tour of Homes and Gardens** – a tradition for more than 60 years – takes place in late Mar–early Apr. Contact Historic Savannah Foundation, 18 Abercorn St, Savannah, GA 31401; tel: (912) 234-8054. The Coastal Heritage Society; tel: (912) 651-6895, schedules historical re-enactments associated with Civil War battles.

NIGHTLIFE

River St's cobblestones are the place for living it up in Savannah. Container ships and luxury yachts sail by on the river and lively music belts out of restaurants, taverns and shops in converted cotton warehouses. Some restaurants, especially those in City Market, offer weekend entertainment. To hear what's hot from local bands, try **Velvet Elvis**, 127 W Congress St; tel: (912) 236-0665.

Savannah Pops concerts, tel: (912) 236-9536, are regular performances of 1920s–1940s popular music. The **International Arts Festival**, tel: (912) 236-5745, holds 40 arts events and concerts in historic downtown venues, many events free.

ST PATRICK'S DAY SOUTHERN STYLE?

It's not known how or why Savannah's became the second largest St Patrick's Day celebration in the country, but it has been for more than 150 years. Beer, food and anything else you can think of is dyed green – even the 40,000 people on parade. One year locals tried to dye the river green. The parade begins at 1015, with live music at the City Market, and the festivities go on until midnight; tel: (912) 232-4903.

Orlando was once a sleepy Southern town surrounded by orange groves and pine forests. Then Walt Disney turned 43 square miles of swampland into the Magic Kingdom and life has never been the same. The orange groves have given way to a multitude of hotels and motels, shopping malls, and many non-Disney theme parks. Orlando is for tourists seeking sun, fun, shopping and more than a dash of fantasy.

Downtown Orlando itself sprawls north of the East-West Expressway (Hwy 408) but many of the attractions are spread over a wide area to the south, along International Drive (the locals call it I-Drive) and down to Kissimmee. Walt Disney World is at Lake Buena Vista, 20 miles south of Orlando. Big improvements in public transport, shuttle buses, monorails and the like mean that the attractions can be seen without a car, but no matter how you get to an attraction, there will be a fair amount of foot-slogging.

GETTING THERE AND GETTING AROUND

AIR Orlando International Airport (MCO), tel: (407) 825-2001 or (407) 825-2352, is 9 miles south of the city. The airport is served by cheap buses to both downtown and the International Dr. area. The service operates daily, but is reduced at weekends. The stop for both services is on the airport's 'A' side, and the trip takes about 70 mins.

THE MARK OF THE PAW

Lynx, the regional transport authority, operates on the basis of a cheap flat fare (exact money only) – check out cheap transfers, multi-ride tickets and other discounts available from the Downtown Bus Station, 445 North Garland Ave. Lynx bus stops carry a paw mark logo.

Also try I Ride, the International Drive Resort Area Shuttle, a privately run company. These trolley buses run along the tourist strip, from SeaWorld at the south end to Wet 'n' Wild at the north – a great way to get to Beltz Outlet Mall and other discount emporiums. Again, there's a flat fare, and children under six travel free.

RAIL/BUS Amtrak stations are at 1400 Slight Blvd, Orlando (about 23 miles from Disney World) or 111 Dakin Ave, Kissimmee (about 15 miles from Disney World). Greyhound buses pull into 103 E Dakin Ave, Kissimmee; van shuttle to and from the Kissimmee terminal is available from most hotels and motels.

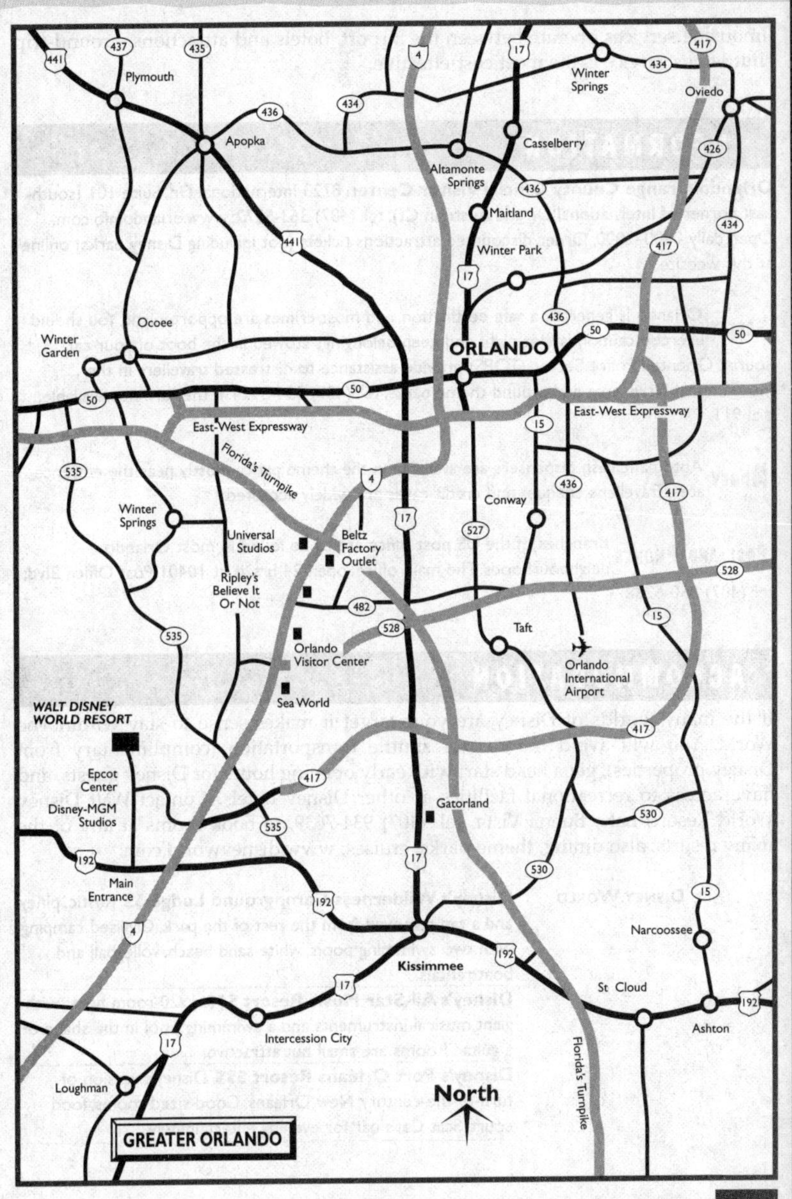
441
437
435
Plymouth
4
17
Winter Springs
417
434
Oviedo
434
436
Apopka
Casselberry
426
Altamonte Springs
436
Maitland
441
434
417
Winter Park
17
436
50
50
Ocoee
Winter Garden
ORLANDO
50
50
East-West Expressway
15
East-West Expressway
Florida's Turnpike
535
4
436
417
Winter Springs
Conway
17
527
Universal Studios
Beltz Factory Outlet
528
Ripley's Believe It Or Not
482
15
528
535
Taft
Orlando Visitor Center
Orlando International Airport
Sea World
WALT DISNEY WORLD RESORT
417
Epcot Center
417
Disney-MGM Studios
Gatorland
530
535
192
17
530
Main Entrance
192
15
4
Narcoossee
192
Kissimmee
17
St Cloud
192
Ashton
Intercession City
17
Florida's Turnpike
Loughman
North
GREATER ORLANDO

limousine services operate between the airport, hotels and attractions – round-trip shuttle bus service is the most cost-effective.

INFORMATION

Orlando/Orange County Official Visitor Center, 8723 International Dr., Suite 101 (south-east corner of International Dr. and Austrian Ct); tel: (407) 363-5872; www.orlandoinfo.com. Open daily 0800–2000. Order discounted attractions tickets (not including Disney parks) online at this website.

SAFETY Orlando is generally a safe destination, and most crimes are opportunistic. You should exercise caution late at night and keep belongings stowed in the boot of your car. Tourist Oriented Police Sector (TOPS) provide assistance to distressed travellers in the International Drive area and around theme parks; tel: (407) 354-3924. If they are not available, dial 911.

MONEY Automatic cash dispensers are available in the theme parks, mostly near the entrance area. Traveller's cheques and credit cards are widely accepted.

POST AND PHONES Branches of the US post office are to be found in most Orlando neighbourhoods. The main office, open 24 hrs, is at 10401 Post Office Blvd; tel: (407) 850-6288.

ACCOMMODATION

If the many worlds of Disney are your target it makes sense to stay within The World. You will avoid the cost of shuttle transportation (complimentary from Disney properties), get a head start with early opening hours for Disney guests, and have access to recreational facilities at other Disney hotels. Contact Walt Disney World Resort, Lake Buena Vista, tel: (407) 934-7639, to book rooms at any of the many resorts; also dining, theme parks, cruises; www.disneyworld.com.

DISNEY WORLD

Disney's Wilderness Campground Lodge $$. Rustic, piney and a tad removed from the rest of the park. Civilised camping with two swimming pools, white sand beach, volleyball and boat rentals.

Disney's All-Star Music Resort $$$. 1920-room hotel with giant musical instruments and a swimming pool in the shape of a guitar. Rooms are small but attractive.

Disney's Port Orleans Resort $$$. Disney's version of turn-of-the-century New Orleans. Good-sized rooms, food court, Scat Cat's bar for evening entertainment.

Outside, almost every international hotel chain has at least one property in the area (see p. 52).

OUTSIDE DISNEY WORLD

Orlando/Kissimmee Resort Hostel $–$$ 4840 West Irlo Bronson Highway; tel: (407) 396-8282 or (800) 909-4776, access code 33. Motel-style hostel with dormitory and private room accommodation. Set on a lake (don't swim in it), with a swimming pool, barbecue grill, and laundry facilities. Shuttle from airport and to Disney theme parks.

Comfort Inn $$ 8442 Palm Pkway; tel: (407) 996-7300 or (800) 999-7300. Located only 2.5 miles from the Disney Worlds, and with free shuttle transport, this clean, if spartan, motel is a good deal. Facilities include two swimming pools, washer/dryers and a video game arcade.

Fairfield Inn by Marriott $$ 8432 Jamaican Ct; tel: (407) 363-1944 or (800) 228-2800. In a safe and quiet location, with restaurants within walking distance (mind the traffic crossing I-Drive!), free newspapers and continental breakfast.

Perrihouse B&B Inn $$$ 10417 Centurion Ct; tel: (407) 876-4830 or (800) 780-4830; email: Birds@Perrihouse.com. Set in an orange grove 3 mins from the Disney Main Gate. Transport to the B&B can be arranged in advance.

CAMPSITES

Kampgrounds of America (KOA), Kissimmee/Orlando KOA, 4771 W Hwy 192, Kissimmee; tel: (407) 396-2400. Tent village, RV pitches and cabins, close to Walt Disney World (shuttle service to the attractions).

Fort Wilderness Campground and Lodge. The campground ($$) has restrooms, showers, lifeguards, canoe rentals, grocery shopping and restaurants nearby. Over 700 sites are available; for reservations tel: (407) 824-2900. The lodge ($$$) is a magnificent multi-storey log cabin, replete with totem poles and a massive stone fireplace. Complimentary transport to and from Disney theme parks.

FOOD AND DRINK

International Dr. has the widest choice, but the Church St area downtown and Hwy 192 out towards Kissimmee are also well served. Each of the area's major attractions has a host of restaurants, cafés and food stalls. You can bring your own snacks into the various theme parks but picnic facilities are not available, and the park operators frown if you eat your own food at restaurant tables.

The B-Line Diner at the Peabody Hotel $ 9801 International Dr.; tel: (407) 345-4460. Serves classic burgers,

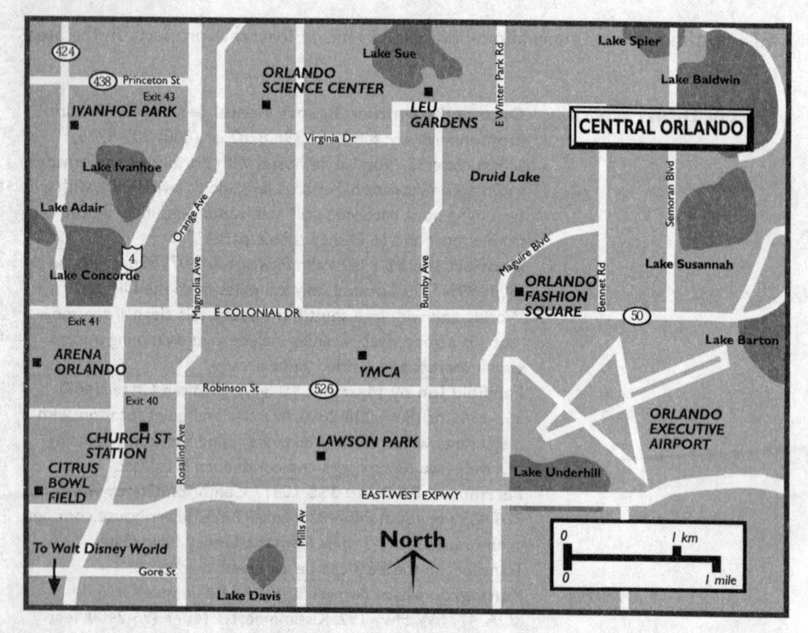

steaks, seafood and home-made ice cream in the chrome and pastel décor of the 1950s.

Guitar-shaped Hard Rock Café Universal City Walk; tel: (407) 351-7625. The Hard Rock Café has been renovated and relocated here. For those who care more about rock 'n' roll than food.

Ming Court $$$$ 9188 International Dr.; tel: (407) 351-9988. A favourite with Orlando business folk; pricey, but the Chinese dishes are legendary.

HIGHLIGHTS

THEME PARKS **Universal Studios Florida** is a working production studio with movie-theme attractions and daredevil stunt shows. Ride the Movies features take you right inside blockbuster films like *Jurassic Park*, *Earthquake* (feel the heat of the flames), *King Kong* (smell his banana breath), *Back to the Future* (hurtle through fog made of liquid nitrogen), *Jaws* (hang on tight as he tries to capsize your boat) and *ET* (travel through space amid hundreds of planets and thousands of stars). **Universal's Islands of Adventure** bases nearly all rides on Universal movies or Marvel comic books. Among them, 'Jurassic Park Island' is a jungly ride with

WALT DISNEY WORLD

The Magic Kingdom

The first of the Walt Disney World theme parks features nearly 50 major shows and adventures divided into seven fantasy lands. Cinderella's Castle is its most famous landmark, and this is where Mickey and friends hang out. Ride the Skyway from Tomorrowland to Fantasyland as the fireworks begin and you will feel as though you are flying through the stars.

Disney-MGM Studios

This is a working film, TV, radio and animation studio as well as a theme park. Experience the Indiana Jones Epic Stunt Spectacle, the Twilight Zone Tower of Terror. Each evening ends with Fantasmic, a laser, fireworks and water animation spectacular.

Epcot

Epcot is a celebration of technological and social achievements. There are whizzbang effects at Future World, a chance to see and use the products of tomorrow at Innoventions and a global tour in World Showcase's 11 national pavilions. Don't miss the nightly laser light show over the lagoon (for a good view in comfort, grab an outside table at the UK pavilion's Rose and Crown).

Disney's Animal Kingdom

This latest extravaganza is filled with real and fabricated critters. Rescue dinosaurs from extinction, or take a photo safari. The Tree of Life dominates the park and houses a riotous 3-D film, *A Bug's Life*. Go early or stay late as many animals are nocturnal and not particularly active during the heat of the day.

Downtown Disney

This is where to head at night. It pulses with all the energy of a metropolis on New Year's eve, every night of the year. You'll find oodles of restaurants and shopping; save time for a performance of Cirque du Soleil's 'La Nouba'.

Visitors have a memorable time, but not a cheap one – a one-day admission to an individual theme park is upwards of $50, with little discounted for children. It may be worth investing in a Park Hopper Pass, which permits unlimited entry to all the parks. The passes are sold in 3, 4 and 5 day segments and do not expire, so any unused days on your present trip will remain good for a future experience.

The bus tours and IMAX® cinema are understandably popular – book for these as soon as you arrive, so you don't miss out.

animatronic lizards; 'Dueling Dragons' is a rollercoaster which takes riders on dual tracks hurtling towards each other at 60 mph and missing by heart-stopping inches; and 'The Amazing Adventures of Spider Man' combines 3-D film, live action and moving audience seats to engage guests in the superhero's battle against evil. The Bates Motel Gift Shop is a must for *Psycho* fans. $$$$ (parking extra); opening times vary according to the season.

More than 20 major shows and displays are featured at **SeaWorld** (7007 SeaWorld Dr.). This long-established marine life park enables you to enter the underwater world of whales, dolphins, manatees and other marine mammals, and there are daily shows. $$$$ (plus parking); open daily 0900–1900 (hours vary during summer and holidays).

More than 5000 alligators and crocodiles inhabit **Gatorland**'s extensive marshes. There is alligator wrestling, a marsh with an observation tower, a natural cypress swamp and lots of other animals, birds and reptiles. When hunger strikes, try alligator cooked Southern style. $$$, 14501 S Orange Blossom Trail; open daily 0900–dusk.

Splendid China has replicas of 60 Chinese historical and cultural landmarks and sites, most – like the Great Wall of China and the Terracotta Warriors – miniaturised. $$$, 3000 Splendid China Blvd, Kissimmee; open daily 0930–1900. **Chinatown**, the dining, shopping and entertainment area, open 0930–2200, is free.

MUSEUMS The **Orlando Science Center**, downtown at 777 E Princeton St, is likely to be crowded with children trying out the interactive exhibits *you* would like to try. $$, open Mon–Thur 0900–1700, Fri–Sat 0900–2100, Sun 1200–1700; CineDome and parking extra.

North of the centre is the **Orlando Museum of Art**. Its pre-Columbian gallery houses more than 250 pieces from Mexico, Guatemala, Colombia, Costa Rica, Panama and Peru dating from 1200 BC to AD 1500. Among its permanent collections is an exhibition of

ALMOST FREE

Turkey Lake Park, 3401 Hiawassee Rd; tel: (407) 299-5594. Picnic tables, bicycle and hiking trails, beaches, swimming pool, fishing pier, canoe rentals and pet zoo. $, open daily 0930–1900.

Disney's Boardwalk Entertainment Complex, Walt Disney World; tel: (407) 824-4321. Waterfront village in the style of the 1930s Atlantic coast resorts, offers shopping, restaurants and nightlife.

Downtown Disney, Walt Disney World; tel: (407) 939-7727. Shopping in the market place, upmarket restaurants, cinema complex and bustling street life.

Farmers Markets, I-4 and Church St, Sat mornings. Fresh produce, baked goods, plants and flowers. Tel: (407) 623-3200.

City Walk, Universal Studios, is filled with restaurants and music venues. Admission is free, but the price for individual venues varies. You'll find the Hard Rock Café Orlando, Jimmy Buffet's Margaritaville, NASCAR Cafe, City Jazz and the Latin Quarter; tel: (407) 363-8000. Now that there are two Universal Studios theme parks, a multi-day theme pass is even more important than ever.

20th-century American and African art. $, 2416 N Mills Ave; open Tues–Sat 0900–1700, Sun 1200–1700. In less reverential mood, **Ripley's Believe It Or Not!** has hundreds of unbelievable exhibits in an eccentric showplace. $$, 8201 International Dr.; open daily 0900–2300. **Titanic, Ship of Dreams** is an interactive museum which features over 200 artefacts and memorabilia from the film *A Night To Remember*; White Star 'staff' welcome you aboard. $$, Mercado Mall, International Dr.; tel: (407) 248-1166; open daily 1000–2200.

WILDLIFE In addition to showpieces like SeaWorld and Gatorland (see p. 284), and Disney's Discovery Island, Orlando has a couple of animal attractions. **Jungleland Zoo** has alligators, crocodiles, birds, big cats and monkeys. $$$, 4580 W Hwy 192; open daily 0900–1800. Out at Maitland, **Audubon of Florida** is the headquarters of the Florida Audubon Society, one of the state's oldest and largest conservation organisations. At the Audubon House visitors view live bald eagles, owls, hawks and other birds of prey. Guided tours are conducted. 1101 Audubon Way, Maitland (take I-4 east to Lee Road exit); tel: (407) 644-0190; open Tues–Sun 1000–1600; entry by donation ($5 suggested for adults, $4 for children).

SPORT AND ACTIVITIES Like the rest of Florida, Orlando is golf and tennis crazy and many facilities are available to visitors. There are five major splash parks in the Orlando area, of which Disney operates three – River Country, Typhoon Lagoon and Blizzard Beach. **Wet 'n' Wild**, $$$$, 6200 International Dr., has 25 acres of rides, slides and flumes, and **Water Mania**, $$$$, 6073 W Hwy 192, adds outdoor concerts for pool occupants and picnic grounds by the water rides.

The adventurous and early risers may like to take to the air. For an expensive but exciting experience, a number of companies offer hot-air balloon flights over the theme parks and lakes. Contact Aviation Services, 11475 Rocket Blvd, tel: (407) 841-8787, or Rise and Float Balloon Tours, 5767 Major Blvd; tel: (407) 352-8191.

SHOPPING

The area's largest factory outlet (over 180 stores) is **Beltz Factory Outlet World**, 5401 W Oakridge Rd (at the north end of International Dr.); tel: (407) 352-9600; open Mon–Sat 1000–2100, Sun 1000–1800. **The Florida Mall**, 8001 S Orange Blossom Trail, tel: (407) 851-7234, is open daily and houses major department stores and speciality shops, an excellent choice for inclement weather.

NIGHTLIFE

Orlando is devoted to entertainment, day and night. The daily newspaper, *Orlando Sentinel*, lists concerts, operas, recitals, ballets, plays and other entertainment and cultural activities in its calendar section, published on Friday. For theatre lovers, Orlando Broadway Series presents a late Oct–May season of national and touring productions of Broadway plays and musicals at the 2500-seat **Bob Carr Performing Arts Centre**, 201 S Orange Ave; tel: (407) 423-9999. The professional **Orlando Opera Company** performs at 1111 N Orange Ave; tel: (407) 426-1717.

City Walk, located between Islands of Adventure and Universal Studios, tel: (407) 363-8000, is a collection of shops, eateries and theatres pleasantly arranged around a lagoon. Nightclubs, which make a cover charge, include Cityjazz, the groove, Hard Rock Live and Jimmy Buffet's Margaritaville.

At the **Cricketers' Arms**, 8445 International Dr., tel: (407) 354-0686, there's budget eating and drinking with an English pub atmosphere and nightly entertainment. Open daily 1100–0200.

New Year's Eve is celebrated every night of the year at **Pleasure Island**, part of the Walt Disney World complex. Lots of music here: rhythm and blues, modern jazz, rock 'n' roll, and country and western. The nightly 'New Year' is announced with cannon fire, bells, fireworks and dancing in the streets. Open daily 1900–0200; admission for all clubs $$$.

DINNER SHOWS

Dinner shows form a major part of Orlando's night-time entertainment programme, and if you like your dinners packaged and served in a regimented, if lively, fashion, there are several to choose from. $$$$ (inclusive prices).

Arabian Nights Dinner Attraction, 6225 W Hwy 192, tel: (407) 239-9221 or (800) 553-6116, combines virtuoso horsemanship with a four-course prime rib dinner. Italian fare accompanies speakeasy entertainment with gangsters, molls and cops at **Capone's Dinner and Show**, 4740 W Hwy 192; tel: (407) 397-2378.

WHERE NEXT?

When Mickey et al. have exhausted you, Florida has an abundance of resorts and wildlife and, of course, the Kennedy Space Center Visitor Complex (see p. 287).

FLORIDA BEYOND THE THEME PARKS

There is a great deal more to Florida than sunshine and hype, retirees and refugees. The beaches *are* superb – high society made Palm Beach an exclusive winter retreat long before the masses discovered Fort Lauderdale or the Gulf Coast – and the winter sun is a bonus (don't forget, winter is the *high* season here). There is a downside – parts of Miami, hurricanes, mosquitoes, overdevelopment – but there's also dramatic wildlife, some charming towns and non-theme park attractions from prehistoric caves to the launch pads of Cape Canaveral.

GETTING THERE AND GETTING AROUND

The major Florida airports are Miami International, Orlando International and Tampa International. Fort Lauderdale-Hollywood, West Palm Beach, Jacksonville and Key West all have smaller international airports.

Amtrak Silver Services run three times daily between New York and Miami with a number of stops along the Florida Atlantic Coast.

Greyhound buses link most of the main centres and make the run right down Hwy 1 to Key West. The nearest stop to the Everglades is Homestead, 10 miles north. The St Augustine stop is centrally located in a busy area, and the stop for Tampa is located downtown in a relatively safe area.

JOURNEY INTO SPACE

Take one small step into both the history and the future of space travel at the **John F Kennedy Space Center**. The Mission Countdown, Gallery of Space Flight and the Galaxy Center with its IMAX® cinema ($) are just some of the hands-on attractions at Spaceport USA. Launch schedules permitting, there are bus tours ($$) of the working areas of the Center and out to Cape Canaveral, taking in the Saturn V rocket and a simulated *Apollo 11* moon launch. Spaceport USA is an all-day experience that will bring you closer than you ever dreamt to the excitement of space exploration; amazingly, bus tours and the IMAX® cinema apart (book immediately upon arrival), it is all *free*.

i **The Space Coast Office of Tourism**, 2725 Judge Fran Jamieson Way, Viera; tel: (800) 872-1969; www.space-coast.com/florida; also has a visitor centre at the Space Center. Interested in seeing a space shuttle or rocket launch? Call: (800) KSC-INFO.

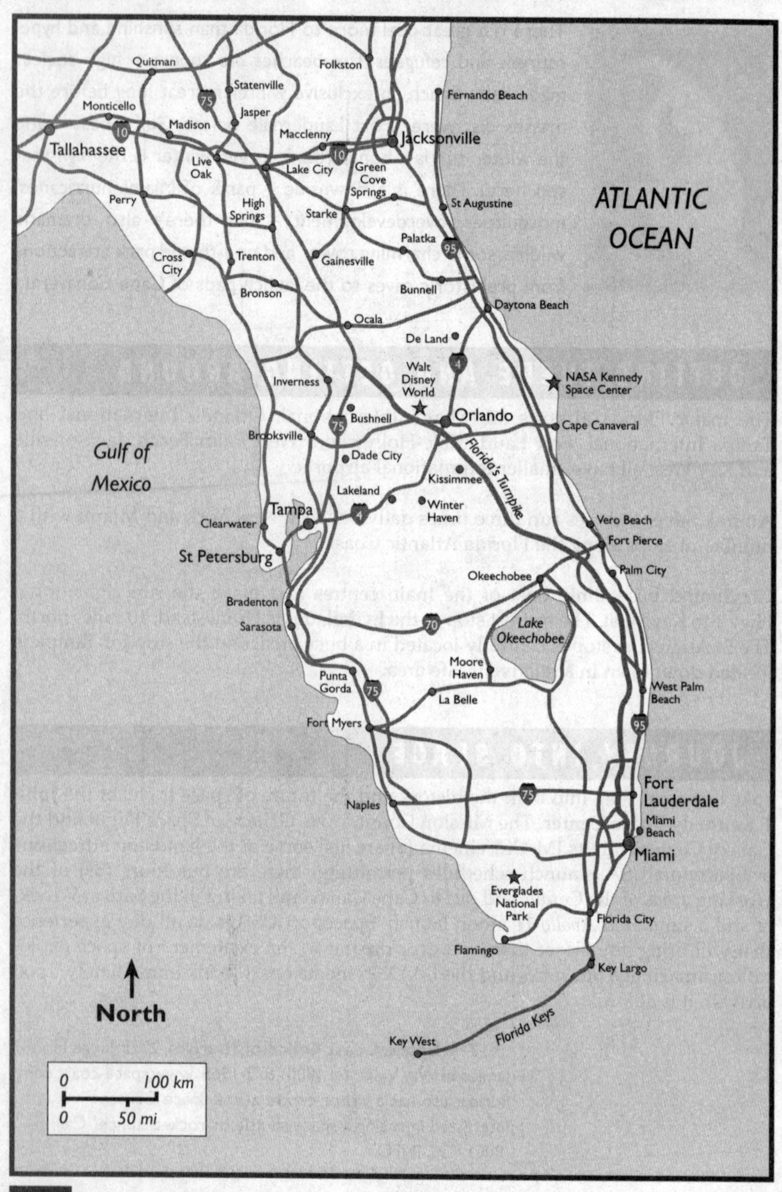
ATLANTIC OCEAN
Gulf of Mexico
Quitman
Folkston
Statenville
Fernando Beach
Monticello
Jasper
Madison
Macclenny
Jacksonville
Tallahassee
Live Oak
Lake City
Green Cove Springs
Perry
High Springs
Starke
St Augustine
Palatka
Cross City
Trenton
Gainesville
Bronson
Bunnell
Daytona Beach
Ocala
De Land
Walt Disney World
NASA Kennedy Space Center
Inverness
Bushnell
Orlando
Cape Canaveral
Brooksville
Dade City
Florida's Turnpike
Kissimmee
Lakeland
Winter Haven
Tampa
Clearwater
St Petersburg
Vero Beach
Fort Pierce
Palm City
Okeechobee
Bradenton
Sarasota
Lake Okeechobee
Moore Haven
Punta Gorda
La Belle
West Palm Beach
Fort Myers
Fort Lauderdale
Naples
Miami Beach
Miami
Everglades National Park
Florida City
Flamingo
Key Largo
North
Key West
Florida Keys
0
100 km
0
50 mi

TALLAHASSEE

The state capital has the gracious atmosphere of a Southern country town quite different from the resort world of peninsular Florida. It's a useful base for exploring the Panhandle and the white Gulf of Mexico beaches, 25 miles south. The area is lush with rolling hills, towering pines and cypress, fragrant magnolias, shimmering lakes, swamps and sink holes.

Tallahassee's historic district glimpses into yesteryear with *antebellum* (pre-Civil War) mansions and nostalgic **Old Town Trolley**; tel: (850) 891-5200, providing free transit Mon–Fri 0700–1800. **The Old Capitol Museum**, S Monroe St, tel: (850) 487-1902, has been restored to its 1902 appearance, complete with red striped awnings, stained-glass dome and classic rotunda. The **Governor's Mansion**, 700 N Adams St, tel: (850) 488-4661, is a Georgian-style mansion, and **Knott House Museum**, 301 E Park Ave, tel: (850) 922-2459, is a Victorian delight, filled with whimsical rhymes.

Near Tallahassee is **Wakulla Springs State Park**, $, tel: (850) 224-5950, one of the world's deepest freshwater springs featuring glass-bottom and river boat tours, swimming trails and a fine-dining restaurant.

BY RAIL

Amtrak station is 5 minutes from downtown on Gaines and Railroad Ave, tel: (800) 872-7245, connecting Tallahassee with east–west service via the 'Sunset Limited'.

i **Tallahassee Area Visitor Information Center**, 106 E Jefferson St, tel: (800) 628-2866, (850) 413-2900 or www.see-tallahassee.com, open Mon–Fri 0800–1700, Sat 0900–1300.

Collegiate Village Inn $$–$$$ 2121 W Tennessee St; tel: (850) 576-6121. Located near the Universities, with colour TV, air conditioning and free continental breakfast.

Microtel Inn & Suites $$ 3216 N Monroe St; tel: (850) 562-3800. Refrigerators, microwave and coffee-makers, complimentary continental breakfast, exercise facility, and cookies and milk every evening.

Local specialities include the famous Apalachicola oysters and Panacea blue crabs.

Boss Oyster $–$$1830 Monroe St N; tel: (850) 385-8734. Apalachicola Bay oysters, shrimp, crayfish and barbecue. Open-air porch to catch the breezes.

Nino $$–$$$ 6497 Apalachee Pkwy; tel: (850) 878-8141. Unique blend of Italian and German cuisine in a charming old house. Pasta, seafood and an extensive winelist.

Po' Boys Creole Café $–$$ 224 E College Ave; tel: (850) 224-5400. Cheap, cheerful and serving up lots of red beans and rice.

ST AUGUSTINE

Though Native Americans might quibble, attractive little St Augustine considers itself the oldest city in the USA. Spaniards, who settled here as early as 1565, built a star-shaped fort whose walls still stand. Though the town has become quite touristy, riverside Castillo de San Marcos ($) remains worth a look. Other attractions are only moderately interesting, but the Spanish Quarter Village ($) is entertaining for children – there's a blacksmith who works a forge, for example.

St Augustine Visitor Information Center, 10 Castillo Dr.; tel: (904) 825-1000; www.oldcity.com.

Anastasia Inn $$–$$$$ 218 Anastasia Blvd; tel: (904) 825-2879. Basic motel convenient to sights. All rooms are equipped with microwaves and refrigerators.

Econo Lodge $$$ 311 A1A Beach Blvd; tel: (904) 471-2330. Chain motel out by the long beach. Some rooms have kitchenettes.

International Haus $–$$ 32 Treasury St; tel: (904) 808-1999 or (877) 466-3864. Amazingly central hostel with private rooms and dorms worthy of a B&B. Rooftop terrace, kitchen and lounge.

A1A Ale Works $$ 1 King St; tel: (904) 829-2977. Decent microbrewery with Caribbean-influenced menu of fish dishes and grand views of sunset and Lion's Gate Bridge.

King's Head British Pub $$ 6460 Hwy 1 N; tel: (904) 823-9787. British pub serving bangers 'n' mash, pasties and shepherd's pie. Good selection of draft beers.

Theo's Restaurant $ 169 King St; tel: (904) 824-5022. Popular luncheonette reflecting the city's Minorcan (Greek) community. Breakfast and lunch only.

TAMPA BAY

Florida's Gulf Coast is one of its quieter areas. Tampa, the largest city, retains a strong Cuban heritage from its days as an early centre of cigar manufacture; the Ybor City Museum at 1818 E 9th Ave ($) relates this history. To the west, Clearwater's beaches are long, clean and powdery. In St Petersburg, the main draw is the surprisingly complete Salvador Dalí museum at 1000 3rd St S ($$).

St Petersburg/Clearwater Visitors Bureau, 14450 46th St N, Clearwater; tel (800) 345-6710 or (727) 464-7200; www.floridasbeach.com.

NATURE AND WILDLIFE

Think of Florida wildlife and you conjure up the **Everglades**: careening across the water in an airboat at 60 mph, floating silently past 'gators basking among the mangroves, marvelling at pink clouds of flamingoes and roseate spoonbills. A proportion of this rich wildlife habitat, a relic of the swamps and seas of reeds that once covered southern Florida, is preserved within the Everglades National Park and Big Cypress National Preserve. You'll need a vehicle for access, but there are plenty of opportunities for boat tours, canoeing and ranger-led walks. Winter is the best time to visit, when the bird population is at its height and the air mercifully free of the mosquitoes that plague the area from Apr to Nov (but beware of the hunting season mid-Nov–Dec).

Tampa Bay Visitor Center, 3601 Busch Blvd; tel: (813) 985-3601; www.visittampabay.com.

AmeriSuites Tampa Busch Gardens $$$–$$$$ 11408 N 30th St; tel: (813) 979-1922 or (800) 833-1516. Reliable chain hotel; good for families, as all rooms have kitchenettes.
Clearwater Beach Hostel $–$$ 606 Bay Esplanade, Clearwater; tel: (727) 443-1211 or (800) 909-4776 ext. 16. Well-run dorms and motel rooms close to the beach. Self-catering kitchen, pool, common room, television.
Gram's Place $$–$$$ 3109 N Ola Ave; tel: (813) 221-0596. Not your typical B&B, this one has musical theme rooms, a 16-track recording studio, a bar and a whirlpool.

Don Quixote Cafetería $ 1901 13th St in Tampa's Ybor City. Bustling joint serving huge portions of inexpensive Cuban food. Open Mon–Fri 1030–1500.
Frenchy's Saltwater Café $$ 419 Poinsettia Ave, in Clearwater Beach. Cheerfully laid-back eatery with freshly caught and fried seafood. Indoor and outdoor dining.
Thai Basil $$ 4445 E Bay Dr., Largo (south of Clearwater). Unpretentious family-run restaurant serving terrific Thai meals.

FORT LAUDERDALE

The spectacular beach is the big draw, but Fort Lauderdale gives tourists other reasons to visit.

The **Museum of Discovery and Science and Blockbuster IMAX® 3-D Theater**, open Mon–Sat 1000–1700, Sun 1200–1800 ($$), has the only interactive IMAX® cinema ($$) in the region as well as seven interactive exhibit areas. The **Seminole Okalee Village & Museum** ($) on Rte 7 south. tel: (954) 792-0745, on the Hollywood Reservation, explores the Native American side of Broward County. A small cultural museum is augmented by craftspeople and alligator wrestling demonstrations.

Everglades Holiday Park $$$, on Griffin Rd, tel: (800) 226-2244 or (954) 434-8111, offers airboat tours of the Everglades outside the National Park boundaries. Airboats also stop at a hammock (stretch of dry land with grass and trees) for alligator wrestling and trinket

A GRAND BAHAMA INTERLUDE

For a break with a Caribbean feeling, Grand Bahama is still an unspoiled getaway that offers snorkelling, kayaking and miles of uncrowded beaches, easily and inexpensively accessible from Fort Lauderdale. *Discovery Sun* takes a 5-hour day cruise to Freeport for as little as $129; two-night/three-day packages from $149 include cruise and lodging on the island. The gourmet dining package for an additional $21 per person, a five-course extravaganza, is outstanding. Discovery Cruise Line, 1775 NW 70th Ave, Miami, FL 33126; tel: (800) 866-8687, (305) 597-0336, www.discoverycruise.com. At **Paradise Cove**, Deadman's Reef, Grand Bahama, tel: (242) 349-2677, fax (242) 352-5471, www.deadmansreef.com, you can rent a two-bedroom villa or one-bedroom apartment with fully equipped kitchen and living room, only feet from sandy beaches, perfect snorkelling and kayak tours.

sales. There is also fishing, with or without a guide, picnicking and an RV park.

Jungle Queen Cruises $$$, tel: (954) 462-5596, cruise the inland waterways daily, complete with vaudeville entertainment and sing-songs that pre-date many of today's grandparents. The nightly four-hour dinner cruise includes an all-you-can-eat barbecue on a private island.

Getting around is difficult without a car. Taxis are pricey for any but the shortest of excursions. **Water Taxi**, tel: (954) 467-6677, picks up passengers at more than 80 marinas, hotels, beaches, restaurants, museums, shopping malls and cinemas near the water. The bright yellow boats cost $7.50 one way, $14 return, or $16 for an all-day pass.

i **Greater Fort Lauderdale Convention & Visitors Bureau**, 1800 Eller Dr., Suite 303, Ft Lauderdale, FL 33316; tel: (800) 356-1662 or (800) 22-SUNNY. Open Mon–Fri.

There are 30,000 hotel rooms in the area, concentrated near the beach close to Rte A1A, on the harbour and near the airport. All major chains are represented, usually with several properties each, including:

Doubletree Oceanfront Hotel $$$$ 440 Seabreeze Blvd; tel: (800) 222-8733 or (954) 524-8733, at the busiest section of the beach.

Marriott's Harbor Beach $$$$ 3030 Holiday Dr., tel: (800) 222-6543 or (954) 525-4000, has one of the longest hotel beaches in the area.

Radisson Bahia Mar $$$$ 801 Seabreeze Blvd, tel: (800) 531-2478 or (954) 764-2233, has splendid water views.

Shopping on Las Olas Blvd, where settlers once traded with Native Americans, draws a lively crowd to tiny boutiques, art galleries and outdoor cafés. Many shops are closed on Sundays.

Ft Lauderdale claims more than 3000 restaurants, from the Polynesian kitsch of **Mai Kai** $$$$ 3599 N Federal Hwy, tel: (954) 563-3272, to **15th Street Fisheries** $$ 1900 SE 15th St, tel: (954) 763-2777,

overlooking the harbour, a local favourite for fish and alligator.
Bar Amici $$ 1301 E Las Olas Blvd, tel: (954) 467-3266, moderate, has delicious fish.

MIAMI

Miami's mass-media image as a stylish, dangerous town is mostly accurate. While most of the high-rollers live in Miami proper (also home to a fascinating Latin American community), Miami Beach is the place to vacation: think long beaches, attractive sunbathers and streets of bars, Cuban diners, neon and throbbing all-night clubs.

Reaching the beach without a car can be tricky and dangerous; take a taxi from the airport or train station. Once here, however, you're rewarded by nonstop action. Pedestrian-only Lincoln Rd is the place to shop, eat or sip a coffee, while Washington Ave concentrates the best clubs; Collins Ave is lined with diners and Art Deco hotels; and Ocean Dr. is the domain of fashion models and the like. The beach is also a magnet for gay culture.

Greater Miami Convention and Visitors Bureau, 701 Brickell Ave; tel: (305) 539-3063 or (888) 76-MIAMI; www.gmcvb.com.

Choicest lodgings are all in Miami Beach, though prices become unreasonably high between Christmas and Easter.
Clay Hotel & International Hostel $–$$$ 1438 Washington Ave; tel: (305) 534-2988 or (800) 379-2529. Sprawling pink complex with a range of hotel rooms, dorms and an attractive interior courtyard.
Mermaid Guesthouse $$$–$$$$ 909 Collins Ave; tel: (305) 538-5324. Steps from the beach. Guest rooms have a tropical feel, enhanced by a lush garden and colourful owners.
Villa Paradiso $$$–$$$$ 1415 Collins Ave; tel: (305) 532-0616. Apartments rented nightly, weekly or longer. Most have kitchenettes; there's a laundry on site.

La Sandwicherie $ 229 14th St; tel: (305) 532-8934. Tasty baguette sandwiches good for taking to the beach.
Puerto Sagua $ 700 Collins Ave; tel: (305) 673-1115. Cuban food at rock-bottom prices. Wake up with a Cuban espresso and go to bed with a midnight sandwich.
Wolfie's $$ 2038 Collins Ave; tel: (305) 538-6626. Classic, 24-hr Jewish diner serving huge, pricey menu of pastrami, brisket and towers of pie.

The Conch Tour Train, tel: (305) 294-5161, and the Old Town Trolley, tel: (305) 296-6688, offer 90-minute rolling tours of Old Town. The Tour Train stops at the corner of Duval and Front Sts and the Key West Welcome Center on N Roosevelt Blvd. The Trolley makes 14 stops along a more complete route through Old Town. Riders can leave and reboard their tour at any stop.

Key West International Airport is 3 miles (10 mins) from the historic district. A taxi to city centre hotels costs $6–$8.

US Hwy 1 is the only road in, or out, of Key West and leads to the historic Old Town district. The Greyhound Bus Lines depot is at 615-1/2 Duval St; tel: (305) 296-9072.

KEY LARGO AND KEY WEST

The Keys is a fascinating chain of islands linked by US Hwy 1. **Key Largo** is one of the world's most popular scuba-diving destinations, and most of the islands offer diving or snorkelling, or a trip in a glass-bottomed boat, to glimpse the fragile coral reef and old shipwrecks.

Key West, the land's-end community of bohemians, is where you can join the locals at Mallory Square to watch the sun go down as you sip your margarita. It has three sightseeing areas: the Old Town, the Dry Tortugas islands (70 miles west) and the beaches.

Discovery Tours, tel: (305) 293-0099, has daily glass-bottomed boat tours of nearby reefs out of Land's End Marina while the **Old Island Restoration Foundation**, Old Mallory Sq., tel: (305) 294-9501, has created a 50-stop walking tour of Old Town.

The oldest building in Key West is the 19th-century **Wrecker's Museum**, $, 322 Duval St; tel: (305) 294-9502, open daily 1000–1600. **Key West Lighthouse**, $, 938 Whitehead St; tel: (305) 294-0012, open 0930–1630, follows the evolving history of the Keys lighthouses that eventually put the wreckers out of business.

Limited space keeps Key West lodging prices high. The most desirable addresses are around lower Duval St, near Front St.
Casablanca **$$–$$$** 900 Duval St; tel: (305) 296-0637.
Pilot House **$$–$$$** 414 Simonton St; tel: (800) 648-3780.
Courtney's Place **$$–$$$** 720 Whitmarsh Lane; tel: (800) 869-4639 or (305) 294-3480.

Casablanca **$$–$$$** 914 Duval St; tel: (305) 296-0637, has some of the tastiest seafood and best service.
Blue Heaven **$–$$** 729 Thomas St; tel: (305) 296-8666, has excellent Caribbean fare and outside tables.
El Siboney **$–$$$** 900 Catherine St; tel: (305) 296-4184, may be the best Cuban restaurant in Key West.
Louie's Backyard **$$–$$$** 700 Waddell Ave; tel: (305) 294-1061. A sunset drink on the oceanside deck is a more affordable alternative to dinner.

While it was New Orleans that unleashed jazz on the world from the mouth of the Mississippi, Memphis, upriver, is the home of the blues and its offspring, rock 'n' roll. Music is its heart and soul. Memphis is also known in many Americans' minds as the place where civil rights leader Martin Luther King Jr was assassinated in 1968. The city has converted the site to a civil rights museum.

Downtown is the obvious place to start, with a number of museums on and around Beale St, though this whole area is clearly tourist-oriented. Midtown Memphis offers good dining and some excellent museums. The city's other top tourist draw is about 10 miles south of the city centre: Elvis Presley's suburban home, Graceland.

MUST SEE/DO IN MEMPHIS

Eat pit barbecue and listen to blues on Beale St

Take the Monorail and Walkway to Mud Island and absorb river lore at the museum there

Pay respects to the King at Graceland

Take a paddlewheeler cruise on the Mississippi

GETTING THERE AND GETTING AROUND

Memphis International Airport is a major regional hub. Northwest and KLM have daily flights to Amsterdam. The airport shuttle DASH serves all downtown hotels. The Amtrak station is in a slowly regenerating part of town just south of the centre at 545 S Main St; Memphis connects with Chicago and New Orleans (see p.344).

Greyhound buses stop at the central terminal at the corner of Union Ave at Hernando St and 4th St. Most sites are close together; you can hop on the historic Main St Trolley to shuttle you north–south across the centre. Buses serve sites further out.

INFORMATION

The **Memphis Convention and Visitors Bureau** is very convenient at 119 N Riverside Dr.; tel: (901) 543-5333 or (800) 873-6282, www.memphistravel.com; open daily 0900–1800. Regional information is available here also. The city's other site, www.memphisguide.com, has a thorough rundown of the history and sites of Beale St.

MONEY Banks with automatic cash dispensers abound. Travelex is situated at 84 N Evergreen, No. 4; tel: (901) 276-6060; about 2 miles east of the centre.

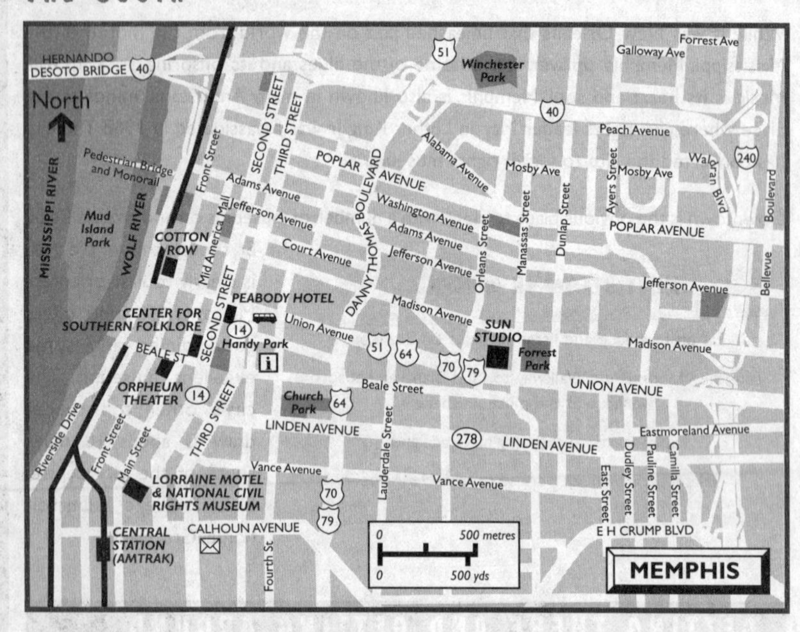

POST AND PHONES Post offices are at 555 S 3rd St and at Front & Madison St. Both open Mon–Fri 0830–1730, Sat 1000–1400. For poste restante, include the zip code TN 38101.

ACCOMMODATION

The **Peabody Hotel**, 149 Union Ave, is distinguished not only by its costly rooms, but its marching ducks, who promenade to a Sousa march up to the hotel fountain at 1100, where they swim until roused up to return home promptly at 1700. This silly scene has drawn huge crowds since the 1930s.

Your best bet for centrally placed budget rooms is the chain hotels (see p. 52). Days Inn, Best Western and Comfort Inns are all in central locations. Elvis Presley Blvd, which runs south to Graceland, also has several motels and camp sites to choose from. For more homely accommodation, B&B in Memphis, tel:(800) 206-5829, can set you up in (mostly suburban) pensions.

FOOD AND DRINK

Pit barbecue is big time in Memphis, and the combination of blues and BBQ downtown is an essential ingredient in the city's social life. Beale St and Union Ave are good streets to wander when you're hungry, though the area is really quite touristy. To get away from the crowds, try the Pinch Historical District. Midtown Memphis, which includes 3 miles or so east of centre, is also becoming a hip place to eat and drink. Pick up the *Dining out in Memphis* guide from the visitor centre for more listings.

CENTRAL	**Rialto** $ 135 S Main St. Italian bistro, bakery and café – good for lunch or a snack.
	Huey's Restaurant $ 77 S 2nd St. Well regarded for its burgers and a wide selection of beers.
	Automatic Slim's Tonga Club $$ 83 S 2nd St. A fun blend of Southwestern and Caribbean cuisine – wild lunchtime sandwiches are a speciality.
	The Little Tea Shop $–$$ 69 Monroe Ave. Extremely popular lunch-only spot since 1918 – southern cuisine.
	The Rendezvous $–$$ 52 S 2nd St. A local favourite for fantastic charbroiled ribs.
	Blues City Café $$ 138 Beale St. Jumbo shrimp, huge steaks and ribs are their speciality.
	Elvis Presley's Memphis $$ 126 Beale St. Kitschy Elvis-themed American restaurant.
	King's Palace Café $$–$$$ 162 Beale St. Cajun/Southern/BBQ place with late-night jazz and blues.
	Sleep Out Louie's $$–$$$ 88 Union Ave. Great oyster bar with live music on weekends.
MIDTOWN	**The Cupboard** $$ 1400 Union Ave, and **The Cupboard, Too**, 149 Madison Ave. Home-cooked meals, including vegetarian specials.

HIGHLIGHTS

Beale St is synonymous with Memphis blues, arguably the city's greatest contribution to world culture, and surely the heart of any visit to Memphis. Today's Beale St Historic District is far cleaner and more polished than in its colourful past.

Beale St's real heyday was the 1910s and 1920s, when segregation and prohibition were in full force, and Beale St became a centre of commerce for blacks and at night a haven for rowdy pleasure-seekers and various vagabonds. In the 1960s a depressed economy and subsequent bulldozers wiped out most of the street. Shops and bars retain or imitate the original flavour, and a number of good museums keep the culture alive, as do live blues, soul and rock 'n' roll.

One building spared from demolition was the **Orpheum Theatre**, at the corner of Beale and S Main Sts. Once the home of Memphis's vaudeville theatre, it now stages plays and musicals. At no. 163 Beale St, **A Schwab's Dry Goods Store** has been in operation since 1876, stocking the same articles it always has, such as voodoo potions: its motto is 'If you can't find it at Schwab's, you're better off without it'. Open Mon–Sat 0900– 1700; like most shops in the Bible Belt, it's closed on Sunday.

Continuing east down Beale St, you pass **W C Handy Performing Arts Park**, a gathering spot for amateur street musicians named after the man who, in 1909, wrote what is considered the first blues tune. His house, a few steps down the street at no. 352, is a little turn-of-the-century home converted into a **museum** to the father of the blues. $, open Tues–Sat 1000–1700, Sun–Mon closed. Right around the corner from the Music Hall of Fame the pedestrianised **Main St Mall** stretches for several blocks, and you can take a ride on the restored antique Main St Trolley to bring back a taste of the old days.

The **Center for Southern Folklore** has an entertaining collection of photos and films of Memphis and Southern culture in general. $, 119 South Main St; open Sun–Wed 1100–1900, Thur–Sat 1100–2300.

Since African-Americans contributed so much to Memphis's riches, it is telling that Martin Luther King Jr chose to participate in a black workers march here in 1968. On the evening before the march, 4 April, King was shot by James Earl Ray while standing on the balcony outside his room at the Lorraine Motel. The site is now preserved as the **National Civil Rights Museum**, a few blocks south of Beale St at 450 Mulberry St.

THE BLUES

It's only natural that the blues should emanate from Memphis. The city grew rich in the 19th century from the cotton trade, and the blood, sweat and tears of the slaves who harvested that cotton also produced a rich, spiritual mourning music as they incorporated the sounds and styles of African music into their experience in America. The blues developed into a uniquely American form of music, gaining a hard edge in the raucous corridors of downtown Memphis, particularly Beale St. In the 1950s, the blues fused into a new style popularised initially by Elvis Presley – rock 'n' roll – and kick-started a new generation of Memphis musicians.

TOURS

Sample Memphis Tours, tel: (901) 274-9473, offers three different insightful tours of downtown Memphis, with peeks into hidden places, Elvis's favourite hangouts, and tales of the ghost of Beale St.

Heritage Tours, tel: (901) 527-3427, offers good cultural and historic group tours of all of Memphis's main sites, including many important off-the-beaten-track places such as the Alex Haley House Museum and various Civil War sites.

Blues City Tours, 325 Union Ave, tel: (901) 522-9229, does much the same, and is a little more geared to the showy side, with tours including casinos and riverboat show cruises.

FOR FREE

Beale St and the pedestrianised S Main St are good for simple strolling, and you can pop over to one of the parks along the river with your picnic lunch.

Highlights include a bus (from Montgomery, Alabama) commanding black riders to sit in the rear, and the balcony and room where MLK was shot. $, open Mon, Wed– Sat 0900–1700, Sun 1300–1700.

Sightseeing cruises of the mighty Mississippi are given from Apr to Nov on **Memphis Queen Line** paddlewheelers, lasting 1½ hours. They also have dinner cruises and moonlight music cruises: tel: (901) 527-2628 or (800) 221-6197; www.memphisqueen.com.

Memphis not only of preserves its unique past, but also pushes forward with modern architecture such as the unmissable **Pyramid**, on the river just past the I-40 overpass. The tourist office calls this 32-storey stainless steel model of the Great Pyramid in Egypt 'a tribute to Memphis's Egyptian heritage', though that heritage really is in the city's name and the similarity it shares in lying on a great river. Inside is a 22,000-seat arena used for concerts and sporting events.

THE MISSISSIPPI

The river itself is a prime destination in town, and **Mud Island** in the middle of it has plenty of leisure and educational attractions. Getting there is fun too, on the new **Monorail and Walkway** from Adams Ave. Mud Island is part city playground – with an amphitheatre and the World War II B-17 bomber the *Memphis Belle* – and part river history lesson, with a large-scale model of the Mississippi and the entertaining **Mississippi River Museum**, documenting the great waterway's geographic features, folklore and importance in American commerce. Grounds open daily 1000–2000 (June–Aug); 1000–1700 (Apr–May and Sept–Nov).

MIDTOWN

Overton Park is a lovely stretch of near-forest, and contains the very good **Memphis Zoo**, which has been recently revamped and houses several exotic and endangered species. $$, open daily 0900–1800 Mar–Oct and 0900–1700 Nov–Feb. Also in the park, the **Memphis Brooks Museum**, at 1934 Poplar Ave, features fine and decorative arts from antiquity to the present. Open Tues–Fri 1000–1600, Sat 1000–1700, Sun 1130–1700. Bus no. 50 runs down Poplar Ave from the city centre. Another good art museum in the area is the small **Dixon Gallery and Gardens** at 4339 Park Ave, with Impressionist works by Renoir, Degas and Monet, plus some lovely gardens. $, open Tues–Sat 1000–1700, Sun 1300–1700.

Quick tours of the real **Sun Studio**, **$$**, at 706 Union Ave, are given daily, 1000–1800. Sam Phillips opened a small recording studio here in 1950, and over the next 20 years helped launch the careers of Elvis Presley, Jerry Lee Lewis, B B King, Howlin' Wolf, Johnny Cash, Carl Perkins and Roy Orbison, to name a few. Out-of-hours it still functions as a studio.

GRACELAND

Billing itself as 'the most famous home in America after the White House', **Graceland**, 10 miles south of downtown on Elvis Presley Blvd, is the beloved home of the king of rock-'n'-roll. Regardless of your level of devotion to Elvis – his fanatical followers make regular pilgrimages here – you'll probably be pleasantly surprised. There

THE UNDERGROUND RAILROAD

The *antebellum* **Slavehaven/Burkle Estate Museum**, several blocks north at 826 N 2nd St, was originally a station on the 'Underground Railroad', one of many throughout the South owned by sympathetic whites who provided secret tunnels and hiding places for runaway slaves during their quest northwards. The house also contains exhibits on the slave era. Tours must be booked in advance through Heritage Tours (see p. 298).

are a number of sites on the estate, and it's all nicely packaged, with personal headphones that tell the stories and play the music.

In the home itself you can visit the King's kitchen, living room, dining room, music room, TV room, and 'jungle' den – complete with floor-to-ceiling carpets. Other buildings house his own racquetball court, business office, trophy collection – including his huge collection of gold records – and various articles of his elaborate stage costumes and jewellery. Elvis's cars, including the famous 1955 pink Cadillac, and motorcycles, are there, along with his luxuriously equipped private planes. The Sincerely Elvis museum portrays Elvis's more personal side through candid photos and a 22-minute film tracing highlights of his career. Finally, the Meditation Garden contains the remains of Elvis and his immediate family. $$–$$$, open Mon–Sat 0900–1700, Sun 1000–1600 (Mar–Oct), Wed–Mon 1000–1600 (Nov–Feb). 1000–1600 every day. The house and each museum require a separate ticket, and the house tour is closed on Tues Nov–Feb.

NIGHTLIFE

Beale St is still the place to head for live music, and if you've only got one night in Memphis, you shouldn't miss this.

B B King's Club, 143 Beale St. An obvious starting point, with live jamming almost every night – and occasional appearances by the man himself. Pork barbecue and fried catfish are among the house specialities.

Rum Boogie Café and Blues Hall, 182 Beale St. Another hot spot, decorated with memorabilia from lots of blues greats.

Silky O'Sullivan's Patio, 183 Beale St. Popular Irish saloon with live pop-blues and outdoor seating.

Beale Street Barbecue and Piano Bar, 205 Beale St. A restaurant with a stage featuring blues, country, and rock 'n' roll.

The Lounge @ the Gibson Guitar Factory, 145 Lt George W Lee Ave (one block south of Beale St). Live entertainment in an ultra-hip setting.

Isaac Haye's Music, Food, Passion, 150 Peabody Place (one block north of Beale St). Soul food specialities and live music, as promised.

One of America's foremost 'comeback communities', Chattanooga, Tennessee, has emerged from its environmentally polluted past with a spectacular degree of success. Two decades ago, steel foundries alongside the Tennessee River spewed fumes, often heavy enough to cause afternoon dim-outs. Now clear skies prevail in this not-so-big city (population 155,000), tucked into hilly terrain near the Tennessee–Georgia state line. Lookout Mountain, 2391 ft high, looms over the metro area's southern outskirts. Major Civil War battles erupted on that promontory and adjacent ridges. Incorporated in 1839, Chattanooga's location guaranteed rapid growth stimulated by river transport and railroad expansion, linking raw-materials producers in the South with manufacturers in the North (cross-currents that led to the mid-19th century's wartime confrontations).

GETTING THERE AND GETTING AROUND

Chattanooga Metropolitan Airport is 13 miles east of downtown. The shuttle service to/from city-centre locations costs $14; a taxi fare is $20 for two passengers and the hourly bus no. 19 costs $1. If you're travelling by car, come via Interstate highway 24, 59 or 75. The Greyhound/Trailways bus station is situated near the airport, not downtown. Nor is Chattanooga directly on Amtrak's rail route. Passengers arriving from, for example, Atlanta or Charleston must transfer to downtown by bus. Chattanooga Area Regional Transportation Authority (CARTA) operates the city's public-transit system; tel: (423) 629-1473. CARTA's Downtown Shuttle employs battery-powered electric buses on a 20-stop route, Mon–Fri 0600–2130, Sat 0900–2130, Sun 0900–2030.

INFORMATION

The **Chattanooga Visitors Center** is located on a riverfront plaza at the north end of Broad St; open daily 0830–1730. For advance planning, contact the **Chattanooga Area Convention & Visitors Bureau**, 2 Broad St, Chattanooga, TN 37402; tel: (800) 322-3344 or (423) 756-8687; www.chattanoogafun.com.

ACCOMMODATION

Urban revitalisation has spawned an agreeable mix of hotels; the Chattanooga Area Convention & Visitors Bureau offers a comprehensive listing. Low- to mid-price motels are abundant at I-75 exits near the airport.

Chattanooga Clarion $$–$$$ 407 Chestnut St; tel: (423) 756-5150 or (800) 252-7466. Close to downtown attractions; outdoor pool, fitness centre.

TOURS

For escorted sightseeing, contact **All Aboard Chattanooga Travel**, 5512 Ringgold St; tel: (800) 499-9877 or (423) 499-9977. **Chattanooga Horse Trams** take passengers on easygoing downtown rides; tel: (423) 265-6544. *Southern Belle* cruises depart from the Ross's Landing dock; tel: (423) 266-4488. Or, at Coolidge Park, board the *Chattanooga Star* paddlewheeler; tel: (423) 265-4522. A fleet of **Chattanooga Ducks** consists of World War II amphibious landing vehicles, used for river-navigating tours; tel: (423) 756-3825.

FOR FREE

Passengers ride free on the **Downtown Shuttle's** ecologically trend-setting electric buses. They cover north–south routes through central Chattanooga.

Read House Hotel & Suites $$–$$$ M L King and Broad Sts; tel: (423) 266-4121. Circa 1926 landmark, renovated and filled with Civil War memorabilia.

Chattanooga Choo Choo Holiday Inn $$$ 1400 Market St; tel: (423) 266-5000 or (800) 872-2229. Named after the Glenn Miller band's 1941 hit song; in rejuvenated Terminal Station. Meals served aboard a Victorian-era railcar.

FOOD AND DRINK

Revitalized Chattanooga's restaurants suit all tastes. Downtown's Broad and Market Sts offer varied choices; ditto for Frazier Ave across the river.

Northside Lunch $ 202 Frazier Ave; tel: (423) 756-9799. Cubbyhole diner in business since 1889. Famous for Alma's homemade chili.

Pickle Barrel $ 1012 Market St; tel: (423) 266-1103. Make-your-own sandwiches. Spiral stairway leads to a roof deck.

Schlotzky's Deli $ 701 Broad St; tel: (423) 267-8484. A no-frills favourite for sandwiches, soups and salads.

Stone Cup Roasting Company $ 224 Frazier Ave; tel: (423) 265-5010. Choices of grilled panini sandwiches, fresh-roasted coffees. Rear deck for views of Coolidge Park and city skyline.

Altruda's $$ 138 Market St; tel: (423) 267-6145. Downtown's moderate-price Italian eatery.

Big River Grille & Brewing Works $$ 222 Broad St; tel: (423) 267-2739. Typical American brewpub; billiard tables and king-size bar.

HIGHLIGHTS

Chattanooga's resurgence is symbolised by the **Tennessee Aquarium**, an architectural showpiece surrounded by riverfront Ross's Landing Park and Plaza. Inside the world's largest freshwater aquarium, skylights illuminate brooks and streams, ponds, living forests and a Delta Country swamp – habitats for 9000 creatures ranging from catfish to snapping turtles, Amazonian piranhas to Surinam toads, Gila monster lizards and 'eyelash' vipers, plus otters and a giant alligator. $$ One Broad St; tel: (423) 266-3467; open daily 1000–1800.

Ross's Landing 'anchors' the 7-mile **Riverwalk**. Stairways get you up to the **Walnut Street Bridge**. The century-old structure was reopened as a pedestrian-only span in

1993, reaching the river's opposite (north) bank, where **Coolidge Park** features an antique carousel 'populated' by 52 hand-carved animals.

Follow the Riverwalk eastward towards a zigzagging ascent to reach the **Bluff View Art District**, locale of Chattanooga's prestigious **Hunter Museum of American Art**. $ 10 Bluff View; tel: (423) 267-0968; open Tues–Sat 1000–1630, Sun 1300–1630.

The circa 1909 Terminal Station has been transformed into a complex called **Chattanooga Choo Choo** – evoking memories of swingtime-era band leader Glenn Miller's rendition of the then-popular song. The high-domed depot houses a hotel, restaurants and shops. Also on site are rose gardens and the **Model Railroad Museum**. $, 1400 Market St; tel: (423) 266-5000; open Thur–Sun 1000–1800, Fri–Sat 1800–2000.

The Incline Railway climbs the world's steepest passenger railway (the gradient reaches 72.7%) to Lookout Mountain's summit. $$, Lower Station–Upper Station; round trips daily 0830–2100 summertime, 0900–1700 rest of year; tel: (423) 821-4224.

The Battles for Chattanooga Electric Map & Museum recapitulates 1863's Civil War engagements culminating 'above the clouds' on Missionary Ridge. Adjacent to **Point Park**, with memorials recalling the area's military campaigns. $, 1110 E Brow Rd; tel: (423) 821-2812; open daily 0900–1830 summertime, 1000–1700 rest of year.

HIGH ABOVE CHATTANOOGA

At **Ruby Falls** on Lookout Mountain, a waterfall plunges 145 ft into a crystal-clear pool, deep inside a cavern encrusted with eerie mineral deposits; $$, tel: (423) 821-2544. Nearby **Rock City Gardens** is a fantasyland of odd-shaped, lichen-covered sandstone formations; $$, tel: (423) 820-2531.

SHOPPING

Occupying recycled railroad storage buildings, **Warehouse Row** attracts bargain-hunters to dozens of factory-outlet stores purveying top brand-name merchandise. 1110 Market St; tel: (423) 267-1111.

NIGHTLIFE

Performing arts venues include the **Soldiers & Sailors Memorial Auditorium**, **Theatre Center** on the riverfront, **Backstage Playhouse** and Broad St's lavish **Tivoli Theater**, opened in 1926 as a movie palace, now home of the **Chattanooga Symphony, Opera and Ballet.**

NEW ORLEANS

The Big Easy, the Crescent City, the Birthplace of Jazz – New Orleans is a city unlike any other, moving to its own sultry beat. The elegance of its colonial buildings, Spanish moss dangling from massive oak trees, the mysteries of jazz, blues and voodoo, along with the scents of spicy shrimp and roasted chicory, mingle with the ever-present swelter of the Mississippi delta to create an aura of constant excitement and expectation.

The city's unique atmosphere stems from a rich and complex heritage. At the end of the 17th century the first French colonists (dubbed 'the kids' – *las criollas* or Creoles – by rival Spanish merchants) began to penetrate the Louisiana swamps, establishing the trading post of New Orleans on a bend in the Mississippi in 1718. The site, bordered by the Mississippi River, Lake Pontchartrain and endless swamps in the hinterlands, was not a healthy one, and even today the summer heat and humidity in the city can be unbearable. Traders and slaves added Spanish, Caribbean and African influences to the cultural mix, and this complex personality gives New Orleans a peculiar disjointedness: stunning architectural beauty rubs shoulders with abject poverty, while blacks and whites still maintain an uneasy coexistence.

Due to the devastation inflicted by **Hurricane Katrina** and to the time it will take the city to recover, it has not been possible to check the current status of places featured in this chapter. See p.258 for further information

MUST SEE/DO IN NEW ORLEANS

Stroll along the quaint streets of the French Quarter, admiring the old architecture and ironwork balconies

Grab a drink and run the gauntlet through the carousing crowds on Bourbon St

Drop in to hear real New Orleans jazz at the Preservation Hall

Drive along Hwy 90 to see some authentic *antebellum* plantations.

Visit Cajun country for great food and even better music

GETTING THERE

New Orleans International Airport is about 21 miles west of centre in nearby Kenner just off I-10, the interstate that cuts east–west through New Orleans. Taxis from the airport to the French Quarter are about $24, and a van shuttle service is available from a number of competitors.

The Amtrak and Greyhound stations are next door to each other at 1001 Loyola Ave near the Superdome, a shortish walk from the French Quarter - though this is very definitely inadvisable at night.

INFORMATION

The official **Visitors Center** is at 529 St Ann St, on Jackson Sq. They have a recorded message on their visitor information line, tel: (504) 566-5003 or (800) 672 6124, and a good website: www.neworleanscvb.com. Another decent source of online information is www.thetrip.com. The Louisiana State Museum, in the Cabildo on Jackson Sq., has stacks of tour brochures.

Safety New Orleans has a reputation as one of the USA's more dangerous cities, but is improving. You're best advised to drive or take a taxi just about anywhere outside the French Quarter or Uptown/Garden District areas. Even an empty streetcar isn't completely safe at night.

Money There is no shortage of banks in the Central Business District, and the French Quarter and Garden District. Several have foreign currency exchanges. There are plenty of automatic cash dispensers – though charges range on average about $2 for the service.

Post and Phones The main post office is at 701 Loyola Ave, in the Central Business District: open Mon–Fri 0800–1630, Sat 0800–1300. Poste restante is handled here (zip code LA 70140). There's also the French Quarter Postal Emporium, at 828 Royal St; open Mon–Fri 0930–1800, Sat 1000–1500.

ACCOMMODATION

Rooms don't come particularly cheap in New Orleans, and for Mardi Gras you'll pay even more and have to book several months in advance. Many visitors aim straight for the French Quarter, though some good budget possibilities - such as several B&Bs - exist Uptown within an easy ride on the St Charles Streetcar. The visitor centre can help with budget accommodation, and many of the national chain hotels have rooms at fairly good prices outside the French Quarter. Another good source is Bed & Breakfast, Inc., 1021 Moss Street; tel: (504) 488-4640 or (800) 729-4640; fax: (504) 488-4639; e-mail: bedbreak@gnofn.org, an accommodation service for all price ranges.

French Quarter

New Orleans Guest House $$$ 1118 Ursulines St; tel: (504) 566-1177 or (800) 562-1177; fax: (504) 566-1179. Pleasant enough establishment with decent rates.

French Quarter Courtyard Hotel $$$–$$$$ 1101 N Rampart Street; tel: (504) 522-7333 or (800) 466-1408; fax:

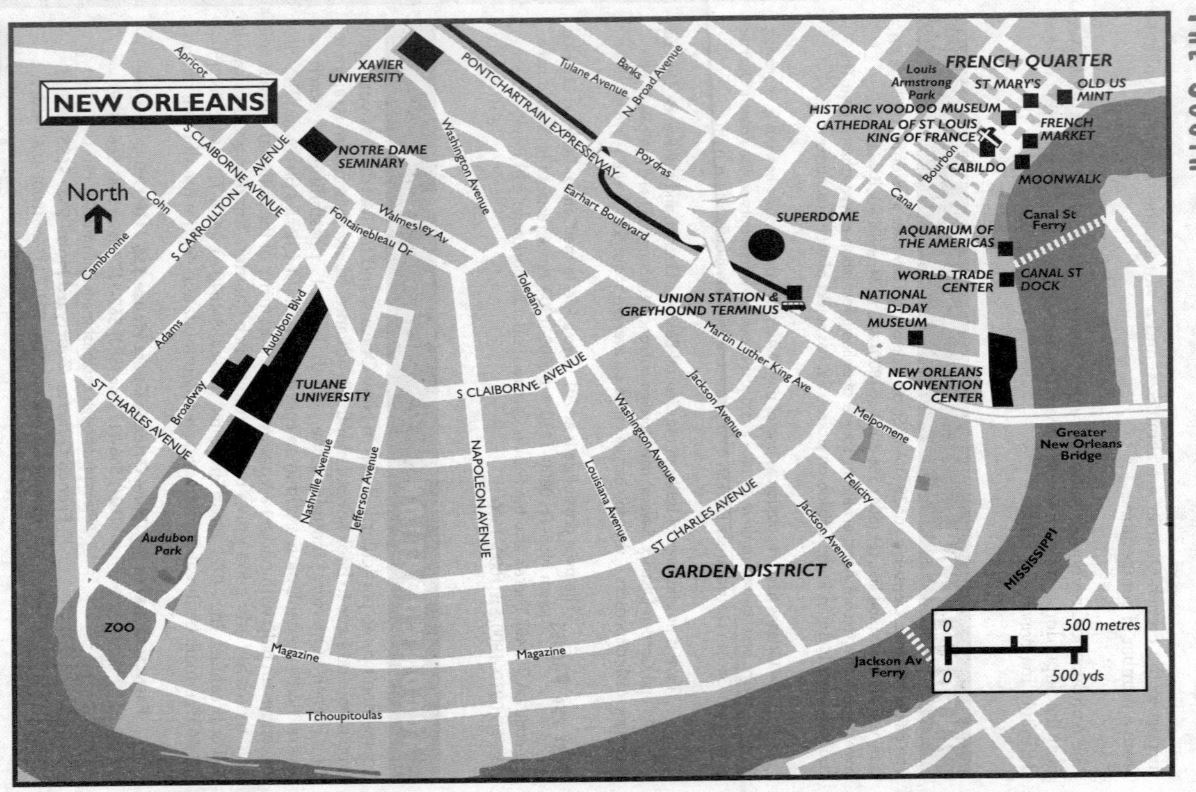
NEW ORLEANS
North
Apricot
XAVIER UNIVERSITY
PONTCHARTRAIN EXPRESSWAY
Tulane Avenue
Banks
N. Broad Avenue
FRENCH QUARTER
Louis Armstrong Park
ST MARY'S
OLD US MINT
HISTORIC VOODOO MUSEUM
CATHEDRAL OF ST LOUIS KING OF FRANCE
FRENCH MARKET
Bourbon
CABILDO
MOONWALK
Canal
S CLAIBORNE AVENUE
NOTRE DAME SEMINARY
Washington Avenue
Poydras
Earhart Boulevard
SUPERDOME
Canal St Ferry
AQUARIUM OF THE AMERICAS
Cohn
S CARROLLTON AVENUE
Fontainebleau Dr
Walmesley Av
CANAL ST DOCK
WORLD TRADE CENTER
Cambronne
Toledano
UNION STATION & GREYHOUND TERMINUS
NATIONAL D-DAY MUSEUM
Adams
Audubon Blvd
Martin Luther King Ave
NEW ORLEANS CONVENTION CENTER
TULANE UNIVERSITY
S CLAIBORNE AVENUE
Jackson Avenue
Broadway
ST CHARLES AVENUE
Washington Avenue
Melpomene
Greater New Orleans Bridge
Nashville Avenue
Jefferson Avenue
NAPOLEON AVENUE
Louisiana Avenue
Felicity
ST CHARLES AVENUE
Jackson Avenue
Audubon Park
MISSISSIPPI
GARDEN DISTRICT
ZOO
Magazine
Magazine
Jackson Av Ferry
0
500 metres
0
500 yds
Tchoupitoulas

(504) 522-3908; www.fqch.com. On the northern edge of the Quarter.

Le Richelieu $$$$ 1234 Chartres St; tel: (504) 529-2492 or (800) 535-9653; fax: (504) 524-8179; www.lerichelieuhotel.com. With its fine furnishings, pool and garden courtyard, this is one of the better value up-market hotels in the French Quarter.

DOWNTOWN

LaSalle Hotel $$–$$$ 1113 Canal St; tel: (504) 525-4188, or (800) 733-4188; fax: (504) 525-2531. Simple budget hotel near the Quarter and downtown.

Days Inn Canal $$–$$$ 1630 Canal St; tel: (504) 586-0110 or (800) 242-1945; fax: (504) 581-2253; www.daysinnneworleans.com. Eight blocks north of the French Quarter downtown; not the most beautiful setting, but cheap enough.

UPTOWN AND THE GARDEN DISTRICT

Hostelling International-New Orleans $–$$ 2249 Carondelet St; tel: (504) 523-3014; fax: (504) 529-5933; HI hostel located in a grand *antebellum* house one block from the St Charles streetcar. Some simple double rooms.

Best Western Patio Downtown Motel $$–$$$ 2820 Tulane Ave; tel: (504) 822-0200 or (800) 270-6955; fax: (504) 822-2328. Decent uptown location; standard chain hotel décor.

Quality Inn Midtown $$–$$$ 3900 Tulane Ave; tel: (504) 486-5541; fax: (504) 488-7440. This national chain won't win any award for atmosphere, but the location and price are fine.

St Charles Guesthouse Bed & Breakfast $$–$$$ 1748 Prytania St; tel: (504) 523-6556; fax: (504) 522-6340, www.stcharlesguesthouse.com. Yet another Garden District B&B, with very reasonable rates.

FOOD AND DRINK

Cajun/Creole cuisine has its home in the Louisiana bayous, and New Orleans capitalises on this festive and flavourful food with a broad array of restaurants. The two are in fact distinct: Creole cuisine derives from the French and Spanish colonists, with African and native Choctaw Indian influence, and is quite refined; while Cajun is a spicier, more soulful, poor-folks' food. Restaurants today usually combine them into one, as the ingredients are almost identical: chicken, shrimp harvested from the Gulf of Mexico, red beans and rice, onions, garlic and lots of hot peppers. Some of the more unusual local fare includes crawfish and alligator, which is quite tough and fatty; both are culled from the inland swamps and bayous. A lot of the food is deep fried, though the perennial favourites, **gumbo** (a thick stew of shrimp, chicken, and vegetables in a tomato and okra base) and **jambalaya** (a rice dish made from any of the above) are healthy and hearty. For the sweet-toothed, chicory coffee and pralines – pecans glazed with butter and sugar – are consumed in large amounts.

The South

Snack and lunch food is a treat: fabulous sandwiches such as **muffulettas** (Italian sandwiches with savoury meats, cheeses and olive relish and garlic-olive oil dressing), and their poor cousin, the **po-boy** (a French bread sandwich stuffed with fried oysters or shrimp), are ubiquitous. A string of places along Decatur St in the French Quarter is perfect for picking up a takeaway lunch. The traditional Monday lunch is red beans and rice, and while most local restaurants serve it up, locals claim with all honesty that the best to be had are at any Popeye's Chicken fast-food chain.

Dining out can be a real experience, though the best restaurants take full advantage of the New Orleans image – you can quite easily shell out $50 for a full meal with drinks. Cheaper options are abundant, however, and a solid Cajun meal can easily be had for under $10. The French Quarter is an obvious place to start looking for food – most of which is Cajun/Creole – but shop carefully for value. There are lots of good options in the Garden District and Uptown as well – St Charles Ave around Jackson St, and Magazine St between Washington Ave and Louisiana Ave, and between Napoleon Ave and Jefferson Ave, are good hunting grounds.

French Quarter	**Café Du Monde** $ 813 Decatur St. Settled comfortably into the French Market, and *de rigueur* for chicory coffee, people-watching and beignets, special doughnuts.
	Central Grocery $ 923 Decatur St. One of several good delis along here serving up massive, mouthwatering muffulettas.
	Johnny's Po-Boys $ 511 St Louis St. Simple, tasty, greasy-fried, order-at-the-counter New Orleans eats.
	Napoleon House Bar and Café $$ 500 Chartres St. Unique European-style café, with great po-boy sandwiches and excellent prices.
	The Gumbo Shop $$–$$$ 630 St Peter St. Lively Cajun/Creole place serving up everybody's favourite po-boys and gumbo.
	Acme Oyster and Seafood House $$$–$$$$ 724 Iberville St. A New Orleans institution: start off with raw oysters on the half-shell, then move on to fried seafood platters.
Uptown and the Garden District	**Dante's Kitchen** $$ 736 Dante St. Serving innovative seafood and new American cuisine, located in the Riverbend.
	Semolina International Pastas $$–$$$ 3226 Magazine St. Trendy place at several locations, featuring variations on favourites like jambalaya pasta, pasta with pesto, and pad Thai.
	Vaqueros $$–$$$ 4938 Prytania St. Just off the St Charles Streetcar line, and popular for its Mexican, Southwestern and native American cuisine, as well as its huge margaritas.
	Café Atchafalaya $$$ 901 Louisiana Ave. Excellent alternative to the Quarter's much-hyped fine dining; quality New Orleans cuisine at competitive prices.

GETTING AROUND

The French Quarter is small enough to be enjoyed on foot, but to get almost anywhere else you'll need to take advantage of the city's buses or, to head to the Garden District and Uptown, the magnificent St Charles Streetcar. This restored relic follows St Charles Ave westward in a swoop from the French Quarter to Audubon Park; rides cost $1.25 and correct change is required.

HIGHLIGHTS

THE FRENCH QUARTER

The real highlight of New Orleans is the **French Quarter**, filled with 18th-century colonial buildings and hopping to the beat of jazz and blues joints on and around **Bourbon St**. Unless it's night-time and you're bent on drinking, the best thing to do is simply to wander and admire at random. It's a surprisingly small part of town, the heart of the old city, though you'll want to visit it at various times of day and night to catch its different colours and flavours.

The Quarter, as it's referred to by the locals (or Vieux Carré in the original French), is ethereal in the early morning, when the streets are almost unnaturally quiet and you can admire the smart homes, intricate balconies, dangling fuchsia and crape myrtle, and cobbled courtyards, unfettered by tourist hordes and the late-night partying crowd. During the day you're likely to wander through a Dixieland band blowing in Jackson Square, and at night the bars and clubs spill onto the streets, doing their best to fulfil the image that visitors have of New Orleans.

JACKSON SQUARE AND THE RIVER

Unassuming **Jackson Square** is the city's focal point, a pleasant, grassy park which anchors the French Quarter to the Mississippi River. It takes its name from Andrew Jackson, seventh president of the United States, who as a military general defeated the British here in 1815. A giant equestrian statue of the man sits proudly in the centre. American hero that he was, Jackson was also responsible for flushing out native American tribes throughout the South, so his legacy is somewhat tainted in modern historical interpretations.

ON THE RIVER

Take a riverboat tour *Cajun Queen* ($11) or *Creole Queen* ($16), tel: (504) 524-0814 or (800) 445-4109, departing from the Canal St Dock, or the *Steamboat Natchez* ($17), tel: (504) 586-8777 or (800) 233-2628, from Toulouse Wharf at Jackson Sq. All also offer a jazz dinner cruise ($$$). Or take the free commuter ferry from Canal St to Algiers, on the west bank – catch it just before sunset or at night for the most exhilarating views of the city's skyline.

The **St Louis Cathedral** presides over the square; it's actually rather small. The

JAZZ

Jazz was cultivated in New Orleans around the turn of the 20th century, fuelled by the funky mix of ethnic influences. Because of its humble origins in rowdy bars in black neighbourhoods, it was long looked down upon by the music establishment. Jazz is based upon improvisation and a deep-down homey and exuberant attitude; its first big stars included Louis Armstrong and Joe 'King' Oliver, and its presence is integral to the city's identity.

The **Old US Mint**, 400 Esplanade Ave, tel: (504) 568-6968, houses the jazz museum ($), open Tues–Sun 0900–1700.

interior is ornate and beautiful, and the building has a few secrets, related on free guided tours throughout the day.

The **Louisiana State Museum**, also on the square, provides a good background to the history and culture of the city and region. $, open Tues–Sun 0900–1700. Next door to the cathedral, the **Cabildo** is an impressive former city hall, built by the Spanish and then altered to look more French after the Louisiana Purchase, which was signed here in 1803. Today it houses a museum on the city's history, a fascinating look at its complicated and often turbulent cultural and physical development. It's not all pretty, either: while Africans, Caribbean islanders and native Americans are woven into New Orleans's ethnic quilt, the story of the city has often been one of oppression and war, floods and disease.

The **Presbytere**, on the other side of the cathedral, is home to the Louisiana Portrait Gallery as well as an elaborate exhibit on Mardi Gras. The **1850 House** ($) at 523 St Ann St is a restored Creole family mansion, displaying its flamboyant housewares; open Tues–Fri 0900–1700.

A quick walk straight out of the square, across Decatur St and over the streetcar tracks, brings you to the mighty Mississippi. Some 2200 miles downstream from its source, the great river broadens through New Orleans before ploughing into the Gulf of Mexico. Stroll through the shopping mall within the old Jax Brewery and out onto the **Moon Walk** to see the busy riverside.The nearby **Audubon Aquarium of the Americas** is one of the country's best, with massive glass tanks housing sharks, penguins and alligators. $$$, open daily 0930–1900 end May–early Sept, rest of year Sun–Thur 0930–1800, Fri–Sat 0930–1900.

VOODOO

Appropriate to this often bizarre city, the **VooDoo Spiritual Temple**, 828 Rampart St, tel: (504) 522-9627, www.voodoospiritualtemple.com, tries to teach the basic tenets of this religion. There is an eclectic collection of rabbits' feet, bats' heads, herbs, oils, and depictions of voodoo ceremonies, as well as a surprising interspersing of more traditional religious objects, all overseen with good grace and humour by Priestess Miriam. Scattered around the French Quarter are shops filled with voodoo paraphernalia; beware, though, of tacky souvenir shops trading on the more sensationalist aspects. Walking tours that feature New Orleans's extraordinary above-ground cemeteries also include some explanation of this hybrid religion.

TOURS

Several companies, e.g. **New Orleans Spirit Tours**, tel: (504) 314-0806, offer walking tours of the French Quarter and the Garden District. Themed offerings include a day tour of cemeteries with a bit of voodoo thrown in, and a night haunt with tales of ghosts and vampires. **Gray Line**, tel: (800) 535-7786, (504) 587-0733, offers bus tours of just about everything, from city sweeps, including a day-long hop-on–hop-off deal, to rural plantation and swamp tours ($$$).

FOR FREE

Free guided tours of the French Quarter are offered daily at 0930 by the National Park Service, 419 Decatur St – but get there early, they fill up fast. Strolls through the French Quarter, Garden District and Audubon Park are delightful as well as being easily digestible lessons in history (collect the free brochures on self-guided walking tours at the tourist office on Jackson Sq.). For free music, you can usually hear makeshift street bands in front of the cathedral and in Louis Armstrong Park, or just stroll past the bars on Bourbon St.

Downstream from Jackson Square (away from downtown) on Decatur St passes wonderful cafés before veering off to the **French Market**. Active since the 1720s, this is the place to load up on local specialities such as hot pepper sauce and voodoo dolls. The Farmer's Market and the weekend flea market, just beyond, are great for fresh produce and antiques, respectively. The **Ursuline Convent** ($), 1100 Chartres St, is a lovely little piece of French colonial architecture dating from 1745 – one of the oldest buildings in the city. For tours, tel: (504) 529-3040.

BEYOND THE QUARTER Just north of the French Quarter, **Louis Armstrong Park** was once the location of the city's slave market. Though it may appear benign, this is one of the city's worst crime zones after dark. Nearby, the eerie **St Louis Cemetery No. 1** is New Orleans's oldest graveyard. As it sits below sea level, above-ground graves are used to prevent the grotesque occurrence of floating corpses. The dead are placed inside stone tombs, many of which crumble over time, so it is not unusual to come across the remains of a forearm or vertebra. Again, wander with a group, and only during the day.

This part of town, particularly around Basin St, was where jazz flourished in the early 20th century. Known as **Storyville**, it used to seethe with bars and bordellos – the city realised it couldn't control the illicit sex and booze, so it set aside this area for them. Today the scene has moved to the Quarter, the I-10 overpass barrels through, and it's dangerous.

News in 2005 was the opening of **The National D-Day Museum** ($$$ 945 Magazine St; tel: (504) 527-6012; www.ddaymuseum.org, open daily 0900–1700), whose exhibits vividly illustrate the 1944 invasion of Normandy, the Home Front and the Pacific Invasions artifacts, text and personal accounts of WWII veterans and others involved in the war effort. Two films, one on Normandy and one on the Pacific, show daily, alternating at one-hour intervals.

UPTOWN AND THE GARDEN DISTRICT Further west, the graceful swoop of the Mississippi cradles a number of beautiful and lively neighbourhoods collectively referred to as **Uptown**. St Charles Ave is the main thoroughfare, and the lovely **St Charles Streetcar** trundles the length of the crescent-shaped avenue, a great way to see the area and worth the trip for the atmosphere itself.

The city's most intriguing area after the French Quarter is the luscious and ostentatious **Garden District**, home to New Orleans's rich and famous. Magnificent homes line the streets, their subtropical gardens designed partly for aesthetics and partly to help keep the inhabitants cool in the stifling summer months. None is open to the public, though it's fun just to wander the streets, and self-guided walking tour maps are available from the tourist office. The official borders of the Garden District are St Charles Ave to the north, Magazine St to the south, and Jackson Ave and Louisiana Ave on either end, but the elaborate Victorian style spreads throughout much of Uptown. Among the most notable mansions to look out for are the so-called Wedding Cake House, at 5809 St Charles Ave, and the 'Gone with the Wind' house, modelled after Tara from the film, a block in at 5705 St Charles Ave.

The St Charles Streetcar passes Audubon Park in its wonderful urban green setting, the unusual geographic features of southern Louisiana condensed into one location. Magnificent overgrown oaks and weeping willows swoop down from overhead, and murky pools and walking paths lead to the excellent **Audubon Zoo**; $$ tel: (504) 581-4629 or (800) 774-7394, www.auduboninstitute.org; open daily 0930–1700 Mon–Fri, 0930–1800 Sat–Sun, mid-March–late Oct; 0930–1700 rest of the year. Among the rare species on display here is a white alligator, and the zoo has gone to great lengths to recreate a local swamp.

NORTH OF CENTRE Contained amongst the shady lagoons of the New Orleans City Park is the very good **New Orleans Museum of Art**, tel: (504) 488-2631, www.norma.org, open Tues–Sun, 1000–1700, whose collection includes, appropriately, an array of French and Spanish paintings and sculptures. What is perhaps surprising is that among these are a number of works by Rodin and Picasso, and also Degas, who lived here in the 1870s.

SHOPPING

You'll surely want to poke around the jewellery and antique shops in the French Quarter and Garden District. Most visitors come away from New Orleans with pralines, chicory, and hot pepper sauce – you won't believe the variety available. The French Market is a good place to look, as is the shopping centre in the Jackson Brewery building, on the river in the French Quarter.

Nightlife

The French Quarter bops and grinds well into the night. Most places keep their doors open, so you can stroll about until you hear something you like, though anywhere you go, your drinks won't be cheap. One way to cut costs while roaming is to buy big plastic cups of beer from the many street stands: this is the only city in America where open containers on the street are legal, so take advantage.

Mardi Gras in New Orleans

New Orleanians throw the biggest carnival of the year outside Rio – a genuine local outpouring of fun and passion that goes back several centuries. 'Fat Tuesday', as Mardi Gras translates from the French, is the last day to make merry before the sombre Lenten fast. Spectacular parades, masked balls and general drinking and dancing in the streets go on for a full week leading up to the day itself. While it's all in good fun, locals complain that Mardi Gras has been tainted in recent years by too many out-of-town visitors.

The name **Bourbon Street** inspires images of sweaty 1920s jazz and blues clubs and raunchy bordellos, and today it thrives on this reputation – which produces a sort of mass-market sterile sleaze. The place is actually pretty tacky, crammed with souvenir stalls and striptease joints, so scout out entertainment on the other streets as well. It is still packed to the hilt with live music venues, though much of the stuff spewing out of the guitars and drums is commercialised and tainted by a bland rock-'n'-roll influence. Given the city's tolerance of public drunkenness, it can be rowdy down here well into the wee hours.

Faubourg Marigny, a funky district just east of the Quarter, is an up-and-coming club spot, and there are lots of places spread across the Uptown area – Magazine St around Louisiana Ave and Napoleon Ave is always good. *The Gambit* is a good little free paper with entertainment and club listings.

French Quarter

Preservation Hall, 726 St Peter St, tel: (504) 522-2841 or (888) 946-JAZZ. Still the original and best for live jazz, kept purposefully dingy to prove it. Neither drinks nor seating available but you'll still have to show up early to catch the music. Small cover charge.

Old Absinthe Bar, 240 Bourbon St. One of the few places along this street with good R and B in a genuine setting, but no longer serving absinthe.

Molly's, 1107 Decatur St. Popular Irish bar with New Orleans-style pub grub.

The Funky Butt, 714 N Rampart St. Music true to its name.

Donna's, 800 N Rampart St. Simple place with occasional zydeco in addition to jazz and blues.

Just outside the Quarter

Snug Harbor, 626 Frenchman St. Cosy, established jazz and blues club a few streets east of the Quarter in Faubourg Marigny.

Café Brasil, 2100 Chartres St, tel: (504) 522-949-0851. Off-beat coffee shop with a wide variety of musical styles from eclectic to mainstream.

UPTOWN

Tipitina's, 501 Napoleon Ave, tel: (504) 895 8477. Biggish theatre/dance hall which occasionally draws some big names in rock and blues; good local stuff otherwise.

Maple Leaf Club, 8316 Oak St, tel: (504) 866-9359. Usually a good selection of live Cajun, blues and zydeco in an appropriately dusty venue.

BEYOND THE CITY

THE NORTH SHORE

Across Lake Pontchartrain, in St Tammany Parish, gracious towns stretch along lazy rivers, wildlife thrives deep in the bayous, and good food is a way of life. New Orleans residents cross the 24-mile causeway for the fine dining at non-tourist prices. St Tammany is perfect for hiking, cycling on the **Tammany Trace**, paddling, antiquing or just enjoying the easy landscapes and off-beat attractions.

A highlight is **Dr Wagner's Honey Island Swamp Tour**, a bayou boat that sneaks up on alligators and turtles sunning on cypress roots; tel: (504) 242-5877 or (985) 641-1769; $$$. Over 2200 animals roam free at the 900-acre **Global Wildlife Center** ($$) in Folsom. Hand feed giraffes, zebras and exotic deer from open-sided wagons; tel: (985) 624-9453, www.globalwildlife.com. To see baby alligators and learn how they are hatched and raised, visit **Insta-gator Alligator Ranch** ($$) in Covington; tel: (985) 892-3669. **Pontchartrain Vineyards**, in Bush, offers tours and tastings, tel: (985) 892-9742, www.pontchartrainvineyards.com.

Fine southern mansions line the lakefront promenade in **Mandeville**, where you should ask directions to the 1000-year-old **Seven Sisters Oak**, the largest live oak in North America. Shoppers and browsers head for pretty **Covington**, whose tree-draped streets are lined by antique shops that won't break the budget, and art studios and boutiques. For just plain fun, see the quirky, funky **UCM Museum** ($), 22275 SR 36 in Abita Springs, the work of artist/inventor John Preble; tel: (985) 829-2624, open daily 1000–1700.

THE TAMMANY TRACE

Cyclists, runners and rollerbladers love the wide, paved 31-mile rail-trail from Abita Springs through Mandeville and Lacombe. Shaded by moss-draped live oaks, it passes through Fontainebleau State Park and bayous and past Abita Brewery (tours Sat–Sun). Hire bikes at Abita Art Gallery; tel: (985) 867-3323.

i **St Tammany Parish Tourist & Convention Commission**, 68099 Hwy 59, Mandeville, LA 70471; tel: (985) 892-0520 or (800) 634-9443; www.NewOrleansNorthshore.com. The area suffered some damage from Hurricane Katrina – see p.258.

MUSIC AND DANCING

Don't miss a chance to hear the music that made this area famous. Dine on crayfish ($$–$$$) and two-step to Cajun fiddlers at **Randol's** in Lafayette; tel: (337) 981-7080. At **Grant Street Dance Hall**, Lafayette, you can hear live music and dance all night to every rhythm from two-step to swamp pop; tel: (337) 237-8513. Zydeco Breakfasts bring crowds to Breaux Bridge's **Café des Amis** $–$$ on Saturday mornings for dancing and listening; tel: (337) 332-5273, www.cafedesamis.com.

Budget chain motels cluster at Exit 266 of I-10 in Slidell.

Little River Bluffs $$$ 11030 Garden Lane, Folsom; tel: (985) 796-5257. An idyllic woodland retreat; three self-catering cottages overlook the river, where free kayaks await. Weekly $$–$$$.

Although fine dining is never cheap, this is the place to sample some of the finest New Orleans chefs, outside the hyper-priced French Quarter.

The Broken Egg Cafe $–$$ 200 Gerard St, Mandeville; tel: (985) 624-3388. Feast on copious omelets, blackberry grits and other local specialities 0730–1400 Tues–Sun.

La Provence $$–$$$ 25020 Hwy 190, Lacombe; tel: (985) 626-7662, offers an exceptional three-course early dinner for $15, Wed–Sat 1600-2200, 1200-2100 Sun.

CAJUN COUNTRY

About 130 miles west of New Orleans, **Lafayette** is a stop on Amtrak's *Sunset Limited*. If driving, follow Hwy 18 from New Orleans to see beautifully restored plantations (those open to tour are signposted), before following Hwy 1 to I-10. Lafayette is in the heart of the area settled by French Acadians ('Cajuns') deported from Nova Scotia by the British in the 1700s. Their French language, *joie de vivre*, food and music offer a down-home contrast to touristy New Orleans. Get used to the infectious beat of zydeco, born here, and to the French two-step played on a fiddle.

Mulate's, 325 Mills Ave, Breaux Bridge, near Vermilionville, www.mulates.com (with another branch in New Orleans), offers live music nightly, excellent gumbos and jambalayas; the atmosphere is of a party in itself.

Begin at **Vermilionville** ($$), a beautiful living history village, where you meet the Acadians and their Creole neighbours as they lived in the 18th and 19th centuries; tel: (337) 233-4077, www.vermilionville.org, open Tues–Sun 1000–1600. The first Acadians settled St Martinsville, on Bayou Teche, considered the setting for Longfellow's fictional epic *Evangeline*. The **Evangeline Oak** shades an excellent **Heritage Museum** ($), relating both African-American and Acadian experiences. Nearby is a moving memorial to the original 'Cajun' immigrants.

Visitor Center, 1400 NW Evangeline Thwy (I-10/I-49 intersection), Lafayette; tel: (337) 232-3737, (800) 346-1958; www.LafayetteTravel.com. Mon–Fri 0830–1700, Sat–Sun 0900–1700.

MOBILE

The graceful city of Mobile has a particular southern charm which makes it a fine place to relax for a day or two. Ancient oak trees form a lush canopy over central boulevards, providing much needed shade from the blistering summer heat. Mobile is sometimes referred to as the Azalea City, for more than 50 varieties bloom here.

It's also known as the Port City: while profiting as a commercial and manufacturing centre thanks to its location on Mobile Bay, the rich ecology of the delta and the Gulf of Mexico offers a host of outdoor attractions, including thick swamps, nature reserves and lovely beaches. The city escaped the worst of Hurricane Katrina, but suffered some damage (see p. 258).

The pronunciation of the name, *Mobeel*, derives from the French – the first to settle here three centuries ago, in 1702. It was traded with the British and Spanish before being seized by the US during the war of 1812. This combined heritage is celebrated in an extravagant Mardi Gras which precedes the more famous one in New Orleans by several decades.

Mobile has a few specific sights – highlights include Fort Condé, built by the French in 1718, a series of retired battleships and warplanes, and several antebellum (pre-Civil War) homes and gardens – but really, the things to do are to stroll through the pretty historic districts and take a tour around the entire bay area.

GETTING THERE AND GETTING AROUND

Amtrak and Greyhound both have centrally located stations. Trains pull into 11 Government St, and buses use the terminal at 2545 Government Blvd.

The centre of the city can be covered on foot, and city buses run to outlying sites. As always in America, though, you can see much more by car.

INFORMATION

The **Mobile Area Convention and Visitors Bureau**, tel: (800) 5-MOBILE, has a visitor centre in Fort Condé, 150 South Royal St.. Open daily 0800–1700; tel:(251) 208-7304; www.mobile.org.

MONEY There are plenty of banks with automatic cash dispensers in the centre.

POST AND PHONES The main post office is in the centre at 250 St Joseph St; open Mon–Fri 0830–1730.

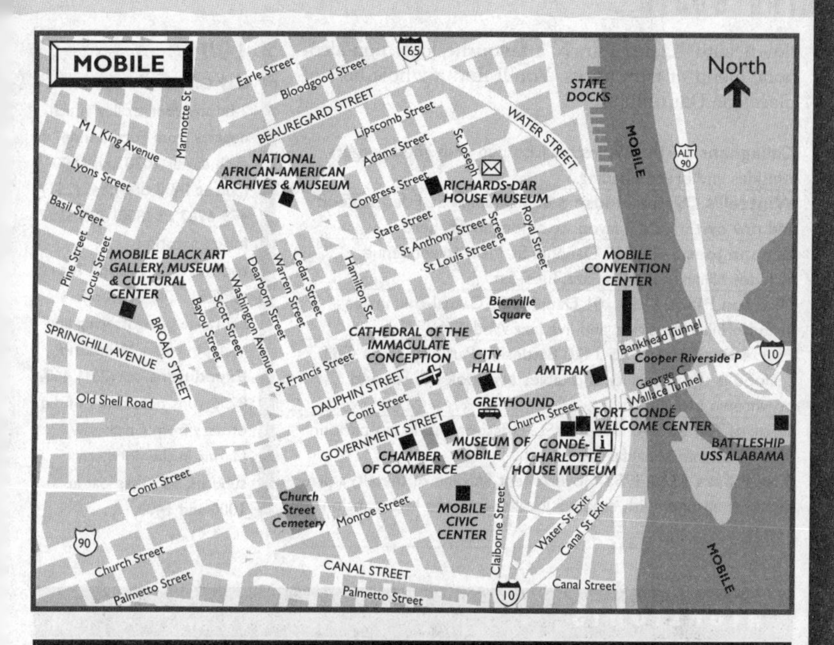

ACCOMMODATION

Check with the visitor centre for a full rundown of the budget options. Mobile's pretty streets mean a fair number of B&Bs in historic homes, with prices for most hovering around $100 per double room. Your true cheap options are the chain motels (see p. 52) on the main roads west of centre.

Olsson's Motel $–$$ 4137 Government Blvd; tel: (251) 661-5331. Simple and friendly, although some distance from the centre.

Malaga Inn $$ 359 Church St; tel: (251) 438-4701. Gorgeous Southern inn with large rooms and swimming pool, centrally located.

Riverview Plaza $$–$$$ 64 S Water St; tel: (251) 438-4000. Modern high-rise towers above the Mobile Bay waterfront. Three appealing restaurants; 376 rooms-with-a-view; walkably close to all city-centre attractions.

FOOD AND DRINK

Seafood, whether steamed, fried or raw, is a real speciality this close to the Gulf of Mexico, with Gulf shrimp leading the parade. Southern cooking, in the form of steaks, pork chops and lots of fresh vegetables, is also generously served. Wash it all down with Azalea Punch, a favourite local non-alcoholic blend of fruit juices. You'll find a whole host of places on Dauphin St.

Callaghans $ 916 Charleston. Irish pub with good burgers, whiskies and bread pudding.

Wintzell's Oyster House $ 605 Dauphin St. Fried seafood and raw oysters are a favourite among locals here.

Banana Joes $–$$ 219 Dauphin St. Main street venue includes billiards and live jazz, Tues–Sat.

Drayton Place $–$$ 101 Dauphin St. Casual-chic image includes billiards, cigars and live jazz Wed–Sat.

Pier 4 Restaurant $$ 1420 Battleship Parkway. Fresh Gulf seafood is the speciality, and tables overlook the bay and downtown Mobile.

Spot of Tea $$ 310 Dauphin St. A Victorian-style tea parlour, serving elegant breakfast and lunch.

The Pillars $$$$ 1757 Government St. One of the city's premier restaurants with creative local specialities in a mansion setting.

Tours

Bay City Tours operates a 2-hr city tour trolley which departs from Fort Condé each day at 1030 and 1400 (Sun at 1400 only); tel: (251) 479-6962 or (800) 338-5597 for information. **Memorable Mobile Tours**, tel: (251) 344-8687, offers a full range of sightseeing and in-depth tours. **Wildland Expeditions**, tel: (251) 460-8206, runs boat tours of the estuary from Chickasaw Marina in the northern suburbs, $$$ Tues–Sat at 1000 and 1400.

HIGHLIGHTS

Fort Condé is as good a place to start as any, as it offers good views of the city from its reconstructed walls, and contains a museum with dioramas depicting the city's French, British and Spanish eras. Open daily 0800–1700.

From here it's a short walk to the pretty central area. Government St is a major thoroughfare with a number of noteworthy buildings. **City Hall**, at no. 208, dates from around 1855 and sports an architectural style drawn from the West Indies. In the same building, the **Museum of Mobile** provides a good historical background to the area including exhibitions relating to the city's uneasy relationship with slavery. Open Mon– Sat 0900–1800, Sun 1300–1700.

Just around the corner on 65 Government St is the **Gulf Coast Exploreum Science Center**. Filled with amazingly creative themed interactive features, the exhibits, although primarily geared for children, are great fun for adults as well. Open Mon–Fri 0900–1600, Sat 1000–1700, Sun 1200–1700. There is a domed Imax cinema adjacent.

Dauphin St is Mobile's 'Main St' and a pleasant and lively stretch of pavement, and from here you can get a good taste of the area. The city's identity as a grand dame of the South is revealed through its many ***antebellum* homes**. These magnificent houses were the pleasure palaces of rich landowners who revelled in their Southern

MOBILE BAY

South-west of Mobile is the colourful fishing village of **Bayou le Batre**. East of here is **Bellingrath Gardens**, a beautiful 64-acre landscaped semi-tropical garden; a viewing of the **Bellingrath Home** is included in the tour. $$$, open daily, gardens 0800–1700, house 0900–1600. At the mouth of Mobile Bay accessible via the bridge on Hwy 193, **Dauphin Island** has pretty beaches and the 164-acre **Audubon Bird Sanctuary**. The **Estuarium** displays sea life in the Gulf. $, open Mon–Sat 0900–1700 (until 1800 in summer), Sun 1300–1700. **Fort Gaines** is a neo-Renaissance construction which figured prominently in the defence of Mobile during the Civil War. $, open daily 0900–1700, summer 0900–1800. **Fort Morgan,** opposite, can be reached by car ferry, $$. From here, it's an easy drive to the tourist town of **Gulf Shores**, famed for its marvelous white-sand beaches. The trip north up the Eastern Shore offers pretty views of the calm waters while passing quaint villages, including **Fairhope**, lined with art galleries and antique shops.
The return to Mobile is via a low causeway rising barely above the water.

grace; all relied in large part on slave labour, and the stories of African-Americans are as fascinating as those of their masters, though for different reasons. Styles vary, but common features are two-storey columns supporting a massive front porch; the furnishings inside are always exquisite. The following are quite central and open to the public.

The **Condé-Charlotte Museum House**, 104 Theater St and next door to Fort Condé, was Mobile's first jail and is one of the city's oldest buildings; each room is furnished according to different eras in city history. $, 104 Theatre St; open Tues–Sun 1000–1600. The **Richards-DAR House Museum** is a large Italianate townhouse in the attractive de Tonti Square area: $, 256 N Joachim St; open Mon–Fri 1100–1530, Sat 1000–1530, Sun 1300–1600. The **Oakleigh Historic Complex** includes three adjacent residential museums. The main house was built in 1833 in the Greek Revival style. $, 350 Oakleigh Pl.; open Mon–Fri 0900–1600.

One of the city's real tourist attractions is the **Battleship Memorial Park**, along Mobile Bay. This is the appropriate final resting place of the USS *Alabama*, the World War II battleship that led a US fleet into Tokyo Bay to accept the surrender of Japan in 1945. Also on site is the USS *Drum* submarine. $$, open daily 0800–1800; winter 0800–1600.

The **National African-American Archives/Museum** documents the lives of blacks in Alabama - Mobile was a major port during the slave trade. Free, 564 Martin Luther King Ave; open Mon–Fri 0900–1400.

NIGHTLIFE

Mobilians don't go in for much rollicking on Saturday nights, so you're somewhat limited to the bars around Dauphin St. Check the *Mobile Register* for theatre and concert listings.

Banana Joe's (see under Food and Drink) has billiards and live jazz.

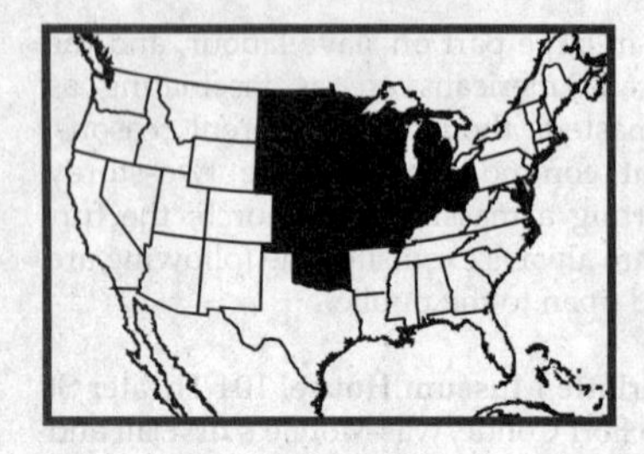

So vast is the area that Americans call their Midwest that almost any generalization you read about it is bound to be incomplete. In fact, the variety of landscapes, cities and ways of life encompassed by this central area is as great as its expanse. That said, the Midwest does set itself apart from the rest of the country in many ways. The first is its topography.

Lying between the east's Appalachians and the Rocky Mountains of the west, the area has no great mountain ranges. But don't think that its terrain is all flat prairies. The Black Hills in the Dakotas, Mississippi River bluffs, the Wisconsin Dells and other natural features lend an interesting and scenic vertical dimension. Rolling hills characterize much of the area, and through its centre runs the mighty Mississippi River.

The Great Lakes offer miles and miles of scenic driving, with water vistas, beaches and attractive lakeside cities where those who enjoy water sports will find plenty to keep them busy. The Mississippi River offers both water travel – be sure to take a steamboat ride somewhere along its length – and a swathe of historic settlements that reflect both America's history and its heartland.

Heartland is the word you will most often hear in describing this part of America. If things in the Midwest seem a little slower and a little less up-to-date than on either coast, it is a reflection of the basic conservatism of middle America.

While both the east and west coasts are known for their cutting-edge lifestyles and for being the first to try new ideas, the Midwest has always represented the epitome of small-town attitudes. Missouri says this right up front, in its nickname of 'The Show Me State', and a common question asked in boardrooms is 'Will it play in Peoria?' This is another way of asking how an idea or product will be received by mainstream Americans.

Although there are a number of busy modern cities in the Midwest, Chicago, Illinois, is the area's largest and most dynamic city. In the mind of most Americans it is the unofficial capital of the entire land between the ocean coasts.

This showplace of the Midwest was originally an army post, chosen for its strategic location as early as 1803. It quickly became the transportation hub for the expanding westward frontier and the shipping centre for the agricultural goods from the fertile Midwest farm and ranch lands. The poet Carl Sandburg called it 'Hog butcher to the world'. You can still find fine steak dinners in the restaurants clustered around the city's stockyards.

Although Chicago has a good share of 'new American' restaurants serving avant-garde cuisine, it is also rich in ethnic foods. These restaurants are often centred in neighbourhoods outside the Loop (Chicago's business centre), and include Chinatown, Bronzeville (one of the final stops on the Underground Railroad), Little Italy and Greek Town.

Middle European and Scandinavian immigrants settled throughout the Midwest and today their cooking styles and tastes still influence the foods of America's heartland. 'Home cooking' is a complimentary term in the Midwest and is represented by such substantial all-American dishes as Indiana fried chicken, pork sausages seasoned with sage, baking-powder biscuits (non-yeast bread rolls) and dumplings.

Team sports are important in the Midwest. Several cities have well-known professional baseball teams (Chicago has two) and this is the perfect area in which to find traditional American sandlot baseball. Motor-racing fans will already know that the Indianapolis 500 is held in that Indiana city on Memorial Day (31 May) each year – a good time for those not interested in racing to avoid the city. But the big news there is the return of the Formula One race, for the first time in a decade, in September 2000, to be held there for the foreseeable future.

Although Broadway and Hollywood get more headlines, the Midwest has its own lively arts and entertainment scene. World-class symphony orchestras, professional theatre companies, blues venues and great jazz are in good supply.

After all, Chicago was one of the three 'capitals' of the Jazz Age, Detroit is the home of Motown music, and comedians such as *Saturday Night Live*'s Gilda Radner and Dan Aykroyd began their careers here. Chicago was also brought into the television entertainment spotlight by the popular *Oprah Winfrey Show*. The Midwest may be flat, but it is certainly not boring.

Nor is its history dull. During America's Prohibition era of the 1920s and 1930s, Chicago was the no-holds-barred centre for gangsters and rum-running. Infamous characters like Al Capone weave through the city's history and the legends of the Chicago gangsters are recalled in special tours that visitors enjoy today. The writer Mark Twain chronicled another age, the romantic steamboat era, with the stories of Tom Sawyer and Huck Finn, recalling days when the Mississippi River was America's greatest highway.

This waterway, along with the Great Lakes, provided the transportation link that made the Midwest America's breadbasket, brought raw materials to the steel mills and car factories of Cleveland and Detroit, and shipped the finished products all over the world.

Five of these Midwestern states – Ohio, Indiana, Illinois, Michigan and Wisconsin – made up the original Northwest Territory, which the United States acquired in 1783 under the Treaty of Paris. This is the area bounded by the Great Lakes to the north, and by the Ohio and Mississippi Rivers to the south and west.

The Midwest stretches almost endlessly with its fields of golden grains, and indeed transcontinental travellers may wish to cover part of this ground by overnight train. Keeping these long distances in mind, those who chose to cross the Midwest by car should be aware of the hazards of falling asleep at the wheel. Roads are long, straight and flat without much change in scenery to divert the driver's attention. It is always wise to have someone else awake in the car, keep the radio going and have a good supply of fresh fruit or sweets for a quick pick-me-up. The United States truck drivers' associations have stressed the importance of drivers pulling over for a nap if needed, so don't feel awkward if you need to find a parking lot to snooze in.

In the plains states, winter driving can be hazardous during snowstorms, so keep a close ear to the weather. Often, highway signs will tell you which radio stations broadcast regular travel and weather information. Those travellers using public transport will find long-distance routes between cities to be convenient and efficient. Travellers intent on seeing those areas where 'big sights' are closer together may wish to fly from coast to coast and view this area from the air.

The best time to visit America's heartland is in the spring and autumn. Summer is also pleasant if you don't mind taking a chance on heatwaves in the southern Midwest that can push daily temperatures just short of 38°C (100°F). Wisconsin and Michigan are usually spared these summer 'scorchers', and their mile after mile of cool green forests and many lakes make them popular places for southern Midwesterners to escape the heat of their cities.

These same states, as well as Brown County in southern Indiana, are known for their spectacular autumn foliage colours. Beginning in the far north, the height of colour moves southwards from the middle of September to the middle of October. Try to avoid Chicago in the depths of winter – January and February – when icy winds off Lake Michigan leave no question as to how it got its nickname as the Windy City. The two northernmost states are also very cold in the winter with snowstorms that can complicate winter driving, but leave a snowcovered landscape that cross-country skiers will appreciate. Although outside temperatures are icy in midwinter, the arts and entertainment season is in full swing then.

OUR CHOICE

Chicago Art Institute and Field Museum

Chicago's architecture viewed from a skyscraper

Boat tour on the Chicago River

Chicago's ethnic neighbourhoods

Gateway Arch

Victorian neighbourhoods of St Louis

The Mississippi River

Michigan's or Wisconsin's autumn foliage

HOW MUCH YOU CAN SEE IN A ...

WEEK (7 DAYS)

Chicago, St Louis and the Mississippi River

Niagara Falls, Lake Erie, Cleveland and Chicago (via train)

Washington DC, Western Pennsylvania and Chicago (train, returning by air)

FORTNIGHT (14 DAYS)

Chicago, St Louis, the Mississippi and Lake Michigan

Chicago, Lake Michigan and the Wisconsin Dells to Minneapolis

Washington DC, Western Pennsylvania, Chicago, Lake Erie and Niagara Falls (by train and local bus)

Chicago, St Louis, the Mississippi River, Memphis and New Orleans

The Second City is in fact second to none with its spectrum of sights, sounds and activities. Nestled on the shores of Lake Michigan is everything from ethnic neighbourhoods to esteemed educational institutions, from commerce to culture, from skyscrapers to stupendous shopping. Even the shadows of Chicago's notorious past – the great fire of 1871, 'hot air' politicians who gave Chicago its 'Windy City' nickname, the Capone/Dillinger gangster era of the 1920s and 1930s, and the Democratic National Convention and race riots of the 1960s – can't diminish its positives.

Chicago has been the birthplace and home of famous people and famous things – novelists Ernest Hemingway and Dos Passos and poet Carl Sandburg, McDonald's, Cracker Jacks and deep-dish pizza, steel-framed skyscrapers, Walt Disney and the zipper. Corporate giants like Sears, Amoco, Motorola, Sara Lee, Caterpillar and United Airlines call it home, as do famous personalities such as Oprah Winfrey and basketball's Michael Jordan. And the wheels of a global economy whirl on the trading floors of its exchanges.

Trade has been at the core of Chicago since its meagre beginnings. Jean Baptiste Point du Sable, a French-African Haitian, built a fur trading post here when he saw the potential of the site beside great Lake Michigan, with access to the Chicago River and the Des Plaines River which flowed into the Mississippi. In 1803, the US Army also appreciated its strategic value and built Fort Dearborn, the core of what is now downtown Chicago.

MUST SEE/DO IN CHICAGO

Take an architectural tour by boat

Explore the city with a native from Chicago Greeters

Immerse yourself in one of the city's ethnic neighbourhoods

People-watch and browse in shops along Michigan Avenue

Have a deep-dish pizza at Pizzaria Uno, where the original was invented

Eat a real Chicago-style hot dog

Take a walk along the lake shore

But history is a small part of the story. A visit to Chicago, preferably between April and November (winters are bitter), can be as varied as the city. Architecture and art, culture and cuisine, sports and sandy beaches, water and watering holes: you will find them all here.

GETTING THERE AND GETTING AROUND

FOR KIDS
On the International Terminal's lower level is **Kids on the Fly**, a branch of the Chicago's Children's Museum.

AIR **O'Hare International Airport** is the busiest in the world. Its Airport Transit System connects the terminals to each other and to economy parking lots. Information booths are located on the lower levels of the domestic terminals and the upper and lower levels of the International Terminal. For Travelers Aid at O'Hare, tel: (773) 894-2427.

The Chicago Transit Authority (CTA) Blue Line provides a cheap, rapid 24-hr service (45 mins) between the airports and downtown (connections between other CTA trains are $0.25). Departures are every 8–10 mins ($1.75). Airport Express ($20) is a frequent shuttle service that runs to downtown hotels, the North Shore and Oak Brook suburbs ($18–20) (purchase tickets at counters located across from the baggage claim). A taxi to downtown Chicago will cost around $40–50 (flat Shared-Ride rate – $19).

Midway Airport is located 30 mins from downtown and has the same local transport as O'Hare. The CTA Orange Line leaves from the east side of the airport, and Continental Airport Express ($16) leaves every 15 mins; taxis into the centre are around $40–50 (Shared-Ride flat rate – $14). An information booth is located in the main lobby.

RAIL/BUS Chicago's Union Station, 225 S Canal St, is the arrival and departure point for long-distance trains such as *The Southwest Chief*, *The Empire Builder*, *The Texas Eagle* and *The California Zephyr* as well as more services to Milwaukee, Detroit and Pontiac. It is also used by some METRA local rail services.

The Greyhound main terminal is at 630 W Harrison St.

ROAD Because of Chicago's strategic position, many of the nation's interstates lead to it. Interstate 90/94 runs about a mile west of downtown Chicago. Interstate 90 runs from Boston, Buffalo and Cleveland and passes through Chicago on its way to Billings and Seattle. Take I-90 from Milwaukee or I-94 from O'Hare or Madison, Wisconsin or Minneapolis. The Eisenhower Expressway (290) enters the Loop from the west. Nostalgic Route 66, the old cross-country route from California, ends downtown at Adams and Michigan Avenues, across from the Art Institute.

A citywide and suburban bus and train system is provided by the CTA, PACE (which covers the suburbs) and Metra (commuter trains). Locals call the CTA elevated train the 'L'. The tracks circle the city centre and have given it its nickname, 'the Loop'. For information tel: (888) 968-7282. A day pass ($$) on a Chicago Motor Coach Double Decker bus or on Chicago Trolley's San Francisco type streetcars will give you unlimited stops in the Loop area. Drivers carry no change, so check on the current fare (usually a flat rate, and senior citizens and children pay less) and have the right money ready.

Guided tours ($$–$$$) are run by **Gray Line of Chicago**; tel: (312) 251-3107.

INFORMATION

CITY MAP
– inside back cover

Chicago Convention and Tourism Bureau; tel: (312) 567-8500.

Chicago Office of Tourism (COT), Chicago Cultural Center, 77 E Randolph St; tel: (877) 244-2246. For the hearing impaired, tel: (866) 710-0294, www.877chicago.com. Open Mon–Fri 1000–1800, Sat 1000–1700, Sun 1200–1700. Outside North America, tel (312) 201-8847.

Visitor Information Centers at Chicago Water Works, 163 E Pearson Street at Michigan Avenue, open daily except Thanksgiving and Christmas, 0730-1900, and Illinois Market Place (Navy Pier, 700 E Grand Ave), open Sun–Thurs 1000–2100, Fri and Sat 1000–2400.

For a free visitor information pack, tel: (800) 2CONNECT or visit http://cityofchicago.org/tourism. Free weekly publications like the *Reader*, found at restaurants and local businesses, and *Key: This Week In Chicago*, available at hotels, include lists of attractions and activities.

SAFETY As in any large city, caution is the key. Avoid areas west of downtown (beyond the south branch of the Chicago River) and walking alone in parks, unfrequented streets after dark, on the South Side and on the subway, especially at off-peak hours. For those times, a car or taxi is advised. Since 11 Sept 2001, bag, coat and purse searches are common.

MONEY Banks are plentiful in downtown Chicago. Cash dispensers are everywhere. Travelex foreign exchange offices are located at 19 S LaSalle St in the American Airlines office; tel: (312) 807-4941; open Mon–Fri 0900–1730; and Naperville, 150 N Naper Blvd, Suite 152, Naperville; tel: (630) 955-0536; open Mon–Fri 0900–1730, Sat 0900–1500.

POST AND PHONES The main post office is at 433 W VanBuren St; open Mon–Fri 0700–1730, Sat 0800–1730; 24-hr self-service window.

ACCOMMODATION

Downtown hotels are expensive. Check hotels for special rates, promotions and cheaper winter rates at (877) 244-2246. To make hotel reservations, contact **Illinois Reservation Service**, tel: (888) 733-7666. **Accommodations Plus**, tel: (800) 733-7666, does advance bookings and is able to secure downtown locations for under $100. For B&Bs try **At Home Inn Chicago**, tel: (800) 375-7084. Hostels are not recommended except for the new Hostelling International ones.

DOWNTOWN

Northwestern University Dormitory Housing $ 850 N Lake Shore Dr.; tel: (312) 503-8514. Dorm rooms available May–July, seven-night minimum stay required.

Days Inn Lincoln Park North $$$ 644 W Diversey Parkway; tel: (773) 525-7010 or (888) LPN-DAYS; www.lpndaysinn.com; e-mail: daysinn.lpn@worldnetatt.net. Old World charm close to lake, zoo, the theatre and restaurant district. Special rates.

Essex Inn $$$–$$$$ 800 S Michigan; tel: (800) 621-6909; tel: (312) 939-1605 fax. Check special promotional rates.

Ho Jo Inn $$$–$$$$ 720 N LaSalle St; tel: (312) 664-8100; fax (312) 664-2356. Meagre but adequate hotel about five blocks west of the Magnificent Mile.

Hostelling International $ 24 E Congress Parkway; tel: (312) 360-0300; fax: (312) 360-0313; www.hichicago.org.

Red Roof Inn $$$–$$$$ 162 E Ontario St; tel: (312) 787-3580; fax: (312) 787-1299. Charming European-style hotel one block east of Michigan Ave, near shopping, museums and Navy Pier.

Ohio House Motel $$$–$$$$ 600 N LaSalle St; tel: (312) 943-6000. Located about six blocks west of Michigan Ave, near Rainforest Cafe.

Congress Plaza Hotel $$$ (winter) – $$$$ (summer); 520 S Michigan Ave; tel: (800) 635-1666; fax: (312) 427-7264. Older hotel with small but adequate rooms. Located across from Grant Park.

NEAR NORTH

The House of Two Urns Bed & Breakfast $$$–$$$$ 1239 Greenview; tel: (312) 810-2466 or (800) 835-9303; www.twourns.com; email: twourns@earthlink.net. Close to downtown.

The Willows Hotel $$$–$$$$ 555 W Surf; tel: (773) 528-8400; fax: (773) 528-8483. Small, attractive property with English ambience near the lake in the Lakeview area.

The Majestic $$$ 528 Brompton Place; tel: (773) 404-3499 or (800) 727-5108; fax: (773) 404-3495. Quaint hotel located in the Lakeview area, not far from downtown.

EVANSTON

This northern suburb has some reasonable places within walking distance of downtown and about 40 mins from the city centre.

Seabury-Western Seminary $$ 2122 Sheridan Rd, Evanston; tel: (847) 328-9300; fax: (847) 328-3367. Located across from Northwestern University, near the lake and within walking distance of public transport, the school offers a limited number of rooms for guests.

FOOD AND DRINK

Chicago is most famous for hot dogs (wieners) and Chicago-style pizza. Its multicultural roots also mean a rich pool of culinary delights, from Vietnamese and South American to Polish and Irish, so in addition to the selective listing here, explore the diverse cuisines of the old Chicagoan neighbourhoods (see pp. 334–336).

Gold Coast Dogs $ – 4 Loop locations: 175 N Wabash Ave; 2 N Riverside Plaza, Fl 2; 225 S Canal St; 418 N State St. Locals love their hot dogs.

Adobo Grill $$ 1610 N Wells St; tel: (312) 266-7999. An Old Town 'recommendable' for traditional cooking that typifies various regions of Mexico. Dinner only.

Amarit $$ 1 E Delaware; tel: (312) 649-0500. Tasty Thai food in an informal setting with good service.

Amitabul by Jim's Grill $$ 3418 N Southport. Buddhist vegetarian restaurant specialising in steamed stir-fry. Open for lunch and dinner.

Artopolis Bakery & Cafe $–$$ 306 South Halsted St. The good things in life at a cheap price – a bistro, coffee house, Greek restaurant, bakery and gift shop. Open for lunch and dinner.

The Berghoff $$–$$$ 17 West Adams, tel: (312) 427-3170. Downtown Chicago's best-known German restaurant, family operated since 1898. Specialties include Sauerbraten and Wiener Schnitzel. Also, of course, sausages and imported beers.

Hi Rickey's Noodle Shop and Satay Bar $$ 941 W Randolph and two other Near North locations; tel: (773) 276-8300. Asian noodles and rice dishes. Open for lunch and dinner.

Lou Mitchell's Restaurant $$ 565 W Jackson (by the Amtrak station); tel: (312) 939-3111. For large portions, good food and service. This place is always busy, and free ring doughnuts are served while you wait to be seated. Ladies get a free box of Milk Duds (caramels).

Pizzeria Uno $$ 29 E Ontario and **Pizzeria Due**, 619 N Wabash. One can't visit Chicago and not go to the places where deep-dish pizza originated.

Tango Sur $$–$$$ 3763 North Southport Ave; tel: (773) 477-5466. Huge Argentine and American steaks. Argentine take-away service at the adjacent grocery store. Dinner only.

Heaven on Seven $$$ 111 N Wabash, 7th floor (breakfast and lunch) and 3478 N Clark (lunch and dinner); tel: (312) 280-7774. A favourite with the locals, who like Cajun and Creole cuisine. Each table comes with salt, pepper and 26 different hot sauces.

Russian Tea Time $$$$ 77 E Adams; tel: (312) 360-0000. Expensive, but portions are large enough to share. Try the chicken breast roulade with oyster mushrooms à la St Petersburg. Its accompaniments, beet caviar and carrot salad, are extremely tasty. Dinner reservations advised.

HIGHLIGHTS

From 'Prairie' style to sleek skyscraper, the Chicago skyline casts a stunning silhouette against Lake Michigan. The Windy City's exterior is a tribute to the design brilliance of such notable architects as Louis Sullivan, Helmut Jahn, Frank Lloyd Wright and Ludwig Mies van der Rohe.

Those who like to see the skyline from cloud level can view the lake and the city

FRANK LLOYD WRIGHT

Fans of the distinctive work of perhaps the best known name in modern American architecture can visit the remodelled lobby of the **Rookery Building** and **Robie House**, near the University of Chicago, both fine examples of his Prairie school of architecture, as well as the **Frank Lloyd Wright Home and Studio** in Oak Park ($$–$$$), tel: (708) 848-1976.

from the 1000-ft high skywalk at the **Hancock Observatory** ($$) or go higher and see it from the **Sears Tower Skydeck.** Besides the amazing view, the Sky-deck features an interactive history exhibit ($$).

The steel, glass and concrete towers look very different when cruising past their foundations and viewed from pylon level. **The Chicago Archi-tectural Foundation,** tel: (312) 922-3432, and **North Pier Architectural and Historical Cruises**, tel: (312) 527-2002, give tourists that opportunity on their informative 90-min guided cruises along the Chicago River. The Architectural Foundation runs more than 50 bus, walking and river tours, affording a good prospect of the city's unique heritage. Walking tours allow a more intimate peek at the more eminent structures.

The 100-year-old **Chicago Cultural Center** is a good place for self-guided architectural aficionados to start. The rich detail of its interior is crowned by the world's largest Tiffany glass dome. **The Museum of Broadcast Communications,** part of the facility, contains the late comedian Jack Benny's vault and the Kraft TV studio. Become an aspiring news anchor and tape a news programme ($$$).

The Cultural Center is also home to the Chicago Office of Tourism. Mid-June–mid-Oct the COT offers a free Loop history and historical tour aboard the L. Visitors can rent ($) a self-guided walking tour tape, *Audio Architecture,* which highlights the highest building in the western hemisphere, the Sears Tower, the Federal Plaza and the rooftop gargoyles of the new public library.

OUTDOOR ART

Many of downtown's architectural gems are graced by the creations of world-renowned artists. Masterpieces include the six-storey-high Picasso at the Civic Center, Joan Miró's *Miró's Chicago* at the Brunswick Building Plaza, and Jean DuBuffett's *Monument With Standing Beast* at the State of Illinois Building. Marc Chagall's *The Four Seasons* can be found at Dearborn and Monroe, and Claes Oldenburg's huge baseball bat, *Batcolumn*, and Alexander Calder's red *Flamingo* are at the Chicago Federal Center. All can be discovered on a leisurely stroll around the Loop.
A free booklet which gives details of all these sculptures is available from the COT. **Millennium Park** offers an outdoor ice rink along with a public art plaza, Frank Gehry-designed orchestra pavillion and gardens at the north-west corner of Grant Park.

THE LOOP Downtown Chicago is designated by the encircling loop of the 'L' tracks. World-class museums and galleries abound in Chicago, and many of the best are located near downtown.

Artefacts, photographs and exhibits at the **Chicago Historical Society** (at Clark and Dearborn) trace the city's roots from frontier days to the present. $ (Mon free); open Mon–Sat 0930–1630, Sun 1200–1700. Art lovers may already be acquainted with the **Art Institute of Chicago.** The fine collection of French Impressionist paintings and drawings, as well as sculptures, textiles and art treasures that date from 3000 BC to the 1990s, reinforces its well-deserved reputation. $ (free Tues); 111 S Michigan St; open Mon, Wed, Thur, Fri 1030–1630; Tues 1030–2000; Sat–Sun 1000–1700. Unique hanging mobiles, paintings and sculptures created since 1945 make up the exhibits at the **Museum of Contemporary Art**. Works by Calder, Magritte and Warhol are well represented. Check out Cattlelan's *Novecento*: it is a horse hanging from the ceiling. $$ (free first Tues of each month); 220 E Chicago Ave; open Wed–Sun 1000–1700 (Tues until 2000).

THE LAKESIDE Between Michigan Ave and the lake lies **Grant Park**, venue for dancing waters on summer evenings and a series of food and music festivals (see p. 337). Walk through the park towards the lake and a little north and you'll see **Navy Pier**, 600 E Grand. It stretches for 50 acres out into the lake, making it easy for tour boats, dinner cruises and visiting vessels to dock there. The pier includes the unique – fried dough, sand-bottle 'art', squeezable eyeballs – and the entertaining – **Chicago Shakespeare Theater**, IMAX theater, one of the world's largest McDonalds, beer garden, merry-go-round, shops and restaurants. Stained-glass windows at the

KIDS' STUFF

Chicago abounds with activities and museums that are geared towards children or those who act like them. Besides **Chicago's Children's Museum** there is the **Kohl Children's Museum**, where the young ones will come away happy and with cheeks covered with face paint. $, 165 Green Bay Rd, Wilmette; open Tues–Sat 0930–1700, Sun 1200–1700.

The **Art Institute of Chicago** (see above) has a children's area and a magnificent collection of miniatures, The Thorne Rooms. Budding physicists can witness a nuclear chain reaction at **ComEd's Powerhouse Museum,** 100 Shiloh Blvd, in the far north suburb of Zion; open Mon–Sat 1000–1700. Free.

Something wild is always going on at the city's **Lincoln Park Zoo**. Over 1000 animals live in this lovely setting alongside the lakefront. Cannon Dr. at Fullerton Pkwy; open 0900–1900 (until 1700 in winter). Free.

From late spring to early autumn, **Brookfield Zoo** transports visitors on motorised safari vehicles through a swamp, a 5-acre savannah and past many different creatures. $, 8400 31st St, Brookfield; open daily 1000–1700.

The giant chills and thrills amusement park **Six Flags Great America** is north of Chicago, at Gurnee (off I–94). Bugs Bunny and friends hang out around the park's attractions and its 130 rides, which include eight roller-coasters and a 227 ft free-fall tower. $$$, open special weekends in May and Oct and daily June–Aug.

TOURS WITH A DIFFERENCE

To see the city from the water, try the popular **Windella Boat Tour**. It leaves from Wacker Dr. and Michigan and runs end Apr–Oct. $$$

Native Chicagoans look to do the unusual. Some visit the famous people who have made their eternal home at Graceland Cemetery. The 2-hr **Chicago Architectural Foundation Graceland Cemetery Tour** describes the former notables and their unique tombstones and mausoleums. $, Clark and Irving Park; daily at 1400 (Aug–Oct).

Pier's Smith Museum of Stained Glass reveals Chicago's history from the 1870s to the present (free). The enclosed Ferris wheel moves so slowly even the worst acrophobe will feel safe, and kids love the exhibits at the **Chicago Children's Museum** such as the Art and Science of Bubbles, PlayMaze and the Stinking Truth About Garbage. $$, open Tues–Sun 1000–1700, plus Thur 1700–2000, when it is free.

If going from the depths of the ocean to the outer limits of space, with a look at life through the ages in between, seems more appealing, visit the Museum Campus, 1200–1300 S Lake Shore Dr. Dolphins and beluga whales perform five times a day at the **Shedd Aquarium**, while over 6000 creatures lurk in the world's largest aquarium and in the facility's newest exhibit, Amazon Rising: Seasons of the River. $$, open 0900–1800. Reach for the stars at the world's first interactive Star Rider Theater or the 60,000 square-foot Sky Pavilion of the **Adler Planetarium:** $ (free Tues); open daily 0900–1800; Fri 0900–2100; weekends and holidays 0900–1800. Mummies and the bones of Sue, the largest T. Rex ever discovered, are some of the former living creatures at the **Field Museum of Natural History**: $$ (free Wed); open 0900–1700. To save money for six of Chicago's most popular attractions (Adler Planetarium, Art Institute, Field Museum, Museum of Science and Industry, Shedd Aquarium and Sears Tower Skydeck) purchase a CityPass ($30.50); www.citypass.com.

The temptation to reach out and touch the elusive, three-dimensional pictures at the **Museum of Holography** escapes no one. Museum director Loren Billings enthusiastically explains the basic principles of this technical science which has helped to further advances in medicine, engineering and entertainment. $ 1134 W Washington Blvd; open Wed–Sun 1230–1700.

Science and nature connect at the new **Notebaert Nature Museum** with exhibits such as Butterfly Haven, City Science and Wilderness Walk. $$, Fullerton Pkwy and Cannon Dr.

Many Chicagoans love to walk, bike and rollerblade down the **lakeshore path** where, at every turn, there is another postcard view of the city. That's one reason it is so crowded on weekends. Though the path actually starts on 71st St, it is safer to use only the section north of Navy Pier. For those who prefer wheels to feet, rollerblades and bikes can be rented ($$) at any one of Bike Chicago's four locations, weather permitting; tel: (800) 926-BIKE.

Another favourite walk starts along the lake at Fullerton, goes to the LaSalle St overpass and then back to Fullerton through Lincoln Park Zoo. In the summer walkers also stroll along the lake north from Monroe St, to the Merchandise Mart and along the Chicago River, passing murals and sculptures along the way. They climb back up to the hustle and bustle of street level at Michigan and Wacker. These walks are not safe after dark.

SOUTH OF THE LOOP Tucked away at 1801 S Indiana is the **National Vietnam Veteran Art Museum**. This treasure contains over 500 pieces of haunting artwork created by both allied and enemy Vietnam veterans. Its newest exhibit, 'Above and Beyond', is a wind-chime-like sculpture of imprinted dog tags that memorializes the 58,000 'vets' who lost their lives. A blend of art and artefacts helps the visitor to understand the Vietnam conflict from the perspective of those who experienced it. $, open Tues–Fri 1100–1800, Sat 1000–1700, Sun 1200–1700.

Further south is the **Museum of Science and Industry**. Its multitude of hands-on and permanent exhibits – the space capsule, vintage aeroplanes, *Pioneer Zephyr* train, Colleen Moore's fairy castle, coal mine, model railway, Omnimax Theatre and a U-505 submarine – leave no doubt as to why it is considered one of the 15 best museums in the world. $ (Thur free; some exhibits extra); S Lake Shore Dr. and 57th St; open 0930–1600 (weekends and holidays until 1750).

At the south end of the museum, in Jackson Park, is the **Japanese Garden**. Lily pools, arched bridges, dwarf pines, stone lanterns and a ceremonial bamboo tea house are designed to evoke tranquillity.

Situated on the University of Chicago campus is the **Oriental Institute Musuem**, 1155 E 58th St; tel: (703) 702-9514. Open Sun 1000–1600, closed Mon, Wed 1000–2030, other days 1000–1600, free. University archaeologists have gathered this fine collection of Egyptian sculpture, jewellery and statues as well as other Middle Eastern artefacts.

NORTH SHORE It is worth renting a car to visit Chicago's North Shore. Take the Outer Drive and continue down Sheridan Rd to the first suburb, Evanston. Walk along the paths of the beautiful lakeside campus of **Northwestern University**. There are only about 25,000 native Americans residing in Chicago, but the **Mitchell Museum – American Indian** at Central Park and Central has a fine collection of over 2000 pieces of Indian artefacts, including pottery, textiles, basketry from the Plains, Western Great Lakes, Pueblo and Navajo Indians. $, open Tues–Sun 1000–1800.

Continue on to Wilmette's delicately sculptured **Bahai Temple**, one of seven in the world and the North Shore's foremost landmark. Its summer gardens are lovely. Follow Sheridan Rd through ravines and past beautiful homes to Lake Cook Rd.

Turn left to the **Chicago Botanic Gardens** (East of Edens Expressway); free, but there is a charge for parking. You can meander along its numerous promenades around the lake and through English gardens, Japanese bonsai, expanses of roses and changing landscapes.

The drive further north will take you past Ravinia Park, to Lake Forest's elegant mansions. The north-west suburb of Des Plaines is the **McDonald's Museum**. Big Mac lovers will enjoy seeing the original golden arches, cooking equipment, advertising and even the 'Speedee' road sign at the 1955 restaurant: 400 Lee St, Des Plaines; open Wed, Fri, Sat 1000–1600 (free).

THE NEIGHBOURHOODS If Chicago's architecture is its skin, and the Loop its brain, then the city's heart lies in its myriad cultures. Maybe poet Carl Sandburg named it 'the city of big shoulders' because of the strength it takes to support all that diversity. The flavour of the roots that have made up Chicago permeates the city – visit the neighbourhoods and see the world. Do it on your own or take one of the **Chicago Neighborhood Tours** that depart from the Chicago Cultural Center every Sat ($$$). If you plan to explore on your own, do it during daylight hours as some areas are not always safe after dark, especially the South Side.

NEW CHINATOWN

The red pagoda at the Argyle L stop signals New Chinatown, the Argyle/ Broadway/Sheridan Rd area that has become a new hot spot for locals and visitors seeking Korean, Thai, Filipino, Vietnamese and Cambodian grocery stores, gifts shops and restaurants.

To reach **Chinatown**, take CTA Red Line south to 22nd St/Argyle. Asia is well represented here, just south of the Loop in Chinatown Sq. Messages of peace, harmony and co-operation welcome visitors at the **Chinatown Gate** (Wentworth and Cermack). Exotic aromas emanate from the Chinese herb stores, bakeries and groceries housed in the brightly coloured Asian architecture. They whet one's appetite for dim sum. Served at local restaurants between 1000 and 1400, this parade of carts brimming with tantalising oriental delicacies adds a finishing touch to an interesting afternoon. Try the **Three Happiness Restaurant** $, 2130 S Wentworth.

Bronzeville is reached via no. 4 bus south to 56th St and Cottage Grove. For African-Americans, one of the final stops on the Underground Railroad was the **Olivet Baptist Church** (35th and King Drive) in what came to be known as Bronzeville. Life in Bronzeville between 1919 and 1948 rivalled New York's Harlem. Many of its buildings have attained National Historic Landmark status, and the once vibrant community is coming back to life.

The **DuSable Museum of African American History** details points of interest such as Martin Luther King's living quarters during his campaign for open housing and equal justice. $ (free on Sundays) 740 E 56th Place; open 0900–1700, Sat–Sun 1200–1700. The Chicago Historical Society and other major museums often feature exhibits on African

IRISH BROGUE

Take the Red Line to 35th St to visit one of the city's foremost Irish neighbourhoods. Anyone who knows Chicago knows that the Irish have long dominated its politics – there has been an Irish mayor for most of the last 45 years. The tree- and bungalow-bordered streets of South Side Bridgeport (Pershing/Stevenson Expressway/Princeton and the river) were home to long-time late mayor, Richard Daley.

John Comiskey built the White Sox ball park as a monument to the Bridgeport Irish. Traditional Irish pubs, gift shops and restaurants are plentiful throughout the city and suburbs.

America. And ethnic restaurants, featuring ribs and soul food, are found throughout the city.

To travel from Africa to Europe, take the Blue Line west to Cicero/ Polk. **Little Italy and Greektown** are just west of the Loop and south of the Congress St Expressway, especially around the University of Illinois– Chicago (UIC) area. Italian roots go back to the turn of the century. At first it was extortions and murders, then it was the 'booze wars' of the Twenties. The North Side Italian Community (bounded by Goose Island, North and Chicago Aves) became known as Little Hell. Later, Italian immigrants settled Little Italy around Taylor and Halsted. Though the UIC campus has taken over much of the neighbourhood, many original buildings have been preserved. The early 20th-century structures and the old country cuisine of the Taylor St restaurants make the neighbourhood appealing.

UIC also swallowed up most of the original Greektown, but a two-block segment of Halsted St west of the Loop is still devoted to bellydancers and cries of 'Opaa!' To make the area more of a tourist attraction, there are three 45 ft columns, each representing a high point in Greek culture. A spit-roasted lamb in the window of the **Parthenon Restaurant** ($$) 314 S Halsted St stimulates nostalgia, as do several other traditional Greek restaurants. The 1927 **St Basil's Greek Orthodox Church**, 733 Ashland, was once a Jewish synagogue. Though the church has recently been renovated, it has maintained the stained-glass windows and the seat-name plaques of the original congregation.

One of the main Jewish shopping areas during the late 1940s to the early 1960s was **Rogers Park**, between 2300 and 2900 blocks of Devon Ave. Since then, the kosher delicatessens, butcher shops and bakeries of Rogers Park have been replaced by a hodgepodge of Pakistani, Israeli, Russian, Assyrian, Thai, Korean and Indian ethnic groceries, bookshops and restaurants. This United Nations is a bargain hunter's paradise for electronics, jewellery and saris. To get there, take the Red Line north to Sheridan, then bus 155 west.

UIC expansion halted the pushcarts and peddlers of Maxwell St, which was a staple to Jewish immigrants. Most of the urban Jewish communities have made an exodus to the suburbs, but religious artefacts, paintings, sculpture and costumes pertaining to Judaic culture are regular exhibits at **Spertus Museum of Judaica** $, 618 S Michigan Ave; open Sun–Wed 1000–1700, Fri 1000–1500, Thur 1000–2000 (Fridays free).

'**Polish Main Street**' is Milwaukee Ave, directly northwest of the Loop; take the Green Line to Milwaukee and Augusta. The **Polish Museum of America** features permanent exhibits of Casmir Pulaski, ethnic and military costumes and a Maritime Room; Milwaukee and Augusta; open daily 1100–1600; free. The 3000 block of Milwaukee Ave is a potpourri of authentic bakeries, gift shops, delis and restaurants where pierogi are plentiful. Enjoy tasty and authentic Polish cuisine at **Orbit Restaurant and Lounge**, 2954 N Milwaukee, or at **Grota**, 3112 N Central Ave. It is cheap.

FOR FREE

Several television shows originate in Chicago, the most popular being the *Oprah Winfrey Show*. To obtain free tickets for her show, out-of-towners must contact the ticket hotline at least a month in advance; tel: (312) 591-9222. If you can't get to see Oprah, you might try to get tickets for the outrageous *Jerry Springer Show*, tel: (312) 321-5365; or the *Jenny Jones Show*, tel: (312) 836-9485.

TRADING PLACES

Get your ups and downs at Chicago's commerce exchanges. All have videos explaining how the exchanges work and a visitors' gallery where you can watch the frenzy of trading options, foreign currency, stock or agricultural commodities.

It is a good idea to call ahead since the exchanges may be closed for security reasons.

Choose from the **Chicago Board of Options Exchange**, 400 S LaSalle St; tel: (312) 786-7492; **Mercantile Exchange**, 30 S Wacker; tel: (312) 930-8249; and the **Chicago Stock Exchange**, 440 S LaSalle St; tel: (312) 663-2222. All are open 0730–1530 (Mercantile closes 15 mins earlier).

Lincoln Square Mall is Chicago's **Germantown**. A huge mural depicting the German countryside colours the 4600 block of 'Sauerkraut Boulevard' (Lincoln Ave). Although 'the boulevard' does not always reverberate with oom-pa-pa, there is an abundance of ethnic restaurants, delis and shops. Take the Blue Line north to Montrose, then no. 78 bus east to Lincoln Sq.

Scandinavian settlement in the northern part of the city in **Andersonville** (Foster to Bryn Mawr near Clark St; no. 22 bus north to Clark and Foster) peaked about 1930. The **Swedish American Museum Center** (5211 N Clark St and the **Ebenezer Lutheran Church** (1650 Foster) remain. Descendants of the original immigrants still run the Clark St craft and food establishments, and a visit to Andersonville would be incomplete without sampling **Ann Sather's** mouthwatering cinnamon buns at 5207 N Clark, plus five other locations.

The *corazón* of Mexico beats in the **Pilsen/La Villita** area (no. 60 Cermack bus west to Lawndale). A pink gateway arch at Albany and 26th welcomes visitors to La Villita. Ethnic music and the murals that decorate 25th and 26th St groceries, shops, newsstands and restaurants give Chicago's South of the Border residents a sense of the homeland. Prominent Mexican artists perform concerts, folk music, children's theatre, readings and display art at the **Museum of Mexican Fine Arts Center**, 1852 19th St; open Tues–Sun 1000–1700; free.

TAKE ME OUT TO THE BALLGAME

Sportsmania is part of the Chicago scene. Didn't ex-Bull basketball player Michael Jordan put Chicago on the world map? Whatever the time of year a professional team is playing. In the cooler months, it is the **Bulls** (basketball), **Bears** (football), **Chicago Blackhawks** or **Wolves** (hockey). Summer is the baseball season, and you'll find the **White Sox** at Comiskey Park and the **Cubs** at Wrigley Field. It's fun just to watch the fans. Wrigley Field, one of the grand old ballparks, is where you'll find 'bleacher bums' swigging beer, yelling and predicting the plays.

Since game tickets are expensive, many fans opt instead for sports bars. You can find dancing and big screens at the **Alumni Club**, 15 W Division. The college-aged crowd likes **Hi-Tops** by Wrigley Field (3551 N Sheffield), where by 2300 you can expect people to be dancing on the tables. From the windows of **Cubby Bear**, on Addison and Clark, you can see the famous Wrigley Field moniker, plus they have live music on most non-game nights. Another local Wrigley Field pub is Bernie's on Clark and Grace, which serves decent food and has an atmosphere more like a backyard patio than a bar.

SHOPPING

Speciality boutiques, Water Tower Place, and the best upmarket department stores are on N Michigan Ave's **Magnificent Mile**. From just over the Chicago River Bridge to Oak St, it is one of the city's best places to people-watch. Stop off at FAO Schwarz, the giant toy store: the electronic keyboard on the floor plays every note you step on (like the one on which Tom Hanks danced in the film *Big*). Turn down Oak St to check out the international designers like Ultimos, Armani and Versace. A new Michigan Ave shopping venue, **The Shops at North Bridge**, anchored by Nordstroms, features speciality shops such as Armani and Hugo Boss.

If you don't have the wallet for designer labels, shop in **State St**. It is Chicago's original shopping mecca, with the original Marshall Field and Carson, Pirie, Scott. There are great deals on designer merchandise at T J Maxx. Filene's Basement also has a branch on Michigan Ave, but it takes time to rummage through the merchandise.

EVENTS AND FESTIVALS

Chicagoans love to celebrate - anything. There are ethnic festivals and parades throughout the year (the Chicago River is even dyed green for **St Patrick's Day**, 17 March). Check with the COT to see where the party is.

In Grant Park the sounds of great classical, jazz, country, gospel and blues ride the summer breezes on warm summer nights against a backdrop of coloured spotlights and the dancing waters of the Buckingham Fountain. Grant Park hosts three great celebrations under the stars. The **Blues Festival** (early June) and the **Jazz Festival** (early Sept) are free. Food can be costly at the week-long **Taste of Chicago** celebration, a hodgepodge of speciality and ethnic cuisines that culminates with a gala 4 July fireworks display.

In late July, Lake Michigan is aglow with boats, planes and fireworks as the city celebrates **Venetian Night** at Monroe Harbor. The Monroe Avenue Yacht Club hosts a free open house.

If you are a hearty soul, come to Chicago during the Winter Delights promotion - 1 January and 28 February. Get a free Value Card for discounts on food, attractions and lodging; 2tel: (866) 2CHICAGO, 710-0294; www.877chicago.com.

NIGHTLIFE

From autumn through to spring the world-class **Chicago Symphony** performs at Symphony Center, 220 S Michigan. Solo jazz greats such as Dave Brubeck and classical artists such as cellist Yo-Yo Ma or violinist Pinchas Zuckerman also play there. In the summer the musicians take their acts on the road and perform outdoors at Ravinia Park in the northern suburb of Highland Park. Reduced price 'rush' tickets for students and those aged 64 and over go on sale for $12.50 at the box office 2 hrs before the concerts at Symphony Center.

Theatres offer everything from lavish productions to intimate pieces – many small theatres and great restaurants have sprouted up in a 2-mile section around the Lincoln/Halsted Ave area. Half-price, day-of-performance tickets are available at Hot Tix booths, tel: (312) 977–1755.

PLAY THE CASINOS

There are several riverboat gambling venues outside Chicago at the Empress Casino, Joliet, the Grant Victoria Casino, Elgin, and the Hollywood Casino in Aurora. In Indiana, there is Harrah's in Hammond and the Majestic Star Casino in Gary.

The **Second City,** 1616 N Wells St, is the socio-political, satirical comedy club where such notables as John Belushi, Alan Arkin, Gilda Radner, Bill Murray and Dan Aykroyd started out. It is one of the great places for improvised comedy. For tickets, tel: (312) 377-3992 or (877) 778-4707.

Chicago has some great jazz and blues clubs. Expect to pay a cover charge in most.

Buddy Guy's Legends, 754 S Wabash. Arrive early to get a good seat for local and top name blues performers.

Dick's Last Resort, 435 E Illinois St. Billed as having no cover, no dress code and no class, this is the place to watch the boats float by North Pier at sunset and listen to live Dixieland music.

Green Dolphin Street, 2200 N Ashland. Hip jazz if you can stand the cigar smoke.

Green Mill, 4802 N Broadway. There is great jazz here, but the neighbourhood warrants caution.

House of Blues, 329 N Dearborn, at the base of Marina City. Features rhythm and blues music with New Orleans-style cuisine. Cover for live music and concert. At the Sunday Gospel Brunch, 0930–1430, wild designs and African-American folk art surround patrons as their ears and stomachs are filled with soul food and sacred music.

If you fancy dancing the night away, try:

Hangge-Uppe, 14 W Elm. Dance mixes played upstairs, while downstairs the 1950s-through-1970s music prompts singalongs. Ceilings are decorated with old 45 records. Free popcorn, but a cover charge.

Where the locals go:

Clark Street, south of Wrigley Field, has really developed in the past few years, becoming a lively night scene. Along this strip are dozens of new bars and restaurants, including **Goose Island Brewery** and **Bar Louie**.

WHERE NEXT?

The whole US transport network radiates out from Chicago like a spider's web. In addition to the transcontinental routes, Amtrak routes trace the course of the Mississippi down to New Orleans (see p. 304) or cross the vast grain fields of Kansas and Oklahoma to San Antonio (see p. 377) and Santa Fe (see p. 385). Discover more of the Great Lakes with a visit to the Erie Canal and Niagara Falls (see p. 100). From Chicago the 'Texas Eagle' rolls through the flat prairieland of Illinois to quiet Little Rock. From there it cuts through tall pine forests to glitzy Dallas, where sightseers can take in the memorabilia of the Kennedy assassination, and then to the city's historical competitor, nearby Fort Worth. The university city of Austin is the next main stop before the train reaches its final destination of San Antonio (see p. 377).

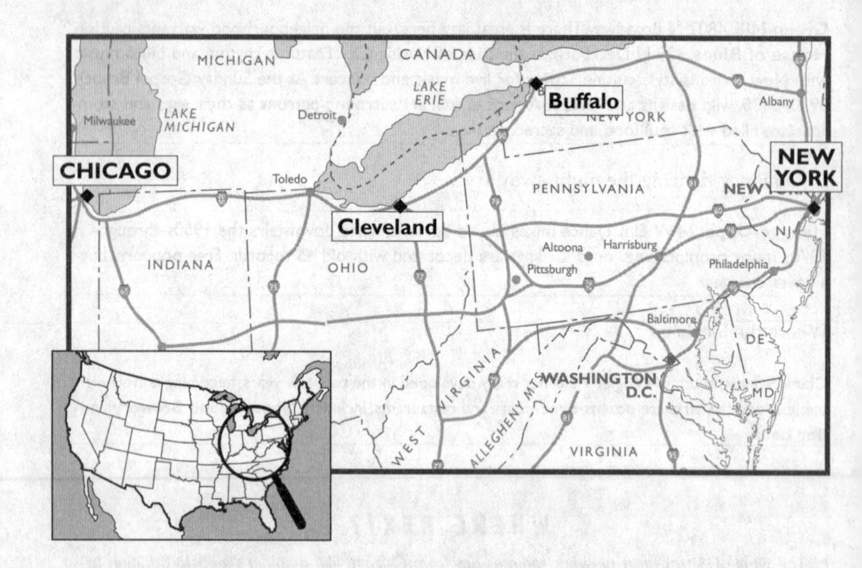

CHICAGO — NEW YORK

OTT Tables 301/315/333/501/524/530/531/532

Service	Bus	Bus	Bus	Bus	RAIL	RAIL	RAIL	RAIL	Bus	RAIL	RAIL	RAIL
Days of operation	Daily	Daily	Daily	Daily	ex⑥⑦	Daily	Daily	⑦	Daily	ex⑥	daily	⑦
Special notes	B	C	F	E	H	A			D		G	
Chicago d.	1145	0730	....	....	....	1955	....	....	....	....	....	....
Cleveland d.	2035	1750	....	....	....	0410	....	....	....	....	....	....
Buffalo d.	|	2150	....	....	0535	0710	....	0845	0855	0945	1325	1550
Albany d.	|	....	0935	0930	1100	1230s	1300	1415	|	1515	1915	2115
Boston a.	|	....	1315	|	|	|	1820	|	|	|	|	|
New York a.	0620	....	....	1215	1325	1525	....	1640	1740	1755	2145	2345

Special notes:

A–The Lake Shore Limited. This train has sleepers and a dining car available, and all journeys should be reserved in advance.

B–Additional trips: 1700, 2330.

C–Additional trips: (all require a change of bus at Cleveland) 1145, 1700, 2045, 2330.

D–Additional trips: 0015, 0300, 0950, 1130, 1350, 1615, 1930, 2215, 2245.

E–Additional trips: 0140, 0330, 0600, 0730, 1130, 1230, 1330, 1530, 1730, 1830, 2130, 2230.

F–Additional trips: 1330, 1645, 2010.

G–The Maple Leaf. This train starts in Toronto.

H–Runs 1 hour later on ⑥.

ON THE 'LAKE SHORE LIMITED'

Of the two Chicago–New York rail routes, the Lake Shore Limited is the more roundabout, following the shores of Lake Erie right up to Buffalo and touching the southern shore of Lake Ontario before dropping south 100 miles along the Hudson River valley to New York. The extra mileage is worth it, though, especially when the stunning autumn foliage turns the entire Hudson valley a rich golden red.

The route is interesting for its cross-sector views of American life, from smooth, easy agricultural lands to newly fashioned industrial cities and well-heeled rural serenity. Cleveland, only recently considered a place with absolutely no redeeming qualities, has suddenly come into its own with a tidied-up downtown and the great new Rock and Roll Hall of Fame. Buffalo has the massive draw of Niagara Falls, while Albany, the state capital, is the gateway to New England.

CLEVELAND

Like many cities in America's so-called Rust Belt, Cleveland has made great strides since its economic collapse of the 1960s and 1970s, to become a much more livable and enjoyable place. One of America's great industrial centres, along with the likes of Philadelphia and Pittsburgh, Cleveland hit rock bottom in the early 1970s, when the Cuyahoga River actually caught fire, so polluted was it from decades of heavy metal waste. But now it is often cited as the best example of urban renewal, and other cities model their programmes on Cleveland's success.

The city's urban renewal drive reached full tilt in the mid-1990s, when Cleveland opened its showpiece, the **Rock and Roll Hall of Fame**. On the spanking new North Coast Harbor, the Hall of Fame is a hugely popular testament to the musical genre. Tracing the roots of rock back to influences as diverse as blues and bluegrass, the museum has exciting interactive exhibitions on great names such as Chuck Berry, Elvis Presley, Aretha Franklin and John Lennon. The building itself is a striking piece of work by I M Pei, and contains wacky displays such as stage items from Rolling Stones tours. Because of the museum's popularity, it's a good idea to reserve tickets in advance. $$$, tel: (888) 764-7625 or (216) 781-7625; open daily 1000–1730.

After the novelty of Cleveland's claim to fame, take time to wander around more of the city. **Public Square** is a rather grand statement of its former wealth and enduring working-class pride. Meander south-west towards the notorious Cuyahoga River to drink up the gritty exuberance. The **Historic Warehouse District**, once busy with crates and forklifts, is now a lively row of shops, eateries, dance clubs and live music venues leading towards **The Flats**, an active riverside hotchpotch of grandiose century-old mills and bridges; this is the place to come at night.

CHICAGO – NEW YORK (LAKE SHORE)

Another good way to spend a lazy afternoon or evening is at a baseball or football game. Baseball's Cleveland Indians, after decades of dormancy, are now one of the league's best, and their home is the beautiful new **Jacobs Field** stadium downtown. The Cleveland Browns, after decades as the city's – and the nation's – favourite hard-luck football team, relocated to Baltimore in 1996, but a new team made its debut in 1999, in the new, state-of-the-art Cleveland Browns Football Stadium. Check with the tourist office for schedules and tickets.

The Convention and Visitors Bureau of Greater Cleveland is at the epicentre, in the Terminal Tower at 50 Public Sq.; tel: (216) 621-5555 or (800) 321-1004.

Amtrak lets you off on the cusp of the downtown area and the lakefront on Hwy 2.

For B&B reservations, call **Private Lodgings**, tel: (216) 321-3213. Aside from this, cheap rooms are scarce.

Comfort Inn $$–$$$ 1800 Euclid Ave; tel: (216) 861-0001 or (800) 228-5150. The most central budget place.

Cleveland is known for its ethnic diners, particularly in the Warehouse District and The Flats, along the Cuyahoga River. In addition, there is a plethora of bar and grill joints, enough to keep you full of burgers and beer.

The Watermark Restaurant $$$ 1250 Old River Rd. Known for its excellent seafood and ambience.

Winking Lizard Tavern $$ 811 Huron Rd. Downtown pub with a huge beer menu.

THE GREAT LAKES

The five Great Lakes – Ontario, Erie, Huron, Michigan and Superior – together total nearly 100,000 square miles. Linked by short waterways, they form one enormous water system, and as such they are the largest composite body of fresh water in the world. They also form one of the world's busiest shipping arteries: the Erie Canal connects Buffalo and Lake Erie to New York City and the Atlantic, and the Illinois Waterway links Chicago and Lake Michigan to the Mississippi and the Gulf of Mexico.

This extensive network was largely responsible for the USA's tremendous rise in agricultural and industrial might in the 19th century. Chicago is the world's biggest agricultural commodities market, and iron-and-steel-cities such as Cleveland have benefited from their accessibility to shipping. Likewise, Milwaukee's prominent breweries are well situated to exploit the area's rich grain fields, and Detroit became automobile capital of the world – Motown – in large part because of its ease of receiving raw materials, and of sending the finished product both nationwide and overseas.

BUFFALO

Perhaps more than any city in the region, Buffalo's fortunes have risen and fallen with the lake on which it stands. The completion of the Erie Canal (see p. 100) was a boon to the city's emerging shipping industry, as goods could now be transported between the Great Lakes cities and New York. Buffalo handled grain, iron ore, limestone, coal and oil, and although its importance has diminished in recent decades, it is still an economic force.

As a primarily commercial city, Buffalo lacks the cultural attractions of other mid-size cities. But if you're heading for **Niagara Falls** (see p. 100) Buffalo makes a good base, and its passable arts and entertainment scene will seem particularly appealing after the crass and unavoidable tourist exploitation at the famous falls.

The most noteworthy building is the tall **City Hall**, while the most interesting is the **Albright-Knox Art Gallery**, at 1285 Elmwood Ave in Delaware Park. Its rich collection from the late 19th and 20th centuries is well worth a look. $, open Tues–Sat 1100–1700, Sun 1200–1700.

NOTE

Those stopping in Buffalo for a side trip to Niagara Falls should note the westbound train's 0054 arrival and plan their stop on the eastbound trip.

The **Greater Buffalo Convention and Visitors Bureau**, 617 Main St, tel: (800) 283-3256 or (716) 852-2356, has information on the city and Niagara Falls.

Amtrak has stations in the suburbs of Depew and at Exchange St. The two stations are several miles apart. *The Lake Shore* only calls at Depew. The westbound train arrives at Buffalo at 2330.

There is an excellent **HI Youth Hostel** $ with double rooms close to the Visitors Bureau, at 667 Main St; tel: (716) 852-5222; or you could head a few blocks further north to the **Buffalo Tourist Lodge** $$, a budget chain motel at 1159 Main St; tel: (716) 882-3490.

You have to try the nationally renowned local speciality, buffalo wings: spicy chicken wings in a hot pepper sauce with blue cheese dressing, messy but scrumptious. The **Anchor Bar**, at 1047 Main St, serves them up by the dozen.

WHERE NEXT?

At Albany (see p. 99) the route divides, and instead of continuing on to New York, you have the choice of taking a separate train across Massachusetts to Boston (see p. 113).

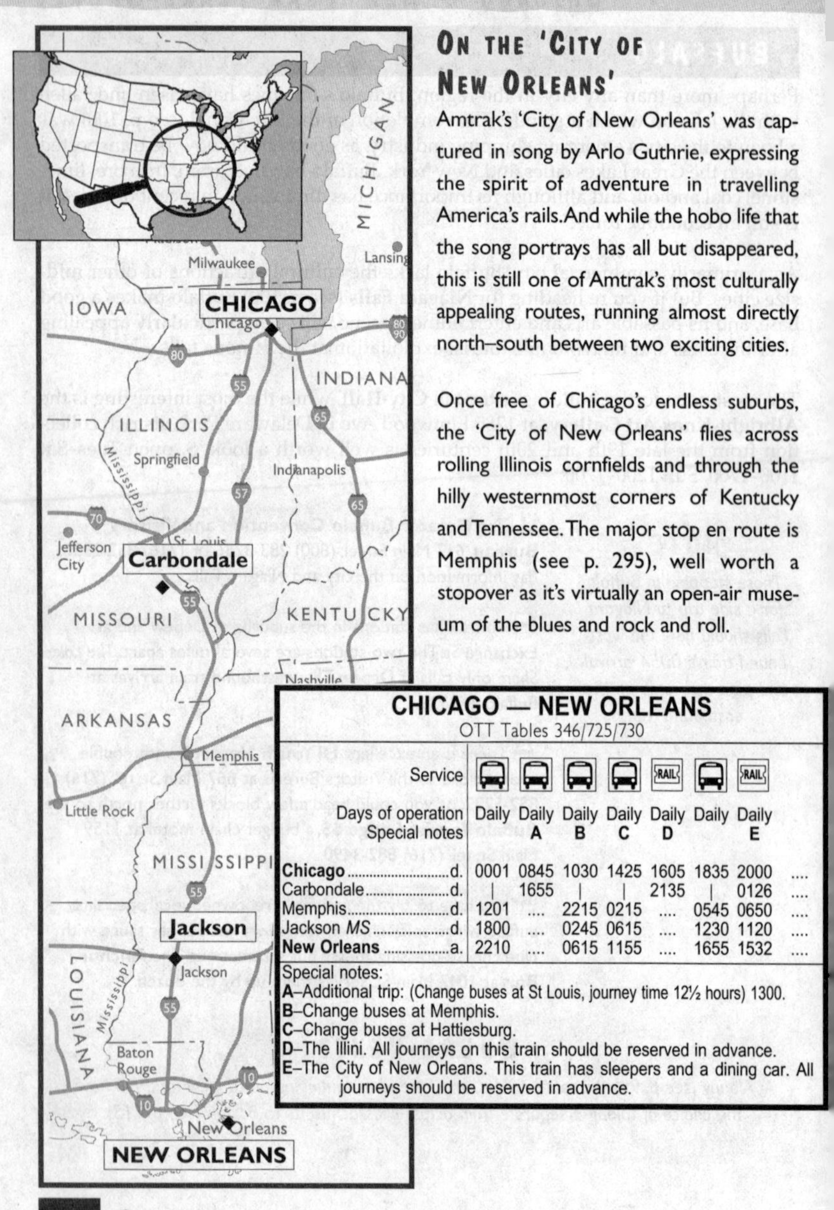

On the 'City of New Orleans'

Amtrak's 'City of New Orleans' was captured in song by Arlo Guthrie, expressing the spirit of adventure in travelling America's rails. And while the hobo life that the song portrays has all but disappeared, this is still one of Amtrak's most culturally appealing routes, running almost directly north–south between two exciting cities.

Once free of Chicago's endless suburbs, the 'City of New Orleans' flies across rolling Illinois cornfields and through the hilly westernmost corners of Kentucky and Tennessee. The major stop en route is Memphis (see p. 295), well worth a stopover as it's virtually an open-air museum of the blues and rock and roll.

CHICAGO — NEW ORLEANS

OTT Tables 346/725/730

Service	Bus	Bus	Bus	Bus	RAIL	Bus	RAIL	
Days of operation	Daily	Daily	Daily	Daily	Daily	Daily	Daily	
Special notes		A	B	C	D		E	
Chicago d.	0001	0845	1030	1425	1605	1835	2000	....
Carbondale d.	|	1655	|	|	2135	|	0126	....
Memphis d.	1201	....	2215	0215	....	0545	0650	....
Jackson *MS* d.	1800	....	0245	0615	....	1230	1120	....
New Orleans a.	2210	....	0615	1155	....	1655	1532	....

Special notes:

A–Additional trip: (Change buses at St Louis, journey time 12½ hours) 1300.

B–Change buses at Memphis.

C–Change buses at Hattiesburg.

D–The Illini. All journeys on this train should be reserved in advance.

E–The City of New Orleans. This train has sleepers and a dining car. All journeys should be reserved in advance.

The rails just nudge the Mississippi River here before levelling out across the flat, hot cotton fields of the state of Mississippi, where you gain a perspective on a very different life and culture. Jackson, the state capital, has two good museums on the state's turbulent history and culture. The train then rolls on down to New Orleans (see p. 304).

The Blues Train

The 'City of New Orleans' links Chicago and New Orleans via Memphis – all cities that have been pivotal in the creation and development of jazz and blues. It is not coincidental that the tracks trace the path that hundreds of thousands of migrant black workers took northwards in the late 19th and early 20th centuries, bringing with them the experience and the sound that gave rise to the music.

CARBONDALE

At Carbondale, Illinois, an Amtrak Thruway Bus connects to St Louis (see p. 347), a Mississippi riverside city with plenty of exciting monuments and museums to explore.

JACKSON

The small city of Jackson, Mississippi, provides a foretaste of the grand Old South. A city of grace, Jackson also recognises the appalling conditions wrought here by slavery and segregation. Start at the **The Old Capitol**, built in the Greek Revival style and converted into a museum, which now has a very good permanent exhibition entitled 'Native American, European, and African Cultures in Mississippi, 1500–1800'. Open Mon–Fri 0800–1700, Sat 0930–1630, Sun 1230–1630; free.

Just near the new capitol, at 528 Bloom St, is the highly informative **Smith Robertson Museum and Cultural Center**, located in the former heart of Jackson's black community. Displays portray the lives of blacks during the slave era and the equally difficult Reconstruction, when severe racism effectively kept blacks as second-class citizens. Photographs and artefacts bring the experience to life. $, open Mon–Fri 0900–1700, Sat 0900–1200, Sun 1400–1700.

i The train station and tourist office are both very central. Tourist information from **Metro Jackson Convention and Visitors Bureau** 921 N President St, PO Box 1450, Jackson, MS 39125-1450; tel: (601) 960-1827; Mon–Fri 0800–1700 or (800) 354-7695; www.visitjackson.com.

THE MISSISSIPPI RIVER

The mighty Mississippi holds a special point of reverence for those who live within its powerful tug of influence. The river is a way of life for millions of people in the Midwest and South, providing major shipping opportunities and helping create the conditions for America's rich farm belt. It also effectively marks the east–west boundary of the country.

The name comes from the Algonquin Indian *Misi sipi*, meaning 'big river', and one of its many nicknames is Big Muddy, derived from its incredible breadth (over a mile at some points) and brown, earthy make-up. 'Old Man River' has its own lore, captured in literature by Mark Twain, who was raised on the waters and based his two most famous rabble-rousing characters, Tom Sawyer and Huckleberry Finn, on his own boyhood adventures. (Twain, whose real name was Samuel L Clemens, worked as a pilot on the Mississippi and took his *nom de plume* from the boatmen's call as they plumbed the river's depth.)

The river is, by any measure, an awesome sight. The colourful steamboats that were once a mainstay for shipping and passenger transport are still around, many converted to casinos or pleasure cruise ships. Nostalgic (not to mention pricey) tours of up to two weeks can be arranged with companies such as the **Delta Queen Steamboat Company**, tel: (800) 543-1949, whose boats ply the waters between all the major southern cities. If your budget doesn't allow for this, you can gain good vantage points, and take hour-long sightseeing rides, on the river in Memphis (p. 295), St Louis (p. 347) and New Orleans (p. 304).

EN ROUTE

South of Jackson the route skirts the vastness of the Mississippi Delta, through the bayous and swamps of Louisiana. Look out of the left-hand side of the train for Lake Pontchartrain as the train approaches New Orleans.

Accommodation is plentiful and you should have no difficulty finding somewhere to stay. Try the **Old Capitol Inn** $$ 226 N State St; tel: (601) 359-9000 or (888) 359-9001.

Field's Café $$ 100 W Griffith St. Offers live music and dancing Fri and Sat nights to go with your meal.

St Louis is best known for the Gateway Arch and its outstanding professional sports teams. But St Louis offers more: the busy commercial city has a surprisingly active cultural life. Just downstream from the confluence of the Mississippi and Missouri rivers, it became a profitable base for fur traders, westward pioneers and steamboat shippers, drawing a mix of French, German, black and Italian immigrants. Summers can be hot and humid.

The sights are scattered throughout the city. The famous Arch sits on the riverfront, near the historic Laclede's Landing entertainment district – good at night, when the restaurants and clubs come to life. Forest Park, 8 miles west of downtown, contains many good museums, and working-class South St Louis has several ethnic enclaves, such as Soulard and the Hill.

MUST SEE/DO IN ST LOUIS

Wander Laclede's Landing in the evening

See the Gateway Arch at sunset

Catch some local spirit at a Cardinals game

Take advantage of all the free museums

Stroll past the 'painted ladies' around Lafayette Park

Eat gelato at a sidewalk café on The Hill

GETTING THERE AND GETTING AROUND

Lambert–St Louis International Airport is 13 miles north-west of centre, easily accessible by local bus or by the MetroLink light-rail system. MetroLink runs from the airport and museums to downtown and sporting venues. Rides cost just $1.25.

Amtrak trains pull in at a small station at the corner of S 16th and Market Sts. A block north of here, you can visit the St Louis Union Station, once the largest railway station in the world, rejuvenated to its former grandeur and filled with shops and restaurants.

INFORMATION

Visitor centres are open daily at both the Main and East Terminals at Lambert-St Louis International Airport and two downtown locations – Kiener Plaza at Broadway at Chestnut, America's Center at 7th and Washinton. Information is also available at www.exlorestlouis.com and at tel: (314)-421-1023 or tel: (800) 916-0040.

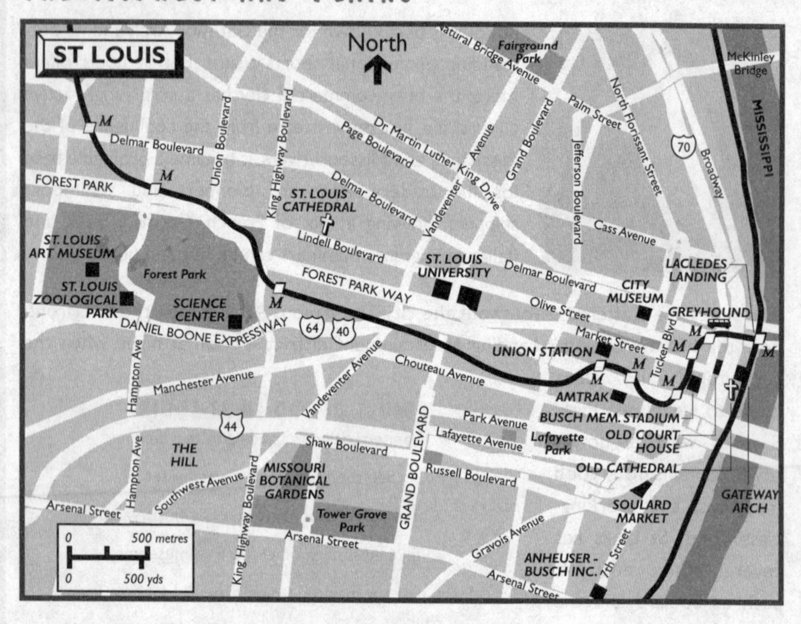

SAFETY St Louis is fairly safe as far as cities go, but don't wander around empty streets at night.

MONEY There are banks and cash dispensers in central and shopping areas.

POST AND PHONES The main post office is next to Union Station at 1720 Market St; open Mon–Fri 0700–1700, Sat 0700–1200. The zip code for poste restante is MO 63155.

ACCOMMODATION

Check with the visitor centre for special hotel rates. **St Louis Convention and Visitors Commission**, tel: (314) 421-1023 or www.explorestlouis.com, can help with budget accommodation, including B&Bs.

St Louis RV Park, 900 N Jefferson. Surprisingly central camping ground, geared toward RV travellers.

Gateway Council of Hostelling International $$$ 7187 Manchester Rd, tel: (314) 644-4660; www.gatewayhiayh.org.

Huckleberry Finn Youth Hostel $ 1904–08 S 12th St (at Tucker Blvd); tel: (314) 241-0076 or

(800) 909-4776 code 70; fax: (314) 436-0170; email: huckfinn@mindspring.com. HI hostel in three historic brick buildings in Soulard (closed 20 Dec–20 Jan). Bus no. 73 from the Arch or no. 21 from Locust St and 12th St.

Hampton Inn at the Arch $$–$$$ 333 Washington Ave; tel: (314) 621-7900. Very good prices for the location.

EconoLodge $ 1100 N 3rd St; tel: (314) 421-6556. Just off Laclede's Landing, and one of the cheapest places in town.

Lister House $$–$$$ 4547 McPherson Ave; tel: (314) 361-5506. Reasonable B&B near Forest Park.

Best Western at the Park $$ 4630 Lindell Blvd, tel: (314) 367-7500 or (800) 373-7501. Simple chain hotel in the Central West End.

Lafayette House $$–$$$$ 1718 Missouri Ave; tel: (314) 772-4429 or (800) 641-8965. Charming Victorian home in the Lafayette Sq. area.

FOOD AND DRINK

The Hill neighbourhood is great for authentic Italian food, particularly around the 5200 block of Shaw Ave. For a trendy blend of Asian, African and neo-American, there's a stretch of N Euclid Ave in the Central West End between about the 100 and 500 blocks; also the University City, particularly around the 6200–6500 block of Delmar Blvd.

Central/Central West End

Balaban's $$$ 405 N Euclid Ave. Continental cuisine, extensive wine list.

Laclede Street Bar & Grill $–$$ 3818 Laclede Ave. Voted the 'best happy hour in St Louis', karaoke Wed–Sat.

Fat Freddie's Pub & Grub $–$$ 3834 Laclede Ave, two-level bar, pool and darts, outdoor patio, dancing.

Kopperman's $ 386 N Euclid Ave. Grocery store and deli with excellent breakfast and lunch platters. Outdoor seating, or you can wrap it up and take it to the park for a picnic.

Wild Flower Restaurant & Bar $$ 4590 Laclede Ave; tel: (314) 367-9888. Rustic, comfortable, artistic atmosphere with creative cuisine.

Bar Italia $–$$ 4656 Maryland. Genuine Italian cuisine, and serving up coffee and desserts on weekend evenings. Closed Mon.

Duff's $$ 392 N Euclid Ave. Neo-French/international cuisine with no pretensions and good prices; a reliable local favourite.

Crazy Fish Fresh Grill $$–$$$ 15 N Meramec St. Popular new place serving up – yes, fresh grilled fish, as well as pasta and vegetarian meals.

South St Louis

The Bevo Mill $$ 4749 Gravois. German cuisine in a reconstructed Dutch windmill, near the Anheuser-Busch brewery.

Day Trips

St Charles, 25 miles south of St Louis, is a charming little riverside town, well preserved despite numerous floods. And if for you the Mississippi is synonymous with Tom Sawyer and Huckleberry Finn, make the 100-mile trek north to Hannibal, where Mark Twain's boyhood home and a museum dedicated to him are the main draws.

Charlie Gitto's 'On the Hill' **$$–$$$** 5226 Shaw Ave. Creative Italian dishes such as toasted ravioli and home-made tiramisù. Dinner only; closed Tues–Wed.

Giovanni's on the Hill **$$–$$$** 5201 Shaw Blvd. Casual-dressy Italian restaurant in the Hill neighbourhood which has won several local awards for its pasta. Dinner only; closed Sun.

HIGHLIGHTS

St Louis's defining feature is the magnificent **Gateway Arch**, a graceful 630-ft half-loop of stainless steel that symbolises the city's role as gateway to the West during the 19th century. It sits in the Jefferson National Expansion Memorial, honouring President Thomas Jefferson's Louisiana Purchase, which opened the way for westward expansion in the 19th century. The Arch is particularly striking at dawn and at sunset when it catches the sun's rays. A specially designed lift takes you to the top, stopping every few moments to reposition itself in the curve of the Arch. It's justifiably popular, so you may wish to purchase tickets ($) early in the day and return at your allotted time. The lift runs 0900–1800 in winter, 0830–2130 in summer. The visitor centre (open 8000–2200 daily) underneath shows films about the Arch's construction and about the journey of Lewis and Clark, who set sail from St Louis up the Missouri in 1804 to explore the newly purchased western territory. The Museum of Westward Expansion further documents this extraordinary voyage.

Laclede's Landing Historic District, just beyond Eads Bridge, is a restored waterfront named after Pierre Laclede, founder of the city. It's hard to get a feel for how bustling the city was in its heyday as the area has been prettified and converted to shopping, restaurant, bar and club space, but it has its own atmosphere none the less: cobblestone streets and cast-iron lamps add authenticity. The **Basilica of Saint Louis** (the 'Old Cathedral' as the locals call it), at 209 Walnut St, was built in the 1840s, the first cathedral west of the Mississippi. Its presence is overshadowed – literally – by the I-70 over-pass and the colossal **Busch Stadium** nearby, which devours several city blocks. There's little reason to visit the ballpark unless you're intent on catching a Cardinals baseball game – not a bad idea, as the fans here are known for their exuberance. Right behind it at 8th and Walnut Sts, the **St Louis Cardinals Hall of Fame** shares premises with the **International Bowling Hall of Fame** – both of which are more interesting than they sound. Bowling, it turns out, goes back 5000 years, while the Cardinals have been around more than 100. $, open Mon–Sat 0900–1700, Sun 1200–1700 (all until 1900 in summer).

One of St Louis's newest and best attractions is the **City Museum**, 701 N 15th St. A great place for kids, it explores art, science and history with lots of interactive displays. $, open Wed–Fri 0900–1700, Sat–Sun 1000–1700.

WEST OF CENTRE Much of St Louis's appeal lies in its arty and ethnic neighbourhoods, so don't limit yourself to a quick trip to the Arch. About 4 miles west of the city centre, the Central West End is a hip mix of speciality shops, outdoor cafés, art and antique galleries, and imaginative restaurants. The tree-lined streets are pleasant for a stroll, and the highlight is the wonderful **Cathedral Basilica of Saint Louis** at 4431 Lindell Blvd, the 'New Cathedral' to the locals. The design is nouveau-Romanesque with Byzantine influence, and the interior contains the largest collection of mosaic art in the world.

DRED SCOTT AND THE SLAVE CASE

Dred Scott was a slave whose master took him to the northern (non-slave) states of Illinois and Wisconsin. Upon his return, Scott argued that because he had spent time in the north, he ought by law to be considered a free man. In 1847 he won his court case, and the restored courtrooms in which this pivotal trial took place can be seen at the grand **Old Courthouse** (once used for slave trading) at 11 N 4th St; open daily 0800–1630; free.

The verdict given here, however, was overturned by the US Supreme Court, which ruled that because he was born in a slave state, he was forever the property of his owner. The decision helped bring the issue of slavery to the fore, leading to increasingly fractured governmental debate until the Civil War broke out ten years later.

The Central West End abuts the expansive **Forest Park**, a classic late-19th-century urban park. Small lakes dot the green space where you can rent boats and take gondola cruises, and the park contains a large amphitheatre for summer concerts. It is also home to many of the city's best museums, all of which are open free of charge.

St Louis Cardinals paraphernalia – baseball caps, jerseys, etc. – are worn with pride by the locals and make fun souvenirs. Cardinals' first baseman Mark McGwire captivated the nation in 1998 as he set a new single-season home-run record.

Towards the western end, the impressive **Saint Louis Art Museum**, built in the *beaux-arts* style for the 1904 World Fair, houses a good collection of works from the Renaissance, pre-Columbian Mexico and the German expressionist era. Open Tues 1330–2030 and Wed–Sun 1000–1700. The **Missouri History Museum**, along the park's northern strip, tells the tale of this state, whose identity is part Midwest and part South. Among its famous sons are Charles Lindbergh, who made the first solo transatlantic flight in the *Spirit of St Louis* in 1927. Other exhibits cover life on the Mississippi and the city's rich history of black music: Scott Joplin, Chuck Berry, Miles Davis and Tina Turner all were born or lived here. Open Tues–Sun 0930–1700. The **St Louis Science Center and James S McDonnell Planetarium**, at the southern edge of the park, features displays on ecology, aviation, architecture and the human body. Open Mon–Thur and Sun 0930–1700, Fri–Sat 0930–2100; free except for Omnimax Theater, Discovery Room and McDonnell Planetarium. The **St Louis Zoo** is similarly

TOURS

The visitor centre has information on various **neighbourhood walking tours** and, because the city is so spread out, bus tours taking in the main sites. **Gateway Arch Riverboat Cruises**, tel: (800) 878-7411, offer a 1-hr narrated tour of the Mississippi River, as well as Dixie dinner cruises with live bands. For something really substantial (and expensive) take a 2- to 12-day **steamboat tour** aboard the *Delta Queen*, the *Mississippi Queen* or the *American Queen*; tel: (800) 543-1949.

FOR FREE

A lot can be done with no money in St Louis, and a good place to start is Forest Park and its free museums. Other free visual entertainment abounds – just strolling down Euclid Ave in the Central West End, Delmar Blvd in University City, the Soulard Farmers Market, or Shaw Blvd in the Hill, is fun in itself, though the many shops and cafés can be tempting.

child-friendly: in addition to a number of rare animals, the zoo has high-tech exhibits and a petting zoo. Open daily 0900–1700 (until 2000 on Tues in summer).

Beyond Forest Park, **University City**, also known as 'U-City' and 'the Loop', is a good place to find lively bars and cafés. Here, too, is the **St Louis Walk of Fame**, a series of 100 plaques in the 6500 block of Delmar Ave commemorating famous St Louisans like T S Eliot, Chuck Berry and Tina Turner.

SOUTH ST LOUIS St Louis's ethnic neighbourhoods are really on display in the working-class south side, particularly in Soulard and the Hill. **Soulard** is noted for its signature 19th-century red-brick buildings, and is a favourite local spot for live jazz, blues and casual dining. The Soulard Farmers Market, at Broadway and Lafayette, has been in existence since 1779, and from Wed to Sun teems with fresh produce and bric-à-brac.

A half mile or so west of Soulard Market, **Lafayette Park** is a nice swathe of urban green, surrounded by wonderful, colourful Victorian homes referred to as the 'painted ladies' for their effusive displays of pastel orange, yellow, purple and green. A little further west, **Tower Grove Park** has been designated a national historic landmark for its ornate bandstands and gazebos. Linked to its northern edge on the 4300 block of Shaw Blvd, the **Missouri Botanical Garden** is a fantastic landscaped park, considered one of the world's top three in display and design, with a Japanese tea garden, an English rose garden and a tropical rainforest greenhouse. $, open daily 0900–1700 (winter); 0900–2000 (summer).

The Hill district, a few streets further west down Shaw Blvd, is St Louis's Italian neighbourhood, distinguished by its red-white-and-green fire hydrants. This is the place to come for *gelato*, espresso, fresh baked bread and great Italian restaurants.

Colour Section

(i) St Louis Gateway Arch and skyline (p. 347); New Orleans (pp. 304–315), Natchez paddle steamer; Bourbon street musician

(ii) San Antonio (pp. 377–382), Mission San José; The Alamo; inset: Santa Fe trail sign

(iii) Taos pueblo (p. 401); Albuquerque, old town (pp. 402–405)

(iv) Tombstone, Arizona (p. 410); Yellowstone National Park (pp. 448–455), Old Faithful geyser; inset: bison

NATCHEZ
STEAMER
NATCHEZ
NATCHEZ.

OLD SANTA FE TRAIL

INDIAN JEWELRY & LEATHER KING
201

John B
STETSON
4X 5X 10X Quality
BEAVER HATS
SINCE
SALOON

The Germans made their presence felt in St Louis as well, and the area south of Soulard still has a slightly continental flavour. The air is also tinged with the scent of malt from the **Anheuser-Busch brewery** at Broadway and Pestalozzi St – the largest in the world. Budweiser and its many watery cousins are produced here *en masse*, and tours give the history of the family, some insight into beer-making, and free samples at the end. Tours run Mon–Sat 0900–1730, Sun 1130–1730.

Nightlife

St Louis has a jazzy, bluesy soul: it's been home to many esteemed musicians, and bars and clubs around town turn out some great performances. There are several places to scout out: Laclede's Landing tends toward the ritzy, but is alive at night; Soulard thumps with live blues, and Delmar Blvd in University City lives and breathes the student life. St Louis also has an excellent symphony orchestra, and concerts are held at the lovely restored **Powell Concert Hall**, 718 N Grand.

Downtown	**Trainwreck on The Landing**, 720 N First St; tel: (314) 436-1006; www.trainwrecksaloon.com. Live music, sports bar and 20 domestic beers on tap.
	Mississippi Nights, 914 N 1st St. Great place to catch biggish-name rock, reggae and heavy metal bands.
	Jazz at the Bistro, 3536 Washington Ave.; tel: (314) 531-1012; www.jazzatthebistro.com. Features both local and international jazz artists.
Soulard	**BB's Jazz, Blues and Soups**, 700 S Broadway. Upmarket blues club with Cajun cuisine.
	Broadway Oyster Bar, 736 S Broadway. Cajun cooking and St Louis blues.
	1860s Hard Shell Café and Bar. Seafood restaurant turning into an energetic dance floor at night, with live blues and rock.
	Mike and Min's, 925 Geyer. Local bar with honest blues bands at night.
Central West End and University City	**Club Viva**, 408 N Euclid St. World beats from Brazil, Senegal and the Mississippi delta.
	Delmar Lounge, 6235 Delmar Blvd. Good place for martinis and other mixed drinks.
	Blueberry Hill, 6504 Delmar Blvd. Part burger place, part dance club, and part gallery of American pop culture; live pop/rock bands most nights, and Chuck Berry performs at least monthly.

CHICAGO – SANTA FE

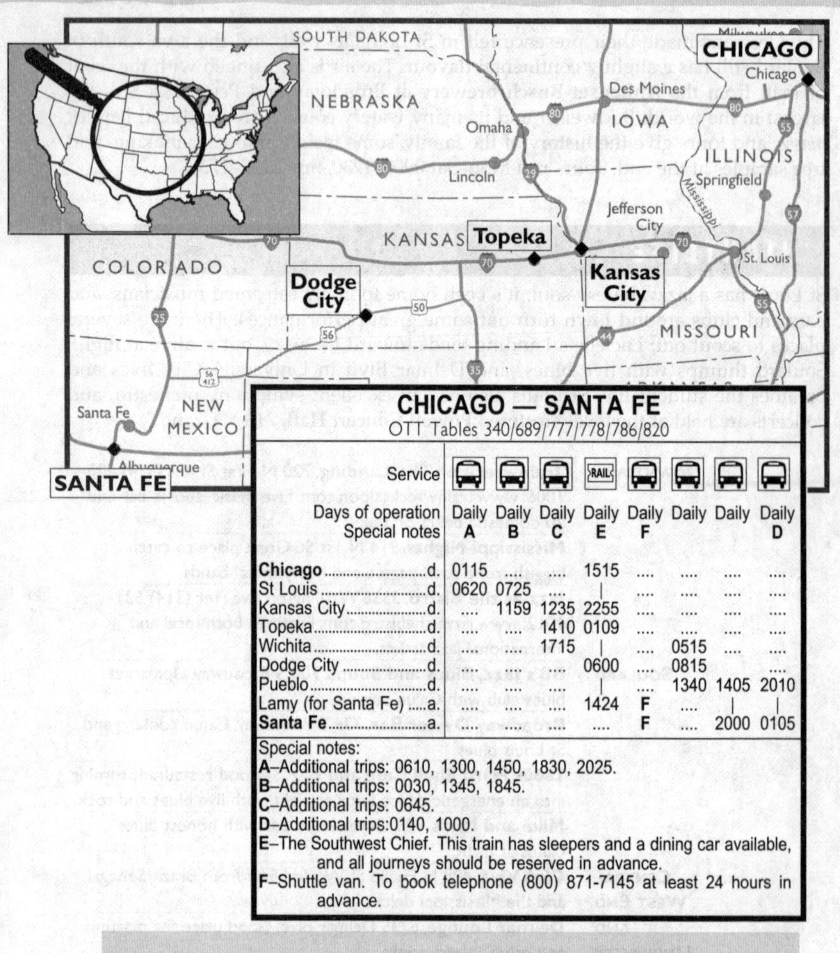

CHICAGO — SANTA FE

OTT Tables 340/689/777/778/786/820

Service	Bus	Bus	Bus	Rail	Bus	Bus	Bus	Bus
Days of operation	Daily	Daily	Daily	Daily	Daily	Daily	Daily	Daily
Special notes	A	B	C	E	F			D
Chicago d.	0115	....	....	1515	....	....	....	....
St Louis d.	0620	0725	....	|	....	....	....	....
Kansas City d.	....	1159	1235	2255	....	....	....	....
Topeka d.	....	....	1410	0109	....	....	....	....
Wichita d.	....	....	1715	|	....	0515	....	....
Dodge City d.	....	....	....	0600	....	0815		....
Pueblo d.	....	....	....	|	....	1340	1405	2010
Lamy (for Santa Fe) a.	....	....	....	1424	F	....	|	|
Santa Fe a.	....	....	....	....	F	....	2000	0105

Special notes:

A–Additional trips: 0610, 1300, 1450, 1830, 2025.
B–Additional trips: 0030, 1345, 1845.
C–Additional trips: 0645.
D–Additional trips:0140, 1000.
E–The Southwest Chief. This train has sleepers and a dining car available, and all journeys should be reserved in advance.
F–Shuttle van. To book telephone (800) 871-7145 at least 24 hours in advance.

Notes

Night travel is mostly across the expanses of the Corn Belt, the attraction of which soon palls. The nearest Amtrak stop to Santa Fe is Lamy, from which the Lamy Shuttle Service runs into Santa Fe (included with the Amtrak USA or North America Rail Pass, otherwise a fare is payable. Note: the stop before Lamy is Las Vegas – but not *the* Las Vegas…). There are buses from Kansas City to Topeka at 0715, 0815, 1230 and 1925; journey time 1½ hrs.

On the 'Southwest Chief'

The changing landscape of America looms outside the windows of the 'Southwest Chief'. The train leaves the urban sprawl of Chicago in its dust as it rolls past Illinois's prairies and over two great rivers, the Missouri and the mighty Mississippi. In western Missouri, the railway begins to trace the Santa Fe Trail. Opened in 1821, the trail blazed the way for pioneers, missionaries, trappers and traders from Franklin, Missouri to Santa Fe. It crosses the spacious wheatfields of Kansas, and the legendary Old West until it ascends the towering Sangre de Cristo Mountains and the Ratón Pass into New Mexico's high country near Santa Fe.

KANSAS CITY, MISSOURI

Art deco architecture, culture, fountains, jazz and barbecues lure today's tourists to the 'Heart of America' city. In the 19th century travellers came here for supplies before embarking on the Santa Fe, Oregon or California trails. Provisions are now available amid the unique Moorish architecture of the **Country Club Plaza**, the nation's first outdoor shopping mall (Broadway and Ward Parkway). Speciality shops, restaurants, theatres and the new City Science Museum are on the menu at the newly opened Beaux Arts-styled **Union Station**.

The **Hallmark Visitors Center**, Crown Center, tells you everything you ever wanted to know about greetings cards. Its inventive Kaleidoscope Workshop entices creative kids, and is free. 8450 Grand Blvd; open Mon–Fri 0900–1700, Sat 0930–1630. Former president Harry Truman lived nearby in **Independence** (take the KC Trolley, see below). His life and times are detailed at his home ($, 223 N Main St; open daily except Mon), the Harry S Truman Courtroom and Office ($, City Sq.; open Fri–Sat, Mar–Nov), and the Truman Library and Museum ($, Hwy 24 and Delaware; open Mon–Sat 0900–1700 (Thur until 2100), Sun 1200–1700.

For Free

Free attractions include tours of the State Capitol (10th and Jackson Sts, Mon–Fri 0800–1600, Sat–Sun 0900–1500) and the Tiffany windows at the First Presbyterian Church, 817 SW Harrison St (opening hours vary).

i **Kansas City Visitors Center**, 4709 Central in Country Club Plaza; tel: (800) 767-7700; info@visitkc.com; has Metro bus timetables. The **KC Trolley** goes to a number of attractions and out to Independence; tel: (816) 221-3399.

The Amtrak station is located at Main and Pershing Sts.

Rodeway Inn City Center $$ 3420 Broadway.
Best Western Seville Plaza $$$ 4309 Main St.
Holiday Inn Express $$$ 801 Westport.
Contact all three by their central booking numbers – see p. 52.

Barbecue food is what Kansas cuisine is all about.

Phoenix Piano Bar and Grill $–$$ 302 W 8th St. Features live KC Swing.

Gates Barbecue $$ 3201 Main St. Good-value, mid-town.

Winslow's City Market Barbecue $$–$$$ 20 E 5th St. For barbecue and blues.

TOPEKA

Kansas's state capital played a large role in the prelude to the Civil War. Not only was it a stop on the Underground Railroad (the route used to smuggle runaway slaves north), but the slavery issue became so intense that the controversy here became known as 'Bleeding Kansas'. The free **Kansas Museum of History** traces the state's roots from Bleeding Kansas to Karl Menninger (founder of one of America's foremost mental treatment facilities) and from wagon trains to McDonald's: 6425 SW 6th St; open Mon–Sat 0900–1630.

WHERE THE BUFFALO ROAM

Bison still live at the Finney Game Refuge in Garden City, 50 miles west of Dodge City, or the next train stop. Free tours by Friends of Finney Game Refuge: tel: (888) 445-4663, ext. 9400.

Topeka Convention and Visitors Bureau, 1275 S Topeka Blvd; tel: (785) 234-1030 or (800) 235-1030; www.topekacvb.org; has public transport timetables and other tourist information.

The Amtrak station is located on 5th and Holiday Sts.

Heritage House Historic Inn $$$ 3535 SW 6th St; tel: (785) 233-3800. The original Menninger Clinic is now a charming B&B with fine dining.

Capital Plaza Hotel $$$ 1717 SW Topeka Blvd; tel: (785) 431-7200 or (800) 579-7937. Topeka's newest hotel, near the Expo Center.

Paisano's Italian $$ 4043 SW 10th St; tel: (785) 273-1011. Traditional Italian dishes.

Blind Tiger Brewery and Restaurant $$$ 417 SW 37th St. Juicy Kansas wood-grilled steak, ribs and pork chops.

DODGE CITY

Fort Dodge, established in 1865 to protect voyagers on the Santa Fe Trail, still exists 5 miles east of the modern city, on Hwy 154, and just west of the city, along Hwy 50, original wagon ruts are still visible at **Santa Fe Tracks**. Dodge City's lawlessness became legendary and so did its lawmen – Bat Masterson, Wyatt Earp and Charlie Basset among them. Boot Hill, the cemetery where cowboys were 'buried with their boots on', is here and all this history comes alive at the **Boot Hill Museum** (3rd and

Wyatt Earp Sts) and **Front Street** (Front and 5th Sts). Buffalo, wagon and horseback riding, a cattle drive and a chuck wagon dinner show bring legendary Dodge City alive at Marchel Ranch, 10873 West Hwy 50; tel: (877) 631-6196; e-mail: Marchelranch@hotmail.com. The sites ($) can be visited aboard the Dodge City Trolley (end May–1st week Sept, $). Even Andrew Carnegie left his mark here: the **Carnegie Center for the Arts** at 701 2nd Ave features Kansas artists (open Tues–Fri 1200–1700, Sat 1100–1500; free).

JESSE JAMES

The boyhood home of cowboy outlaws Frank and Jesse James is now the **Jesse James Farm and Museum**, 25 miles north of Kansas City in Kearney, Missouri; $, open Mon–Fri 0900–1600, Sun 1200–1600.

i **Dodge City Convention and Visitors Bureau**, 400 W Wyatt Earp Blvd; tel: (800) OLD-WEST; www.dodgecity.org.

The Amtrak station is located at Central and Wyatt Earp. General public transport runs only Mon–Fri 0800–1600. The town has no taxi service, but almost everything is easily walkable. Unfortunately westbound trains arrive very early in the morning. If you are hiring a car, Hertz and Avis will arrange pick-up, as will hotels.

Lodgings offer free shuttle service from the station.
Best Western Silver Spur $$ 14th and Wyatt Earp Sts.
Boot Hill B&B $$ 603 W Spruce St; tel: (316) 225-7600; www.bbonline.com/ks/boothill. Across from Boot Hill.
Dodge House $$ 2408 Wyatt Earp St; tel: (316) 225-9900.

Mic-Leo's $ 2nd and Wyatt Earp Sts. For sandwiches.
Casey's Cowtown Club $$ 507 E Trail. Juicy Kansas steaks.
Café Potpourri $$$ 2nd and Wyatt Earp Sts. Features continental cuisine.

THE TRAIL WESTWARDS

Time stands still at **Ratón**, one of Santa Fe Trail's original stops, and its Historic District allows a peek into the past. Sugarite Canyon and Cimarron Canyon state parks are nearby. Ratón Chamber of Commerce: tel: (800) 638-6161; www.raton.com. You can fish or explore the high country of the **Pecos Wilderness** by foot or by horse. Contact Las Vegas/San Miguel Chamber of Commerce: tel: (800) 832-5947; www.worldplaces.com.

WHERE NEXT?

Stay in Santa Fe to explore some of the Southwest's fascinating attractions (see p. 385), or get back aboard the 'Southwest Chief', which continues westwards for almost another thousand miles, arriving in Los Angeles the following morning (see p. 430). A Thruway coach links Flagstaff to the Grand Canyon (see p. 435).

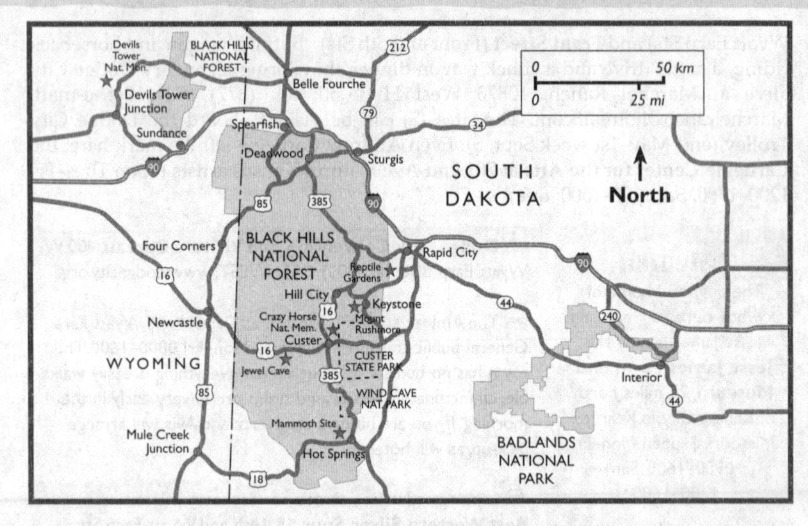

A wealth of beauty and frontier history is buried in the **Black Hills** of South Dakota. Its two giant monuments, **Mount Rushmore** and **Crazy Horse**, pay homage to those who shaped this country. The hills began as an erupting bubble of magma, which grew into spires and caves. Earlier, dinosaurs dwelled here; the largest *Tyrannosaurus rex* ever unearthed was discovered in the nearby **Badlands**. Names like Crazy Horse, Calamity Jane, General Custer and Wild Bill Hickok echo through its canyons, along with memories of the Native American slaughter at the Battle of Wounded Knee.

GETTING THERE AND GETTING AROUND

I-90 leads to the north-west corner of South Dakota. Sightseeing tours are available from Rapid City. Follow Hwy 16 south to 16A for Mount Rushmore, Custer State Park, Hot Springs and Crazy Horse.

Travellers arriving by bus can tour the **Black Hills** area with **Affordable Adventures** in Rapid City; tel: (605) 342-7691; e-mail: carol@rapidcity.net.

INFORMATION

For general information contact Black Hills, Badlands & Lakes Association, tel: (605) 355-3600; www.blackhillsattractions.com. Rapid City Convention and Visitors Bureau, tel: (800) 487-3223, www.rapidcitycvb.com.

MONEY There are banks in Rapid City and ATMs at many of the parks, but it is unlikely that local banks will be prepared for foreign currency exchange.

SAFETY Care is essential on the trails, especially on climbs. The unstable Badlands formations are unsuitable for rock climbing and water there is unsafe. Do not approach or feed wild animals, no matter how tame they appear.

ACCOMMODATION

Cedar Park Lodge $$ Badlands National Park, open Apr–Oct, reservations necessary; tel: (605) 433-5460.

Budget Host Inn $$ 2101 Mt Rushmore Rd on Hwy 16, Rapid City; tel: (800) 456-5126, includes continental breakfast.

EconoLodge $$–$$$ 625 E Disk Drive, Rapid City; tel: (800) 424-0221, new facility.

Holiday Inn Express $$–$$$ 750 Cathedral Dr., Rapid City; tel: (800) 465-4329. Indoor pool, hot tub and continental breakfast.

Super 8 $$ 2520 Tower Rd, Rapid City; tel: (800) 800-8000. Free continental breakfast.

CAMPING Sites available on a first-come-first-served basis.

Badlands–Cedar Pass $ and **Sage Creek Primitive Campground**, free.

Custer State Park $ tel: (800) 710-2267, reservations recommended.

FOOD AND DRINK

Cedar Park Lodge $–$$ Badlands National Park. Specialises in Indian tacos.

Fireside Inn $$–$$$ 810 Main St, Rapid City. Tasty food; a very popular restaurant.

Flying T Chuckwagon $$ 8971 S Hwy 16, next to Reptile Gardens, Rapid City; reservations (888) 256-1905. Barbecue supper, baked beans, cowboy music and corny jokes.

HIGHLIGHTS

Rapid City is centrally located, a good base for seeing the Black Hills. Visit the historic **Hotel Alex Johnson**, whose ceiling designs are based on Indian beadwork, and

Prairie Edge Trading Co. & Galleries, just across Sixth St, its rooms overflowing with Native artwork and sweet Lakota flute music. At **The Journey Museum**, interactive exhibits transport visitors back through 2.5 million years of history; $$, open Mon–Sat 1000–1700, Sun 1300–1700. An albino boa constrictor, cobra and crocodiles live 6 miles south on Hwy 16 at **Reptile Gardens**, 'the world's largest reptile collection'; $$, open Apr–Oct; www.reptilegardens.com.

Continue on Hwy 16 south to **Mount Rushmore National Monument**, where 60-foot faces of US presidents George Washington, Thomas Jefferson, Teddy Roosevelt and Abraham Lincoln pay tribute to America's first 150 years. The monument's original plaster-cast model is housed in the Sculpture Studio, on the 2-mile paved Presidential Trail that runs along the base of the mountain. The park's restaurant has a stunning view of the mountain and good food, $$. Park admission is free, but parking is $8; Tel: (605) 574-2523, www.nps.gov/moru. No pets are allowed in the park.

Mount Rushmore pales in size compared to **Crazy Horse Memorial**, off Highway 16. After 50 years of daily dynamite blasting, only the Oglala Sioux's 90-foot face is carved. Upon completion, the late Korschak Ziolkowski's mountain masterpiece will depict the great warrior on horseback, pointing to the former lands of his people, and will be the world's largest sculpture. The tribute to Native American heroes contains the sculptor's home and workshop, plus an Indian museum and culture centre. Crazy Horse, SD off Hwy 16 on Hwy 385. Open all year, 0700 until dark, $$; tel: (605) 673-2185; www.crazyhorse.org.

Crazy Horse probably hunted in what is now **Custer State Park**. To see the buffalo roam and the antelope play, explore the park by foot, bike, horseback ($$$) or jeep safari ($$$). Former buffalo are stew ($) at the park's **Blue Bell Lodge**. More upscale dining is available in the **Pheasant Dining Room** ($$$) at **The State Game Lodge & Resort**. The lodge was used as a summer White House for presidents Eisenhower and Coolidge. Custer, SD, $4.00 per person or $10.00 per car; general information tel: (605) 255-4515, www.sdgfp.info/parks.

Jewel Cave ($$), where you can explore and see the calcite crystals that line the walls, is also in Custer, daily summer hours: 0800–1930, visitor centre winter hours: 0800–1630; tel: (605) 673-2288; www.nps.gov/jeca.

Wildlife abounds at nearby **Wind Cave National Park**. Underneath the prairies, unusual honeycomb-like formations hang from the rooms of the US's third largest cave. Hot Springs, free but $ for cave tours. Open year round; tel: (605) 745-4600; www.nps.gov/wica.

Hot Springs is also the home of **Mammoth Site** where 26,000-year-old mammoth bones were unearthed, and archeological digs continue. Admission includes tour, $. Open year-round, hours vary but usually 0900–1700; www.mammothsite.com.

Early settlers found difficulty in navigating the soft composition of the land east of Rapid City. It became known as the **Badlands**. The many pullouts and trails along the steep and winding **Badlands Loop** disclose its ever-changing banded spires and canyons. Fossil replicas dot the ¼-mile paved walkway of **The Fossils Exhibit Trail**. Buried in the Badlands is the world's richest collection of mammal relics. At **Prairie Wind Overlook** the grasslands seem never-ending, while **Pinnacles Overlook** is a vista of misshapen canyons and colourful hills. **Ben Reifel Visitor Center** is open all year, but the **White River Center** is open only in summer. No public transportation is available to the park. Fee $10.00 per car; www.nps.gov/badl.

'Visit Wall Drug' signs are seen all over the west. Located on the 'wall' of the Badlands, **Wall Drug** got its start by supplying free ice water to travellers on their way to Yellowstone. Water is still free at the block-long superstore, but animated displays like T Rex, a shooting gallery, pharmacy museum, chapel, restaurant and lots of merchandise have been added. Free: 510 Main St, Wall, South Dakota, exits 109 or 110 off I-90; www.walldrug.com.

To the west of Rapid City, the old frontier is alive and well. In **Deadwood**, ladies and casinos beckon tourists. Movie actor Kevin Costner owns one of South Dakota's most upscale ones, **The Midnight Star Casino**. It has a five-star restaurant and movie memorabilia. Costner's movie *Dances with Wolves* was filmed in the Black Hills area.

West of Deadwood, **Devils Tower National Monument** looms hauntingly above surrounding grasslands, where prairie dogs romp. Indian legends say that the 865-ft column of hardened magna was created when seven little girls jumped on a rock to avoid a pursuing bear. The rock pushed upward, and the girls became the stars in the constellation Pleiades. Indians, who still believe in its sanctity, pray near the quiet trail walks, the 1½-mile Red Rocks Trail and the shorter 1⅓-mile Tower Trail, that encircle it. Devil Tower climbers are required to register and check in immediately upon their return. Fee $8.00 per vehicle; tel: (307) 467-5370; www.nps.gov/deto.

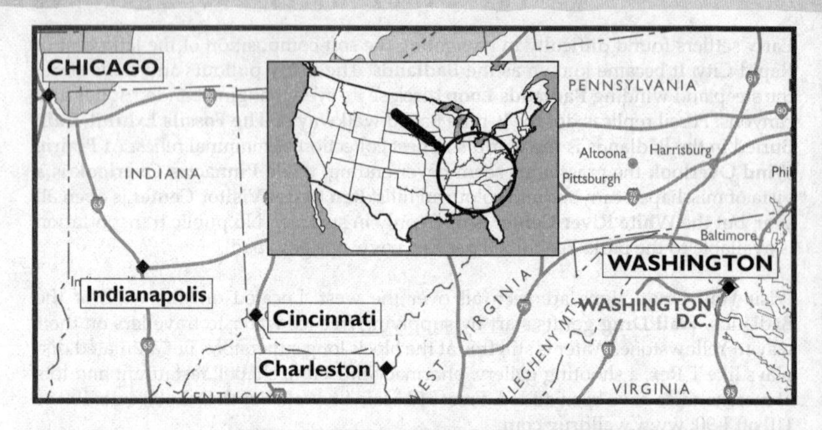

On the 'Cardinal'

WASHINGTON — CHICAGO OTT Tables 331/563/583/617/630/631/673							
Service	Bus	Rail	Rail	Bus	Bus	Bus	Bus
Days of operation	Daily	③⑤⑦	Daily	Daily	Daily	Daily	Daily
Special notes	A	B	C	D	E	F	G
Washington d.	0930	1315	....	....	....	....	....
Charlottesville d.	1220	1550	....	1650	....	....	....
Charleston *WV* d.	....	2205	....	0125	0145	....	....
Cincinnati d.	....	0305	....	....	1000	1220	....
Indianapolis d.	....	0550	0550	....	....	1330	1400
Chicago a.	....	1040	1040	....	....	....	1755

Special notes:
A–Additional trips: 0150, 1330, 1715.
B–The Cardinal. This train has sleepers and a dining car available. All journeys should be reserved in advance.
C–All journeys on this train should be reserved in advance.
D–Change at Lynchburg and Wythville. Additional trips: 0625 (change at Wythville), 2020 (change at Wythville).
E–Additional trips: 0940 (change at Lexington), 1845.
F–Additional trips: 0125, 0530.
G–Additional trips: 0055, 0300, 0500, 0745, 1125, 1715.

The 'Cardinal' certainly gives scenic value for money, perhaps to make up for its winding route. The most direct way to Chicago would be due west from DC, but the train swoops south-west through magnificent Virginia countryside and the forbidding hills of West Virginia. Stops en route include Jefferson's Charlottesville and West Virginia's capital, Charleston, but the highlight is stunning New River Gorge.

Beyond West Virginia lies serene Kentucky bluegrass country, famed for its horses and for the odd tint of blue in the grass. The 'Cardinal' crosses the Ohio at lively Cincinnati, by far the most worthwhile big city en route to explore. It then cuts diagonally across Indiana, through eminently missable Indianapolis and across fields of grain to Chicago.

CHARLESTON

Surrounded by neatly-clipped lawns, dotted with fountains and statues (spot Abraham Lincoln and Stonewall Jackson), the **Capitol Complex** at Kanawha Blvd houses the Cultural Center, the Governor's Mansion (a fine Georgian Colonial building), open 0930–1130, and the WV Veteran's Memorial Plaza. The Capitol Building itself is the largest in the country, and was designed by Cass Gilbert. Open Mon–Fri 0900–1515.

Downtown Charleston, the **Village District** stands out as a beautifully restored turn-of-the-century shopping area with a tempting array of clothing and speciality stores. For information, call Charleston Renaissance Corporation, tel: (304) 345 1738.

The curious will be enthralled by the **Sunrise Science Hall and Art Museum Complex**, $, 746 Myrtle Rd, Charleston, tel: (304) 344 8035. There are over 30 interactive exhibits and programmes, as well as a Planetarium. Open Wed–Sat 1100–1700; Sun 1200–1700.

i Tourist Information at the **Charleston Convention and Visitors Bureau**, 200 Civic Center Dr.; tel: (304) 558 0220 or (800) 733-5469; www.charlestonwv.com.

Charleston is not short of cheap motor inns just on the outskirts of the town: try MacCorkle Ave, lined with budget accommodation.

Embassy Suites Hotel $$$$ 300 Court St, Charleston, tel: (304) 347-8700 or (800) 362-2779, is a more luxurious option, primarily geared for the business traveller although they do offer some good short-break deals.

Microtel Inn $$ 600 2nd Ave, Charleston, tel: (304) 744-4900 or (800) 248-8879, is located five minutes from the centre of Charleston, at exit 56, Hwy 64.

Fairfield Inn $–$$ 1000 E Washington St, E Charleston, tel: (304) 343-4661 or (800) 228-2800. This chain hotel is minutes from the centre and the town mall.

EN ROUTE

The 50-mile-long canyon of New River Gorge can only be crossed by rail – or by raft on the water itself. This can be done in the picturesque town of Hinton, where the train stops before the gorge. Motel accommodation is available here.

The Wren's Nest Restaurant $$, 1 mile out on Coal River Road, St Albans, tel: (304) 727-3224, is a charming log cabin roadside supper club, where you can dine, listen and dance to the best of wartime songs.

Fifth Quarter $$ tel: (304) 345-2726, is a steakhouse located on the corner of Clendenin and Quarrier Sts, specialising in tender prime rib and seafood, and with an award-winning 65-item salad bar.

Southern Kitchen, $, MacCorkle Ave and 53rd St, tel: (304) 925 3154, for nourishing home-style cooking. Open 24 hours every day.

BLUEGRASS

The 'Cardinal' could just as well have been named the 'Bluegrass', as it cuts a line through Appalachia, the home of bluegrass music. Characterised by fast-picking banjoes, mandolins, fiddles and twangy, high-pitched vocals, bluegrass emerged from the lives of coal miners and farmers in Virginia, West Virginia, Kentucky and Tennessee. Today's distinctive style was developed by Bill Monroe and imitators in the 1940s, and deeply influenced the rise of rock'n'roll a decade later: one of Elvis's first hits was Monroe's 'Blue Moon of Kentucky'. Often derided as hillbilly wailing, bluegrass remains popular as a uniquely American folk element.

CINCINNATI

Europeans settled here on the banks of the Ohio in the late 18th century, building on a native American trading post, and hilly Cincinnati soon became a major Midwest commercial centre. This wealth is evident today in the city's attractive buildings, and with its excellent art galleries, 'Cincy' makes a good break on the route. Its energetic centre appeals primarily for its setting, with a lively riverfront, rolling hills and gleaming skyscrapers striking a good balance. **Fountain Square** is the heart of it all, at 5th and Vine Sts, named for its massive spewing fountain. Imposing **Carew Tower** has an observation deck on its 48th floor. The riverfront has some nice open space upstream past the stadium and highway overpass. There are steamboat tours of the river from here at BB Riverboats, $$; tel: (859) 261-8500.

A few streets in from the river, at Pike and 4th Sts, the **Taft Museum** has beautiful glassware, china, and paintings from the likes of Rembrandt and Goya. $, open Mon–Sat 1000–1700, Sun 1300–1700. Fine art at the **Cincinnati Art Museum**, 2 miles or so north-east, runs from the ancient Middle East to impressionist France. $$, open Tues–Sat 1000–1700, Sun 1200–1800. Back towards Fountain Sq., the **Contemporary Arts Center** houses cutting-edge modern art; $, 115 E 5th St; open Mon–Sat 1000–1800, Sun 1200–1700.

i **Greater Cincinnati Convention and Visitors Bureau,** 300 W Sixth St; tel: (800) 246-2987; www.cincyusa.com. Information booth at Fountain Sq. open Mon–Sat 0845–1700.

Amtrak's station is about a mile north-west of centre in the Union Terminal, with an easy bus link to the centre.

Chains are best for a cheap sleep (see p. 52).

Holiday Inn $$–$$$ 800 W 8th St; tel: (513) 241-8660 or (800) HOLIDAY. Good position and fair prices, particularly at weekends.

Symphony Hotel $$$–$$$$ 210 W 14th St; tel: (513) 721-3353. European style B&B near the Music Hall.

Delis, pizzerias, bars and grills are abundant downtown.

Schlotzsky's Deli $$ 415 Vine St; tel: (513) 421-4480. Downtown hotspot for fresh-baked bread, big sandwiches and individual pizzas.

Arnold's Bar and Grill $$ 210 E 8th St; tel: (513) 421-6234. Claims to be Cincinnati's oldest inn; solid food and live music at night.

INDIANAPOLIS

Hardly a tourist destination of the first order, Indianapolis nevertheless has a spot or two of interest, and is host to the annual Indianapolis 500 stock car race. Race fans turn up en masse – to the tune of nearly a half million people – for the Memorial Day-weekend extravaganza, traditionally the biggest event of the American car-racing season. Outside of this, Indianapolis is basically just a quiet place. Recent attempts to bring life to things are evident in the Circle Center mall, a haven of shops and restaurants downtown. One unusual thing about the city is its lack of a river: the site was chosen as state capitol merely for its centrality.

Some of the city's earliest wooden buildings survive in the **Lockerbie Square Historic District**, just east of downtown at East and New York Sts. On the other side of town, the **Eiteljorg Museum of American Indians and Western Art** is a grand collection of everything to do with the Wild West. Native American artefacts and an evocative group of paintings conjure up the romance and adventure. The museum is located at 500 W Washington St; tel: (317) 636-9378; $$, open Tues–Sat 1000–1700, Sun 1200–1700.

Indianapolis Convention & Visitors Association, in the billowy white RCA Dome stadium at 2nd St and S Capitol Ave; tel: (317) 237-5200 or (800) 958-4639; www.indy.org; icva@indianapolis.org. can help out with accommodation.

Rooms are fairly cheap, with many chains (see p. 52).

Comfort Inn City Centre $$–$$$ 530 S Capitol Ave; tel: (317) 631-9000 or (800) 228-5150. Well equipped and close to the RCA Dome.

You can settle your food and drink needs in the **Alcatraz Brewing Co.** $–$$ Circle Centre, 49 W Maryland St. tel: (317) 488-1230, which makes its own beers and serves up pizzas, sandwiches and steaks.

THE SOUTHWEST

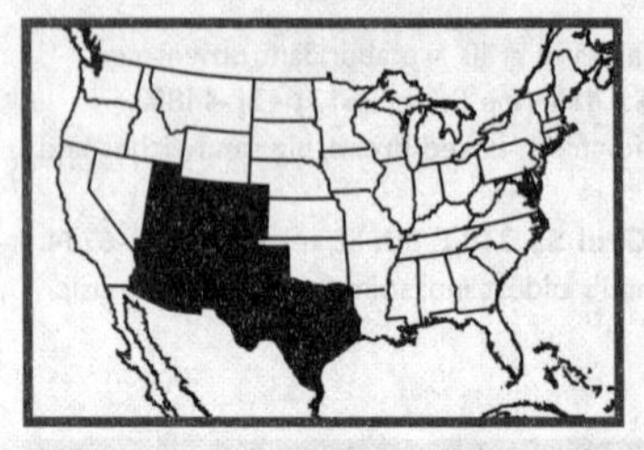

'I want to ride to the ridge where the West commences, gaze at the moon until I lose my senses…'. So began a popular song of the 1940s, and it's this romantic image of the Wild West that still characterises the Southwest to many visitors. Here is the America that the world knows – or thinks it knows – through generations of Westerns, both films and television shows.

And although this idealized Wild West of the movies never really existed, the real west was very wild indeed, and its wildness is still real today. The traveller who looks beyond the theme-park re-enactments will find ghost towns, abandoned mines, cattle ranches, round-ups, rodeos and well-worn ten-gallon hats – in a setting that makes the visitor half expect to see John Wayne riding into town, or hear Roy Rogers break into song.

The Southwest is all the 'wide open spaces' anyone could ask for, and visitors may find the task of seeing the Southwest a large bite to chew. Which version of the Southwest should you choose? The vast open landscape with the solitary figure of the Marlboro man in the distance? The rugged mountains of Colorado and New Mexico? The sub-sea-level deserts of southern Arizona or the majesty of the Grand Canyon? Or the Wild West of Wyatt Earp and Billy the Kid? They are all there. So are interesting cities such as Santa Fe and San Antonio, the former with its traditional adobe architecture and the latter with the historic symbol of Texas itself in a setting of a vibrant up-beat cityscape.

The Southwest is a composite of three main cultures: Native American, Hispanic and Anglo, which, for the most part, exist in harmony. While they may have adopted aspects from each other's cultures, they remain quite distinct. In the larger cities of Tucson, Phoenix, Santa Fe and Albuquerque it is easy to find evidence of all the influences. However, in the smaller cities and towns one culture is most likely to dominate.

THE SOUTHWEST

Some of the best-known and most distinctive Native American cultures are those of the Southwest. Various tribal groups are known for their silver and turquoise jewellery, woven rugs, elegant traditional pottery and *kachina* figures (representing their ancestors). Adobe dwellings built high in cliff-top caves, as well as entire pueblos of adobe homes, represent native cultures of long ago and of today. The former are protected in a National Park, the latter welcome visitors to living communities.

Part of the drama of the Southwest is its geographic rawness, and a distinct sense that the past is not so long ago. Raft through the Grand Canyon and it appears to have been recently carved, hike trails and you are likely to find trilobites or other fossils. Drive through the winding mountains of Colorado across the Continental Divide and you will come across remains of mining gear, left there when the mines were worked out nearly a century ago.

America has a fascination with a new facet of the Southwest: its decorating and architectural styles. These are exemplified in the city of Santa Fe and, in fact, this adobe-and-terracotta look is often called Santa Fe Style. Parlours from Miami to Boston may be decked in Navaho rugs, with bold bouquets displayed in giant terracotta pots against cream-coloured stucco walls. It is a look that is native to this region, and you will notice the distinctive architecture throughout the Southwest. Buildings seem to have grown out of the earth itself. Which is not surprising, since adobe bricks are made from the local clay.

The cuisine is a blend of the cultures that settled here. You will find true Mexican dishes and the sophisticated southwestern take on New American. More commonly you will encounter Tex-Mex and chuckwagon favourites and hearty, spicy Texas barbecue. Phoenix, San Antonio, Santa Fe, Taos and Telluride have the most cosmopolitan variety of restaurants. For down-home traditional food try Albuquerque, Durango and Tucson.

Planning an itinerary in this vast territory is much more challenging than planning a tour of the *antebellum* (pre-Civil War) South or New England. The traveller cannot simply hop from place to place in an hour or so; getting there takes time. But the scenery between the 'sights' is like having a vintage Western film roll by, and just being in the middle of it is a thrill of its own. There's plenty of breathing space 'out west'.

The Southwest

Take two days to see San Antonio, strolling its effervescent Riverwalk, visiting HemisFair and stepping back into the most turbulent drama of all Texas history at the Alamo, to many Texans the most sacred shrine in their state. 'Remember the Alamo' became the rallying cry of the Lone Star Republic, and the stronghold's history is in its very stones. Tucson and Tombstone deserve a day each – in Tucson, make sure that you make room for another kind of 'day' – a night for astronomical observing. Stay at the Stargazers Inn and combine a B&B with a night of stargazing in the company of trained observers, who will make sure you discover all the secrets of the crystal-clear night sky.

Take a week to drive the San Juan Skyway from Durango to Telluride and beyond to Mesa Verde (Mesa Verde could take two days depending upon how many of the tours you would like to do – they are all first come, first served, and fill up quickly). From Mesa Verde and the Four Corners area you can drop down into Arizona to visit the Barringer Meteor Crater and Petrified Forest, and then continue on to the Grand Canyon. This American icon should take a minimum of two days, longer if you want to hike or ride a mule to the bottom, or to take the river raft rides.

Crossing the Southwest is a bit like riding a roller coaster – from New Mexico's high elevations you drop down into Arizona, which in places like Tucson is actually below sea level. Remember the lower you sink, the higher the temperature will be – although it is a dry heat. These sudden and dramatic changes in elevation – hence temperature – mean that you will need to bring a variety of clothing. In the morning you may need a pullover and jacket in the mountains, only to be too warm in shorts in the afternoon at below sea level.

If you want to experience a real time capsule of American history, take time for Route 66. Immortalised in song and in the mythology of the West, this cross-country route was 'the way west' before the interstate highway system made it redundant. Bypassed sections still retain the feel of their glory days of the quirky motels built like tepees, rattlesnake museums and glimpses of 'Ship Rock' in the distance. This rock is so big it looms ahead looking like a ship under full sail, a really impressive sight that modern interstate travellers don't see.

The best seasons to visit the Southwest are spring and autumn, when temperatures are neither too hot nor too cold. In spring the vegetation takes on more colour, and you may find desert plants in bloom. In the higher elevations winter can be, well … wintry.

OUR CHOICE

San Antonio River Walk

The Alamo

Santa Fe

The Museum of New Mexico complex

The Rocky Mountains

Grand Canyon

San Juan Skyway

Mesa Verde National Park

Taos

Pueblos

Stargazing in Tucson

Durango and Silverton Railroad

Pagosa Springs

Zion National Park

Bryce Canyon National Park

HOW MUCH YOU CAN SEE IN A ...

WEEK (7 DAYS)

Durango, Silverton Railroad, Mesa Verde and Pagosa Springs

Mesa Verde, Meteor Crater and the Grand Canyon

San Antonio (two days)

Albuquerque, Taos, Santa Fe and the pueblos

Phoenix, Tucson and Tombstone

FORTNIGHT (14 DAYS)

San Juan Skyway (Durango to Telluride), Mesa Verde, the Four Corners area, Barringer Meteor Crater, Petrified Forest and the Grand Canyon

Washington by train to Chicago, on to Santa Fe via Kansas City and Topeka, Albuquerque, Taos and the pueblos (return by air)

Chicago to Los Angeles by train, stopping at Santa Fe for Taos and the pueblos and at Flagstaff for the Grand Canyon (return by air)

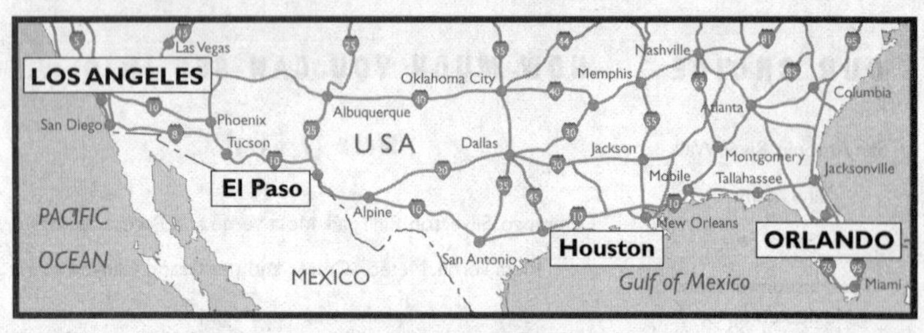

LOS ANGELES — ORLANDO

OTT Tables 327/350/643/645/855/914

Service	Bus	Bus	Bus	Bus	Bus	RAIL	Bus	Bus
Days of operation	Daily	Daily	Daily	Daily	Daily	③⑤⑦	Daily	Daily
Special notes				**C**		**B**	**A**	
Los Angeles d.	0130	....	0830	....	1100	1430	1825	2340
El Paso d.	1840	....	0400	....	0625	0900	1125	0505
San Antonio d.	0730	....	1630	....	|	0100**a**	2330	....
Houston d.	1110	1201	1945	2030	1215	0615	0400	....
New Orleans d.	....	|	....	|	....	2230**b**	1215	....
Jacksonville d.	....	|	....	|	....	1700	|	....
Orlando a.	....	1030	....	2045	....	2045	0545	....

Special notes:
A–Total journey time is 56½ hours and you have to change buses 3 times.
B–The Sunset Limited. This train has sleepers and a dining car available. All journeys should be reserved in advance. Total journey time is just over 78 hours. **a**–Arrives at 2225. **b**–Arrives at 1600.
C–Additional trips: 1810.

On the 'Sunset Limited'

Following the former Southern Pacific railroad's historic 'Sunset Route', the tri-weekly 'Sunset Limited' is Amtrak's only true transcontinental train. Leaving Los Angeles Wednesday, Friday and Sunday afternoons (a schedule subject to change), the train crosses the deserts of Arizona and New Mexico, stopping at Tucson (p. 406), before arriving in the morning at the border city of El Paso, Monday, Thursday and Saturday. The train crosses West Texas, arriving in the Alamo city of San Antonio (p. 377) during the night. It departs the following day in the early hours and continues eastward through to sprawling Houston and across the Louisiana bayous to a spectacular crossing of the Mississippi River into New Orleans late afternooon Tuesday, Friday and Sunday (p. 304). The train continues on to Mobile (p. 316), Tallahassee (p. 289) and Jacksonville (p. 261) before arriving in Orlando (p. 278) the following evening, Monday, Wednesday and Saturday.

EL PASO

The west Texas city of El Paso, located directly across the Rio Grande from Mexico, is the second oldest settlement in the USA. It is also the jumping-off point for **Big Bend, Carlsbad Caverns** and **Guadalupe Mountains National Parks**. There is no public transport to or from the parks but car hire is available at El Paso International Airport, 20 mins by taxi from the city centre.

El Paso's main interest is two noteworthy museums and a chance to walk over the border to Mexico. **El Paso Museum of Art** features the Kress Collection of 13th–18th-century European paintings, plus American, Mexican and Southwestern art, $, 1 Arts Festival Plaza; open Tues, Wed, Fri and Sat 0900–1800, Sun 1000–1700. The **Americana Museum** showcases the Pre-Columbian, tribal, historic and western art of the Americas, $, 5 Civic Center Plaza; open Tues–Fri 1000–1700. You can cross the Santa Fe St Bridge into **Ciudad Juarez, Mexico**, and walk past nightclubs, restaurants and curio shops before coming to the old mercado and the Cathedral of Our Lady of Guadalupe, established in 1659. Or hop on the **Border Jumper Trolley** ($$) for a guided circular loop through Juarez that lets you debark and re-board along the way. The trolley departs hourly from the El Paso Convention and Performing Arts Center, 1000–1700 daily (1000–1600 Nov–Mar). To see three states and two countries, take the Wyler Aerial Tramway to Franklin Mountain Peak ($$).

Amtrak stops at 700 San Francisco Ave in the city centre, within walking distance of the border. **Sun Metro**, tel: (915) 533-1220, operates city buses, including two useful trolley routes. **The Art Museum Trolley** (bus 4) operates every 15 mins from Amtrak to points throughout the city centre Mon–Fri 0615–1850, Sat 0845–1815 and Sun 1145–1715. The **North/South Trolley** (bus 8) operates every 10 mins from San Jacinto Plaza to the International Bridges Mon–Fri 0615–2015, Sat 0745–2015 and Sun 0845–1915.

El Paso Convention and Visitors Bureau, 1 Civic Center Plaza, El Paso TX 79901-1187; tel: (800) 351-6024, www.visitelpaso.com, is open Mon–Fri 0800–1700.

Camino Real Hotel $$$$ 101 S El Paso St, tel: (915) 534-3000, fax (915) 534-3024, www.caminoreal.com. A luxurious 1912 gem located in the city centre.
Gardner Hotel $$ & **El Paso International Youth Hostel** $ 311 E Franklin St, tel: (915) 532-3661, fax (915) 532-0302, www.gardnerhotel.com. Located near San Jacinto Plaza in the city centre.
Sunset Heights Bed & Breakfast Inn $$$ 717 W Yandell Dr., tel: (915) 544-1743. Located ½ mile from city centre. Will pick up from Amtrak.

Azulejos $$ Camino Real Hotel, 101 S El Paso St. Tex-Mex and regional fare is the speciality.

H & H Coffee Shop & Car Wash $ 701 E Yandell. Mexican-style breakfasts.

The Dome $$$ Camino Real Hotel, 101 S El Paso St. Fine dining in opulent decor.

CARLSBAD CAVERNS NATIONAL PARK

Located 233 km north-east of El Paso via Hwy 62/180, Carlsbad Caverns is one of the world's largest caves with 5 km of trails through underground corridors and huge chambers filled with stalactites and stalagmites.

Park Headquarters Visitor Center, tel: (505) 785-2232, www.nps.gov/cave, is open daily 0800–1900 summer, 0800–1700 the remainder of the year. Closed 25 Dec.

GUADALUPE MOUNTAINS NATIONAL PARK

Located 161 km north-east of El Paso via Hwy 62/180, on the way to Carlsbad Caverns, the park features hiking trails leading to 2667-m Guadalupe Peak, the highest point in Texas. More popular, and less strenuous, is the relatively flat 11-km trail through McKittrick Canyon, passing from bare desert to lush mountain forests beside sheer canyon walls. This walk is particularly spectacular in autumn, when the trees take on brilliant colours.

Park Headquarters Visitor Center, located on Hwy 62/180 at the top of Guadalupe Pass (Pine Springs); tel: (915) 828-3251, www.nps.gov/gumo, is open daily 0800–1800 summer and 0800–1630 the remainder of the year. Another visitor centre is located at McKittrick Canyon. Closed 25 Dec.

HOUSTON

Sprawling Houston is the fourth largest city in the USA and the centre of the oil industry. **Old Market Square**, bounded by Milam, Travis, Congress and Preston Sts, is Houston's original business district, containing a number of historic buildings offering an assortment of taverns and restaurants. A few blocks east is Enron Field, a new baseball stadium that recently replaced the Astrodome as home for the Houston Astros. **Sam Houston Historical Park** on Bagby St features eight historic structures dating from 1823 to 1905. The **Theatre District**, west of Milam St between

Preston and Rusk, is home to the acclaimed Alley Theatre which offers last-minute discount seats, and the Wortham Theatre Center houses opera and ballet. **Bayou Place**, at Bagby between Texas and Capitol Sts, has dining, live music, billiards and the Angelika Film Center.

The oak-lined boulevards of the **Museum District**, 8 km south-west of the city centre, are enjoyable to explore on foot. The 11 museums that make up the district offer everything from fine art exhibitions to hands-on activities for children. Take METRO buses 8, 15 or 65 on Main St to reach the area. **Six Flags Astroworld** has 100 rides, shows, and attractions, including the Texas Cyclone, rated one of the world's best roller coasters; $$$, 9001 Kirby Dr.; opening hours vary. Take METRO bus 18 on Walker. **Space Center Houston** features hands-on exhibits and behind-the-scenes tours: 1601 NASA Rd; open daily 0900–1900 summer and Mon–Fri 1000–1700, Sat–Sun 1000–1900 the remainder of the year. Take METRO bus 246 on Milam.

Amtrak arrives at 902 Washington Ave, west of the city centre. Public transport and taxis are scarce but METRO buses 36 and 85 provide some service.
Houston METRO, tel: (713) 635-4000, www.ridemetro.org, operate bus services throughout the city. Five colour-coded Trolley routes circulate in the city centre. The most useful is Route A (Green), stopping at the Convention Center, Visitor Center, Theatre District, Old Market Square and Enron Field every 10 mins, Mon–Fri 0630–1930. In the evening and at weekends Route N (Black) runs 1930–2230 Mon–Fri, 1700–2230 Sat.

Houston Convention & Visitors Bureau, 801 Congress St, Houston TX 77002; tel: (713) 227-3100, www.houston-guide.com, is open Mon–Fri 0830–1700.

Grant Motor Inn $$ 8200 S Main St; tel: (713) 668-8000. Near the Astrodome and METRO bus 8.
Houston International Hostel $ 5302 Crawford St; tel: (713) 523-1009, www.houstonhostel.com. Conveniently located near the Museum District and METRO buses 1 and 2.
Lovett Inn $$$ 501 Lovett Blvd; tel: (713) 522-5224, www.lovettinn.com. Offers first-class service and Southern hospitality. METRO bus 82 is nearby.

Clives $$$$ 517 Louisiana. A good pre-theatre stop with a well-stocked wine cellar.
Treebeards $ 315 Travis St. Cheap and tasty Cajun food.
This Is It $$ 207 W Gray St. Soul food at budget prices.

DALLAS AND FORT WORTH

The Metroplex, as Texans call the area that stretches between the cities of Dallas and Fort Worth, is one of America's largest urban areas. Dallas sizzles as a busy centre of business and finance, with a deep interest in sports as well as western culture. Fort Worth, although it was always a cattle town and sits in the midst of vast agricultural areas, is far from rustic. A cosmopolitan city, it is rich in museums and fine art, thanks to the wealth the great cattle drives brought to the city.

DALLAS

Central Dallas is littered with skyscrapers and neon lights. Shopping is a luxurious experience: sample the **Neiman Marcus Department Store** on Main St. Walk south down St Paul St into Marila St and you will see **City Hall**, film-star famous as the police station in *Robocop*.

The **Dallas Museum of Art** is in the northern part of downtown, at 1717 N Harwood St. European works are downstairs; upstairs are the American exhibits, including a special collection of pre-Columbian memorabilia. Open daily 0900–1800, to 2000 Thurs; free.

Worldwide, the city is also famous for being witness to President Kennedy's assassination in 1963, and being the host of the *Dallas* TV serial and the Cowboys football team.

Deep Ellum is the old warehouse district, made famous by its music in the 1920s. It is now the fashionable place to go, with galleries, trendy clothes stores, cafés and clubs. The **Pegasus Theater**, 3916 Main St, tel: (214) 821 6005, puts on modern plays and original productions.

A City of Conspiracy?

Dealey Plaza is quickly recognised and needs no introduction. Only a little imagination can take you to 12.30 pm, 22 November 1963, when John F Kennedy toured the streets of Dallas and was shot here by Lee Harvey Oswald. Nearby, at 411 Elm St, you will find the **Texas Schoolbook Depository** from which Oswald fired. The Sixth Floor Museum houses a recreation of the gunman's nest, some moving displays and the infamous film of the assassination. $, open daily 0900–1800.

It is generally accepted that Oswald acted independently (he in turn was shot in a police station by nightclub owner Jack Ruby to avenge the killing), but conspiracy theories still flourish. Some witnesses say they heard shots that day from the grassy knoll just to the north of Elm St. These theories and others are discussed in detail at the **Conspiracy Museum**, $$, 110 S Market St, open daily 0900–1800. Close by you will find the **Kennedy Memorial**, located in the Dallas Historical Plaza.

South of Deep Ellum is **Fair Park**, a plaza originally built to house the Texas Centennial Exposition. Inside you will find several fine museums: the **Dallas Museum of Natural History**, tel: (214) 670-8400, open Mon–Fri 1000–1300 ($, free Mon); the **Dallas Aquarium**, $, open daily 0900–1630; and a recent addition, the **Museum of African Art**.

Southfork Ranch, 25 miles out of town, at 3770 Hogge Road, Parker, is the television home of the fictional Ewing clan. It has been kitted out as a mini-theme park, with a museum where tourists can have their photograph taken in a cowboy hat at JR's desk.

i **Dallas Visitors Center**, 1303 Commerce St, tel: (214) 712-1944 or (800) 232-5527, is open daily 0800–1700 (Sat, Sun until 1600).
North Park Center, 1201 Elm St, tel: (214) 746-6677, is open Mon–Sat 0830–1700.

The Amtrak service stops at Union Station, just west of downtown, at 400 S Houston St.

Central Dallas has high prices aimed at the business traveller, but if you phone in advance you may be able to obtain good weekend deals. There is also a B&B reservation service: (800) 899-4538; **B&B Texas Style**, 4224 W Red Bird Lane; tel: (214) 298-8586. There is camping at **Lewisville Lake Park** ($); tel (972) 219-3742.
Adolphus Hotel $$$ 1321 Commerce St; tel: (214) 742-8200 or (800) 221-9083.
Stoneleigh Hotel $$ 2927 Maple Ave; tel: (214) 871-7111.

Café Brasil $ 2815 Elm St; tel: (214) 747-2730.
Blind Lemon $$ 2805 Main St; tel: (214) 939-0202.
Dinger's Catfish Café $$ 2706 Elm St; tel: (214) 741-9012.

FORT WORTH

Built from fortunes in the cattle trade, Fort Worth was the home of the Sundance Kid and of Bonnie and Clyde, and in the late 19th century was the last stop on the great cattle drive to Kansas, the Chisholm Trail.

Leafy downtown is centred on **Sundance Square**, encircled by shops, restaurants and bars between 2nd and 5th, Calhoun and Throckmorton Sts. It is overlooked by two glass skyscrapers, City Center Towers, and flanked by the **Bass Performance Arts Hall**. Notice the walls covered with murals, and the topiaries of longhorns and cowboys.

Around Exchange Ave, 2 miles north, **The Stockyards National Historic District** is an area of western restaurants, saloons and shops (like the quaint M L Leddy's Saddle Shop) nestling together on the brick streets to form a nostalgic cowboy heaven. **Cowtown Coliseum** holds a championship rodeo every Fri and Sat at 2000.

Fort Worth Herd longhorn cattle drives move along Exchange Ave in the stockyards at 1130 and 1600 daily. For animals of a wilder kind, the **Fort Worth Zoo** has an 8-acre exhibit called **Texas Wild!** that shows the state's fauna in native settings.

If cowboy celebrations are your style, time your visit for the **Chisholm Trail Round-Up** in mid-June, or **Pioneer Days** (in mid-September), western-style celebrations in the Stockyards.

i **CVB**, 415 Throckmorton St; tel: (817) 336-8791 or (800) 433-5747; www.fortworth.com; open Mon–Fri 0830–1700. **Stockyards Visitor Center**, 130 E Exchange Ave; tel: (817) 624-4741; open Mon–Fri 0900–1800, Sat 0900–1900, Sun 1100–1900. **Cultural District Visitor Center**, 3401 Lancaster Ave; tel: (817) 882-8588.

The Amtrak station, at the historic former **Santa Fe Railroad Depot**, is downtown at 1001 Jones St; tel: (800) USA RAIL or (800) 875-7245.

Sundance Sq. and the Stockyards are the most lively areas of the city. Motels can be found on the freeways both north and south of the city.

Park Central Hotel $ 1010 Houston St; tel: (817) 336-2011 or (800) 848-PARK.

Ramada Plaza Downtown $$ 1701 Commerce St; tel: (817) 335-7000 or (800) 228-2828.

Etta's Place B&B $$$ 200 W 3rd St; tel: (817) 654-0267. Named after the schoolteacher girlfriend of the Sundance Kid.

Steak barbecue and Tex-Mex are the specialities at Fort Worth, and the best steakhouses can be found at the Stockyards.

Flying Saucer $ 111 E 4th St.; tel: (817) 336-7468.

Cabo's Grill $$ 115 W 2nd St; tel: (817) 348-8226.

Cattlemen's Steak House $$$ 2458 N Main St, tel: (817) 624-3945.

Risky's Barbecue $ 300 Main; tel: (817) 877-3306, in Sundance Sq. and 140 East Exchange; tel: (817) 626-7737, in the Stockyards.

SAN ANTONIO

San Antonio has always been a crossroads and a meeting place. Old Mexico, Native Americans, African Americans, Germans, the Wild West, the Deep South and the Republic of Texas: all have mingled and merged to produce San Antonio. It is a city of sensations – taste, feel, sights and sounds – that are both familiar and exotic.

In 1836 Texas shook off the yoke of colonialism – this was the year of the Alamo (see p. 380) and Sam Houston's subsequent victory – and for ten years the territory existed as an independent republic. Surprisingly, it was the Europeans who flocked here after the revolution, and by 1850, Mexicans and Anglos were outnumbered in San Antonio by continental Europeans, especially Germans.

San Antonio's multi-ethnic roots are reflected in its varying architectural styles. More recently the city has returned to its Hispanic roots, and new buildings flaunt red-clay roofs, Saltillo tile floors and central patios. San Antonio is a tale of two cities. The compact, downtown area with the River Walk, Alamo and business district will keep a visitor contented for days; beyond the centre the city sprawls in several directions, laced together by an extensive freeway system.

MUST SEE/DO IN SAN ANTONIO

Pay tribute to the martyrs of the Texas Republic at the Alamo

Enjoy the best San Antonio has to offer, day and night, at the River Walk

Take a break from downtown to visit the artisans of La Villita

Shop for Mexican crafts at El Mercado, stop for a bite at Mi Tierra

Enjoy some peace and tranquillity while learning about San Antonio's origins at the Missions National Historic Park

Visit the whales, sea lions, otters and walruses at SeaWorld

Ride some of the world's tallest and fastest roller coasters at Six Flags Fiesta Texas

GETTING THERE AND GETTING AROUND

AIR San Antonio International Airport is located 8 miles from downtown. Transport is available by bus, taxi or van shuttle.

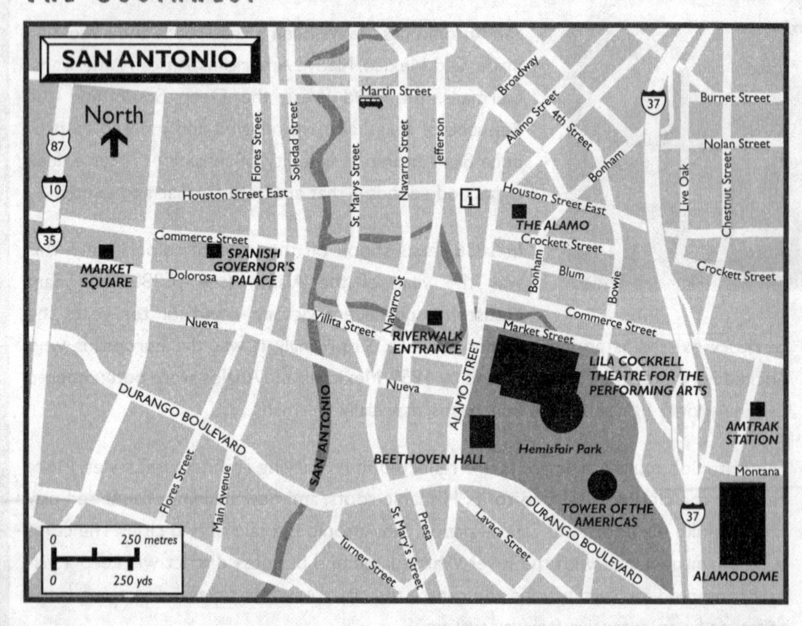

TRAIN/BUS The Amtrak station is at 350 Hoefgen Ave, tel: (210) 223 3226 or (800) 872-7245, on the east side of downtown, near the Alamodome. Hop on a VIA streetcar to your downtown hotel. Taxis are also available. The Greyhound terminus is downtown, at 500 N St Mary's St, two blocks from the River Walk; tel: (210) 231-2222. The station is within walking distance of many hotels, and streetcar and bus transport are nearby.

VIA Metropolitan Transit Service, tel: (210) 362-2020, operates 105 routes to every major tourist attraction, including express routes from central San Antonio to SeaWorld San Antonio and Six Flags Fiesta Texas.

VIA San Antonio Streetcars are open-air, authentic reproductions of the rail streetcars that plied the streets of San Antonio more than 50 years ago. They now shuttle tourists and residents alike through downtown. Stops include the Alamo, La Villita, St Paul Sq. and the King William area, for a flat fare.

INFORMATION

Visitor Information Center, 317 Alamo Plaza; tel: (210) 270-6748 or (800)THEALAMO, ext. 10; www.SanAntonioVisit.com. Open daily 0830–1800. Closed at Thanksgiving, Christmas and New Year.

POST AND PHONES The downtown post office is at 615 E Houston St (across from the Alamo); tel: (210) 275-8777.

SAFETY The usual precautions apply, especially at night. Rangers patrol the River Walk and public parks.

ACCOMMODATION

San Antonio International Hostel $ 621 Pierce St; tel: (210) 223-9426. Next to the Bullis House Inn, this has a reading room, small kitchen, dining areas, swimming pool and picnic tables. Pleasant but not very convenient for public transport.

Bullis House Inn $$ 621 Pierce St; tel: (210) 223-9426. Best B&B bargain in town, if you don't mind sharing a bathroom. Just down the street from Fort Sam Houston and filled with oak panelling, parquet floors and crystal chandeliers. Near I-35 and Hwy 281.

Menger Hotel $$$ 204 Alamo Plaza; tel: (210) 223-4361 or (800) 345-9285. Good location between the Alamo and the River Center Mall. Decor ranges from Victorian to Oriental, with a smattering of unknown periods that possess kitchenettes and balconies. If Victorian is your choice make sure to specify when booking.

Arbor House Suites Bed and Breakfast $$$ 540 S St Mary's; tel: (210) 472-2005 or (888) 272-6700. Neither quite a hotel nor a B&B (although croissants, muffins and juice are delivered to your door); five historic buildings surrounding a garden courtyard. Close to the River Walk, La Villita and the Convention Center.

La Mansión del Rio $$$$ 112 College St; tel: (210) 518-1000 or (800) 292-7300. Spanish hacienda-style hotel converted from a 19th-century seminary. The balconies overlooking the River Walk are worth the price.

FOOD AND DRINK

Dining options run the gamut from burgers to fine French cuisine, Chinese to Cajun, and soul food to German specialities. San Antonio, however, is Tex-Mex. Try the queso flameado, chilli relleno, enchiladas, chalupas, menudo (chilli-hued stew of tripe, pig's foot and hominy, acclaimed as a hangover cure) and sopapillas. And, of course, the chilli. Note: chilli with beans is for wimps and 'con carne' (with meat) is redundant: chilli here means just that.

Mi Tierra $ 218 Produce Row, Market Sq.; tel: (210) 225-1262. Open 24 hours, and allegedly the best place to go when you've had too much to drink, or when you must have eggs and chorizo at 2 am. Fabulous bakery on site.

El Mirador $$ 722 St Mary's St; tel: (210) 225-9444. Creative cooking, presenting Tex-Mex favourites with some new twists.

Paseano's River Walk $$ 111 W Crockett St; tel: (210) 22-PASTA. Because you can't eat Tex-Mex all the time! Huge portions at reasonable prices. The cheese tortellini with artichokes, spinach and cream is a delight.

Rosario's $$ 910 S. Alamo; tel: (210) 223-1806. Great atmosphere, good food, and possibly the best margaritas in San Antonio.

Boudro's $$$ 421 E Commerce St; tel: (210) 224-8484. Drift down the river while you feast on Tex-Mex specialities. Servers whip up fresh guacamole en route.

HIGHLIGHTS

Amid all the revolution, rebellion and reconstruction, the heart of San Antonio was, and is, the river. No other part of the city so accurately reflects its multiple personality as the **River Walk**, where European-style cafés serving Tex-Mex specialities blend smoothly with cobblestone walkways, night clubs, art galleries and gleaming high-rise hotels.

The River Walk – or Paseo del Rio – is the city's core, and its pride. First called 'Yanaguana' by the Payaya Indians, meaning 'place of refreshing waters', the description is no less accurate today. Lush green foliage lines the banks of this calmly flowing river. Cobbled walkways lead visitors to the river-level restaurants and shops. This is *the* place to walk, eat, cruise the river, gaze at the stars and drink in the soul of San Antonio. Its 2½-mile stretch can be thronged with crowds around the restaurants or cafés, or quiet and peaceful just a short walk away.

Beyond the River Walk there is much to explore. Downtown you will find La Villita, with its shops and artisans; the King William Historic District lined with Victorian homes, some of them now B&Bs; and, of course, the Alamo.

Located in the heart of the city (300 Alamo Plaza), the **Alamo** is a monument to the 189 men, including Davy Crockett, who sacrificed their lives during the famous battle here in 1836. Housed in the grounds of the historic mission, the museum exhibits artefacts from the battle and the period of the Republic of Texas, including manuscripts, maps and weapons. The shrine (free) is open Mon–Sat 0900–1730, Sun 1000–1730. Closed 24–25 Dec.

REMEMBER THE ALAMO

In 1718 Father Antonio Olivares founded the mission of San Antonio de Valero. Within little more than a decade the outpost had become a complex of missions, settlements and a military garrison known as the Alamo, defending itself first against hostile Indians and later from large numbers of immigrating Anglos.

The name of the Alamo became etched into American history when, in 1836, it stood against some 4000 of General Antonio Lopez de Santa Anna's Mexican troops, sent to take Texas for newly independent Mexico. The 189 defenders held out for 13 days before falling. One month later, Sam Houston spurred his troops on at the Battle of San Jacinto with the rallying cry of 'Remember the Alamo'. His victory secured independence for the new Republic of Texas.

The **Spanish Governor's Palace**, 105 Military Plaza, has been called 'the most beautiful building in San Antonio' by the National Geographic Society. It once housed the officials of the Spanish Province of Texas. Distinguishing features include period furnishings and a cobblestone patio with fountain and foliage. Open Mon–Sat 0900–1700, Sun 1000–1700; tel: (210) 224-0601.

La Villita is a lovely oasis in the city centre – a unique arts and crafts community with shops, working artists, restaurants and a post office. The Old San Antonio Exhibit in the museum houses a collection of artefacts relevant to its history. Open daily 1000–1800.

Step back into San Antonio's rumbustious past with a visit to **Buckhorn Saloon and Museum**. Walk into a recreation of a 120-year-old saloon and take a tour of Texan history and local entertainment. A restaurant, arcade and curio stores share space with the Hall of Horns, Fins and Feathers. Quirky, but fun. $, 318 E Houston; tel: (210) 247-4000. Open daily 1000–1800.

The 32 shops of **El Mercado**, in Market Sq., are modelled on a Mexican market. In addition, there are over 80 speciality shops in the Farmers Market Plaza. The square hosts many Hispanic festivals, where food and beverage booths sprout alongside the Victorian lamps and strains of mariachi music are heard. Open daily (except major holidays) summer 1000–2000, winter 1000–1800.

The cool greenscapes and water features of **HemisFair Park** (200 S Alamo St) provide a refreshing retreat from the city streets. The park was the site of the 1968 HemisFair, celebrating the progress made by the confluence of civilizations in the western hemisphere. The playground is near the Alamo St entrance, and the park includes the University of Texas Institute of Texan Cultures at San Antonio, Instituto Cultural Mexicano and the **Tower of the Americas**. This tower, 750 ft tall, was the theme structure for the fair, and you can ride up to the top for panoramic views of San Antonio and the surrounding area. There is a restaurant that serves lunch and dinner (great view, mediocre food), and after dark the lofty bar is a lovely way to drink in the sparkling array of city lights. The observation deck ($) is open Sun–Thur 0900–2200, Fri–Sat 0900–2300; tel: (210) 207-6815.

LIFE BEYOND DOWNTOWN

Southtown, once depressed, is now teetering on the verge of trendy, and has a good mix of Hispanic shops, coffee houses and galleries. Monte Vista, north-west of the city centre, is a transitional area largely occupied by student housing for nearby Trinity University. To see how the other half lives, head for Alamo Heights, home to the city's wealthy residents and filled with expensive shops and trendy restaurants. Alamo Heights is where yuppies call home in San Antonio.

Rebellion and railways aside, San Antonio has prospered in part by a continuing military presence. The Alamo became a quartermaster depot for the US Army, and in 1876 **Fort Sam Houston** was built. The Apache war chief, Geronimo, was held prisoner here in

1886 and it was from Fort Sam that Teddy Roosevelt equipped his 'Rough Riders'. In 1910 the first military flight by an American took off from here and in subsequent years it was the location for early aviators, such as Charles Lindbergh, to sharpen their skills. By 1941, four air force bases had sprouted, making San Antonio the largest military complex in the USA, outside Washington DC. It is now the home of the Army Medical Command and Headquarters, Fifth Army. The fort is located between I-35 and Harry Wurzbach Hwy. The museum is in Building 123 and offers a leaflet giving a self-guided tour. Open Wed–Sun 1000–1600, closed holidays. Free; tel: (210) 221-6358.

The chain of missions established along the San Antonio River in the 18th century now collectively forms the **San Antonio Missions National Historical Park**. Reminders of one of Spain's more successful attempts to dominate the New World, the missions were more than just churches: they served as vocational and educational centres, and bastions of trade. They formed the basis for what is San Antonio today. Within the park are the Missions Concepción, San Jose, San Juan and Espada. The visitor centre is at Mission San Jose, 6701 San Jose Dr., tel: (210) 932-1001; www.nps.gov/saan. Open daily 0900–1700; free.

A highlight of visiting San Antonio is to take a gentle cruise on the river in flat-bottomed, environmentally friendly barges. Tours operate every day and last 35–40 mins. Take a tour ($), or for less than the cost of two tickets buy a shuttle pass for the day and ride as frequently as you like. A special treat is a dinner cruise. Rio San Antonio Cruises, 315 E Commerce St; tel: (210) 244-5700 or (800) 417-4139 (reservations); www.sarivercruise.com.

NIGHTLIFE

San Antonians love a fiesta and are ready to party at the drop of a sombrero. You'll find a fiesta occurring every month of the year. At the top of the list is Fiesta San Antonio, held in the third week of April. Other celebrations include: Cinco de Mayo, celebrating Mexico's independence from France in May; Oktoberfest, celebrating San Antonio's German roots; and Fiesta de las Luminarias, when the River Walk is lit by thousands of candles on the weekends before Christmas.

The rest of the year, see something of San Antonio's nightlife at:

Jim Cullum's Landing, 123 Losoya, River Walk; tel: (210) 223-7266. Traditional jazz from big band to Dixieland.

Blue Star Brewing Company, 1414 S Alamo; tel: (210) 212-5506. Good beer brewed on site for a largely collegiate crowd.

Durty Nelly's Irish Pub, 715 River Walk; tel: (210) 222-1400. Quaff a lager with lime, throw your peanut shells on the floor and join the gang for a sing-along. Trite, but good fun.

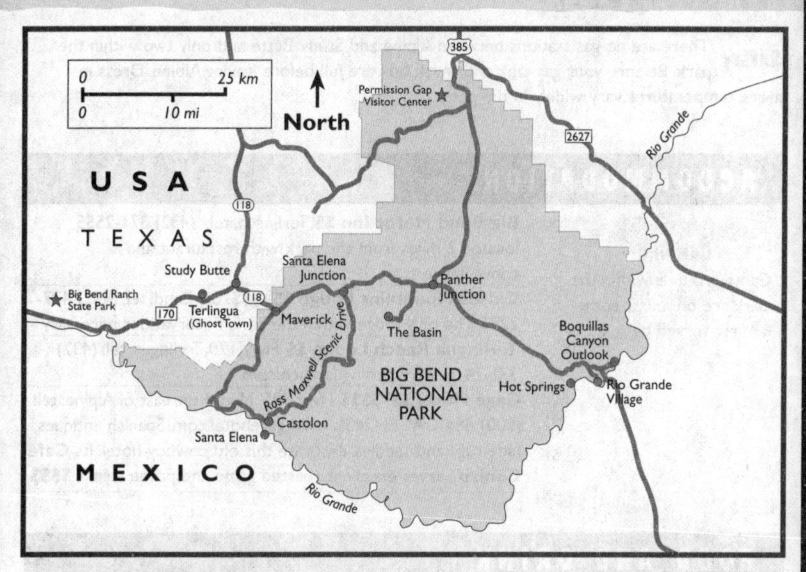

Big Bend National Park is on a horseshoe curve of the **Rio Grande River** by the Mexican border. Remote, but the stark contrasts of the Chisos Mountains and unending Chihuahuan desert make it unforgettable.

GETTING THERE

RAIL Amtrak's 'Sunset Limited' access is from San Antonio or El Paso to Alpine.

BUS/CAR All Aboard America and Greyhound buses run to Alpine. The park is accessible only by car from El Paso, via 1-10 east to Rte 90, to Alpine. From Alpine, the park headquarters is 120 miles; , but there is no public transport to Big Bend. The best option is to rent a car in El Paso (325 miles) or Midland/ Odessa (230 miles). From Alpine take Texas Hwy 118 to the west entrance. From Marathon take US 385 to the north entrance.

INFORMATION

General information: www.visitbigbend.com. **Big Bend National Park**; tel: (432) 477-2251; www.nps.gov/bibe. **Alpine Chamber of Commerce**; tel: (432) 837-2326 or (800) 561-3755.

MONEY The closest ATM is at Study Butte at the park's west entrance.

SAFETY There are no gas stations between Alpine and Study Butte and only two within the park. Be sure your gas tank and snack box are full before leaving Alpine. Dress in layers; temperatures vary widely in the park.

ACCOMMODATION

CAMPING
Camp grounds within the park are on a first-come-first-served basis, $.

Big Bend Motor Inn $$, Terlingua; tel: (432) 371-2555, located 2 miles from the park with restaurant and convenience store.

Chisos Mountains Lodge $$–$$$, Big Bend; tel: (432) 477-2291. The only lodge within the park. Reservations necessary.

Terlingua Ranch Lodge $$ Hwy 170, Terlingua; tel: (432) 371-2416; www.terlinguaranch.com

Gage Hotel $$–$$$$ Hwy 385, Marathon, east of Alpine; tel: (800) 884-GAGE(4243); www.gagehotel.com. Spanish antiques, hide rugs and saddles decorate this old cowboy hotel. Its **Café Cenizo** serves excellent roasted game and prime steaks $$$$.

FOOD AND DRINK

Chisos Mountains Lodge Dining Room, the park's only restaurant, has very ordinary food $–$$.

HIGHLIGHTS

Start at the **Panther Junction Visitor Center** for maps, orientation and full details of all attractions. Take **Ross Maxwell Scenic Drive** to discover the red and beige mule-ear shaped mountains, steep canyons and scrub landscape that make up the park. Head south at the **Santa Elena Junction** and turn left at **Castolon** to explore the old army outpost. The road ends at the **Santa Elena Canyon Overlook,** where steep, colourful walls erupt 1500 ft above the Rio Grande.

Other attractions include jeep expeditions; rafting and a visit to the McDonald Observatory, one of the largest in the USA, situated 26 miles north-west of Alpine on Hwy 118.

Santa Fe will take your breath away! This may be because of its altitude – around 7000 ft above sea level – but more likely because it is one of America's most charming and attractive cities. It feels like one giant, outdoor, interactive museum of art and history, with the magnificent Sangre de Cristo Mountains as a backdrop. Adobe-lined streets are seasonally adorned with fresh lilacs, poppies, sunflowers or a dusting of snow.

MUST SEE/DO IN SANTA FE

Get into the local art spirit at the Georgia O'Keefe Museum

Savour the Museum of Fine Arts

Take the Canyon Road Arts Walk

Admire the staircase at the Loretto Chapel

By the time the Pilgrims set foot on Plymouth Rock, Santa Fe was already firmly established, and over the centuries it has been the capital for the Spanish kingdom of New Mexico, the Mexican province of Nuevo Mejico, the American territory, and later the state, of New Mexico. Native Indians, Spanish conquistadores, mountain men, gamblers, writers, artists and musicians have all contributed to making Santa Fe the cultural heart of the Southwest. Nearby, there are forests, parks, monuments, ancient Indian ruins, Indian pueblos and Los Alamos to explore. Hiking trails, kayaking, river rafting, biking, horse-riding, tennis and golf will keep the active traveller happy.

GETTING THERE AND GETTING AROUND

AIR Albuquerque International Airport (renamed Sunport) is 65 miles south-west of Santa Fe. The Sandia Shuttle costs $23 per person, one way (reservations recommended); tel: (888) 775-5696; www.sandiashuttle.com. Sandia Shuttle makes ten trips daily. Santa Fe Municipal Airport, tel: (505) 955-2900, has services to Denver and Phoenix.

RAIL/BUS Amtrak's 'Southwest Chief' stops in Lamy, 14 miles east of Santa Fe (see p. 354). Call (800) 871-7415 to arrange the van connection to Santa Fe. Bus depot tel: (505) 471-0008.

Greyhound and TNM&O (Texas, New Mexico and Oklahoma) buses arrive at 858 St Michael's Dr.; tel: (505) 471-0008 or (800) 528-0447, quite a distance from the central plaza and relatively safe during the day, but exercise caution in the evening.

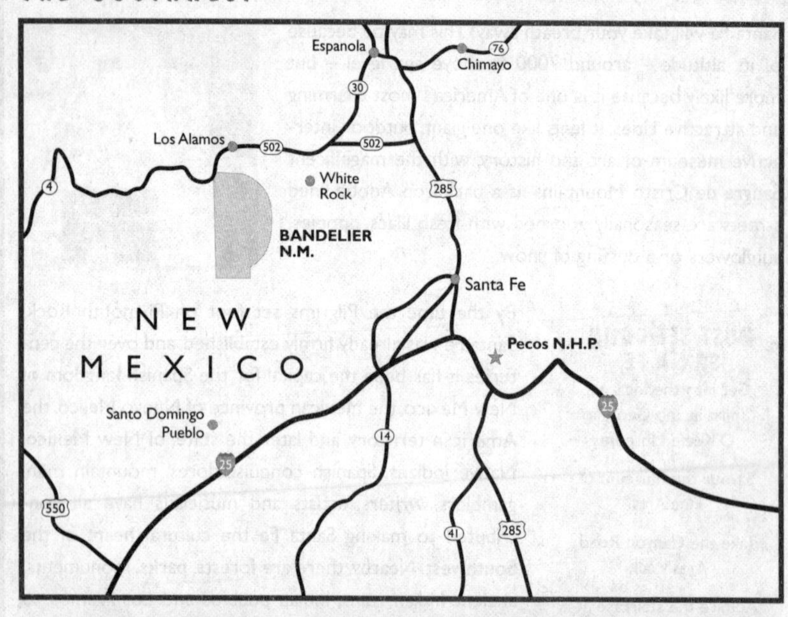

INFORMATION

Santa Fe Convention and Visitors Bureau, 201 W Marcy St, Santa Fe, 87504-0909; tel: (505) 955-6200 or (800) 777-CITY; www.santafe.org.

Santa Fe is the highest city in the United States at 6970 ft. Allow yourself time to adjust – the altitude can leave you breathless. Rest, drink plenty of water and limit alcohol to avoid the drowsiness, dizziness, headaches and nausea that come with altitude sickness.

SAFETY Despite its benign appearance, Santa Fe has in the past had its problems of petty theft in hotels and bag grabbing, although these incidents have now dropped noticably.

MONEY Automatic cash dispensers abound throughout the city. You can exchange foreign currency at Nationsbank, 1234 St Michael's Dr., and First Security Bank, 121 Sandoval St.

POST AND PHONES The main post office is at 210 S Federal Place (two blocks north and one block west of the plaza); tel: (505) 988-6351. Open Mon–Fri 0730–1745.

ACCOMMODATION

Budget Inn $$ 725 Cerillos Rd; tel: (505) 982-5952. Central, but ask for a room at the back to avoid the street noise.

El Paradero $$ 220 W Manhattan St; tel: (505) 988-1177. An eccentric, rambling old farmhouse dating from the 1880s. Rooms have skylights and fireplaces. A full breakfast is served.

Travelodge $$ 646 Cerillos Rd; tel: (505) 982-3551 or (800) 578-7878. Rooms have mini-refrigerator and coffeemaker.

The Inn of the Animal Tracks $$–$$$ 707 Paseo de Peralta; tel: (505) 988-1546. A restored pueblo-style home in the centre of town, filled with hardwood floors and platform beds with feather mattresses.

Four Kachinas Inn $$$ 512 Webber St; tel: (505) 982-2550; www.fourKachinas.com. B&B in a turn-of-the-century house. Some rooms have their own patio.

La Fonda $$$$ 100 E San Francisco St; tel: (505) 982-5511 or (800) 523-5002. The oldest hotel in Santa Fe. Guests have included John F Kennedy and Robert Redford. Elegant, expensive and worthy of the splurge.

Alexander's Inn $$$–$$$$ 529 E Palace Ave.; tel: (505) 986-1431 or (888) 321-5123. Charming, romantic B&B in Santa Fe's historic neighbourhood.

A TAXING EXPERIENCE

No matter where you stay in Santa Fe, you will be charged a hefty 10.25 per cent hotel tax.

FOOD AND DRINK

Plaza Diner $ 54 Lincoln Ave (on the Plaza); tel: (505) 982-1644. Classic diner where New Mexican, Greek and American foods top the menu. The Kahlua flan calls for second helpings.

Downtown Subscriptions $ 376 Garcia St; tel: (505) 983-3085. Giant lattes, shady patio and the largest selection of international newspapers and magazines in town.

Celebrations $–$$ 613 Canyon Rd; tel: (505) 989-8904. Yummy huevos rancheros, eggs Benedict and home-made cinnamon rolls served all day long. Lovely place to stop and nibble between gallery stops on Canyon Rd.

Santacafé $$$ 231 Washington St; tel: (505) 984-1788. The Southwest meets South-East Asia. Expensive but interesting, with a twist on local cuisine. Reservations recommended.

HIGHLIGHTS

Santa Fe's plaza, surrounded by narrow streets filled with adobe houses, has retained its historic role as the focus of town life, and is the place to begin your explorations.

In the centre of the plaza, a monument commemorates Santa Feans' valour in repelling various 19th-century invaders, such as Confederate troops and [ ] Indians (locals have eradicated the word 'savage' from the plaque, as they point out that these were not local Indians but rather Comanches who came from Texas – as, for that matter, did the Confederate soldiers).

Forming the north side is the **Palace of the Governors,** housing the New Mexico Museum of History. Built in 1610 as the original capital of New Mexico, it has been in continuous public use longer than any other structure in the United States. The museum highlights the colonial and territorial eras, with exhibits such as the beautiful full-scale reconstruction of a Penitente chapel. Under the museum's porticos Indians sell jewellery and pottery, an 'exhibit' of the museum, which regulates the works' quality and authenticity.

GETTING AROUND

Santa Fe is easily explored on foot, but **Santa Fe Trails**, the public bus system, may be a welcome aid in the summer heat. It runs Mon–Fri 0630–2230; Sat 0800–2000 (no service Sun or public holidays); tel: (505) 955-2001.

One block west is the **Museum of Fine Arts** built in 1917, sparking a resurgence in the architecture that characterizes Santa Fe today. The upstairs galleries house classic paintings from early 20th-century Santa Fe and Taos. (Allow at least 2 hours to see both museums. See box on p. 389.)

Santa Fe's leading attraction is the **Georgia O'Keeffe Museum** on Johnson Street. The abstract artist O'Keeffe was drawn to New Mexico's desert landscapes for inspiration, and was a resident of Santa Fe at the time of her death in 1986.

The Historic Styles Act, passed in 1957, legislated that all new structures built within the downtown area must be either Spanish pueblo or territorial in appearance. Large electrical signs are prohibited and even the building height and window sizes are regulated. The result? A low-rise, earth-toned city that is easy on the eye.

Diagonally across the plaza is **La Fonda**, Santa Fe's oldest hotel. Browse through the lobby to view its unusual décor. West, up San Francisco St, is **St Francis Cathedral**, built in 1869, with *La Conquistadora,* a blue-clad willow-wood statue of the Virgin, carried by Spanish in their flight from the Pueblo Revolt of 1680. The statue is carried in a thanksgiving procession that has been held annually since 1716.

Sena Plaza, just north of the plaza on E Palace Ave, is one of the city's most beautiful and secluded historic sites. Once the central court of a 33-room hacienda, it has been transformed into an intimate garden.

One block south of La Fonda, on the Old Santa Fe Trail, is the 1873 **Loretto Chapel** (chapel of Our Lady of Light) in the grounds of the Hotel Loretto. The chapel is patterned after Sainte Chapelle church in Paris. Its best-known feature is its 'miraculous staircase', a remarkable spiral staircase that makes two complete 360° turns with no central or other visible means of support. Many legends surround its construction, but the only element upon which all the stories agree is that a mysterious carpenter completed the work and vanished without waiting to be paid.

> **THE MUSEUM OF NEW MEXICO**
> Of the four individual museums that make up the **Museum of New Mexico**, the **Palace of Governors** and the **Museum of Fine Arts** are in the heart of Santa Fe. The **Museum of International Folk Art** and the **Museum of Indian Arts and Culture** are located just a few miles away.
> All are open Tues–Sat 1000–1700. You can pay separate admission to each ($) or, for the cost of two admissions, obtain a four-day pass, valid for both the museums.

Across the river is the historic **Barrio de Analco**. Past the **San Miguel Mission** and the **Oldest House** is the **Roundhouse**, the New Mexico State Capitol, completed in 1966. The only round capitol building in the USA, it was designed to reflect the shape of a Zia Pueblo, the Circle of Life. Surrounded by a lush garden of 100-plus varieties of plants and trees, with plenty of benches and sculptures, the outside is much more interesting than its functional interior.

FIESTA TIME The most famous of Santa Fe's many festivals is the **Santa Fe Fiesta**, held annually in September. This four-day celebration begins with dancing, fireworks and the burning of the 40-ft figure of Zozobra or Old Man Gloom.

SHOPPING

Native American artefacts and traditional crafts, western paintings, contemporary Indian art and 'wearable art' (western fashions with an *haute* twist) will all combine to put a major dent in your budget. If you are in the market for a painting that costs more than a car, you will find many here.

> Canyon Rd is the art and soul of Santa Fe. This mile-long road was once travelled by Pueblo Indians, Spanish explorers and pioneers. In recent history the path has been trodden by artists and writers from around the world. Dozens of galleries, studios, shops and restaurants are now housed within the historic buildings. Wear comfortable walking shoes: the pavement is uneven.

DAY TRIPS

Pecos National Park, 20 miles east of Santa Fe (head northbound on I-25), is the site of a 17th-century Spanish mission and a major pueblo ruin that dates from the 13th century. The Pecos pueblo was abandoned in the mid-19th century after Comanche raids left but few survivors. The E E Fogelson Visitors Center relates the history of the Pecos people with exhibits and dioramas. A 1½ mile loop trail takes you past the excavation of the Misión de Nuestra Señora de Los Angeles de Porcincula, all that remains of what was once the most magnificent church north of Mexico City. $, open daily 0800–1700.

RIDING INTO THE SUNSET

The **Santa Fe Southern Railroad** will take you on an evening ride to Lamy. This five-car train with restored cars represents different eras of railway history. Seats covered in green velvet and walls of gleaming wood highlight the New Jersey Car of the 1920s, and the Plaza Lamy car, built in the 1950s as a lounge car, has a domed roof. The caboose was originally built in the 1940s as part of a livestock train.

To visit the **Bandelier National Monument** take Hwy 84/285 north approximately 16 miles to Pojoaque, then head west on Rte 502. The monument, named after pioneering Swiss archaeologist Adolph Bandelier, reflects his perseverance in 34 years of excavation. Only a stone floor plan remains of what was once a three-storey, castle-like walled town. To appreciate the ruins fully climb to the Ceremonial Cave for the best view. The area is also a hiker's paradise. $$ (per car); open daily during daylight hours.

LOS ALAMOS Further along Rte 502 is **Los Alamos**, perched atop the 7300 ft Pajarito Plateau. Best known for its secret project to develop the atom bomb in World War II, Los Alamos was home to Pueblo tribes for well over a thousand years. The fascinating **Bradbury Science Museum** puts a very positive spin on nuclear energy and the 18-min film, *The Town That Never Was*, tells how this community evolved in secrecy: 15th St and Central Ave; tel: (505) 667-4444; open Tues–Fri 0900–1700, Sat–Mon 1300–1700; free.

The **Los Alamos Historical Museum** is a massive vertical log building showing the area's history, from prehistoric cave dwellers to a more realistic view of the devastating effects of nuclear weapons: 1921 Juniper St; tel: (505) 662-4493; open Mon–Sat 0930–1630, Sun 1100–1700 (summer); Mon–Sat 1000–1600, Sun 1300-1600 (winter); free.

BLACK HOLE

Do not take an engineer or technophile anywhere near 4015 Arkansas, Los Alamos, if you have anything else planned for that day! This store/museum is filled with the remains of the nuclear age: Geiger counters snuggle up to giant blenders and every other sort of technical gizmo (the owner has supplied props to many sci-fi movies). Bring a jacket or sweater as the temperature inside hovers at about 40°F/5°C.

WHERE NEXT?

The drive north from Santa Fe to Taos (see p. 397) will take you along a spectacular 80-mile route through mountains, red painted desert, villages bordered by apple and peach orchards and the foothills of the 13,000 ft peaks of the Sangre de Cristo Mountains. Equally dramatic is the Durango Driving Loop (see p. 391). Amtrak's 'Southwest Chief' will take you west to Los Angeles (see p. 430) or north all the way to Chicago (see p. 325).

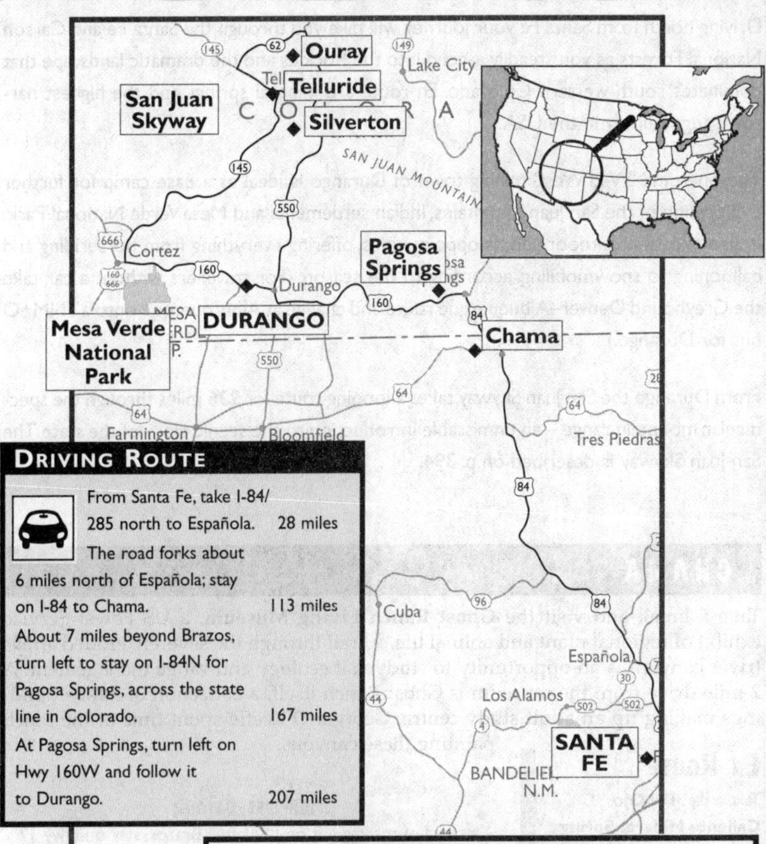

Driving Route

From Santa Fe, take I-84/285 north to Española. 28 miles

The road forks about 6 miles north of Española; stay on I-84 to Chama. 113 miles

About 7 miles beyond Brazos, turn left to stay on I-84N for Pagosa Springs, across the state line in Colorado. 167 miles

At Pagosa Springs, turn left on Hwy 160W and follow it to Durango. 207 miles

SANTA FE — SILVERTON

OTT Tables 377/820/859

Service	Bus	Bus	Bus	Bus		Bus	Bus	Rail
Days of operation	Daily	Daily	Daily	Daily		Daily	Daily	A
Special notes								A
Santa Fe d.	0105	....	....	0730	....	1530	2005	....
Albuquerque d.	0215	0255	....	0845	....	1650	2120	....
Durango d.	....	0810	0820	....	....	....	....	A
Silverton a.	....	....	0945	....	....	....	....	A

Special notes:
A–Durango and Silverton Railroad. See OTT Table 377. Operates steam-hauled tourist trains during the summer.

The Southwest

Driving north from Santa Fe your journey will take you through the Santa Fe and Carson National Forests as you steadily ascend into the Rockies and the dramatic landscape that dominates south-western Colorado. En route are mineral springs and the highest narrow-gauge railway in the USA.

The one-time 'Wild West' mining town of Durango is ideal as a base camp for further exploration of the San Juan mountains, Indian settlements and Mesa Verde National Park. It also excels in outdoor sports opportunities, offering everything from horseriding and ballooning to snowmobiling, according to the season. (For travellers without a car, take the Greyhound Denver–Albuquerque route and change at Alburquerque onto a TNM+O bus for Durango.)

From Durango the San Juan Skyway takes a looping route for 236 miles through the spectacular mountain range – an unmissable introduction to the scenic glory of the state. The San Juan Skyway is described on p. 394.

CHAMA

Take a break and visit the **Ghost Ranch Living Museum**, a US Forest Service exhibit of regional plant and animal life. A trail through the severely eroded *arroyo* (river canyon) is an opportunity to study soil ecology and range management. A 2-mile drive from the museum is Ghost Ranch itself, a collection of adobe buildings making up an adult study centre. Georgia O'Keeffe spent time at the ranch painting these canyons.

En Route

Take a dip! The **Ojo Caliente Mineral Springs**, 50 miles north-west of Santa Fe, were considered sacred by prehistoric tribes and are now a National Historic Site. No other hot spring in the world has Ojo Caliente's combination of iron, soda, lithium, sodium and arsenic. The dressing rooms are in good shape, but it could use an overall sprucing up. Open daily 0800–2000.

High-life Detour

Instead of turning left on I-84 after Brazos, stay on Hwy 17 N to the Cumbres and Toltec scenic railway. This is the longest and highest narrow-gauge railway in North America. The journey ends in Antonito, Colorado, and is a day trip of tunnels, gorges and mountains; tel: (719) 376-5483 or (505) 756-2151.

PAGOSA SPRINGS

Pagosa is an Ute Indian name given to the hot mineral springs renowned for their healing qualities. The relaxing hot mineral baths and 12 swimming pools are open all year round. After a refreshing soak – and a massage perhaps? – visit the Fred Harman Art Museum, Rocky Mountain Wildlife Park, and Chimney Rock Indian Ruins. In winter you will find great powder skiing at Wolf Creek Ski Area.

i **Pagosa Springs Chamber of Commerce**, Box 787, Pagosa Springs, CO 81147; tel: (800) 252-2204; www.pagosaspringschamber.com.

DURANGO

Durango began its life as a frontier mining town. Today the romance of the Old West remains in Durango's century-old saloons, Victorian architecture and narrow-gauge railway. This lively town snuggled into the shadows of the San Juan Mountains has a wide selection of accommodation and restaurants, and activities such as river rafting, jeep tours and relaxing hot springs.

i **Durango Chamber Resort Association**, 111 Camino del Rio, Durango; tel: (800) 525-8855. Plenty of ATMs and local banks will do currency exchanges, but you will have difficulty locating bureaux de change.

Siesta Motel $$ 3475 Main Ave; tel: (970) 247-0741. Clean and quiet, with cooking facilities and jacuzzi.
Jarvis Suites $$$ 125 W 10th St; tel: (970) 259-6190 or (800) 824-1024. Studios and suites with kitchens, a barbecue on the patio and outdoor hot tubs.
Strater Hotel $$$$ 699 Main Ave; tel: (970) 247-4431 or (800) 247-4431. A taste of the Old West, but with hot tubs/jacuzzis, television and laundry. It also has a restaurant (see below).
Rochester Hotel $$$ 726 2nd Ave.; tel: (800) 664-1920; www.rochesterhotel.com. A bit of the Old West with high ceilings and 19th-century decor.

Durango has even more restaurants per capita than Santa Fe but no distinctive regional cuisine. For a special treat you might dine in the Victorian atmosphere of **Henry's** in the Strater Hotel – a bit of a splurge, but you won't find another restaurant as splurge-worthy for many miles.

HIGHLIGHTS

Durango's premier tourist attraction is the **Durango and Silverton Narrow-Gauge Railroad**, a puffing steam train that travels a spectacular route through the Animas river valley and San Juan National Forest. The journey will transport you through an unspoilt wilderness of waterfalls, meandering creeks and dense forests. The train has been pursued by bands of 'outlaw' Hollywood extras, while its passenger cars have echoed to the footsteps of such actors as David Niven in *Around the World in 80 Days*. Four round-trip trains operate daily between late Apr and Oct; reservations are essential. $$$$+; tel: (970) 247-2733.

UTE INDIAN RESERVATION

Ignacio, south-east of Durango on Rte 172, is the home of the Southern Ute tribe. The reservation, covering more than 680,000 acres, was established in 1886. Explore the tribe's history at the Sky Ute Event Center and Cultural Center Museum, or try your hand at limited-stakes gambling at the Sky Ute Casino or Ute Mountain Casino. In town you will find art, crafts, native pottery and jewellery in the shops and galleries that feature the work of these Native American artisans.

Durango celebrates the active life. You can take to the air with a glider ride over the scenic Animas valley (Durango Soaring Club, 3 miles north on Highway 550) or lift your spirits with a hot-air balloon trip. More earthly pursuits include horseriding, hayrides, hiking, fishing and biking. During the winter season you can try sleigh rides and snowmobiling.

THE SAN JUAN SKYWAY

This breathtaking 236-mile loop on paved highways through the San Juan mountains begins and ends at Durango. Designated an 'all-American road', the Skyway travels through alpine forests and towering mountains, some as high as 14,000 ft, and past Native American cliff dwellings. The most spectacular segment, between Ouray and Silverton, is nicknamed the Million Dollar Highway.

From Durango follow Hwy 550N to Silverton (45 miles). Continue north on Hwy 550 to Ouray (15 miles) and on to Ridgway (10 miles). At Ridgway turn west on Hwy 62 to Placerville (24 miles), then turn east on Hwy 145 south to Telluride (15 miles). Continue south on Hwy 145 past Ophir, Rico and Dolores (60 miles). Past Dolores Hwy 145 ends at the junction with Hwy 160. Turn east towards Mesa Verde National Park and Mancos, and so back to Durango – a total of 236 miles.

SPECIAL DRIVING NOTE

Your journey will take you over some of the steepest mountain passes in North America. Be careful not to overheat your engine and especially careful not to 'ride the brakes': this may cause them to overheat and fail.

From Telluride the route is quite remote, and from a scenic viewpoint a little dull. It's better to turn tail at this point and head back to Durango, enjoying the scenery from the other direction.

SILVERTON

One of Colorado's most scenic settlements lies at the end of the narrow-gauge railway from Durango. Its wide, dirt-paved streets and false-fronted Victorian-era stores along once notorious Blair Street, known for its bordellos, evoke the 'shoot 'em up' days of the Wild West when Bat Masterson was the city marshall.

Teller House Hotel $$ 1250 Greene St; tel: (970) 387-5423 or (800) 342-4338. Built above the French Bakery, it needs refurbishing, but has a quirky charm. Rooms have private or shared bath.

Wingate House B&B $$ 1045 Snowden St; tel: (970) 387-5220 or (800) 484-9547-5520. Snuggle under a satin comforter (quilt) or elk hide. Non-smoking.

Romero's Cantina and Restaurant $ 1151 Green St; tel: (970) 387-0213. Enjoyable Mexican cuisine in an authentic cantina setting.

OURAY

The 24 miles between Silverton and Ouray are along the heart-stopping Million Dollar Highway. Ouray is a charmer – the entire town is listed on the National Register of Historic Districts – and also has an abundance of hiking trails and mineral hot springs.

Box Canyon Lodge $$ 45 Third Ave; tel: (970) 325-4981. Relax in mineral hot tubs on a redwood deck. Fireplace suite available, but otherwise pretty standard accommodation.

Historic Western Hotel $$ 210 Seventh Ave; tel: (970) 325-4645 or (888) 624-8403. Wooden building with an upper-storey verandah that overlooks the former stagecoach stop. It has 12 rooms with shared bath, two suites with private bath.

TELLURIDE

Tucked into a box canyon 120 miles north of Durango, Telluride's beauty is legendary. This resort town was briefly home to a young Butch Cassidy, who robbed his first bank here. Today, Telluride's reputation is based on its outstanding ski trails and Hollywood residents. The wide main street, designated a National Historic District, heads directly towards one of the most spectacular views of the Rockies.

Telluride Visitors Bureau, 700 W Colorado Ave. Open Mon–Fri 0800–2000, Sat–Sun 1000–1600.

Ridgway/Telluride Super 8 Lodge $$, 373 Palomino Trail, Ridgway, Colorado 81432. Tel: (800) 363-5444 or (970) 626-5444. Reasonable, quiet, clean and surrounded by breathtaking scenery. A fireplace large enough to park a Buick!

MESA VERDE NATIONAL PARK

The cliff dwellings and artefacts of the Anasazi (a Navajo word meaning 'ancient ones') were accidentally discovered in 1888 and are a must-see.The Anasazi, the ancestral Puebloans, began building communities on the plateaux of Mesa Verde as early as AD 550. After more than 600 years of living on the mesa they began to build structures in the alcoves of the sandstone cliffs. Despite decades of research and archaeological excavations, the exact reason for their departure remains unknown. Most experts speculate that a combination of overpopulation, crop failure and drought may have caused them to abandon the area.

Today's visitors will find themselves awestruck at what they accomplished. The access road to Mesa Verde is 10 miles south of Cortez on Hwy 160, 36 miles west of Durango. Entrance fee ($$) is per vehicle, and guided tours, both full day and half day, are available ($$$$). The park is extremely crowded in summer, and the best months to visit are May, Sept and Oct. Wear comfortable, non-slip shoes and make sure you take a hat and water bottle. Facilities within the park include an archaeological museum lodge, several restaurants, gift shops, petrol stations and a 425-pitch camp site.

It's a 15-mile drive from the entrance to the Far View visitor centre, and immediately beyond, the road divides for the two areas of remains: **Chapin Mesa** to the south and **Wetherill Mesa** to the west. You will not manage to do both on the same day, so Chapin Mesa is your best bet, with tours of both the Cliff Palace and Balcony House. Tours ($) run every hour during peak season. **Cliff Palace**, the largest Anasazi cliff dwelling to survive, is tucked 200 ft below an overhanging ledge of sandstone. Its 217 rooms once were home to over 200 people. Inside you will walk through empty plazas, mysterious *kivas* (underground rooms) and gaze on fading murals. **Balcony House**, a little further on, is not for the faint of heart. Access is very difficult and involves climbing ladders and crawling through a narrow tunnel. It's not visible from above, so the only way to view Balcony House is to take the tour.

To make reservations for tours of the park, tel: (800) 449-2288 or (970) 529-4421. Take a look at the park's website: www.visitmesaverde.com. Here you can also learn about the nation's newest national park at the nearby Black Canyon, a 2700-ft deep gorge in the Gunnison River.

Taos began as the northernmost outpost of Spanish colonial America. Founded five years after Santa Fe, it was the third permanent Spanish settlement in what is now the United States. Bypassed by the railways in the 1880s, the economy languished until the end of the 19th century, but in 1898 two American artists, bound for Mexico on a sketching trip, made it only as far as Taos before their wagon broke down. Enchanted by the land and the exotic, vivid quality of its light, Bert Phillips and Ernest Blumenschein stayed to form the nucleus of Taos's active artist community. After World War I more artists arrived and by the end of the 1920s the area became known as 'the left bank of the American Frontier'.

A quirky little town set in the middle of a sage-covered valley, Taos is filled with narrow streets punctuated by artists' galleries and artisan shops. At first glance, the dusty streets populated with funky residents may strike the visitor as Key West moved inland. Take time to sweep the dust from your eyes and you will discover a thriving arts community with an awe-inspiring mountain-range background.

MUST SEE/DO IN TAOS

Watch the sunrise cast pink light over Taos pueblo's age-old adobe buildings

Browse the town's galleries and artisans' studios for insights into famously bold Taoseño creativity

Farther afield, hike or bike across the high bridge spanning the Rio Grande Gorge. You'll be awestruck by the natural grandeur, Southwest USA-style.

GETTING THERE AND GETTING AROUND

AIR Taos has its own airport, about 8 miles north on US 64, but a more comprehensive service is to Albuquerque International Airport, about 2.5 hours away. For transit into town, take Twinhearts Shuttle, tel: (505) 571-1201 or (800) 654-9456, or Faust's Transportation, tel: (505) 758-3410, (888) 830-3410.

BUS/TRAIN Amtrak does not run through Taos, but TNM&O (Texas, New Mexico & Oklahoma) coaches arrive at 1213A Gusdorf; tel: (505) 758-1144.

Taos Transit, tel: (505) 751-4459: the Chile Line runs from from Kachina Lodge on Paseo del Pueblo Norte to the Ranchos Post Office on the south side of town and from Taos to Taos Ski Valley. The flat fare is very cheap, even for an all-day or 7-day pass.

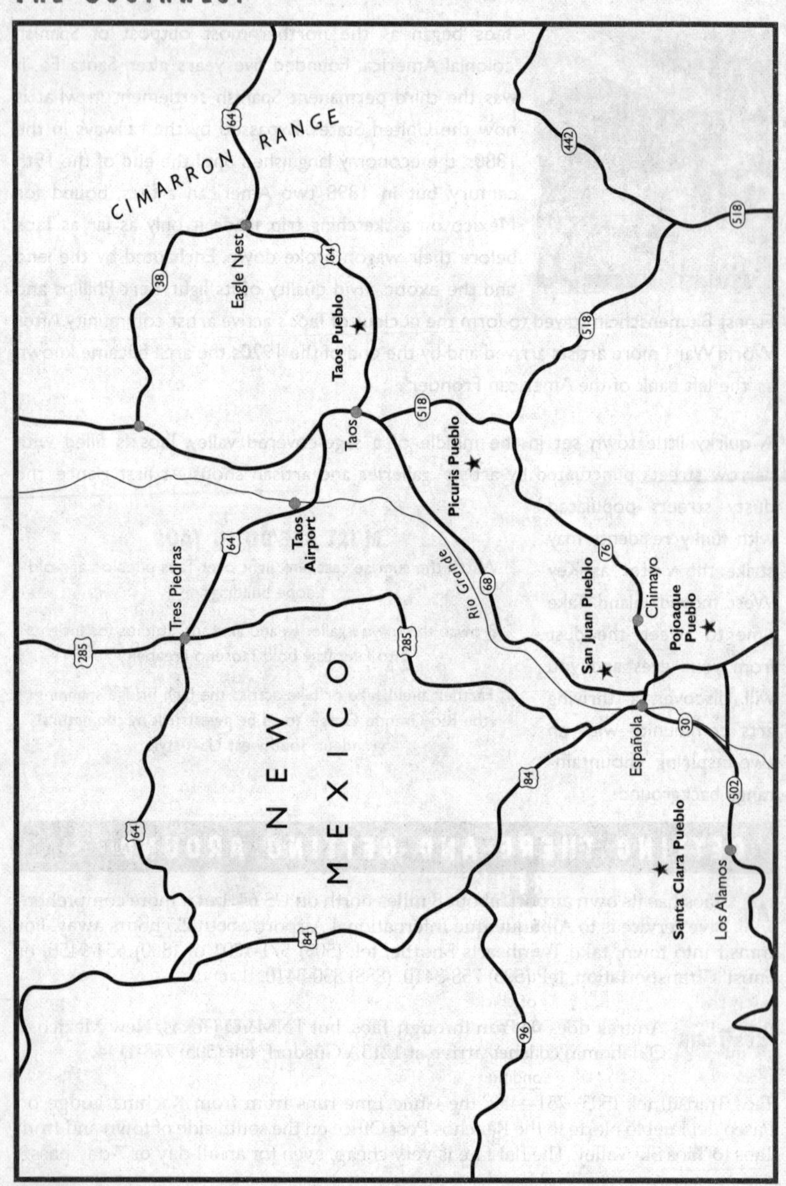
CIMARRON RANGE
Eagle Nest
Taos Pueblo
Taos
Picuris Pueblo
Taos Airport
Tres Piedras
Rio Grande
NEW MEXICO
San Juan Pueblo
Chimayo
Pojoaque Pueblo
Española
Santa Clara Pueblo
Los Alamos
64
442
518
38
285
68
76
30
502
84
96

INFORMATION

Tourist Office: Taos County Chamber of Commerce, junction of US 64 and NM 68; tel: (505) 758-3873 or (800) 732-TAOS; www.taoschamber.com. Open daily 0900–1700; closed on major holidays.

POST AND PHONES Taos Post Office is at 318 Paseo del Pueblo Norte; tel: (505) 758-2081.

ACCOMMODATION

Most hotels, motels and inns are located along Paseo del Pueblo Norte and Sur, with a few scattered east of the town centre. B&Bs can be found in various back streets. Condo accommodation is available in outlying ski areas only.

American Artists Gallery House $$–$$$ 132 Frontier Lane; tel: (800) 532-2041; www.taosbedandbreakfast.com. Romantic and private setting. Great breakfasts, fireplaces, jacuzzis, unobstructed views. Centrally located.

La Doña Luz $$ 114 Kit Carson Rd; tel: (505) 758-4874 or (800) 758-9187. You will feel part of the Taos art community in this B&B with its painted murals on the doors, wood carvings and set tiles.

Fechin Inn $$$ 227 Paseo del Pueblo Norte; tel: (505) 751-1000 or (800) 811-2933; www.fechininn.com. Adjacent to artist Nicholai Fechin's home/studio museum. Fechin works adorn guests' rooms. Fitness facilities, open-air whirlpool.

Hotel La Fonda $$$ 108 South Plaza; tel: (505) 758-2211 or (800) 833-2211; www.hotellafond.com. Prime plaza location, intricately carved woodwork, colorful murals and decorative motifs. Rare collection of novelist D H Lawrence's erotic art.

Taos Inn $$$ 125 Paseo del Pueblo Norte; tel: (505) 758-2233 or (888) 519-8267; www.taosinn.com. National Historic Landmark. Most of its 36 rooms have kiva fireplaces. Lively Adobe Bar, amiable Doc Martin's Restaurant.

FOOD AND DRINK

Bent Street Deli and Café $ 120 Bent St; tel: (505) 758-5787. Homely atmosphere with hearty breakfast burritos, home-made granolas and a picnic to take away.

Bravo! $$ 1353-A Paseo del Pueblo Sur; tel: (505) 758-8100. Casual atmosphere for salads and sandwiches, also huge servings of chicken pasta.

Michael's Kitchen $$–$$$ 304 Paseo del Pueblo Norte; tel: (505) 758-4178. Breakfast burritos and enchiladas, fresh-baked breads and baguettes. Lunch sandwiches, full Tex-Mex dinners. Rustic décor includes a mint-condition pot-bellied stove.

HIGHLIGHTS

D H Lawrence, whose books stirred such controversy on both sides of the Atlantic, took refuge in Taos during 1924–5 to escape notoriety. However, while here, he tried his hand at painting, and the results earned him an obscenity prosecution (and drove him from Britain one last time). You can view the naughty pictures in the back room of **Hotel La Fonda** on the Plaza.

The **Kit Carson Home and Museum of the West** is just east of the Plaza. The 12-room adobe dwelling was purchased by the famous mountain man, Indian agent and scout as a wedding present for his young bride, Josefa, and was their home for 25 years. Furnishings, antique firearms and memorabilia are on display. The museum bookshop is very comprehensive on New Mexico history. $, 113 Kit Carson Rd; tel: (505) 758-4741; open daily 0800–1800.

South of the Plaza is the 1797 adobe **Blumenschein Home**, the residence and studio of Ernest Blumenschein, a founder of the Taos Society of Artists. Changing exhibits, European antiques and hand-made Taos furniture are on display. $, 222 Ledoux Dr: tel: (505) 758-0505; open daily 0900–1700.

It would be a shame to visit Taos without browsing in the art galleries that line the streets. Foremost among these are the **Michael McCormick Gallery**, with 4500 sq. feet of display space, and the **Variant Gallery**, also on the plaza.

You can buy a joint ticket to cover entrance to all the Kit Carson Historic Museums: the Kit Carson Home, the Blumenschein Home and the Martinez Hacienda.

Martinez Hacienda is the only remaining Spanish colonial hacienda in New Mexico. Built in 1804 as a refuge from Comanche raids, it is remarkably beautiful for a building of thick adobe walls with no exterior windows. $ Lower Ranchitos Rd, Hwy 240; tel: (505) 758-1000; open daily 0900–1700.

Four miles north of Taos (off NM 522) is the **Millicent Rogers Museum**, housing one of the most extensive private collections of Indian art in the Southwest. Featured are Navajo and Pueblo jewellery, textiles, Pueblo pottery and painting, and Zuni and Hopi *kachinas* (images of supernatural ancestors), as well as some Spanish colonial folk items. $, tel: (505) 758-2462; open daily 1000–1700 (closed Mon Nov–Mar).

Heading south about 4 miles out of Taos, at Rancho de Taos, you will find **San Francisco de Asis Church**. This adobe edifice with no windows or doors has been the subject of many photos by Ansel Adams and paintings by Georgia O'Keeffe. It contains the phenomenon of 'The Shadow of the Cross' by Henry Ault. Under ordinary light it portrays a barefoot Christ at the Sea of Galilee; in darkness, however, the portrait becomes luminescent and a shadow of the cross appears over the left shoulder of Jesus's silhouette. The artist claims this was not of his doing, and it remains a mystery why these illusions appear. Open Mon-Sat 0900-1200 and 1300-1600, and for Mass: Sat 1800 (English), Sun 1900 and 1130 (Spanish).

The Pueblos Taos Pueblo – the oldest and best known of the Rio Grande Indian pueblos – is a National Historic Landmark, 3 miles northwest of town. Preserved here is the multi-storey architectural style that dates back over 1000 years.

About 1400 people live in the pueblo today, existing as their ancestors did centuries ago, baking bread in traditional *hornos*, drinking water that flows from the sacred Blue Lake. It is a quiet life, with an emphasis and dependence upon nature.

Pueblos

More than just a tourist attraction, pueblos are microcosms of Native American culture – the past, present and future all uniquely represented in tight, family-oriented communities. These villages manage to welcome tourists while conducting their daily lives. The pueblos have been thriving since the time of the Battle of Hastings (1066). Harvest celebrations, ceremonial dances and sacred rituals offer an intriguing glimpse into pueblo culture. Each tells a different story, with the costumes brilliant with beads and headdresses and punctuated by the insistent cadence of drums. Pinon smoke fills the air and the chatter of strange native dialects will transport you to another century, with sights, sounds and smells that are a feast for the senses.

New Mexico is home to 19 Indian pueblos; Acoma, Cochiti, Isleta, Jemez, Laguna, Nambe, Picuris, Pojaque, Sandia, San Felipe, San Ildefonso, San Juan, Santa Ana, Santa Clara, Santo Domingo, Taos, Tesuque, Zia and Zuni, most are within a 2-hour radius. Each is unique. Some pueblos have strict rules governing photography, sketching and tape recording, so you should always ask permission and be prepared to pay. All visitors must abide by the laws and rules of the pueblo they visit, most pueblos have a tribal office to answer any questions. Remember when touring the pueblos that these are peoples' homes. No peeking in windows, no wandering through open doors, and at all times behave in a respectful manner.

Ceremonies and dances held at the pueblo include the Fiesta de San Antonio in June, a corn dance in late July and the Fiesta de San Geronimo in late September. The Taos Pueblo is open to the public daily 0900-1630. Parking fees and photography fees are charged. No cameras may be used during any ceremony.

ALBUQUERQUE

Up, up and away! Albuquerque is a city that feels as free-spirited as the hot-air balloon festival it hosts each year. Even if you cannot visit the city in October when the International Balloon Festival is held, you won't go far without seeing the ubiquitous hot-air balloon motif. And on almost every weekend morning you will spot up to 50 hot-air balloons floating above the city, roaring like dragons as they sometimes bounce off suburban rooftops.

Albuquerque's heritage can be traced to early Spanish settlers, Native Americans and merchant Anglo settlers. The city never went through the lawless days of many south-western frontier towns, and by the last quarter of the 19th century Albuquerque was already well established as a rail trade centre. Historic Route 66 weaves through the 100 square mile sprawl of modern Albuquerque, connecting the threads of its historic past.

MUST SEE/DO IN ALBUQUERQUE

Take to the skies in a hot air balloon

Get some kicks driving Route 66

Sample New Mexican specialities at Maria Teresa's

Learn about Native Indian history at the Indian Pueblo Cultural Center

GETTING THERE

Air Albuquerque International Airport (now known as the Sunport), in the south central part of the city, is served by most major carriers. Sun Tran buses, tel: (505) 843-9200, make airport stops, but the service is somewhat limited. Efficient taxi service and Checker Airport Express ferry passengers to and from city hotels.

Rail/Bus Amtrak is located at 214 First SW; tel: (800) USA RAIL or (800) 872-7245. The Greyhound terminal is close by, at 330 Second St NW; tel: (505) 243-4435. Sun Tran serves the city bus network. Its Sun Trolley service ($0.75 fare) operates 1000–1800 and runs every 30 mins.

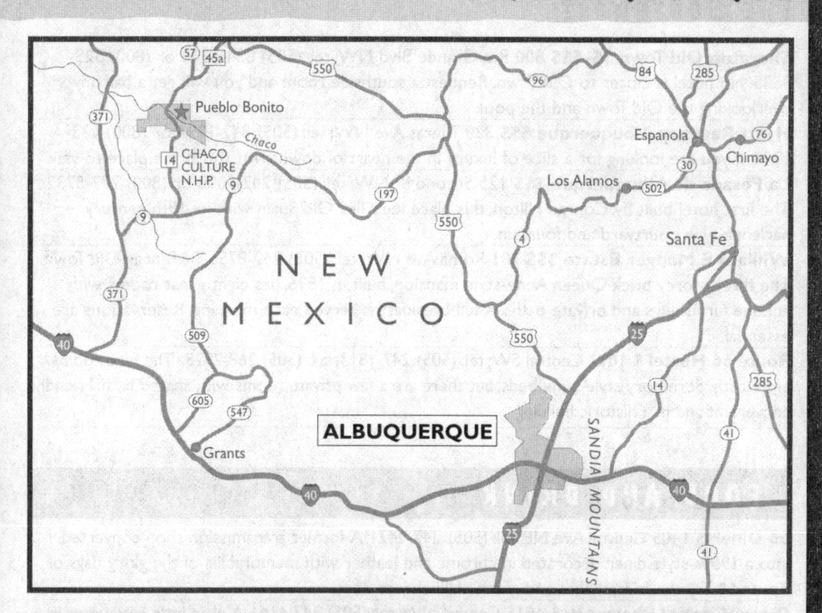

INFORMATION

Albuquerque Convention and Visitors Bureau, 20 First Plaza NW; tel: (505) 842-9918 or (800) 284-2822; www.itsatrip.org; open Mon–Fri 0800–1700. An Old Town visitor centre, at 303 Romero St NW, is open daily 0900–1700. The daily *Albuquerque Tribune* and the evening *Albuquerque Journal* are both useful sources of information.

POST AND PHONES The main post office, 1135 Broadway NE, tel: (505) 245-9561, is open daily 0730–1800. There are 25 branches throughout the city.

SAFETY Avoid the cluster of motels at the east edge of the town along Route 66 – this is a bad area, frequented by prostitutes and unsavoury types.

ACCOMMODATION

Downtown or Old Town are the best places to stay. Albuquerque adds a 10.562% occupancy tax to every hotel bill.

Best Western Rio Grande Inn $$–$$$ 1015 Rio Grande Blvd NW; tel: (505) 843-9500 or (800) 959-4726. Handcrafted furniture and original artwork in all guestrooms. Beautiful outdoor pool.

Sheraton Old Town $$–$$$ 800 Rio Grande Blvd NW; tel: (505) 834-6300 or (800) 325-3535. No hotel is closer to Old Town. Request a southside room and you will get a balcony overlooking the Old Town and the pool.

Hyatt Regency Albuquerque $$$ 330 Tijeras Ave NW; tel: (505) 842-1234 or (800) 233-1234. If you are looking for a slice of luxury in the heart of downtown, this is the place to stay.

La Posada de Albuquerque $$$ 125 Second St NW; tel: (505) 242-9090 or (800) 777-5732. The first hotel built by Conrad Hilton, this place feels like Old Spain with its 19th-century hacienda-type courtyard and fountain.

William E Mauger Estate $$$ 701 Roma Ave NW; tel: (505) 242-8755. B&B near Old Town. The three-storey brick Queen Anne-style mansion, built in 1896, has eight guest rooms with antique furnishings and private baths. A full breakfast is served each morning. Reservations are essential.

Route 66 Hostel $ 1012 Central SW; tel: (505) 247-1813, fax: (505) 268-2825. The nine rooms are mostly dormitory style bunk beds, but there are a few private rooms with shared bath. Friendly, convenient and in a historic building.

FOOD AND DRINK

66 Diner $ 1405 Central Ave NE; tel: (505) 247-1421. A former transmission shop converted into a 1950s-style diner, decorated in chrome and leather with memorabilia of the glory days of Route 66. Try the fries, shakes and green chilli cheese dogs.

Duran Central Pharmacy $ 1815 Central NW; tel: (505) 247-4141. A plain little restaurant in the back serves up authentic northern New Mexico food. Try the blue-corn enchilada plate or the huevos rancheros smothered in green chilli.

Maria Teresa $$-$$$ 618 Rio Grande Blvd; tel: (505) 242-3900. This restored 1840s adobe home a block north of the Plaza holds one of Albuquerque's most appealing restaurants. You'll find beef, chicken and seafood on the menu, as well as New Mexican specialities. Reservations are recommended.

HIGHLIGHTS

The heart of Old Town, Albuquerque's original **Plaza**, dating back to 1706, has remained remarkably intact even as high-rise buildings have sprouted all around it. It is an oasis of antiquity. Browse in the art galleries and shops, bargain for handicrafts with the Pueblo Indian vendors, or pause for a quiet moment in the 18th-century San Felipe de Neri church.

The **New Mexico Museum of Natural History** contains exhibits about New Mexico's human and animal inhabitants in the last Ice Age, and a large display about the Rio Grande, including aquariums of fish that live in the river. The most unusual exhibit is a simulation of a journey into the depths of a volcano. $, 1801 Mountain Rd NW; tel: (505) 841-8200; open daily 0900–1700.

Across the road, the **Albuquerque Museum** features an impressive permanent exhibit on the History of Albuquerque and the largest collection of Spanish colonial artefacts in the USA: 2000 Mountain Rd NW; tel: (505) 243-7255; open Tues–Sun 0900–1700; free.

The **Indian Pueblo Cultural Center** is modelled after Pueblo Bonito, a 9th-century ruin in Chaco Culture National Historic Park, and has a series of exhibit halls, screening rooms and hands-on interactive displays. The huge gift shop is filled with moderately priced items, and galleries selling Indian arts and crafts surround a central open-air dance plaza. Indian dances and craft demonstrations are held here at most weekends. $, 2401 12th NW; tel: (505) 843-7270 or (800) 766-4405; open daily 0900–1730. A moderately priced restaurant specialises in Native American cuisine (a great place for a lunch stop).

Free walking tours of Old Town start from the Albuquerque Museum, Tues–Sun at 1100.

Just off the Old Town plaza, the **American International Rattlesnake Museum** has living specimens of common, uncommon and very rare rattlesnakes – more than 30 species in all. $$ 202 San Felipe NW; tel: (505) 242-6569; open daily 1000–1800.

A fun half-day can be spent riding the **Sandia Peak Tramway**, a journey of 2.7 miles to the top from its base station at 10 Tramway Loop NE. The views from the peak are extraordinary, especially at night. At the summit you can dine in the very pricey High Finance restaurant, or picnic along one of several hiking trails (La Luz Trail is partly flat and easy). The schedule varies and the tram can be particularly crowded during the skiing season. For operating times, tel: (505) 856-7325; $$$ (special rates with dinner at High Finance).

The walls of **Tinkertown** are lined with 55,000 glass bottles and inside are collections of wedding cake couples and hand-carved performers in a miniature big top circus. Located 20 minutes away on the Turquoise Trail National Scenic Byway in Sandia Park. $, open 0900–1800 daily Apr–Oct; tel: (503) 281-5233, www.tinkertown.com.

BALLOON FIESTA

The **Kodak Albuquerque International Balloon Fiesta**, held every October, is the largest hot-air balloon festival in the world. Mass Ascensions are held on all four weekend mornings of the fiesta, just after dawn, when the sight of several hundred balloons taking flight with the sunrise is stunning.

If you can't resist the temptation, several balloon operators can take you up into the clear blue skies (about $130 per person per hour). Contact Rainbow Riders, 11520 San Beinardillo Ave NE, tel: (505) 823-1111 or World Balloon Corporation, 4800 Eubanks Blvd NE; tel: (505) 293-6800. Be prepared for an early morning take-off.

TUCSON

Tucson (pronounced *TOO-sawn*) shines like an undiscovered gem in the Arizona desert, ringed by mountains and flanked on both east and west by the thousands of acres of Saguaro National Park.

Possessing a strong Spanish, Mexican and Native American heritage, Tucson is more than just a pretty face. It is the oldest continuously inhabited settlement in the USA – remnants of the Hohokam Indian civilisation found here date back to the 1st century AD.

Tucson is also where you find the real and 'reel' Old West. The Earps and the Clantons, Cochise and Geronimo, dance-hall girls, gunfighters and sheriffs were all part of the untamed frontier, and it's here that Hollywood created its own version of the Wild West. Countless westerns have been filmed with the saguaro-covered landscape and mountains as a backdrop.

The sun shines here 350 days a year, more than any other city in the USA. Although blessed with a more temperate climate than Phoenix because of its higher elevation, it does get a bit toasty in the summer. The clear skies, dry air and multiple mountain peaks have also made Tucson the astronomy capital of North America.

MUST SEE/DO IN TUCSON

Visit El Presidio Historic District

Hike and picnic amid the cactus at Saguaro National Park West

See the 'Old West' at Old Tucson Studios

Stargaze at Kitt Peak Observatory

GETTING THERE AND GETTING AROUND

AIR Tucson International Airport, tel: (520) 573-8100, is 6 miles south of the city. Taxis, shuttle vans and some hotels offer transport into the city.

TRAIN/BUS The Amtrak station, 400 E Toole Ave, tel: (800) USA RAIL or (800) 875-7245, is relatively convenient for the city centre but not safe at night; the station is as dilapidated as the neighbourhood. Although close to the Downtown Arts District and the Hotel Congress, the Greyhound terminus, at 2 S Fourth Ave, tel: (520) 792-3475, is another area in which to be extremely wary.

Sun Tran, tel: (520) 623-4301, the local bus service, operates routes within the city and to the airport. The service does not extend to such attractions as the Saguaro National Park, Old Tucson Studios or the foothills area - better to take an organised tour or hire a car.

INFORMATION

Metropolitan Tucson Convention and Visitors Bureau, 100 S Church Ave.; tel: (800) 638-8350; www.visittucson.org. The visitor centre is open Mon–Fri 0800–1700, Sat–Sun 0900–1600.

SAFETY Tucson is relatively safe for a city of over half a million people. Be careful after dark in the Downtown Arts District, except on Downtown Saturday Nights. To the south of downtown is a poorer area that is best avoided.

When driving be aware that many streets in Tucson are subject to flash flooding conditions in summer. Heed warnings, find an alternative route if possible and do not attempt to cross a low-lying area that has been flooded.

MONEY Automatic cash dispensers are everywhere. Traveller's cheques are widely accepted; be prepared to present your driving licence for identification.

POST AND PHONES The main post office, at 141 S Sixth Ave, is open Mon–Fri 0830–1700, Sat 0900–1200.

ACCOMMODATION

Hotel Congress $$ 311 E Congress St; tel: (520) 622-8848 or (800) 722-8848. Great for the younger set, with shared hostel rooms available. The Cyber Bar, Cup Café and Library of Congress make this the coolest spot in Tucson. Convenient for the railway and bus stations.

Clarion Hotels and Suites $$$ 88 E Broadway; tel: (520) 622-4000 or (800) CLARION. Around the corner from the Arts District, its Café Poca Cosa is a good bet for lunch.

Arizona Inn $$$$ 2200 E Elm St; tel: (520) 325-1541 or (800) 933-1093. Old Arizona charm with all the modern conveniences. Filled with furniture made by disabled veterans of World War I. Some rooms have fireplaces. The dining room is one of the finest in the state.

FOOD AND DRINK

La Indita $ 622 N Fourth Ave; tel: (520) 792-0523. Family-run restaurant with cheap, authentic Tex-Mex. Chicken mole, mushroom tacos, and spinach and nut enchiladas are worth a try.

Garcia's $$ 419 E Congress St; tel: (520) 628-1958. Mexican food; fajitas and huge salads top the menu.

Cafe Poca Cosa, $$ 88 E Broadway Blvd, tel: (520) 620-6400. Lively atmosphere, terrific food and lethal margaritas.

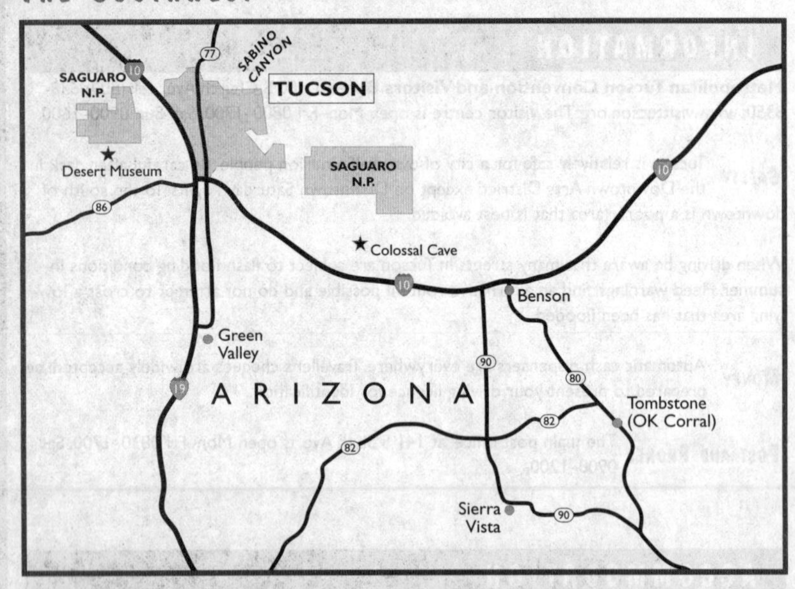

HIGHLIGHTS

Downtown Tucson is quite compact and easily explored on foot. The narrow streets within the historical neighbourhoods are filled with reminders of life in the Old West. A walking tour of the **Tucson Museum of Art**, 140 N Main Ave, will introduce you to the El Presidio Historical District, five historic properties that house many of the museum's permanent collections: the Fish House, Steven's House, Corbett House, Manning House and La Casa Codova were all built in the 19th century.

Old Town Artisans, 201 N Court Ave, tel: (520) 623-6024, is a historic 1850s adobe building, housing shops and a restaurant. Just north of here was where Tucson's élite built their homes; still fascinating to stroll by.

Between downtown and the university district you will find **Fourth Avenue** and its eclectic collection of shops. More than 100 shops, galleries and restaurants are nestled into buildings from the 19th century.

The University of Arizona is home to the **Arizona State Museum**, the **Flandrau Science Center and Planetarium** and the **Center for Creative Photography**. If you've ever yearned to see an Ansel Adams or Harry Callahan original photograph, this is the place.

BEYOND THE CITY About 25 minutes from downtown, 'Old Tucson Studios' was built as a set for the 1939 epic western *Arizona*. Today, **Old Tucson Studios**, 201 S Kinney Rd, is a working studio and theme-park recreation of an 1880s frontier town. Take Speedway Blvd west of I-10 over scenic Gates Pass and through Tucson Mountain Park. The road ends at Kinney Rd. Turn south, and Old Tucson is about ¼ mile on. $$$, tel: (520) 883-0100; open daily 1000–1800.

South-east, along Old Spanish Trail, lies **Saguaro National Park**. The saguaro cactus, the 'monarch of the desert', is found only here in the Sonoran Desert, and the impressive stand of the saguaro gives a prehistoric feel to the landscape. You can picnic, photograph or hike within the park; tel: (520) 733-5100.

From 5900 N Sabino Canyon Rd you can take a breathtaking tram ride up the 3.8 mile **Sabino Canyon**. The tram stops at nine locations, allowing time to get off and explore. If you have limited time, the Phone Line Trail is good even if you have only an hour before you must go back. $, tel: (520) 749-2861. Open daily dawn–dusk; the tram operates 0900–1600.

STARGAZING The climate and terrain around Tucson combine to provide ideal stargazing conditions. Kitt Peak Observatory, Fred Whipple Observatory on Mount Hopkins, Vatican Observatory (yes, the scientists from Rome are all practising Jesuit priests), and the University of Arizona's facilities are all nearby. Stellar research is so important to the area that Tucson even passed a city ordinance to limit light pollution.

The **Kitt Peak National Observatory**, 56 miles west of Tucson on Route 86, has the greatest concentration of telescopes for stellar, solar and planetary research in the world. Guided tours are held daily, and Kitt Peak also offers an evening of stargazing beginning at sunset, including dinner, that lasts 3 hours. Reservations are required; $$$$+; tel: (520) 318-8726.

Skywatchers Inn in the grounds of the private Vega-Bray Observatory offers not only a bed for the night but a blanket of stars. The observatory's telescopes can be rented for individual use, or you can join an astronomer-assisted programme. (With sufficient notice, Dr Vega can arrange transfer from the Amtrak station.) $$$ (including full breakfast); 420 S Essex Lane, Benson (between Tucson and Tombstone); tel: (520) 745-2390; www.skywatchersinn.com.

NIGHTLIFE

Do not let the preoccupation with history and astronomy lead you to think that Tucson ignores the arts! There are over 215 arts groups and organisations and over 35 galleries in the city. Add to that its own symphony, ballet, opera and theatre companies and you will understand why Tucson has been dubbed a mini-mecca for the arts.

The first and third Sat of each month Tucson throws a party – Downtown Saturday Night. It's part of the Tucson Arts District's efforts to show off downtown's many amenities. Street bands, street vendors and performance artists enhance the existing array of shops, cafés and galleries. It's free, and great for people-watching.

DAY TRIP

Tombstone, 'the town too tough to die', lies 65 miles south-east of Tucson. Most famous for the Gunfight at the OK Corral, Tombstone retains all the old charm of its Wild West heritage, with frontier architecture and raised wooden sidewalks. Take a stagecoach tour of the historic district to get an overview of the OK Corral, Bird Cage Saloon and Museum of the West.

TOMBSTONE GUNFIRE

Films such as *High Noon* and *Gunfight at the OK Corral* have painted a picture of the 'Old West' that has endured for decades. The real gunfight took place on 26 October 1881 in downtown Tombstone, Arizona, then a town of 15,000 people. Even the name of the cemetery, Boothill, evokes the image.

The OK Corral was not a corral at all but rather a 15-ft-wide strip of land between two buildings near the corner of Fourth and Fremont Streets. When the outlaw Clanton Gang announced that they would come to Tombstone to kill law men Wyatt Earp, his brothers Virgil and Morgan and the notorious 'Doc' Holliday, Earp and his deputies stayed to meet them, ending in the deaths of gang members Billy Clanton and Tom and Frank McLaury.

Look for re-enactors who advertise hangings and gunfights.

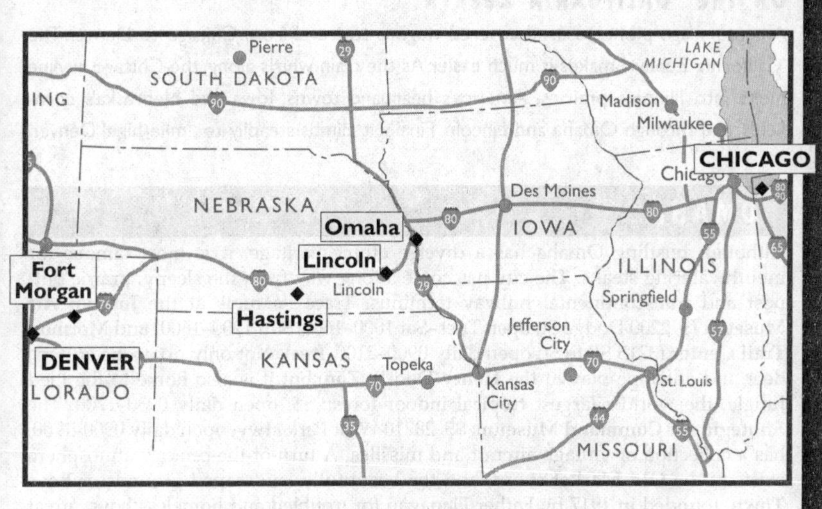

CHICAGO — DENVER

OTT Tables 342/781

Service	Bus	Rail	Bus	Bus
Days of operation	Daily	Daily	Daily	Daily
Special notes		A		
Chicago d.	0630	1350	2145	....
Omaha d.	2045	2239	0900	1615
Lincoln d.	2150	0029	1020	1725
Hastings d.	|	0202	|	....
Fort Morgan d.	0440	0520	1845	....
Denver d.	0600	0730	2000	....

Special notes:
A–The California Zephyr. This train has sleepers and a dining car available. All journeys should be reserved in advance.

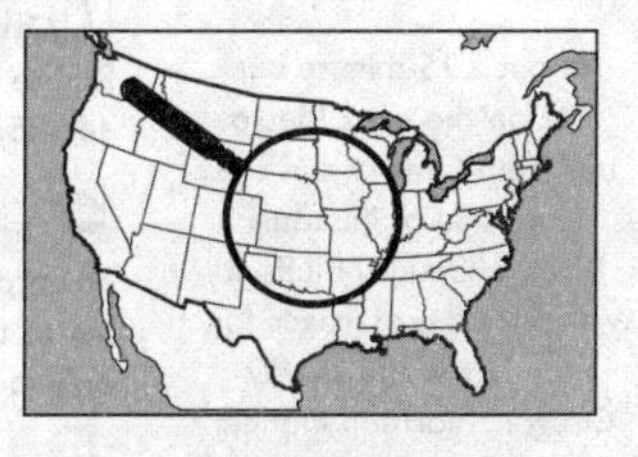

Notes

The 'California Zephyr' arrives at Omaha at 2219.

ON THE 'CALIFORNIA ZEPHYR'

A century ago pioneers used covered wagons to travel from Chicago to Denver. The 'California Zephyr' makes it much easier. As the train whirls along, the Chicago skyline melts into Illinois's prairies, America's heartland towns, Iowa and Nebraska's cornfields, and through Omaha and Lincoln. Finally it climbs steadily to 'mile-high' Denver.

OMAHA

Although bustling Omaha has a diverse ethnic heritage, it is most famous for mouthwatering steaks. The city has come a long way from the sleepy, prairie outpost and transcontinental railway terminus. Trace its roots at the **Joselyn Art Museum** ($, 2200 Dodge St; open Tues–Sat 1000–1600, Sun 1200–1600) and **Mormon Trail Center** (3215 State St; open daily 0900–2100, free). Not only do exotic critters, deer and antelope play at the **Henry Doorly Zoo**, but it is also home to the Lied Jungle, the world's largest tropical indoor forest: $$, open daily 0930–1700. The **Strategic Air Command Museum**: $$, 28210 West Park Hwy, open daily 0900–1700, has a collection of vintage aircraft and missiles. A turn-of-the-century atmosphere exists at the **Old Market** shops, and the beautifully landscaped grounds of **Boys Town**, founded in 1917 by Father Flanagan for troubled and homeless boys, are at 138th and Dodge Sts; open daily 0800–1630.

About a 15-minute bus ride on the no. 2 Metro bus from Omaha, and the Iowa side of Missouri River, is Council Bluffs. It was once a crossroads for the Lewis and Clark, Oregon, Mormon Pioneer and California Trails; crowds nowadays migrate to the gaming tables of its three casinos.

i **Omaha Convention and Visitors Bureau**, 6800 Mercy Rd Ste 202; tel: (402) 444-4660 or (800) 332-1819; fax: (402) 444-4511; www.visitomaha.com.

The Amtrak station, at 9th and Pacific, is a mile from downtown. Metro Area Transit schedules are available here, but as the train arrives in the middle of the night, taxis are the only means of transport from the station.

Best Western Metro Inn $$$ 3537 W Broadway.
Hampton Inn-Central $$$ 301 S 72nd St.
Holiday Inn $$$ 3321 S 72nd St.

Gorats $$$ 49th and Center Sts; tel: (402) 551-3733.
Johnny's Café $$$ 4702 S 27th St; tel: (402) 731-4774.
Adjacent to this café are remnants of the old stockyards.

LINCOLN

Nebraska's capital shares much of its history with Omaha. Its crowning glory is the **Capitol** at 15th and K Sts, with its 400 ft gold dome: mosaics, marble and murals depicting Nebraska's history blanket almost every part of its interior. Entrance is free. Also free: a three-dimensional **brick train mural** on the wall at Haymarket and Iron Horse Park; **restored warehouses** with speciality shops and microbrewery (9th and P Sts), and the funky **Sheldon Museum and Sculpture Garden** (12th and R Sts). The new **Lincoln Children's Museum** ($$, 1420 P St; open Sun–Mon 1300–1700, Tues–Sat 1000–1700) presents some exciting learning exhibits, including Prairie Dog Town, the 'Big Splash' and the Sky High Airport.

The most interesting attractions are in Nebraska. For information, tel: (800) 228-4307 or visit www.visitnebraska.org. One quirky sight en route, though, is in Iowa: Burlington's 275-foot Snake Alley is considered to be the crookedest street in the world.

i **Lincoln CVB**; tel: (402)434-5335 or (800) 423-8212; www.lincoln.org. The Amtrak station is at 7th and P Sts, and the **Visitors Center**, which has public transport timetables (StarTran) is on the other side of the building; tel: (402) 476-1234.

Cornhusker $$$$ 333 S 13th St; tel: (800)793-7474.
Holiday Inn $$$$ 13th and M Sts; tel: (800) 405-4329. Walking distance from the station.

Valentine's Pizza $$ Local chain with four locations in town. Try the runzas, spices, ground beef, cabbage and onions baked inside homemade bread, a Nebraskan speciality.
Billy's Restaurant $$$ 1301 H St. One of Lincoln's finest, named after its native son William Jennings Bryan.
The Green Mill $$$ at the Holiday Inn (see above). Has some of the best food in town.

HASTINGS

This little town has a great museum with an IMAX® cinema, planetarium, whooping cranes and a large exhibit on Edwin Perkins, inventor of Kool Aid drinks. Another Hastings speciality, Eileen's Colossal Cookies, gives Mrs Fields competition.

i **Adams County Convention and Visitors Center**, tel: (800) 967-2189; www.visithastingsnebraska.com.

FORT MORGAN

Fort Morgan Museum commemorates the life of big band leader Glen Miller, who spent his youth here. **Pawnee National Grassland**, about 50 miles north, has abundant wildlife and two huge buttes that erupt from shimmering grass-filled flatlands.

i Fort Morgan Chamber of Commerce, tel: (800) 354-8660; www.fortmorganchamber.org.

WHERE NEXT?

After Denver (see p. 414), the 'California Zephyr' snakes through the Rockies and across northern California to San Francisco (see p. 426).

DENVER

The Mile High City is dwarfed by the Rocky Mountains but stands out in history as one of the main gold-rush centres of the 1860s. In fact, it was the first spot where small quantities of gold were discovered in the Colorado River. Back in those days, the town buzzed with fickle fortune-seekers. As it turned out, there was very little gold in Denver itself, and they left immediately when word came of a massive gold strike in Central City. Silver in the mountains caused the town to prosper again.

Nowadays Denver is both welcoming and enjoyable, a cosmopolitan city with a fine choice of recreational and cultural activities. Downtown Denver is formed from a regimental grid of tightly packed streets, and Lo Do, or Lower Downtown, is a focus for shops, bars and cafés. To one side of the Civic Center Park, the State Capitol provides a stunning view of the Rockies, and to the other side the Denver Art Museum and the Colorado History Museum are two of the area's finest. Denver is not without its more curious attractions either: the Molly Brown House was home to 'unsinkable' Molly Brown, famous for surviving the *Titanic*, and Buffalo Bill's grave and museum at Lookout Mountain, in nearby Golden, mark the final resting place of the famous showman William Cody.

MUST SEE/DO IN DENVER:

See the State Capitol, copy of the one in Washington DC

Visit the 'unsinkable' Molly Brown's House

Stroll through the historic district of 'Lo Do', choose somewhere to eat

Go to Lookout Mountain and see Buffalo Bill's grave

Catch the Colorado Rockies Baseball team at Coors Field

See a rock concert at the stunning outdoor amphitheatre at Red Rock

Get out of town into the mountains

Take the train from Union Station and spend the day skiing

GETTING THERE AND GETTING AROUND

Amtrak trains arrive on the north-west side of Denver, at Union Station on Wynkoop St. Regular free buses run up and down 16th St pedestrian mall, one block away from the station, through the downtown area. There is also a tram line which runs for 5 miles linking downtown and Broadway.

INFORMATION

Denver Visitor Information Centers, tel: (303) 892-1505 or toll free (800) 2DENVER, www.denver.org, are at three locations: Denver International Airport main terminal, 918 16th St (Downtown) and Cherry Creek Shopping Center at the information booth.

SAFETY Denver is generally safe and friendly, but as with any other large city, take the usual common-sense precautions, such as not straying out of the well-lit downtown area at night. In case of emergency, the Denver Police Department is at 1331 Cherokee St, tel: (303) 640-2011. Denver also has a large Department of Safety, with an information service, tel: (303) 640-5356.

MONEY Travelex has a foreign exchange office at 299 Detroit St.

POST AND PHONES A conveniently-located post office, fairly close to the State Capitol building is 8275 E 11th Ave, tel: (303) 377-1016. Alternatively, try 1823 Stout St, or 951 20th St.

ACCOMMODATION

There is plenty of accommodation in Denver, ranging from budget hostels and historic B&Bs to freeway motels and luxury hotels.

Adam's Mark Hotel $$$$ 1550 Court Place; tel: (303) 626-2543, www.adamsmark.com. Vast, luxurious establishment right in the centre of town.

Hostel of The Rockies $ 1530 Downing St; tel: (303) 861-7777, www.hiayh.org. Clean and cozy accommodation just north of downtown. Bus and train pick-ups.

Melbourne Hostel $ 607 22nd St; tel: (303) 292-6386, www.denverhostel,com. Clean, comfortable and secure; six blocks to the bus station.

Queen Anne Inn $$ 2147 Tremont Place; tel: (303) 296-6666, www.queenannebnb.com. With 14 rooms and 4 suites, this Victorian-themed downtown lodging exemplifies the more elegant American version of the bed and breakfast idea.

FOOD AND DRINK

Denver has many themed Western steak and barbecue places, as well as many cosmopolitan restaurants. Try the Larimer Square Lo Do area for a wide selection, or some of the city's brewpubs for good quality meals.

Josephina's $$$ 1433 Larimer St; tel: (303) 623-6939, www.josephinas.com. Lively Italian restaurant with adjoining bar.

Tommy Tsunami's $$ 1432 Market St; tel: (303) 534-5050. Oriental cuisine, with trendy sushi and Thai.

St Mark's Coffeehouse $ 1416 Market St; tel: (303) 446-2925. Small but popular café good for cheap snacks and drinks.

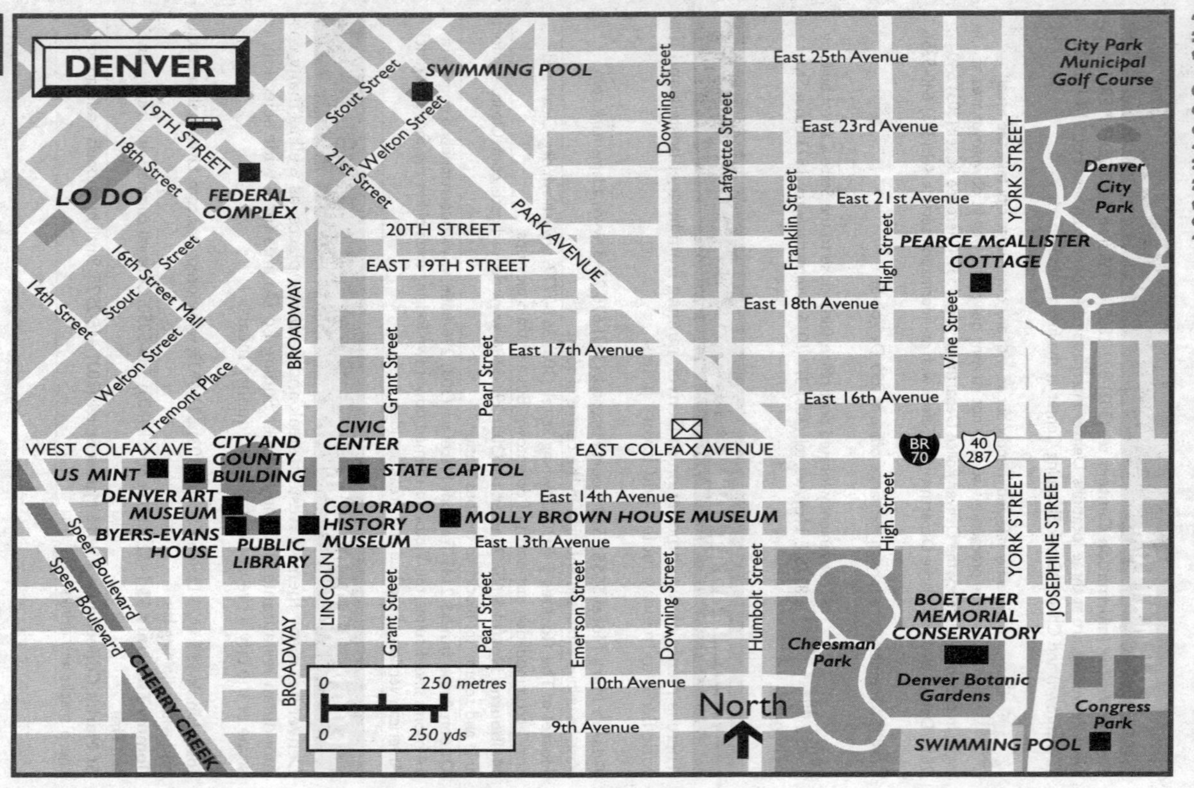
DENVER
SWIMMING POOL
East 25th Avenue
City Park Municipal Golf Course
Stout Street
19TH STREET
Welton Street
21st Street
Downing Street
Lafayette Street
East 23rd Avenue
YORK STREET
Denver City Park
18th Street
LO DO
FEDERAL COMPLEX
PARK AVENUE
Franklin Street
East 21st Avenue
High Street
PEARCE McALLISTER COTTAGE
20TH STREET
EAST 19TH STREET
16th Street Mall
Stout Street
14th Street
East 18th Avenue
Vine Street
BROADWAY
Grant Street
Pearl Street
East 17th Avenue
Welton Street
Tremont Place
East 16th Avenue
WEST COLFAX AVE
CITY AND COUNTY BUILDING
CIVIC CENTER
EAST COLFAX AVENUE
BR 70
40 287
US MINT
STATE CAPITOL
DENVER ART MUSEUM
East 14th Avenue
COLORADO HISTORY MUSEUM
MOLLY BROWN HOUSE MUSEUM
BYERS-EVANS HOUSE
PUBLIC LIBRARY
East 13th Avenue
JOSEPHINE STREET
Speer Boulevard
LINCOLN
Emerson Street
Humbolt Street
BOETCHER MEMORIAL CONSERVATORY
Cheesman Park
CHERRY CREEK
0 250 metres
0 250 yds
10th Avenue
Denver Botanic Gardens
North
9th Avenue
Congress Park

HIGHLIGHTS

Standing proudly marking the centre of Denver is the **State Capitol** with its bright golden dome. Sited between Broadway and E Colfax Ave, it is a copy of the one in Washington DC. For a 'mile high' view of the stunning Rocky Mountains, climb to the thirteenth step, which is exactly one mile above sea level. Inside, free 45-minute tours are held every half hour Mon–Fri 0900–1530 June–Aug, 0915–1430 Sept–Dec, 0900–1430 rest of the year; tel: (303) 866-2604.

Mixed among the offices and shops of downtown Denver are some delightful original Victorian buildings, each with its own fascinating history. **Molly Brown House Museum** was the home of an extraordinary survivor of the *Titanic*, who went on to become a suffragette and then ran for senator. Pictures taken in 1910 were used to restore the home with original family possessions and replicas. $, 1340 Pennsylvania Ave; tel: (303) 832-4092, www.mollybrown.org. Open Tues-Sat 1000–1530, Sun 1200–1530. Also open Mon 1000–1530 June–Aug.

The two namesakes of **Byers–Evans House**, John Evans and William Byers, were instrumental figures in the early growth of Denver. Byers was publisher of the *Rocky Mountain News* and Evans was Colorado's second territorial governor. They both worked tirelessly to ensure that the railway came to the city. The house was originally the property of Byers, but was sold to Evans's son in 1889. Today it contains most of the original elegant furnishings, and a tour of the house commences with a short film about the careers of these successful men. $, 1310 Bannock St; tel: (303) 620-4933. Open Tues- Sun 1100–1500.

At 320 W Colfax Ave is the **US Mint.** For security reasons, tours are offered on a limited basis only, tel: (303) 405-4761, recorded message: (303) 405-4765, or www.usmint.gov for details. In the meantime, a gift shop offers souvenirs and more information on the presses, where millions of new coins are minted before they are sorted, counted and bagged. Underneath the mint is the National Treasure of $100 million in solid gold bars, hidden securely in the basement behind steel framework. Don't get too many ideas, though – outside the mint machine-gun turrets still guard, left over from when they were set up in the Depression.

THE LEGEND OF BUFFALO BILL

William F Cody was a true character of the Wild West. Better known as Buffalo Bill for the thousands of buffalo that he killed, Cody became a national hero as a pony express rider, army scout and showman. Legend has it that early in his life he asked to be buried in Cody, but that its rich neighbour Denver 'stole' his body to bury it on Lookout Mountain. It is at this site today, above the Coors brewery, where you can find his grave and a modern museum alongside. The mountain affords some impressive views, and the museum displays buffalo rifles, clothing and Native American artwork.

THRILLS AND SPILLS

On the western edge of the city the **Six Flags Elitch Gardens theme park** provides entertainment for children and adults alike, and has an extensive water park. Open daily 1000–2200 June–Aug (check for operating hours at other times of the year, tel: (303) 595-4368). It is surprisingly close to the city, and can be reached either by a bike path along Cherry Creek or on the Cultural Connections Trolley. The park has some scary rides, the Tower of Doom, a freefall vertical drop of 70 ft, being a particular favourite.

Denver also has a wealth of museums. The **Denver Art Museum** in Civic Center Park holds examples of Native American craftwork and pre-Columbian art, with many pieces by the Plains and Hopi tribes; $, open Tues–Sat 1000–1700, except Wed 1000–2100, Sun 1200–1700. At 1300 Broadway, the **Colorado History Museum** has several dioramas in the lower galleries depicting historical scenes, including pictures of the Anasazi of Mesa Verde, and of trappers meeting with Indians at a 'Wilderness Fair'. $, open Mon–Sat 1000–1630, Sun 1200–1630.

Two or three miles east of central Denver, between 17th and 23rd Aves and York St and Colorado Blvd, en route to the airport, is City Park. Here is undoubtedly the cream of the museums, the inventive **Denver Museum of Nature & Science** ($) 2001 Colorado Blvd; tel: (303) 322-7009, www.dmns.org, open 0900–1700 daily. It is internationally recognised for its travelling exhibits and scientific research programmes, and has over 90 wildlife habitat dioramas. Take a peek at the Watering Hole exhibit in the Botswana African Hall, or sample another extreme of the globe at the Alaskan exhibit. Entering the Hall of Life you will receive a 'life card', which will activate various interactive displays showing how life begins. In the Dinosaur Hall, fossils draw you back to the times of the stegosaurus, tyrannosaurus rex and friends. The IMAX® theatre adds to the sense of adventure – it creates a breathtaking illusion of trips around the world, including stunning shots of the Grand Canyon and Stonehenge. Elsewhere in this large museum, the Planetarium shows displays of the night sky through the seasons.

A BASEBALL FRENZY

Baseball is an American institution and is one of the cheapest sports to watch (usually well under $15 for a seat). The pitcher begins play when he throws the ball at lightning speed towards the catcher, who crouches behind 'home plate'. A batter from the opposing team, positioned before home plate, then tries to intercept the ball and hit it into 'fair territory'. With a successful hit the batter races through the sequence of bases, set 90 ft apart at the corners of a diamond, before the opposing team can touch the base or runner with the ball (the game has echoes of rounders and cricket). There are nine players on each side, who bat in rotation; games usually last two to three hours and are kept lively by the incessant chanting, singing and waving from the enthusiastic crowd.

Denver's own major league baseball team is the Colorado Rockies, whose home is Coors Field, 2001 Blake St, a 50,000-seat stadium opened in 1995. For ticket information, tel: (303) ROCKIES.

Also in City Park is **Denver Zoo**, well on the way to becoming a first-class natural environment park. Animals are housed in their natural habitats, rather than in traditional cages. $, tel: (303) 376-4800. Open daily Apr–Sept 0900-1700, Oct–Mar 1000-1600. Visitors are greeted by a simulated African savannah scene, dotted with giraffes, zebras and warthogs; there are also two okapis, a species rarely seen in North America. You cannot avoid Bear Mountain, which offers all the home comforts that Grizzly and Himalayan Black Bears need. The zoo also has a large selection of primates, a tantalising Tropical Discovery feature and an Australian wildlife exhibit. Check feeding times when you arrive at the park. There is a Zooliner train for non-stop guided tours of the zoo's 76 acres.

Zoo lovers will enjoy the **Ocean Journey Aquarium**, a world-class aquarium that covers the areas from the continental divide in Colorado to Mexico's Sea or Cortez, and the Indonesian rainforest to the Pacific Ocean. $, 700 Water St, tel: (303) 561-4465, www.oceanjourney.org.

NIGHTLIFE

At night, the brewpubs in Lo Do (Lower Downtown) open up and the city centre becomes a hive of activity. At **Breckenridge Brewery**, 2220 Blake St, you can watch the beers being brewed on site as you drink. Nearby **El Chapultepec**, 20th and Market St, is a tiny, popular venue, where there is nightly live jazz and the occasional visit from a big name.

Twelve miles west of Denver is **Red Rocks Amphitheater**, which has been the setting for thousands of rock and classical concerts. A huge new state-of-the-art Visitor Center has just opened for those tourists who'd like to see the park during the day.

THE BEST POWDER SNOW IN THE WORLD

Averaging 20 or 30 ft of snow and 300 days of sunshine a year, Colorado has a total of 27 ski areas and a ski season that runs from end Nov to mid-Apr. Two of the most popular resorts are Aspen and Vail: celebrities and film stars flock to enjoy the steep, lengthy runs and powder snow that have made the slopes world famous. Fashionable **Aspen** has four mountains dedicated to skiing which cater for all grades of skier, from Aerobic Avenue for the fitter enthusiasts to the beginners' favourite, Snowmass. **Vail**, king of the North American ski hills, also has a special park for snowboarders (see also p. 424).

DAY TRIPS

Travelling around Colorado is easy: many bus services link Denver airport to the most popular resorts, including **Aspen**, **Colorado Springs**, **Rocky Mountain National Park** (see p. 425) and **Vail**. Book them as far in advance as possible: for information on Denver transport check the following: for Aspen and Vail: Colorado Mountain Express, tel: (800) 525-6363, www.cmex.com; for Colorado Springs (and connections to most other parts of the country): Greyhound, tel: (800) 231-2222. There is no public transport to Rocky Mountain National Park, but private companies offer guided and non-guided ways to the park: phone General Park Information, tel: (970) 586-1333 for details.

For a one-day ski trip catch the morning Ski Train, tel: (303) 296-4754, from Union Station in Lo Do at 1701 Wynkoop St to **Winter Park** for a selection of slopes varying in difficulty, or to pick up the basics at the innovative Discovery/Learn-to-Ski Park.

COLORADO SPRINGS

Colorado Springs was originally developed as a vacation spot in 1871 by the railway tycoon William Jackson Palmer. Nowadays it is the most popular city in south-east Colorado and provides excellent access to the gold mining country around. There are a number of cheap flights from Denver International Airport, or you can use the Greyhound Bus service, which stops downtown at 327 Weber St. On the western edge of the city, the amazing **Garden of the Gods** is a twisted park of red sandstone rockery which has been eroded into finely balanced overhangs, pinnacles and pedestals. Entry to the site is free. Open 0500–2300 May–Oct, 0500–2100 rest of the year. Colorado Springs sits at the foot of **Pikes Peak**. Ride up to the summit, at 14,110 ft, on the cog railway from late April to December (see p. 422).

CRIPPLE CREEK

Cripple Creek, named after a calf that broke its leg trying to jump over a tumbling stream, was a gold camp which rests in a grim volcanic bowl just by Pikes Peak. In 1890, with the discovery of gold, Cripple Creek became a boom town. In its heyday it boasted two opera houses, a stock exchange, 75 saloons, eight newspapers and a large variety of brothels. Nowadays visitors still try to strike it rich at Cripple Creek's gambling casinos, but its most famous brothel is now the Homestead Museum. Ride the **Cripple Creek and Victor Narrow Gauge Railroad** into the heart of the gold mining district, $, open daily 0930–1730 (June–mid-Oct); or descend 1000 ft underground into the **Molly Kathleen Mine** ($) to learn what the rush was all about; open daily 0900–1700 May–Oct. Take your own walk into the past or join a **Ghost Walk Tour** of Cripple Creek or Mount Pisgah Cemetery Tour ($).

i **The Colorado Springs Convention and Visitors Bureau**, 515 S Cascade; tel: (719) 635-7506, www.coloradospringstravel.com, is open Mon–Fri 0830–1700, and has details of hiking trails. For tours and maps of Cripple Creek check out the **Cripple Creek Welcome Center**, 5th St and Bennett Ave; tel: (877) 858-GOLD; www.cripple-creek.co.us.

WHERE NEXT?

The Colorado Driving Loop (see p. 421) explores more of the state's dramatic landscape. Denver is a major stop on the 'California Zephyr' which runs westwards to San Francisco or east to Chicago and navigates the Rockies by day (see pp. 411 and 543).

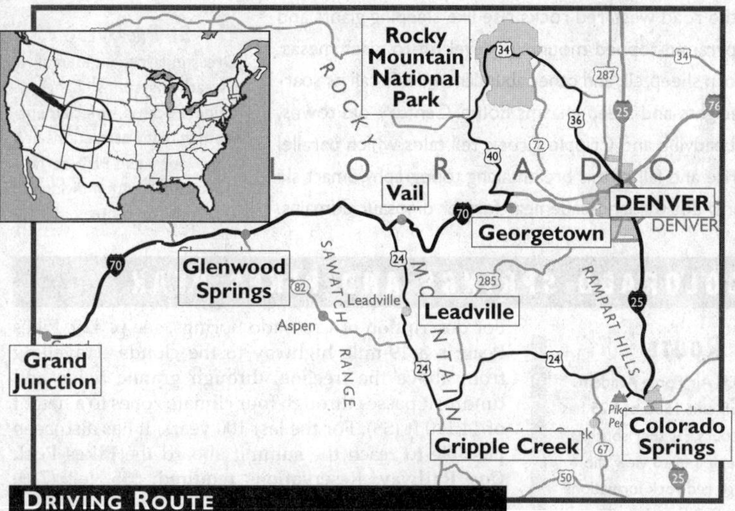

DRIVING ROUTE

From Denver, take I-25 south to Colorado Springs. 54 miles

Follow Rte 24 to the south entrance of Pikes Peak (toll road). 62 miles

Return to Hwy 24 to Hwy 67, south to Cripple Creek. 90 miles

Double back on Hwy 67 to Hwy 24 and follow it west and north, along the Top of the Rockies Scenic Byway, to Leadville. 191 miles

Continue north on Hwy 24 from Leadville to I-70. 224 miles

Turn west through Glenwood Springs to Grand Junction. 370 miles

Go east on I-70 past Vail through the Eisenhower Tunnel to Georgetown. 426 miles

Continue east, then north on Hwys 40 and 34, around Rocky Mountain National Park to Hwy 36. 489 miles

Follow Hwy 36 south to Denver. 549 miles

DENVER — GRAND JUNCTION

OTT Tables 342/786/820/831

Service	Bus	Rail	Bus	Bus	Bus
Days of operation	Daily	Daily	Daily	Daily	Daily
Special notes	A	B		C	
Denver d.	0545	0805	0815	0900	1815
Colorado Springs d.	0745	|	|	|	|
Vail d.	....	|	1025	|	2020
Glenwood Springs d.	....	1353	1150	|	2140
Grand Junction a.	....	1610	1325	1320	2315

Special notes:

A–Additional trips: 0700, 0715, 1100, 1600, 1730, 2320.

B–The California Zephyr. This train has sleepers and a dining car available. All journeys should be reserved in advance.

C–Additional trip: 0001.

The Southwest

On the road west, red rocks rise like sleeping giants and the pyramid-topped mountains level off to giant mesas. Bighorn sheep, elk and other abundant wildlife call its soaring heights and steep chasms home. Century-old towns, like Leadville and Cripple Creek, tell tales which parallel the rise and fall of this breathtaking topography. Smart ski resorts dot the landscape near former dinosaur domains.

Be Prepared

Dress in layers – mountain weather systems change rapidly. Because of inclement weather, many attractions are only open end May–early Oct; check with individual visitor centres.

COLORADO SPRINGS AND PIKES PEAK

En Route

The US Air Force Academy just off exit 156B of I-25 has free tours. Further south, take exit 146 to view the strange red rock formations at the Garden of the Gods (also free).

After Colorado Springs, possible stops along the way include the Anasazi Cliff Dwellings at Manitou Springs ($$) and the Cave of the Winds ($$).

For description of Colorado Springs, see p. 420. Pikes Peak is a 19-mile highway to the clouds. Travelling from above the treeline, through granite fields and tundra, it passes through four climate zones to a height of 14,110 ft ($$). For the last 100 years, it has also been possible to reach the summit aboard the **Pikes Peak Cog Railway**. Reservations required; $$$, tel: (719) 685-5401; www.pikes-peak.com.

CRIPPLE CREEK

A detour south along Hwy 67 will take you to the old gold-mining town of Cripple Creek. Casinos are now the main game in town since gambling was legalised here a decade ago (see p. 420).

LEADVILLE

Another boom town, Leadville certainly has had its ups and downs. At 10,152 ft above sea level, it is the highest incorporated town in the USA. In the 1860s, when over $5 million of gold was extracted from the nearby California Gulch, it became a town of high crime and high rollers. Gunman-gamblers like Bat Masterson, Wyatt Earp and Doc Holliday came here to ply their trade. J J Brown, husband of 'the unsinkable' Molly, made his fortune from the mines, and Meyer Guggenheim maintained a residence here. The downs came when the minerals ran out. Now Leadville is a working man's town with only memories of its glory days. The **National Mining Hall of Fame and Museum**, $, 120 W 9th St, showcases Leadville's mining past. **The National Historic District** and other historic buildings and recreational trails are well worth a visit.

i **Leadville Chamber of Commerce**, tel: (888) LEADVILLE or (888) 532-384553; www.leadvilleusa.com.

The Delaware $$$ 700 Harrison Ave.; tel: (800) 748-2004. Charming century-old hotel echoes Leadville's glory days – Butch Cassidy was once a guest. Breakfast included in cost.

GETTING INTO HOT WATER

Natural springs abound in Colorado, and one of most unassuming and inexpensive resorts is the Cottonwood Hot Springs Inn & Spa (west of Buena Vista which is south of Leadville), tel: (719) 395-6434, www.cottonwood-hot-springs.com. Located almost 9000 ft high yet still nestling at the base of a mountain, this place has a real 1960s flavour. Access fees are low (a dip in the communal pool costs $15 in summer, $10 in the winter) and therapies are offered at reasonable cost. Private and dorm rooms are available.

GLENWOOD SPRINGS

The hot springs that gave this town its name are welcome after a strenuous hike. Soak away aches and pains in the **Glenwood Springs Hot Springs Pools**, $$, N River St; tel: (800) 537-7946; open daily 0730–2200 in summer; 0900–2200 in winter. If that is not enough, visit **Yampah Spa**, $$; tel (970) 945-0667 - their vapour caves were once a Ute Indian hot spot. There are also full spa services - their herbal wraps ($$$) will make you feel like a human burrito. Inside Glenwood's **Fairy Caves**, delicate crystal formations adorn limestone walls. $$, tel: (970) 945-6511; open late May–early Sept; reservations required.

Visitor Centre at 1102 Grand Ave; tel: (970) 945 6589; or try www.glenwoodguide.com.

Ramada Inn and Suites $$$–$$$$, exit 16 of I-70; tel: (888) 4GLENWOOD. Lovely rooms and friendly atmosphere, with continental breakfast.

GRAND JUNCTION

There are diverse attractions hidden in the valley of the Grand Junction area, from award-winning wineries (near Hwy 6 in Palisade) to dinosaur remains. The **Dinosaur Journey Museum** ($) in Fruita (Rte 6) chronicles history from 4.5 billion years ago to moon rocks. Huge creatures move and moan as hands-on exhibits familiarise kids with the extinct giants. The whimsical variety of Main Street's **Art on the Corner** sculpture in Grand Junction itself runs the gamut from bike-riding dinosaurs to a huge junk-crafted motorcycle.

The big draw of the region, however, is its natural beauty. From the Colorado River's Grand Valley, **Rim Rock Drive** (Rte 340) ascends the high country of **Colorado National Monument** ($$$). Its 23-mile journey around steep canyons and red rock sculptures is reminiscent of both the Grand Canyon (see p. 435) and Bryce national parks. Dinosaur fossils were found on Dinosaur Hill (Rte 340), so undiscovered treasure may still await any hiker or cyclist.

The **Grand Mesa Scenic and Historic Byway** (exit 46 from I-70) curves alongside imposing rock formations, then gradually ascends to the world's largest table mountain. Snow, trails and 300 lakes cover Grand Mesa's 10,839 ft summit.

WHERE NEXT?

If you want to head west from Grand Junction instead of returning to Denver, it is 100 miles to Arches National Park (see Southern Utah National Parks, p. 510). Take I-70 for 80 miles to Crescent Junction, then head south along Hwy 191.

i **The Visitor Center** is found at I-70 and Horizon Dr., tel: (970) 244-1480. Open daily 0830–1700 (–2000 in summer).

Los Altos B&B $$$–$$$$ 375 Hillview Dr.; tel: (888) 774-0982; www.colorado-bnb.com/losaltos. Perched atop a high mesa, this solitary B&B offers spectacular views, great breakfasts and friendly atmosphere.

The Winery $$$ 642 Main St. Excellent food (dinner only) in an attractive atmosphere.

Crystal Café and Bake Shop $$ 314 Main St. Yummy Portobello mushroom sandwiches with pesto mayonnaise, cinnamon rolls and scones. Friendly service. Open Mon–Sat for breakfast and lunch only.

Rock Slide Brew Pub $$ 401 Main St. Tasty food and beer.

VAIL

Vail is not left out in the cold after the ski season: hikers, mountain bikers and whitewater rafters still populate the area in summer. Within the quaint village itself is the **Ski Museum Hall of Fame**, while the **Betty Ford Alpine Gardens**, near S Frontage Rd, has over 2000 species of native plants; both free. **Gerald Ford Amphitheater**, next to the gardens, hosts music festivals, ballets and free Tues night concerts.

EN ROUTE

The Eisenhower Tunnel penetrates the mountains near the watershed of the Continental Divide. All North American waters and melting snow west of the Divide flow towards the Pacific, and those on the east side flow towards the Atlantic.

Much of Vail's landscape is being lost to million-dollar homes but the sweeping beauty of the Gore Range is unsullied as it unfurls at **Eagle's Nest**. The ride up is via the Vista-Bahn Express chairlift (free; closed late Apr–June).

i **Contact Vail Valley Tourism and Convention Bureau**, 100 E Meadow Dr.; tel: (800) 525-3875; www.visitvail-valley.com for reservations, rafting companies and tourist information.

During spring, summer and fall seasons, many restaurants offer half-price menus.

GEORGETOWN

Past and present merge in Georgetown (exit 228 from I-70). Mining brought money, and the railway from Denver brought the people. It is still the ordinary Western town it was a century ago – that is its charm. Visitors can ride into yesterday aboard the **Georgetown Loop Railroad** which climbs 600 ft on its way to Silver Plume ($$$). Antique shops, boutiques and art galleries are housed within 6th St's renovated Victorian buildings. The furnishings and exhibits in the once-smart **Hotel de Paris** $, at the street's east end, reflect century-old business life. Catch a glimpse of how Georgetown's wealthy lived at **Hamill House**, where original furniture and wallpaper still adorn the rooms; $, 3rd and Argentine Sts. The **Bowman-White House Museum** depicts a middle-class lifestyle; open Sat–Sun 1100–1600 (free). The **Georgetown Energy Museum**, at the east end of 6th St, is within the plant which has powered the town since 1900 (free).

Most attractions operate only late May–early Oct. Over the first two weekends in Dec, an arts and crafts Christmas Market, carollers and holiday foods bring the town back to life.

i For tourist information which has lodging and dining details tel: (800) 472-8230; www.georgetowncolorado.com.

1025 Rose Street $$$. Tasty food at reasonable prices. **Happy Cooker $$** 6th St. Snacks and sandwiches.

ROCKY MOUNTAIN NATIONAL PARK

The park ($$ per car) is a mecca for hikers, bikers and drivers who enjoy stunning scenery. Alpine lakes, steep canyons, tundra, towering mountains, wild flowers and wildlife embellish **Trail Ridge Rd**, a byway traversing the park that has been used for about 10,000 years. Bighorn sheep graze near **Sheep Lakes**. Viewpoints on **Many Parks Curve** reveal mountain meadows vistas, and 2500 ft below Forest Canyon there is a spectacular view of a glacier-chiselled valley. Walk slowly at Rock Cut (altitude 12,110 ft) to **Toll Memorial Mountain Index**. A dazzling 360° view, strange rock formations, tundra and craggy peaks await you.

Lulu City is the site of an old mining town, while the **Moraine Park Museum** offers regional history. The 7-mile **Wild Basin Trail** takes you along the St Vrain Creek, around waterfalls and through spruce forests. Because of extensive road construction, the hikers' paradise **Bear Lake** is only accessible by shuttle. Open June–mid-Sept. Dogs are not permitted on the trails.

i **Rocky Mountain National Park**, Estes Park, CO 80517; tel: (970) 586-1333 or (970) 586-1200. Visit www.nps.gov/romo or www.estesparkresort.com.

DENVER – SAN FRANCISCO

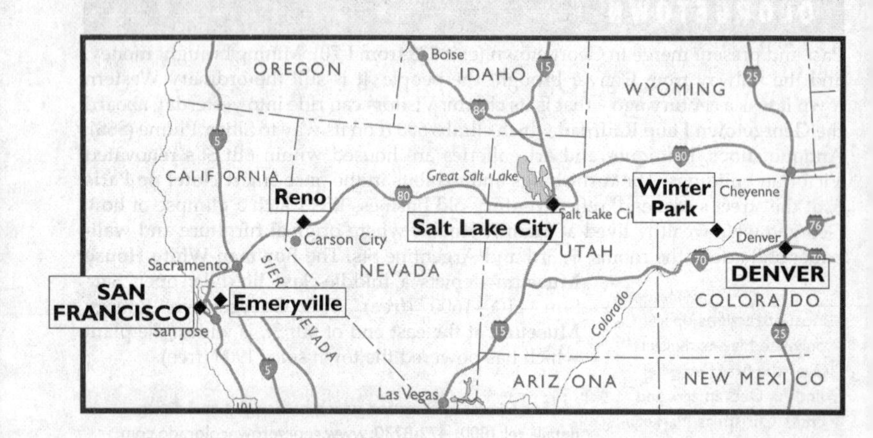

DENVER — SAN FRANCISCO
OTT Tables 342/358/781/851

Service		RAIL	Bus	Bus		RAIL
Days of operation		Daily	Daily	Daily		Daily
Special notes		A				B
Denver	d.	0805	0015	1215	....	....
Winter Park	d.	1007	|	|	....	....
Salt Lake City	d.	2359	1100	2345	....	....
Reno	d.	0914	2040	0745	....	B
Emeryville	d.	1649	|	|	....	B
San Francisco	a.	**1740a**	0140	1255	....	B

Special notes:
A–The California Zephyr. This train has sleepers and a dining car available. All journeys should be reserved in advance.
B–Reno to San Francisco connections available using a combination of Amtrak trains and Thruway buses. See OTT Table 358.
C–Change buses at Salt Lake City.
a–Emeryville to San Francisco (Fisherman's Wharf) connection by Amtrak Thruway bus.

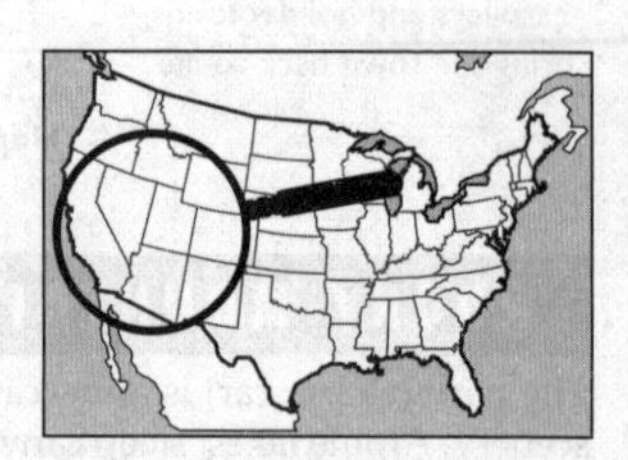

Notes

The train terminates at Emeryville, and Amtrak Thruway buses connect with Oakland and downtown San Francisco.

The Denver and Rio Grande Western railroad also operates a weekend service from Denver to Winter Park Dec–Apr.

ON THE 'CALIFORNIA ZEPHYR'

The western half of the 'California Zephyr' route winds through the glorious mountain and desert scenery of Colorado, Utah, Nevada and California; it's pure joy just to sit and gape at the stunning panorama of the western USA. From Denver, the train wiggles uphill into the Rockies, where the first port of call is the ski centre of Winter Park. Westwards, the train follows the majestic Colorado River before crossing into Utah. Salt Lake City, the prosperous Mormon-built metropolis, is a good place to break the journey. Piling on across the salt flats, the 'Zephyr' slips into the haunting brown hills of Nevada, where the all-absorbing desert maintains a firm grasp on the eyes, all the way to the casinos of Reno. Sierra Nevada peaks loom to the west, and the train rolls through Californian Gold Rush country on its way to Oakland, on San Francisco Bay.

WINTER PARK

Excellent skiing and luxuriant summer hikes are eminently achievable by public transport in the Rockies. The train stops in Fraser, in the hills some 60 miles northwest of Denver, and shuttle buses connect to Winter Park, 5 miles south, and surrounding resorts. Contact the **Winter Park/Fraser Valley Chamber of Commerce**, tel: (800) 903-7275, www.winterpark-info.com, to help plan a visit.

SALT LAKE CITY

Utah's capital is easily the biggest city within a radius of several hundred miles. A relaxed, friendly place founded by independent-minded Mormons in 1847, it has little to detain the average visitor, but those with an interest in the Mormons' history and faith will find plenty of museums and monuments. Its position, at the base of the gorgeous Wasatch Mountains, and its pleasant climate, make it a superb base for nearby ski resorts - part of the reason it was chosen for the 2002 Winter Olympics.

The city centre is compact, with the greatest concentration of sights in Temple Square. This landscaped park contains the city's most noteworthy building, the **Salt Lake Temple**, spiritual heart of the Mormon Church. Only Mormons can go inside, and then only at high ceremonies, but the grandiose stone spires do instil inspiration. Also on the square, the **Mormon Tabernacle** is the domed home of the Mormon Tabernacle Choir, whom you can hear singing on Sun mornings at 0930, or during evening rehearsals (Thur from 2000). For more on the Mormons, visit the **Museum of Church History and Art**, which lays out the trials and travails of these dynamic people. Open Mon–Fri 0900–2100, Sat–Sun 1000–1900; free. Salt Lake City's tallest building, appropriately enough, is the **Latter-day Saints Church Office Building** at 50 E North Temple St, with an observation deck on the 26th floor.

THE MORMONS

The Mormon faith, or the Church of Jesus Christ of Latter-day Saints, has a fascinating history. The church was founded in 1830, when Joseph Smith claims to have discovered a set of golden tablets in upstate New York. From these, he transcribed the Book of Mormon, which the faith holds to be a restoration of the Bible in a purer form. His successor, Brigham Young, set up colonies in New York and further west, but was constantly hounded by more entrenched religions and the government. After a skirmish in St Louis, Young led his flock to the Salt Lake basin, where they established a semi-autonomous territory.

The Mormons are often misunderstood, largely because their services are strictly reserved for church members only, and because many people associate Mormonism with polygamy – Brigham Young had no fewer than 55 wives – though the practice was banned within the church over a century ago. Young Mormon missionaries actively travel the world, and the Mormon trademarks of clean living and a friendly, welcoming spirit endure.

Just north of Temple Square, the **Utah State Capitol**, 400 N State St, is a fine example of Renaissance revival architecture, and contains exhibits on Utah's history. On the edge of town, towards the hills, **This is the Place Heritage Park**, 2601 Sunnyside Ave, reconstructs early Mormon life in the area. $, open Tues–Sat 1100–1700 (Thur until 2000).

SIDE TRIPS

The Great Salt Lake itself, north-west of the city, is the second saltiest reservoir in the world after the Dead Sea. With a car, you can visit the shores at Great Salt Lake State Park, west on I-80, or Antelope Island via I-15N.

Utah sports some of the very best skiing in the world, and Salt Lake City is wonderfully close to the slopes. **Park City** and **Alta**, among others, are within easy striking distance, and the Utah Transit Authority, tel: (801) 262-5626, provides bus service to various resorts in winter.

Visitor Information Center, 90 S West Temple; tel: (801) 521-2822 or (800) 847-5810; open Mon–Fri 0800–1700 (until 1800 in summer), Sat and Sun 0900–1700. A useful web-site to inspect is www.visitsaltlake.org.

The Amtrak station is fairly central, at 320 S Rio Grande St, but as both eastbound and westbound trains arrive at unsocial hours, take a taxi from the station.

Salt Lake City has a good variety of accommodation, but you should book in advance, especially in winter.

Camp VIP camp site is a longish walk from the centre: 1400 W North Temple; tel: (801) 328-0224 or (800) 226-7752.

The Avenues Hostel $ 107 F St; tel: (801) 359-3855 or (888) 884-4752. HI hostel five blocks east of Temple Sq.; can help with bike and ski rental.

Anton Boxrud B&B $$–$$$$ 57 S 600 E St; tel: (801) 363-8035 or (800) 524-5511. Pleasant and just east of Temple Sq.

Peery Hotel $$$ 110 W 300 S St; tel: (801) 521-4300 or (800) 331-0073. Registered historic hotel, completely renovated.

Squatters Pub Brewery $ 147 W Broadway. Salt Lake's premier brew pub.

Martine $–$$ 22 E 100 South. Café and tapas.
Oasis Café $$ 151 S 500 East. Marvellous outdoor vegetarian dining.
Red Iguana $$–$$$ 736 W North Temple. Great authentic Mexican food, appropriate to this part of the Southwest.
Old Salt City Jail Restaurant $$$–$$$$ 460 S 1000 East. In the former city penitentiary; steaks and salad bar a speciality.

RENO

Reno's slogan, 'The Biggest Little City in the World', blazes from a neon arch downtown casino district. Little, but growing rapidly thanks to casinos and commerce, Reno is a mini-Las Vegas. If you're not hitting the casinos, you could take a stroll down the prettily developed central riverfront, or learn more about this rather exotic state in the **Nevada Historical Society Museum**, 1650 N Virginia St, which displays Native American artefacts, pioneer relics, antique furniture, guns and minerals.

SIDE TRIP

Lake Tahoe is one of the playgrounds of the West, sitting at the crook in the California–Nevada border. Only a few miles southwest of Reno, Tahoe's clear, cold waters are rimmed with world-class resorts, and skiing and boating opportunities abound. Reno visitor centre is really helpful in arranging visits.

The **Visitor Center** at 3rd St and Virginia Ave, tel: (888) HIT-RENO, www.visitrenotahoe.com, is great for general information and advice on accommodation.

The Amtrak station is downtown, at 135 East Commericial Row; tel: (800) 872-7245.

There are plenty of central places to stay in all categories along Virginia Ave and Lake St. Casinos offer good room values midweek, but prices jump dramatically at the weekend. The leading light is **El Dorado** $$$–$$$$ 4th St and Virginia Ave; tel: (800) 648-5996.

The local speciality cuisine, oddly enough, is Basque, thanks to generations of Basque shepherds who have settled across Nevada. The best is:
Louis' Basque Corner $$–$$$ 301 4th St.

SIERRA NEVADA AND THE GOLD RUSH

Gold was first discovered in the Sierra Nevada in 1848, prompting a massive surge westwards that turned San Francisco and other cities into frenzied supply stops. Towns popped up overnight as fortune-seekers panned the rivers and bored deep into the hills in search of the precious metal, but the cost of mining rose to such a high that within 20 years most towns had gone bust and were abandoned. Many of these remain as ghost towns today – some restored, some simply faded relics, amid the dry brown Sierra Nevada hills.

Notes

You have to leave the train at Lamy, from where you catch a shuttle van to Santa Fe. Call (800) 871-7145 in advance to arrange collection or drop-off. There is also an Amtrak Thruway bus to Phoenix and the Grand Canyon from Flagstaff. The bus service takes two routes, one via Phoenix and the other via Flagstaff.

LOS ANGELES — SANTA FE

OTT Tables 340/820/855/864

Service		Bus	Bus	Bus	Rail	
Days of operation		Daily	Daily	Daily	Daily	
Special notes		**A**	**A**	**B**	**C**	
Los Angeles	d.	0130	0830	1350	1845	....
Phoenix	d.	0900	1620	2235	|	....
Flagstaff	d.	1240	2000	0205	0501	....
Albuquerque	d.	2035	0630	1120	1255	....
Lamy	a.	|	|	|	1400	....
Santa Fe	a.	2205	0740	1235	**a**	....

Special notes:

A–Change buses at Phoenix and Albuquerque.

B–Change buses at Albuquerque.

C–The Southwest Chief. This train has sleepers and a dining car available. All journeys should be reserved in advance.

a–Lamy to Santa Fe connection by shuttle van. Telephone (800) 871-7145 at least 24 hours in advance to arrange collection.

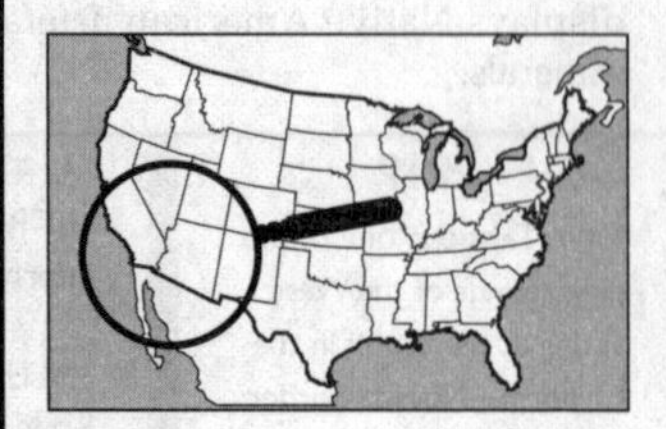

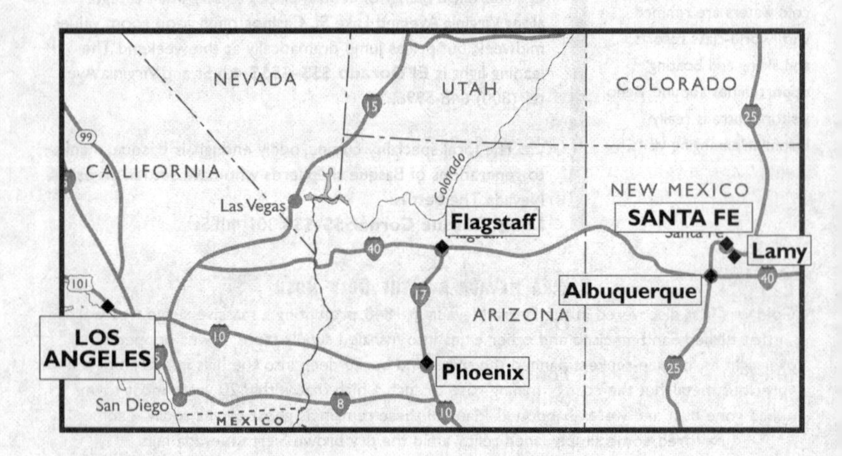

ON THE 'SOUTHWEST CHIEF'

There are some wonderful sights on this journey as it traverses the arid land of Arizona: pueblos hundreds of years old, lava flows, weird geological formations and extraordinary desertscapes. Breathtaking canyons are just a few feet wider than the train. The scenery is no less awesome as you continue eastwards into New Mexico and Santa Fe.

The main stop en route is Flagstaff, to visit the Grand Canyon (p. 435). Take a detour for the day to Phoenix (p. 433) to see the famous America West Arena or enjoy some exclusive shopping in Scottsdale.

FLAGSTAFF

Flagstaff is a university town, a rail and trucking hub, and prosperously dependent upon the tourist trade visiting the Grand Canyon and coming to ski in winter. Historic **Route 66** still wends its way through downtown, where small cafés and bookshops foster a lively music scene at night. Flagstaff's jewel is the **Museum of Northern Arizona**, on Hwy 180. A brightly lit but cool building houses a major collection of doll-size *kachina* figures (fetishes) and an outstanding display of pottery from different archaeological eras, excavated on the Colorado Plateau. Open Wed–Sun 0900–1700; tel: (520) 774-5213.

The **Riordan Mansion State Historic Park**, 409 Riordan Ranch St, is a 40-room home covering 13,000 sq. ft, shared by two families in 1904. It is open for tours; tel: (520) 779-4395. You can also take a tour of the world-famous **Lowell Observatory**, from which Pluto was discovered in 1930; tel: (520) 774-2096; open daily 0900–1700 (summer), 1200–1700 (winter).

The outstanding natural feature of the area is, of course, the Grand Canyon (see p. 435), but the landscape around Flagstaff has other wonders to offer. Snow-capped **Humphrey's Peak**, Arizona's highest point at 12,663 ft, is just north of the city, visible for a hundred miles in any direction. Unexpectedly wild scenery awaits at **Sunset Crater Volcano** and **Wupatki National Monuments**; tel: (602) 556-7042. Black lava is strewn about the one-mile circular trail near a cinder cone which last exploded in 1100 AD. Plan to arrive at the end of the day to see the sun set over the Wupatki ruins (there are several sites along the route), or the Sinagua or Anasazi villages, whose crumbling remains resemble Crusader castles. To the north, on the Navajo Nation reservation, is the **Painted Desert**.

In the **Coconino National Forest** you will see pygmy trees where high altitude and winds have stunted the conifers' growth. En route, as the highway descends to Valle, huge statues of Fred, Barney, Wilma and the rest of the *Flintstones* TV cartoon gang lure visitors into **Bedrock City**.

Flagstaff Visitor Center, One E Route 66 and Beaver St (in the railway depot); tel: (800) 842-7293 or (520) 774-9541; www.flagstaff.az.us. Open daily.

Be warned that because of its proximity to the Grand Canyon, Flagstaff is liable to book up several months in advance. The Grand Canyon Railway office makes bookings.
Grand Canyon International Hostel $ 19 S San Francisco St; tel: (520) 779-9421. Adequate lodgings at budget prices.
Hotel Monte Vista $$$ 100 N San Francisco; tel: (800) 545-3068 or (520) 779-6971. Dates from around 1927, with cosy lobby and moderate rooms.

Flagstaff will always be popular, whether as a stopover for tourists traversing Rte 66, or for those visiting the Grand Canyon; so there is more than enough money to support several upmarket restaurants and some hearty steakhouses.
Black Bart's $$–$$$ 2760 E Buner Ave, tel: 520 779 3142, is a themed Western Steakhouse where the staff amuse you by singing and dancing while you eat. Try their 'Big Ribs'.
Beaver Street Brewery $–$$ 11 S Beaver St, tel: (520) 779-0079. Quirky, quaint and housed in an old supermarket, this microbrewery serves up suds (beer) and some of the best burgers in town.
Alpine Pizza $ 7 N Leroux St, tel: 520 779 4109, serves beer and cheap pizzas, and is a student favourite.

WHERE NEXT?

The 'Southwest Chief' stops at Albuquerque (see p. 402) and Lamy for Santa Fe (see p. 385) before making its long journey across the Midwest to Chicago (see p. 354). Greyhound buses serve Phoenix from Flagstaff (see p. 433) or you can hire a car for the 2-hr journey.

Make no mistake. Phoenix is a tourist town. Its mild winter climate and 300 days of sunshine have lured travellers and health-seekers since the turn of the 20th century. The sixth largest city in the USA is an oasis of golf courses (180 of them) and spas in the south-west desert. Located on the banks of the Salt River, where early Hohokam Indians first settled, Phoenix is hugged by dramatic mountain ranges to the north, south and east. This 'Valley of the Sun', or 'The Valley' as locals call it, is a spectacular setting for a city.

With so many sun-filled days it's no wonder that there are so many outdoor activities and adventures for a metropolitan area. Phoenix is a haven for horseriding, hot-air ballooning and rafting on the Salt River.

If you'd rather spectate than participate, Phoenix is among a handful of cities in the USA to have professional teams in four major sports. The Arizona Diamondbacks (baseball), Phoenix Coyotes (hockey), Phoenix Suns (basketball) and Arizona Cardinals (football) all play in the metropolitan area.

GETTING THERE AND GETTING AROUND

AIR Sky Harbor Airport is 4 miles east of downtown, with limited connecting bus service. Very few hotels offer complimentary shuttle, but taxis are plentiful.

RAIL Amtrak, tel: (800) 872-7245, provides bus transfers to Phoenix from train stations in Flagstaff and Tucson, arriving at the Greyhound Bus Depot, 2115 E Buckeye Rd, or the Phoenix Metro Center, 9617 N Metro Parkway West; tel: (602) 568-2208.

BUS Bus service by Valley Metro, tel: (602) 253-5000, is very limited after 2230, with no service on Sunday. DASH (Downtown Area Shuttle) runs between the Arizona Center and the State Capitol; its bright purple minibuses charge $0.35.

INFORMATION

Arizona Office of Tourism, 1110 Washington St, Suite 155 is open weekdays 0800–1700; tel: (602) 230-7733 or (888) 520-3444, www.phoenixcvb.com.

SAFETY As with all large metropolitan areas visitors should exercise caution in unfamiliar surroundings. While downtown Phoenix is experiencing a renaissance, there remain pockets of dismal districts. Be especially careful in the south-central area of the city.

MONEY Most local banks can handle currency exchange for a fee. ATMs are plentiful.

ACCOMMODATION

Phoenix has more hotels and resorts than any other city in the USA, but you'll need reservations months in advance to visit Feb–Apr. Also, because of its popularity, it is one of the most expensive places to stay. The best bargains can be found in the downtown area at weekends when the business travellers have gone home.

ON THE RANCH

Ready to trade your city-slicker status for that of a real cowboy? For about $100 you can be part of a breakfast cattle drive with **Rocky Mtn Cattle Moo-vers**, tel: (800) 826-9666, and get a glimpse of the cowboy life. If you've got more money, and you aren't too weary, you can stay on and ride herd for both lunch and sunset.

Lexington Hotel $$ 100 W Clarendon Ave; tel: (602) 279-9811, has a 45,000 sq ft fitness facility including a large outdoor waterfall pool. You'll find a wide variety of dining options, but this is the place to try a genuine mesquite grilled cowboy steak.

Quality Hotel & Resort $$ 3600 N Second Ave; tel: (602) 248-0222. Rooms are simply furnished but the rooftop pool has a spectacular view of the downtown skyline.

Willow House $–$$ 149 McDowell Rd; tel: (602) 252-0272. Enjoy coffee and a snack in one of the nine rooms of an early 1900s residence. Local artists showcase their work, used books are for sale, and the garage has been turned into a small theatre for poetry readings. Very cool. Very retro.

HIGHLIGHTS

The **Phoenix Art Museum**, 1625 N Central Ave, tel: (602) 257-1212, is considered the major visual arts institution in the Southwest. The nearby **Heard Museum**, 2301 N Central Ave, tel: (602) 252-8848, features one of the world's foremost collections of Native American and Southwest artefacts.

Downtown, take time to visit **Heritage Square**, Sixth and Monroe Sts, the cornerstone of a city block of museums, gift shops and restaurants housed in buildings that date back to the late 1800s. When walking leaves you weary, head to **Encanto Park** on Seventh Ave, near the Heard Museum. This tropical oasis in the middle of a city has a lagoon and islands for waterfowl, boat rentals and a small music shell for concerts.

South Mountain Park, 10919 S Central Ave, tel: (602) 495-0222, is the largest municipal park in the world, a 16,500-acre home to more than 300 specimens of plant life. Drive to the summit on the challenging twisting and winding road for fantastic views of the entire Valley of the Sun.

A short bus journey from Phoenix is **Old Town Scottsdale**, a cluster of early 20th-century buildings and more recent ones styled to look like those of the Old Southwest. Scottsdale itself is pricey, but has the best shops and restaurants in the area. The **Scottsdale Centre for the Arts** has galleries, a sculpture garden and live performing artists.

'The region . . . is altogether valueless. It can be approached only from the south, and after entering it, there is nothing to do but leave. Ours has been the first, and will doubtless be the last, party . . . to visit this profitless locality.'

That 1858 US government survey estimate on the number of people who might visit the Grand Canyon was out – by more than five million visitors annually. The enormous gorge displays two billion years' worth of history, recorded in layer upon layer of red, white, buff, grey, yellow, orange, brown, pink and black rock. The first outsider to see the Grand Canyon from below was Major John Wesley Powell, who successfully navigated more than 1000 miles of the Colorado River in 1869. Powell's notes from the trip, and a second in 1871–72, remain invaluable guides for modern river rafters braving the same white-water rapids.

The Grand Canyon is even larger than it appears. From the popular South Rim straight across the canyon to the less frequented North Rim measures 10 miles; go round from one to the other by road and you will cover 215 miles.

It's possible to see the Grand Canyon in a day, less if you take a flightseeing package from Las Vegas, but the ever-changing colours and the utter vastness of the canyon beg to be absorbed at leisure, far from the millions of visitors who will stop at the South Rim and Grand Canyon Village each year. At the very least, skirt the crowds by walking or cycling the South Rim Trail from Hopi Point east to Grand Canyon Village and Mather Point; a free shuttle eases the return.

GETTING THERE

Grand Canyon Village (South Rim) is located 60 miles north of Interstate 40 at Williams via Hwy 64, and 80 miles north-west of Flagstaff via Hwy 180. Only 10 miles from rim to rim as the crow flies, the North Rim is 215 miles (about 4½ hours) from the South Rim by car. The North Rim is 44 miles south of Jacob Lake, AZ, via Hwy 67. For information on road conditions, tel: (928) 638-7888. The parking fee is $20 for private vehicles, valid for seven days on both rims.

The Grand Canyon Railway, 233 N Grand Canyon Blvd, Williams, AZ 86046, OTT table 375, runs to the South Rim from Williams, 65 miles south of the park. The 1901

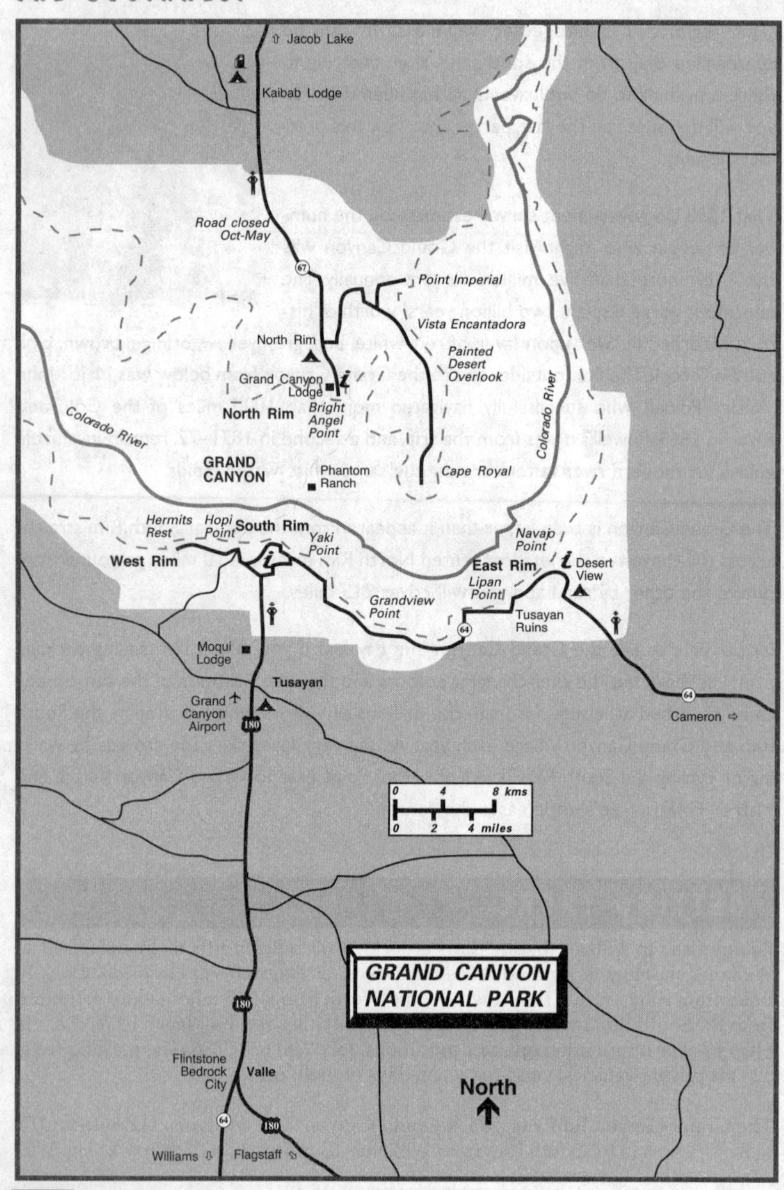

Jacob Lake
Kaibab Lodge
Road closed Oct-May
67
Point Imperial
Vista Encantadora
North Rim
Painted Desert Overlook
Grand Canyon Lodge
Bright Angel Point
North Rim
Colorado River
Colorado River
GRAND CANYON
Phantom Ranch
Cape Royal
Hermits Rest
Hopi Point
South Rim
Yaki Point
Navajo Point
West Rim
East Rim
Desert View
Lipan Point
Grandview Point
Tusayan Ruins
64
Moqui Lodge
Tusayan
Grand Canyon Airport
180
64
Cameron
0 4 8 kms
0 2 4 miles
GRAND CANYON NATIONAL PARK
180
Flintstone Bedrock City
Valle
North
64
180
Williams
Flagstaff

line, originally run by the Santa Fe Railway, provided the easy access that turned the Grand Canyon from geographic curiosity into an American icon. A vintage steam locomotive pulls the rake of restored 1920s Harriman carriages, Memorial Day to September, while a 1950s diesel does the duty in winter. $$$ Contact 1201 West Route 66, Suite 200, Flagstaff, AZ 86001; tel: (928) 773-1976 or (800) 843-8724; fax: (928) 773-1610; www.thetrain.com.

Commuter lines fly daily from Los Angeles and Las Vegas to Grand Canyon Airport in Tusayan, 8 miles south of the Visitor Centre. Scenic Airlines, tel: (800) 634-6801 or (702) 638-3300, offers flights from several Southwest destinations. Shuttles run hourly from the airport to Grand Canyon Village; taxi service is also available.

Amtrak, tel: (800) USA-RAIL or (800) 872-7245 serves Flagstaff and Williams. Connecting bus service to the Grand Canyon from Flagstaff is available through Open Road Tours, tel: (602) 997-6474.

The Grand Canyon is a National Park, so there is an entrance fee ($$$) however you arrive.

INFORMATION

Grand Canyon National Park, Box 129, Grand Canyon, AZ 86023; tel: (520) 638-7888; www.nps.gov/grca.

The **Canyon View Information Plaza** is located at Mather Point. Access is via shuttle bus. Ride either the Village Route bus or the Kaibab Trail Route bus. The **Desert View Information Center** is located at the park's east entrance on the South Rim. The North Rim Visitor Center is adjacent to the parking lot on the Bright Angel Peninsula. Ask for the *Grand Canyon Magazine*, free at all visitor centres.

National Park Service Information Desk, Grand Canyon Lodge lobby, North Rim. Open daily 0800–1800 (mid-May–Oct).

MONEY There is a bank (with a 24-hr cash dispenser) and post office on both the North and South Rims. Bank One will cash traveller's cheques, exchange currency, and handle wire transfers and charge card advances.

ACCOMMODATION

Xanterra Parks and Resorts, tel: (303) 600-3400, fax: (303) 600-3600, www.xanterra.com, operates all park accommodation and restaurants. Book as early as possible (6–12 months ahead) to ensure a place to sleep at one of America's most popular national parks. **Grand Canyon National Park Lodges**, tel: (928) 638-2631, handles information and same-day bookings; South Rim is open year-round; North Rim is open May–Oct. Williams and Flagstaff, an hour south of the canyon, both offer a wide variety of accommodation. There is no youth hostel in Grand Canyon National Park.

TIP

If you are flexible on dates, you'll stand a better chance of getting a room at short notice. Room availability changes constantly, so phone frequently for the latest room status. Many lodges release blocks of rooms held by tour wholesalers 21 to 30 days prior to arrival. Mark your calendar to place a direct call to a specific lodge for available space. Be patient, telephone hold times can be lengthy.

SOUTH RIM **Tusayan**, the park's dedicated 'village' located 7 miles south of the southern entrance to the park, has an RV park and motels. **Mather Campground**, tel: (800) 365-2267, (301) 722-1257 outside US, has non-hookup pitches, and **Desert View Campground**, 26 miles east of Grand Canyon Village, usually opens mid-May–mid-October, though this depends on weather conditions.

Maswik Lodge $$ and **Yavapai Lodge** $$. Removed from the village.

Bright Angel Lodge $$$. Located on the rim.

Thunderbird Lodge $$$ and **Kachina Lodge** $$$. Offer a choice of canyon-side or park-side rooms on the rim.

El Tovar Hotel $$$. Historic lodge on the rim, located near the railway station.

NORTH RIM The **National Forest Service** operates first-come, first-served camp sites: the 25-pitch **DeMotte Park Campground**, 5 miles north of the boundary, and the 50-pitch **Jacob Lake Campground**, 30 miles north of the park. **Jacob Lake RV Park**, tel: (928) 643-7804, has RV hookups and tent pitches, and the **North Rim Campground**, tel: (800) 365-2267, has 82-pitch, non-hookup sites; stays are limited to seven days, and the camp site closes 16 Oct.

Grand Canyon Lodge $$$ tel: (928) 638-2611. Xanterra; tel: (303) 297-2757. Open May–Oct.

Kaibab Lodge $$ tel: (928) 638-2389; 5 miles north of the park boundary. **Kaibab National Forest** permits camping at will in designated areas near roads and water sources.

FOOD AND DRINK

The Grand Canyon is ideal for picnicking – almost any spot along the rim has a scenic rock on which to dine and enjoy the vista.

SOUTH RIM

El Tovar Dining Room $$$ tel: (928) 638-2631. 'Fine' dining à la meat-and-potatoes and sweet desserts.

Arizona Room $$$ at Bright Angel Lodge. Serves dinner only. Open year round.

Bright Angel Restaurant $$. Breakfast to dinner.

Bright Angel Fountain (next to the South Rim). The place for ice cream. Open May–Sept.

Hermit's Rest Snack Bar $$ end of West Rim Dr.

General Store Delicatessen, at The General Store. Snack bar located across the street from the Visitor Center. There are also cafeterias at the Maswik and Yavapai lodges. Maswik Cafeteria open all year. Yavapai open Mar–Dec.

NORTH RIM

Grand Canyon Lodge Dining Room $$$, tel: (928) 638-2611, ext. 160. The main dining venue in the park, open for breakfast to dinner, for which reservations are required. There is also a tea room and a snack shop in the Lodge complex. A general store serves the North Rim Campground.

HIGHLIGHTS

SOUTH RIM West Rim Drive, Hermit Rd, Yaki Point and the South Kaibab trailhead are accessible *only* by shuttle, tour bus, taxi or on foot. For tour information, tel: (928) 638-2631 for same-day bookings; tel: (303) 297-2757 for advance reservations.

> **FREE SHUTTLES**
>
> The park runs a free shuttle bus system year-round through the village and the West Rim. The **Hermit Rd Scenic Shuttle** runs from several lodges to Yaki Point on the East Rim. The **Tusayan Shuttle** runs hourly from the village south of the park. Information from the Visitor Center, Bright Angel Lodge and Yavapai Lodge.
>
> On the North Rim, the shuttle is non-operational until the North Kaibab Trail is reconstructed beyond Cottonwood.

The **Canyon View Information Plaza** has excellent explanations of early expeditions on the Colorado River, the effects of environmental pollution on air quality (242-mile visibility is occasionally reduced to 76 miles), and flora and fauna on both sides of the canyon.

Bright Angel Trail began as a native American trail from the rim down to the springs at Indian Gardens. Private developers widened the trail in 1891 and began the mule rides that remain one of Grand Canyon's most popular organised activities (see p. 441).

The most popular hike along the Bright Angel Trail is rated very strenuous. The trailhead, at 6860 ft, is next to the Kolb Studios (near Bright Angel Lodge). To hike the 9.3 miles to Bright Angel Campground/Phantom Ranch is to descend to the canyon floor's 2480 ft elevation via a switchback trail, pass Indian Gardens previously tended by indigenous Havasupai, and cross the Colorado River. It is hiking in the open, aided by stops for water at Mile-and-One-Half Resthouse and

Three-Mile Resthouse between May and Sept. Hiking just a portion of this trail is a challenging experience.

GRAND CANYON VILLAGE HISTORIC DISTRICT

Ask at one of the park lodge concierge desks for a copy of the brochure, *Self-Guided Walking Tour of Grand Canyon Village Historical District*. Covering the tiny area around El Tovar and Bright Angel Lodge, the tour takes in the **1909 Santa Fe Railway Depot** (still used by the Grand Canyon Railway), as well as the log and stone **El Tovar Hotel**, the adobe Southwest-style **Hopi House** and **Verkamp's Curios** (successor to a canyon floor trading post; see Shopping, p. 443), all completed in 1905.

For those wishing to stay here, the 1890 **Bucky O'Neill Cabin** near Bright Angel Lodge can still be rented. The **Red Horse Station**, once a two-storey hotel, is now a two-room guest cabin. In 1935, **Bright Angel Lodge** was opened to provide for tourists' modest accommodation near the rim. The 10-ft-tall lounge fireplace is designed to show the many layers of geological strata in the canyon.

South Rim Trail runs 9 miles between 7120 ft Mather Point and 6640 ft Hermits Rest, with access at any point along the route. This is the path to see Yavapai Observation Point, and the lodges, restaurants and curio shops by El Tovar and Bright Angel; you can also stop at 7043 ft Hopi Point for a view of 45 miles of canyon expanse. The trail is flat and easy, skirting the edge of the canyon and offering many photo opportunities. Walk west towards Hermits Rest in the morning or east in the Mather Point direction in the afternoon for the best views with the sun behind you. Much of the trail is not fenced or barricaded, so beware – a dozen or so people fall over the rim edge each year, drawn by the majesty of the scenery or while posing for photographs.

For more information on hikes and camping permits, consult a ranger. *The Official Guide to Hiking the Grand Canyon* by Scott Thybony (1994), Grand Canyon Natural History Association, Grand Canyon, AZ 86023, is an excellent guide to hiking trails on and between both rims.

Just inside the eastern boundary of the park, a three-storey golden rock tower hovers above the canyon. The **Watchtower** was built in 1932 to approximate prehistoric buildings in the region. Pay a few cents to walk up the tower stairs for magnificent views from windows in the wall, set between Native American-style murals.

Eight centuries ago, a local band of Native Americans, the Anasazi, abandoned a village along the East Rim of the canyon which they had inhabited for 1300 years. The **Tusayan Ruins** are what remain. There is a small museum, and rangers lead interpretative walks on the ¼ mile of paths around the ruins.

NORTH RIM

The North Rim, 1000 ft higher than the South Rim, is a different world. While the South Rim bakes in desert heat, the North Rim enjoys a cooler, mountain summer with spruce, fir and quaking aspen. And when the South Rim is dusted with snow, the North Rim is frozen beneath 25 ft of white. Although the Grand

Canyon Lodge and other North Rim facilities are closed Nov–Apr, the park itself remains open to Dec, snow permitting.

A shorter season and more roundabout access mean that North Rim crowds are only about 10% the size of South Rim mobs. Hwy 67 takes you south to the promontory at **Bright Angel Point**; Grand Canyon Lodge sits close by. The Cape Royal/Point Imperial turn-off before the point is a winding road through forest which stays well away from the rim. At the T-junction, left will take you north towards the picnic area and viewpoint for **Point Imperial**; right leads south on a twisting road past rimside picnic areas at **Vista Encantadora** and the **Painted Desert Overlook**. Continue south on the Walhalla Plateau to the tip of Cape Royal.

The quickest way to enjoy the relative serenity is on foot. The canyon's north side has excellent hiking and trail rides along rim trails and routes to the canyon floor. The easiest walks are the ½ mile **Bright Angel Point Trail** and the 1½ mile **Transept Trail**. From the 0.6 mile **Cape Royal Trail** on the Walhalla Plateau, the Colorado River appears closer than from any other spot on the rims. The hardy can hike part

MULE RIDES

Descending into the canyon on mule back has been popular for generations, and a traditional alternative to hiking on foot; aches and pains at the end of the day are comparable.

From the South Rim, one-day trips travel from the stone corral at the head of Bright Angel Trail to Tonto Platform and Plateau Point, 3200 ft below. The blue-green Colorado River twinkles another 1300 ft down. The ride takes about 7 hrs. Phantom Ranch rides stay overnight at Phantom Ranch cabins on Bright Angel Creek at the bottom of the canyon. The trip can be made in two ache-provoking days in the saddle or stretched to three days mid-Nov–mid-Mar.

You should book 9–12 months in advance, or get on the standby list at Bright Angel Transportation Desk the day before an intended ride. A one-day ride costs $100-plus; an overnight to Phantom Ranch with meals nearly three times as much. Contact **Mule Rides**, Grand Canyon National Park Lodges, Reservations Dept, 6312 South Fiddlers Green Circle, Suite 600N, Greenwood Village, CO 80111; tel: (888) 297-2757 or (928) 638-2525. One-day and overnight rides can also be arranged year-round through **Xanterra Parks and Resorts**; see under Accommodation, p. 437. Mid-Nov–mid-Mar they also do three-day Phantom Ranch rides.

On the North Rim, **Canyon Trail Rides**, based at Grand Canyon Lodge, tel: (435) 679-8665, offers several possibilities. A one-hour ride goes along the North Rim; a half-day ride explores the rim more fully or ventures a short way down towards the canyon floor; while the full-day ride goes into the canyon. Prices range from under $30 for an hour on mule back, to around $105 for a full day, including lunch.

Riders must be at least 4 ft 7 in tall, weigh under 200 lb (clothes and equipment included), and be fluent in English (for riding directions).

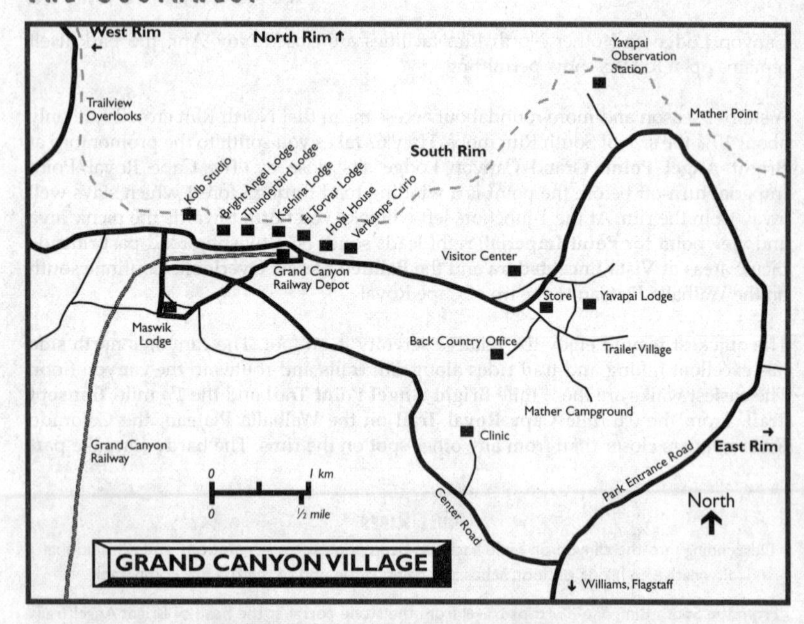

or all of the **North Kaibab Trail** into the canyon, starting on the North Rim at 8250 ft. The multi-day return trip down to the Colorado River covers 28 miles and a 5750 ft drop. Accommodation is available at Phantom Ranch or at the Bright Angel Campground with the same reservation/permit requirements outlined for the South Rim (see p. 440).

There are several alternatives to all this foot slogging. A mule trek could take anything from an hour to several days (see p. 441). From June to mid-Oct **Canyoneers**, tel: ((520) 526-0924, organises guided rides of the Kaibab Plateau and North Rim from a base at the Kaibab Lodge. For the winter, the lodge has created both tracked and marked backcountry trails for **cross-country skiing** (the area is reached using heated vans); tel: (520) 526-0924 or (800) 525-0924.

WHEELCHAIR ACCESS

Wheelchair-accessible tours can be requested in advance. The Grand Canyon National Park Accessibility Guide can guide visitors who may use free wheelchairs, available from the park rangers upon request.

Rafting the Colorado River remains the most adventurous way to see the Grand Canyon. Allow a full day for a smooth-water float, including a picnic lunch. White-water trips last from three days to three weeks. Most departures are from Lees Ferry, upstream from the park, but a shorter trip starts at Phantom Ranch.

Contact the park, tel: (520) 638-7888, for a free trip planner that includes contact information for approved concessionaires, or check with local chambers of commerce. A good link to river adventure companies is www.gcroa.org; www.grand.canyon.national-park.com is also filled with helpful information. Summer trips get fully booked early in the season, although a few concessionaires ride the river all year. The waiting time for private river-running permits is six to eight years.

SHOPPING

Curio shops are everywhere on the South Rim, mostly open from 0700 or 0800 until well into the evening. Hopi House, across from El Tovar, has native American rugs, pottery, *kachina* (fetishes) and souvenir jewellery for sale; upstairs you will find museum-quality jewellery and ceramic work by contemporary native American artists.

The General Store, across the road from the South Rim visitor centre, is well stocked with provisions, and camping and hiking equipment. The visitor centres on both rims, the Kolb Studio at Bright Angel Trailhead, the Yavapai Observation Station and many of the curio shops all stock maps and books.

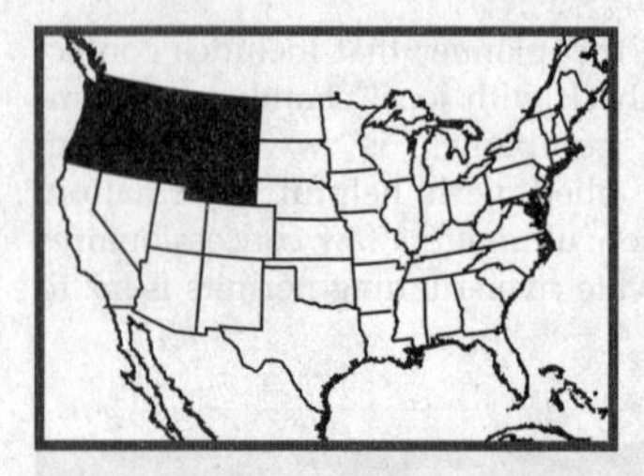

The Northwest region of the United States is divided into two parts by the Cascade Mountains. This range, which spans from the northern border of California through Oregon and Washington to Canada, is made up of many volcanic mountains, most of which are completely inactive. Most peaks of this range are covered with snow or topped with glaciers which feed the many rivers and tributaries that carve little gorges down the sides of the mountains. The Cascades have an almost Alpine look to them, and are considered some of the most breathtakingly beautiful peaks in the country.

The Cascades were created by the drift of continental plates which pressed them higher and higher to peaks of nearly 15,000 feet. The barrier created by the Cascades between the coastal regions of the two western states and the land of the interior is more than just a feature on a map. It defines the character and climates of the two regions, as well. The mountains keep the heavy moisture of the coast from passing into the inner regions, and also seem to create a social barrier between the liberal west coast and the conservative farmlands of the eastern sections of Washington and Oregon as well as Idaho, Montana and Wyoming.

Along the coast, visitors will be amazed by the lush vegetation and thick green landscape. This is a result of the heavy and frequent rainfall of the area, and perhaps one of the reasons residents can find the almost interminable rain tolerable. This section of the country is known for its grey skies and damp Pacific climate, yet is loved by all who live there. They cite its mild temperatures and rich green landscapes.

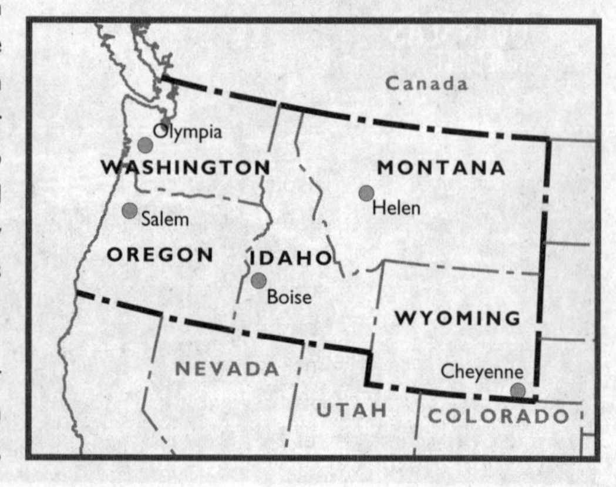

The coast is well known for its thick forests filled with ponderosa pine, Douglas fir, red cedar, spruce and western hemlock. The humidity makes this area a perfect habitat for the moss which seems to hang everywhere, adding a thick bright green canopy over all it touches. Those who have never walked beneath Douglas firs are often struck speechless at the size and height of these grand old trees. Stands of these are referred to as the 'cathedral forests' for their awe-inspiring grandeur as they soar to the canopy far overhead.

Within the ancient forests live the northern spotted owls, which have been a source of heated and lengthy local controversy. After many years of political struggle between conservation groups and the logging companies, the habitat of this threatened species is finally being protected.

This area is endowed with a multitude of fossils, which show that the region was once tropical, home to many varieties of tropical plants. State parks protect the areas that house the most incredible of these fossil collections. Today, the Olympic rainforest has the last growing specimens of flora from this era, testifying to the humidity level of the region.

The Pacific coast and waters have their own share of the Northwest's natural wonders. The Puget Sound is a prime spot to see the yearly migration of the grey whales, as they make their way south to give birth to their calves in warmer waters. This area is also a great place to see groups of killer whales playing, with their toothy smiles.

Seattle is best known for its coffee and its liberal, youthful and often brash attitude. The city is a hub of some of the country's best-known coffee producers, as well as a plethora of 'micro-roasters' who specialize in small-scale production of gourmet beans. No trip to Seattle is complete without a coffee tasting, taken every bit as seriously as wine tastings in the Napa Valley. The area's economic boom is largely due to its successful and still growing software industry. By far Seattle's most popular sight for visitors is the Space Needle, a standout for its bizarre form.

After the bustle of busy Seattle, a passenger ferry can bring you to the tranquil shores of the San Juan Islands, located in the Puget Sound, close to the Canadian city of Victoria. Although the summer months are busy here, the best time to see the whales that cavort in the waters of the sound is May through to August. The museums and nature interpretation centres that abound on the islands will tell you all about these yearly migrations. The waters of the sound are also home to playful seals, and the skies are thick with the national symbol, the bald eagle. It would be a shame to visit Seattle and not take at least a day to hop over the border to the lovely Canadian city of Vancouver, set in the water, overlooked by mountains. Or to the even closer Vancouver Island, to enjoy British Columbia's charmingly Victorian capital, Victoria, and nearby Butchart Gardens, among the finest in North America.

West of the Cascades, the weather is drier and much warmer. This creates a habitat rich in wild flowers. In the spring and sometimes through to late summer (the season is influenced by the melting of glaciers), meadows and mountainsides may be solid in bright red Indian paintbrush or covered in the peaceful blue of penstemon or the tall spikes of lupins. These colourful displays paint a beautiful foreground for the ice-capped mountains beyond, making train travel through this region a spectacular experience. Elsewhere in the Northwest, plant lovers will see rhododendron, creeping phlox and fireweed colour the landscapes, each in its season.

Along the eastern slopes of the Cascades and down into the forests of western red cedar, which reach all the way to Idaho, elk and mule deer roam, nibbling on tender vegetation. During the hot summer months of the interior, the deer can be seen high up on the mountainsides. Black bear and cougar also make this region their home, and the former are occasionally seen in camp sites foraging for food (see p. 50 in A–Z of Travel basics for how to react when bears are present.) Birdwatchers will enjoy the frequent sight of eagles.

At the far eastern side of this region, without a lot of other sights around it, is Yellowstone National Park. In Wyoming, but lying along the borders of Idaho and Montana, this park covers an area nearly 50 miles wide. Like the Cascades, this striking region was created by volcanic activity, although here the result was a crater instead of mountains. Inside this giant boiling pot, the volcanic action deep within the earth's crust fuels Yellowstone's breathtaking geysers, steam vents and hot springs. Despite the devastating forest fire of 1988, Yellowstone still hosts America's highest concentration of wildlife. Bird lovers will find more bald eagles here, in addition to ospreys and trumpeter swans. Not far south of Yellowstone is Grand Teton National Park.

It was into this rich and uncharted land of the Northwest that the explorers Lewis and Clark ventured in the early days of the republic, sent by President Thomas Jefferson. The modern-day explorer in this larger-than-life landscape still has the sense of its raw grandeur, unspoiled habitats and great diversity, some of the same qualities that Lewis and Clark observed there two centuries ago. And finally ... at the end of our Northwest section we briefly introduce Alaska, the ultimate wilderness state way way up north. Get there from Seattle or Vancouver and view from a cruise ship; see p. 495.

OUR CHOICE

Seattle's streets

Pike Place Market

The Space Needle

San Juan Islands

Whale-watching trip

Hoh Rain Forest and Olympic National Park

Yellowstone and Old Faithful

Grand Teton National Park

North Cascades National Park

Mount Rainier

Mount St Helens

Crater Lake

Glacier National Park

Vancouver, British Columbia

HOW MUCH YOU CAN SEE IN A ...

WEEK (7 DAYS)

Seattle, the San Juan Islands and the Olympic Peninsula

Seattle, the San Juan Islands and Vancouver Island

Seattle, the San Juan Islands, Vancouver (the city) and Victoria

Seattle, the Olympic Peninsula and North Cascades National Park

San Juan Islands, Olympic Peninsula, North Cascades National Park and Mount St Helens, from a base in Seattle

Olympic Peninsula, North Cascades National Park, Mount St Helens and Mount Rainier, with a short time in Seattle

Seattle, Glacier National Park and Chicago by train (return by air)

San Juan Islands, Victoria and Vancouver circuit

FORTNIGHT (14 DAYS)

Seattle, Spokane, Glacier National Park, Yellowstone and Grand Tetons by car

Seattle, San Juan Islands, Olympic Peninsula, North Cascades National Park, Mount St Helens and Mount Rainier, with a short time in Vancouver or Victoria

San Francisco, Mendicino and the northern California coast, Redwood National Park, Olympic Peninsula, Seattle and San Juan Islands

Seattle, North Cascades National Park, Glacier National Park, Yellowstone to Chicago by car (return by air)

YELLOWSTONE NATIONAL PARK

Yellowstone is nature's giant cauldron. It steams, spits, bubbles and burps amid an untamed landscape of deep canyons, craggy peaks, petrified trees, vast woodlands, alpine lakes and rushing waterfalls.

It took two million years and three volcanic eruptions to produce the world's oldest national park. Volcanic activity caused the central portion to collapse, and a caldera (depression) 28 miles by 47 miles was created. The same magnetic heat that caused previous eruptions continues to energise Yellowstone's hot springs, fumaroles (steam vents), spewing mud pots and geysers today. The entire park's instability makes it all the more interesting.

In 1988 a great fire torched about 800,000 acres. It opened the forest canopy, and gave Yellowstone's ecosystem a new start. Vegetation has regenerated, and Yellowstone still has the greatest variety of wildlife in the lower 48 states. Mule deer, bighorn sheep, moose, bald eagles, ospreys, trumpeter swans, elk, wolves, bison and grizzly bears reside amid a diverse landscape. Keep cameras handy; roads are narrow and laybys few.

GETTING THERE AND GETTING AROUND

Tucked away in the north-west corner of Wyoming, the park has five entrances:

North Entrance, along Hwy 89 from I-90 at Livingston, Montana;
Northeast Entrance, along Hwy 212 from I-90 at Billings, Montana, or Hwy 296 from Cody, Wyoming;
West Entrance, from Hwy 191 from Bozeman, Montana, or US Hwy 20 from Idaho Falls, Idaho;
East Entrance: US Hwy 16 from Cody, Wyoming;
South Entrance: US Hwy 89 from Jackson, Wyoming.

Entrance passes ($$–$$$ per person, per vehicle or per snowmobile) are for seven days and include Grand Teton National Park (see p. 453).

There is no public transport available within the park, but from the end of May to mid-Sept, Yellowstone National Park Lodges, operated by Xanterra Parks & Resorts, provides motorcoach tours from lodges, camp sites, Mammoth and Gardiner, Montana ($$$). Self-guided auto audio tours can be rented for a half-day or for 24 hours ($$$). Trekking some of the 1000 miles of hiking trails, climbing aboard a stagecoach at Roosevelt Lodge Corrals ($$$), horse-riding ($$$) and cycling are

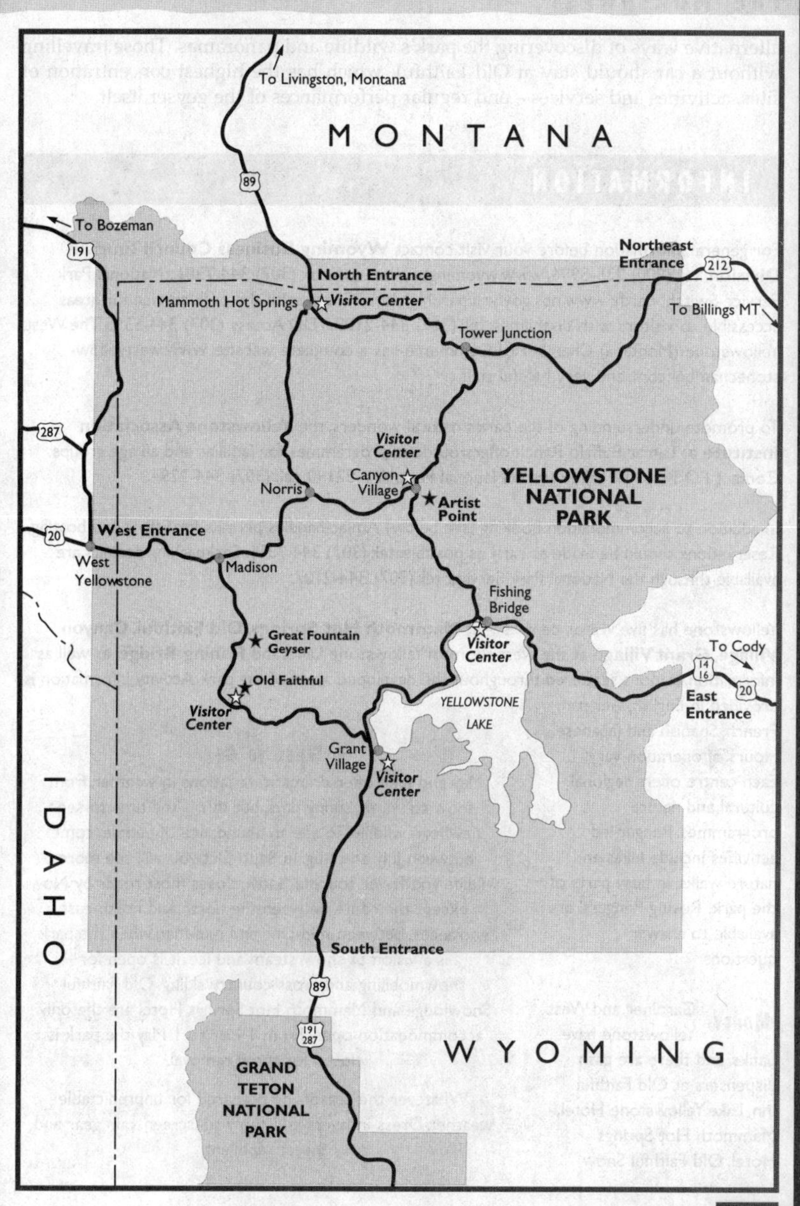
To Livingston, Montana
MONTANA
89
To Bozeman
191
Northeast Entrance
212
North Entrance
Mammoth Hot Springs
Visitor Center
To Billings MT
Tower Junction
287
Visitor Center
Canyon Village
Norris
YELLOWSTONE NATIONAL PARK
Artist Point
20
West Entrance
West Yellowstone
Madison
Fishing Bridge
Visitor Center
Great Fountain Geyser
To Cody
14
16
20
Old Faithful
Visitor Center
YELLOWSTONE LAKE
East Entrance
Grant Village
Visitor Center
IDAHO
South Entrance
89
191
287
WYOMING
GRAND TETON NATIONAL PARK

alternative ways of discovering the park's wildlife and panoramas. Those travelling without a car should stay at Old Faithful, which has the highest concentration of sites, activities and services – and regular performances of the geyser itself.

INFORMATION

For general information before your visit contact **Wyoming Business Council Tourism Division**, tel: (800) 225-5996, www.wyomingtourism.com, or (307) 344-7381 (National Park Service Switchboard); www.nps.gov/yell/parkhigh.htm. Check with the park service for areas accessible to visitors with disabilities; tel: (307) 344-2109. TDD Access (307) 344-5395. The West Yellowstone (Montana) Chamber of Commerce has a complete website, www.westyellowstonechamber.com, and very helpful staff.

To promote understanding of the park's natural wonders, the **Yellowstone Association Institute** at Lamar Buffalo Ranch offers outdoor programmes for families and all age groups. Contact PO Box 117, Yellowstone National Park, WY 82190; tel: (307) 344-2294.

In addition to accommodation booking (see below), Amfac handles permits for fishing and boating. Reservations should be made as early as possible; tel: (307) 344-7311. Backpacking permits are available through the National Park Service; tel: (307) 344-2107.

Yellowstone has five visitor centres – at **Mammoth Hot Springs**, **Old Faithful**, **Canyon Village**, **Grant Village** at the west shore of Yellowstone Lake, and **Fishing Bridge**, as well as information stations scattered throughout the developed areas of the park. Activity information is provided in English, German, French, Spanish and Japanese. Hours of operation vary. Each centre offers regional cultural and nature programmes. Ranger-led activities include hikes and nature walks. In busy parts of the park, 'Roving Rangers' are available to answer questions.

When to Go

May and June offer dramatic variations in weather, from snow to warm, sunny days, but this is the time to see newborn wildlife. To see an abundance of people, come between July and Aug. In Sept–Oct you will see more wildlife and fewer tourists. Snow closes most roads by Nov, except the route between the north and north-east entrances. Between mid-Dec and mid-Mar, when the park is a vision of snow, steam and ice, it is open for snowmobiling and cross-country skiing. Old Faithful Snowlodge and Mammoth Hot Springs Hotel are the only accommodation open. From 1 Mar to 1 May the park is closed for snow removal.

Whatever the season, be prepared for unpredictable weather. Dress in layers and carry sunscreen, rain gear and insect repellent.

Money Gardiner and West Yellowstone have banks, and there are cash dispensers at Old Faithful Inn, Lake Yellowstone Hotel, Mammoth Hot Springs Hotel, Old Faithful Snow

Lodge and Canyon Lodge. Foreign currency exchange is available at park lodges Mon–Fri 0800–1700.

SAFETY Touching thermal pools or getting too near geysers is dangerous. Lake, river and stream water is unsafe to drink without boiling. Do not try to feed the animals or approach for photos – view them from a distance. Stay on the trails to avoid tick bites (see p. 51).

ACCOMMODATION

Although some lodge rooms in the park are cheap to moderate, most are expensive. Cabins range from cheap, with shared bath, to moderate. Contact **Xanterra**, which handles lodging and camping; tel: (307) 344-7311 or book on the web at www.travelyellowstone.com. Outside the north-east gate are several moderately priced motels, including Comfort Inn and four Best Westerns (see p. 52). Lodging is also plentiful in West Yellowstone, near the West Entrance.

Yellowstone Canyon Village Lodge and Cabins $$$–$$$$ Canyon Village. Open May–Sept.

Lake Yellowstone Hotel and Cabins and Lake Lodge Cabins, Fishing Bridge. The 1920s-style sunroom of Lake Yellowstone Hotel's 100-year-old property has a spectacular view of Lake Yellowstone. There are cabins ($$$) or lodge rooms ($$$$). Open May–early Oct.

Mammoth Hot Springs Hotel and Cabins, Mammoth Hot Springs. Choice of cabins ($$) or rooms ($$$–$$$$). Open May–Oct, mid-Dec–mid-Mar.

Old Faithful Inn, Old Faithful. The huge rustic lobby has a massive fireplace. Rooms in the Old House without bath ($$), regular rooms ($$$$), or cabins ($$–$$$). 2003 season only: open June–Aug. Open May–mid-Oct.

Old Faithful Snow Lodge and Cabins, Old Faithful. The newest property has rooms ($$$$) and cabins ($$$). Open May-mid Oct, mid-Dec–mid-Mar.

Roosevelt Lodge Cabins $$–$$$ Tower Junction. A Western ranch atmosphere, geared to families. Tiny cabins. Open May–Sept.

CAMPING

Camp sites ($) are located close to the lodges, but those operated by the National Park Service are on a first-come first-served basis and are usually full by noon. Fishing Bridge has RV hookups, but because it is bear habitat, RVs must be hardsided. For camping information and reservations, tel: (307) 344-7311. Supplies are available throughout the park.

FOOD AND DRINK

Reasonably priced fast food and snack shops are located throughout the park. Lake Lodge, Old Faithful Lodge and Canyon Lodge have cafeterias. Delis or places to buy take-away sandwiches or picnic supplies are hard to find. Grant Village, Old Faithful Inn and Roosevelt have family-style restaurants – Roosevelt sports an 'Old

West' atmosphere. All the hotels except Roosevelt have fine dining restaurants. Except at Snow Lodge, reservations are necessary; $$$-$$$$, tel: (307) 344-7901.

HIGHLIGHTS

Yellowstone has five distinct regions: the hot springs sector that stretches out from Mammoth; the geyser area reaching from Norris south past Old Faithful; the region surrounding Lake Yellowstone; canyon country with the Grand Canyon of Yellowstone and Hayden Valley; and the north-east section, Roosevelt Country, with its petrified forests, waterfalls and feel of the Old West. A 142-mile figure eight, the Grand Loop Road, traverses the park, with spur roads linking with the entrances. This is easily driven as two day-trips.

MAMMOTH COUNTRY

From the north entrance the Grand Loop passes Park Headquarters in Mammoth country. Here the thermal waters undulate over the travertine **Minerva Terraces**. Primitive bacteria and algae living in the water produce the terraces' beiges, browns, greens and reddish-browns. Resident elk and bison couldn't care less about such geothermal phenomena. On the way south to geyser country's steam and dancing waters are the black volcanic glass of **Obsidian Cliff** and snorting fumaroles at **Roaring Mountain**.

GEYSER COUNTRY

Steamboat Geyser is just past Norris. Its 300–400 ft eruptions are the world's tallest, but they are unpredictable. Nearby **Gibbons Falls**, another visitor favourite, drops 84 ft over the caldera rim. A huge amount of burping and spitting makes **Fountain Paint Pot** Yellowstone's most famous mud pot. It is near **Firehole Lake Drive**, where the **Great Fountain Geyser** sometimes blows 200 ft up. At **Midway Geyser Basin**, you'll find the largest of the hot springs – the colourful **Grand Prismatic Spring** is 370 ft wide.

There are 150 geysers within one square mile of the **Upper Geyser Basin**. The most famous is **Old Faithful**. It may not be the highest or the largest, but it is certainly consistent and beautiful. It spews 5000–8000 gallons of water at least 20 times a day. The visitor centre posts expected eruption times. The trail behind Old Faithful crosses Firehole River to **Geyser Hill**. The rotten-egg smell of hydrogen sulphide accompanies walkers past the many geysers and boiling springs to the far end of the basin and **Morning Glory Pool**. The pool got its name from its deep blue-green colour and likeness in shape to the flower. Not far away, in **Black Sand Basin**, the clear water of **Emerald Pool** seems endless. Oranges and yellows border the deep green of the pool, the result of algae growing in the pool's depths.

YELLOWSTONE LAKE

From the Old Faithful area the Grand Loop passes the Continental Divide of the Rockies at Isa Lake, and continues to **West Thumb**. A thermal area of Yellowstone Lake, West Thumb has bubbling pots, hot springs and geysers. Fishermen used to cook their catch in the bubbling waters of the submerged

Fishing Cone Geyser. Yellowstone Lake is the park's fishing and boating area. Cut-throat trout are plentiful at **Fishing Bridge**, where the Yellowstone River runs into the lake. Bison, bear and bald eagles are often spotted along the 100-mile shoreline of America's largest lake above 7000 ft. Bridge Bay ponds are a hangout for moose.

PARK ACTIVITIES

Besides hiking and camping, there is fishing, boating and horse-riding ($$$) from most of the centres, guided fishing trips ($$$), scenic cruises on Lake Yellowstone ($$) and boat rental at Bay Bridge Marina ($$–$$$).

CANYON COUNTRY Elk, deer and buffalo graze on the hillsides, meadows and sagebrush flats of **Hayden Valley**, an old lake bed from the last Ice Age. Have your binoculars handy because its upper meadows are grizzly bear land. Along the Yellowstone River, white pelicans, trumpeter swans and Canada geese hobnob with gulls and ducks. Up the road, nature hurls football-sized mud blobs from **Mud Volcano** and **Black Dragon's Cauldron**. This is also a good place to try your hand at catch-and-release trout fishing.

From Canyon Village Visitors Center, travel to **Canyon Rim Drive**. Trek the 2½ mile one-way loop that leads to **Inspiration Point** for a spectacular view of the canyon and the Lower Falls. Cataracts tumble, foam and strike the canyon floor with great force on their 308 ft descent. The trail chiselled by the turbulent Yellowstone River reaches a depth of 1540 ft near **Artist Point**, and the vertical landscape drops 700 ft to the canyon's bottom. Bright-coloured canyon walls are the result of heat and chemical action on their rhyolite rocks. The layers of colour in the Grand Canyon of Yellowstone go from black to pink to orange to yellow – it was the bright yellow hue that gave the river and the park their name. The path continues to **Upper Falls**, where the waters plunge 109 ft into a deep green pool. This is the most dramatic section of the park.

ROOSEVELT COUNTRY Subalpine fir and whitebark pine border the road from the canyon to Roosevelt Country as it ascends Dunraven Pass. **Mt Washburn**, at 10,243 ft, forms the northern boundary of the caldera. This is grizzly bear country, so watch for cars parked along the road. At **Tower Junction**, just past the volcanic pinnacles that surround the 132 ft **Tower Falls**, is a one million year-old tree stump. **Specimen Ridge** contains petrified redwoods, spruce, fir and a hundred other plant species that have been preserved by multi-million-year-old volcanic ash. Towards the north-east entrance the climate is drier, and the sagebrush and grassy valleys are the winter home for many of the area's large animals. It was a favourite area of Teddy Roosevelt.

OUTSIDE THE PARK

GRAND TETON NATIONAL PARK The Tetons lie just south of Yellowstone, and the lack of foothills dramatically underscores the range's dramatic climb from evergreen forests, alpine meadows and blue glaciers to bare granite peaks. **The Snake River** slithers through its valley floor. Buffalo, moose, Canada geese, sandhill cranes, trumpeter swans, beavers, elk and deer all inhabit the area's wetlands. **Teton Park Road** rises from the river to a sage-covered flat where it reveals the whole Teton Range. There is a first-class view of **Mount Moran's** massive sandstone peak at **Oxbow Bend**. **Jackson Lake** is inside a depression that was scooped out by an Ice Age glacier. One of the park's most popular areas is **Jenny Lake**. Walkers can take a boat ($) across the lake to **Cascade Canyon Trail** for the 1/2-mile walk to **Hidden Falls**. The delicate cascade resembles foaming tresses. **Inspiration Point**, just up the trail, overlooks the entire lake.

The highlights of Grand Teton National Park are an easy day-trip loop drive from the Old Faithful area of Yellowstone. Follow Route 89/191 south along the shores of Jackson Lake, turning right onto Teton Park Rd to visit Jenny Lake. Continue south to Moose Park entrance, where you rejoin Rte 89/191, this time heading north along the Snake River, and eventually backtracking along Jackson Lake for the return to Yellowstone.

Besides hiking, camping, horse-riding and biking, there are nature seminars and Snake River float trips; $$$, contact Teewinot; tel: (307) 733-3316. Park visitor centres are at Colter Bay, Jenny Lake and Moose Village.

Menor's Ferry and the **Chapel of the Transfiguration** are some of the historic settlements at **Moose Village**. There are great panoramas of the Tetons aboard the aerial tram. $$$ Jackson Hole Ski Resort; tel: (307) 733-2292.

The Old West or a tourist version of it is alive and well around the antler arches of **Jackson Hole** square. There are saddle seats and country and western music at the Million Dollar Cowboy Bar, just off the square ($$) and within it at the Jackson Hole Shoot-out (Mon–Sat 1830, free). Fine art galleries contribute to making Jackson Hole a sophisticated little ski town.

North and west of the park, a dozen National Forest campgrounds are located betweem 3 and 20 miles from park entrances, and these offer large, well-spaced tent pitches, fewer crowds and a far more pleasant experience for caravan or tent travellers. Visit http://www.fs.fed.us and search by name for 'Gallatin' to locate these.

i **Jackson Hole Chamber of Commerce**, tel: (307) 733-3316; **Grand Teton National Park Information**, tel: (307) 739-3300; www.nps.gov/grte. One entrance-pass covers Grand Teton and Yellowstone for seven days. There are cash dispensers at most lodges. The closest bank is in Jackson.

Colter Bay & Cabins $$–$$$ Tent cabins do not have sleeping bags; tel: (307) 543-3100 or visit www.gtlc.com. Camp sites are usually filled by noon.

HENRY'S LAKE STATE PARK Wildlife and wild scenery follow Hwy 20 west out of the park to Henry's Lake State Park and Island Park Reservoir, Idaho. This is also the place for fly fishermen to have a bout with a cut-throat trout. Along Mesa Falls Scenic Byway (Hwy 47) the thunder of the **Upper and Lower Mesa Falls** resonates at Henry's Fork as the Snake River crams itself into a gorge that drops 65 ft. A mile south of the falls is **Harriman State Park**, a 16,000 acre wildlife reserve. Trumpeter swans make their home here, as did the Harrimans – a tour of their 1950s **Railroad Ranch** gives the impression they have only just left it. For tour reservations, tel: (208) 558-7368 ($).

i Tel: (800) VISITID (847-4843); www.visitid.org.

BEARTOOTH Breathtaking vistas accompany the **Beartooth Highway** (Hwy 212) from the north-east entrance. A series of switchbacks climbs 11,000 ft to Beartooth Pass on its way to Red Lodge, Montana. The pass's metamorphic rocks are some of the earth's oldest.

i Tel: (800) VISITMT (800-847-4868); www.visitmt.com.

CODY, WYOMING The **Buffalo Bill Historical Center** is the home of a huge collection of Western Americana. It includes Bill Cody's personal memorabilia, the Whitney Gallery of Western Art, the Plains Indian Museum and the Cody Firearms Museum. $$, 720 Sheridan Ave, Cody (two-day admission).

i Cody, Wyoming Chamber of Commerce; tel; (307) 587-2777; www.codychamber.org.

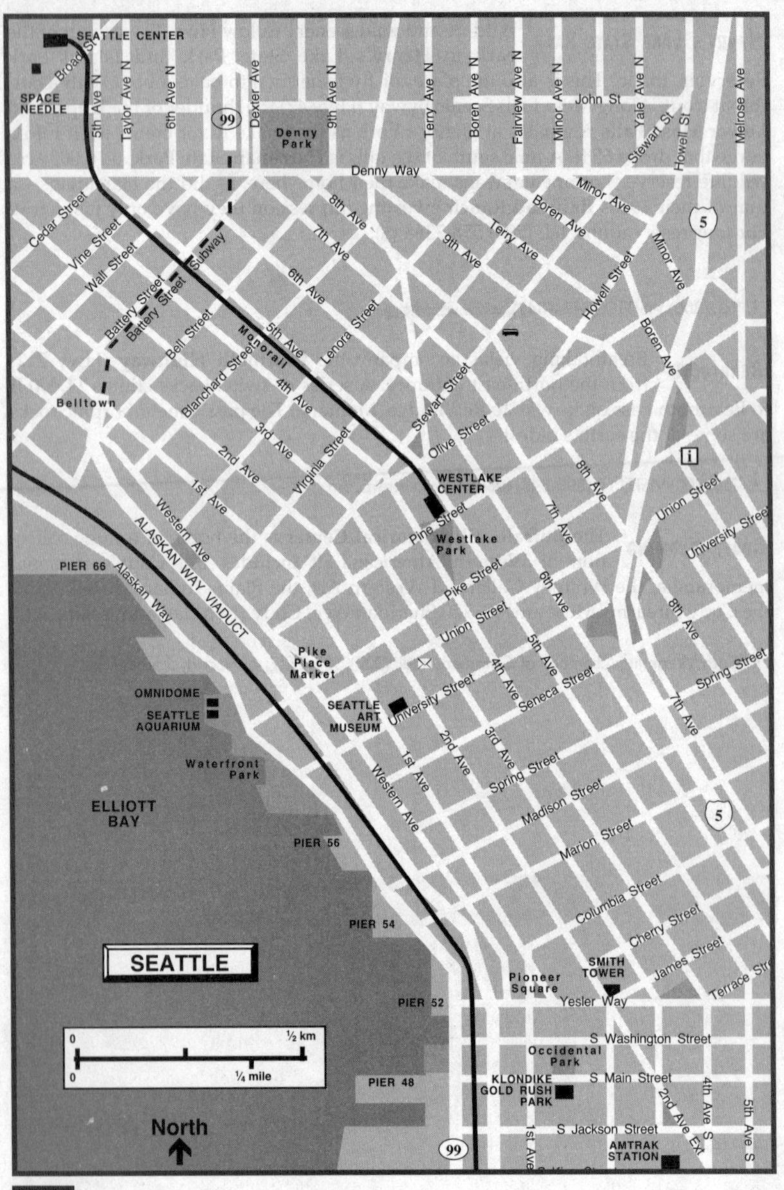
SEATTLE CENTER
SPACE NEEDLE
Broad St
5th Ave N
Taylor Ave N
6th Ave N
99
Dexter Ave
Denny Park
9th Ave N
Terry Ave N
Boren Ave N
Fairview Ave N
Minor Ave N
John St
Yale Ave N
Stewart St
Howell St
Melrose Ave
Denny Way
Minor Ave
Boren Ave
Terry Ave
9th Ave
8th Ave
7th Ave
6th Ave
5th Ave
4th Ave
3rd Ave
2nd Ave
1st Ave
Western Ave
Cedar Street
Vine Street
Wall Street
Battery Street
Battery Street
Subway
Bell Street
Blanchard Street
Monorail
Lenora Street
Virginia Street
Stewart Street
Olive Street
Howell Street
Minor Ave
Boren Ave
5
Belltown
WESTLAKE CENTER
Pine Street
Westlake Park
Pike Street
Union Street
Union Street
University Street
ALASKAN WAY VIADUCT
PIER 66
Alaskan Way
Pike Place Market
OMNIDOME
SEATTLE AQUARIUM
SEATTLE ART MUSEUM
University Street
Seneca Street
Spring Street
Spring Street
Madison Street
Marion Street
Columbia Street
Cherry Street
James Street
Terrace Stre
Waterfront Park
ELLIOTT BAY
PIER 56
PIER 54
PIER 52
PIER 48
SEATTLE
SMITH TOWER
Pioneer Square
Yesler Way
S Washington Street
Occidental Park
KLONDIKE GOLD RUSH PARK
S Main Street
S Jackson Street
AMTRAK STATION
1st Ave
2nd Ave Ext
4th Ave S
5th Ave S
0
½ km
0
¼ mile
North

Rainfall and mist-grown trees make Seattle the Emerald City. Puget Sound's deep blue waters combine with lead-grey skies and green-dappled parks in a lush, hilly city by the sea. A society built on commerce, timber and fishing is being transformed by the computer software industry and the aerospace giant, Boeing. Grunge bands put the city on the pop music map in the early 1990s, and gourmet coffee shops stoke the locals with caffeine. The result is a youthful population of forward looking independent thinkers, rooted in pragmatic capitalism, living the good life at the north-western corner of the USA.

Seattle is known not so much for its wealth of sights as for its particular atmosphere and spectacular emergence as America's city of the 1990s. Pioneer Sq. downtown is a good place to get your bearings, and the new Seattle Arts Museum nearby is well worth a visit, while to the north the crazy, now-notorious Space Needle commands your attention. Most important, though, is to stroll the waterfront and the atmospheric Pike Place Market.

MUST SEE/DO IN SEATTLE

Absorb local colour at Pike Place Market

Stroll the waterfront as the sun sets; climb the viewing deck at the north end for spectacular city views

Stop for coffee – and maybe a poetry reading – at Elliott Bay Book Company and Café

Ride the Monorail, for a retro view of yesterday's 'futuristic'

Ride a ferry to Bainbridge Island or take a harbour cruise to see the city from the water

GETTING THERE AND GETTING AROUND

AIR Seattle-Tacoma International Airport (Sea-Tac) is about 10 miles from the centre. Gray Line Airport Express buses operate 0540–2335 every 20 mins between two Sea-Tac terminal stops and eight downtown hotels for $8.50. Metro Transit bus no. 194 runs every 30 mins from the lower level baggage claim.

RAIL/BUS Amtrak trains from Chicago, Vancouver and Los Angeles arrive at King St Station, 3rd Ave and S Jackson St in southern downtown. Greyhound and regional buses use the terminal at 8th Ave and Stewart St.

BOAT Coming from Canada, one viable option is to travel by boat. **Clipper Navigation**, tel: (206) 448-5000 or (800) 888-2535, runs passenger ferries between Victoria, British Columbia and Seattle's Pier 69. **Black Ball Transport**, tel: (250) 386-2202 or (360) 457-4491, sails a car-and-passenger ferry year-round from Victoria to Port Angeles, Washington. From Port Angeles, **Olympic Bus Lines**, tel: (800) 457-4492 or (360) 417-0700, www.olympicbuslines.com, has a twice-daily service to Seattle.

For most trips, use **Metro Transit buses** (cheaper out of peak hours and for under-17s any time). You can buy a weekend and holiday All-Day Pass for the cost of two off-peak journeys. Travelling *towards* downtown, pay the driver as you enter; *from* downtown, pay as you exit. Buses are free Mon–Fri 0600–2300, Sat 0600–1900, within the Downtown Seattle Ride Free Area (between 6th Ave, S Jackson St, Alaskan Way and Battery St). A 1.3-mile tunnel speeds the passage of electric buses through downtown under 3rd Ave.

The **Waterfront Street Car** (same prices as buses) runs every 20 mins daily along Alaskan Way downtown; these historic green-and-cream trolleys are imported from Melbourne, Australia. A legacy of the 1962 Seattle World's Fair, the **Monorail** is a fast way to travel from Westlake Center to Seattle Center and the Space Needle, but it makes no stops.

INFORMATION

The Seattle-King County Convention and Visitors Bureau, 8th Ave and Pike St, tel: (206) 461-5840, fax: (206) 461-5855, www.seeseattle.org, is open Mon–Fri 0830–1700, Sat–Sun Apr–early Sept 1000–1600, closed weekends early Sept–May, and can give leads to the numerous walking, cycling and boat tours of the Seattle area.

SAFETY At night caution is advised outside the downtown and in the waterfront areas – take a taxi if you are dining away from downtown. Ask advice from the hotel concierge about which specific areas you should avoid.

MONEY Travelex has a foreign exchange office downtown at Westlake Center (4th Ave and Pine St), open Mon–Sat 1000–1800, Sun 1200–1700, also offering sightseeing and transport information. There is another location at 906 3rd Ave, open Mon–Fri 0900–1700, Sat 1000–1400. Automatic cash dispensers abound throughout Seattle.

POST AND PHONES The main post office is at 301 Union St, open 0800–1730.

ACCOMMODATION

The visitors bureau has an extensive *Lodging Guide*, and the **Seattle Hotel Hotline**, tel: (206) 461-5882 or (800) 535-7071, books accommodation free of charge. Summer prices are high, but Nov–Mar the visitors bureau organises the Seattle Super Saver Package with discounts of up to 50%. **Seattle Bed & Breakfast Association**, tel: (206) 547-1020 or (800) 348-5630, www.lodginginseattle.com, has information on a dozen historic inns. At the bottom end, there is a good selection of hostels and a fair number of B&Bs, particularly in Capitol Hill. There are a few cheapish places in Belltown, north of Pike Place Market.

International Hostel $ 84 Union St; tel: (888) 622-5443 or (800) 909-4776 ext. 08; fax: (206) 682-2179. Within easy reach of the waterfront and Pike Place Market.

Commodore Motor Hotel $$ 2013 2nd Ave; tel: (206) 448-8868 or (800) 714-8868; fax: (206) 269-0519. Easily the best hotel value downtown, just to the north-west of Pike Place Market. Dorm beds also available ($).

Kings Inn $$ 2106 5th Ave; tel: (206) 441-8833 or (800) 546-4760; fax: (206) 441-0730. In Belltown, basic but cheap.

Pensione Nichols $$$–$$$$ 1923 1st Ave; tel: (206) 441-7125. Great location near Pike Place Market, with views of Puget Sound.

Tugboat *Challenger* Bunk & Breakfast $$$–$$$$ 1001 Fairview Ave N; tel: (206) 340-1201; fax: (206) 621-9208. At the south end of Lake Union near Capitol Hill.

Best Western Pioneer Square $$$$ 77 Yesler Way; tel: (206) 340-1234. Classy and an excellent location; good value.

FOOD AND DRINK

Dining can be a sublime art here. The pan-Asian dining trend is rooted in Seattle: the Pacific Rim includes both shores, and Seattle chefs invite adventurous dining. Seafood and Asian restaurants are easily found – for the best of these, head for the Waterfront and the International District respectively. For snacks and light meals, aim for the many food stalls in Pike Place Market.

Seattle is one of the few American cities that embraces European-style café culture, and trendy coffee spots all over town are well frequented day and night for a caffeine fix. Many also serve up beers and a variety of entertainment. Microbreweries are plentiful, and speciality bars are rampant.

Le Panier Very French Bakery $ 1902 Pike Pl.; tel: (206) 441-3669. Claims to have the best baguettes outside Paris.

Grand Central Bakery $$ 214 1st Ave S; tel: (206) 622-3644. Eat delicious roast vegetable sandwiches by a fireplace, or outdoors overlooking totem poles in Occidental Park.

icon Grill $$ 1933 5th Ave; tel: (206) 441-6330. Casual place for basic regional American dishes, nicely updated. Try bacon-wrapped meatloaf with treacle gravy.

Sit and Spin $$ 2219 4th Ave; tel: (206) 441-9484. An urban launderette, where excellent budget vegetarian food meets counter-culture furniture and patrons.

Ivar's Acres of Clams $$–$$$ Pier 54, Alaskan Way; tel: (206) 624-6852. Traditional clam house, bustling and basic.

Elliott's Oyster House and Seafood Restaurant $$$ Pier 56, Alaskan Way; tel: (206) 623-4340. Fine for shellfish and relaxing on the pier.

Wild Ginger Asian Restaurant and Satay Bar $$$–$$$$ 1400 Western Ave; tel: (206) 623-4450. Has perhaps the tastiest marriage of fresh ingredients in Pacific Rim recipes.

The Sky Lounge $$$–$$$$ Seattle Center, 219 4th Ave N; tel: (206) 905-2100. Two dining rooms revolving 500 ft above ground level: the casual Space Needle Restaurant and the slightly more expensive formal Emerald Suite.

TILLICUM VILLAGE

For a truly memorable evening, book a cruise to Tillicum Village on Blake Island. After boarding at Pier 55, you travel through the sound to Blake Island State Park, where a Native American centre provides a traditional dinner of steamed clams and plank-grilled salmon, followed by a programme of dance and story-telling, reliving ancient legends. There's time to walk the park trails or shop for native crafts before the cruise back in the sunset. $70, good value for dinner, cruise, theatre and cultural experience; tel: (206) 933-8600, (800) 426-1205, www.tillicumvillage.com.

HIGHLIGHTS

DOWNTOWN Hills, skyscrapers, espresso bars, sculptures and the presence of the sea define downtown Seattle. The central area's two foci are Pioneer Sq. and the area around Pike Place Market. In between, the city's skyline reaches upward, dominated by the 76-storey Columbia Tower. Back down on the ground, the Waterfront is a lively run of ferry docks, shops and restaurants. In fact, the city's greatest attractions are its streets and marketplaces, and much of Seattle is simply best explored outdoors – it is a joy to wander around, and all for free.

Pioneer Square is the place to head for a taste of Seattle's not-so-ancient roots in the timber trade and gold rush. In its early years, local businessman Henry Yesler built a lumber mill in the square, at the bottom of the so-called 'Skid Road', a long, narrow path down which logs were slid. The square now anchors the **Pioneer Square Historic District**, with its 1909 pergola, a replica totem pole from a nearby Tlingit Indian village and a bust of Chief Sealth, all surrounded by graceful period red brick and stone buildings.

Seattle's precarious setting on the edge of Puget Sound has meant periodic flooding, and occasional landslides, so much of the original city is now well below the present street level. One of Seattle's real highlights is **Bill Speidel's Underground Tour**, tel: (206) 682-4646, a fascinating trip through the district's subterranean passages. What are now drainage and cabling channels were once street-level shops, lumber yards and brothels, and this 90-min tour, led by informed and amusing guides, reveals much of the history, squalor and colour. Tours ($$) leave regularly from Doc Maynard's pub at 601 1st Ave (on Pioneer Sq.).

The 42-storey Smith Tower nearby was built in 1914 as the tallest building outside New York City. The bright, crusty white structure is more appealing for its oddity than its beauty, and has an observation deck nominally open 1000–1900.

The **Klondike Gold Rush National Historic Park**, a few blocks south of Pioneer Sq. at 117 S Main St, chronicles the general panic and the role of Seattle as the prospectors' jump-off point on their journey north. Open daily 0900–1700; free.

SEATTLE IN WOOD AND GOLD

From the original 1851 landing at Alki Bay, settlers moved to Elliott Bay and named their town Seattle after a friendly Duwamish chief, Sealth. The timber industry hit full stride almost immediately: millions of logs from the vast neighbouring forests were shimmied down the city's steep hills to sawmills near the water's edge. But it took Yukon gold to turn Seattle into a boom town. As the nearest sizable port city, it swelled overnight with fortune seekers and local merchants eager to make a buck. While most prospectors returned in financial ruin, Seattle reaped the spoils of the Klondike Gold Rush.

Just south of here is **Safeco Field**, Seattle's main sports complex. Abutting its eastern edge, the **International District**, formerly called Chinatown, is a focal point for Asian immigrants. Shabby and quiet, it's nevertheless a fun place to scout out Chinese groceries and Vietnamese restaurants – head for Jackson St between 5th and 8th Sts.

A huge black Hammering Man sculpture marks the **Seattle Art Museum** (SAM) at 100 University St, completed in 1991. This is one of the best places to see north-west Native American art, which is complemented by African masks, East Asian scrolls, a swathe of European fine arts and contemporary American pop art. $, open Tues– Sun 1000–1700 (Thur until 2100).

Harbor Steps Park connects the art museum to Alaskan Way in 104 wide steps with eight fountains. Alaskan Way runs along the **Waterfront**, the most interesting stretch of which is between about Pier 50 and Pier 70. Bell Street Terminal is where cruise ships dock. Between shops and restaurants, open piers provide fine views of both the city and the water. Stop at the **Seattle Aquarium** at Pier 59 for large window views of Puget Sound fish. Highlights include adorable sea otters and the fascinating Pacific salmon, which swim – leaping over falls where necessary – hundreds of miles upstream to inland spawning waters. $$, open 1000–1700 (until 1900 in summer). Waterfront Park has nice spots for picnicking and summer concerts, and the **Pike Place Hill Climb** stairs ascend to Pike Place Market.

Gray Line, tel: (206) 626-5208, offers narrated bus tours of the city's main sights.

Seattle's bounty overflows at **Pike Place Market**, 7 acres of food stalls, restaurants, crafts, produce and flower sellers, gift shops and fishmongers. Open year-round, the market draws thousands of residents at weekends; arrive early on Sat morning to see the finest produce and fish. A stroll along Pike St towards the water brings you to the entrance, where you'll see the famous yell-and-fish-throw performed by fishmongers at Pike Place Fish whenever a customer places an order.

BELLTOWN A skid row for decades between the waterfront, Seattle Center and downtown, Belltown is now filled with small restaurants, clubs, galleries and consignment clothing shops a hip magnet for the young set.

The 1962 Seattle World's Fair forced the little-known city to polish its attractions and add the **Space Needle** as its icon. Now horribly anachronistic, the needle none the less offers spectacular 360° views from its 520-ft high observation deck – when the weather is good. $$, open 0800–midnight.

Other sights of interest here include the **Pacific Science Center**, **Children's Museum** and **Fun Forest Amusement Park** (collectively the Seattle Center). Along with the Space Needle, the futuristic **Monorail** has dated badly over the past 40 years, but is still the best way to get here from the centre.

Fantastic views of the striking Seattle skyline are best had from ferries serving Puget Sound islands such as Bainbridge and Vashon. Washington State Ferries, tel: (206) 464-6400 or (800) 843-3779, has regular commuter ferries from Piers 50 and 52.

CAPITOL HILL AND THE UNIVERSITY DISTRICT Further east, elegant Capitol Hill holds some lovely mansions, and is Seattle's center of gay life, with good restaurants, coffeehouses and shops. **Volunteer Park** is a lazy green space with a conservatory and 75 ft moss-covered water tower. It contains the **Seattle Asian Art Museum**, with excellent Pacific Rim collections; $, open Tues–Sun 1000–1700, Thur 1000–2100. The Kado Tea Garden within the museum is open at weekends for teas and pastries. North of Capitol Hill. The University District is a great place for chic boutiques and cafés.

FREMONT Across the Lake Washington Ship Canal, Fremont is a self-appointed Seattle Left Bank, where a salvaged 53 ft rocket steams up at what residents consider the centre of the universe. 'Republic of Fremont' mottos like *delibertas quirkas* and 'Freedom to be Peculiar' flaunt the humour of this ultra-trendy district. Lenin's statue watches over the **Sunday Flea Market** on Fremont Ave N, and nearby a sculpture, the **Fremont Troll,** munches a Volkswagen Beetle under the Aurora Bridge. **Redhook Ale Brewery**, a few streets west on N Canal St, is an institution over 'a huge natural reservoir holding the largest proven beer reserve in the world'.

SHOPPING

Local crafts such as Pacific Northwest art and replica totem poles can be obtained in several shops. Pike Place Market and the streets north are good for these; try Made in Washington, 2221 2nd Ave, and Stonington Gallery, 2030 1st Ave. Also in this area is the Westlake Center, the indoor heart of downtown shopping. The Waterfront is handy for souvenir shopping, particularly around Pier 54. Pioneer Sq. is a good browsing zone and Pioneer Sq. Mall has antiques. Elliott Bay Book Company and café, 101 S Main St, is Seattle's rainy-day magnet, famed for author readings.

BOEING BOEING

In 1916, the Boeing Company began making military planes; today it is by far the world's largest passenger aircraft manufacturer. Its century of achievement is showcased at the **Museum of Flight** some 30 mins south of central Seattle at 9404 E Marginal Way S. More than 50 aircraft are on display, including the Boeing 707 Airforce One used by Presidents Eisenhower and Johnson. $$, open daily 0900–1700 (Thur until 2100). To see where Boeing puts its planes together, make for the **Boeing Tour Center** near Everitt, about 30 miles north of Seattle. Tours take you through nearly 100 acres of assembly plant, and are popular, so call ahead: tel: (800) 464-1476; www.boeing.com.

NIGHTLIFE

The Seattle music scene has produced such names as Jimi Hendrix in the 1960s, and Nirvana and Pearl Jam in the 1990s; the 'Seattle Sound' has much to do with the city's current identity, though grunge bars are already out. Pop and rock 'n' roll have their own interactive museum, the **Experience Music Project**, www.emplive.org. Theatre and classical music are also well represented. The **Seattle Symphony**, tel: (206) 215-4747, has a new home, Benaroya Hall downtown at 2nd Ave and University St, while the **Seattle Opera**, tel: (206) 389-7699, puts on grand spectacles at Seattle Center. Several free papers list cultural and nightlife events, including *Seattle Weekly*'s Wed 'Going On' section, *Eastside Week* and the bi-weekly *The Rocket*.

Central Café, 207 1st Ave S; tel: (206) 622-0209. Popular century-old bar near Pioneer Sq., with occasional live bands.

Bohemian Café, 111 Yesler Way; tel: (206) 447-1514. A variety of jazz, blues and rock acts most nights.

Speakeasy Café, 2304 2nd Ave; tel: (206) 728-9770. Belltown café/bar with light food and events including concerts, poetry readings and films.

Dimitriou's Jazz Alley, 2033 6th Ave; tel: (206) 441-9729. Seattle's leading jazz club, featuring national acts.

Vogue, 1516 11th Ave; tel: (206) 324-5778. Established part of the city's club scene, amid the galleries and bars of Belltown.

Virginia Inn, 1937 1st Ave; tel: (206) 728-1937. Lively beer place near Pike Place Market.

Redhook Ale Fremont Brewery and **Trolleyman Pub**, 3400 Phinney Ave N; tel: (206) 548-8000. Good budget food and brews in this nationally known microbrewery.

Less than a half-hour's ferry ride from busy Seattle lie several big, quiet islands that still – against the odds – retain a rural charm.

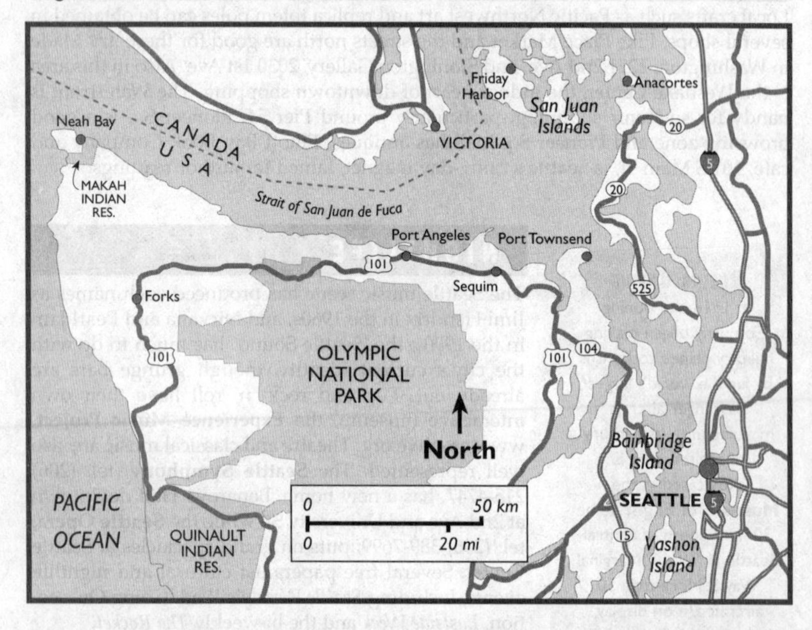

SAN JUAN ISLANDS

It takes a high tolerance for tranquillity to enjoy the San Juan Islands between Sept and May, and an equally high tolerance for queues in summer. Some 700 islands dot the sparkling blue waters of Puget Sound. Only San Juan Island has an incorporated town, named Friday Harbor. This is also the most accessible and varied of the islands: wild flowers carpet forest meadows in spring, while orchards gone wild

Getting There

Victoria Clipper has a daily passenger ferry from Seattle's Pier 69 to Friday Harbor May–Sept (weekends only Oct–Apr). Advance booking is recommended (strongly so in summer). If you're bringing a car, take the Washington State Ferries service from Anacortes, a 2-hr drive north of Seattle. San Juan Central Reservations, tel: (360) 378-8773, handles accommodation bookings for the entire island, which include everything from camp sites to motels to a luxurious isolated resort. Be sure to call before arriving.

produce apples, pears and cherries. The waters are busy with seals and the largest population of orcas (killer whales) in the world; America's largest concentration of bald eagles keeps company overhead.

San Juan's claim to historical fame is its role in the so-called Pig War, a British-American skirmish over possession in which the only casualty was a pig. Reconstructed fortresses at the southern and western edges of the island tell the tale. Friday Harbor has a **Whale Museum**, and the easiest way to see the real thing is to cross the island west to **Lime Kiln Point State Park**; prime time for whale-watching is May–Aug. Bicycles can be rented from Island Bicycles, 380 Argyle; tel: (360) 378-4941.

OLYMPIC PENINSULA

Seattleites look west towards the Olympic Peninsula with awe. Jagged mountain-tops are riddled with glaciers – 10 miles of them on Mount Olympus – and the rain here is a part of the scenery, creating an unusual northern rainforest.

Getting There

Olympic Bus Lines, tel: (360) 417-0700, run twice daily between Seattle and Port Angeles, a 3½ hr-trip, but transport around the park is scarce. A number of motels line the main streets in Port Angeles. Clallam Transit, tel: (360) 452-4511, runs buses Mon–Sat from Port Angeles to Neah Bay and Hurricane Ridge (ski season only); tel: (800) 858-3747, www.clallamtransit.com.

Much of the peninsula is contained within the **Olympic National Park**, the main point of entry to which is Port Angeles. The main visitor centre, which dispenses good driving and hiking maps, is on Race St; open daily 0900–1700 in summer, to 1600 rest of the year.

Port Angeles is a compact town at the start of a dramatic upward drive along **Hurricane Ridge**, whose views of the Strait of Juan de Fuca are breath-taking. In the north-west corner of the park, **Sol Duc hot springs** is a resort at which you can soak in mineral baths (daily mid-May–Sept, Thurs–Sun spring and autumn). The astonishing **Hoh Rain Forest** lies on the western slopes of the mountains, which are lashed by massive Pacific storms. Over 200 ins of precipitation per year feed a virgin temperate rainforest, perpetually blanketed in a greenish twilight.

At the north-western tip of the peninsula, beyond park boundaries, Neah Bay is the only town on the **Makah Reservation**, a salmon fishing port and home of the Makah Indians. It's out on Cape Flattery, the absolute outermost tip of Washington state. For 500 years, the tribe kept the secret of Ozette Village, which was buried beneath a landslide. Artefacts uncovered in the 1970s now contribute to exhibits at the **Makah Museum**; $ open Wed–Sun 1000–1700 (daily in summer).

South of **Neah Bay**, US Rte 101 takes you to Forks. The town, best known for the local timber museum, brags that it's the world's lumber capital. You'll very quickly notice lots of flannel shirts, diners, logging trucks – and anti-environmentalist bumper stickers. From here south on Rte 101, the peninsula is mostly empty roads passing through Native American reservations.

GETTING THERE

Olympic Bus Lines, tel: (360) 417-0700 or (800) 457-4492, www.olympicbuslines.com, serves Discovery Bay, about 7 miles west of Port Townsend, to Seattle's Greyhound Station.

PORT TOWNSEND

First settled in 1792, Port Townsend, with its large, calm harbour, rests in the rainshadow of the Olympic Peninsula. In the mid-19th century, bars, brothels and gambling were a social mainstay. Red-brick buildings from the time are now preserved as hotels, restaurants and shops, while high society Victorian homes, on a bluff above, offer magnificent vistas of the still-busy docks.

Port Townsend bursts with accommodation, but the city is very popular with weekenders. Port Townsend Visitors Center, 2437 E Sims Way, tel: (360) 385-2722 or (888) 365-6978, www.porttownsend.com can help. There's a hostel at nearby Fort Worden, tel: (360) 385-0655 or (800) 4776 ext. 37.

Silver Salmon Resort $$ 1280 Bayview Ave, Neah Bay; tel: (360) 645-2388 or (888) 713-647. Right on the water, cheap, and Native-run.

Hostelling International–Narrowstone $ 10621 Flagler Rd, Port Townsend; tel: (360) 385-1288. This hostel, located in a state park, is 20 miles away on a nearby island connected by causeway. It's quiet, but sometimes booked with groups.

Hostelling International–Olympic Port Townsend $ 272 Battery Way, Port Townsend; tel: (360) 385-0655. Located on the former Naval grounds, it offers spartan rooms, matchless views and a lively communal feeling.

The Smokehouse Restaurant $$ 193161 Hwy 101, Forks. Serves some of the finest salmon meals on the peninsula, smoked with alder fires in the little smokehouse right out back.

Elevated Ice Cream $ 627–631 Water St, Forks; tel: (360) 385-1156. This huge place scoops some of the finest locally made ice cream in the Northwest.

Three Crabs $$$ 11 Three Crabs Road, Sequim. Focuses on the world-famous local Dungeness crab; can get a bit pricey.

VASHON AND BAINBRIDGE ISLANDS

On 12-mile-long **Vashon Island**, farmhouses alternate with fishing shacks and, in the interior, fruit orchards and fruit-packing operations, including well-known Wax Orchards and the lesser-known Maury Island Farming Company, a smaller firm specializing in currant jelly. The mixed character of old-line farming and fishing families with urban professionals building second homes has created an odd amalgam of practical and pretentious.

Bainbridge Island is wealthier - you're more likely to find a European-import wine shop than a bait shack on the main street. Home to the Suquamish Indians for thousands of years, the island was 'discovered' by Europeans in 1792. Settlers soon built a shipyard and what was, for a time, the world's biggest sawmill. Today the quiet island has private homes, a few restaurants, beaches, a nature reserve and a good little vineyard that offers tastings.

Getting There

Ferries run on seasonally varying schedules. The **Bainbridge ferry** runs hourly from Pier 52 on the Seattle waterfront – an especially scenic way to view the Seattle skyline on the return trip – carrying cars, foot passengers and bicycles.

Cars must take the **Fauntleroy ferry** to **Vashon**, reached by taking Rte 99 south. Passengers and cyclists can take a more direct ferry from the waterfront piers, but once on Vashon there's no public transport save occasional taxis. Contact Washington State Ferries at (800) 843-3779 for all schedule details.

Bainbridge Island Chamber of Commerce, 590 Winslow Way E; www.bainbridgechamber.com.

Bainbridge is loaded with B&Bs, plus some much more expensive inns. Vashon is shorter on accommodation, but there is a rustic hostel that's fun for kids.

Cedar Meadow B&B $$$ 10411 NE Old Creosote Hill Rd, Bainbridge Island; tel: (206) 842-5291. Owners will pick you up at the dock if you book in advance.

Island Country Inn $$$ 920 Hildebrand Lane on Bainbridge Island; tel: (206) 842-9808. Less than a mile from the dock.

On Bainbridge Island:

Café Nola $$$, 101 Winslow Way E; tel: (206) 842-3822. Multi-ethnic cuisine, including Thai, Italian and French.

Harbor Public House $$ Winslow Way; tel: (206) 842-0969. Pub grub such as burgers, fish, chops and chicken. Seattle beers on draught.

La Belle Saison $$–$$$ 278 Winslow Way; tel: (206) 780-4064. French cooking with a touch of Americana thrown in; the homemade croissants are always good. Breakfast and lunch only.

Island Ice Cream & Coffee 584 Winslow Way E; tel (206) 842-2557. Perfect for a quick treat or caffeine lift. Open daily 0800–1600.

The Streamliner $ 397 Winslow Way. Typical Northwestern diner, with low prices and huge, filling portions of flapjacks, seafood, burgers. Open 0700–1430.

THE NORTHERN CASCADE MOUNTAINS

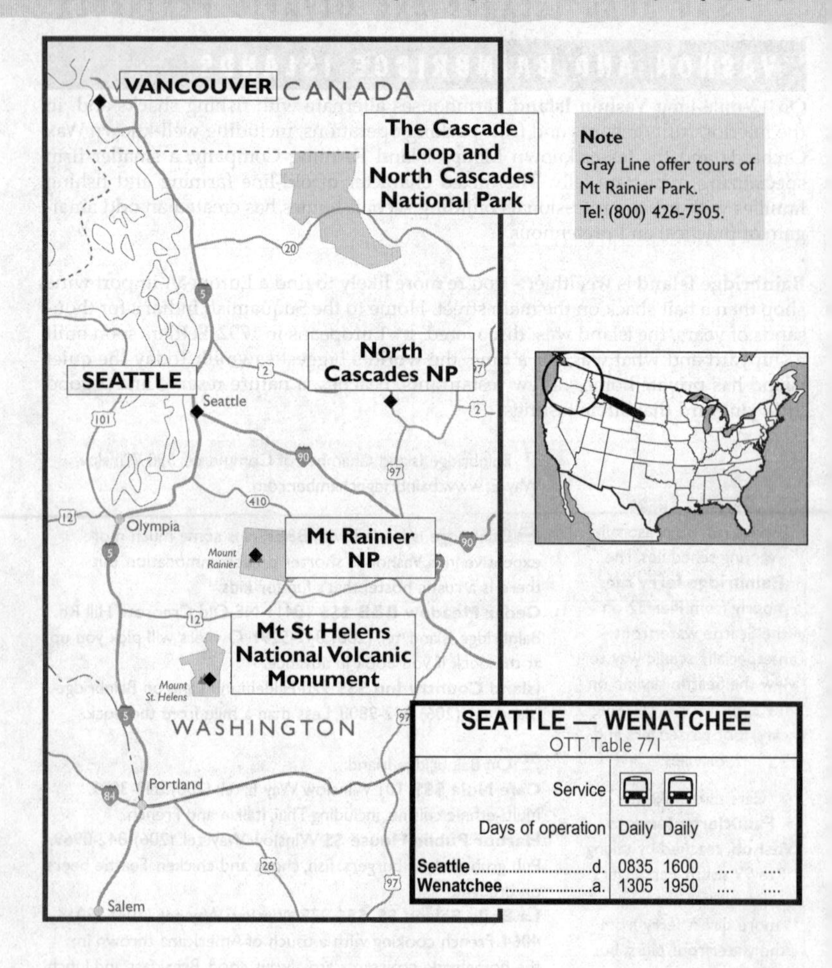

Note
Gray Line offer tours of Mt Rainier Park.
Tel: (800) 426-7505.

SEATTLE — WENATCHEE
OTT Table 771

Service	🚌	🚌		
Days of operation	Daily	Daily		
Seattle ....d.	0835	1600	....	....
Wenatchee ....a.	1305	1950	....	....

Within an hour's drive east of Seattle, the dramatic, brooding Cascade Mountains offer a surprising swathe of snow-covered peaks on a par with the Rockies. On clear days (rare as they are) you can see Mount Rainier from Seattle, and townies make a beeline for this part of the mountains. Further south, Mount St Helens' notorious 1980 volcanic eruption lends a certain volatility to the range.

The northern Cascades are far less visited, and the Cascade Loop, a circular highway route, slips through the upper reaches and the beautiful North Cascades National Park. Stop for fresh apples, for which Washington state is famous – and juicy cherries in season

Exploring on Public Transport

It is possible, though time-consuming, to get to the area by public transport. Northwestern Trailways buses run from Seattle along Hwy 2 through Leavenworth and on to Wenatchee. No public transport reaches the national park, but towns to the south offer equally wonderful scenery: local bus companies serve Chelan on Lake Chelan, across which a boat takes you to Stehekin.

THE CASCADE LOOP AND NORTH CASCADES NATIONAL PARK

Three linked highways north-east of Seattle create the 400 mile Cascade Loop. Two parallel roads lead off I-5 north of Seattle – a southern stretch, Hwy 2, and a northern stretch, Hwy 20 – both of which connect to Hwy 97 towards north central Washington. The Cascades are so twisty that no single highway could traverse the range; instead, one must tack back and forth for hours. It's probably easiest to take I-5 to the entry point of your choice, then explore from there.

Leavenworth, surrounded by mountains on Hwy 2, re-invented itself as a Bavarian village after losing its lumber industry. They've done it up so grandly that only the signs in English remind you where you are. Beautifully painted buildings, carved balconies and ornate signs line streets filled with German restaurants and cute shops, and Bavarian band music drifts into the evening. The Enzian Inn has an alpenhorn 'concert' from its balcony each morning.

En Route

Just 25 miles east of Seattle off I-90, Snoqualmie Falls is a fantastically misty waterfall, familiar to many from David Lynch's TV series *Twin Peaks*. Short hikes lead from the falls, including one up Mount Si, for great views of the Cascades.

On around the loop, **Chelan**, on Hwy 97, is a pretty place from which you can catch a morning ferry across beautiful Lake Chelan, surrounded by stunning purple-green mountains. On the northern tip of the lake, the village of **Stehekin** makes a launch pad for the northern Cascades, with a ranger's station, bicycle rental and shuttle buses to take you further into the hills.

Reaching to the Canadian border, **North Cascades National Park** is far less frequented than Mount

Rainier, partly because of its isolation and lack of tourist facilities. This renders its high glaciers and nearly impenetrable forest all the more enticing.

i **Leavenworth Chamber of Commerce**, PO Box 327, Leavenworth, WA 98826; tel: (509) 548-5807; www.leavenworth. org.

North Cascades National Park Visitor Center, Sedro-Woolley, tel: (360) 856-5700, isn't even in the park, but way back west on Hwy 20. It's open Mon–Thurs 0800–1630 (Fri to 1800 in summer). A small ranger's station on Hwy 20 in the park provides maps and wild camping permits.

Evergreen Motor Inn $$–$$$ 1117 Front St, Leavenworth; tel: (509) 548-5515.

Cabana Motel $$–$$$ 304 Wapato Ave, Chelan; tel: (509) 682- 2233 or (800) 799-2332. Basic motel offering simple rooms.

Enzian Inn $$–$$$ Hwy 2, Leavenworth; tel: (509) 548-5269. Spacious rooms in an alpine theme and bountiful breakfast buffet.

Silver Bay Inn $$$–$$$$ 10 Silver Bay Rd, Stehekin; tel: (509) 682-2212. A finely situated B&B.

MOUNT RAINIER NATIONAL PARK

Think of Mount Rainier, and think of 100 inches of snow, frequent rain, fog, mist, and even occasional brilliant sunshine or starshine glinting from the summit. Of two million annual visitors, 10,000 hikers attempt the snowy 14,411 ft summit – the highest in the Cascades and a world-class climb. For the less vertically inclined, subalpine wild flowers are profuse throughout the summer months, and the lower slopes of the mountain are cloaked in Douglas fir.

The main point of access to the park in which Mount Rainier sits so haughtily is Hwy 706 (off Hwy 7 from Tacoma) through the Nisqually entrance. Roads through the park are deliberately narrow, slowing traffic and preserving scenic vistas in a timeless setting. A few miles into the park, **Longmire** is a collection of buildings including a museum, general store, lodge and restaurant. Further up the slopes of Mount Rainier, the few buildings in **Paradise** include a year-round visitor centre, lodge, restaurant and facilities for hikers, climbers and snowshoers. Rainier Mountaineering, tel: (360) 569-2227, can help with equipment, passes and guides. Nearby **Narada Falls** is a sheer 168 ft drop of clear water into a pool below, and beyond, the winding **Nisqually Glacier** is known to move 3 ft per day.

In summer you can drive on around the base of Mount Rainier and link up with Hwy 410, which leads through the park's north-eastern White River entrance; the route is usually closed during the winter months. This is a staging area for short hikes to **Emmons Glacier**, and from here a narrow, switchback highway ascends to **Sunrise**, a summer-only visitor centre at 6100 ft.

i **Mount Rainier National Park Headquarters**, Ashford; 9 miles west of the Nisqually entrance; tel: (360) 569-2211 for information.

Jackson Visitor Center, Paradise, is open daily mid-May–Oct, Sat–Sun the rest of the year; tel: (360) 569-2211 ext. 2328.

There are cheapish motels in Ashford, and **Mount Rainier Guest Services**, tel: (360) 569-2275, fax: (360) 569-2770, books rooms at lodges in Longmire and Paradise (both $$$–$$$$). There are campsites, all with RV hookups, near each park entrance, all first-come, first-served. Each of the park's developed areas mentioned above has dining facilities, though only Longmire remains open year-round.

MOUNT ST HELENS NATIONAL VOLCANIC MONUMENT

If there was ever any doubt that the white-capped Cascade Range was formed by shattering volcanic upheaval, Mount St Helens dispelled it with a terrifying explosion on 18 May 1980. The blast was the latest in a series of Mount St Helens eruptions, many of which had been viewed by Klickitat Native Americans. The mountain has been a justifiably popular destination since its grand statement, and scientists have been surprised by the speed of nature's regeneration. Insects, small animals, birds and seeds survived under the pyroclastic flow or in caves; this and the mountain's gaping wound, plus the sight of acres of stunted trees, make it an extraordinary sight. The visitor centre in Amboy issues permits for volcano climbing. A long trail encircles the mountain, and there are many shorter hikes to take in the unusual scenery.

THE ERUPTION

A lateral blast lopped the peak's height from 9677 ft to 8383 ft in minutes, spewing a hazy, smoking grey vertical plume 11 miles high, and sending half a cubic mile of pumice, ash and glacial ice down the north face. The Toutle River to the west clogged and the 40 ft deep Columbia River Channel was mired in rock and debris. Trees 150 ft tall toppled like straws up to 17 miles from the explosion, and ash rained down for hundreds of miles. Dust and gases from the eruption affected weather around the globe.

i **Visitor Center**, Amboy (south of the volcano, off Hwy 503 and I-5, closer to Portland); tel: (360) 247-3900. There are several visitor centres along Hwy 504 (which heads east off I-5) leading to the mountain.

There are several motels in the town of Kelso (off I-5 west of the mountain), such as the **Best Western Aladdin** $$ 310 Long Ave; tel: (360) 425-9660 or (800) 764-7378. A number of camp sites surround the mountain.

Driving Route

From Portland take US 30 west to Astoria. Follow US 101 south through Seaside, Tillanook and Florence to Brookings.

Continue on US 101 south to Crescent City, California.

Take US 199 north-east to I-5 at Grants Pass.

Follow I-5 south (really east in this stretch) to Medford.

Take Oregon 62 to the Crater Lake Park access road.

Exit the Park north of Crater Lake and follow Oregon 138 east to Crater-Diamond Lake Junction.

Take US 97 north to Bend, continuing north to Madras.

Take US 26 north-west through Warm Springs Indian Reservation lands, climbing 3949-ft Wapinita Pass over the spine of the Cascades.

Turn north (right) onto Oregon 35, quickly ascending the even higher (4670 ft) pass to Mount Hood.

Continue north on Oregon 35 to I-80 A, taking it west to Portland, or crossing the Columbia River into the state of Washington at Hood River and following Washington 14 west to I-5 and recrossing the river into Portland.

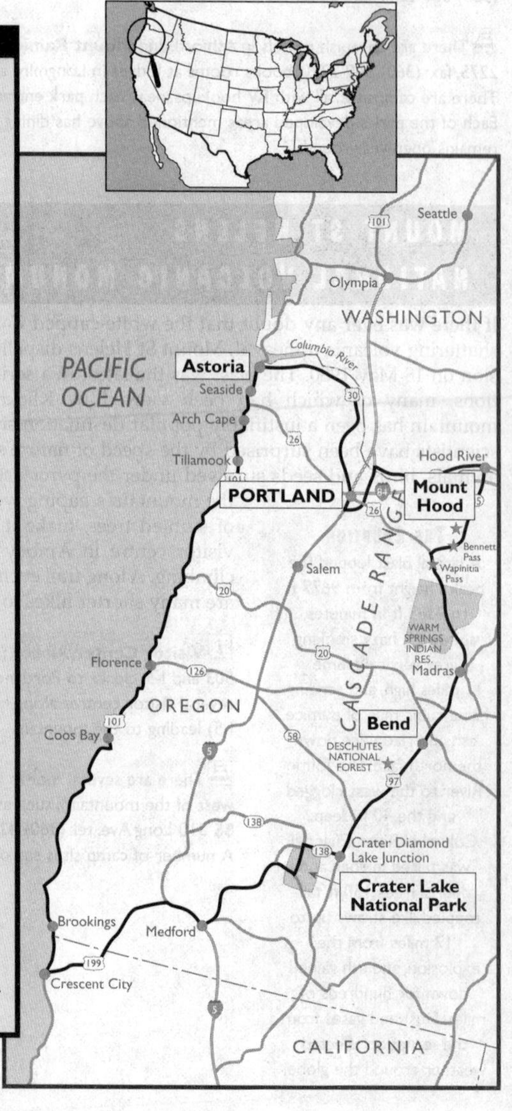

Portland's man-made attractions have to vie hard for your attention as the natural wonders that surround the city will leave your jaw dragging. A hint of the scenic attractions of the surrounding landscapes rises above the city, whose skyline is crowned by majestic Mount Hood. Beyond is the volcanic crater of Mount St Helens. A drive along the Oregon Coast is among the highlights of a trip to the Northwest, with beaches, ocean vistas and unusual rock formations keeping the scenery changing mile by mile.

PORTLAND

Portland, officially known as the 'City of Roses', is certainly the place to wet your whistle. This city has more microbreweries and brewpubs than any other city in the USA, plus a bevy of coffeehouses and some of the most elegant public water fountains to grace a metropolis. Perched on the banks of the Willamette River, Portland is a city of natural wonders and man-made whimsy. Where else can you find sidewalks paved with famous quotes, a book store that encompasses an entire city block, and a 25-ft-tall sculpture that predicts the weather with a fanfare of trumpets every day at noon?

Raise a Glass to Portland's Microbreweries!

For more than a decade Portland has been hailed as the epicentre of the craft-brewing renaissance with more microbreweries, brewpubs and outlets per capita than any other American city. If you've never tasted a craft brew, these hints may help you enjoy your experience even more.

The darker the skies, the darker the beer in your glass (winter is the perfect time for stout, porter or bock).

Microbrews tend to be stronger than mass-produced beer; beware the 'buzz factor'.

Never be afraid to ask what a local would recommend. In Portland the locals love to talk about beer!

Getting There and Getting Around Portland International Airport (PDX), approximately 12 miles from downtown, is served by most US carriers. Tel: (877) 739-4636. City buses, hotel shuttle buses, taxis and limos service the airport. MAX Red Line light rail operates between PDX and downtown.

TriMet, 4012 SE 17th Ave, tel: (503) 238-7433 or www.tri-met.org, operates the local bus and light rail service, the MAX train. For exploring downtown you can't beat the 'Fareless Square', a 330-block zone in which bus, light rail, trolley and streetcar passengers ride for free.

Portland Streetcars travel a 4.8-mile loop through downtown Portland, the art-gallery laced Pearl District, Nob Hill and the Portland State University campus.

Driving? Most streets downtown are one-way only and Fifth and Sixth Streets are limited to bus traffic between West Burnside and Southwest Madison.

INFORMATION Portland Information Center, Pioneer Courthouse Square, 701 SW Sixth Ave; tel: (800) 962-3700; www.travelportland.com.

MONEY Foreign currency exchange is available at the airport and major banks such as Wells Fargo and US Bank. There are plenty of ATMs downtown, in hotels and shopping malls.

ACCOMMODATION Most of the moderate hotel chains are represented such as Econo-Lodge, Holiday Inn and Ramada. Particularly good value, at both the airport and Gresham locations, are the **Pony Soldier Inns**, $$–$$$, tel: 800-634-7669; www.ponysoldierinns.com; the price includes a generous breakfast buffet and free shuttle from the airport.

Hostelling International $ 3031 SE Hawthorne, tel: (503) 236-3380, is situated in one of the best neighbourhoods in Portland with plenty of restaurants and shops. Reservations are recommended for private rooms.

FOOD There is a distinct Pacific Rim flavour and flair to Portland's cuisine, and a very local one as well, with salmon a staple on most menus.

Portland Saturday Market, 108 W Burnside, is the nation's largest continuously operating open-air market for hand-crafted goods, open both Sat and Sun from Mar to 24 Dec. The work of the artisans is top-notch and the overall flavour is straight from the 1960s.

Noho's Hawaiian Café $ SE Clinton and 26th, tel: (503) 233-5301, features large portions of ribs and Hawaiian stir-fry.
Saigon Kitchen $ 835 NE Broadway, tel: (503) 281-3669 makes a lemon-grass soup that feeds several.
Horse Brass Pub $–$$ 4534 SE Belmont St, tel: (503) 232-2202, serves traditional British specialities: ploughman's lunch, scotch egg, sausage rolls or fish and chips.
Huber's $–$$, 411 SW 3rd St; tel: (503) 228-5686. Portland's oldest restaurant is famous for Spanish coffee: right before your eyes they combine coffee, Kahlua, Bailey's, a splash of 151 Rum and light it on fire. Very impressive finish to an evening.

HIGHLIGHTS The City of Roses is famous for, of course, its **International Rose Test Garden**, 400 SW Kingston Ave in Washington Park, open year round. This is the oldest test garden in the USA and features 9000 rose plantings, representing 560 varieties spread over a 4.5-acre site. The terraced garden offers a splendid view of downtown Portland, majestic Mount Hood and the volatile Mount St Helens.

Pittock Mansion, $, 3229 NW Pittock Dr., tel: (503) 823-3624, was completed in 1914. This elegant mansion showcases antique furnishings and fine art.

The 62-acre Catholic sanctuary, **The Grotto – National Sanctuary of Our Sorrowful Mother**, NE 85th Ave and Sandy Blvd, tel: (503) 254-7371; www.thegrotto.org, is one of Portland's most visited attractions. This natural gallery in the woods features a marble replica of Michelangelo's *Pietà*, carved into the base of a 110-ft cliff. Ride the elevator ($) to the top of the bluff for an impressive panoramic view of the Columbia River Valley.

Several of Portland's museums are well worth a visit – **Portland Art Museum** features masterpieces by Monet, Renoir and Picasso as well as Native American and Asian art; the **Oregon Museum of Science and Industry (OMSI)** is an interactive science experience for all ages; and the **Oregon Maritime Museum** features ship models, photos and the sternwheeler *Steamer Portland*, used in the Mel Gibson film *Maverick*.

Pioneer Square Courthouse, SW Broadway and Yamhill, is known as 'Portland's living room'. This public plaza in the heart of the city is paved with bricks inscribed with the names of the donors who contributed to its construction. Surrounding the square are upscale shope, such as Nordstrom's, Swatch and Abercrombie & Fitch. A wonderful place to meet and linger.

Portland's new **Eastbank Esplanade**, a 1.5-mile pedestrian/cycling trail that extends along the east side of downtown Portland's Willamette River from the Steel Bridge to the Hawthorne Bridge, includes a 1200-ft-long floating walkway, a public boat dock and art. With connections from four bridges, visitors are able to complete a 3-mile loop that offers unparalleled views of downtown.

One of the best-kept secrets for travellers is the **Portland Farmer's Market**, which features fresh flowers, seafood, breads, nuts, produce and locally prepared foods. On Saturday, May to October, the market is held in the South Park Blocks on the campus of Portland State University from 0800–1300.

Young visitors will delight in the newly relocated **Children's Museum 2nd Generation**, or CM2 as known by the locals. The museum has taken up residence in Washington Park, just across from the Oregon Zoo. Known for hands-on exhibits that integrate play and learning, the facility is a big hit with the under-12 set. Among the museum's new exhibits are a magical forest for babies and toddlers and the 'Vroom Room' where kids can make things really move.

Ready for a river adventure? Try a wet and wild jetboat ride with **Willamette Jetboat Excursions**; tel: (503) 231-1532; www.jetboatpdx.com. This is an exciting way to view Portland's historic shipyards, waterfront and bridges. Tours operate from late April to mid-October. Call for schedules and boarding location directions.

THE OREGON COAST

One of the West Coast's most pleasant drives runs the length of the Oregon coast, a total distance of some 350 miles or so – and slow miles, at that. During the summer months, every last Winnebago in North America seems to have plotted a direct course for this stretch of US Highway 101, so don't expect or hope to complete the journey in a day. Take heart, though. Views of the ocean, lighthouses, fog, boats, tiny towns, beaches and weird 'sea stacks' (stone formations) are so beautiful that you won't mind the extra time.

It's easiest to get here by coming directly from the Olympic Peninsula (see pages 464–467); at the little town of Chinook in far south-western Washington, cross the toll bridge to Astoria and proceed due south along US 101. If you're coming from Seattle, exit I-5 at Longview (about one hour south of Olympia) and cross the bridge into Oregon, turning west on US 30 for Astoria.

From Portland, take US 26 west to the ocean, about a ½ hour drive. Finally, from California and points south, either continue north along US 101 from Eureka, or take I-5 to Eugene or Corvallis, then turn west along the twisting two-lanes of Oregon 126 or US 20 until you reach the sea.

GETTING THERE Greyhound runs a service along the length of Hwy 101, but only once a day each direction (north and south); its schedule varies. Contact Greyhound, tel: (800) 229-9424; www.greyhound.com.

ASTORIA TO TILLAMOOK This is probably the best stretch of the coast, and consequently the slowest. Every turn seems to reveal a new view of the Pacific breaking far below against the rocks.

Astoria, the northern gateway to Oregon's coast, is a sturdy and historical old town with fishing and trapping origins; its position at the mouth of the giant Columbia River once made it a salmon capital, though today the river has been tamed in the name of barges and hydroelectric power. This is the area where explorers Lewis and Clark made their winter camp near the Pacific after a year and a half of difficult journeying from St Louis by horse and foot. To the south, **Fort Clatsop** recreates what life might have been like in the spare, long-gone wooden barracks the party built.

Seaside is, frankly, a beach resort town but there's more than a little history here too: Lewis and Clark's party obtained salt from boiling seawater here (the salt works are still partly visible); you're more likely to swim at the good beach or wander the boardwalk. A mile south, there's good climbing through towering spruce trees.

Cannon Beach earns its name with pounding waves. The beach is fine, and the town is more eclectic than most in these parts, but most travellers pass this way to gawk at the enormous rock known as the **Haystack**, and it really does look like one. **Arch Cape**, just south, is another fantastic rock formation glimpsed from on high – very high. By the time you've dropped back down to the turnoff for the sea-level town of **Manzanita** you might well be ready for a short walk on the small, pretty beach.

Rockaway Beach has yet another strip of sand, plus a great local smokehouse right on the highway selling expensive but delicious cuts of cured salmon.

It's 23 more miles of scenic driving to **Tillamook**, nationally famous for its orange-coloured smoked local cheeses. Several emporiums on the east side of the highway lay out free samples in an effort to make the sale, and they lay the cow business on a little thick, but there's no harm nibbling.

Seaside Visitors Bureau, 71 North Roosevelt St; tel: (888) 306-2326 or (503) 738-3097. One of the best sources of information along this stretch of the coast.

Hostelling International–Seaside $ 930 Holladay Dr. in Seaside; tel: (800) 909-4776 ext. 46 or (503) 738-7911. One of the better West Coast hostels, with an espresso bar, river deck, barbecue and motel-style double rooms. The owner is a cycling enthusiast and advises on local biking.

The Stand $ at Avenue U near the beach in Seaside, serves authentic and delicious Mexican food that's West Coast enough to lose most of the grease.

TILLAMOOK TO FLORENCE This section, relatively flat, sees the cliffs and sea stacks of the northern coast giving way to sand dunes and beaches. The stretch is dense with seaside state parks, a few with campgrounds attached – a good thing, as accommodation in this area is mostly priced above budget level.

After a stretch of good beaches, one comes to the two commercial hubs of this resort area: first comes **Lincoln City**, with all the obligatory services and accommodation. Then it's another 25 miles along to **Newport**, larger and with more attractions – among them the Yaquina Bay Lighthouse, the Oregon Coast Aquarium ($$) and the Oregon History Center.

Then begins a much wilder and less populated stretch, wedged between the increasingly rocky coast and the big Siuslaw National Forest. **Yachats** is well known for its seasonal fishing and pretty coastline, and is a good base for dramatic **Cape Perpetua**, a park ($) with a high overlook onto the coast and an explanatory visitor centre. The **Haceta Head lighthouse** and sea lion caves bring you to Florence.

Lincoln City Visitor and Convention Bureau, 801 SW Hwy 101; tel: (800) 452-2151 or (541) 994-8378. Largest tourism office along this middle stretch of coast.

Cape Perpetua Interpretive Center is west of Yachats, on the ocean; tel: (541) 547-3289.

EconoLodge $$ 606 Highway 101, Newport; tel: (541) 265-7723. Predictable chain hotel in a strip of similar contenders.
Days Inn $$ 544 Highway 101; tel: (541) 265-5767. The cheapest option in an area where summer prices are artificially inflated.

Mo's $–$$ 657 Southwest Bay Boulevard, Newport, seems like the original Northwestern diner, and is something of a legend in these parts. Thick tasty bowls of clam chowder are the speciality, though the restaurant does other items as well. There's a newish annex across the street, but eat at the original (still no credit cards accepted) for more atmosphere.

FLORENCE TO BROOKINGS

The final stretch south, from Florence to Brookings, begins with dunes but quickly changes to the sort of headlands that characterize the northern portion of the coast. It begins with **Oregon Dunes National Recreation Area**, a stunning collection of 200-ft-plus dunes that extends nearly 40 miles in all. There's an overlook area about 10 miles south of Florence.

Reedsport, a fishing town with some of the coast's least expensive hotel beds, is next, then miles more of the dunes, which continue almost to the doorstep of even more working-class **Coos Bay**. Rather than stopping here, continue approximately 15 more miles south on Highway 101.

Bandon's main street looks like any other's, but a block away there's a good sandy beach with stunning rock formations warped by thousands of years' worth of wind and water. It's definitely worth a look. The area is also known for its cranberry harvest; most of it ends up in commercial juice products.

The last 90 miles are quiet, with more beaches and headlands and less traffic. **Brookings**, just before the California state line, offers little excitement beyond its curiously warm climate, even in winters, which is due to an upsurge of moist southerly winds; they grow astounding varieties of flowers here, but the town is a less-than-grand finish to the coastal tour.

The Oregon Dunes National Recreation Area Visitors Center in Reedsport dispenses information about dunes to the south. Tel: 541-271-3611.

Anchor Bay Inn $$ 1821 Highway 101 in Reedsport; tel: (541) 271-2149. Some rooms at this simple motel have kitchenettes.

Economy Inn $$ 1593 Highway 101 in Reedsport; tel: (541) 271-3671. Inexpensive, characterless motel.
Motel 6 $$ 1445 Bayshore in Coos Bay; tel: (541) 267-7171. Not all that bad a budget option if you've come this far south.
Sea Star Hostel $ 375 2nd St in Bandon; tel: (541) 347-9632. A converted motel, definitely a bit down-at-heel but certainly adequate enough at a pinch – and it's only a few blocks from the beach.
Westward Motel $$ 1026 Chetco Ave, Brookings; tel: (541) 469-7471. Still another no-frills motel along Highway 101.

Bandon Baking Co. and Deli $ 160 Second St, Bandon; tel: (541) 347-9440. Casual breakfast and lunch place serving homemade granola, soup and sandwiches. Open 0800–1700 daily.
City Sub $ 149 N 4th St in Coos Bay. Just what it promises: filling sandwiches at a sub-fancy price. A winner with the locals.

CRATER LAKE NATIONAL PARK

Nearly a perfect circle, and blue as the sky, Crater Lake is justifiably popular during the short summer season when it's snow-free. Don't expect solitude when you get here.

After paying the admission fee ($$, but valid for one week), collect maps and information at the visitor centre. Just below, a small house with a balcony overlooks the lake, whose bottom lies nearly 2000 ft beneath the rim; inside, some of the history and natural history – including an explanation of the long-extinct volcano that once erupted here – is laid out in exhibit form.

Most visitors then choose to circle the caldera via the 35-mile-long Rim Drive, a clearly marked drive with turnings to high cliff paths with splendid views, and other walks to such sights as Wizard Island, a weird rock formation that interrupts the lake's western shore. (Many of these trails and roads are impassable due to snow during the long winter, however.)

Accommodation is limited to a few lodges and motels, plus a collection of campgrounds; most are located south of the actual park boundaries at Rte 62. Note that many of the services – including all lodgings and gas stations – close for the season at the end of October, not to reappear until late the following May at the earliest.

Reach the park directly from Portland by taking I-5 to Roseburg, then exiting onto Rte 138 and climbing east approximately 85 miles through the pretty Umpqua forest, past lakes and falls to the park turnoff.

ℹ **The Rim Village Visitor Center**, about 5 miles north of the Hwy 62 turnoff, is the central clearinghouse for park information. Tel: (541) 594-2211.

Crater Lake Lodge $$$$ 585 Rim Village Dr.; tel: (541) 830-8700 is the only lodging within park boundaries, and just what one would expect: an old-fashioned wilderness lodge of simple, wooden furnishing and few distractions save the stupendous lake views.

BEND AND THE CENTRAL CASCADES

Tucked beneath the eastern brow of the mountains, and thus much drier than its counterparts on the western side, Bend, Oregon, makes a good overnight stop for excursions into the central Cascades.

The huge Deschutes National Forest lies just west. Among the choicest other options are a drive west up scenic Route 242 (open only in summer), which climbs from the town of Sisters to a pass and then follows the McKenzie River down to the sea; a look at the lava caves, craters and petrified forest just south; or a drive along the Cascade Lakes Highway with its mountains, lakes, and sports centres.

The city itself is part logging-town and part base camp for outdoorsy types; there are few true attractions save the High Desert Museum. Accommodation is plentiful, however, and there are numerous campgrounds in the Cascade Lakes and hotels in Sisters, as well.

ℹ The headquarters for Deschutes National Forest is located at 1645 Hwy 20 E in Bend; tel: (541) 383-5300. Other ranger stations are located in Crescent and Sisters.
For tourism information in the Bend area, contact the Bend Chamber of Commerce, located at 63805 N Hwy 97; tel: (541) 382-3221.

Bend Cascade Hostel $ 19 SW Century Dr.; tel: (800) 299-3813 or (503) 389-3813. Homey little hostel near the woods, with good management and sturdy bunks.

MOUNT HOOD

Just south of the Columbia River gorge (which is also the dividing line where Washington ends and Oregon begins), Mount Hood rises steeply from the river, nearly at sea level, to more than 11,000 feet high – easily the roof of Oregon. Reach it directly from Portland by driving due east on US 26 about 50 miles or, far more interesting, the scenic Loop Highway from Hood River south along Oregon Route 35 through orchards, foothills and a good lookout point.

There's more than just the peak, however. The huge Mount Hood Wilderness Area, comprising more than a million acres, is split into several parts: ski lodges, developed resort areas, campgrounds, and then wilder backcountry. Skiing is the prime draw – you can do it year-round – but you'll also find plenty of hiking trails on the lower slopes that are full of appreciative locals who want a taste of the mountain's meadows during the summer months.

Camping is concentrated on the eastern flanks of the mountain (Rte 35) and also around Timothy Lake, just to the south.

i The park information station is located on US Route 26 near the turnoff to the park. Tel: (888) 622-4822.

Mount Hood Inn $$$$ 87450 Government Camp Loop, Government Camp, OR; tel: (503) 272-3205. Fairly plush and expensive, though definitely geared toward skiers, with a waxing room, lockers, laundry, whirlpool and restaurant.
Schoolhouse Hostel $ PO Box 855, Bingen, WA; tel (509) 493-3363. Just across the Columbia River, about 25 miles north of Mount Hood, this simple hostel caters mostly to windsurfers.

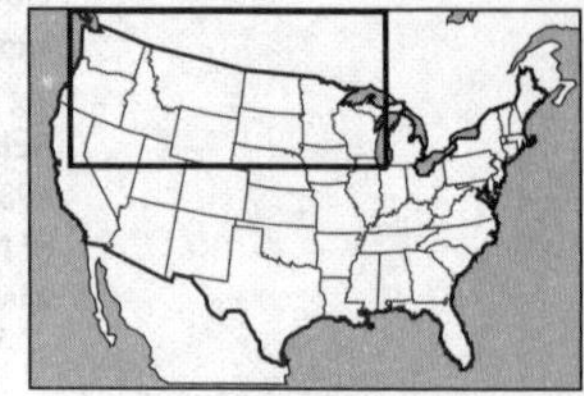

SEATTLE — CHICAGO

OTT Tables 341/769/770/771

Service	Bus	Bus	RAIL	Bus	Bus
Days of operation	Daily	Daily	Daily	Daily	Daily
Special notes		C	A		B
Seattle D .... d.	1030	1420	1645	2330	....
Spokane .... d.	1715	2125	0115	0615	....
Butte .... d.	0130	....	|	1445	....
Glacier Park .... d.	....	....	0954	|	....
Bismarck .... d.	....	....	|	1000	....
Minneapolis .... d.	....	....	0735	1010	1300
Milwaukee .... d.	....	....	1400	0445	2015
Chicago D .... a.	....	....	1540	0630	2200

Special notes:

A–The Empire Builder. This train has sleepers and a dining car available. All journeys should be reserved in advance.

B–Additional trips: 0700, 0900, 1500, 2210, 2345⑤⑦.

C–Additional trip: 1800

D–This route crosses three times zones. All times shown are local times.

On 'The Empire Builder'

Traversing a vast northern stretch of the USA, Amtrak's 'Empire Builder' makes a two-day journey across some of the country's most dramatic mountain scenery, most desolate prairies and richest farmland. From Seattle, the train flies through the snowy Cascade Mountains and across central Washington. After Spokane, the route takes in a piece of northern Idaho and more mountain scenery follows in western Montana. The train slips along the southern boundary of Glacier National Park, one of the very finest in the land.

En Route

Before it turns on its long journey eastward, look out of the left-hand side of the train to see the jagged mountain tops of Olympic National Park, across Puget Sound.

On the Portland route, keep your eyes open (right-hand side of the train) for the plunging cascades of Bridal Veil and Multnomah Falls and the graceful contours of Mount Hood as the train runs through the Columbia River Gorge.

Montana's northern Rocky Mountains are as haunting as any, but between eastern Montana and Minnesota, as the train sprawls across the empty North Dakota plain, the trip can drag a bit if you're not simply dazzled by the vastness of it all. Wisconsin and Minnesota form part of America's heartland, and the tracks cross rolling fields of corn and beans, skirting thousands of lakes. There are two cities of note. Milwaukee, a blue-collar town on the shores of Lake Michigan, is one of the country's beer-brewing capitals, while Minneapolis and St Paul (known as the Twin Cities) share some excellent museums, fine architecture and a balanced flavour.

SPOKANE

Home to the first non-native settlement in the Pacific north-west, Spokane has become the only genuine city in Washington east of the Cascades. Built at the largest falls on the Spokane River, it's the commercial and cultural capital of the Inland Empire, a vast area stretching north into British Columbia, east to the Rocky Mountains, south to the Columbia River and west to the Cascades. Lumbermen, fur traders, farmers, barkeepers, prostitutes and missionaries followed the railway to Spokane, and the economy was fuelled by rich mining strikes in nearby Idaho and British Columbia. It remains a thoroughly pleasant city.

Riverfront Park is Spokane's defining feature, and was the site of the 1974 World's Fair. **Spokane Falls**, in the centre of the park, were an important Native American fishery and settlement, and later became the base from which a sawmill developed into today's city. Best viewing spots are from the gondola cable cars ($; running daily 1100–2100 except in winter) or the footbridge directly over the falls – though the spray can be drenching.

Many fine brick and stone buildings from the ebullient industrial years survive in the city centre. The sparkling **Northwest Museum of Arts and Culture** is one any city would be proud of, with excellent displays interpreting history and culture of the Northwest. It includes the historic Campbell House mansion, open Tues–Sun 1100–1700. $$, 2316 W First Ave, tel: (509) 456-3931, www.northwestmuseum.org.

i **The Convention and Visitors Bureau**, 926 W Sprague St; tel: (800) 248-3230 or (888) 776-5263; or the **Visitor Information Center**, 201 W Main Ave; tel: (509) 747-3230.

Amtrak pulls in at 221 W First St.

Advance booking is strongly recommended. The closest camp site is at Riverside State Park, 6 miles north.

Howard Johnson $$ 211 S Division St; tel: (509) 838-6630 or (888) 271-4190. Simple budget rooms near the centre.

Fotheringham House $$$–$$$$ 2128 W 2nd Ave; tel: (509) 838-1891; fax: (509) 838-1807. An 1891 house, easily the city's most comfortable B&B with the tastiest breakfast.

Northwest cuisine (especially salmon) features prominently.

Frank's Diner $$ 1516 W 2nd St; tel: (509) 747-8798. Classic American fare (breakfast, burgers, milkshakes) in a 1906 railroad car. Meals daily to 2100.

Steam Plant Grill $–$$$ 159 S Lincoln St; tel: (509) 777-3900. In a historic building, this hip restaurant features inexpensive New American dishes and beer brewed on site.

GLACIER NATIONAL PARK

One of the National Park Service's jewels, Glacier National Park ($) is a wilderness of rocky peaks, cold glacial lakes, thousands of waterfalls and dense pine forest. By far the heaviest tourist season is summer, when the park's one through-road is open.

Amtrak stops at East Glacier Park (summer only), and at Essex and West Glacier Park (year round). The park service runs shuttle buses along this route between East Glacier and West Glacier, but there is no other transport into or within the park. Coming by train, West Glacier is your most viable option, as it's only 2 miles from here to the Apgar Visitor Center on beautiful **Lake McDonald**.

The area around Lake McDonald is as good a place as any to spend time if you're without a vehicle; it has camping, lodging and dining facilities. You can take sunset cruises on the lake or rent your own rowing boat, and the lower slopes of the park can be explored on foot from here. Unless you want to embark on a several-day hike, though, **Going to the Sun Road** is the only way to attain the park's upper reaches. Despite the heavy traffic, the ribbon of highway elicits oohs and aahs at every turn, as it weaves a path along mountain slopes. The views are simply awesome, and the ecology of the park - purple wild flowers, mountain goats - and Montana's famous big sky can leave you breathless. With the right equipment, it's easy to slip off travelled routes and escape. The road emerges at St Mary entrance, where another visitor centre and basic facilities are available.

i Glacier National Park, PO Box 128, West Glacier, Montana 59936; tel: (406) 888-7800.

It is essential to book a room before arriving. All reservations are handled by **Glacier Park Inc.**, tel: (406) 756-2444, and these include lodges and cabins at the main entrances and in more remote sections. There is an **HI hostel** in East Glacier on Hwy 49; tel: (406) 226-4426; handy for the train station, but not so accessible to the park without your own car. There are more than a dozen camp sites near the entrances and main road, and these fill up fast in summer.

MINNEAPOLIS AND ST PAUL

The twin cities of Minneapolis and St Paul, on opposite sides of the Mississippi River, exemplify the sense of cleanliness, order and general wholesomeness of the American Midwest. Both are attractive and have plenty to offer culturally, as well as pretty lakes nearby for a swim in summer.

Minneapolis is affectionately referred to as the 'Minneapple' by its residents, and has a nice stretch of parkland along the Mississippi to complement several good museums. Downstream a few miles and on the opposite bank, central St Paul is presided over by the stern state capitol and its grand cathedral. The two city centres are linked by express bus 94BCD.

A good place to start is the **Riverfront** in Minneapolis, a scenic stretch known alternatively as the Mississippi Mile. The city was founded by a fur trader in the 1840s, and the cobbled streets and restored buildings give a feel of the time. A modern glass-and-steel skyline now overshadows the 1929 **Foshay Tower** (821 Marquette Ave), which has an observation deck. Several blocks south-west of centre, Vineland Pl. and Lyndale Ave S, the **Walker Art Center** is a great contemporary arts gallery with a huge sculpture garden. $, open Tues–Sat 1000–1700 (Thur until 2000), Sun

> Winters in the Midwest are severe. You will need to come equipped with padded waterproof layers for sightseeing out of doors, but the trappings of modern comfort in the Twin Cities have bestowed both cities with a skyway system of glass passages linking downtown office buildings.

1100–1700. An equal distance south of downtown, the excellent **Minneapolis Institute of Art**, 2400 3rd Ave S, has art from virtually all corners of the globe covering five millennia. In addition to the Rembrandts, Van Goghs, Cézannes and Mirós, the gallery has fine collections of African, East Asian and Peruvian artefacts. Open Tues–Sat 1000–1700 (Thur until 2100), Sun 1200–1700; free.

St Paul preserves its feeling of grandeur with stately monuments and fine Victorian mansions. The art deco **City Hall and Courthouse** near the Wabasha St Bridge are complemented by a three-storey white onyx statue, the 'Vision of Peace'. The **Minnesota History Center**, 345 Kellogg Blvd, presents the lakes, dairies and heavily Scandinavian-influenced culture of the state. Open Wed–Sat 1000–1700 (Tues until 2000), Sun 1200–1700; free. Uphill to the north is the **State Capitol**, while to the west the **Cathedral of St Paul**, built in 1915, is modelled after St Peter's in Rome. Summitt Ave winds down and around the cathedral's base, past beautiful old homes of some of the wealthier early 20th-century citizens.

South of town near the airport, at the intersection of Hwys 5 and 55, **Fort Snelling** was built in 1819 as a wilderness outpost; today it does a good job of presenting early Minnesota history. $, open May–Oct, Wed–Sat 1000–1700, Sun 1200–1700. Take bus no. 7 from Minneapolis or no. 9 from St Paul.

People come from around the world to visit the outrageous **Mall of America**, easily the world's largest shopping mall. Serious shoppers won't want to miss the 500-plus stores and amusement park rides. Express bus no. 80 from Minneapolis, and bus no. 54 from St Paul, make the run regularly.

i **The Minneapolis Visitor Information Center** is at 40 S 7th St; tel: (612) 335-5827 or (800) 445-7412; www.minneapolis.org. **The St Paul Convention and Visitors Bureau** is at 175 W Kellogg Blvd; tel: (651) 265-4900 or (800) 627-6101; www.stpaulcvb.org.

The Amtrak station, 730 Transfer Rd, near University Ave, is about midway between the city centres on the St Paul side.

The Twin Cities' welcoming Midwest style carries over into its gracious B&Bs. Always ask about weekend rates at hotels.

MINNEAPOLIS

City of Lakes International House/Hostel $ 2400 Stevens Ave S; tel: (612) 871-3210. Budget dorm beds and private rooms in historic mansion. Bus nos. 10, 17 or 18 southbound to 24th Street and Nicollet Ave.

Hotel Amsterdam $$ 828 Hennepin Ave; tel: (612) 288-0459 or (800) 649-9500. Reasonable downtown establishment with a largely gay clientele.

Evelo's B&B $$–$$$ 2301 Bryant Ave S; tel: (651) 374-9656. Victorian B&B within walking distance of Walker Art Center.

ST PAUL **Chatsworth B&B** $$$ 984 Ashland Ave; tel: (651) 227-4288 or (877) 978-4837. Victorian home near the governor's mansion.

Although standard Midwest fare is readily available, the Twin Cities have a cosmopolitan array of cuisines from which to choose. The best places to look are the Warehouse District (around 3rd St S and Hennepin Ave) and Nicollet Mall in Minneapolis, and along St Peter's St in St Paul.

MINNEAPOLIS **8th St Grill** $$ 800 Marquette Ave; tel: (612) 349-5717. Popular downtown Minneapolis bar and grill.

Ben Coleman's Caribbean Splash $$–$$$ 106 N 3rd St; tel: (800) 706-3871. A surprise in these parts: Jamaican jerk chicken and ginger beer.

Café Brenda $$–$$$ 300 1st Ave N Warehouse District café specialising in vegetarian and seafood dishes.

ST PAUL **Babani's Kurdish Restaurant** $$–$$$ 544 St Peter St. America's first Kurdish café, a pleasant downtown St Paul affair.

Taste of Scandinavia $$$–$$$$ 2232 Center Ave; tel: (651) 645-9181. Appropriately for the cities' rich Scandinavian heritage, an ever-changing array of salmon, venison and meatballs.

MILWAUKEE

To most Americans, Milwaukee means one thing: beer. However, the industry has gone through some big shakeups in the past few years, with corporate buyouts siphoning off business, and the city is no longer the beer centre it once was. Milwaukee's character derives from its largely German immigrant, working-class population, and this influence is evident today in the city's neighbourhoods and many bars. Active ethnic communities hold more than a dozen festivals along the lakefront each year and visitors are almost sure to happen upon one of these.

Although Milwaukee is not a major tourist destination, a few sites do merit your attention. The **Riverwalk** development improves the city's otherwise drab downtown, a stretch of the Milwaukee River devoted to shops, restaurants and strolling space. On the lakefront, the **Milwaukee Art Museum** features European and American paintings and sculpture, decorative arts and a good collection of American and Haitian folk art. $, 750 N Lincoln Memorial Dr.; open Tues–Wed and Fri–Sat 1000–1700, Thur 1200–2100, Sun 1200–1700.

To understand the importance of beer in Milwaukee's economy and social life, visit the **Captain Frederick Pabst Mansion**. The founder of the Pabst brewery (no longer in Milwaukee) built his home in the Flemish Renaissance style; the opulent interior attests to his wealth. $$, 2000 W Wisconsin Ave, west of centre; open Mon–Sat 1000–1530, Sun 1200–1530. Free samples are given out after the **Miller Brewing Company** tour. The huge brewery, at 4251 W State St, is open Mon–Sat 1200–1530; tel: (414) 931-BEER; free. Take bus no. 71 west from the centre.

Milwaukee's friendly **Visitor Information Center** is located at 510 W Kilbourn Ave; tel: (800) 231-0903; www.milwaukee.org. Open Mon–Fri 0800–1700.

The Amtrak station is about a mile west of centre at 433 W St Paul Ave.

Business travellers are the city's main hotel draw, but there are also plenty of B&Bs. The only hostel is way out of town.

Red Barn Hostel $ 6750 W Loomis Rd, Greendale; tel: (414) 529-3299 or (800) 909-4776 ext. 28. Open May–Oct only. Accessible by bus no. 10 from W Wisconsin Ave; change to bus no. 35 at Southway and Loomis Rd. Bicycles and canoe rental available.

Ambassador Hotel $$–$$$ 2308 W Wisconsin Ave; tel: (414) 342-8400; fax: (414) 342-0238. Art deco central hotel.

County Clare $$$–$$$$ 1234 N Astor St; tel: (888) 942-5273 or (414) 272-5273; fax: (414) 290-6300. Irish-style B&B near the lake.

MADISON

Wisconsin's capital, Madison, is a lively, pretty college town an hour west of Milwaukee. Frequent buses make the trip daily.

German cuisine meets the Midwest on happy plates of meat and potatoes. Fish from a multitude of nearby lakes is another speciality. Wash it all down with beer, of course.

Milwaukee Ale House $$–$$$ 233 N Water St; tel: (414) 226-2337. Pushing the local tradition, this small brewery serves German and Cajun food to go with its ales, riverfront views and live music.

Karl Ratzsch's Restaurant $$$ 320 E Mason St; tel: (414) 276-2720. Central European schnitzels and sausages are highlights of the menu.

Third Street Pier $$$ 1110 N Old World 3rd St; tel: (414) 272-0330. Seafood and steaks downtown on the Milwaukee River.

WHERE NEXT?

There are frequent buses to Madison, Wisconsin's lively, pretty capital an hour west of Milwaukee. See p. 325 for the city guide to Chicago. If doing this journey in reverse, see pp. 457 and 469 for Seattle and the Northern Cascade Mountains.

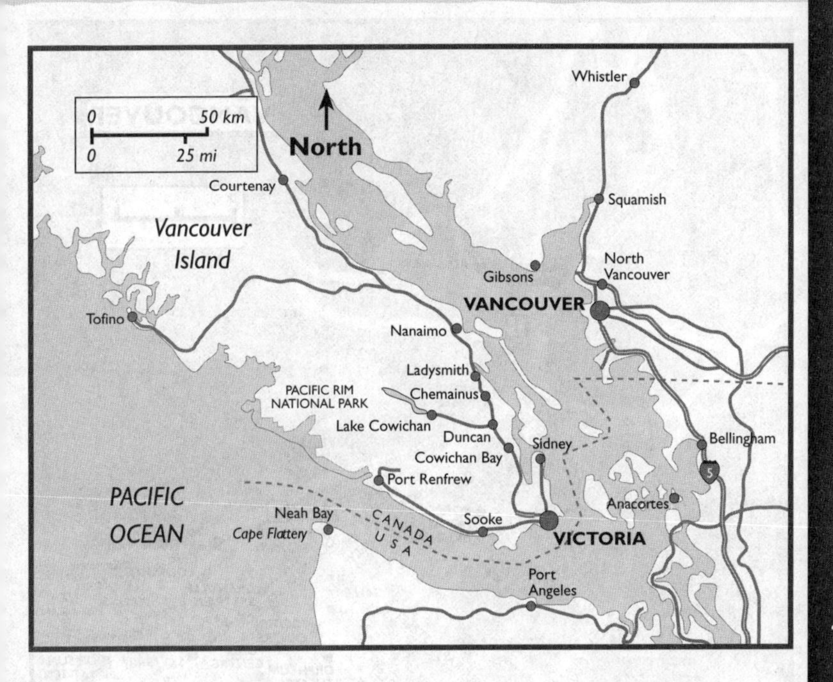

Confusingly, the city of Vancouver is on the mainland, while Victoria is on Vancouver Island.

Travellers in the far Northwest are rightly tempted to add another country and two delightful cities to their itinerary. It's easy to do, and the temptation becomes even greater when travellers realise that they can do so in a circuit that includes scenic ferry rides. Vancouver and Victoria, both in the Canadian province of British Columbia and a short ferry ride apart across the Strait of Georgia, are among North America's most pleasant cities to visit. Both are beautifully situated, Victoria around its Inner Harbour and Vancouver caught between the mountains and the water that nearly surrounds it.

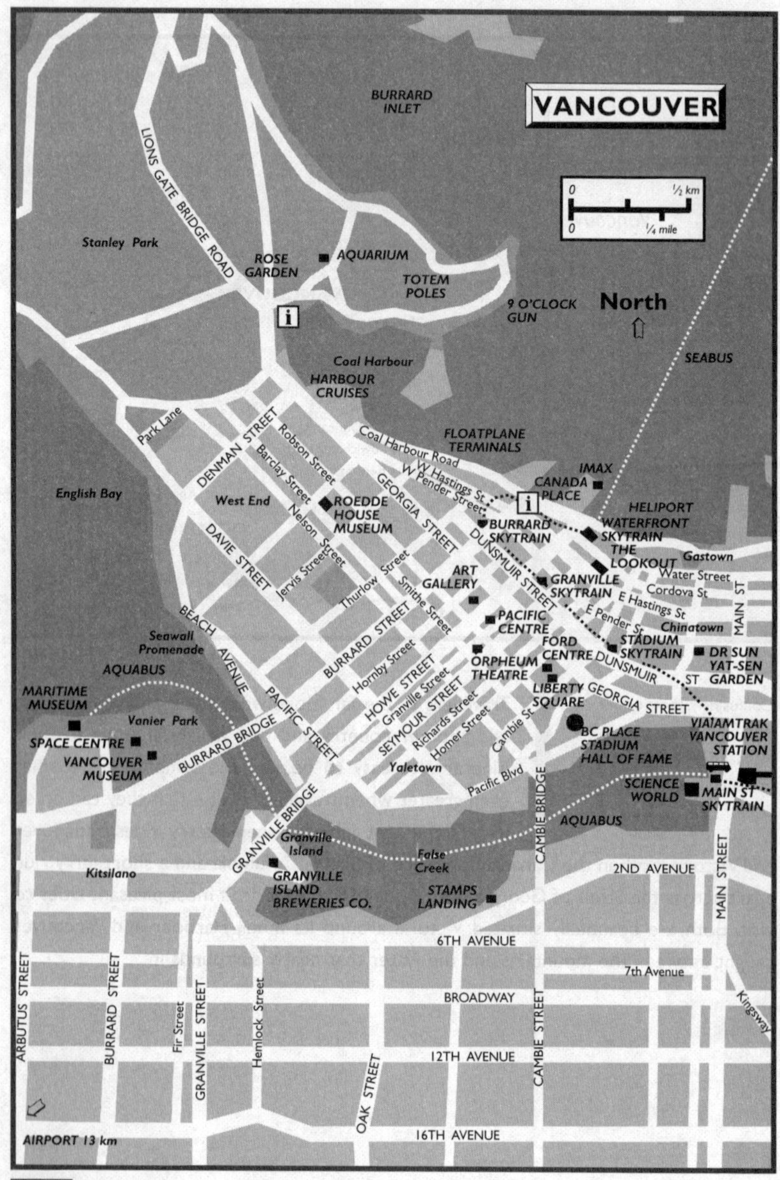
VANCOUVER
BURRARD INLET
0 ½ km
0 ¼ mile
North
Stanley Park
LIONS GATE BRIDGE ROAD
ROSE GARDEN
AQUARIUM
TOTEM POLES
9 O'CLOCK GUN
SEABUS
Coal Harbour
HARBOUR CRUISES
FLOATPLANE TERMINALS
Coal Harbour Road
Park Lane
DENMAN STREET
Robson Street
Barclay Street
W Hastings St
W Pender Street
IMAX
CANADA PLACE
HELIPORT
English Bay
West End
ROEDDE HOUSE MUSEUM
Nelson Street
GEORGIA STREET
BURRARD SKYTRAIN
WATERFRONT SKYTRAIN
THE LOOKOUT
Gastown
DAVIE STREET
Jervis Street
Thurlow Street
DUNSMUIR STREET
ART GALLERY
GRANVILLE SKYTRAIN
Water Street
Cordova St
E Hastings St
MAIN ST
Smithe Street
PACIFIC CENTRE
E Pender St
Chinatown
BEACH AVENUE
Seawall Promenade
BURRARD STREET
FORD CENTRE
STADIUM SKYTRAIN
DR SUN YAT-SEN GARDEN
AQUABUS
Hornby Street
ORPHEUM THEATRE
DUNSMUIR ST
MARITIME MUSEUM
HOWE STREET
Granville Street
LIBERTY SQUARE
GEORGIA STREET
VIA/AMTRAK VANCOUVER STATION
Vanier Park
PACIFIC STREET
SEYMOUR STREET
Richards Street
Homer Street
Cambie St
SPACE CENTRE
BURRARD BRIDGE
BC PLACE STADIUM HALL OF FAME
VANCOUVER MUSEUM
Yaletown
Pacific Blvd
SCIENCE WORLD
MAIN ST SKYTRAIN
GRANVILLE BRIDGE
CAMBIE BRIDGE
AQUABUS
Granville Island
False Creek
Kitsilano
GRANVILLE ISLAND BREWERIES CO.
STAMPS LANDING
2ND AVENUE
MAIN STREET
6TH AVENUE
7th Avenue
BROADWAY
Kingsway
ARBUTUS STREET
BURRARD STREET
Fir Street
GRANVILLE STREET
Hemlock Street
CAMBIE STREET
12TH AVENUE
OAK STREET
AIRPORT 13 km
16TH AVENUE

GETTING THERE AND GETTING AROUND

Vancouver is about 144 miles north of Seattle via I-5, a 3-hr drive with border formalities. More scenic is the route from the Olympic Peninsula via car-ferry from Port Angeles to **Victoria**, and ferry to Tsawwassen. Clipper Navigation operates the Victoria Clipper between Seattle and Victoria, the most direct way to reach the island from the US; tel: (206) 448-5000 in Seattle, (250) 382-8100 in Victoria, (800) 888-2535 elsewhere; www.victoriaclipper.com.

Greyhound buses and Amtrak connect Seattle and Vancouver, arriving at 1150 Station St; the elevated **SkyTrain** takes you downtown.

Vancouver Translink buses operate 0400–2400; tel: (604) 953-3333, www.transitbc.com. Their **SeaBus** crosses Burrard Inlet to North Vancouver, a scenic excursion (avoid commuting hours). Hip **Granville Island** is reached by tiny ferries or by bus.

BC Ferries suggests vehicle reservations between Tsawwassen and Vancouver Island; tel: (604) 444-2890, (888) 223-3779, www.bcferries.bc.ca. Bus/ferry service is by **Pacific Coach Lines**; tel: (800) 661-1725.

VANCOUVER

As Canada's gateway to the Pacific, Vancouver relishes its tremendous ethnic variety. Chinatown (Pender and Keefer Sts) and newer Japantown (Powell St) join Little Italy (East Vancouver), which itself now includes many other ethnic communities, and Little India's bright Punjabi Market.

Its natural setting, too, is diverse. Water almost completely surrounds the city, and snow-capped mountains are so close that you could ski in the morning and sail in the afternoon. The variety continues into the evening, especially Oct–Apr, when the choices include 18 dance companies, 32 theatre groups and the Vancouver Symphony Orchestra (www.allianceforarts.com).

i Super Natural British Columbia; tel: (800) 435-5622 or (250) 387-1642, www.hellobc.com; Vancouver Tourism (800) 667-3306, www.tourismvancouver.com.

Super Natural British Columbia (above) makes hotel reservations, essential May–Sept.

VANCOUVER'S ETHNIC FESTIVALS

January (or early **February**): Chinese New Year, with a Dragon Parade
April: Basakhi Day, the Indian New Year
May: Sikh Sports Festival
June: Canadian International Dragon Boat Festival
July: Caribbean Days Festival
July: Greek Days
July: Italian Days
August: Squamish Band (First Nations) Pow Wow
August: Powell Street Festival (Japanese)
November: Festival of Lights in Little India

GOTTA DANCE?
Harbour Dance Centre in downtown Vancouver will let you drop in for ballet, jazz, modern and other dance classes. 927 Granville St, Third Floor, tel: (604) 684-9542; www.harbourdance.bc.ca.

Days Inn Vancouver Downtown $$–$$$$, 921 W Pender St; tel: (604) 681-4335 or (800) 325-2525.
Global Village Backpackers $ 1018 Granville St; tel: (604) 682-8226, (888) 844-7875, www.globalbackpackers.com. Bright, colourful, funky and highly social, this hostel has dorms and private rooms, in an excellent location.
University of British Columbia $$ Student Union Blvd; tel: (604) 822-2901. Dorm rooms May–Aug.

Menus blend traditions from all over the world with local ingredients, creating a unique western Canadian style.
White Spot $–$$, several locations, is the local burger and comfort-food source, with good fish and chips.
Raintree at the Landing $$$ 375 Water St (Gastown); tel: (604) 688-5570. Local delicacies include smoked salmon and fiddleheads.
Villa del Lupo $$–$$$ 869 Hamilton St (Yaletown); tel: (604) 688-7436. Try steelhead trout with crabmeat-mashed potatoes.

HIGHLIGHTS Ride the glass elevator to **Lookout! At Harbour Centre** for a 360-degree view, then explore the brick and cobblestone streets of old **Gastown**, a lively shopping and restaurant quarter. Every 15 mins the **Steam Clock** whistles, puffing steam.

Stanley Park, North America's largest city park, has 999 acres (400 hectares) of woodland, gardens and water to tour by horse-drawn carriage or miniature steam railroad, daily in summer. Here also are the **Children's Zoo** and the **Vancouver Aquarium**, featuring 9000 fishes and 360 amphibians ($$), open daily.

The **UBC Museum of Anthropology**, on the University campus, shows Native American arts, totems and carved Haida buildings ($$), open Tues–Sun. The striking **Vancouver Maritime Museum**, near the Burrard St Bridge, encloses a restored sailing schooner ($$), open daily. Adjacent **Vancouver Museum** shows life-sized exhibits of city history, including an entire trading post ($$), open daily. The **Dr Sun Yat Sen Classical Chinese Garden** in Chinatown was the first authentically constructed outside China.

Capilano Suspension Bridge ($$), tel: (604) 985-7474, www.capbridge.com, swings over the rushing waters of **Capilano Canyon** in North Vancouver. Nearby **Grouse Mountain Sky Ride** ($$) climbs Grouse Mountain, where you can dine or just enjoy the panorama. In winter, ski trails lead back down.

In West Vancouver, explore the 3-mile **Lighthouse Park** trail on your own or with Rockwood Adventures, tel: (888) 236-6606 or (604) 926-7705. This rare northern coastal rainforest of giant cedars and majestic Douglas firs dates back 2500 years. Picnic on a rocky cliff and watch bald eagles fish.

WHISTLER In 2010 Whistler will welcome the world to the Winter Olympics held on the breathtaking slopes of Whistler and Blackcomb Mountains. This honour is well deserved and Whistler is rightly renowned for its excellent skiing and winter sport facilities, with ski trails dropping into the resort village and more than 2800 hectares of ski-able terrain. The 1600 metres of vertical drop is the highest of any North American ski area, and the high-speed lift system is the continent's largest.The gondola ride to the top operates year-round. However, locals know the true secret of Whistler – it's a year round destination with plenty of trails to hike, hot tubs in which to soak, fine restaurants to sample and, in summer, outdoor music and entertainment. Whistler, 75 miles (121 km) north of Vancouver on Rte 99, is also reached by **BC Rail**, tel: (604) 984-5246, or **Maverick Coach**; tel: (604) 662-8051.

Whistler Central Reservations can find lodgings; tel: (800) 944-7853 or (604) 664-5625, or try **Eidelweiss Pension Inn** $$, tel: (604) 932-3641.

The **West Coast Railway Heritage Park** in Squamish, 25 miles (40km) north of Vancouver has over 60 pieces of heritage rolling stock, dating back to the 1890s and being lovingly restored. A star attraction is the Royal Hudson steam loco. The Park ($$) is open all year, 1000–1700; tel: (604) 898-9336; www.wcra.org; e-mail: park@wcra.org. Details of West Coast Rail Tours are posted on the website.

VICTORIA

The provincial capital centres around its historic Inner Harbour. In fact, British Columbia's Parliament Building faces it, outlined at night in lights that reflect in the water. **Victoria Harbour Ferry** circles on a continuous tour. Victoria has a distinct British feel, with its tidy downtown, pubs, teashops, public gardens, double-decked buses and bagpiper parading the esplanade in the afternoon.

Tourism Victoria; tel: (250) 953-2033 www.tourismvictoria.com.

The Empress Hotel $$$$ 721 Government St; tel: (250) 384-8111 or (800) 257-7544, www.fairmont.com, is a harbour landmark; elegant afternoon teas, $$$$.

Shoal Harbour Inn $$$$ Sidney; tel: (250) 656-6622 or (887) 956-6622. Small log estate with beautiful guest-rooms and fine dining.

Cherry Bank Hotel $$–$$$$ 825 Burdett Ave.; tel: (250) 385-5380. Comfortable older hotel in a quiet neighbourhood.

Il Terrazzo $$–$$$$ 555 Johnson St; tel: (250) 361-0028. Italian delicacies in a charming courtyard.

Spinnakers Brewpub $$–$$$ 308 Catherine St, Victoria; tel: (250) 384-2739. Local ales, excellent seafood.

Blethering Place Tea Room and Restaurant $$–$$$ 2250 Oak Bay Ave; tel: (250) 598-1413 or (888) 598-1413. Cosy for breakfast, lunch or dinner.

HIGHLIGHTS Fine 1800s homes line Victoria's streets, several open as museums. The outstanding **Royal British Columbia Museum** brings history to life with carved and painted Haida boxes and totems, a reconstructed mining camp and entire 19th-century high street; $$, open daily. The **Maritime Museum**, on Bastion Sq., houses two sailing vessels, ship models and marine artefacts; $$, open daily. To the north, **Chemainus** is a giant outdoor art gallery where artists have recorded the area's rich history in 33 outdoor murals. **Cowichan Native Village** ($$$) in Duncan, tel: (250) 746-8119, is a living cultural museum. Watch totem carving, see Native dances and lunch on cedar-planked salmon.

Butchart Gardens, built to beautify an unsightly stone quarry, blooms throughout the seasons with acres of showy daffodils in March to late autumn chrysanthemums. This is one of North America's premier gardens, rivalling any in Europe. The gardens are 14 miles (22 km) north of Victoria, accessible by frequent bus; $$$, open daily.

UP ISLAND

Don't make the mistake of thinking Victoria is the only destination to visit on Vancouver Island. Roads lead north to some of the most glorious scenery and funky towns in the province.

Chemanius, about an hour north of Victoria, is the home of the world-famous outdoor murals. More than 30 larger-than-life works adorn the buildings of this small town. Simply follow the footprints to view the art that depicts the history of the Chemanius Valley.

Nanaimo, once a thriving coal town, is the second largest gateway to the island with not one but two ferry terminals linking the island to the mainland. Nanaimo hosts a Jazz Festival in September. Could this be where Diana Krall got her start?

Cathedral Grove, on Highway 4 heading west to Port Alberni, is one of the finest stands of old growth forest on the island. Eight hundred-year-old Douglas firs and west coast cedars are just a short walk from the highway edge. The grove is within MacMillan Provincial Park, which also includes Cameron Lake.

The road west leads to Port Alberni, a thriving mill town, and then along a torturously twisting road to **Pacific Rim National Park**. When you stand facing the Pacific on Long Beach, almost 34 km in length, almost all of Canada is at your back. The park is a haven for wildlife; you may spot bears, black-tailed deer, bald eagles, porpoises, pods of orcas and during the summer, whales.

Are you ready for a 'wild' time? Embark on an Alaska cruise and watch eagles swoop, whales breach and chunks of glacier crash into the sea – all from the comfort of your deck chair. The lure of Alaska, that remote, enormous, isolated US state at the top left of North America, is its vast wilderness, abundant wildlife, snow-capped mountains, glaciers, endless forests and beautiful streams and waterfalls. Cruise ships offer comfortable access to the wilderness, often at reasonable prices, and the Alaska Marine Highway connects towns on this ragged coast via ferry.

GETTING THERE AND GETTING AROUND

Most Alaska destinations are only accessible by air or sea. Vancouver and Seattle are the major departure points for Alaska cruises. Many major cruise lines, such as Princess, offer excellent itineraries with a wide variety of shore excursions (see below for details).

If you want to see every nook and coastal cranny, choose a small ship - Cruise West has particularly good itineraries - or take the Alaska Marine Highway. This ferry system begins in Washington State and sails to most Alaska ports. Unlike a cruise ship, the ferry system is basic, but don't expect major savings, since you'll pay extra for sleeping accommodation and meals, unlike cruises.

INFORMATION

Alaska Travel Industry Association, 2600 Cordova St, Suite 201, Anchorage, AK, 99503, tel: (800) 862 5275, www.travelalaska.com, is open 0800–1700 Mon–Fri.

MONEY Most major cruise lines can exchange most major currencies on board ship. There are also currency exchanges at most cruise stops and plenty of ATMs.

CRUISES **Cruise West** sails small ships on nature-oriented itineraries, tel: (888) 851-8133, www.cruisewest.com. **Princess Cruises** ply Alaska waters in large, more luxurious ships with full cruise-ship facilities, tel: (800) 744-6237, www.princess.com. Take waterproof clothing; you can expect cold rainy weather on one or more days of your visit.

ACCOMMODATION AND FOOD AND DRINK

As most visitors arrive by cruise ship, towns have no need for large hotels. Although hotels are smaller, older and usually quite basic, prices are very high because of the short tourist season. The same applies to restaurants. As most visitors' meals are eaten on board, only basic restaurants are found at most stops. If you eat locally, try the seafood, especially the salmon, shrimp, trout and halibut, or game such as venison, moose and bear.

HIGHLIGHTS

When choosing a cruise, consider whether you are most interested in getting as close as possible to the natural wilderness or in seeing local culture in the towns. While it's possible to do some of both, certain ships are better suited to one or the other. Smaller exploration-type ships, such as those of Cruise West, are able to sail deep into places like Tracy Arm and right up to calving glaciers. They can move close to shore for bear watching and stop quickly to observe otters, seals and bald eagles. The emphasis is on nature, and experts are on deck at all times to explain it. Larger ships, such as the Princess ships, bring you to the scenic highlights and allow you to explore the coastal towns with their frontier look and rollicking gold-rush ambience.

JUNEAU The capital of Alaska, once a thriving mining town, is today mostly government offices and souvenir shops. But just outside the city is the **Mendenhall Glacier**, the major local attraction. A comprehensive interpretive centre is at the base of the glacier and tour buses run from the port. The **Red Dog Saloon** is a remnant of Juneau's frontier past. Walk in through the swinging doors, cross the sawdust floor, sit down to enjoy a wet one. Take in the ambience, which includes live entertainment, tongue-in-cheek menu, and walls covered with dusty local artefacts, such as stuffed animals and life preservers from lost ships.

SITKA Until the Russians sold Sitka to the Americans in 1867, it was their headquarters for trapping and trading sea otter pelts. The city maintains its Russian heritage with some original buildings such as St Michals, a beautiful Russian Orthodox church. Locals perform Russian dances for cruise ship visitors. Local waters are always alive with whales and other sea life, a good place for a 'Whale Watch'. Visit the **Alaska Raptor Center**, a rescue hospital for injured birds of prey, which are returned to the wild after treatment if possible. Those that cannot survive in the wild remain for display or go to zoos.

KETCHIKAN Ketchikan started life as a native fishing village, and grew into the 'Salmon Capital of the World'. Most of the fishing boats are gone, but the world's largest collection of totem poles remains. **Totem Heritage Center** is in town, **Totem Bight State Park** is north of town, and **Saxman Village and Totem Park** is south of town. At the latter, see new totems being carved, a longhouse, native dancing and displays of native life. **Creek Street** is not actually a street, but small buildings joined with a narrow wooden boardwalk built over a steam that is still an active salmon spawning ground. In Ketchikan's glory days, this was a red light district, and **Dolly's House** has been maintained as a museum in its original décor, but now the gussied up ladies only tell bawdy tales and sell souvenirs.

Colour Section
(i) The Grand Canyon (pp. 435–443); Natural Bridge, Bryce Canyon National Park (pp. 513–514)
(ii) The Strip, Las Vegas (pp. 516–517); San Diego's Gaslamp Quarter (pp. 524–525)
(iii) Santa Barbara (p. 584); inset: Hollywood, Mann's Chinese Theater (p. 508)
(iv) Cable car on Powell St, San Francisco (pp. 543–552).

UNION
Plaza
GOLDEN GATE
CASINO
HOTEL
Carl's Jr.
CASINO
Carl's Jr.
FROZEN YOGURT
Coin Castle
GLITTER GULCH
TOPLESS
GIRLS OF
GLITTER
DOUBLE

GASLAMP
QUARTER
HISTORIC HEART OF SAN DIEGO
GASLAMP
QUARTER

EL CAMINO REAL
MISSION SANTA BARBARA
FOUNDED DECEMBER 1786
MISSION SAN BUENA VENTURA 30
MISSION SANTA INEZ 48
AUTO CLUB OF SO. CAL.

MARKET STREET &
POWELL AND MARKET
HYDE AND BEACH
FISHERMANS WHARF
27
blame us.
EYEWITNESS NEWS
FISHERMANS WHARF

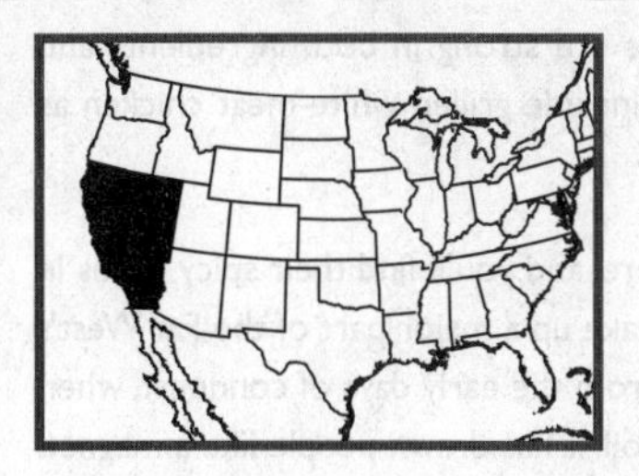

California looms larger than life, not only as the second largest of the continental states, but as a way of life. Were it not for the glitter of the Las Vegas casinos, Nevada – the other state in this section – might be lost entirely.

No other state – even Texas – has come to epitomize a style of its own as California has. Throughout the US, you will see it on menus (California-style sushi, for example, is a vegetarian sushi containing avocado) and in advertising for clothing, home furnishings and other goods. And although most Americans know what it means, it's hard to quantify exactly what makes 'California style'.

Begin with the way people dress. You'll see fewer jackets, neckties and 'dressy' dresses here. Silicon Valley – the booming computer-driven and computer-driving techno-centre of America – set the style for jeans and T-shirts in the office.

You'll meet more vegetarians per table than anywhere else. You'll meet people who care and talk a lot about food and wine. The American wine revolution began here, with the rise of the Napa Valley and Sonoma vineyards. Quality is the key, and California now produces wines that can beat the French at their own game. It was in California that wine first replaced the sacred American cocktail before dinner, and wine bars were common here before Chicago and New York heard of them.

'California cuisine' is a term you may see describing restaurants all over America, and it means light, fresh and a little sassy, rather like the state's population. The emphasis will be on fresh vegetables and fruits, on white meat instead of red, on seafood instead of meat. Asian influences are strong in both ingredients and preparation styles. Salads are bountiful, and may include grilled white-meat chicken as a main dish, especially at lunch.

Along with Asian influences, Mexican is strong here, and you'll find their spicy foods in many neighbourhood restaurants. Both groups make up a major part of the Far West's ethnic mix. California is a world of newcomers. From the early days of conquest, when the flag of Spain was first planted in Californian soil, it has drawn people like a magnet.

Among the first was Junipero Serra, the Spanish Franciscan friar who established the first of California's famous missions in the 1700s. Many of these beautiful buildings still stand, and the history-minded may want to follow their trail, called El Camino Real, the length of the state. Others may wish to see only the best known – Carmel, San Juan Capistrano and Santa Barbara.

In 1849 the 'Forty-niners' came, seeking gold, which had been discovered the previous year at Sutters Mill. California would never be the same. Over land and by boat they came, a rough-and-ready lot of men from points east, followed by an equally odd-lot bunch of 'ladies'. Not everyone struck gold – the mineral – but in the boom time that followed more fortunes were made in commerce than in the gold fields.

This was the beginning of the Chinese immigration to the west coast, and more followed as workers on the railroad, which soon tied California to the east coast by a silver ribbon of steel. This new access brought more and more people from the east, seeking the dream that California seemed to conjure up.

The tides of immigration to California didn't stop, and its population doubled each decade for more than a century. In the 1960s it was said that if any more people fled the east to go there, the country would tip into the Pacific Ocean from their weight.

Perhaps it was true since pieces of California have slid into the Pacific, on a fairly regular basis, and its dramatic coastal cliffs are works in progress. Because of its size and its location, the scenic contrasts of the state are stunning. From these steep ocean cliffs the land rises to the Coastal Range and the Sierra Nevada – 'snowy mountains' in Spanish. But California also includes the most desolate of deserts at Death Valley and rich green rainforests in the north. It has the highest and lowest points in the 48 contiguous states.

Some of the west's most breathtaking scenic wonders are in California. It is a land of superlatives. At King's Canyon is the deepest gorge on the continent, deeper even than the Grand Canyon. Yosemite Falls drop further than any other waterfall in North America. The giant redwood trees are the largest living things on the planet. Texas may be the bigger state, but California has the biggest sites.

The drive along the Big Sur is on a road carved into the rock cliff, and the area is pure Pacific, with steep rock faces, crashing surf and a string of idyllic beaches. It's one of the most memorable stretches of coastline in America. And in Sequoia National Park you can see awe-inspiring trees several thousand years old.

Californians' love for fresh vegetables and fruits may stem from the state's vast agricultural regions, centred in the 450-mile-long valley between the state's two mountain ranges. Here the long growing season produces everything from citrus fruits to asparagus; California leads the United States in agricultural production.

Although distances are long, California's freeway system is so outstanding that you can drive more than 500 miles north from San Diego, near the Mexican border, without encountering a traffic light or stop sign. The comedian Bob Hope once observed that the miracle of California's roads was that you could get on a freeway and drive half the length of the state – whether you wanted to or not. If you do, you will certainly not be alone. California has the highest concentration of motor cars of any place in the world, and traffic jams are legendary.

But despite its traffic and its long distances, California is a wonderful place to travel. It offers a clear contrast to the east coast, both in its scenery and its lifestyle. Several of the great American icons are here: Disneyland – the original Disney theme park – Hollywood, the Golden Gate Bridge, Yosemite, the giant redwoods. And right next door, nestled in the crook of California's half-flexed elbow, is spacious Nevada, with the brilliant lights of Las Vegas sparkling in its lower corner.

Unlike New England or the Midwest, California is neither a microcosm of America nor representative of its mainstream. Whatever else California – and the entire west coast – is, it is decidedly not mainstream. Ideas begin here, take hold here and are often discredited here before they are adopted elsewhere. But its brash, open, liberal, full-steam-ahead momentum is just as much a part of the American national character as the staid and measured step of New England, and no one can truly claim to know America without meeting California firsthand.

THE FAR WEST

When? Preferably not in the winter, when it drizzles monotonously, and the fog, as the poet Carl Sandburg described it, 'creeps in on little cat feet'. Summer weather is dependably dry. You can plan a camping trip or a picnic with the certainty that rain will not interrupt it. But it is also hot and parched, and the green valleys and mountainsides may have turned to brown. Spring – which begins early here – and early summer are perfect, with fields red with poppies, gardens at their best and temperatures comfortably warm. You can join young Californians in their beloved surf, camp in the spectacular mountain parks and ride San Francisco's fabled cable cars for glorious views of the bay under a blue sky.

There's no place like it on earth; if you don't believe us, ask any Californian.

California or Las Vegas, Nevada, are jumping-off points for the Hawaiian islands way out in the Pacific Ocean, a US state nonetheless but with a very different feel. Check our introduction to Hawaii on pp. 585–586.

OUR CHOICE

San Francisco

Fisherman's Wharf

Golden Gate Bridge

Cable cars

Chinatown

Hollywood

California Missions (Carmel, San Juan Capistrano, Santa Barbara)

SeaWorld

San Diego Zoo

San Diego's Old Town

Hearst Castle

Big Sur

Yosemite National Park

Sequoia National Park

King's Canyon National Park

Sonoma and Napa Valley wineries

HOW MUCH YOU CAN SEE IN A ...

WEEK (7 DAYS)

San Francisco and the wine country

Monterey, Carmel, the Big Sur and Hearst Castle

San Francisco and Yosemite

Los Angeles and San Diego, via San Juan Capistrano

San Francisco, Old Faithful and Napa Valley

King's Canyon and Sequoia National Park

San Diego and Santa Barbara via the southern beaches

Santa Barbara to San Francisco via Hearst Castle and Big Sur

All the major sites in Yosemite National Park

San Francisco to the Redwood Parks via Mendocino

FORTNIGHT (14 DAYS)

San Francisco, Yosemite, King's Canyon and Sequoia National Park

San Francisco, Yosemite, Sacramento and Gold Country

San Francisco, the wine country, Monterey, Carmel, the Big Sur and Hearst Castle

Los Angeles, San Diego, San Juan Capistrano and Palm Springs

San Francisco, Hearst Castle, the Big Sur and all the major sites in Yosemite National Park

San Francisco, Hearst Castle, the Big Sur and highlights of Yosemite and King's Canyon National Park

LOS ANGELES

As your plane approaches Los Angeles International Airport, the flat sprawl which houses 9.8 million souls within Los Angeles county is ended only by the great Pacific Ocean. The denizens of the amorphous neighbourhoods, urban villages, slums, beach towns and creative colonies all co-exist: Angelenos are an upbeat, eternally optimistic mix. Nearly half are Hispanic, many from Mexico, while a good percentage are African-American or have an Asian or Pacific Island heritage. Angelenos call their home El-Lay – short, snappy, abbreviated, sassy, entertaining, like themselves.

Most of the city's cultural attractions, shopping and nightlife are concentrated on the trendy Westside from Beverly Hills to Santa Monica and along the coast. Other centres of activity include Old Pasadena and the Universal CityWalk area. The strip malls and tract houses of the inland valleys are now home to immigrants from all over the world. Many Angelenos have never been downtown, although there are many interesting sights in the area, and a new metro now links the area with the Hollywood Blvd 'Walk of Fame' in just 15 minutes. Those who do not wish to navigate the LA freeways will find downtown a good base for taking day trips by train and bus although hotels can be expensive and night-time activity is nil. Santa Monica is another good base for seeing the sites on the Westside. The subway now serves the popular Universal Studios and City Walk, making that area an excellent base.

MUST SEE/DO IN LOS ANGELES

Walk around the new Walt Disney Concert Hall, attend a free Saturday concert

Walk down Hollywood Blvd to find your favourite stars

Sample authentic Mexican food in the Olvera St area

Listen to tomorrow's stars at a club on Sunset Strip

GETTING THERE AND GETTING AROUND

Air Los Angeles International Airport (LAX) is 17 miles west of downtown, at 1 World Way; tel: (310) 646-5252; www.lawa.org. Find all outbound transport except taxis on the Lower Level/Arrival islands outside arrival baggage carousels. There is a frequent airport bus service to Buena Park/Knott's Berry Farm, Disneyland and Pasadena, and a free shuttle bus to the Metro Green Line Light Rail Station; take the line to Imperial/Wilmington, then transfer to the Blue Line to 7th St/Metro Center in downtown Los Angeles. There are also free shuttles to hire car locations and airport hotels. A taxi to the downtown area will cost about three times as much as the bus – not expensive considering the distance, and well worth it if there are more than two of you.

RAIL/BUS Amtrak trains pull into cavernous, mission-style Union Station, 800 N Alameda St. From here Metrolink, tel: (800) 371-5465; www.metrolinktrains.com, has its Mon–Fri commuter train hub for routes north-west to Oxnard, north-east to Lancaster, east to San Bernardino and Riverside and south-east to Oceanside. Antelope Valley and San Bernardino trains also operate Sat. San Bernardino trains operate seven days a week.

Greyhound buses arrive at a small terminal at 1716 E 7th and Alameda Sts, about 1 mile east of downtown; tel: (213) 629-8401.

Much of the LA region is served by the MTA Metro rail and bus system, tel: (800) 266-6883; www.mta.net. Metro Rail connects Union Station with North Hollywood (Red Line), Long Beach (Blue Line), the airport area (Green Line) and Sierra Madre Villa in Pasadena (Yellow Line) for a flat fare. Trains operate 0500–2400 daily. Metro buses operate throughout the city and suburbs, some 24 hr (same flat fare as the trains). The cheap DASH bus routes make frequent stops around the centre daily (separate weekday and weekend routes). Six DASH routes operate weekdays 0630–1900, three routes operate weekend 1000–1700.

'Metro Rapid' buses operate frequent, limited-stop service on Wilshire-Whittier Blvd between Santa Monica and Commerce (Line 720), on Ventura Blvd between Warner Center and Universal City (Line 750) along South Broadway (Line 745) and Vermont Ave (Line 754); the last two both connect with Line 720. Line 720 connects with the Metro Red Line at the Wilshire/Western Station. Line 750 connects with the Metro Red Line at the Universal City Station.

INFORMATION

Los Angeles Convention and Visitors Bureau (LACVB) Downtown Visitor Information Center, 685 S Figueroa St; 7th St/Metro Center; tel: (213) 689-8822; www.lacvb.com. Open Mon–Fri 0800–1700. Ask for the Destination LA guide.

SAFETY Avoid areas east of Broadway and south of 7th Street and Wilshire Blvd. Caution is advised in the Hollywood area, especially after dark. Ask at the front desk of your hotel to seek advice on travelling to areas you are uncertain of.

MONEY There is a Travelex foreign exchange bureau at branches of the Bank of Los Angeles at 806 Hilldale Ave, West Hollywood, tel: (310) 659-6093, and at 421 Rodeo Dr., Beverly Hills and 452 N Bedford Dr., Beverly Hills.

POST AND PHONES US Post Office is next to Union Station, at 760 N Main St.

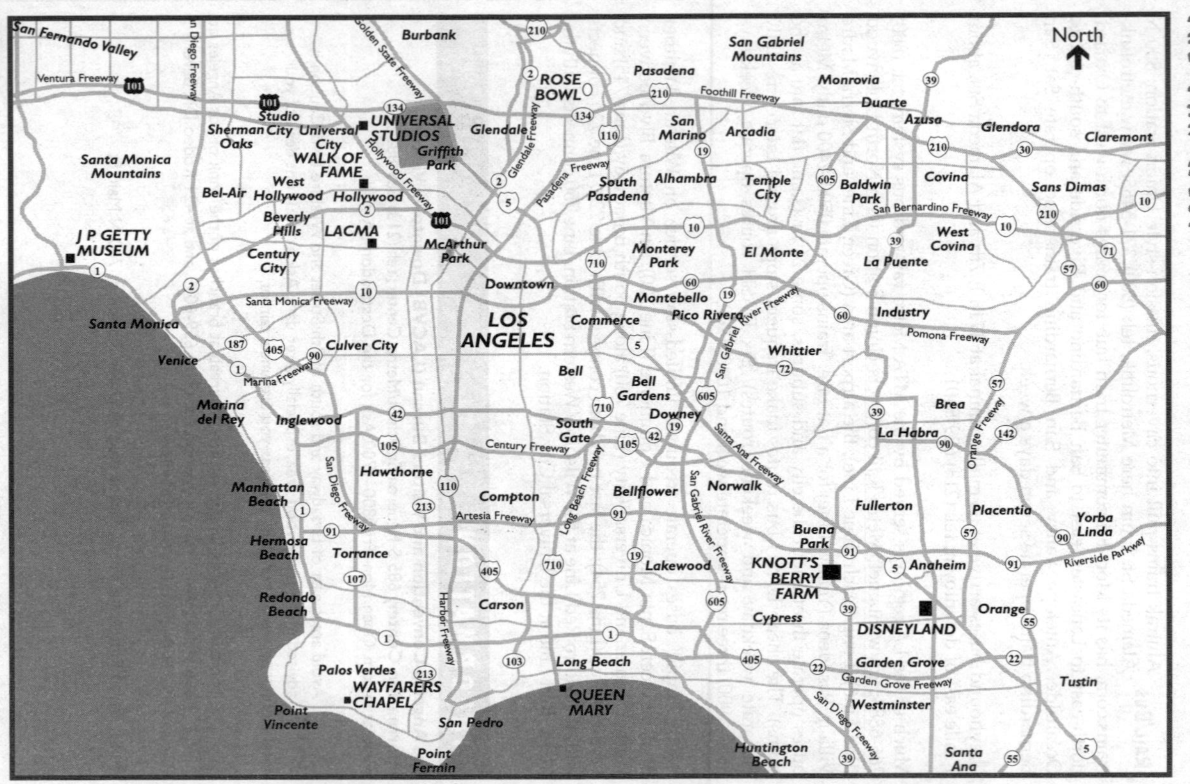
San Fernando Valley
Ventura Freeway
an Diego Freeway
Golden State Freeway
Burbank
San Gabriel Mountains
North
ROSE BOWL
Pasadena
Foothill Freeway
Monrovia
Duarte
Azusa
Glendora
Claremont
Studio City
Sherman Oaks
Universal City
UNIVERSAL STUDIOS
Griffith Park
Glendale
Glendale Freeway
Hollywood Freeway
San Marino
Arcadia
Santa Monica Mountains
WALK OF FAME
West Hollywood
Bel-Air
Hollywood
Pasadena Freeway
South Pasadena
Alhambra
Temple City
Baldwin Park
Covina
Sans Dimas
San Bernardino Freeway
Beverly Hills
LACMA
J P GETTY MUSEUM
McArthur Park
Century City
Monterey Park
El Monte
West Covina
La Puente
Downtown
Santa Monica Freeway
Montebello
Santa Monica
LOS ANGELES
Commerce
Pico Rivera
San Gabriel River Freeway
Industry
Pomona Freeway
Culver City
Venice
Marina Freeway
Whittier
Bell
Bell Gardens
Marina del Rey
Inglewood
Downey
South Gate
Brea
La Habra
Century Freeway
Santa Ana Freeway
Orange Freeway
Hawthorne
Manhattan Beach
San Diego Freeway
Compton
Artesia Freeway
Long Beach Freeway
Bellflower
Norwalk
Fullerton
Placentia
Yorba Linda
Hermosa Beach
Torrance
Buena Park
Lakewood
KNOTT'S BERRY FARM
Anaheim
Riverside Parkway
Redondo Beach
Carson
Harbor Freeway
Cypress
Orange
DISNEYLAND
Long Beach
Garden Grove
Garden Grove Freeway
Tustin
Palos Verdes
WAYFARERS CHAPEL
QUEEN MARY
Westminster
Point Vincente
San Pedro
San Diego Freeway
Huntington Beach
Santa Ana
Point Fermin

IF YOU'RE DRIVING

Traffic does flow – at a few miles per hour in the rush hour – on most LA area freeways. During the rush hour, it may be as efficient to take major surface streets (arterials) in the direction desired.

Parking meters are widely available, take change, and can be a good bargain if parking for less than a couple of hours (hourly restrictions are posted on detailed signs on the kerb). Downtown and in smart areas, car parks may charge several dollars per hour, or may not. For dining in any popular area, especially at night, valet parking is *de rigueur*, from $5 to $15.

ACCOMMODATION

The LACVB lists member hotels in the *Essential Los Angeles* guide, but does not make bookings. To conserve time and energy, base yourself close to attractions you intend to see. Always ask for secure parking.

Hostelling International $1436 2nd St, Santa Monica; MTA bus 33,333, 720 or Santa Monica bus 10; tel: (310) 393-9913; fax: (310) 393-1769; reserve@HILosAngeles.org. Two blocks from the beach, pier and Third Street Promenade; free airport pick-up.

Hostelling International $ 3601 S Gaffey St no. 613, San Pedro; MTA bus 446; tel: (310) 831-8109. In the South Bay community of San Pedro.

Kawada Hotel $$$$ 200 S Hill St; Civic Center Metro; tel: (213) 621-4455. Boutique hotel located near Civic Center.

Student Inn $ 7038½ Hollywood Blvd, Hollywood; tel: (323) 469-6781, (800) 557-7038. With free pickup from LAX airport, free lockers and linen, breakfast included, a full kitchen, internet access and discounted tickets, this hostel is hard to beat. Reservations and international passport required.

Wilshire Grand Hotel and Centre $$$$ 930 Wilshire Blvd at Figueroa; 7th St/Metro Center; tel: (213) 688-7777; fax: (213) 612-3989. In the downtown business district.

Hollywood Roosevelt Hotel $$$$ 7000 Hollywood Blvd; Hollywood/Highland Metro; tel: (323) 466-7000; fax: 462-8056; www.hollywoodroosevelt.com. On Hollywood's Walk of Fame.

FOOD AND DRINK

Local newspapers, and the free monthly *Where Los Angeles* magazine, list restaurants and review trendy newcomers. See also Hollywood, p. 508.

Phillippe the Original $ 1001 N Alameda St; Union Station Metro; tel: (213) 628-3781. Has been serving original French dip sandwiches for over 90 years.

Original Pantry Café $$ 877 S Figueroa St; 7th St/Metro Center; tel: (213) 972-9279. A downtown favourite serving All-American breakfasts and other hearty fare 24 hours a day, seven days a week.

Café Pinot $$$ 700 W Fifth St; Pershing Square Metro; tel: (213) 239-6500. Excellent Cal-French, served inside a see-through box with the lights of downtown all around.

Water Grill $$$ 544 S Grand Ave, between 5th and 6th Sts; Pershing Square Metro; tel: (213) 891-0900. Rated LA's top seafood restaurant. The high quality is reflected in the prices.

HIGHLIGHTS

DOWNTOWN Once shunned as dingy and crime-ridden, today's civic centre has soaring skyscrapers, a fanciful funicular, a strangely familiar City Hall and a wealth of architecture.

The **Biltmore Hotel**, built in 1923, is an LA landmark facing Pershing Sq. – stroll through its ornate Spanish Renaissance-style lobby. Three blocks away, at 304 S Broadway, the **Bradbury Building** features five skylit levels of intricate ironwork and an exposed lift accented by marble, tilework and rich polished wood. This fanciful $500,000 1893 masterpiece is a frequent film location; it is open to the first landing Mon–Fri 0900–1800, Sat–Sun 0900–1700. Opposite is **Grand Central Market** (Pershing Sq. Metro). Since 1917, Angelenos have shopped for ingredients for their kitchens here. Look for the bronze pig heads at the Broadway entrance. Open Mon–Sun 0900–1800, one-hour free parking with a $10 purchase.

CITY HALL

The shimmering white icon of City Hall, 200 N Spring St, served as Superman's *Daily Planet* building.

Pedestrianised Olvera St at the heart of downtown is the centrepiece of the **El Pueblo de Los Angeles Historic Monument** (Union Station Metro). Among the state historic park's 27 buildings is LA's oldest building, **Avila Adobe**, dating back to 1818 and now perfectly restored and furnished as an 1850s *rancho*. A Mexican-style open-air shopping arcade has well-crafted leather goods and Mexican tourist trinkets. Restaurants serve modest, authentic Mexican food. **Sepulveda House Visitors Center** (tel: 213-628-1274) is open Mon–Sat 1000–1500. Free 45-minute guided walking tours are given Tues–Sat on the hour, except Thanksgiving and 25 Dec.

WALKING TOURS

Los Angeles Conservancy Tours, 523 W 6th St, Suite 826; tel: (213) 623-2489, runs guided tours ($) that cover art deco, the Biltmore Hotel, Broadway movie theatres, City Hall, Little Tokyo (Japantown), Pershing Square, Union Station and architecture.

The **Museum of Contemporary Art** (MOCA) on California Plaza (top of Angel's Flight DASH bus 'B' or 'DD') presents the last 60 years of modern art with large sculpture, abstract paintings and prints. There are multimedia and video presentations in lower level galleries. $$, open Mon 1100–1700; also Thur 1100–2000 (free), Fri 1100–1700, Sat–Sun 1100–1800.

The **Music Center**, at N Grand Ave/W Temple St (Civic Center Metro), tel: (213) 972-7211, is the performing arts complex in the heart of downtown. The newest addition here is the stunning Frank Gehry **Walt Disney Concert Hall**. The undulating asymmetrical exterior is sheathed in reflective panels, reminiscent of Gehry's Guggenheim Museum in Bilbao, Spain. The complex also includes the Dorothy Chandler Pavilion, which hosts the Los Angeles Opera. Cutting-edge theatre is presented in the Mark Taper Forum. Broadway plays and mainstream theatre are performed at the Ahmanson

Theater. A Jacques Lipchitz 'Peace' fountain in the courtyard constantly varies its water flow, creating the illusion of an erratic brook in the city centre.

WILSHIRE BOULEVARD This long and famous street runs from the edge of downtown out to Beverly Hills – Metro buses 20, 21 and 720 (Metro Rapid) run along it.

The **Los Angeles County Museum of Art** (LACMA) has a world-renowned Indian and South-east Asian art collection and notable textiles and costumes among its powerhouse collection. The Japanese Pavilion is on two levels of galleries which include magnificent Japanese scrolls in a building designed in the shape of a pagoda. $$, 5905 Wilshire Blvd. Open Mon–Tues and Thur 1200–2000, Fri 1200–2100, Sat–Sun 1100–2000.

TAR BABY

Ice Age fossils about 40,000 years old have been found in bubbling **La Brea Tar Pits**, once mined for natural asphalt. See the discoveries at the **George C Page Museum ($$)** 5801 Wilshire Blvd; open Mon–Fri 0930–1700, Sat–Sun 1000–1700.

For an introduction to LA's love affair and dependence upon the automobile, pay a visit to the **Petersen Automotive Museum**. Cars of the stars, hot rods, sport cars, roadside cafés, service stations – they're all here. $$, 6060 Wilshire Blvd; open Tues–Sun 1000–1800.

The **Armand Hammer Museum of Art** houses the late entrepreneur-philanthropist's third art collection: Old Masters, Impressionists and Post-Impressionist paintings, Dürer watercolours and satirist Daumier's lithographs. $, 10899 Wilshire Blvd; open Tues–Sat 1100–1900 (Thur until 2100), Sun 1100–1700.

BEVERLY HILLS Beverly Hills, west of downtown and Hollywood, is a town and a state of mind. **Rodeo Drive** is three blocks of ultra-smart boutiques dripping with sophistication, where there are more tourists than shoppers. The **Museum of Television and Radio** (Metro bus 20 and 21 and Metro Rapid 720) is the best spot outside the museum's New York City venue to view television clips and listen to historic radio programmes and advertisements. $$, 495 N Beverly Dr.; open Wed–Sun 1200–1700.

The **Museum of Tolerance**, 9786 W Pico Blvd (take Metro bus 3) is a gripping introduction to – or reminder of – the effects of racism and intolerance. $$, open Mon–Thurs 1130–1830, Fri 1130–1500 (1700 summer), Sun 1100–1930. Note that the last admission is 2½ hours before closing.

PASADENA North-east of central LA, Pasadena beams into millions of homes on New Year's Day with the televised Rose Parade preceding the Rose Bowl football match. Metro buses 401, 402 and 483 will take you out there. The **Norton Simon Museum** is a marriage of a millionaire's exquisite taste with gallery display. $, 411 W Colorado Blvd; open Mon 1200–1800, Wed–Sun 1200–1800 (Fri until 2100). Find designer wear and casual dining at Old Pasadena's **One Colorado** complex

HOLLYWOOD

The studio system has gone, the glitz may be tarnished, but Hollywood still means movieland. More than 2000 pink stars – the **Hollywood Boulevard Walk of Fame** – embedded in the pavement of Hollywood Blvd, from La Brea Ave to Vine St, recall stars of film, television, radio, music and the stage. Try out the stars' autographed hand and foot imprints before the exotic pagoda facade of **Mann's Chinese Theater**, 6925 Hollywood Blvd (Hollywood/Highland Metro), and take part in the interactive exhibits of the **Hollywood Entertainment Museum** $, 7021 Hollywood Blvd. Independent films feature in the newly renovated 1922 **Egyptian Theater**, $, 6712 Hollywood Blvd; tel: (323) 466-3456.

A classic view of the 50 ft high letters of the landmark **Hollywood sign**, plastered across the dry hills at the top of Beachwood Canyon (near the corner of Beachwood Dr. and Franklin Ave) is from Griffith Observatory. Griffith Park is also the location of the **Museum of the American West**, which offers a vibrant, honestly captioned collection of Western US art, artefacts and cowboy film memorabilia. $$, 4700 Western Heritage Way; Metro bus 96; open Tues–Sun 1000–1700 (Thur 1700–2000).

Just north of Hollywood proper, **Universal Studios Hollywood**, 100 Universal City Plaza; www.universalstudios.com (Universal City Metro), is one of the world's oldest film studios, and what Hollywood was all about. Surrounded by a cinema-themed amusement park ($$$), it offers a Backlot Tram Tour past actual set locations and sound stages with a bridge drop-out. Brace youself for an encounter with King Kong and a simulated earthquake. Dinosaurs run amok in 'Jurassic Park – The Ride'; prepare to get soaked when a humungous tyrannosaurus rex dunks the ride's car. Open daily various hours. 'Back to the Future – the Ride' is a clever motion simulator with effects of ice cliffs, lava flows and another T-rex, while 'ET Adventure' puts you on a bicycle to save the beloved Extra Terrestrial's home planet. Outside the park entrance gate is the free (with parking) **Universal City Walk**, a pedestrian walking, shopping, dining, entertainment and multiplex cinema area.

Some bargain places to eat in Hollywood:

Shanky's Mexican Grill $ 1716 N Cahuenga Blvd; tel: (323) 461-7881. Some of the best fish tacos in LA.

Chan Dara $$ 1511 N Cahuenga Blvd; tel: (323) 464 8585, north of Sunset Blvd. Draws diners for scrumptious Thai food – especially pad Thai noodles.

Fabiolus Café $$ 6270 Sunset Blvd, east of Vine St; tel: (323) 467-2882. A pasta bowl chain that's popular with low-budget 'moguls' and struggling actors.

Hollywood Hills Coffee Shop $$ Best Western Hollywood Hotel, 1745 N Vermont Ave; tel: (323) 467-7678. American food served in what is best described as a 'scene'.

Musso and Frank Grill $$$ 6667 Hollywood Blvd; tel: (323) 467-7788. The essence of 'old' Hollywood – martinis and chicken pot pie to die for.

(Colorado Blvd and Fair Oaks Ave).

An unexpected facet of LA is also out to the north-east. The **Huntington Library and Botanical Gardens** in San Marino has fine art, lovely gardens, a tearoom and medieval manuscripts. $$, 1151 Oxford Rd; Metro bus 79; open Tues–Fri 1200–1630, Sat–Sun 1030–1630.

INFORMATION

Hollywood Visitor Information Center, The Janes House, 6541 Hollywood Blvd; open Mon–Sat 0900–1700.

Metro Rail Red Line connects Union Station with Hollywood in 15 mins. Greyhound buses stop two blocks north at 1715 N Cahuenga Blvd; tel: (323) 466-6381.

SHOPPING

The LACVB offers a pocket-sized *Shopping in Los Angeles* guide for suggestions of where and what to purchase. Rodeo Drive (Beverly Hills) or the Beverly Center (8500 Beverly Blvd) are starting places for smart-conservative with touches of Academy Award gown thrown in. For the raw materials, a DASH bus will take you to the Fashion District.

NIGHTLIFE

Look in the free weekly newspapers: *LA Weekly*, *New Times* and the mainstream *Los Angeles Times Sunday Calendar* for listings.

Sunset Strip, Sunset Blvd in trendy West Hollywood (Metro bus 2), still offers **Whisky A Go Go**, 8901 W Sunset Blvd, tel: (310) 652-4202; other star-making (Springsteen, Bob Marley) music venues like the **Roxy**, 9009 W Sunset Blvd, tel: (310) 276-2222; or American roots music at the **House of Blues**, 8430 W Sunset Blvd; tel: (323) 848-5100.

WHERE NEXT?

Part of the LA conurbation, but each with a separate identity, are the beach resorts of southern California – Santa Monica, Venice Beach et al. (see p. 532). The Pacific Coast Highway runs down to San Diego (see p. 521) and up to San Francisco and beyond (see p. 537), or take a train up the San Joaquin Valley (see p. 570).

DRIVING ROUTE

You could try to do all National Parks in an exhausting seven-day tour, but it is better to choose just a couple of the parks and enjoy them at a leisurely pace.

Arches National Park is just north of Moab, off Hwy 191.

Canyonlands National Park is south-west of Moab, taking Hwy 313 off Hwy 191.

Hwy 24 leads south off I-70 and crosses Capitol Reef National Park, and from there Hwy 12 leads further south and west, crossing Bryce Canyon National Park.

Hwy 9 passes through Zion National Park, linked north to Hwy 12 by Hwy 89, and east to I-15 which runs north to Cedar City.

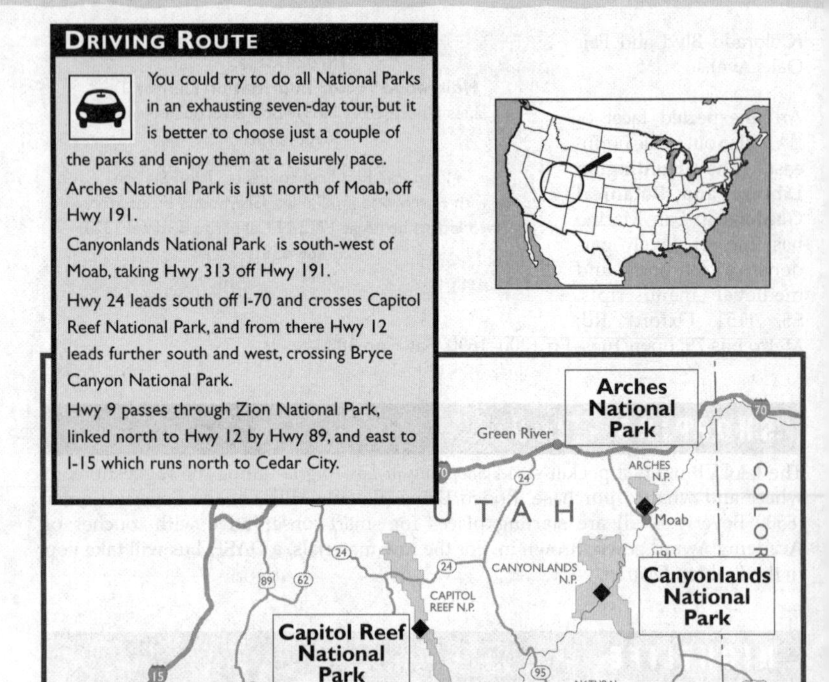

Notes

Greyhound Lines have services from Las Vegas and Salt Lake City that go around the perimeter of this area with stops at St George, Cedar City and Green River. Amtrak's 'California Zephyr' stops at Green River. OTT tables 342, 811 and 831.

SOUTHERN UTAH NATIONAL PARKS

Drive carefully – most accidents in Utah are due to drivers paying more attention to the scenery than to the road. In many of the parks there are small dirt tracks that are best for 4-wheel drive vehicles only. Wide vehicles are not recommended – the National Parks advise that some of these dirt-track drives have a serious risk of vehicle damage.

Geological curiosities, gaping canyons, precipitous ravines, stone arches and needle-like towers eroded by wind and water litter the multicoloured high desert of southern Utah. The only way to see this astonishing landscape is by car, as public transport is extremely limited. Driving through the region's five outstanding national parks will take you from beside the Colorado River across the high red tableland and up into the Wasatch Mountains, through natural phenomena with evocative names like The Devil's Garden, The Maze, Rainbow Point and Weeping Rock.

ARCHES NATIONAL PARK

Travelling from Moab, you will shortly come to Arches National Park, where over 2000 natural arches have been carved into the red stone by erosion – one of the largest concentrations of sandstone arches in the world. The park is 76,519 acres in size, and is dotted with sandstone spires, peaks and strange balanced rocks. An 18-mile road leads into Devil's Garden, where 64 closely grouped arches form a natural backdrop.

The main entrance, with visitor centre, museum and bookshop, is at the park's southern tip, near Moab; shuttles run from here to Green River, on the northern tip, which provides a handy stopping place.

i **Arches National Park Visitors Center,**
Arches National Park, Hwy 191; tel: (435) 259-8161.

Seasonals

Peak Season is between Memorial Day and Labor Day: they are hectic months and best avoided. The parks are visited throughout the year and motels and hotels are open accordingly – prices peak at midsummer and for winter weekends but are lowest in the spring after the skiing season.

Arches National Park Visitor Center is closed only on 25 Dec; park is open throughout the year. Canyonlands: open throughout the year. Capitol Reef Park: open all year. In winter, snowfall is usually light but may close some roads briefly. Zion National Park: open all year. There is often heavy snow in winter, but the main roads are ploughed. Natural Bridges: open all year, although some of the steeper trails are closed in winter as there is often heavy snow. Hovenweep: open all year round. Bryce Canyon: open all year round.

RUN THE RAPIDS
Moab is gaining a reputation as a centre for white-water rafting, and from Canyonlands you can run the rapids of Cataract Canyon. Contact Tag Along Tours and Travel, tel: (435) 259-8946.

There is no accommodation inside the park itself but there are places at both Green River and Moab.

Westwinds Roadway Inn $ 525 E Main St, Green River; tel: (435) 564-3421.

Best Western River Terrace $$ 880 E Main St, Green River; tel: (435) 564-3401.

Castle Valley Inn $$ 424 Amber Lane, Moab; tel: (435) 259-6012.

Ben's Café $ 115 W Main St, Green River, tel: (435) 564-3352.

West Winds Restaurant $$ 545 E Main St, Green River, tel: (435) 564-8240.

CANYONLANDS

Seldom-visited Canyonlands is the preserve of 527 sq. miles of sandstone canyons, where water and gravity have carved flat layers of sedimentary rock into the landscape seen today. Between the deep-cut canyons created by the Colorado River and its tributaries is a towering mesa or tableland. The park is divided up into three land districts which are 2–6 hrs away by car: these are the Needles, named after the tall, thin rock formations that puncture the landscape, Island in the Sky and the Maze.

You can reach the park via buses from Green River, or from Grand Junction, where there is an Amtrak station.

Canyonlands National Park Information, 2282 S West Resource Blvd, Moab; recorded information: tel: (435) 259-7164.

Inside the park there are individual camp sites, which cannot be reserved in advance, at Needles Squaw Flat Campground and at Island in the Sky. Green River and Moab are alternative places to stay and eat (see above).

CAPITOL REEF NATIONAL PARK

Capitol Reef Park provides another set of geological fantasies. A 100-mile long wrinkle in the earth's crust, known to geologists as a monocline and to locals as the Waterpocket Fold, extends from nearby Thousand Lakes Mountain to the Colorado River, which here widens into Lake Powell.

Capitol Reef National Park Information Visitors Center, Hwy 24; tel: (435) 425-3791.

There are plenty of places to stay in towns near the park.
Circle D Motel $ 475 W Main St, Escalente; tel: (435) 826-4297.
Whispering Sands Motel $$ 140 S Highway 95, Hanksville; tel: (435) 542-3238.
Red Rock Restaurant and Campground $ 226 E 100 N, Hanksville, tel: (435) 542-3235.

BRYCE CANYON NATIONAL PARK

Bryce is a 17-mile canyon lined with hoodoos – ancient cliffs that have been eroded into parallel rows of sharp-edged pinnacles tinged with red, gold and chalk. Endless ranks of hoodoos seem to form natural stone amphitheatres, rimmed by guttered minarets, turrets, steeples and towers.

From the park entrance ($) the drive south rises 1100 ft to Rainbow Point. Sunrise is one of the most striking times of day to see the hoodoos and the easiest time of day to park. Park at **Sunrise Point** (less than a mile beyond the visitor centre) to watch the low rays of light begin to pick out the spires, then follow the **Rim Trail** down between the hoodoos to **Sunset Point**, **Inspiration Point** or **Bryce Point**. Return via the main road.

DRIVING TIPS

The road (Hwy 63) offers numerous lay-bys, but parking is extremely limited, so between spring and autumn arrive before 1000 if planning to park and explore from Sunrise, Sunset, Inspiration, Bryce or Paria viewpoints. Caravan trailers are not permitted beyond Sunset Campground, midway along the canyon drive, and RVs longer than 25 ft are prohibited from Paria View, at the end of the road, for lack of turning space. A free shuttle operates mid-May–Sept.

During the day, drive directly to **Rainbow Point**, where visibility can exceed 90 miles and early visitors occasionally spot mountain lions. The one-mile **Bristlecone Loop Trail** threads through stands of rare bristlecone pines, the oldest living organisms on earth.

Sunset Point is the obvious point from which to enjoy the sunset, though parking is a problem in summer. Vistas curve east towards **Queen's Garden**, **Wall Street** and an illusory balanced rock called **Thor's Hammer**. Allow 2 hrs to walk the 1½ mile **Navajo Loop Trail** that wanders past Thor's Hammer, through the narrow clefts separating the hoodoos and through forests of pygmy Douglas fir trees. The easiest canyon trail is a 1½ mile stroll through Queen's Garden from Sunset Point.

Bryce Canyon National Park, Box 170001, Bryce Canyon; tel: (303) 297-2757; www.nps.gov/brca/. The visitor centre is 1 mile south of the park entrance: open daily, 0800–1630 (Oct–Apr); 0800–1800 (late Apr and early Oct), 0800–2000 (May–Sept). Free shuttle is available.

Bryce Canyon Lodge $$ tel: (435) 834-5361. Open mid-Apr–Oct, the lodge is the only non-camping accommodation in the park. Advance booking required.
Best Western Ruby's Inn $$ 1 mile north of the park entrance on Hwy 63; tel: (435) 834-5341 or (800) 468-8660.
Bryce Canyon Pines, 12 miles west on Hwy 12; tel: (435) 834-5441 or (800) 892-7923.
Other accommodation is available in Tropic, east of the park on Hwy 12.

Cowboy's Smokehouse Bar-B-Q $$ 95 N Main St, Panguitch; tel: (435) 676-8030. The best local restaurant, well worth the 6 mile drive for authentic wood-smoked meats and enormous slabs of home-made pie.
Bryce Canyon Lodge Restaurant $$. The only restaurant in the park open all year.
The General Store $$ Sunrise Point. Sells snacks and drinks mid-Apr–Oct.

ZION NATIONAL PARK

The walls of Zion National Park ($) soar hundreds of feet above the river that carved them. Like the Grand Canyon, Zion has two parts: Zion Canyon (south) and Kolob Canyons (north). To protect the park and its tranquillity, private vehicles are no longer allowed on the scenic drive north of Canyon Junction except for lodge guests. The free Zion Canyon Shuttle System operates daily 0630–2130, with the highest frequency around midday. Parking is in Springdale or at the Zion Canyon Visitors Center, and the shuttle makes numerous stops en route.

Kolob Canyons is best known to serious hikers, but the easy 5-mile drive up Hurricane Fault to the picnic area at **Kolob Canyons Viewpoint** is unmissable. Look for stunning views of mesa formations dropping sheer to the Lower Kolob Plateau.

The **Zion Canyon Scenic Drive** up the canyon starts from **The Watchman** (6546 ft), a mountain wedge standing sentinel near the south entrance. A short path leads from the car park to the **Court of the Patriarchs**, with Mounts Abraham, Isaac, Jacob and Moroni to the west.

The natural hanging gardens of **Weeping Rock**, ½ mile from the car park, are watered by mists and rivulets seeping from the sandstone. Take a moment to duck beneath a well-watered overhang to see Zion's serrated peaks shimmer through the mist.

Beyond Weeping Rock, rock climbers cling like ants to cliffs that lead to the **Temple of Sinawava**, end of the road and start of a mile-long **Riverside Walk** along the Virgin River to another hanging garden.

Zion National Park, Springdale, tel: (435) 772-3256; www.nps.gov/zion/. Zion Canyon Visitor Center is ½ mile north of the south entrance; tel: (435) 772-3256. Open daily.

Zion Lodge $$$ 4 miles north of the south entrance; tel: (800) 586-7686. The only indoor accommodation in the park. Reservations are essential, through Amfac Parks and Resorts, 140001 E Iliff Ave, Ste 600, Aurora; tel: (303) 297-2757; fax: (303) 237-3715.
Other accommodation is available in Springdale, just beyond the south entrance, and the nearby towns of Hurricane or St George. The most convenient accommodation for visitors to Kolob Canyons is in Cedar City.

Zion Lodge Restaurant $$$. The only restaurant in the park. Springdale, just outside the park, has many dining options. Picnic supplies can be purchased in nearby towns, a better alternative than the Lodge snack bar.

Where Next?

South from Zion, across the border in Arizona, is the Grand Canyon. Approaching from the north will bring you to the much less commercial and comparatively unvisited North Rim *(see p. 440)**.*

150 miles south of Moab (Hwys 191 and 163) is ***Monument Valley****, part of the Navajo Indian reservation, and characterised by tall, red sandstone formations. Peer closely at the rock formations: they are noteworthy as they resemble animals – look for the bear and the rabbit. It is also the scene of countless movies, Westerns in particular. Visitor Centre, off Hwy 163, tel: (435) 727-3287.*

Outside the Parks

East of the string of national parks are two remarkable national monuments in the south-east corner of the state.

Remote **Natural Bridges Monument** sits high on Cedar Mesa at 6500 ft. Intermittent streams have cut two deep canyons and sculpted three massive bridges from the white sandstone that once lined the ancient sea bed. The bridges can be viewed from overlooks or you can hike into the canyons to see them from below. Approach it from Hite, on Rte 95.

Hovenweep National Monument is 20 miles north of Aneth on a gravel road. Its incredible towers of pueblo ruins, over 1000 years old, have been compared to European castles. There are six units of towers, the largest of which is Square Tower. Hovenweep has one camp site and there is accommodation in Bluff or Blanding. More information can be obtained from Hovenweep National Monument, Monument Headquarters at The Tower Square Group, tel: (970) 529-4461 or (800) 449-2288.

The ads claim that Las Vegas never sleeps. The lure of easy money, clattering slot machines and flashing neon may slow in the hours just before dawn, but Vegas has barely paused for breath since Nevada legalised gambling in the early 1930s.

GETTING THERE AND GETTING AROUND

McCarran International Airport is 5 miles from the city centre. A taxi to the Strip averages $15; return bus fares are slightly less. Some hotels have free shuttles.

Amtrak buses from LA arrive downtown at the Greyhound bus station.

I-15 and I-40 are the main access routes from southern California. From the Grand Canyon follow Hwys 89/9 to I-15 via Zion National Park or Hwys 89/389/9 to I-15 via Pipe Spring National Monument. Traffic along the Strip grinds to a crawl mid-afternoon to late evening, but parking is plentiful, convenient and cheap. Local CAT (702) 228-7433 buses operate 24 hrs a day, and Las Vegas Trolleys (buses) (702) 382-1404 run up and down the Strip 0930–0200 daily.

Las Vegas may be the best jumping-off place for a trip to Hawaii (see p. 585), with frequent bargain air fares on offer at www.alohaairlines.com.

INFORMATION

Las Vegas Convention and Visitors Authority, 3150 Paradise Rd, tel: (702) 735-1616, reservations: (702) 892-7575, www.visitlasvegas.com, is open 0800–1700 daily.

SAFETY Casinos are extremely security-conscious, and the Strip and 'Glitter Gulch', the casino strip on Fremont St, are safe day or night. However, avoid car parks at night (use the free valet parking every hotel offers) and don't take late-night strolls away from the casino areas. Also beware the hustlers (of either sex) who work the casinos.

MONEY Foreign Money Exchange, 101 Convention Center Dr, Plaza 122; tel: (702) 791-3301.

ACCOMMODATION AND FOOD AND DRINK

Vegas is the hotel capital of the USA, mostly concentrated along the Strip and downtown (Fremont St and nearby). New Strip hotels are most luxurious; downtown hotels less expensive. Visit Mon–Thur for the best value.

Dining has become a priority in Las Vegas, with some extremely fine restaurants for special occasions. Casino buffets such as Le Village Buffet at Paris or the Village Seafood Buffet at the Rio are still excellent value. The Palms, Golden Nugget and Main Street Station score well for both food and prices.

Tie The Knot

Las Vegas is the wedding capital of the world: styles range from formal black tie to exchanging vows on the back of a motorcycle at a drive-up chapel window. Neither blood tests nor waiting periods are required but the woman must be 18 years old. Obtain a licence, for $55, at the Clark County Courthouse, 1st Floor, 200 S 3rd St, tel: (702) 455 4416, www.co.clark.nv.us/clerk/marriage-information. The Marriage License Bureau is open 0800–2400 daily, and 24 hrs on legal holidays.

Out of Town

Out in the desert, **Red Rock Canyon** (20 miles west of Las Vegas) is spectacular. Visitor centre opens 0830–1630. 50 miles north-east of Las Vegas is the flame-red sandstone **Valley of Fire**, and 30 miles east on Hwy 93 is the mighty **Hoover Dam**. The **Grand Canyon** is a 4½-hr drive or short flight away; see pp. 435–443.

HIGHLIGHTS

The Razzmatazz For most visitors **The Strip** - Las Vegas Blvd S - *is* Las Vegas. From the **Stratosphere** to **Mandalay Bay**, its 3 miles are lined with more than 40 hotel-casinos and acres of neon. Mobster Bugsy Siegel's **Flamingo** opened here on New Year's Eve 1946 and every year seems to see a bigger, more flamboyant arrival.

'Europe' has recently invaded Las Vegas. **The Paris**, with its replicas of the Eiffel Tower and Arc de Triomphe vie with **The Venetian**'s canals and gondolas.**The Bellagio** imparts an atmosphere of the Italian Lake District and presents a spectacular nocturnal water show at 15-minute intervals. **Caesars Palace** is a constantly evolving classic, its Forum lined with 100-plus brand name shops and restaurants - and 'living statues'. The **Luxor**'s exact replica of King Tutankhamun's tomb, **New York, New York's** Statue of Liberty and an erupting volcano, a rain forest and white tigers at the **Mirage** are only a sampling of the hotel excesses. The **Imperial Palace**'s Antique and Classic Auto Collection features a 1928 Delage limousine owned by the late King of Siam and Eisenhower's parade limo.

Spectacular shows for all tastes are a major attraction. **Cirque de Soleil,** with the awe-inspiring **Mystere** at **Treasure Island**, the beautiful water-based **O** at the **Bellagio** and the X-rated **Zumanity** at **New York, New York** involve prodigious feats of balance and skill. Downtown, 2.1 *million* lights nightly create the **Fremont Street Experience**. For family-oriented entertainment, try **The Adventure Dome** indoor theme park at 'CircusCircus'. Merlin oversees a **Tournament of Kings,** complete with jousting, at the **Excalibur,** and there's a free outdoor pirate-themed **Sirens of TI** show at **Treasure Island**.

Gambling The lure of gaming - as it's euphemistically referred to in the industry - starts with slot machines at the airport. If you're an innocent abroad, take a free lesson in the basics or browse in the Gambler's Bookstore (630 S 11th St).

Away from the Tables The **Las Vegas Natural History Museum** is a good introduction to Nevada's indigenous plants and animals. $, 900 Las Vegas Blvd N; open 0900–1600. Be dazzled in close-up by the **Liberace Museum**: $, 1775 E Tropicana Ave; open 1000–1700 Mon–Sat, 1300–1500 Sun.

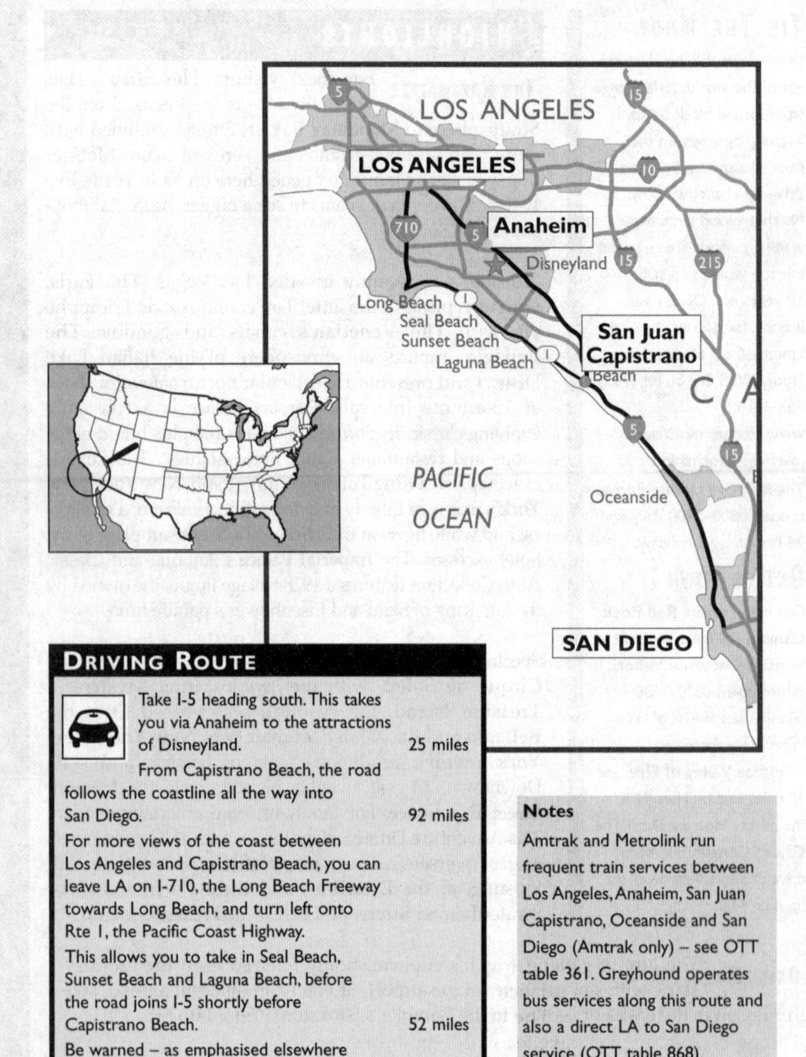

Driving Route

Take I-5 heading south. This takes you via Anaheim to the attractions of Disneyland. 25 miles

From Capistrano Beach, the road follows the coastline all the way into San Diego. 92 miles

For more views of the coast between Los Angeles and Capistrano Beach, you can leave LA on I-710, the Long Beach Freeway towards Long Beach, and turn left onto Rte 1, the Pacific Coast Highway.

This allows you to take in Seal Beach, Sunset Beach and Laguna Beach, before the road joins I-5 shortly before Capistrano Beach. 52 miles

Be warned – as emphasised elsewhere in this chapter, all of these roads are often very congested.

Notes

Amtrak and Metrolink run frequent train services between Los Angeles, Anaheim, San Juan Capistrano, Oceanside and San Diego (Amtrak only) – see OTT table 361. Greyhound operates bus services along this route and also a direct LA to San Diego service (OTT table 868).

From Los Angeles south to San Diego the coast is a sunny, sandy haven for the rich and tanned. The train is a relaxing alternative to the often slow and congested highways, and the stretch between Capistrano Beach and Del Mar, in particular, affords wonderful views of the Pacific. Stops along the way include Anaheim (for Disneyland) and the old mission town of San Juan Capistrano.

ANAHEIM

All of Los Angeles has been accused of being a gigantic theme park, but even here some places are less real than others. Anaheim is the stop for **Knott's Berry Farm**, the USA's original theme park, and for Disney's first dreams-come-true creation, **Disneyland**. Amtrak trains pull into the Anaheim Stadium, about 1 mile east of Disneyland (taxis available at the station).

Just beyond Disneyland's main entrance ($$$$), 1313 Harbor Blvd; tel: (714) 781-4565, **Main Street USA** is lined with Victorian-style shopfronts. Beyond, the dreamland opens up: **Adventureland, Frontierland, Critter Country, Fantasyland** (anchored by the Disney signature Sleeping Beauty's Castle), **Toontown** and the rest. **Tomorrowland** was rebuilt in 1998 to be more futuristic – 'Honey, I Shrunk the Audience' is a chance to wear 3D glasses. Evening parades and fireworks are worth waiting for, but find a vantage point early.

Across from the Magic Kingdom is **Disney's California Adventure** ($$$$) with three themed areas – **Hollywood Pictures Backlot**, **Paradise Pier** and **Golden State** – designed to give visitors a taste of the California Experience. Attractions include **Soarin' Over California**, a simulated hang-glider ride over the state and **California Screamin'**, a roller coaster with a loop-de-loop around a glimmering silhouette of Mickey Mouse's head. Open daily, hours vary.

Located between the two theme parks and the Disneyland, Grand Californian and Paradise Pier hotels is admission-free **Downtown Disney**, an entertainment, shopping and dining centre. Attractions include a new **House of Blues**, **Ralph Brennan's Jazz Kitchen**, **Rainforest Café**, **ESPN Sports Zone** and multiplex cinema. Open daily 0700–0200.

You may not bring food and drink into the park, but cafeterias and fast-food outlets are (of course) here in abundance, from breakfast in Main Street's **Carnation Café** to dinner in 'New Orleans' at **The Blue Bayou**. Official hotels offer children Character Dining ($$$) – they can have tea with Minnie and friends.

About 20 mins away (tel: (714) 220-5200), **Knott's Berry Farm** ($$$$) actually did begin life as a berry farm. The Knott family sidelined into chicken dinners to counteract the 1930s Depression, and the wagon rides they started up to entertain the ever-increasing number of visitors were the forerunners of the hair-raising amusement rides here today. The Wild West – from the partly authentic **Ghost Town** to the Bigfoot Rapids of **Wild Water Wilderness** – is a running theme. Knott's is also the home of Charlie Brown, Lucy, Linus and the rest of the Peanuts gang, with their headquarters at **Camp Snoopy**. The wooden 'Ghost Rider' is a favourite with roller-coaster enthusiasts. And, yes, you can still get a Mrs Knott's Chicken Dinner here.

Disneyland Resort Hotels (tel: (714) 956-6425) include **Disneyland Hotel** ($$$$), **Grand Californian** ($$$$) and the **Paradise Pier** ($$$), across from the park entrance.

SAN JUAN CAPISTRANO

Each year, on St Joseph's Day (19 Mar), legend decrees that the swallows return to Mission San Juan Capistrano. Unfortunately, the nests were taken down during renovations in the 1990s and the swallows started nesting elsewhere. The large mission site is beautiful with fountains, lush gardens, and peaceful courtyards. The Serra Chapel (1777) is the oldest building still in regular use in California, and the ruins remain of the Great Stone Church, which collapsed during morning mass in an 1812 earthquake. $, open daily (except Good Friday, Thanksgiving and Christmas) 0830–1700; tel: (949) 248-2048 or (949) 248-2049.

See fine American antique jewellery, silver, glass, china, saddles, dolls, books and Orange County fruit box labels at **Old Barn Antiques Mall**, 31792 Camino Capistrano, a co-operative of antique dealers; open daily 1000–1700. The 31 structures within **Los Rios Historic District** include adobe houses, a pet farm and the 1894 Santa Fe Railroad Depot.

San Juan Capistrano Chamber of Commerce, 31871 Camino Capistrano, Ste 306; tel: (949) 493-4700; www.sanjuanchamber.com.

Amtrak station is in the historic town, next to the Mission. 26701 Verdugo St.

Laguna Inn and Suites $$$$ 28742 Camino Capistrano; tel: (949) 347-8520.

Café Capistrano $ Camino Capistrano and Ortega Hwy. Features burgers of all kinds.
Ramos House Café $$ 31752 Los Rios St. Breakfast and lunch on an outdoor patio.

EN ROUTE

Around Oceanside is a curious mix of attractions: a surfing museum as well as real surf; tours of the Marine Corps amphibious training base, Camp Pendleton; and, just south at Carlsbad, drag racing, motocross and Legoland California.

MUST SEE/DO IN SAN DIEGO

Step back into the 19th-century Old Town – and have a Margarita before you leave

Meet the pandas and their friends at the San Diego Zoo

Ride a ferry to Coronado Island for the sunset

San Diego is as tropical as California gets. Bright sun and ocean breezes combine with the influence of Mexico, 20 miles south, to concoct a casual, easy-going atmosphere in California's second largest city. Visually, San Diego is uncongested; homes and businesses do not pile above or against one another. East over the mountains is desert; north along the coast are round, eroded cliffs and beaches of golden sand. Coronado Island, in San Diego Bay, offers resort dining and shopping a few minutes from downtown, while Mission Bay has beaches, SeaWorld and marinas filled with pleasure boats. Downtown bustles with business, gracefully proportioned high-rises lining the waterfront. And just 10 inches of annual rainfall encourages al fresco dining most of the year.

GETTING THERE

AIR **San Diego International Airport, Lindbergh Field**, tel: (619) 231-7361, is 3 miles north of downtown. San Diego Transit (MTS) bus 992 will take you into the city centre, but taxis are cheap – as cheap if there are three or four of you. Hotels and other shuttles also operate from between Terminals 1 and 2.

RAIL/BUS Amtrak trains connect Los Angeles and San Diego 11 times daily; the journey takes 2½ to 3 hrs. The terminus at the Spanish Mission-style Santa Fe Depot (1050 Kettner Blvd) has transit connections north to Oceanside on the Coaster commuter service, and via trolley to Old Town, Mission Valley, Seaport Village and the Mexican border. Greyhound stops downtown at 120 W Broadway; tel: (619) 239-3266.

ROAD San Diego is 120 miles south of Los Angeles via I-5; allow 3 hrs to drive from centre to centre, more in the rush hour.

BOAT The Cruise Ship Terminal is across N Harbor Dr. from the Santa Fe Depot.

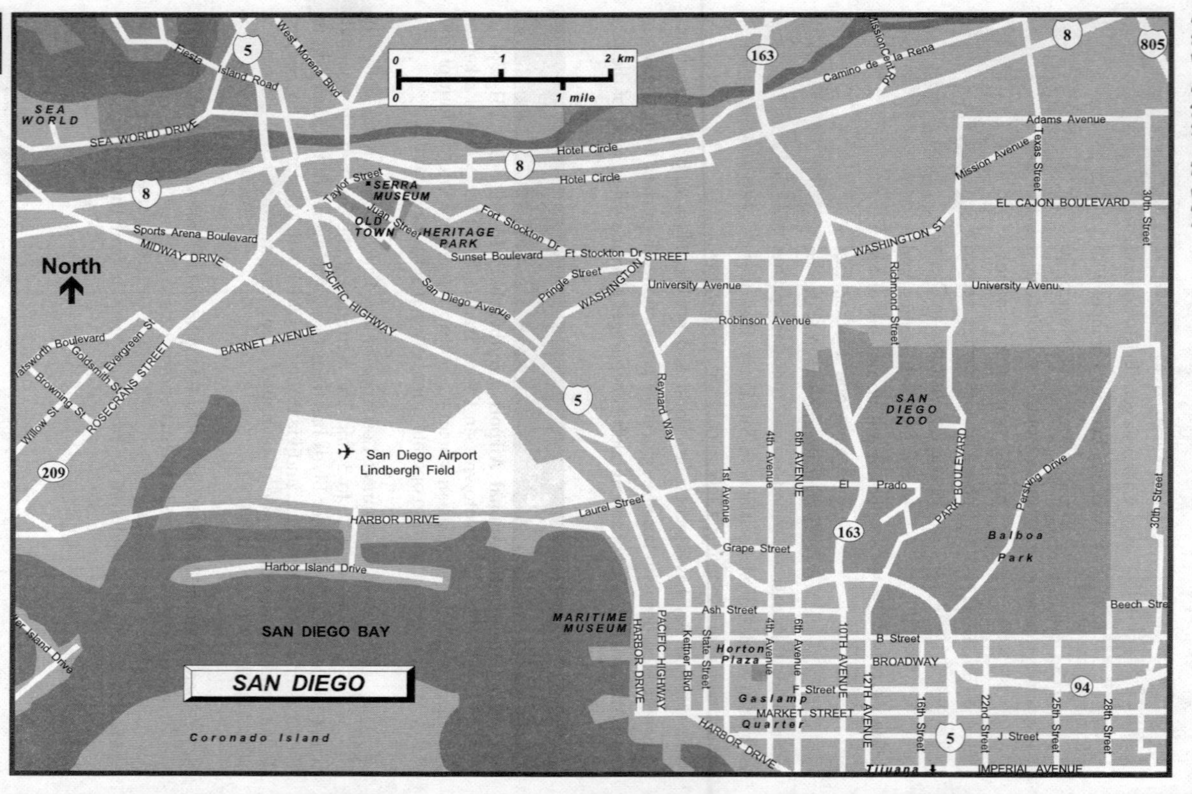

SAN DIEGO
North
0 1 2 km
0 1 mile
SEA WORLD
SEA WORLD DRIVE
Fiesta Island Road
West Morena Blvd
Camino de la Rena
Hotel Circle
Hotel Circle
Taylor Street
SERRA MUSEUM
OLD TOWN
Juan Street
HERITAGE PARK
Fort Stockton Dr
Ft Stockton Dr
Sunset Boulevard
Sports Arena Boulevard
MIDWAY DRIVE
PACIFIC HIGHWAY
San Diego Avenue
Pringle Street
WASHINGTON STREET
WASHINGTON ST
Adams Avenue
Mission Avenue
Texas Street
EL CAJON BOULEVARD
30th Street
University Avenue
University Avenu
Robinson Avenue
Richmond Street
BARNET AVENUE
Boulevard
Goldsmith St
Evergreen St
Browning St
Willow St
ROSECRANS STREET
Reynard Way
San Diego Airport
Lindbergh Field
SAN DIEGO ZOO
1st Avenue
4th Avenue
6th AVENUE
El Prado
PARK BOULEVARD
Pershing Drive
Laurel Street
HARBOR DRIVE
Harbor Island Drive
Grape Street
Balboa Park
Ash Street
Beech Street
MARITIME MUSEUM
SAN DIEGO BAY
HARBOR DRIVE
PACIFIC HIGHWAY
Kettner Blvd
State Street
Horton Plaza
4th Avenue
6th Avenue
10TH AVENUE
12TH AVENUE
B Street
BROADWAY
F Street
Gaslamp Quarter
MARKET STREET
16th Street
22nd Street
25th Street
28th Street
J Street
Tijuana
IMPERIAL AVENUE
Island Drive
Coronado Island
5
8
163
805
209
94

INFORMATION

International Visitors Information Center, 11 Horton Plaza (1st Ave at F St); tel: (619) 236-1212; www.sandiego.org, is open Mon–Sat 0830–1700; also Sun 1100–1700 (June–Aug).
San Diego Visitor Information Center, 2668 E Mission Bay Dr. (I-5 Clairemont Dr. exit); tel: (619) 276-8200; fax: (619) 276-6041; www.infosandiego.com. Open daily 0900–dusk.

SAFETY Avoid areas east of Fifth Ave and south of Imperial.

MONEY Travelex foreign exchange office at 4417 La Jolla Dr., Suite N17; tel: (619) 457 2366.

POST AND PHONES The main post office is at 815 E St.

ACCOMMODATION

Coronado, Mission Bay, coastal and downtown hotels are pricey; look for large rooms, value and easy freeway access from I-8 in Mission Valley's Hotel Circle, a 15-min drive to downtown. Prices drop 15–40 per cent Nov–Mar; what's pricey in high season may be offered at discount later. For discounted hotel rooms, visit www.infosandiego.com.

Hostelling International Downtown San Diego $ 521 Market St; Convention Center Trolley; tel: (619) 525-1531; fax: (619) 338-0129. In the heart of the historic Gaslamp Quarter.

Hostelling International Point Loma $ 3790 Udall St; bus 35 from Old Town Trolley; tel: (619) 223-4778; fax: (619) 223-1833. Near Ocean Beach.

Heritage Park Inn $$$$ 2470 Heritage Park Row; Old Town Trolley; tel: (619) 299-6832 or (800) 995-2470. Victorian cosseting two blocks from Old Town State Historic Park.

Hotel del Coronado $$$$ 1500 Orange Ave, Coronado; bus 901; tel: (619) 522-8000 or (800) 468-3533. The grande dame, picture-postcard resort hotel, complete with ghosts.

Town and Country Resort Hotel $$$$ 500 Hotel Circle N; bus 6 from Fashion Valley Trolley; tel: (619) 291-7131 or (800) 772-8527. Convenient, large convention hotel with posh rooms, cheerful staff and easy freeway access.

FOOD AND DRINK

San Diego's proximity to Mexico makes it easy to find a variety of Mexican food, from bland to chilli-pepper spicy, especially in Old Town. San Diego is also getting a reputation for fusion cuisines, mixing California's fresh produce with delicate recipes, sauces and presentation from Asia. The Gaslamp Quarter has a good choice of restaurants, from moderate to pricey, many with live music in the evening. Seaport Village's several bayside seafood restaurants allow you to enjoy views of gleaming white boats nestled in marinas in Mission Bay.

Croce's $$ 5th Ave and F St; tel: (619) 233-4355. A choice of three venues: Top Hat Bar and Grille has nightly rhythm and blues; Upstairs at Croce's has Southwest cuisine; and Croce's Restaurant and Jazz Bar has all-American cuisine with live jazz.

Buffalo Joe's $$ 600 5th Ave; tel: (619) 233-2678. The place to try baby back ribs.

Casa de Bandini $$ 2754 Calhoun St; tel: (619) 297-8211. An adobe in Old Town serving a variety of tortillas.

Sadaf Restaurant $$ 828 5th Ave; tel: (619) 338-0008. Draws a loyal crowd for Persian dishes.

Hornblower $$$ 1066 N Harbor Dr.; tel: (619) 686-8700. Dinner-dance and Sun Champagne brunch cruises in the Bay.

GETTING AROUND

San Diego's public transport is inexpensive, seamless and a good alternative to city driving. Different transport systems are co-ordinated by the San Diego Metropolitan Transit System (MTS), tel: (619) 233-3004; www.sdcommute.com.

The bright red **San Diego Trolley** connects the Santa Fe Depot with Mission Valley and Old Town (Blue Line) and San Ysidro/Tijuana (Blue Line). Trolleys operate 0430–0100 daily; fares vary by distance.

San Diego Transit buses run from downtown and trolley stations to points throughout the city. Buses operate 0430–0030 daily for a flat fare.

The **Coronado Ferry** departs from Broadway Pier (across Pacific Hwy from Santa Fe Depot) on the hour 0900–2100 (2200 Fri–Sat) and returns from Coronado on the half-hour 0930–2130 (2230 Fri–Sat).

Day Tripper Passes, valid on all MTS bus and trolley routes for one, two, three and four days, are available from selected trolley ticket machines and the **Transit Store**, 102 Broadway at 1st Ave; tel: (619) 234-1060, open 0900–1700 Mon–Fri.

HIGHLIGHTS

DOWNTOWN Opulent late Victorian architecture and street lamps grace downtown's 16-block **Gaslamp Quarter** (between Broadway and Harbor Dr., and 4th and 6th Aves). Alone among California's major cities, this civic and business centre has remained visually intact since its beginnings as 'New Town' in 1887, when San Francisco merchant Alonzo E Horton bought up the waterfront and moved the action from Old Town. The 1850s **William Heath Davis House** was an early merchant-developer's residence; $, 410 Island Ave; open Mon–Fri 1000–1400, Sat 1000–1600, Sun 1200–1600.

Through the next century, the boom town catered to lawman Wyatt Earp's three gambling halls, bordello patrons, sailors and homeless men, evolving into an infamous skid row as population and business shifted north and east. Some homeless missions remain, but the Gaslamp Quarter's 1970s restoration continues, cemented by great music clubs, fine dining and a cheerful ambience of rediscovery. A new stadium for the San Diego Padres is being built just to the south of the Gaslamp, near the trolley station.

Horton Plaza, at the north edge of the Gaslamp Quarter (Gaslamp or 5th Ave Trolley), has 140 shops, including FAO Schwarz for toys and Nordstrom and Macy's department stores. Geometric wedges, odd angles, tilework, the eagle-topped Jessops San Diego Time Clock and 41 cheerful colours make this chic shopping mall a popular destination for San Diegans. Open Mon–Fri 1000–2100, Sat 1000–1900, Sun 1100–1800.

The **Maritime Museum of San Diego** ($$) on N Harbor Dr. (Civic Center Trolley) is dominated by the majesty of the *Star of India*'s square rigging. One of three ships open for touring, the oldest merchant vessel still afloat has been restored to the condition of her launch from the Isle of Man in 1863. The 1898 *Berkeley* ferry boat is the sister ship of the *Eureka*, displayed along the Hyde Street Pier of the National Maritime Museum in San Francisco (see p. 549). Both ferries plied San Francisco Bay. The steamer *Medea*, a Scottish-built luxury yacht, is tied up alongside.

If You're Driving

Freeways may clog abysmally in the rush hour. Hwy S21 is the much slower scenic alternative to I-5, running along the coast from Carlsbad to Mission Bay/Mission Beach.

Many city-centre streets are one-way; follow directional signs to attractions. Downtown parking meters are inexpensive: Horton Plaza offers 3 hrs' free parking with any mall purchase, a cheaper alternative to valet parking at trendy 5th St restaurants. Seaport Village has 2-hr validation.

Old Town North-west of downtown (Old Town Trolley Station), a larger area of motels, restaurants and shops serves visitors to the city's 19th-century settlement. In **Old Town San Diego State Historic Park** three original family adobes, **La Casa de Estudillo, Machado y Stewart**, and **Machado y Silvas** are beautifully restored house museums. At weekends, volunteers dressed in mid-19th-century military uniforms are inspected in front of the **Robinson-Rose House** (also the visitor centre), then drill on the green and parade around the park. A blacksmith demonstrates his skills near **Seeley Stables Museum.** Carriages and stagecoaches are on display inside, supplemented by a film on transport in California. The **First San Diego Courthouse**, the first *San Diego Union* (newspaper) building, a school and a dental museum offer insights into daily life, while the **Wells Fargo Museum** in the reconstructed **Colorado House** explains the economics of stagecoaches and the Gold Rush in California. The park is open daily 1000–1700. For a self-guided walking tour, purchase *Old Town San Diego State Historic Park Tour Guide and Brief History* at Seeley Stables, or take a ranger-led tour. **Old Town Trolley Tours** $$, tel: (619) 298-8687, operate a hop-on hop-off tour in orange and green motorised trams. Board at Twiggs St or any of eight other stops for a 2-hr narrated circuit. Tours run 0900–1600 (last tour).

San Diegans visit Old Town to enjoy margaritas and warm tortillas at several good restaurants, such as those in the courtyard of **Bazaar del Mundo**'s hibiscus-entwined shopping arcade, complete with dancers and mariachi bands.

On the edge of Old Town, **Heritage Park** preserves six Victorian mansions and a Jewish synagogue arranged along a pedestrian walk. All the buildings are still in use, and popular with wedding parties at weekends. A turret marks the Heritage Park Bed and Breakfast Inn in the 1889 Queen Anne style **Christian House**, and there are Victorian-style souvenirs in the 1893 classical revival **Burton House**. The clean classical revival lines of the 1893 **Temple Beth Israel** appealed to Christian congregations, which also used the building before they had permanent sites for their churches.

The **Mormon Battalion Memorial** at 2510 Juan St, between Old Town and Heritage Park (Old Town Trolley), celebrates the arrival in 1847 of Mormon troops to support American troops in the fight against Mexico. North of Old Town, **Presidio Park** was the site of the original 1769 fort and mission. The **Junipero Serra Museum and Tower Gallery** artefacts and scale models explain San Diego's pre-American history.

BALBOA PARK

The city park, Balboa Park is 1400 acres of greenery north-east of downtown (Bus 7 on Broadway). The collection of plants, trees, Californian-Spanish Baroque architecture, museums and the world-renowned zoo (see box on p. 527) have rendered its original 1868 chaparral and cacti desertscape unrecognisable outside the sculptured **Desert Garden** (on the east side of Park Blvd). Many of the Baroque buildings were installed for the 1915 Panama-California Exposition. The park is full of interesting museums, botanical displays, artists' studios and performing arts venues. Many museums are free one Tues each month, but the seven-day, 12-museum **Passport to Balboa Park** provides bargain admission at other times and 13 cultural facilities. There is a visitor centre at 1549 El Prado, and a free **Balboa Park Tram** from the Inspiration Point car park makes a circuit of 11 stops. Visit www.balboapark.org.

Along El Prado, in the western segment of the park, is a varied assembly of sights and entertainments. The **Museum of Man** at no. 1350 is an eclectic, fun collection of ethnic artefacts from all over the world – don't miss the mummies; $ open 1000–1630. The **Mingei International Museum**, at no. 1439, displays worldwide folk arts; $, open Tues–Sun 1000–1600. From the formal arcaded **Alcazar Garden** behind the museum there is a picture-postcard view of California Tower's tile dome. The European art collections at the **Timken Museum of Art** (no. 1500) include magnificent Russian icons. Open Tues–Sat 1000–1630, Sun 1330–1630; closed Sept. Youth productions of ballet, theatre and dance can be enjoyed at **Casa del Prado Theater**; $$, tel: (619) 239-8355. Its elegant façade could be in Spain.

The **Museum of Photographic Art** ($), 1649 El Prado, has changing exhibits of contemporary and historic photography and film, open daily 1000–1700; tel: (619) 238-7559. The building's lower level, however, is heaven for train buffs. The **Model Railroad Museum** has six scale-model mini-gauge train circuits, enhanced by realistic sound effects. $, open Tues–Fri 1100–1600, Sat–Sun 1100–1630 with extended hours during summer.

Transport in all forms is well represented in the park. The combined influence of naval aviation and the aerospace industry in San Diego make the 66 aircraft on display in the doughnut-shaped Ford Building of the **San Diego Aerospace Museum** one of the best introductions to the history of flight. $$, open 1000–1430 with extended hours during the summer; free fourth Tues of the month. The **San Diego Automotive Museum** rotates exhibits of southern California's *raison d'être* from a fine collection of historic vehicles. $$, 2080 Pan American Plaza; open 1000–1600. There are hands-on exhibits and an OMNIMAX® Space Theater at the **Reuben H Fleet Science Center**, 1875 El Prado. Open daily from 0930 - closing times vary. $$, tel: (619) 238-1233.

SAN DIEGO ZOO

This world-famous zoo was among the first to pioneer habitats for its birds and 4000 animals, freeing them from traditional caged confinement.

On several levels of jungle-type vegetation, the zoo wanders through Cat and Bear Canyons and Horn and Hoof Mesa. Queue up early for a glimpse of two pandas on research loan from China who had a cub a few years ago. The Polar Bear Plunge is happily incongruous in the balmy climate, but Gorilla Tropics and the South African klipspringer habitat feel like authentic exotic locations. There's also a Children's Zoo.

Guided tours in double-decker buses get round most of the zoo; Kangaroo Bus Tours provide eight drop-off points. Both depart from Flamingo Lagoon in the main area. The Skyfari Aerial Tram gives a gondola overview with a quick hop to the other side of the park. $$$, open 0900–1700 (last entry 1600), extended hours in summer; tel: (619) 234-3153; bus 7 on Broadway.

For art lovers, **the San Diego Museum of Art** in Plaza de Panama combines contemporary California art with Chinese, Japanese and 15th–18th-century European works, supplemented by the outdoor Sculpture Garden Café. $$, open Tues–Sun 1000–1630. The **Spanish Village Arts and Crafts Center** has a wide, colourful courtyard full of studios where artists work, display and sell sculpture, jewellery, paintings and other arts. Open 1100–1600. The **Globe Theatre**, a reproduction of the London original, presents Shakespeare's plays and more on several stages.

Other curiosities and attractions in the park include **Spreckels Organ Pavilion**, where 4445 organ pipes thrill music lovers with free outdoor concerts Sun afternoons at 1400 and Mon evenings at 2000, June–Aug; the **Botanical Building**, whose plain name disguises the beautiful orchids and heliconia which bloom amid exotic palms (open daily except Thur 1000–1600); and **Marston House**, in the north-west corner of the park. This craftsman-style mansion has lovely landscaped English-style gardens. $, 3525 7th Ave; open Fri–Sun 1200–1630.

SEAPORT VILLAGE This nautical-theme shopping and dining area just north-west of the San Diego Convention Center lies on the bay south of the Gaslamp Quarter. A bayside boardwalk at the south end of the embarcadero gives access to year-round outdoor music, fashion shows and mimes, and shops are open late (until 2100; 2200 June–Aug). **Wyland Galleries** have the famous artist's whale paintings and marine art, and the **San Diego City Store** proffers local-name souvenirs and T-shirts. Go for a cheerful wake-up breakfast at the **Village Café** and take a spin on the 1890 Looff **Broadway Flying Horses Carousel** on the boardwalk.

CORONADO ISLAND Just a ferry ride across San Diego Bay, Coronado Island is resort, getaway, shopping opportunity, and sunset viewpoint. With the arrival of the railway in the 1880s, San Diego cried out for a resort, and the **Hotel del Coronado** met the need. The white Victorian building with bright red roof and towers still stands as a luxury landmark, a wedding-cake frippery.

The **San Diego-Coronado Bridge** arcs gracefully over the bay, a lovely drive except during the rush hour. Bus no. 901 makes the journey, or catch the **Coronado Ferry** (passengers and bicycles only) from Broadway Pier to Ferry Landing Marketplace. (A fast but pricey alternative is Marriott's Coronado Island Resort's water taxi service: 6 mins to the San Diego Convention Center area.)

On the north side of the island, shops and dining are congregated around Ferry Landing Marketplace which, with four parks ½ mile west, has fine views of the afternoon sun glowing on downtown high-rises to the east. Ocean Blvd, north-west of the Hotel del Coronado, is a superb spot for sunsets. **Orange Ave**, near the hotel, is a trendy area to shop, dine, sip espresso, browse in art galleries and people-watch.

MISSION BAY Mission Bay sprang from the imagination when mud dredged from San Diego Harbor created a huge waterside parkland, with beaches on the bay and Pacific Ocean. The sheltered bay offers hotels and camping, restaurants and children's playgrounds, and every sporting opportunity from swimming, jet skiing and sailing to bicycling, skating, kite-flying, fishing, tennis and golf.

The best-known attraction is **SeaWorld San Diego**. Its denizens of the oceans are dominated by the orca (killer whales). Special effects accompany the Shamu Adventure, with performances by Shamu and Baby Shamu. On Wild Arctic, a simulated helicopter takes off from San Diego and lands in a North Pole scenario with polar bears, beluga whales and walrus going about their business. Florida's gentle herbivores are being rehabilitated in Manatee Rescue, a 215,000-gallon freshwater tank with viewing of the sea cows from above and below. A plastic viewing tube protects visitors from the inhabitants of Shark Encounter. Bottlenose dolphins, pilot whales, sea lions, river otters and large birds perform routines, and aquariums introduce less tractable species. SeaWorld ($$$) is open daily from 0900 June–Sept, from 1000 rest of the year, closing times vary; bus no. 9 from Old Town Trolley.

POINT LOMA In 1542, three Spanish ships under Portuguese commander Juan Rodriguez Cabrillo found a 'closed and very good port' and Kumeyaay Indians. The explorers landed, claimed 'San Miguel' for their Catholic majesties, then sailed north to the Channel Islands. At the end of Point Loma peninsula sheltering San Diego Bay, the clifftop **Cabrillo National Monument** ($) is a majestic, oversized white statue of the explorer flanked by cross, crown and coat of arms of Spain. Cabrillo's head faces east, taking in the sweep of the bay channel, Coronado Island and downtown San Diego to the mountains flanking the Mexican border. Below the statue, an observation area offers stunning vistas of sailing regattas and US naval traffic. Bus 26 from Old Town Trolley.

59-MILE DRIVE

The scenic San Diego 59-Mile Drive is a half-day circuit that begins at the foot of Broadway near the Santa Fe Depot, and includes La Jolla and Coronado. Follow the signs of a flying white seagull on a blue and yellow field.

Old Point Loma Lighthouse, a 5-min walk from the monument, sits whitely 422 ft above the Pacific. Operational from 1855 to 1891, the light tower sits in the middle of the house, furnished as it was for the last keeper's posting.

A 2-mile return **Bayside Trail** winds through prickly pear and succulents, black sage and chaparral as it descends 300 ft. A well-marked path close to the monument entrance gives on to accessible tidepools, and the **Whale Overlook** is ideal for grey whale spotting Dec–Mar. Below Point Loma, the eroded **Sunset Cliffs** are popular at sundown. Monument, visitor centre and lighthouse are open daily 0900–1715 (until 1815 4 July–Labor Day). To reach Point Loma, take Hwy 209 to Cabrillo Memorial Dr., or bus No. 26 from Old Town Trolley.

SHOPPING

Perhaps because of the pleasant climate, it's easy to shop in the San Diego area, and shops are usually open until about 2100 most days. Film and TV merchandising stores in the whimsically coloured **Horton Plaza** include, for something more San Diegan than Disney or Warner, the local educational television station **KPBS Store of Knowledge**, and **Sports Fantasy** for genuine US sports team clothing and accessories. Validated parking helps the cost of window-shopping in the **Gaslamp Quarter**. Look for nautical souvenirs at **Seaport Village**, Mexican at Old Town's

Bazaar del Mundo, or search for unexpected bargains at **Kobey's Swap Meet**, 3500 Sports Arena Blvd; tel: (619) 226-0650; open Fri–Sun 0700–1500. **Fashion Valley Shopping Corner**, 7007 Friars Rd (Fashion Valley Trolley) in Mission Valley is filled with clothing, cosmetic and home furnishing shops, a food court and a multi-screen cinema.

NIGHTLIFE

Local newspapers and the free *San Diego Reader* list clubs, nightlife and restaurants. The **San Diego Performing Arts League** has bi-monthly listings in its free *What's Playing in San Diego Guide.* **Times Arts Tix**, south-west corner of Horton Plaza, tel: (619) 497-5000, offers on-the-day half-price tickets for theatre, dance or concert performances.

Hopping jazz, blues and rock clubs are attached to the **Gaslamp Quarter** restaurants along 5th Ave. The presence of University of California San Diego draws big-name music groups to the area.

The Globe Theatre, Balboa Park; tel: (619) 239-2255. One of the most venerable companies in the country fills three stages with 12 productions a year.

San Diego Lyceum Theatre, 79 Horton Plaza; tel: (619) 235-8025. Comic and classic performances in repertory.

La Jolla Playhouse, 2910 Village Dr.; tel: (858) 550-1010.

OUT OF TOWN

California's first mission seems strangely isolated, 7 miles from the coast or downtown, but the white façade and lush front gardens of **Mission San Diego de Alcalá** are exactly the austere and imposing image the Spanish Church and Empire wished to project. $, 10919 San Diego Mission Rd (Mission San Diego Trolley). A small museum displays vestments and manuscripts written by California Mission's founder Fra Junipero Serra and is open daily 0900–1700.

North of the city on US Route 15 is **San Diego Wild Animal Park**, 15500 San Pasqual Valley Rd, Escondido, tel: (760) 747-8702, where animal lovers can see rare and endangered animals in natural settings in a botanical reserve covering more than 2200 acres.

DAY TRIPS

LA JOLLA Just north of San Diego is La Jolla (buses 30, 34), a popular resort graced with a rocky coast and fine beaches. **La Jolla Cove** affords excellent swimming, beachcombing and diving. Carved out of sandstone cliffs by centuries of wave action, **Sunny Jim Cave** is accessible via a staircase in a souvenir shop at 1325 Coast Blvd. The **Coast Walk** features international shopping and dining with ocean views. **La Jolla Tours** offer 1½–2-hr guided walking tours of historic buildings and scenic areas of the downtown coast, including Sunny Jim Cave. Reservations are required: tel: (858) 453-8219.

BASEBALL AND FOOTBALL VENUES

The San Diegans love sport. The **Padres**, tel: (619) 283-4494, play baseball Apr–Oct, and the **Chargers**, tel: (619) 280-2121, have NFL football combat Oct–Dec/Jan at **Qualcomm Stadium** (9949 Friars Rd, while a new stadium is built). Qualcomm Stadium Trolley.

The excellent **Birch Aquarium at Scripps** is an interactive oceanographic museum with a dazzling variety of local and exotic marine life. $$, 2300 Expedition Way; open daily 0900–1700. The **Museum of Contemporary Art, San Diego** features a permanent collection which includes examples of minimalist, conceptual and California art. $ 700 Prospect St; open daily 1100–1700, until 2000 Thur, closed Wed.

Further along Prospect St, places to eat range from a **Hard Rock Café** ($$) to **George's at the Cove** ($$$), where contemporary California cuisine is served in a stylish dining room or with ocean views on the rooftop terrace.

WHERE NEXT?

A popular 'just to say I've been' trip is to cross the border into Mexico. Tijuana is less than a mile across the border. Have a passport and (for non-US citizens or resident aliens) a multiple entry visa or visa waiver in hand, and, rather than drive, book a guided tour or take the San Diego Trolley to the border and walk across. The Tijuana Visitor Information Center is located at 555 H St, Chula Vista, CA 91910; tel: (888) 775-2417.

From San Diego the Pacific Highway follows the coast all the way up through Santa Barbara (see p. 532), San Francisco (see pp. 537 and 543) and northern California (see p. 574), eventually reaching Seattle (see p. 457) and the Canadian border.

SAN DIEGO — LOS ANGELES — SANTA BARBARA

OTT Tables 360/361/868/937

Service	RAIL	RAIL	RAIL	RAIL	RAIL	RAIL	RAIL	RAIL	RAIL	RAIL	RAIL	RAIL
Days of operation	Daily	Daily	ex⑥⑦	Daily	⑥⑦	ex⑥⑦	Daily	⑥⑦	ex⑥⑦	Daily	Daily	⑥⑦
Special notes												A
San Diego......d.	0612	0705	0810	0930	1035	1050	1200	1255	1325	1500	1600	1750
Oceanside......d.	0700	0755	0858	1018	1124	1139	1249	1343	1413	1552	1650	1838
Anaheim......d.	0807	0904	1005	1126	1229	1247	1359	1448	1523	1657	1758	2004
Los Angeles......a.	0850	0950	1050	1215	1315	1335	1440	1535	1605	1745	1845	2050
Los Angeles......d.	0905	....	....	1230	....	....	1455	....	....	....	1900	2105a
Ventura......d.	1054	....	....	1419	....	....	1649	....	....	....	2057	2315a
Santa Barbara......a.	1133	....	....	1504	....	....	1731	....	....	....	2138	2350a
Service	Bus	Bus	Bus	Bus	Bus	Bus	Bus	Bus	Bus	Bus	Bus	Bus
Days of operation	Daily	Daily	Daily	Daily	Daily	Daily	Daily	Daily	Daily	Daily	Daily	Daily
Special notes	B		C	B	D		B		B		B	
San Diego......d.	....	0425	0630	....	0730	0800	....	1330	....	1530	....	1900
Oceanside......d.	....	0515	0720	....	|	0850	....	1420	....	1620	....	1950
Anaheim......d.	....	0640	|	....	|	1025	....	1555	....	1755	....	2115
Los Angeles......a.	....	0825	0900	....	1025	1159	....	1645	....	1935	....	2210
Los Angeles......d.	0630	....	....	0930	....	....	1240	....	1635	....	2005	....
Ventura......d.	0845	....	....	1130	....	....	1455	....	1900	....	2225	....
Santa Barbara......a.	0925	....	....	1210	....	....	1535	....	1940	....	2300	....

Special notes:
A–Additional trips: 1720⑥⑦, 1820⑥⑦, 2020, 2115⑤⑥⑦.
B–Additional faster services, not calling at Ventura: 0110①⑥⑦, 0315, 2140.
C–Additional trips: 0130, 1030, 1415, 1700, 2030, 2330.
D–Additional trips: 0830, 0930, 1130, 1230, 1330, 1630, 1730, 1930, 2200.
a–Connection by bus.

By Car via Laguna Beach, Santa Monica and Venice Beach

If California has a riviera, this is it. The 30 miles of beach cities between Capistrano Beach and Long Beach are among the most affluent in the world. Million-dollar homes are on display along any street near the shore. This scenic route along the southernmost part of the Pacific Coast Highway continues north along the coast, skirting the sprawl of Los Angeles, to arrive at the attractive old mission town of Santa Barbara (see pp. 582–583). Beauty notwithstanding, be warned that the beaches are jammed in summer; parking meters are *de rigueur*. Traffic crawls at weekends, holidays, and when schools are out (June–early Sept).

Driving Route

Take I-5 from San Diego to Capistrano Beach. 60 miles

Then follow Hwy 1 along the coast via Laguna Beach, Venice Beach and Santa Monica to Oxnard. 189 miles

Continue, joining Hwy 101 to Ventura. 196 miles

Follow 101 to Santa Barbara. 216 miles

LAGUNA BEACH

En Route

The **Sherman Library and Gardens** at Corona del Mar (2647 E Pacific Coast Hwy) is a self-described 'horticultural paradise', a botanical garden with cacti, roses and shade-plant areas supplemented by a tropical plant conservatory, all laid out among gazebos and walks. Open 1030–1600 daily.

Laguna Beach, started as a Plein Air School artists' colony in 1917, has continued its association with art. The **Festival of Arts and Pageant of the Masters**, in which human models enact tableaux of famous paintings, takes place each July–Aug; $$, tel: (949) 494-1145 or (800) 487-3378. The **Laguna Art Museum**, $, 307 Cliff Dr., is a glass-façaded building filled with changing exhibitions of modern art. From the museum, take Cliff Dr. along **Heisler Park** for outstanding views or lawn bowling. At Fairview St, walk down a beautiful path to the water and the **Laguna Beach Marine Life Refuge**. Injured sea lions are nursed back to health at **Friends of the Sea Lions Marine Mammal Center**, 20612 Laguna Canyon Rd.

There is no lack of activities available, all close to the highway, as an antidote to hours in the car. Play basketball, surf, bodysurf, body board or explore tidepools at **Main Beach**; scuba or snorkel at **Diver's Cove**; mountain bike or hike in **Aliso/Wood Canyon Regional Park**. You can take a bus from the bus station up to Dana Point, north of town, for an ocean vista from Top of the World Viewpoint.

i **Laguna Beach Visitor Center**, 252 Broadway; tel: (800) 877-1115 or (949) 497-9229; www.lagunabeachinfo.org. Runs a free accommodation and referral service.

Accommodation rates are moderate–pricey. Most desirable are locations near the beach.

Ruby's $ 30622 S Coast Hwy. One of a chain of 1940s-style diners with excellent all-American burgers, fries and milk shakes, served on an outdoor ocean-view terrace.

LONG BEACH

Economic revival has created soaring new office towers and hotels amid refurbished towers from the 1920s. The new **Long Beach Aquarium of the Pacific**, $$$, 100 Aquarium Way, is a celebration of the world's largest and most diverse body of water. Planet Ocean covers the exterior of the **Long Beach Sports Arena** with the world's largest mural, life-sized paintings of whales and other local sea life.

The free Passport Shuttle connects downtown Long Beach to SS *Queen Mary*, with stops at major hotels, restaurants and attractions. Look for signposts with a seagull on top. The ***Queen Mary*** ($$), permanently docked in Long Beach Harbor, is now part hotel, part museum and a stately reminder of the gracious age of the great transatlantic liners. Tour the bridge, engine room and first-class public areas. From the *Queen Mary* you can take a 1-hr cruise aboard the **Catalina Express** $$$, tel: (800) 833-6685 or (310) 519-1212, out to Santa Catalina Island.

i **Long Beach Area Convention and Visitors Bureau**, One World Trade Center, Suite 300, Long Beach, CA 90831; tel: (562)-436-3645 or (800) 452-7829; www.visitlongbeach.com. Open 0800–1700 Mon–Fri.

Lord Mayor's Bed and Breakfast Inn $$ 435 Cedar Ave; tel: (562) 436-0324. A historical landmark furnished with antiques.
Queen Mary $$$$ 1126 Queens Hwy; tel: (562) 435-3511. A 365-state-room hotel ship.
Renaissance Long Beach Hotel $$$ 111 E Ocean Blvd; tel: (562) 437-5900; fax: (562) 499-2512. Luxuriously furnished.

555 East $$ 555 E Ocean Blvd at Linden Ave; tel: (562) 437-0626. Classic upmarket steakhouse.
Cha Cha Cha $$ 762 Pacific Ave at 8th St; tel: (562) 436-3900. Eclectic Caribbean island cuisine.
L'Opera $$$ 101 Pine Ave; tel: (562) 491-0066. Italian cuisine and live opera performed Sat and Sun nights.
Simon's $$$ 340 Golden Shore Dr.; tel: (562) 435-2333. Fish house with view of harbour and the *Queen Mary*.

VENICE BEACH

Venice Beach is a seven-day circus. Oceanfront Walk is jammed with bicycles, skaters, walkers and gawkers from late morning until dusk. The lure is sun, sand and a constant stream of musicians, comedians, jugglers, mime artists and dancers concentrated around Windward Ave. **Muscle Beach**, just south of Windward, is the original outdoor body-building studio. Mr and Ms Universe wannabes pump iron and build bulk in public. Pick-up basketball games are popular on public courts.

i **Venice Chamber of Commerce**, PO Box 202, Venice, CA 90294; tel: (310) 396-7016; www.venicechamber.net.

26 Beach Café $$ 26 Washington St. Boasts the best burgers in town.

SANTA MONICA

The pier has an antique carousel, bumper cars, roller coaster and the three aquariums of the **UCLA Ocean Discovery Center**, plus more adult pastimes like fishing and dining. The **Third Street Promenade** is a lively indoor/outdoor pedestrian shopping and restaurant mall.

i **Santa Monica Visitor Center**, 1400 Ocean Ave, Santa Monica, CA 90401; tel: (310) 393-7593; www.santamonica.com. Open daily 1000–1600.

Hostelling International $ 1436 2nd St; tel: (310) 393-9913; fax: (310) 393-1769. Two blocks from the beach, pier and 3rd St Promenade; free airport pick-up.
Santa Monica Bayside $$ 2001 Ocean Ave; tel: (310) 396-6000 or (800) 525-4447. Near sandy beach and bike path (free shuttle to 3rd St Promenade).

Some of LA's best restaurants line 3rd St Promenade and surrounding streets. Santa Monica Pier has budget takeaways.

EN ROUTE

The **Santa Monica Mountains National Recreation Area** (SMMRA), tel: (818) 597-9192, stretches 18 miles north along the coast beyond Point Dume. The entire area is dotted with wide public beaches, broad parking lots and summer lifeguard stations.

VENTURA

Ventura is a mission town with broad beaches and suburbs spreading in all directions. The walkable downtown has plenty of parking on the west end of Main St near museums and **Figueroa Plaza**, a pedestrian street filled with fountains and colourful tiles.

Mission San Buenaventura, 211 E Main St, was founded in 1782. A peaceful garden, crowded museum and gift shop are next to the church, completed in 1809. Just along the street, the **Albinger Archaeological Museum** is an archaeological dig covering a full city block. Indoor and outdoor exhibits chronicle five different cultures on the site over the past 3500 years. **Ortega Adobe**, 215 W Main St, is the original home of the giant Ortega Chile Company. The 1857 adobe is typical of early Ventura homes.

Surfer's Point, at the end of Figueroa St, is a great place to watch board devotees and sunsets.

Ventura Visitors and Convention Bureau, 89-C S California St, Ventura, CA 93001; tel: (800) 333-2989 or (805) 648-2075; www.ventura-usa.com. Visitor centre open Mon–Fri 0830–1700, Sat 1900–1700, Sun 1000–1600.

Ventura Beach RV Resort $$ 800 W Main St; tel: (805) 643-9137. Just north of downtown.

Shields Brewing Co. $–$$ 24 E Santa Clara St, is the best bet downtown. An alternative is **Nona's Courtyard Café** $–$$ 67 S California St.

SANTA BARBARA

See p. 582.

WHERE NEXT?

The Pacific Coast Highway continues north to San Francisco (see following chapters), or you could strike inland (by road or the Amtrak Thruway coachlink) to take a train the length of the San Joaquin Valley (see p. 570).

EN ROUTE

Channel Islands National Park is a calm marine sanctuary at the edge of an area of population explosion. The visitor centre is on the harbour at 1901 Spinnaker Dr., and Island Packers, next to it, is the sole concessionaire; tel: (805) 642-1393. Boat trips depart from Ventura Harbor and Oxnard's Channel Islands Harbor daily, and include half-day cruise-bys, hiking excursions, snorkelling and blue and humpbacked whale-watching trips. Ask locally for diving-boat operators.

Truth Aquatics, tel: (805) 962-1127 or (805) 963-3564, at Santa Barbara's Sea Landing, offers island trips to Santa Cruz, Santa Rosa and the San Miguel Islands.

Channel Islands Aviation, tel: (805) 987-1301, in Camarillo offers round-trip flights to Santa Rosa Island.

Ten miles north of Ventura is **La Conchita**, the only commercial banana plantation in the continental United States. Many of the sunny slopes around **Carpinteria** are sown in flowers, grown for nursery stock and seed. Blooms are best in springtime.

Carpinteria State Beach has one of the state's largest concentration of public beach camping facilities.

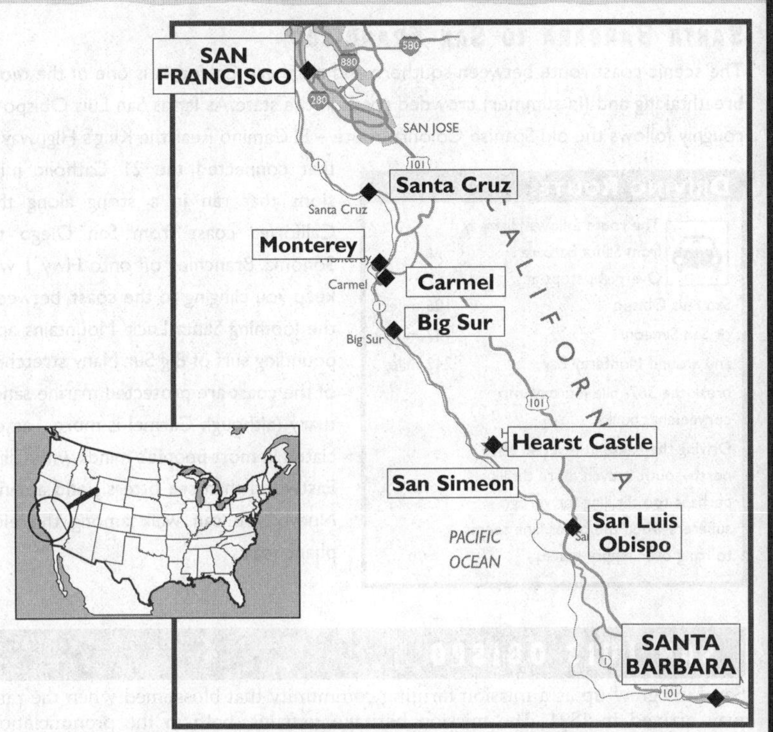

SANTA BARBARA — SAN FRANCISCO

OTT Tables 343/360/926/937

Service		Bus	Bus	Bus	Bus		Bus	Rail	Bus	Bus	Rail	
Days of operation		Daily	①⑥⑦	ex⑦	Daily		Daily	Daily	Daily	Daily	Daily	
Special notes				C				A	B			
Santa Barbara ....d.	....	0005	0305	....	0535	....	0940	1248	....	1225	1731	....
San Luis Obispo............d.	....	0230	0520	....	0815	....	1220	1543	....	1500	2030	....
Salinas............................d.	....	0515	0800	0815	1120	....	1510	1836	....	1805	....	....
Monterey........................d.	....	|	|	0910	|	....	|	|	....	|	....	....
Santa Cruz......................d.	....	0630	|	....	1230	....	1620	|	....	1915	....	....
Emeryville.......................d.	....	|	|	....	|	....	|	2202	2222	|	....	....
San Francisco..............a.	....	0920	1040	....	1520	....	1855	....	2230	2145	....	....

Special notes:

A–The Coast Starlight. This train has sleepers and a dining car available. All journeys should be reserved in advance.

B–Amtrak Thruway bus.

C–Additional trips: 0915ex⑦ and hourly until 1715ex⑦. There is a service via Marina.

The Far West

Santa Barbara to San Francisco

The scenic coast route between southern and northern California is one of the most breathtaking and (in summer) crowded roads in the state. As far as San Luis Obispo it roughly follows the old Spanish Colonial route – El Camino Real, the King's Highway – that connected the 21 Catholic missions that ran in a string along the California coast from San Diego to Sonoma. Branching off onto Hwy 1 will keep you clinging to the coast, between the looming Santa Lucia Mountains and pounding surf of Big Sur. Many stretches of the coast are protected marine sanctuary (although Carmel is more associated in most people's minds with Clint Eastwood than sea otters!) and at Año Nuevo you can walk among the elephant seals.

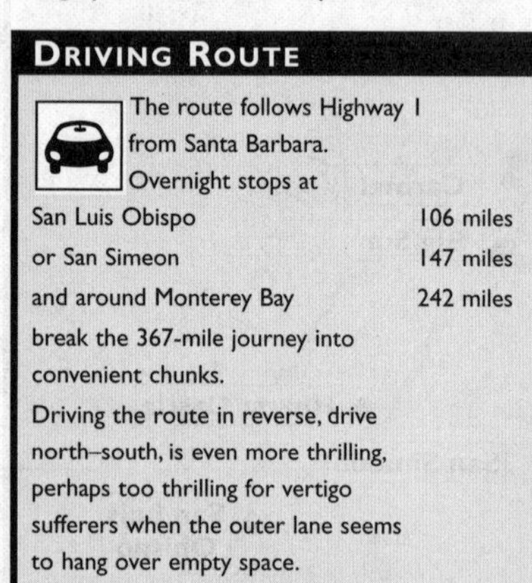

Driving Route

The route follows Highway 1 from Santa Barbara. Overnight stops at

San Luis Obispo	106 miles
or San Simeon	147 miles
and around Monterey Bay	242 miles

break the 367-mile journey into convenient chunks.

Driving the route in reverse, drive north–south, is even more thrilling, perhaps too thrilling for vertigo sufferers when the outer lane seems to hang over empty space.

San Luis Obispo

San Luis grew up as a mission farming community that blossomed when the railway arrived in 1894. The mission heritage remains, both in the pronunciation (Lou-iss, Spanish-style) and the town's common appellation, SLO, as in 'slow', the relaxed pace of life.

The walkable town centre, Higuera and Monterey Sts, contains some of the finest small-town commercial architecture in the state, from adobes to Art Deco and Frank Lloyd Wright. **Mission San Luis Obispo de Tolosa** (Chorro and Monterey Sts) pioneered the red-tiled roof that became the mission hallmark - the 1772 mission needed something more substantial than thatch to withstand fiery attacks by local Native American tribes. Open daily 0900–1700 (till 1600 Oct–Mar). **Mission Plaza**, fronting the Mission, is a shady park sloping down to **San Luis Creek** and the business district. Music wafts through the trees from several restaurant patios that open onto the plaza.

i **San Luis Obispo Chamber of Commerce**, 1039 Chorro St, San Luis Obispo, CA 93401; tel: (805) 781-2777; www.slochamber.org or www.visitslo.com. Open daily (till 2000 Thur–Sat).

Madonna Inn $$$$ 100 Madonna Rd; tel: (805) 543-3000 or (800) 543-9666. A shocking pink temple of kitsch.

SLO Brewing Company $ 1119 Garden St. Enormous servings as well as beer brewed on the main floor.

SLO Perk $ 1028 Chorro St. Breakfast, lunch and coffee stop overlooking the Mission.

HEARST CASTLE, SAN SIMEON

The rolling hills of the Central Coast have long been a magnet for dreamers with money to bring their fantasies to life – none with more extravagance than millionaire newspaper magnate William Randolph Hearst. Hearst called his 165-room Renaissance-Moorish-Medieval holiday house 'The Ranch'. The official name was La Cuesta Encantada, The Enchanted Hill, but the world knew it as Hearst Castle. More estate than castle, Casa Grande, the Big House, is surrounded by guest houses and an outdoor swimming pool complex. The whole is set in lush gardens, complete with a private zoo of free-roaming zebras and other exotic creatures.

The property eventually passed to the State of California and is open by guided tour ($$). **Tour One** is an overview of the property. **Tour Two** concentrates on the unfinished upper floors of Casa Grande, including Hearst's library and bedroom suite. **Tour Three** looks at one of the guesthouses in detail. **Tour Four** (summer only) inspects the grounds and gardens. **Tour Five** (Fri–Sat evenings, spring and autumn) is a 'living history tour' with 'famous guests' and 'servants' from the 1930s. Advance bookings are essential in summer and recommended all year – walk-in space *may* be available midweek out of season. Contact **Hearst San Simeon State Historic Monument**, 750 Hearst Castle Rd, San Simeon, CA 93452; tel: (805) 927-2020 or (800) 444-4445.

The **Visitor Center** is worth a visit even if tours are fully booked. One wall opens on conservation laboratories and the free museum provides a good overview of the Castle and architect Julia Morgan's other and far more original work.

BIG SUR

Big Sur and its series of state parks is one of the most visited parts of California, yet manages to retain an air of isolation, mystery and mysticism. Credit the 90 rugged, craggy miles of Hwy 1 carved into trackless cliffs by convict labour in the 1930s and the scarcity of accommodation. Credit, too, the ethereal magic of the cobalt and turquoise Pacific Ocean battering soaring mountains cloaked in swirling mists and dense forests. The scenery is unendingly stunning, but the winding road demands full driving attention – drivers should wait for the frequent lay-bys.

TROPIC OF CANCER REMEMBERED
The **Henry Miller Memorial Library**, just south of Ventana, is a shrine to the infamous writer who lived in Big Sur for 18 years. The library is filled with Miller memorabilia, much of it for sale. The toilet has erotic tiles by local artist Ephraim Doner; oversized sculptures grace the lawn. Open Tues–Sun 1100–1700.

Big Sur Valley, the centre for tourist services, stretches for six miles along Hwy 1. In the middle sits **Pfeiffer Big Sur State Park**: groves of redwoods, conifers and oaks interspersed with open meadows along the Big Sur River. There are miles of hiking trails and deep, clear river swimming holes among the boulders in summer. Pfeiffer Big Sur is headquarters for all of the Big Sur State Parks, with the best visitor and information centre. **Pfeiffer Beach** is Big Sur's best and hardest-to-find beach. (There's no sign, but take Sycamore Canyon Rd, the only paved road west off Hwy 1 between the Big Sur Post Office and Pfeiffer-Big Sur State Park.) The white strand is dominated by a rock hump that changes from brown to fiery orange as the sun sets.

Some of Big Sur's best coastline and day hikes are within **Julia Pfeiffer Burns State Park**, 12 miles south of Pfeiffer Big Sur itself. Don't miss the easy ½-mile return trail to McWay Waterfall, which drops from a bluff into the ocean. Another easy ½-mile return trail leads from Hwy 1 to Partington Point, overlooking the surging, kelp-filled waters of Partington Cove. Open daily dawn–dusk; $; tel: (831) 667-2315.

Also south of Big Sur Valley, **Nepenthe**, just beyond Ventana, is a restaurant best known for its views. The multistorey structure, 800 ft above the crashing surf, was built in the 1940s by Orson Welles for his bride, Rita Hayworth. Café Kevah has the best views. Open daily for lunch and dinner; $$; tel: (831) 667-2345.

Just beyond Big Sur Valley, the **Andrew Molera State Park** ($) is the largest and least developed of the Big Sur parks. Miles of trails wander its open beaches, meadows and hilltops. **Point Sur State Historic Park** ($), just to its north, contains the **Point Sur Lightstation**, in operation since 1889. The light is automated, but the building interiors are being restored to their turn-of-the-century appearance. The station is open for guided tours as part of a 2½-mile return hike, with moonlight tours in summer. Open Mon (June–Aug), Wed (Apr–Oct), Sat–Sun for guided tours.

i **Big Sur Multi-Agency Station**, ½ mile S of Pfeiffer-Big Sur State Park; tel: (831) 667-2315. Open daily 0800–1800 (till 1700 in winter). The most complete local guide is *El Sur Grande* newspaper, free at ranger stations and shops.

High demand and low supply keep prices high. Advance bookings are essential.

Big Sur Lodge $$$$ Pfeiffer Big Sur State Park; tel: (831) 667-3100; fax: (831) 667-3110. Modern cabins around a swimming pool; the only non-camping accommodation in Big Sur state parks.

Deetjen's Big Sur Inn $$ tel: (831) 667-2377; fax: (831) 667-0466. A rambling, old-fashioned inn popular with long-time visitors.

Post Ranch Inn $$$$ tel: (831) 667-2200 or (800) 527-2200; fax: (831) 667-2824; www.postranchinn.com. A post-modernist retreat below Hwy 1 with stunning views and rooms.

Ventana Inn $$$$ tel: (831) 667-2331 or (800) 628-6500; fax: (831) 667-2419. A rougher-hewn equivalent, above Hwy 1.

At the inns above. **Deetjen's** ($$) serves good Euro-Californian cuisine with larger than average portions. **Sierra Mar** at the Post Ranch ($$$) keeps to cutting-edge California dishes, while the **Ventana** tends to supply traditional California offerings.

EN ROUTE

About 14 miles before you reach Carmel look for the solitary and much-photographed arch of **Bixby Creek Bridge** soaring high above Bixby Creek. **Garrapata State Park**, 3 miles further on, contains 4 miles of undeveloped coast, but has no car parks or other facilities. Park paths from lay-bys around **Soberanes Point** run to ocean beaches through stands of cacti and into dense redwood groves.

CARMEL

In summer and most warm-weather weekends, Carmel-bound traffic backs up on Hwy 1. The town centre, Ocean Ave and its side streets, is filled with antique, art and knicknack shops interspersed with T-shirt emporia, restaurants, ice-cream parlours and hordes of visitors. The area between 5th and 8th Sts and Junipero and the city beach is packed with quaint shingled cottages, dolls' houses loaded with gingerbread details and fake adobe homes.

California's second mission was founded in Monterey in 1770 but moved to Carmel the following year to protect Native American mission women from Presidio soldiers. The **Misión San Carlos Borromero del Rio Carmelo** is at 3080 Rio Rd; mission founder Junipero Serra is buried at the foot of the altar.

Carmel Beach City Park is an alluring crescent of sand the colour of white flour against the aquamarine of Carmel Bay, but the water is too cold and the undertow too fierce for swimming. **Carmel River State Beach**, just south of town, is less crowded, but high surf can be dangerous.

i The **Tourist Information Center** is at Ocean and Junipero Sts; tel: (831) 642-2522 or (800) 550-4333; www.carmelcalifornia.org; open Fri–Sun 1100–1600.

La Playa Hotel $$$$ Camino Real and 8th Ave; tel: (800) 582-8900 or (408) 624-6476. Lush gardens and a memorable restaurant.

Hog's Breath Inn $$ San Carlos, between 5th and 6th Sts. Owned by former Carmel mayor and cinema heavyweight Clint Eastwood.

SANTA CRUZ

Holidaymakers started visiting Santa Cruz during the 1890s and never really stopped. A University of California campus added an ivory tower element in the late 1960s, followed by back-to-the-land refugees from San Francisco and Silicon Valley electronic wizards. The combination keeps local politics and entertainment venues in a ferment.

ELEPHANTS OF THE SEA

The **Año Nuevo State Reserve** at Pescadero is a rare mainland breeding ground for the endangered northern elephant seal. It's the only place in the world where humans can leave their cars and walk among 2–3-ton elephant seals in their natural habitat. Males arrive Nov–Dec and begin fighting for dominance. Females appear in Jan, give birth, and mate again before leaving a month or so later. A few seals remain all year. Winter access is by pre-booked guided tour only; tel: (650) 879-0227 or (650) 879-2025, reservations (800) 444-4445.

Don't miss the **Boardwalk**, south of the Municipal Wharf – the 1924 Giant Dipper roller coaster is usually rated among the country's top ten. The lovingly restored 1911 Charles Looff Carousel has hand-carved horses, chariots and a 19th-century pipe organ. Open daily Memorial Day–Labor Day, weekends and holidays the rest of the year.

Santa Cruz County Conference and Visitors Council, 1211 Ocean St, Santa Cruz, CA 95060; tel: (800) 833-3494 or (831) 425-1234; www.scccvc.org; and Santa Cruz Beach Boardwalk, 400 Beach St, Santa Cruz, CA 95060; tel: (408) 423-5590.

The Bed and Breakfast Innkeepers of Santa Cruz County, PO Box 464, Santa Cruz, CA 95061; tel: (831) 425-8212, offer 12 choices.

The Boardwalk has the largest concentration of restaurants.

Gabriella Café $$ 910 Cedar St. Fanciful pottery to show off fresh northern Italian dishes.

Santa Cruz Brewing Co. and Front Street Pub $ 516 Front St, and **Seabright Brewery** $ 519 Seabright Ave, no. 107, serve popular beers and food to suit tight budgets.

WHERE NEXT?

San Francisco, of course (see p. 543), from where the Pacific Coast Highway continues its journey north (p. 574). Inland across the coastal mountain range is California's capital, Sacramento, and the San Joaquin Valley (see p. 570), with access to Yosemite (see p. 561) and the Sequoia and Kings Canyon National Parks (see p. 555).

For those who live here, San Francisco is never 'Frisco'; it's 'The City', a refuge of civilisation in an otherwise Wild West. The city is an aggregation of minorities who dislike each other but still manage to live together. Precipitous hills, a sparkling bay, bridges, cable cars, 3300 restaurants and benign tolerance for almost anything short of mayhem are eternal touchstones.

Downtown is dominated by the 9 to 5 Financial District, and Upper Market St is not really the place to be after dark. The city's neighbourhoods are where the action is. On Grant Ave, just north of the Financial District, are Chinatown and the Italian North Beach neighbourhood. Walk north along the Embarcadero to the tourist zone at Pier 39 and Fisherman's Wharf. Union St in the Marina District is popular with young heterosexuals, while Castro St and Upper Market cater to the gay population. Haight-Ashbury, near Golden Gate Park, is the area where hippydom's 'Summer of Love' became dominant in the 1960s.

MUST SEE/DO IN SAN FRANCISCO

Ride a cable car

Walk (or drive!) down Lombard St

Walk or bike across the Golden Gate Bridge to Vista Point for sunset views of the city

Ride a blue and gold ferry

Treat your senses to a tasting at a Sonoma winery

GETTING THERE AND GETTING AROUND

Air **San Francisco International Airport** (SFO), tel: (650) 821-8211, is 14 miles south on Hwy 101. The cheapest way into the city is by **SamTrans** bus KX; bus BX goes to the Bay Area Rapid Transit (BART) station. The **SFO Airporter** to downtown hotels or door-to-door van service costs about $10–15, a taxi into town about three times as much. There are free shuttles to car hire locations and airport hotels.

Rail/Bus The Amtrak ticket office and waiting room are at the San Francisco Ferry Building (foot of Market St; the Embarcadero stop on the BART), where Amtrak buses depart for trains calling at Emeryville. Baylink (Vallejo), Golden Gate (Marin County), Oakland/Alameda and Tiburon Commuter Ferries also arrive here. Greyhound buses serve the Transbay Terminal (First and Mission Sts; Embarcadero BART), one block south of Market St.

ROAD The scenic north–south coastal route is Hwy 1. The faster freeway, I-5, is east of the city, with connections to the Oakland–San Francisco Bay Bridge via I-680. I-880 connects from the south, I-80 from the north, and I-580 from the east.

One-way streets, steep hills and lack of parking make driving in the city a challenge. Coloured signs point to key areas: a green outline of Italy for **North Beach;** orange crab for **Fisherman's Wharf;** blue Victorian house for **Union St**; and a white female statue for **Union Sq**. Public parking is scarce – and costs $2–20 per hour. Best bets are Stockton-Sutter Garage near Union Sq.; Fifth and Mission Garage adjacent to Yerba Buena Gardens; Police Garage, 766 Vallejo St; Portsmouth Sq. Garage, Clay and Kearny Sts. Charges are exorbitant at Fisherman's Wharf and Pier 39. Street parking is nearly impossible in the centre and scarce elsewhere. Meters accept only quarters, good for 15–60 mins, depending on the neighbourhood. Try to park and explore on foot, or use MUNI.

FERRIES
Vallejo Baylink, tel: (877) 643-3779 or (707) 643-3779, www.baylinkferry.com departs from the San Francisco Ferry Building, Market St for Vallejo (Solano County, north of San Francisco) with connecting express buses to Sacramento. A Network DayPass allows unlimited use of ferry and all connecting buses. **Blue and Gold Fleet**, tel: (415) 705-5555, www.blueandgoldfleet.com, departs from Pier 41 (Fisherman's Wharf) for Alcatraz, Angel Island, Marine World, Oakland/Alameda, Sausalito, Tiburon and sightseeing cruises. Oakland/Alameda and Tiburon commuter ferries serve the Ferry Building. **Golden Gate Ferry**, tel: (415) 923-2000, www.goldengateferry.org, serves Sausalito and Larkspur from the Ferry Building.

MUNI buses, tel: (415) 673-6864, operate 24 hrs a day, all over the city, following numbered routes. MUNI Metro light rail follows lettered routes underground in the city centre (sharing the Embarcadero, Montgomery, Powell and Civic Center stations with BART) and on the surface in outlying districts.

Restored 1940s/1950s streetcars operate as F-line transportation between the Castro/Upper Market area and the Embarcadero via the Ferry Building and Fisherman's Wharf, daily. The world-famous **cable cars** serve Nob Hill, Fisherman's Wharf, Aquatic Park, Chinatown and the entire uphill/downhill stretch of California St. Bus and streetcar fares ($1.25) and cable-car fares ($3) include up to two transfers. **MUNI Passports**, valid on all MUNI buses, streetcars and cable cars, offer unlimited daily usage (available as a 1-, 3- or 7-day pass).

BART, www.bart.gov, operates via transbay tube from San Francisco to the **East Bay** cities of Richmond (north), Pittsburg/Bay Point (east), Dublin/Pleasanton (south-east) and Fremont (south). The West Bay terminus is at Colma. Trains operate from early morning (0800 on Sun and holidays) through to midnight daily; fares vary. In addition to MUNI and BART, **Caltrain**, 4th and King Sts, tel: (650) 508-6200 or (800) 660-4287, is for commuter rail to Peninsula cities and San Jose;

MUNI links with it. You can buy a weekend pass. **AC Transit**, tel: (510) 891-4706, runs buses from the Transbay Terminal (First and Mission Sts) to East Bay cities via the San Francisco–Oakland Bay Bridge. **Golden Gate Transit** buses, tel: (415) 921-5858, run from Mission St (one block south of Market St) to Marin and Sonoma, via the Golden Gate Bridge. **Samtrans** buses run from the Transbay Terminal to the airport and south to Palo Alto, with two levels of flat fare: local and express. Visit **Bay Area Transit Information**, including fares and schedules, at www.transitinfo.org.

INFORMATION

San Francisco Convention and Visitor Bureau (SFCVB), Hallidie Plaza, Lower Level, Powell and Market Sts; tel: (415) 391-2000; fax: (415) 974-1992; www.sfvisitor.org. Open Mon–Fri 0900–1700, Sat–Sun 0900–1500. Tel: (415) 391-2001 for 24-hr recorded information. The *San Francisco Book* is the complete tourist reference.

SAFETY

Caution is advised south of Market St and in the Civic Center and Tenderloin areas. Golden Gate Park should be avoided after dark.

MONEY

Travelex is located in the financial district, at 100 Spear St at Mission St; tel: (415) 896-1115 or (800) 287-7362; Embarcadero BART. There is also a foreign exchange office near Union Sq., at 75 Geary St at Market St; tel: (415) 362-3452; Montgomery BART.

POST AND PHONES

Centrally located US Post Offices are on the basement level of Macy's department store, 121 Stockton St, Embarcadero Center, near the Ferry Building, and Rincon Center, 180 Steuart St, off Mission St.

ACCOMMODATION

San Francisco has been famous for high prices since Gold Rush days. It's one of America's most visited cities, which keeps hotels and restaurants busy all year round. Always book ahead. **Union Sq.** is the best location without a car, near main shopping, theatres, major tourist sights and public transport routes. Add $20–25 per day for parking. Motels along **Lombard St** (MUNI bus 76) and **Van Ness Ave** (Van Ness MUNI Metro) generally offer free parking; a room at the back minimises street noise. **Fisherman's Wharf** (MUNI buses 30, 42, F-Market Streetcar and Powell-Hyde St Cable Car) is group tour territory. **San Francisco Reservations**, 360 Second St, Oakland, tel: (800) 677-1550, makes free bookings.

HI Hostel $$ Fort Mason, Blg 420; tel: (415) 771-7277. In museum-rich park on cycle path.

Grosvenor Suites $$$ 899 Pine St; MUNI bus 27, California St cable car; tel: (415) 421-1899. Rare affordability on pricey Nob Hill.

Pensione International B&B $$–$$$ 85 Post St; MUNI buses 2, 3, 4, 76; tel: (415) 775-3344. Conveniently close to Union Sq., Chinatown, Civic Center.

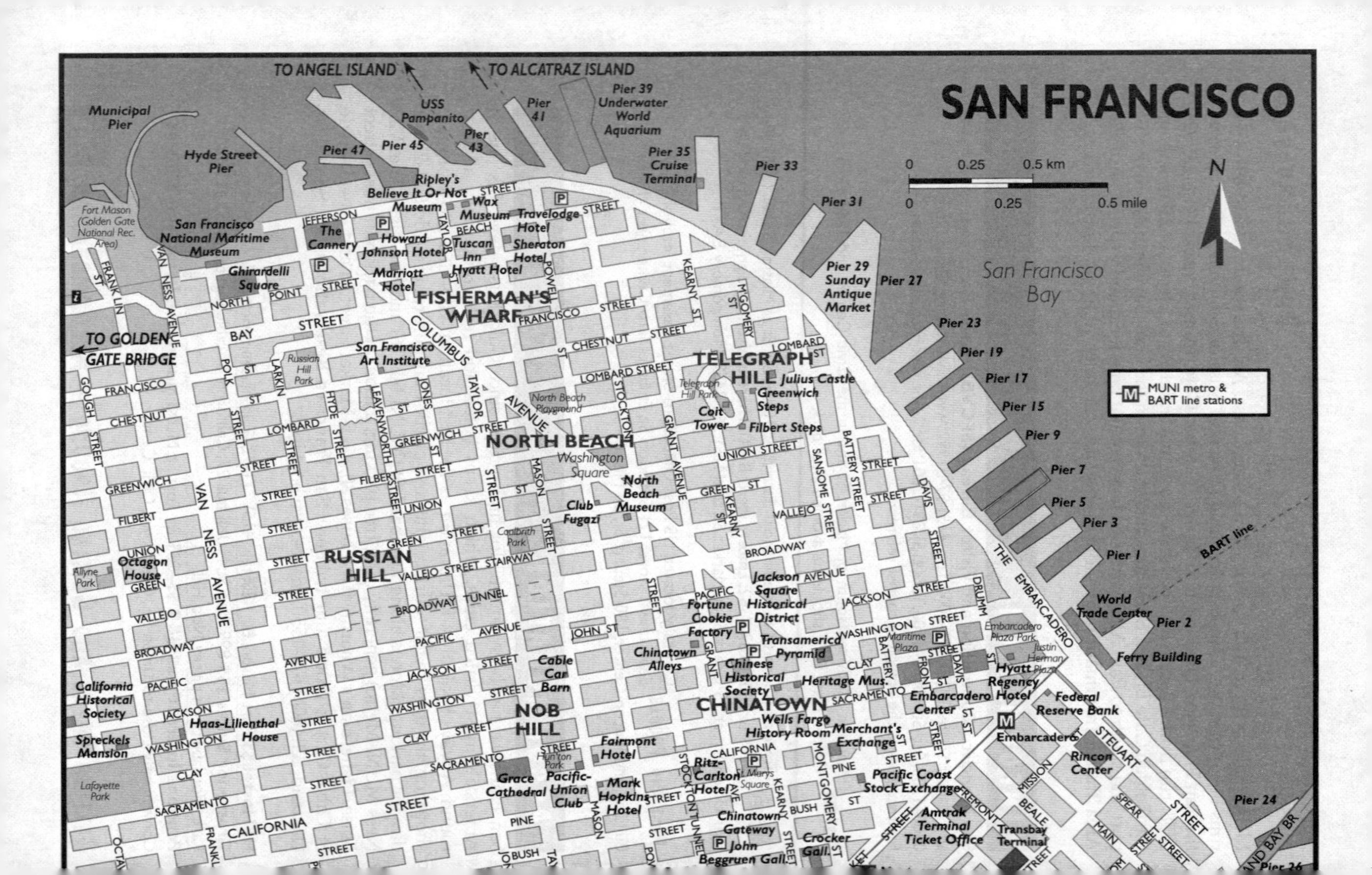
SAN FRANCISCO
TO ANGEL ISLAND
TO ALCATRAZ ISLAND
TO GOLDEN GATE BRIDGE
San Francisco Bay
0 0.25 0.5 km
0 0.25 0.5 mile
N
MUNI metro & BART line stations
BART line
Municipal Pier
Hyde Street Pier
Fort Mason (Golden Gate National Rec. Area)
San Francisco National Maritime Museum
Ghirardelli Square
The Cannery
Howard Johnson Hotel
Marriott Hotel
Ripley's Believe It Or Not Museum
Wax Museum
Tuscan Inn
Hyatt Hotel
Travelodge Hotel
Sheraton Hotel
USS Pampanito
Pier 47
Pier 45
Pier 43
Pier 41
Pier 39 Underwater World Aquarium
Pier 35 Cruise Terminal
Pier 33
Pier 31
Pier 29 Sunday Antique Market
Pier 27
Pier 23
Pier 19
Pier 17
Pier 15
Pier 9
Pier 7
Pier 5
Pier 3
Pier 1
World Trade Center
Pier 2
Ferry Building
Pier 24
Pier 26
FISHERMAN'S WHARF
San Francisco Art Institute
Russian Hill Park
TELEGRAPH HILL
Telegraph Hill Park
Julius Castle
Greenwich Steps
Coit Tower
Filbert Steps
North Beach Playground
NORTH BEACH
Washington Square
North Beach Museum
Club Fugazi
Coolbrith Park
RUSSIAN HILL
Allyne Park
Octagon House
California Historical Society
Haas-Lilienthal House
Spreckels Mansion
Lafayette Park
Cable Car Barn
NOB HILL
Huntington Park
Grace Cathedral
Pacific-Union Club
Fairmont Hotel
Mark Hopkins Hotel
Jackson Square Historical District
Fortune Cookie Factory
Transamerica Pyramid
Chinatown Alleys
Chinese Historical Society
Heritage Mus.
CHINATOWN
Wells Fargo History Room
Merchant's Exchange
Ritz-Carlton Hotel
St Marys Square
Chinatown Gateway
John Beggruen Gall.
Crocker Gall.
Pacific Coast Stock Exchange
Maritime Plaza
Embarcadero Center
Embarcadero Plaza Park
Justin Herman Plaza
Hyatt Regency Hotel
Federal Reserve Bank
Embarcadero
Rincon Center
Amtrak Terminal Ticket Office
Transbay Terminal
THE EMBARCADERO
VAN NESS AVENUE
COLUMBUS AVENUE
GRANT AVENUE
JEFFERSON
BEACH
NORTH POINT STREET
BAY STREET
FRANCISCO
CHESTNUT
LOMBARD STREET
GREENWICH
FILBERT
UNION STREET
GREEN
VALLEJO STREET STAIRWAY
BROADWAY TUNNEL
BROADWAY
PACIFIC
JACKSON
WASHINGTON
CLAY
SACRAMENTO
CALIFORNIA
PINE
BUSH
STOCKTON TUNNEL
GOUGH STREET
FRANKLIN ST
POLK
LARKIN
HYDE
LEAVENWORTH
JONES
TAYLOR
MASON
POWELL
STOCKTON
KEARNY ST
M'GOMERY ST
MONTGOMERY
SANSOME STREET
BATTERY STREET
FRONT
DAVIS
DRUMM
STEUART
SPEAR
MAIN
BEALE
FREMONT
MISSION
JOHN ST

THEATER DISTRICT
Magnin & Co
Marcus
Macy's
Macy's
Arts Gall.
Hotel
Pacific Telephone Building
Frankel Gallery
San Francisco Museum of Modern Art
Pier 30
Pier 32
Pier 34
Pier 36
Pier 38
Pier 40
THE EMBARCADERO
SAN FRANCISCO
80
Hilton Hotel
Powell St Cable Car Turntable
Powell St
Cartoon Art Museum
Yerba Buena Gardens
SF Shop. Center
SF Visitors Information Center
Old United States Mint
Moscone Convention Center
Friends of Photography Gallery
HAWTHORNE ST
HARRISON
JAMES-LICK-SKYWAY
1ST
2ND
3RD
4TH
5TH
6TH
7TH
8TH
9TH
10TH
11TH
12TH ST
South Park
BRANNAN
TOWNSEND
KING
Cartoon Art Museum
China Basin
Caltrain Depot
RAILROAD
SOUTHERN PACIFIC
SOMA
MINNA
MISSION
HOWARD
FOLSOM
BRYANT
HARRIET ST
Hall of Justice
BLUXOM
BERRY
CHANNEL
OWENS
EMBARCADERO
280 F'WAY
3RD STREET
4TH ST
ILLINOIS
GEARY EXPRESSWAY
LAGUNA
SUTTER
POST
GEARY
VAN NESS AVENUE
Sgt John McAuley Park
Great American Music Hall
O FARRELL ST
LEAVENWORTH STREET
ELLIS
EDDY
TURK
GOLDEN GATE AVENUE
St Mary's Cathedral
Jefferson Sq
Hayward Plgd
Hibernia Bank
MARKET STREET
PO/US Court of Appeals
SF Main Library
SF New Public Library
Bus Station
City Hall
CIVIC CENTER
Veteran's Building
War Memorial Opera House
Louise M Davies Symphony Hall
Bill Graham Civic Centre
Civic Auditorium
SF Arts Commission Gallery
Vision Gallery
McALLISTER
FULTON
GROVE
OCTAVIA
HAYES
HAYES VALLEY
SOUTH
HICKORY
Van Ness
GRACE ST
DORE ST
NATOMA ST
KISSLING
JUNIPER ST
NORFOLK ST
OAK STREET
LILY
PAGE
Koshland Park
LAGUNA ST
ROSE
HAIGHT STREET
WALLER ST
BUCHANAN ST
GOUGH ST
MC COPPIN ST
PLUM ST
Univ. of California Extension
HERMANN ST
US Mint
AVENUE
CENTRAL FREEWAY
101
JAMES LICK FREEWAY
DIVISION ST
CHURCH ST
CLINTON PARK ST
DOLORES
14TH
15TH
16TH
17TH
VALENCIA
SHOTWELL
HARRISON
FLORIDA
ALAMEDA
PORTRERO AVE
UTAH ST
VERMONT
KANSAS
RHODE ISLAND
DE HARO STREET
HOOPER ST
IRWIN ST
HUBBELL ST
CONNECTICUT ST
MISSOURI ST
MISSISSIPPI ST
LANDERS
ALERT AL
MISSION
Mission Dolores
PO
TO SAN FRANCISCO INTERNATIONAL AIRPORT
Franklin Square
Jackson Park

The Far West

Petit Auberge $$$$ 863 Bush St; tel: (415) 775-5717, (800) 365-8804, fax (415) 775-5717, www.foursisters.com. Near Chinatown, this classy inn and **The White Swan**, its British-accented sister next door, are far less pricey than most others of this standard.

San Remo Hotel $$–$$$ 2237 Mason St; tel: (415) 776-8688, (800) 352-7366, fax (415) 776-2811, www.sanremohotel.com. Historic, charming and the city's best bargain, this shared-bath pension is close to Fisherman's Wharf.

Queen Anne Hotel $$$$ 1590 Sutter St; tel: (415) 441-2828, (800) 227-3970, fax (415) 775-5212, www.queenanne.com. Victorian hotel with character and amenities far beyond its price.

Food and Drink

San Francisco is one of the food capitals of America. The weekly *San Francisco Bay Guardian* offers current reviews. Local favourites change almost weekly.

Boudin Sourdough Bakery and Café $ 156 Jefferson; tel: (415) 283-1230; MUNI buses 30, 42, F-Market streetcar and Hyde St cable car. The best Fisherman's Wharf sandwiches.

Fog City Diner $$$ 1300 Battery St; tel: (415) 928-2000; F-line streetcar. The Embarcadero's hip version of a folksy US diner, recommendable for creative California cuisine.

Franchino Ristorante $$$ 347 Columbus Ave; tel: (415) 982-2157; MUNI buses 30, 41. Intimate, family-run Italian eatery on North Beach.

Jade Bar 650 Gough St in Hayes Valley; tel: (415) 869-1900. Stylish bar with drinks for $2 during happy hour, Mon–Fri 1700–1900. Try the house concoction Jade Cocktail.

John's Grill $$$ 63 Ellis St; tel: (415) 986-0069; MUNI bus 27. Long-time San Francisco favourite, immortalised in Dashiell Hammet's *The Maltese Falcon* mystery novel and movie.

Lori's Diner $–$$ 501 Powell St; tel: (415) 981-1950; MUNI bus 38, Powell St cable car. All-American fare; 1950s pop memorabilia. Two other locations are near Union Square.

Mama's $$ 1701 Stockton St; tel: (415) 362-6421; MUNI bus 15. Friendly atmosphere, good food; overlooks Washington Sq., North Beach.

O'Reilly's $$ 622 Green St; tel: (415) 989-6222; MUNI buses 41, 45, Hyde St cable car. San Francisco's quintessential Irish pub and restaurant.

Highlights

Fisherman's Wharf This one-time home to San Francisco's commercial fishing fleet now has more touristy T-shirt and souvenir shops than fishing boats. Explore on foot from Pier 39 along to Aquatic Park on the edge of Golden Gate National Recreation Area.

Pier 39 is now converted to shops, entertainment and restaurants with fine views of Alcatraz and Marin headlands and the barking sea lions that have taken over the north side marina. Most ferries leave from Pier 41, just west. **Ghirardelli Sq.** is a bustling retail/entertainment complex – try the hot fudge sundaes at Swensen's. MUNI bus 30, 42, F-Market Streetcar or Powell/Hyde cable car.

WALKING TOURS

City Guides, tel: (415) 557-4266. Culture, history and architecture.

Cruisin' The Castro, tel: (415) 550-8110. The City's gay subculture from 1849 to the present.

Wok Wiz Chinatown Tours, tel: (415) 981-8989. Chinatown alleys, tea and secrets.

Tastes of the City, tel: (415) 665-0480 or (888) 358-8687; www. localtastes ofthecitytours.com; samples breads, chocolates, dim sum and more as they 'eat their way' though varied neighbourhoods.

Italians of North Beach, tel: (415) 397-8530. Italian food, history and culture.

Victorian Home Walk, tel: (415) 252-9485. Explore Victorian architecture, lifestyle and history.

Barbary Coast Trail matches San Francisco history with today's best sights. The CVB has a free self-guiding brochure.

San Francisco National Maritime Historic Park is the nation's only floating national park; $, Beach St; open daily. It includes the **Maritime Museum** in Aquatic Park, and several historic ships docked at **Hyde Street Pier**, open daily for tours. The **USS *Pampanito*** submarine, also open, is moored at Pier 45.

NORTH BEACH

The area has been a nightlife district for more than a century. The topless and nude dancing clubs that have spread across America began at **The Condor** (300 Columbus Ave), now a sports bar, in the 1960s. The Beatnik era survives at poet Lawrence Ferlinghetti's **City Lights Bookstore** (261 Columbus Ave) and **Vesuvio Café** (255 Columbus Ave). It's a short, steep walk from the coffee houses to **Telegraph Hill**, topped by the 212 ft **Coit Tower** (1 Telegraph Hill Blvd, off Lombard St). The interior features splendid Depression-era murals. Parking is limited; walk or take MUNI bus 39.

CHINATOWN

Bounded by Pine, Kearny and Powell Sts (take MUNI buses 1, 15, 45 or the cable car), what began as a shanty town of miners expelled from the gold fields is now one of the largest Chinese communities outside Asia. Sun Yat Sen planned the revolution that became the Chinese Nationalist Republic from a tiny building on Spofford Alley. Waverly Place featured prominently in San Franciscan Amy Tan's novel *The Joy Luck Club*. **Grant Ave** is a tourist trap; **Stockton St**, one block west, is crowded with fresh vegetables, live fish, smoked ducks and colour.

UNION SQUARE AND SOMA

The heart of the shopping and theatre district, Union Sq. has fine department stores, shops and restaurants, and is central for public transport. Two blocks south, Market St cuts diagonally across the city's centre. The formerly industrial **SOMA**, meaning South of Market (St) Area (MUNI bus 30), has become a trendy residential and entertainment neighbourhood.

Yerba Buena Gardens, between Mission and Howard Sts, has become a lively nexus with a performing arts centre, ice rink, Moscone Convention Center, cinemas, shopping, entertainment venues, hotels, restaurants and landscaped gardens. The **San Francisco Museum of Modern Art (SFMOMA)**, 451 3rd St, is northern California's largest collection of modern art, most noted for its distinctive architectural design by Mario Botta. $$, open 1100–1800 (Thur until 2100); closed Wed; free first Tues of each month; half-price Thur 1800–2100. The **Cartoon Art Museum**, 655 Mission St, tel: (415) 227-8666, is one of three museums in America devoted to cartoon art.

SOMA ATTRACTIONS

Young people delve into multimedia learning experiences at **Zeum**, SOMA's new art and technology centre at 4th and Howard Sts alongside the Moscone Convention Center. The complex includes a video production studio, computer animation stations, indoor ice-skating rink, bowling alleys, rooftop gardens and a restored 1906 carousel.

Sony Metreon, also in SOMA, is a complex of 15 movie theatres, restaurants, interactive games and 3-D screens with characters from Maurice Sendak's children's books. The Giants' **stadium**, Pacific Bell Park, King St, is nearby.

MISSION DISTRICT Named after **Mission Dolores**, founded in 1776, the Mission is Latin America come north. Brilliant murals blaze messages of equality, ethnic pride and hope and there's a wide range of Mexican and other Hispanic restaurants. BART 16th St/Mission or 24th St/Mission, or MUNI bus 22.

GOLDEN GATE PARK Not to be confused with the GGNRA (see p. 551), Golden Gate Park stretches west from Haight-Ashbury to the ocean (MUNI buses 5, 6, 7, 21, 71 or Metro N to Stanyan St; 9th Ave is best for access to museums), with 1017 acres of shady forests, winding drives, lakes, open glades and museums. Don't miss jasmine tea and fortune cookies amid exquisite landscaping in the **Japanese Tea Garden**. The **Asian Art Museum** houses the largest collection of Asian art and artefacts in any Western museum. It adjoins the **M H de Young Memorial Museum**, with its collection of 17th–20th-century American art. $$ joint entry (free first Wed of month); open Wed–Sun 0930–1700 (until 2045 first Wed of month).

Just across the Music Concourse stands the **California Academy of Sciences**, with the **Steinhart Aquarium**, the **Morrison Planetarium** and the **Natural History Museum**, all included in a single admission. $ (free first Wed of month); open daily Memorial Day weekend–Labor Day 1000–1700. Don't miss the delightfully retro crocodile pit and underwater views of cavorting seals in the **Aquarium**.

GOLDEN GATE BRIDGE

Opened in 1937, the great bridge linked the gap above the tides churning through the Golden Gate, the narrow passage into San Francisco Bay, named after the Golden Horn in Istanbul by adventurer-explorer John Fremont in 1846. Park at the San Francisco end to walk or cycle across; drive to the vista point just beyond the north end of the bridge to look back toward San Francisco. There is a toll for southbound cars ($), pedestrians and cyclists free. Red-brick **Fort Point** beneath the bridge was built to defend San Francisco during the Civil War, 1861–65.

GOLDEN GATE NATIONAL RECREATION AREA (GGNRA) A string of former coastal defences now forms a vast park stretching west from Aquatic Park and Fort Mason along the Bay to the **Presidio**, then north and south along the Pacific beyond San Francisco. It encompasses the **Marin Headlands**, **Muir Woods National Monument**, **Mount Tamalpais**, and much of **Tomales Bay** shoreline. It gives splendid views of San Francisco and the Bay – especially from Crissy Field, Baker Beach, Lands End (for the best sunsets) and upper Fort Mason. Open daily. Golden Gate Transit bus 50 and MUNI bus 76.

CABLE CARS

San Francisco's original mechanised public transport still climbs half-way to the stars up **Nob Hill** between the Bay and **Hallidie Plaza** and along California St. The **Powell-Hyde St Line** runs to Aquatic Park for easy access to Fisherman's Wharf, the historic ships at Hyde St Pier and Ghirardelli Sq.

Queue up (sometimes for hours) to board at the end of each cable car line or follow the locals who walk a couple of blocks up the street to climb aboard without waiting. To see how the system works, visit the **Cable Car Barn and Museum** (Mason and Washington Sts). Don't miss the gallery overlooking the 14-ft pulleys that haul miles of steel cable beneath city streets to power the cars at a constant 9 mph. Open daily 1000–1700.

The **Exploratorium**, 3601 Lyon St, Marina Blvd (MUNI bus 30) is designed for children, but adults are at least as eager to try the 500 interactive exhibits. It adjoins the **Palace of Fine Arts**, built to resemble a classical ruin for the 1915 Panama-Pacific Exposition. $$ joint entry; open Memorial Day–Labor Day daily 1000–1800 (Wed until 2100); rest of year Tues–Sun 1000–1700 (Wed until 2100). On the west edge of the park, beyond China Beach, is the **Palace of the Legion of Honor** (34th Ave and Clement St; MUNI bus 18). This copy of Napoleon's Palais de la Légion d'Honneur in Paris displays ancient and European art from 2500 BC to the 20th century. $$ (free second Wed of month); open Tues–Sun 1000–1700, Wed to 2100.

OUT IN THE BAY Once the main port of entry from Asia, **Angel Island** ($$) is a rural state park with stunning views, restored immigration buildings, picnic grounds, hiking and cycling trails and a tram ride around the island. Access is by Blue and Gold Fleet ferry from Pier 41. (For cruises see p. 544.)

The list of prisoners incarcerated in the infamous federal penitentiary of 'escape-proof' **Alcatraz Island** reads like a Who's Who of celeb criminals. The tiny island is accessible only by boat; Blue and Gold Fleet operates daily tours ($$). Reservations are advised. Visitors may wander freely, or take a self-guided audio tour narrated by former prison guards.

SHOPPING

Union Sq. has the most expensive marquees, from Disney and Nike to Saks Fifth Avenue and Tiffany. **Post St**'s trendy, pricey shops in stylish Victorian buildings (MUNI bus 76) offer jewellery, clothing, antiques, furnishings and bric-à-brac from around the world. **Haight St** (MUNI buses 6, 7, 71 or Metro N) is an ultra-trendy mix of fashion, food and body piercing. Downtown's **San Francisco Shopping Centre** (65 Market St; Powell BART station, F-line streetcar) contains four levels each of 'name-brand' stores. The chic, skylit **Crocker Galleria** (50 Post St; Montgomery BART station, MUNI buses 2, 4, 5, 15, 30) houses fashion boutiques and speciality stores.

NIGHTLIFE

The Datebook Section in the *San Francisco Sunday Chronicle* is the most complete listing for traditional events; see the *SF Bay Guardian* and *SF Weekly* for avant-garde.

The **American Conservatory Theatre** (ACT), 415 Geary S, Union Sq., tel: (415) 749-2228, is the leading repertory theatre company; **Marines Memorial Theatre**, 450 Post St, tel: (415) 433-9500, is New York's off-Broadway theatre (open Tues–Sun). At **Audium** on Fri or Sat, 1616 Bush St, tel: (415) 771-1616, sound sculptures from 136 speakers surround the audience, sitting in a darkened theatre. **Beach Blanket Babylon**, Club Fugazi, 678 Green St, tel: (415) 421-4222, offers zany cabaret-style musical spoofs of popular culture. Performances Wed–Sun; adults only except Sun afternoon.

The world-class **San Francisco Opera** performs in the newly restored War Memorial Opera House (Van Ness Ave and McAllister St) Sept–Jan; tel: (415) 864-3330. Davies Symphony Hall on Van Ness Ave is home to the **San Francisco Symphony**, tel: (415) 864-6000. Concerts regularly fill **Grace Cathedral**, 1100 California St, California's finest Gothic cathedral, tel: (415) 749-6300, and **Old First Church**, Van Ness Ave and Sacramento St; tel: (415) 474-1608. The **Stern Grove Midsummer Music Festival**, tel: (415) 252-6253, 19th Ave and Sloat Blvd, is a free outdoor summer festival with classical, opera, pop and jazz by top performers. The annual dance season of the **San Francisco Ballet**, 301 Van Ness Ave at Grove St, tel: (415) 865-2000, runs Jan–May.

BEYOND THE CITY

SONOMA COUNTY

California doesn't get any prettier than this region north of the bay, where you can sample redwoods, coastal cliffs, mountain trails, wineries, farms and vineyards, and even an historic mission.

Sonoma's tree-filled plaza is surrounded by vintage adobe buildings that include **Mission San Francisco Solano**, $, tel: (707) 938-9560, open daily 1000–1700, marking the northern end of 'El Camino Real'. **Depot Park Museum**, First St West, tel: (707) 938-1762, open Wed–Sun 1300–1630, several historic homes and the **Sonoma League for Historic Preservation's walking tours**, tel: (707) 938-0510, recall its history.

Glen Ellen, with restored Victorian B&Bs and restaurants, is a good base for exploring the wineries along Rte 12 between Sonoma and Santa Rosa. **Wellington Vineyards** (11600 Dunbar Rd; tel: (707) 939-0708; www.wellingtonvineyards.com) has a tasting room and picnic area. At **The Olive Press** (14301 Arnold Dr; tel: (707) 939-8900; www.theolivepress.com) you can sample fine olive oils. In nearby **Jack London State Park**, $, tel: (707) 938-5216, open daily, 0930–sunset, are scenic hiking trails and the romantic ruins of the early 20th-century author's house.

Free-wheeling **Guerneville** lies along the **Russian River**, in a time-warp that recalls California of the 1960s and '70s. This is Sonoma at its most laid-back. Budget-friendly **Rose Mari's Russian River Spa**,16370 First St, tel: (707) 869-3322, promises spiritual nurturing along with massages and herbal wraps, and nearby you'll find relaxed coffee shops, casual antiques stores and fine chocolates sharing a shop with hemp-woven clothing. At the **Armstrong Redwood State Reserve**, trails wind beneath towering redwood trees. Renowned **Korbel Champagne Cellars**, 13250 River Rd, tel: (707) 824-7000, has a smart little deli-café ($), tastings, gardens and an excellent tour.

Follow the Russian River westwards to **Jenner**, where Pacific Ocean beaches provide a breeding ground for harbour seals, Mar–June. The coastal road north clings to steep mountainsides to reach **Fort Ross** (www.parks.ca.gov), a restored 1812 Russian settlement and trading post. The entire Sonoma coast is refreshingly free of development, with hillsides of sheep-grazed moors overlooking the sea.

i **Sonoma County Tourism**, tel: (800) 380-5392; www.sonomacounty.com. **Sonoma Valley Visitors Bureau**, 453 First St E, Sonoma; tel: (707) 996-1090; www.sonomavalley.com.

El Pueblo Inn $$–$$$ 896 W Napa St, Sonoma; tel: (707) 996-3651, (800) 900-8844. Family-friendly motel with a pool.
Creekside Inn $$$–$$$$ 16180 Neely Rd, Guerneville; tel: (707) 869-3626; www.creeksideinn.com. Sits amid giant trees.

Public transport is not good in Sonoma County, but four daily **Oakland Airport Express Buses** whisk you from San Francisco Airport across the Golden Gate Bridge to Rohnert Park, a central point for claiming rental cars.

Wild Flour Bakery $ Hwy 12, Freestone; tel: (707) 874-2938. Bountiful focaccia, pizza and other hearty breads; you can picnic in the garden.
Applewood Inn & Restaurant $$$–$$$$ 13555 Hwy 116, Guerneville; tel: (707) 869-9093. Exceptional interpretations of locally grown products.
Sonoma Sausage $ 414 First St, on the Plaza, Sonoma: tel: (707) 938-1215; www.sonomasausage.com. Open Tues–Sun, this tiny takeaway shop sells their own delicious, juicy grilled sausages, from proper bangers to German Jagerwurst.
Dempsey's Restaurant and Brewery $$ 50 East Washington St, Petaluma; tel: (707) 765 9694,

www.dempseys.com, open daily. A riverside brewpub with a talented chef – and its own farm, so they know the ingredients are fresh.

NAPA VALLEY Napa is becoming a wine theme park for people with serious money to spend. Prices are higher than in Sonoma County, crowds are bigger, and advance bookings a necessity. You can avoid some of the crowds by following the **Silverado Trail** along the eastern edge of the valley and taking one of the many cross-valley roads back to Hwy 29. Vineyards are thickest around St Helena, Rutherford, Oakville and Yountville; most charge for tasting.

At the northern end of the Napa Valley, **Calistoga** sits atop an active geo-thermal area. The **Sam Brannan Cottage** and the **Sharpsteen Museum** (1311 Washington St) recall Sam Brannan who created the town in 1859, hoping to emulate the highly profitable hot springs of Saratoga, New York (see p. 104). Spa packages start at about $50, depending on resort and options. **Old Faithful Geyser**, 1299 Tubbs Lane, erupts every 4 mins, recent earthquakes permitting, in a 60-ft blast of steam and water.

Napa Valley Conference and Visitors Bureau, 1310 Napa Town Center; tel: (707) 226-7459; www.napavalley.com, has general Napa Valley information. **Napa Chamber of Commerce**, 1556 1st St; tel: (707) 226-7455; www.napachamber.org, is open 0900–1700.
Calistoga Chamber of Commerce, 1458 Lincoln Ave 9, Calistoga, CA 94515; tel: (707) 942-6333.

Napa Valley Reservations Unlimited, 1819 Tanen St, tel: (707) 252-1985, and **Bed and Breakfast Inns of Napa Valley**, tel: (707) 944-4444, can help with bookings. **St Helena Chamber of Commerce**, 1010 Suite A, Main St, tel: (707) 963-4456, is a good information source for B&Bs.
B&B Style, PO Box 28, Calistoga CA, 94515; tel: (707) 942-2888. Camping is at **Napa County Fairgrounds** $ 1435 Oak St, Calistoga; tel: (707) 942-5111.

The Calistoga Inn $$ 1250 Lincoln Ave, Calistoga; tel: (707) 924-4101, www.calistogainn.com, Open 365 days a year, from 1330, this riverside restaurant and brew-pub serves exceptional food, all from fresh locally grown ingredients.

PICNIC PROVISIONS

Napa Valley Olive Oil Manufacturing, Charter Oak Ave, St Helena, sells breads, cheeses, sausages, and fine olive oil. **Guigni's Grocery**, 1227 Main St, Napa, stocks many practical items.

Napa Valley Transit buses from the Baylink Ferry Terminal run north to Napa, Yountville, Oakville, Rutherford, St Helena and Calistoga (a DayPass is good for unlimited travel on the ferry and buses). By car, take I-80 then Hwy 29 north to Napa and the valley.

Robert Louis Stevenson State Park, 10 miles north along Hwy 29, offers the best view of wine country from Mt St Helena. Stevenson honeymooned in an abandoned miner's cabin on the mountain in 1880. The 5-mile return walk to the 4344-ft peak is laborious in summer, but pleasant in autumn or spring. The **Silverado Museum** in St Helena has one of the world's best Stevenson collections.

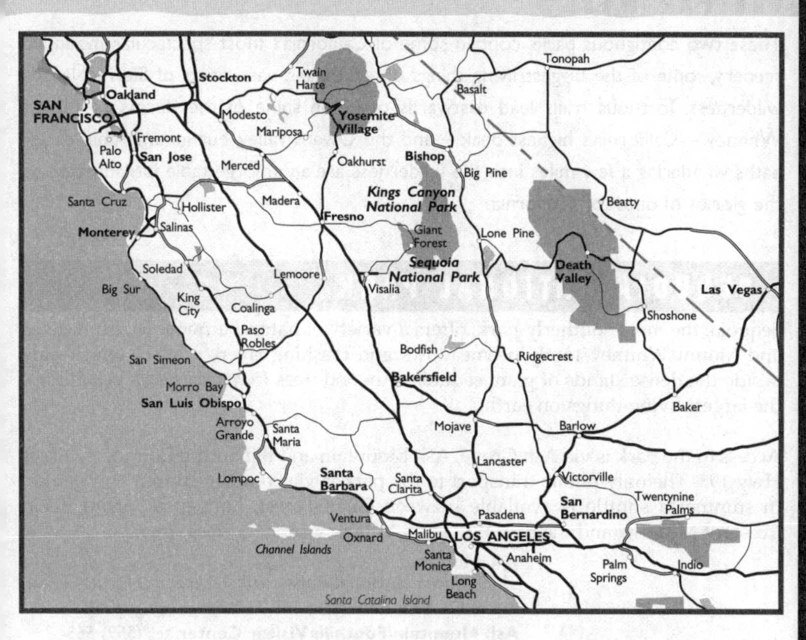

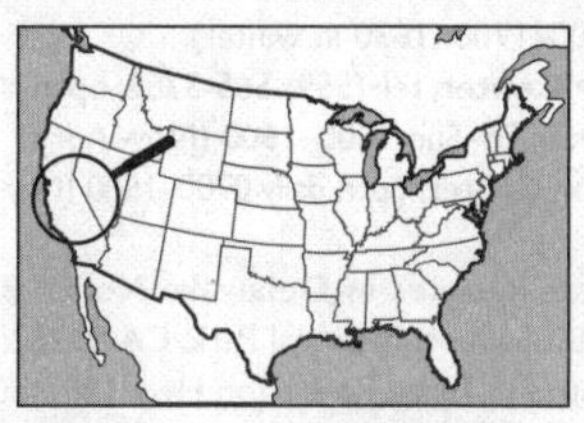

Note
Yosemite VIA and YARTS operate a bus service from Merced to Yosemite National Park.

Driving Route

Hwy 198 leads from Visalia to and through the parks (there is no public transport). Only one road penetrates Kings Canyon Park proper, the Kings Canyon Highway (Hwy 180), open only in summer. Other road access is limited and often closed in winter and barred to RVs: for driving information tel: (559) 565-3351.

SEQUOIA AND KINGS CANYON NATIONAL PARKS

These two contiguous parks contain some of California's most spectacular mountain scenery, some of the biggest living things on earth, and vast tracts of Sierra Nevada wilderness. Tortuous trails lead eastwards over the spine of the sierras to Mount Whitney – California's highest peak – and the Owens Valley, but innumerable easier paths wandering a few miles into the wilderness are an unforgettable introduction to the glories of outdoor California.

SEQUOIA NATIONAL PARK

Sequoia, the more southerly park, offers a variety of natural attractions, from caves and Mount Whitney to alpine meadows and crashing rivers – all of which pale beside the dense stands of giant sequoia redwood trees (*Sequoiadendron giganteum*), the largest living things on earth.

Access to the park is via Ash Grove, Ash Mountain and Big Stump Entrances; all off Hwy 198. The only public transport to the park is via commercial tour companies. In summer a shuttle is available between Giant Forest, Lodgepole, Moro Rock, Crescent Meadow and the new Wuksachi Village Visitor Services Area.

i **Sequoia National Parks**, 47050 Generals Highway, Three Rivers CA 93271; tel: (559) 565-3341; www.nps.gov/seki.
Ash Mountain/Foothills Visitor Center; tel: (559) 565-3135; open daily 0800–1700 (1630 in winter).
Lodgepole Visitor Center; tel: (559) 565-3782; open daily 0800–1800 (May–Oct), Fri–Sun 1000–1600 (Nov–Apr).
Mineral King Visitor Center, open daily 0700–1500 (May–Sept).

All park hotels are operated by **Delaware North Parks Services**, PO Box 89, Sequoia National Park, CA 93262; tel: (888) 252-5757. Motels in Three Rivers (on Hwy 180, south of Ash Mountain Entrance) are open all year; some places in the park open summer only.
Montecito-Sequoia Lodge $$ Generals Hwy (Hwy 180), between Sequoia and Kings Canyon; tel: (559) 565-3388; www.montecitosequoia.com. For advance reservations contact 2225 Grant Rd, Ste 1, Los Altos, CA 94024; tel: (650) 967-8612 or (800) 227-9900. Open all year.
Silver City High Sierra Rustic Family Resort $$ Box 56, Three Rivers, CA 93271; tel: (559) 561-3223 (late May–early Sept); or 2420 E Hillcrest Ave, Visalia, CA 93292; tel: (209) 734-4109 (late Sept–early May). Lantern-lit cabins and chalets on the road to Mineral King in summer.
Wuksachi Village $$. Open all year.

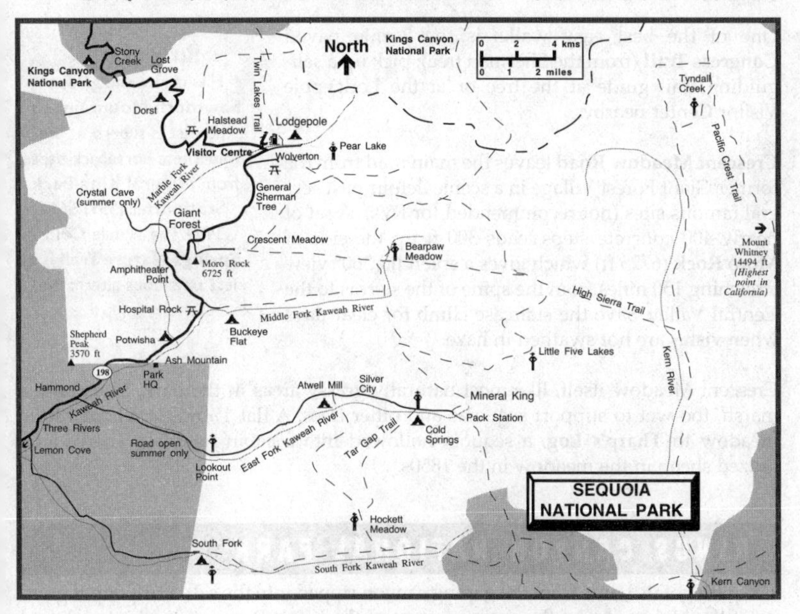

Meals and picnic supplies are available in Wuksachi Village (a new facility near the Giant Forest), Lodgepole and Montecito-Sequoia all year.
Silver City Bakery and Restaurant $$ near Mineral King. Open in summer along with an adjoining general store.

HIGHLIGHTS **Mineral King** (turn-off 5 miles north of Three Rivers; no RVs or trailers) is a scalloped bowl at 7800 ft, the only bit of the park's high sierra country accessible by vehicle. Walt Disney tried to turn the scenic bowl into a ski resort in 1965 – 13 litigious years later it was added to Sequoia National Park instead.

Hospital Rock, 5 miles beyond Ash Grove Entrance towards Giant Forest, marks an ancient Native American village site. Look for pictographs on the surrounding boulders and 71 mortar holes, once used to grind acorns and seeds into flour.

Giant Forest, 30 miles from Big Stump Entrance and 16 miles from Ash Mountain Entrance, was named by John Muir, who first brought Yosemite to the world's attention in the 19th century (see p. 561). Four of the largest known sequoias grow in this grove. The biggest of them all is the **General Sherman tree**, 275 ft tall and 103 ft in circumference.

One of the best easy walks is the 2-mile paved **Congress Trail** (from the Sherman tree); pick up a self-guiding trail guide at the tree or at the Lodgepole Visitor Center nearby.

HIKING TRAILS

Hiking into the golden **Sawtooth Mountains** to the east is superb, as are wilderness horseback trips from **Mineral King Pack Station**, tel: (559) 561-3404. The ¼ mile **Cold Springs Nature Trail** is a less strenuous alternative.

Crescent Meadow Road leaves the main road from the former Giant Forest Village in a scenic detour past several famous sites (not recommended for RVs). A set of nearly 400 concrete steps leads 300 ft up the side of **Moro Rock** (6725 ft) which gives a splendid 360° view stretching 150 miles from the spine of the sierras to the Central Valley. Save the staircase climb for clear days when vistas are not swathed in haze.

Crescent Meadow itself, like most naturally grassy areas in the park, is actually a marsh, too wet to support sequoias and other trees. A flat 1½ mile trail circles the meadow to **Tharp's Log**, a sequoia hollowed into a cabin for Hale Tharp, who grazed sheep in the meadow in the 1850s.

KINGS CANYON NATIONAL PARK

The park got its name from the gaping canyon ripped into the salt-and-pepper granite of the high sierra by the raging torrent of the Kings River, gouged into a broad valley by ponderous glaciers. Just downstream from the confluence of the Middle and South Forks of the Kings River, the canyon plunges 8200 ft from the peak of Spanish Mountain, one of the deepest gorges in North America.

Access to the park is via Hwy 180 from Fresno, and Hwy 198 from Visalia. There are no petrol stations in the park, but Kings Canyon Lodge has a supply at premium prices, and it is also available at Hume Lake.

i **Kings Canyon National Park**, 47050 Generals Hwy, Three Rivers, CA 93271; tel: (559) 565-3341; www.nps.gov/seki.
Grant Grove Visitor Center, Grant Grove Village; tel: (559) 565-4307. Open daily 0800–1800 (summer), 0900–1630 (spring and autumn), 0930–1630 (winter).
Cedar Grove Visitor Center, just west of Cedar Grove Village; tel: (559) 565-3793. Open daily 0800–1800 (late June–Labor Day); Thur–Mon (May and Sept).

All accommodation in the park is booked through **Kings Canyon Park Services**, Box 909, Kings Canyon NP, CA 93633; tel: (559) 335-5500.

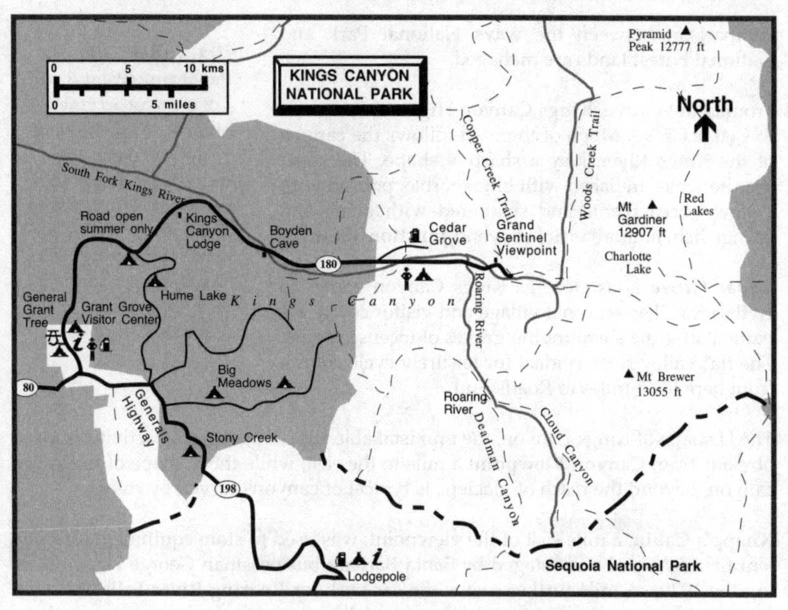

Grant Grove Lodge $$. Open all year.
Cedar Grove Lodge $$. Open in summer.

In summer, picnic supplies and restaurant meals are available in **Grant Grove Village $$, Cedar Grove Village $$,** and **Kings Canyon Lodge $$–$$$**. Grant Grove remains open in winter.

HIGHLIGHTS Kings Canyon's most popular attractions are concentrated around **Grant Grove**, named after the **General Grant Tree**, officially the world's third largest tree at 267 ft tall and 107 ft in circumference. A paved path wanders for 0.3 mile through the grove, passing the **Fallen Monarch**, which has been a house and a stable, and the **Gamlin Cabin**, a rebuilt 1872 logger's cabin. Most of the major trees have been fenced off to protect their shallow root systems from trampling by adoring crowds.

A quieter alternative is the seldom-visited **North Grove Loop**, a 1½ mile trail that begins at the Grant Grove car park. The 2.2 mile **Dead Giant Loop** (from the lower end of the car park) passes a historic lumber mill pond on the way to a giant sequoia killed by girdling, or cutting through the living cambium layer just beneath the bark, which cut the flow of nutrients to the tree. The walk offers an instructive comparison between the ways National Park and National Forest lands are managed.

ON A CLEAR DAY ...
Panoramic Point is one of the most accessible vistas across the spine of the high sierra, with **Hume Lake** to the north below. The 4.7-mile return **Park Ridge Trail** offers views (on clear days) from the high peaks down the descending western ranges into the Central Valley.

From Grant Grove, **Kings Canyon Highway** runs east to Cedar Grove. Much of the road follows the canyon of the Kings River, here a sharp V shape. The sheer granite walls are laced with blue marble, pocked with yellow yucca plants and splattered with green and orange lichen, more visible beyond **Junction View**.

Cedar Grove is as close as Kings Canyon comes to civilisation. The seasonal village and visitor centre are named after the surrounding groves of incense cedars. The flat valley floor is ideal for leisurely cycle rides – from here it's 5 miles to Roads End.

The U shape of Kings Canyon, the unmistakable sign of past glacial activity, is most obvious from **Canyon Viewpoint** a mile to the east, while the V shape of the lower canyon, beyond the reach of glaciers, is typical of canyons carved by rivers.

Knapp's Cabin, a mile east of the viewpoint, was used to store equipment for opulent fishing expeditions staged by Santa Barbara businessman George Knapp during the 1920s. A mile further east is the car park for **Roaring River Falls**. An easy 5-min walk along a paved path leads to the falls.

The 1-mile loop trail through **Zumwalt Meadow** is one of the most scenic walks in either park. The trail crosses a suspension bridge to a view over the grassy meadow and **North Dome** (8717 ft), then descends through the meadow. Expect to see a variety of birds as well as a profusion of wild flowers – leopard lilies, shooting stars, violets, Indian paintbrush, lupins and others. Pick up a self-guiding map at the visitor centre. Just beyond is **Grand Sentinel Viewpoint**, with clear views of one of the most striking rock formations in the area, the Grand Sentinel (8504 ft).

Roads End, literally just that, is the start of a vast network of trails. Gruelling tracks cross the sierra through passes above 11,000 ft into the Owens Valley. The 8-mile return hike to **Mist Falls** is an easier way to see this area. The sandy trail starts relatively flat, but gains 600 ft in the final mile to the largest waterfall in the twin parks. Allow 4–6 hrs for the hike. Return to Cedar Grove on the road, or, more interestingly, via the **Motor Nature Trail** on the north side of the river. This rough corrugated road is passable by passenger vehicles but *not* recommended for RVs.

YOSEMITE NATIONAL PARK

Over 100 years ago a Scottish immigrant and mountain wanderer named John Muir was captivated by Yosemite, carved by waves of glaciers into a colossal landscape, with its wild soaring granite, deep gorges, mountain meadows and silent peaks that seem to touch the sky. Even Yosemite's trees are larger than life – giant sequoias in park groves are among the largest living organisms on the planet. Yosemite Falls, thundering 2425 ft to the valley floor, have a vertical drop greater than that of any other waterfall in North America and the fifth greatest in the world.

In retrospect, Muir was responsible for the steadily growing popularity that has chipped away at Yosemite's beauty. His efforts to preserve and promote Yosemite's spectacular landscape within a national park made him one of the best promoters California has ever seen. Once word got out, people from around the world came to test his tales of astounding beauty, including those on the very first Thomas Cook tour of America in the 1870s. Yosemite became a National Park in 1890. A century ago, it received a trickle of visitors. Today, park rangers warn of 'loving Yosemite to death'.

The problem is that the most famous sights – Half Dome, El Capitan, Yosemite Falls, Bridalveil Fall and others – are in Yosemite Valley, which attracts nearly all of the 4 million-plus people who come each year. The rest of the park is less crowded, including hiking trails barely beyond shouting distance of the gridlocked valley floor. Summer is the busiest time, so if you absolutely must, park your car, hire a bicycle and laugh at the traffic jams. Free shuttles run daily 0700–2200 and make an even easier alternative to driving.

GETTING THERE

From northern California, the park ($$) is reached via Arch Rock Entrance on Hwy 140 from Merced; the most direct route from southern California is Hwy 41 from Fresno, entering at South Entrance. There are also entrances on both east and west sides of the park from Hwy 120, which runs across the park (but is closed in winter).

Amtrak operates Thruway bus services, connecting with the San Joaquin trains at Merced.

Yosemite Area Regional Transportation System (YARTS), tel: (877) 989-2787, www.yarts.com, enables visitors to ride buses from Gateway Communities outside the park to Yosemite Valley. YARTS runs buses year-round on Hwy 140, Hwy 120 East, Hwy 120 West as well as the Wawona Corridor.

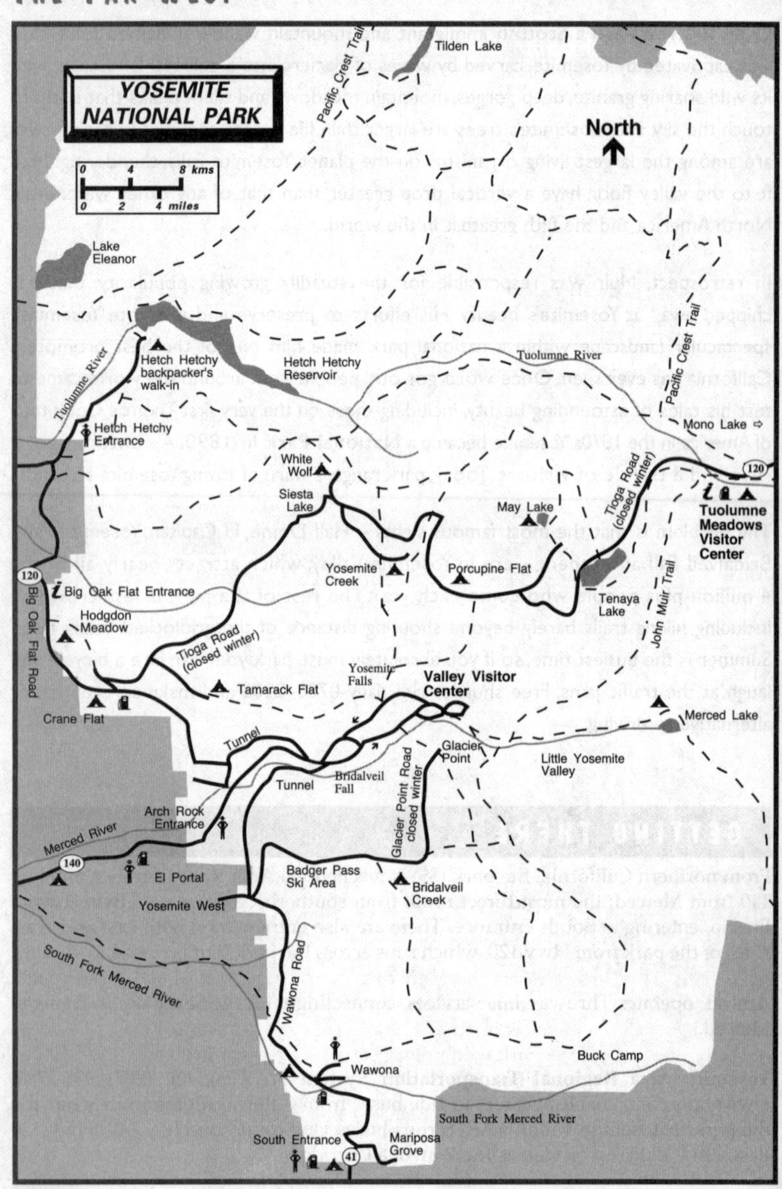
YOSEMITE NATIONAL PARK
0 4 8 kms
0 2 4 miles
North
Tilden Lake
Pacific Crest Trail
Lake Eleanor
Tuolumne River
Hetch Hetchy backpacker's walk-in
Hetch Hetchy Reservoir
Hetch Hetchy Entrance
Mono Lake
Tioga Road (closed winter)
120
Tuolumne Meadows Visitor Center
White Wolf
Siesta Lake
May Lake
Porcupine Flat
Tenaya Lake
John Muir Trail
Yosemite Creek
Big Oak Flat Entrance
Big Oak Flat Road
Hodgdon Meadow
Tioga Road (closed winter)
Yosemite Falls
Valley Visitor Center
Tamarack Flat
Crane Flat
Merced Lake
Tunnel
Glacier Point
Little Yosemite Valley
Tunnel
Bridalveil Fall
Glacier Point Road closed winter
Arch Rock Entrance
Merced River
140
El Portal
Badger Pass Ski Area
Bridalveil Creek
Yosemite West
South Fork Merced River
Wawona Road
Buck Camp
Wawona
South Fork Merced River
South Entrance
Mariposa Grove
41

INFORMATION

Yosemite National Park, Box 557, Yosemite, CA 95389; tel: (209) 372-0200; www.nps.gov/yose. TTY (hearing impaired) tel: (209) 372-4726. Call (559) 255-8345 for reservations and (888) 530-9796 for camping.

The main visitor centre, as well as most accommodation, restaurants and other services, is in Yosemite Village. **Yosemite Valley Visitors Center**, at the west end of Yosemite Village Mall, tel: (209) 372-0200, is open 0900–1700 daily. Must-haves are the park brochure and the newsprint *Yosemite Guide*, both available at park entrances, and the *Yosemite Magazine*, from visitor centre bookshops.

Tuolumne Meadows Visitor Center, Tuolumne Meadows, tel: (209) 372-0200, is open early summer–Sept.

ANIMAL ALERT

Park animals are not domesticated. They may react unpredictably when surrounded or closely approached. Black bears frequent the valley in search of the food visitors bring in – so follow park recommendations for storing food out of bears' way. If a bear is spotted, alert park rangers.

ACCOMMODATION

All accommodation in the park is run by **Yosemite Concession Services**. Advance bookings are essential Apr–Sept and at weekends and holidays all year – contact **Yosemite Reservations**, 5410 East Home Ave, Fresno, CA 93727; tel: (559) 252-4848.

Yosemite Lodge $$ Yosemite Valley. Best value motel accommodation.

Ahwahnee Hotel $$$$ Yosemite Valley. Grand hotel and dining room, worth a visit even if you aren't staying here.

Wawona Hotel $$$ in the south end of the park. Also has camping.

Curry Village $–$$ Yosemite Valley. Tent cabins, cabins and standard rooms available; season begins in late March.

CAMPING Tents, cabins and campsites ($$) are scattered throughout Yosemite Valley. Campsite reservations are handled by the National Park Reservation Service, PO Box 1600, Cumberland, MD 21502; tel: (800) 436-0200 or (301) 722-1257. Advance reservations are essential in all seasons. During May–Sept, the **Camp Curry Campground Reservation Office** sometimes has last-minute cancellations, but demand is intense. Camping away from campsites is by permit only, obtainable from the park wilderness centre. Write as far in advance as possible to Wilderness Permits, PO Box 545, Yosemite, CA 95389, or tel: (209) 372-0200. Half the permits allotted for most wilderness areas are assigned in advance, the other half on a first-come, first-served basis during the season.

FOOD AND DRINK

Village Grill $ Yosemite Village. Basic burgers and sandwiches.

Degnans Deli $ and **The Pasta Place** $ Yosemite Village. Variations on a similar theme.

Yosemite Lodge $–$$ Yosemite Valley. Has a budget-priced cafeteria and a moderate restaurant.

Wawona Hotel Dining Room $$ South Yosemite. Sunday brunch is particularly good.

Ahwahnee Hotel Dining Room $$$ Yosemite Valley. A better bet for breakfast and lunch than dinner – except for special events such as the Vintners' Holidays and the Chefs' Holidays, when dinners are outstanding.

Curry Village and Tuolumne Meadows both have grills open until the first snowfall; the Badger Pass Lodge offers simple meals in winter only. **Village Store** is a full grocery store, but picnic supplies are more expensive than outside the park.

HIGHLIGHTS

There are really three Yosemites within the park: **Yosemite Valley,** with the greatest concentration of attractions and visitors, **South Yosemite** and **Tioga Pass Rd**, which are almost as crowded. The more remote countryside remains relatively untouched.

YOSEMITE VALLEY

Entering the park at the Arch Rock Entrance on Hwy 140, a one-way anticlockwise road loops through the valley. Most of the road is lined with parking spaces on one or both sides. A paved walking/cycling trail runs parallel to the road in the east end of the valley.

The route passes Bridalveil Fall, Sentinel Dome, the wedding chapel and Curry Village before reaching the east end of the valley, with Half Dome in the distance. The road then runs through campsites, passes the Ahwahnee Hotel beneath the valley wall, and comes to Yosemite Village. Yosemite Falls cascade down the valley wall beyond the Village, not far from Yosemite Lodge. The road continues to a connector for the return loop, or beyond, past the sheer rock face of El Capitan, rising 7569 ft, to another return connector.

FREE SHUTTLES

Shuttle buses circle the eastern Yosemite Valley all year, running in non-stop loops from dawn to midnight. Seasonal shuttles serve other attractions such as the Badger Pass ski area, the Mariposa Grove of Giant Sequoias and trailheads between Yosemite Valley and Tuolumne Meadow.

Glacier Point, perched some 321 ft above the valley floor, offers spectacular views of the valley, Yosemite Falls, Half Dome and much of the park. However, it's a circuitous 25-mile drive to get there, and access is

EXPLORING YOSEMITE VALLEY ON FOOT

The most popular walks are the paved ½-mile trails to **Lower Yosemite Fall** and **Bridalveil Fall**, on opposite sides of the valley. The level 2-mile return walk skirts **Mirror Lake**, where the surrounding mountains are reflected in the water. With occasional help, all three trails can be navigated by wheelchairs.

One of the more popular longer valley walks is the 3-mile return hike up the **Vernal Fall Mist Trail** to Vernal Fall. Two miles beyond is **Nevada Fall**. Most visitors take all day over the 7-mile return trip because of the altitude. A special treat for the truly fit and determined is the 17-mile return hike up the granite hemisphere forming the 8842-ft back of **Half Dome**. Steel cables anchored in the rock help the final ascent.

easier from the south. Caravans and RVs are not permitted to use the road, but coach tours run there from the valley in the summer months.

SOUTH YOSEMITE To reach **Mariposa Grove**, travelling from the south, turn right immediately beyond the South Entrance and follow the winding road 2 miles east to the paved parking area. This road is closed to all caravans and RVs more than 25 ft long because of restricted parking space. If parking at the grove is full, drive to Wawona and take the free shuttle back. The grove has toilets, drinking water, a museum and souvenir shop (fencing protects the shallow roots of the giant sequoias that dot the parking area). The **Mariposa Grove Museum** is on the site of a cabin built by Galen Clark, the first official guardian when the Yosemite Valley and Mariposa Grove were set aside as a state reserve in 1864. The museum focuses on the natural history of the sequoias.

The main grove is a 2-min stroll down a walking trail. During the summer an open-top tram tours the grove. Near the start of the trail is the **Fallen Monarch**, immortalised in an 1899 photograph of an entire US Cavalry troop, including horses, posing atop the tree. **Grizzly Giant**, an estimated 2700 years old, is one of the oldest living sequoias. The huge limb far up on the south side of the trunk is nearly 7 ft in diameter, larger than the trunk of any non-sequoia tree in the area.

About 150 ft beyond the Grizzly Giant is the **California Tunnel Tree**, cut in 1895 to allow stagecoaches to pass through. Millions of visitors passed through the Tunnel Tree between 1881, when it was cut open, and 1969, when it collapsed under the weight of a record snowpack. Weakened by the gigantic hole in its base, the tree may have died 1000 years prematurely.

From the park's southern entrance, Hwy 41 runs north, past the entrance to **Wawona Basin**. This valley, now largely taken over by a golf course, was a Native American encampment and site of a roadside hostel built by Galen Clark in 1857 – Clark's Station was an overnight stop between Mariposa and the Yosemite Valley. The white Victorian gingerbread **Wawona Hotel**, built in 1879, is still a popular holiday destination.

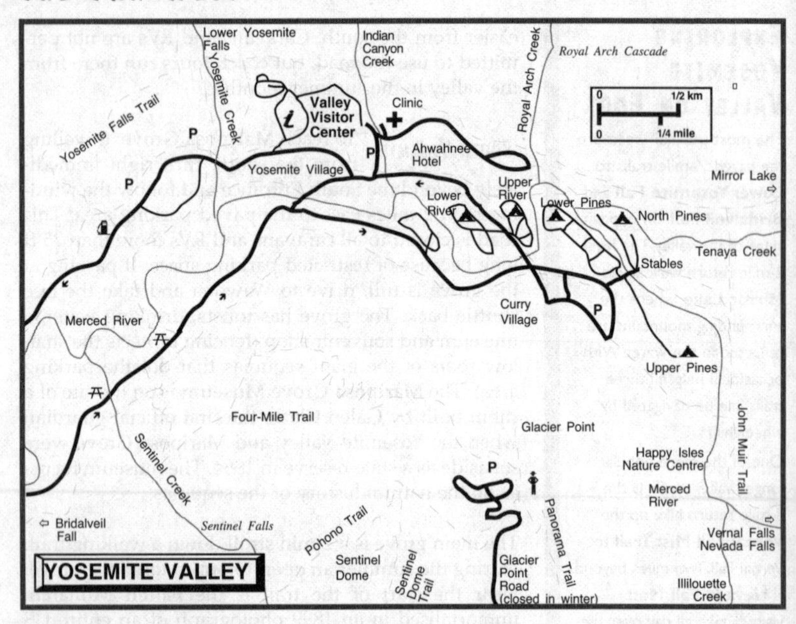

Just beyond the hotel is the **Yosemite Pioneer History Center**, which concentrates on the human history of Yosemite. The museum features a collection of historic cabins and other buildings moved to the site, plus several stagecoaches. There are stagecoach rides and living history demonstrations during the summer months.

Hwy 41 continues north towards Yosemite Valley, 27 miles ahead. It follows the western boundary of the park, winding from the crest of one ridge to the next. Fire scars are visible on both sides of the road in several places, the result of nearly a century of ruthless fire suppression in Yosemite (see box on p. 567).

> **YOSEMITE VILLAGE**
> Village facilities include the Park Headquarters and Valley Visitor Center, stores, restaurants, a medical clinic, bicycle rental (around $20 a day) at Yosemite Lodge, a museum, the Indian Cultural Museum, an art activity centre and other services.

Glacier Point Road is about 12½ miles beyond Wawona, towards Yosemite West, a private development just outside the park boundaries; there is a right turn-off for Badger Pass and Glacier Point. The narrow, winding road (closed to caravans and RVs) twists through forests of pine and fir. It is open all year as far as the **Badger Pass Ski Area**. The remainder of the road is closed in winter, but cross-country skiers can continue all the way to Glacier Point.

The rest of the year it's a short, easy (and well-trodden) walk from the car park at the end of the road. From 3214 ft above, Glacier Point reveals a stunning view of Yosemite Valley. A 1-mile walk from the parking area leads to **Sentinel Dome** (8122 ft), 908 ft above Glacier Point. On full moon nights the valley below becomes a fairyland.

Beyond the Glacier Point Rd turn-off, Hwy 41 turns towards Yosemite Valley. **Inspiration Point**, 6 miles beyond the junction, has a fine view of the Gates of Yosemite. The Cathedral Rocks are on the right, El Capitan on the left, with Half Dome rising in the background. Continuing downhill leads through the tunnel to **Tunnel View**, the official viewpoint into Yosemite Valley. Bridalveil Fall is visible on the right. The view is on the left side of the road, but there is parking on both sides. Watch for pedestrians crossing the highway who are more intent on the view than on traffic. The parking area for Bridalveil Fall, and the beginning of the valley floor loop, is 1 mile further on.

TIOGA PASS The scenic 60-mile Tioga Road rises 3300 ft into the Sierra Nevada on its way east from **Crane Flat** to the Tioga Pass Entrance. **Lee Vining**, just beyond the park's eastern boundary, is one of California's best short drives, threading through lush alpine meadows along the spine of the Sierra Nevada. The road is usually closed by snow in Oct and seldom reopens before the end of May. The best guide to the sights, facilities and geography on the drive is the Yosemite Association's *Yosemite Road Guide*, available on sale throughout the park. Most lay-bys and vista points have picnic tables and explanatory signs keyed to local geography, plants or animals.

From Yosemite Village, follow the valley loop road 6 miles, passing El Capitan on the right. On the left, just beyond El Capitan, is the Merced River and an excellent valley view. At the junction with Hwy 140, bear to the right on Big Oak Flat Rd towards Tioga Pass. The road begins climbing almost immediately, affording broad views across the Merced River canyon; there is an observation point just beyond the

FIRE!

Until the 1960s, forest managers didn't realise that fire is an integral part of sierra forests. Many forest species, including redwoods, need fire to regenerate. Seeds need bare soil created by natural fires and open sunlight to regenerate. When late summer fires swept through these forests every seven to twenty years, burning out undergrowth and fallen branches, a layer of rich ash settled on the bare soil. Years of fire suppression caused a build-up of debris, underbrush and shade-tolerant trees. When fires did start, they burned fiercely through the dense brush and fallen wood. Instead of rejuvenating the forest, fire destroyed everything in its path, leaving vast tracts of charred tree trunks.

The solution is controlled fire, called 'management fires', set by park personnel during damp autumn weather when winds are calm. Watch for signs which warn of management fires ahead. Any other fires should be reported to park personnel by dialling 911 from any telephone.

first tunnel. Turn right onto Hwy 120, following signs for Yosemite Institute, Tuolumne Grove, Tuolumne Meadows and Tioga Pass.

The **Yosemite Institute**, an outdoor education institute, is on the left side of the highway above the **Tuolumne Grove** of sequoias. Walk down to the grove (summer or winter) along a 1-mile return trail. The grove contains 20 sequoias, including the **Dead Giant**, a tunnel tree that broke in two several years ago. Hwy 120 is closed just beyond the grove in winter.

The road continues climbing beyond the grove, following low ridges and shallow valleys between peaks topping more than 10,000 ft. **Siesta Lake**, 14 miles beyond the Tuolumne Grove, is a favourite photographic stop. The shallow lake, on the right-hand side of the road, mirrors the surrounding forests and mountain peaks. **White Wolf**, 1 mile beyond, has summer camping and eating facilities. **Tenaya Lake**, another 14 miles, is a favourite for fishing.

The highlight of the Tioga Pass Rd is **Tuolumne Meadows**, 6 miles from Tenaya Lake. The high country meadows, at an altitude of 8600 ft, are popular for camping, walking and fishing, and as a departure point for mountain climbing and exploration. Rangers at the visitor centre conduct daily walks and evening educational programmes in summer. Petrol, groceries, a restaurant, post office, guides, horses and other services are also available in summer.

The highway continues climbing towards **Tioga Pass** (9945 ft) and the Tioga Pass Entrance just beyond. Food, petrol and accommodation, as overpriced as any inside Yosemite, begin about 2 miles below the park entrance. The last 12 miles of highway take long, sweeping turns down the eastern side of the Sierra Nevada, with magnificent vistas up and down the Lee Vining Canyon National Scenic Byway. Watch for a viewpoint on the right side of the road overlooking Tioga Lake, 5 miles below the park entrance. The panoramas across the Mono Basin and beyond are magical, especially in the warm sunlight of late afternoon.

The steep slope provides an exciting ride, swooping down the mountainside, but it can be extremely hard on the brakes, especially for RVs and caravans. The best driving tactic is to shift into low gear at Tioga Pass and use the brakes sparingly.

Yosemite Out of Season

Hwy 140 from Mariposa into Yosemite Valley seldom closes, but heavy snow closes some of the roads, such as Tioga Rd and Glacier Point Rd, usually mid-Nov–late May. The park may be at its best in winter, when trees and waterfalls are rimmed with ice and the daily visitor count is in hundreds rather than tens of thousands. Badger Pass was the first commercial ski area in California (most runs are beginner and intermediate). Park rangers also lead snowshoe walks into the deep snows that blanket the surrounding forests. In autumn, winter and spring, carry tyre chains in case of unexpected snowstorms.

Notes

Merced is the stop for Yosemite. Reservations for San Joaquin trains can generally be made the same day of travel, except during busy holiday periods.

Hwy 5 from Los Angeles leads to Hwy 99 which connects all the towns mentioned on this route.

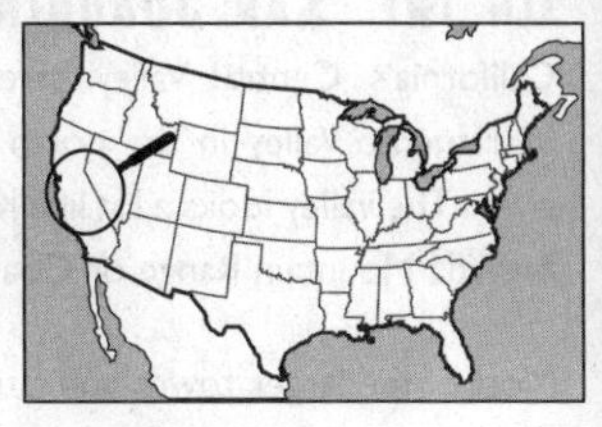

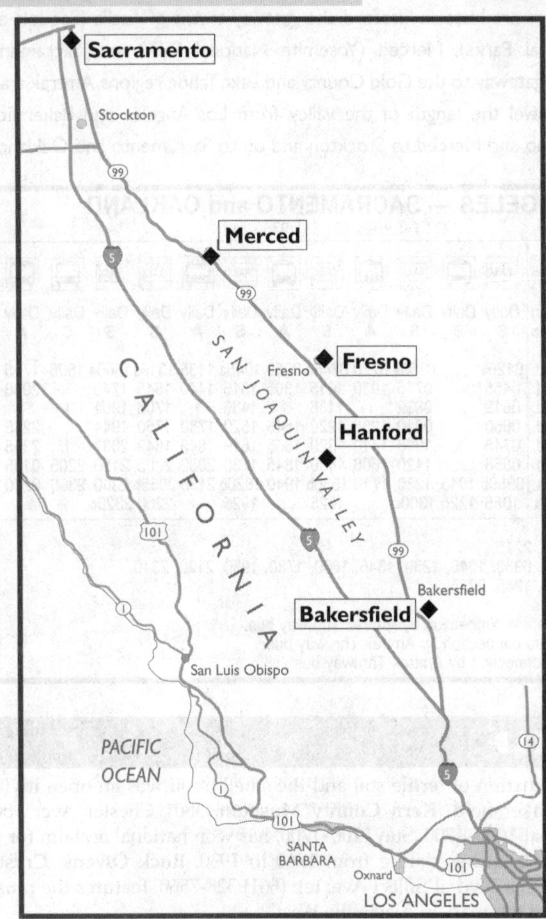

ON THE 'SAN JOAQUINS'

California's Central Valley stretches from Redding to Bakersfield. It is called the Sacramento Valley in the north and the San Joaquin in the south, after corresponding rivers. The valley looks a lot like Kansas... except on clear days when the gently rising Sierra Nevada Mountain Range or Coastal Range is visible in the distance.

Most of the larger towns and cities are located on the eastern side of the valley. Those of most interest to visitors are historic Hanford, the gateway towns of Visalia (Sequoia and Kings Canyon National Parks), Merced (Yosemite National Park) and Sacramento, California's capital and gateway to the Gold County and Lake Tahoe regions. Amtrak trains and Thruway buses travel the length of the valley, from Los Angeles and Bakersfield, through Hanford, Fresno and Merced to Stockton and on to Sacramento and Oakland.

LOS ANGELES — SACRAMENTO and OAKLAND

OTT Tables 356/851/935

Service	RAIL	Bus	RAIL	Bus	RAIL	Bus	RAIL	Bus	RAIL	RAIL	Bus	Bus
Days of operation	Daily	Daily	Daily	Daily	Daily	Daily	Daily	Daily	Daily	Daily	Daily	Daily
Special notes	**S**	**B**	**S**	**A**	**S**	**A**	**S**	**A**	**S**	**S**	**C**	**A**
Los Angeles d.	0125a	....	0355a	0720	0745a	0950	1045a	1135	1315a	1500a	1505	1745
Bakersfield d.	0455	....	0715	1030	1015	1305	1315	1440	1545	1740	|	2030
Hanford d.	0612	....	0832	|	1136	|	1436	|	1706	1901	|	|
Fresno d.	0650	....	0910	1255	1220	1545	1520	1730	1750	1944	|	2245
Merced d.	0745	....	1008	1410	1320	1655	1619	1845	1849	2037	|	2355
Stockton d.	0858	....	1120	1600	1430	1845	1730	2030	2005	2150	2205	0135
Sacramento a.	0950b	1045	1230	1710	1535b	1940	1820b	2135	2055b	2300	2300	0230
Oakland a.	1055	1225	1300c	....	1625	....	1925	....	2200	2320c	....	....

Special notes:
A–Additional trips: 0140, 2215.
B–Additional trips: 0630, 0930, 1045, 1230, 1345, 1600, 1730, 1930, 2120, 2340.
C–Additional trips: 0015, 1245, 2225.
S–San Joaquins services.
a–Los Angeles – Bakersfield connection by Amtrak Thruway bus.
b–Stockton – Sacramento connection by Amtrak Thruway bus.
c–Stockton – Oakland connection by Amtrak Thruway bus.

BAKERSFIELD

The unbeatable combination of fertile soil and the smell of oil was an open invitation for settlers to Bakersfield. **Kern County Museum**, 3801 Chester Ave, open Mon–Fri 0800–1700, Sat 1000–1700, Sun 1200–1700, has won national acclaim for its collection of historic structures dating from 1860 to 1930. **Buck Owens' Crystal Palace**, 2800 Buck Owens Blvd at Sillect Ave; tel: (661) 328-7560, features the music that put Bakersfield on the map as 'Nashville West'.

Visitor Center, 1325 P St; tel: (661) 325-5051; www.bakersfieldcvb.org. Open Mon–Fri 0830–1700.

Amtrak arrives downtown at 601 Truxton St. Adjacent to Centennial Garden Convention Center and hotels.

Downtowner Inn $$ 1301 Chester Ave; tel: (661) 327-7122.

Cottage Sandwich Shop $ 1032 Truxton Ave.
Dewars Candy Shop $ 1120 Eye St. Has served ice cream since 1909.
Uricchio's Trattoria $$ 1400 17th St. Italian family cooking.

HANFORD

Historic Hanford's town square is surrounded by restored buildings including the 1896 **County Courthouse, La Bastille**, shops, restaurants and a carousel. **China Alley** features an 1893 Taoist temple, Temple Theater, herb shop, hand laundry and **Imperial Dynasty Restaurant**, operated by descendants of the once large Chinese community. **Hanford Fox Theater**, 326 N Irwin St, is one of the few remaining Fox 'atmospheric' theatres, with a Wurlitzer pipe organ.

Hanford Visitor Agency, 432 W 7th St; tel: (559) 582-5024, is located in the Amtrak station, three blocks from downtown. Open Mon–Fri 0900–1700.

Irwin Street Inn $$ 522 N Irwin St, tel: (559) 583-8000. B&B near the town square.

FRESNO

Fresno's **Metropolitan Museum of Art, History and Science**, $, 1555 Van Ness Ave, and very own symphony – **William Saroyan Theater**, 700 M St; tel: (559) 498-1524 – mark it as the valley's cultural hub. The art deco **Tower District** (Olive and Wishon Aves) features antique shops, bookshops, restaurants and several live theatres. **Forestiere Underground Gardens** is an underground labyrinth of 50-odd rooms created 1905–46 to protect fruit orchards and other crops from the blistering summer sun. $, 5021 W Shaw Ave; tel: (559) 271-0734; open Wed–Sun 1000–1600 (June–Sept); Sat–Sun 1200–1400 (Oct–Nov). Call for tour reservations.

Fresno Convention and Visitors Bureau, 808 M St; tel: (559) 233-0836 or 1 (800) 788-0836; www.fresnocvb.org; open Mon–Fri 0800–1700. It has an accommodation list.

Amtrak is located downtown at 2650 Tulane St.

George's Shish Kebab $$ 2405 Capitol St; across from Amtrak. Armenian food.
Santa Fe $$ 935 Santa Fe Ave; across from Amtrak. Basque country cooking served family-style.

MERCED

Merced is the transfer point for buses to **Yosemite National Park** (see p. 561). The 1875 **County Courthouse**, 21st and N Sts, houses the county museum. The exterior resembles the State Capitol in Sacramento, and is set in a lovely shady park.

Merced Conference and Visitors Bureau, 690 W 16th St; tel: (800) 446-5353 or (209) 384-3333; www.yosemite-gateway.org. Open Mon–Fri 0830–1700.

The Amtrak station is downtown at 324 W 24th St. Greyhound stops at 710 W 16th St.

Hostelling International $; tel: (209) 725-0407. Call for free pick-up.

The Branding Iron Restaurant $$ 640 W 16th St. A steak house with a collection of cattle branding irons.

SACRAMENTO

California's capital city began at **Sutter's Fort** (27th and L Sts; RT bus 30, 31), built by Swiss immigrant John Sutter, whose Coloma sawmill sparked the Gold Rush. Sutter's adobe administration building is largely original; the rest of the fort ($) is reconstructed. **Old Sacramento** (I–L Sts along the Sacramento River), or 'Old Sac', has brick buildings dating back to the 1850s, skilfully mixed with modern buildings, wooden sidewalks and shade trees. The **California State Railroad Museum** ($) is America's largest railway museum, filled with splendidly restored locomotive engines, luxurious private carriages, sleepers and extensive displays on America's first transcontinental railway. A new **Waterfront Promenade** links Old Sacramento and the **Crocker Art Museum** ($), 2nd and O Sts, the oldest art gallery west of the Mississippi. **Golden State Museum**, 1020 O St, is California's official museum. The domed **California State Capitol** (10th St between L and N Sts) is also an outstanding museum, restored to its turn-of-the-century splendour.

Sacramento Visitor Information Center, 1104 Front St, Old Sacramento; tel: (916) 442-7644; www.oldsacramento.com. Open daily 1000–1700.

Amtrak arrives downtown at 401 I St. Greyhound buses arrive downtown at 715 L St.

HI-Sacramento $ 900 H St; tel: (916) 443-1691. Former mansion, within walking distance of all major attractions.

***Delta King* Hotel** $$$$ 1000 Front St; tel: 1 (800) 825-5464. Restored steam paddlewheel boat on the Sacramento River.

River City Brewing Company $ 545 Downtown Plaza. Offers pub fare.

4th Street Grille $$ 400 L St. Uses pesticide-free produce in salads, pizzas and pastas.

Pilothouse Restaurant $$ *Delta King*; tel: (916) 441-4440. Known for its Sunday brunch.

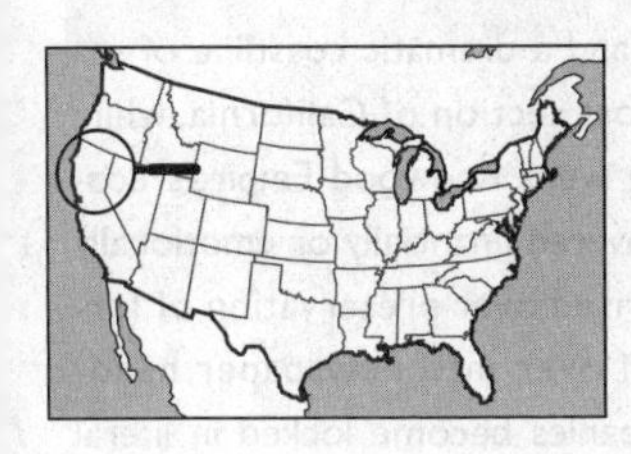

ALTERNATIVE ROUTES

Keeping to Hwy 101 will take you on a slightly shorter inland route (372 miles) that runs roughly parallel to Hwy 1 before the two join at Leggett. On the way, visit quintessentially Victorian American Old Pentaluma, Santa Rosa's Railroad Square Historic District (the station was one of the few buildings to survive the 1906 earthquake) and the northern California wineries between Hopland and Ukiah. Hwy 128, linking Cloverdale on Hwy 101 and Elk on Hwy 1, runs through the vineyards and orchards of Anderson Valley.

If you'd like to let someone else do the driving, the **Amtrak Thruway** bus operates twice daily from Martinez north to Arcata, and the **Greyhound bus** from San Francisco to Portland travels the Redwood Highway daily – OTT table 684.

DRIVING ROUTE

Take Hwy 101 north from San Francisco to the Hwy 1 exit, 3 miles beyond the Golden Gate Bridge.

Follow Hwy 1 north to Leggett.	188 miles
Rejoin Hwy 101 and continue north to Crescent City.	415 miles

For sleep and safety as well as the scenery, allow at least five days for the drive.

PACIFIC COAST HIGHWAY NORTH

Towering forests of coast redwoods, pastoral dairies, and a dramatic coastline of sea stacks and rocky bluffs isolate this north-westernmost section of California, while preserving its regional personality. Timber and fishing were Redwood Empire's economic mainstays, and much of the region has not recovered financially or emotionally from the diminution of both. Local residents are polarised over preservation of forest, fishing and land resources, and animosities spill over into newspaper headlines as environmentalists and huge lumber companies become locked in literal and legal battles.

Despite Ronald Reagan's comment that, having seen one redwood, you've seen them all, the clumps and groves differ in character. Second growth allows much more light to penetrate the canopy, but the size and magnitude of one or more old-growth giants is simply astounding. The stretch of Hwy 101 between Phillipsville and Pepperwood is known as the Avenue of the Giants, while north of Arcata the Redwood National and State Parks collectively conserve some of the tallest, biggest and oldest natural objects on the planet.

Redwood Empire Association, c/o The California Welcome Center, Pier 39, Suite Q-5, San Francisco; tel: (415) 956-3491; www.redwoodempire.com, has information on lodging, dining and attractions in California's coastal areas from San Francisco to southern Oregon.

MENDOCINO

San Francisco artists rescued Mendocino as the lumber industry died in the 1950s. They may have succeeded too well. The town looks like a film set (it has been one, many times), with picture-perfect New England-style buildings perched on the edge of the swirling Pacific Ocean. The whole community is a National Historic Preservation District, its original buildings intact, beautifully renovated, and almost invisible behind the crowds.

Mendocino Art Center, 45,200 Little Lake St, remains the centre for arts and artists throughout the county. The Gallery and the Showcase exhibit local as well as outside artists. If the weather is reasonable, **Mendocino Headlands State Park** is a refreshing respite. Start at park headquarters, the Ford House on Main St, then continue along the sandstone cliffs sculpted by wind and wave. **Russian Gulch State Park**, just north of Mendocino, is another defunct lumber port. The park has 1200 acres of redwoods, rhododendrons, azaleas, ferns, berry bushes, trees, fishing and camping. **Jug Handle State Reserve**, just north of the Caspar Headlands, is a prime example of an ecological staircase. A succession of ancient marine terraces, each about 100 ft above the other, is home to a different set of plants, from salt-tolerant wild flowers near the water to redwoods high above.

Mendocino Coast Fort Bragg Chamber of Commerce, 332 N Main St, PO Box 1141, Fort Bragg, CA 95437; tel: (800) 726-2780 or (707) 961-6300.

Mendocino is filled with B&Bs and restaurants, mostly pricey. Advance bookings essential.

FORT BRAGG

Fort Bragg is Mendocino without culture-vulture crowds and inflated prices. Main St is lined with Victorian buildings, renovated for local use as much as for the tourist trade – merchants decided it was faster, cheaper and more attractive to refurbish than to rebuild. A historic walking guide covers more than two dozen downtown buildings, including the **Fort Bragg Depot, Marketplace and Museum**, a renovated 1924 Ford motor dealership which has railway artefacts, engines, shops and food stalls. The **Skunk Train** ($$$), tel: (800) 777-5865 or (707) 964-6371, still runs through the mountains to Willits on Hwy 101. The **Guest House Museum**, 343 North Main St, displays the history of Fort Bragg and the timber industry.

Fort Bragg-Mendocino Coast Chamber of Commerce, 332 N Main St, Fort Bragg, CA 95437; tel: (707) 961-6300 or (800) 726-2780; www.mendocinocoast.com.

Although Mendocino gets most of the visitors, Fort Bragg is the largest town on the coast between San Francisco and Eureka and prices are considerably more reasonable.

The North Coast Brewing Co. $–$$ 444 N Main St. Usually crowded for the beer and robust meals.

LEGGETT

This small, one-time lumber town is sometimes called the Gateway to the Redwoods. The first of a long string of redwood parks is just north of town, and road signs begin calling Hwy 101 'The Redwood Highway'.

Smithe Redwoods State Reserve, 4 miles north of the town east of Hwy 101, is a preview of the coast redwood giants to come. It is favoured for fishing, picnicking, hiking to a 60-ft waterfall, and summer swimming in the Eel River's South Fork.

About 8 miles short of Garberville, **Richardson Grove State Park** ($), tel: (707) 247-3318, provides services and an early glimpse of major stands of coast redwoods on the Hwy 101 route north. Families swim in the South Fork Eel River in summer; fishers enjoy steelhead later in the year. Camping is popular and cabins are for hire.

Leggett Valley Chamber of Commerce, 66502 Underwood Lane, Leggett, CA 95585; tel: (707) 925-6385.

Eel River Redwoods Hostel, 70400 Hwy 101; tel: (707) 925-6469. Open all year.

GARBERVILLE

AVENUE OF THE GIANTS
Just north of Garberville, coast redwood groves extend for a narrow 31-mile strip along both sides of Hwy 101 from Phillipsville to Pepperwood, cutting left and right over the South Fork of the Eel River. Most are named in tribute to the group or individuals who in the early 20th century worked to save a small number of redwoods before they disappeared. Most groves have a lay-by to park and explore the forest.

Garberville serves as a hub for forestry, and for holidaymakers as a base for exploring the Avenue of the Giants and a convenient stopping point. Environmental protection versus lumbering friction is notable, while musicians and young counterculture types hang out for the atmosphere.

Garberville-Redway Chamber of Commerce, 773 Redwood Dr., Garberville, CA 95542; tel: (800) 923-2613 or (707) 923-2613; fax: (707) 923-4789; www.garberville.org. Open Mon–Fri 0900–1700, shorter hours in winter.

As a services hub, Garberville is well supplied with motels. **Benbow Inn** $$$ 445 Lake Benbow Dr. (1 mile south of Garberville); tel: (707) 923-2124 or (800) 355-3301; fax: (707) 923-2122; www.benbowinn.com. A stunning redwoods version of Tudor, with lovely flower gardens outside and a high-ceilinged lobby and dining room. Open Apr–New Year's Day.

Sicilitos $ 445 Conger St. Old advertising and sports team memorabilia decorate the walls; serves tasty Mexican food and traditional American fare.

HUMBOLDT REDWOODS STATE PARK

Most visitors' encounter with Humboldt Redwoods State Park, tel: (707) 946-2409, is restricted to the Avenue of the Giants, but its 52,000 acres extend to the awesome trees of **Rockefeller Forest**, estimated to represent 10% of remaining old-growth redwoods.

Stop at the convenient and informative visitor centre 2 miles south of Weott, which helps interpret the history of these resilient but endangered trees. A short path from here gives a rare opportunity to see all three species side by side: dawn redwood (*Metasequoia glyptostroboides*), coast redwood (*Sequoia sempervirens*) and giant redwood (*Sequoiadendron giganteum*). The visitor centre is open Thurs–Sun 0900–1700 (Mar–Oct), 1000–1600 (Nov–Feb).

FERNDALE

The town has trademarked its moniker, 'The Victorian Village', but for once the pretentions are justified. Settled in 1852, Ferndale's low-lying, lush pastures were perfect for dairy cattle. It prospered and, by the 1890s, dairymen in Cream City were building heavily embellished Victorian mansions called 'butterfat palaces'. Two subsequent earthquakes wrought havoc, but the homes, mansions, churches and Main St storefronts were repaired and repainted, and once more ooze their charm through sun or frequent fogs.

Main St is the place for shops, galleries, restaurants, bakeries, a meat market, a pioneer museum and the **Kinetic Sculpture Museum**. The **Ferndale Carriage Co.** (from Main and Washington Sts) offers horse-drawn carriage tours of Main St and the mansions. Ferndale is also a walker's paradise.

i **Ferndale Chamber of Commerce**, PO Box 325, Ferndale, CA 95536; tel/fax: (707) 786-4477; www.victorianferndale.org/chamber.

Ferndale has five B&Bs, one hotel, three motels and a county fairground camping area, but book in advance, as the town is popular with tourists from San Francisco and Los Angeles.
Gingerbread Mansion Inn $$$ 400 Berding St; tel: (800) 952-4136 or (707) 786-4000; www.gingerbread-mansion.com. 1899 turreted and gabled Victoriana, with magnificent English formal garden landscaping and a perfect and perfectly incongruous palm tree.

EUREKA

No building in far northern California is more recognisable than the green Victorian **Carson Mansion**, built in 1885 by a lumber baron's employees to fill time. Now a private club, this centrepiece of Eureka's historic **Old Town** (B–I Sts, Waterfront–7th St), shows the 19th-century value of a good fishing harbour with access to lumber. Attractions include horse-drawn carriage rides, galleries, stores, restaurants and B&Bs. Salmon and Dungeness crab are still staples, though fishing is restricted.

i **Eureka! Humboldt County Convention and Visitors Bureau**, 1034 2nd St, Eureka, CA 95501; tel: (707) 443-5097 or (800) 346-3482; fax: (707) 443-5115; www.redwoodvisitor.org. Open Mon–Fri 0900–1200, 1300–1700.

Waterfront Café $$ 102 F St. Fine seafood and salads, a long wooden bar, a stained-glass window with a heron and, most remarkable in this landmark Old Town Eureka building, wall paintings of flowers and natural scenes, even in the loo!
Samoa Cookhouse $ Samoa Bridge, Hwy 255. Large, family-style portions of lumberjack fare served here, in keeping with its status as the last surviving lumber camp cookhouse in the west. Prices are low, and the draw of a free museum to one side with artefacts and old-time pose-with-your-log lumber camp photographs is irresistible.

ARCATA

Youth, counterculture, environmentalism, organic produce and vegetarianism are bywords in this youthful enclave by Humboldt State University. Sand dunes and marshy wetlands are within a mile of an urban forest sheltering magnificent redwoods along trails. Bicycles are common, especially by the marshes and estuaries of the Mad River between Arcata Bay and McKinleyville.

The town square, **Arcata Plaza**, was set aside by original lumber company owners as a park and meeting place. Among well-restored buildings near the plaza are **Jacoby's Storehouse** (1857), 8th and H Sts, its 2-ft-thick stone walls sheltering two restaurants; the 1914 **Minor Theater**, 10th and H Sts, tel: (707) 822-3456, the oldest operating cinema in the USA, enhanced by isinglass door panels; and the 1915 **Hotel Arcata**, 9th and G Sts.

THE KINETIC SCULPTURE RACE

On Memorial Day Weekend (late May) each year, this entertaining and curious spectacle begins at **Arcata Plaza**. Contestants take three days to navigate 38 miles to **Ferndale** on whimsical people-powered contraptions that are the essence of clever design, ornamentation and wackiness. The mechanical sculptures that participate are displayed in Ferndale's **Kinetic Sculpture Museum** (p. 577).

One answer to timber clearing has been to preserve 575 acres on a slope east of Hwy 101 near the university, the **Arcata Community Forest/Redwood Park** (east on 14th St to Redwood Park Dr.). The area includes 10 miles of trails.

Birders are attracted to **Arcata Marsh and Wildlife Sanctuary** year round, but especially mid July–May. River otters and 200 species of birds are visible from trails and blinds on a flat track by grassy uplands, a freshwater marsh, a tidal slough, a brackish lake and mudflats, a system designed to purify wastewater naturally and return it to nature. The **Marsh Interpretive Center**, 600 S G St; tel: (707) 826-2359, is open daily 0900–1700; call for tour information.

i **Arcata Chamber of Commerce/California Welcome Center**, 1635, Heindon Rd, Arcata, CA 95521 (Hwys 101 and 299, exit Giuntoli Ln); tel: (707) 822-3619 or (800) 908-9464; fax: (707) 822-3515; www.arcata.com/chamber/. Ask for the excellent Victorian Building walking tour brochure.

Chain motels cluster around E Guintoli Lane, downwind of fumes from the Louisiana Pacific processing plant. Closer to downtown, a smattering of B&Bs offer Victoriana. Book in advance for Kinetic Sculpture Race weekend in May.

Hotel Arcata $$$ 708 9th St; tel: (800) 344-1221 or (707) 826-0217. Central and cheerful, a 1915 hunting lodge.

Abruzzi $$ 780 7th St (in Jacoby's Storehouse). Italian dinners nightly in historic building on

Arcata Plaza.
Golden Harvest Café $$ 1062 G St. A wide range of dishes with a salad bar, two blocks north of Arcata Plaza.
North Coast Co-Op $ 811 I St. Forthright co-op selling groceries to all. Open 0700–2100.

TRINIDAD

Trinidad qualifies as no more than a hamlet, just south of Patrick's Point State Park, with more than its share of B&Bs and a fishing fleet. Its symbol is the red-roofed replica of the 1871 **Memorial Lighthouse**. A good spot to watch a dramatic sunset behind the Jew's-harp rocks rising from the sea is **Trinidad State Beach** (off Trinity St, north of Main St), with diving and swooping black oystercatchers. Trinidad Scenic Dr., south from Trinity St, parallels Hwy 101 and provides access to **Luffenholtz Beach County Park** and **Houda Point**. **Patrick's Point State Park**, on the west side of Hwy 101 5 miles north of Trinidad, has superb views offshore to whale migrations, northwards to Agate Beach and Big Lagoon and south to Trinidad Head.

i **Greater Trinidad Chamber of Commerce**, PO Box 356; tel: (707) 441-9827.

REDWOOD NATIONAL AND STATE PARKS

The jointly managed state parks, Prairie Creek Redwoods, Del Norte Coast Redwoods and Jedediah Smith Redwoods (east of Crescent City) protect old-growth (over 250 years) coast redwoods. The parks are a World Heritage Site and an International Biosphere Reserve, accessible by car, RV or motorcycle, but much better enjoyed on foot, bicycle, or horseback. Trails are well-marked. Dress for frequent fog and rain. While coast redwoods and elk are the focus, the parks also conserve coastline, tidepools, waterfalls, oak woodlands and prairies. As tame as the stately trees look, it's a wild world out there of ticks, banana slugs, cougars (mountain lions) and bears (see Wildlife, p. 50).

Prairie Creek Redwoods State Park may be best known for the **Roosevelt elk** which roam around three areas (Davidson Rd, Elk Prairie, and remote Gold Bluffs) Aug–Oct. The huge animals cause traffic jams on Hwy 101, and many cars drive through the park without stopping. $, west of Hwy 101, 50 miles north of Eureka; tel: (707) 464-6101, ext. 5301.

Prairie Creek is rich in redwoods, with connecting trails circling through the major groves. Take either Newton B Drury Scenic Parkway exit from Hwy 101. The most dramatic redwoods are near the south exit, where the visitor centre offers previews of what's ahead. Stop and hike to **Big Tree**, a fenced specimen 304 ft high and 216 in in diameter, and to the twined multiple trunks of the **Corkscrew Tree**.

In **Del Norte Coast Redwoods State Park**, 7 miles south of Crescent City, old growth redwoods combine with a spectacular rocky coast and uncrowded trails.

i **Redwood National and State Parks**, 1111 2nd St, Crescent City, CA 95531; tel: (707) 464-6101; www.nps.gov/redw.
Redwood Information Center, Hwy 101, 2 miles west of Orick; tel: (707) 464-6101 ext. 5265. Open daily 0900–1700, with excellent whale-watching.
Prairie Creek/Elk Prairie Visitor Center, 8 miles north of Orick on Hwy 101; tel: (707) 464-6101 ext. 5300. Open 0900–1700 in summer, 1000–1600 in winter.

HI Redwood National Park Hostel, 14480 Hwy 101 at Wilson Creek Rd; tel: (707) 482-8265 or (800) 909-4776, code 74. The Greyhound bus will stop here on request.

CRESCENT CITY

As elsewhere on the north coast, Crescent City, named after the shape of its bay, was long dependent upon fishing and timber. A tsunami tidal wave, caused by a major Alaska earthquake in 1964, wiped out the harbour and downtown, and the rebuilt version gives the town a modern but bland character.

Battery Point Lighthouse, at the west end of Front St, has perched on its well-eroded golden rock since 1856. It has lovely proportions from any angle, and at night its exterior is illuminated. Check in advance to walk the beach to a causeway at low tide. Open for guided tours Apr–Sept.

i **Crescent City/Del Norte County Chamber of Commerce**, 1001 Front St, Crescent City, CA 95531; tel: (707) 464-3174 or (800) 343-8300; www.delnorte.org. Open Memorial Day–Labor Day Mon–Fri 0900–1800, Sat–Sun 0900–1700.

Proximity to Oregon (where prices are lower and there's no state sales tax) keeps prices at Crescent City motels to bargain levels. Hwy 101 divides into north (M St) and south (L St) between Front and 9th Sts; most motels are found here. Others near the harbour at Anchor Rd.

Jefferson State Brewery $–$$ 1151 Lakeview Dr., has a flavourful selection of beers in the 'state of mind' style of this region which, with south-western Oregon, periodically declares its independence from the USA.

WHERE NEXT?

Crescent City is the crossroads for more redwood parks eastwards and the Hwy 199 Smith River Wild and Scenic River drive to the Rogue River Region in Oregon. Up the increasingly wild coastline lies Seattle (see p. 457).

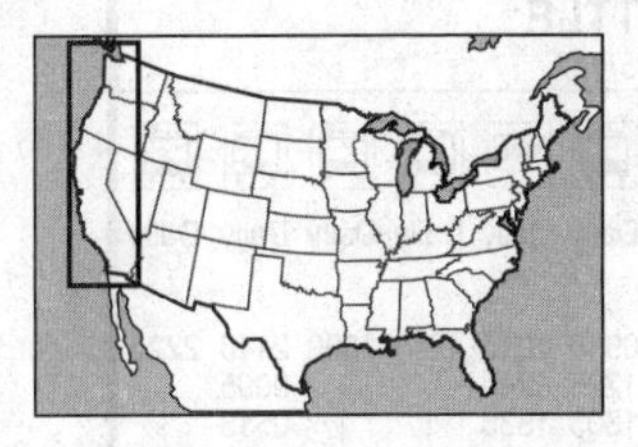

Notes
There is an Amtrak Thruway bus between Salinas and Monterey and Carmel, journey times 40 mins and 1 hr 5 mins. See p. 537.

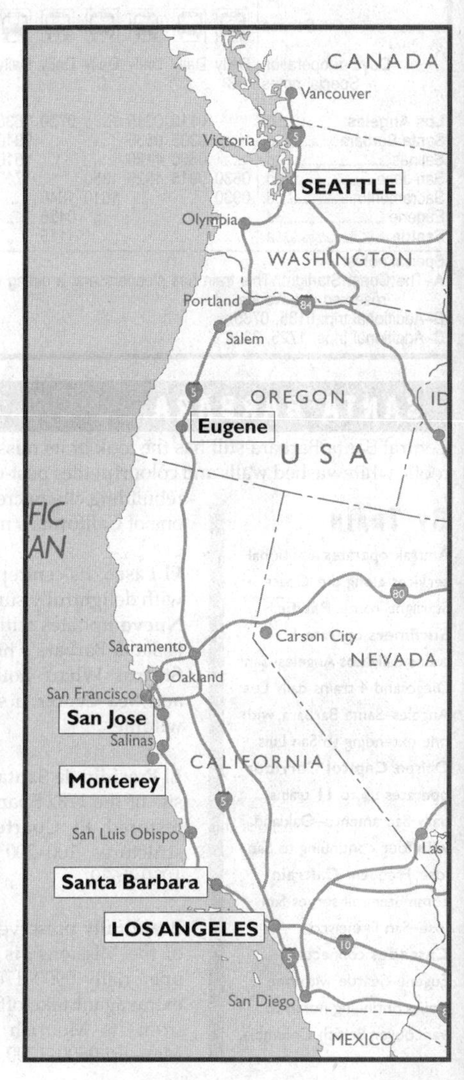

On the 'Coast Starlight'

The 'Coast Starlight' is Amtrak's premier long-distance train, offering spectacular scenery and 'superior service' on the two-day trip from Los Angeles to Seattle. Ride the train northbound for daylight views along 167 km of the Central California coast from Santa Barbara to San Luis Obispo (see p. 538). The following morning, the train crosses the snowy Oregon Cascades before descending into Eugene and Portland (p. 584 and p. 473). After crossing the Columbia River and entering Washington, the train skirts along Puget Sound before evening arrival in Seattle (p. 457).

LOS ANGELES — SEATTLE

OTT Tables 343/906/912/920/935/937

Service	Bus	Bus	Bus	Bus	Bus	Bus	Bus	RAIL	Bus	Bus	Bus	Bus
Days of operation	Daily	Daily	Daily	Daily	Daily	Daily	Daily	Daily	Daily	Daily	Daily	Daily
Special notes	B	①⑥⑦		C				A				
Los Angeles d.	....	0110	0315	....	0720	0630	0930	1015	1245	1500	2140	2225
Santa Barbara d.	....	0305	0535	....	|	0940	1225	1248	|	|	0005	|
Salinas d.	....	0800	1120	....	|	1510	1805	1836	|	|	0515	|
San Jose d.	0630	0915	1320	1350	|	1710	2006	2039	|	|	0720	|
Sacramento d.	0930	....	....	1810	1840	....	....	2359	2035	2340	....	0700
Eugene d.	....	....	....	....	0425	....	....	1244	0550	1010	....	1720
Seattle a.	....	....	....	....	1115	....	....	2030	1400	1735	....	0020

Special notes:

A–The Coast Starlight. This train has sleepers and a dining car available. All journeys should be reserved in advance.

B–Additional trip: 0135, 0735.

C–Additional trips: 1725, 2205

SANTA BARBARA

Central Santa Barbara still has the look of its mission-town origins, but the red-tiled roofs, whitewashed walls and colourful tiles post-date the 1925 earthquake, when the rebuilding city re-created the historic look that makes it one of California's most gracious, attractive cities.

El Paseo, its centrepiece, is an early shopping arcade, with delightfully sunny niches and fountains. **El Paseo Nuevo** updates with the same mission motif; **State St** is Santa Barbara's high street. At its foot, 19th-century **Stearns Wharf** houses speciality shops, restaurants and **Sea Center**, a small museum of Channel Islands wildlife.

El Presidio de Santa Barbara State Historic Park is the site of the 1782 Spanish fort that first lured settlers. Its restored **El Cuartel** is among California's oldest structures. 100–200 E Canon Perdido St; open daily 1030–1630.

Beautifully preserved **Mission Santa Barbara**, 'Queen of the Missions', is at E Los Olivos and Laguna Sts; open daily 0900–1700. The **County Courthouse** is an extravagant take-off on Mission style, with fine views from its Moorish tower: 1100 Anacapa St; open Mon–Fri 0800–1700, Sat–Sun 1000–1700.

BY TRAIN

Amtrak operates additional services along the 'Coast Starlight' route. **Pacific Surfliners** operate 11 trains daily Los Angeles–San Diego and 4 trains daily Los Angeles–Santa Barbara, with one extending to San Luis Obispo. **Capitol Corridor** operates up to 11 trains daily Sacramento–Oakland, with four continuing to San Jose. Frequent **Caltrain** commuter rail serves San Jose–San Francisco. **Cascades** connects Eugene–Seattle with one train continuing north to Vancouver, British Columbia.

FLORA AND FAUNA

The Museum of Natural History specialises in local Native American artefacts, flora and fauna. $$, 2559 Puerta del Sol Rd; open Mon–Sat 0900–1700, Sun 1000–1700. For more local flora, Santa Barbara Botanic Garden, 1212 Mission Canyon Rd, is devoted to native trees, cacti and flowers. $, open daily. Reach both by MTD bus 22.

Santa Barbara Visitor Information Center, 1 Santa Barbara St, Santa Barbara, CA 93101; tel: (805) 965-3021 or (800) 927-4688). Open 0900–1800 summer, 0900–1600 winter.

Amtrak stops at 209 State St.

Santa Barbara Metropolitan Transit District, tel: (805) 963-3364, www.sbmtd.gov, operates a local bus service. Downtown-Waterfront shuttles serve State St and the Waterfront daily 1000–1800.

El Encanto Hotel $$$ 1900 Lasuen Rd; tel: (805) 687-5000 or (800) 346-7039. Sweeping views and a mix of craftsman and Spanish-style cottages.

Hotel Santa Barbara $$$ 533 State St; tel: (805) 957-9300 or (888) 259-7700. A smart stop in the city centre.

The Fish Co. $$ 225 State St. The best fish house in town.

Wine Cask $$ 813 Anacapa St. Excellent Central Coast wine list and five-course Sun–Mon tasting menu.

MONTEREY

State capital under Spanish, Mexican and American flags, Monterey is today a busy tourist capital. **Monterey State Historic Park** offers a self-guided walking tour from 20 Custom House Plaza around 30+ historic buildings dating to 1794.

BOATS AND FISH

Visit Fisherman's Wharf for charter fishing and whale-watching boats and to watch sea lions and sea otters. Cannery Row, immortalised in John Steinbeck's books, has been reborn to process tourists instead of fish. The Monterey Bay Aquarium's three-storey kelp forest is so realistic that wild birds have taken up residence on its artificial ocean.

Monterey Peninsula Visitors & Convention Bureau, 380 Alvarado St, Monterey, CA 93942-1770; tel: (831) 649-1770 or (831) 648-5358, www.monterey.com. Open Mon–Fri 0830–1700.

Motel row, Munras Ave, drifts into the **$$$–$$$$** range.

Room Finders, 140 West Franklin St, tel: (831) 646-9250, makes bookings in all price categories.

Amtrak buses stop downtown at Monterey Transit Plaza, Tyler and Pearl Sts.

Monterey-Salinas Transit, tel: (831) 899-2555, www.mst.org, operates a local bus service, including 'The Wave' shuttle.

For trendy dining, shop Alvarado St, between Del Monte Ave and Jefferson St.

The Poppy $ 444 Alvarado St. A budget breakfast and lunch house.

Rappa's $$ 101 Fisherman's Wharf. Seafood and great early bird specials.

SAN JOSE

Capital of the hi-tech 'Silicon Valley', San Jose was the site of California's first legislature, in 1849. **Peralta Adobe** (circa 1797) and **Fallon House**, an opulent 1850s home, are reminders of this rich past: 175 W St John St; open Tues–Sun 1200–1700. Technology comes alive at **Tech Museum of Innovation**'s interactive exhibits for all ages: $$, 145 W San Carlos St; open daily 1000–1700. Nearby **Children's Discovery Museum of San Jose** offers more than 150 interactive science, art and humanities exhibits: $, 180 Woz Way; open Tues–Sat 1000–1700, Sun 1200–1700.

San Jose Convention and Visitors Bureau, 333 W San Carlos St, Suite 1000, San Jose, CA 95110; tel: (888) SAN-JOSE, www.sanjose.org; information booth in the McEnery Convention Center.

Amtrak and **Caltrain** stop at 65 Cahill St, a few blocks west of city centre, with bus and taxis.
Valley Transit Authority, tel: (408) 321-2300, www.vta.org, operates a 24-hr bus and light rail.

Hotel De Anza $$$$ 233 W Santa Clara St; tel: (408) 286-1000, fax: (408) 286-0500, www.hoteldeanza.com. Elegantly restored 1913 hotel near train station.
Sanborn Park Hostel $ 15808 Sanborn Rd, Saratoga, CA 95070; tel: (408) 741-0166. 1908 log house in a forest. Take VTA bus 54 from Sunnyvale Caltrain station to Saratoga Village; call for a ride.

Gordon Biersch $$$ 33 E San Fernando St. Good quality brewpub fare.
La Taqueria $ 15 S 1st St. 'Killer' soft tacos.

The **Rosicrucian Museum** contains wonderful Assyrian and Babylonian collections, with mummies, a replica tomb and ancient jewellery: $, 1342 Naglee Ave; open daily 0900–1700. Take VTA bus 81. **Winchester Mystery House** is a beautiful but bizarre 160-room mansion: $$, 525 S Winchester Blvd; open daily 0930–1630. Take VTA bus 23 or 24.

EUGENE

Oregon's second largest city is a lively mix of students, professionals and hippies. The Nike running shoe was invented here and miles of running and cycle paths thread through the city and along the **Willamette River Greenway**. Hire bicycles from Pedal Power, 533 High St.

Convention & Visitors Association of Lane County, 115 W 8th Ave, Suite 190, Eugene, or 97440; tel: (541) 484-5307, www.cvalco.org. Open Mon–Fri 0830–1700, Sat 1000–1600.

Hawaii is an offshore US state, a string of eight main islands and over 100 tiny other ones 2500 miles out in the Pacific Ocean, south-west of the USA. Anchoring the string is Hawaii's 'Big Island' in the south-east, with, heading north-west along the line, Maui and Molokai with little Lanai and Kaho'olawe between them, then Oahu, seat of the capital Honolulu, next Kauai and at the far end Niihan.

Formed of ancient volcanoes that have risen out of the sea, the Hawaiian Islands are much more than just sandy beaches and verdant mountain peaks. They are rich in culture and history, fascinating for their nature and geology. Each island is unique, with its own personality. Despite Westernization, the spirit of 'Aloha' survives and Hawaiians welcome visitors warmly.

GETTING THERE AND GETTING AROUND

AIR Hawaii is a 5-hr flight from the Californian coast. Honolulu International Airport on Oahu island is about 5 miles from downtown, 7 miles from Waikiki. Taxis to Waikiki are about $30.00 one way, shuttle buses $8.00.

Most major American airlines, and those from Pacific Rim countries such as Air New Zealand and Qantas, have daily flights to Honolulu. Aloha and Hawaiian Airlines provide several daily flights to each of the other major islands: 35 minutes to Maui, 40 minutes to Hawaii (Kona) and 30 minutes to Kauai. There are no ferries between the islands.

BUS Oahu has an excellent bus system, and for $2.00 you can circle the island; tel: (808) 296-1818.

INFORMATION

Hawaii Visitors and Convention Bureau, 2270 Kalakaua Ave, Suite 801; tel: (808) 923-1811 or (800) 464-2924; www.gohawaii.com. Open Mon–Fri 0800–1630. Check out also www.thisweek.com.

ACCOMMODATION AND FOOD AND DRINK

Most people base themselves on Oahu island. Luxury hotels dominate the prime waterfront areas of popular Honolulu, but good, reasonable accommodation can usually be found just a few blocks from the beaches.

Hale Aloha Hostel $ 2417 Prince Edward St, Honolulu; tel: (808) 926-8313. In a good neighbourhood in Waikiki.
Hokodo Waikiki Beachside Hostel $ 2556 Lemon Rd, Suite 8101, Honolulu; tel: (808) 923-9566. Right at the beach.

Many restaurants have inexpensive buffets; early-bird dinner specials are common.

Wailana Coffee House $ 1860 Ala Moana Blvd at Kalia Rd, Honolulu; tel: (808) 955-1764. This 24-hr 'diner' serves a wide variety of basic American food, as well as Chinese dishes.
Lewers Street Fish Company $$ 247 Lewers St, Honolulu; tel: (808) 971-1000. Excellent seafood at modest prices.

HAWAIIAN FAVOURITES

Try local fish (*ahi* and *mahi-mahi*), *poi* (a condiment with meat or fish), *maui* onion soup, *manapua* (savoury stuffed buns), shave ice, *malassadas* (fried doughnut), or even spam *musubi* (sushi with chopped ham). Don't miss the chance to experience a *luau*, a Polynesian island feast with dancing.

HIGHLIGHTS

OAHU, THE GATHERING PLACE

For most visitors, the first stop is the beach at **Waikiki**. Besides swimming and sunbathing, all sorts of beach toys are available here, for surfing, paragliding, snorkelling, scuba diving, outrigger canoe rides, submarines, and dinner cruises. Waikiki also has easy access to golf, tennis, hiking, bicycling, and horse riding. Beyond Waikiki it is not difficult to find a secluded, empty beach. The **Polynesian Cultural Center**, 55-370 Kamehameha Highway, Laie, www.polynesia.com, is designed as a living museum, with architecture, music, costumes, food and dances from seven major Pacific Island cultures. **Pearl Harbor**, www.pearl-harbor.com, site of the infamous attack that brought the United States into World War II, is still an active naval base. The USS *Arizona* Memorial, the USS *Missouri*, on whose deck the Japanese surrender was signed, and the submarine USS *Bowfin* make Pearl Harbor an all-day excursion.

MAUI, THE VALLEY ISLE

Maui O Ka Noi, 'Maui is Best', is the island's motto, and many visitors agree. A little more laid back than bustling Honolulu, it also offers lots of beaches, hotels and good restaurants. Take an early morning trip to **Haleakala National Park** to watch sunrise over the crater at the 10,000-ft summit of Haleakala.

HAWAII, THE BIG ISLAND

The 'Big Island' makes up about two-thirds of the state's land and, compared to the others, feels like a wide open space. This island is a micro-continent, with snow-capped mountains, active volcanoes, tropical rainforests, prairie ranges and semi-deserts. The main tourist area is the dry west side, known as the Kona Coast. Hawaii's only active volcano is Kilauea, and at **Hawaii Volcanoes National Park** you can see it in action. Better yet, take an evening cruise to watch the glowing molten lava cascade down the side of the mountain and into the ocean, where it creates a steaming cauldron.

KAUAI, THE GARDEN ISLE

Kauai is the quietest, least crowded and has the most spectacular scenery of all of the islands, with just a few well-developed resorts. At **Waimea Canyon State Park**, dubbed the 'Grand Canyon of the Pacific' by Mark Twain, you can drive to the top to the **Kalalau Valley Lookout** for a view of the **Na Pali Coast**. Go early, before the clouds and tourists roll in.

This index lists places and topics in alphabetical sequence. All references are to page numbers. **Bold** numbers refer to map pages. To find routes between cities, see pp. 12–13.

Independent Travellers USA

Feedback Form

Please help us improve future editions by taking part in our reader survey. Just take a few minutes to complete and return this form to us, or even better, e-mail your feedback to *books@thomascook.com* or visit *www.thomascookpublishing.com.*

We'd also be glad to hear of your comments, updates or recommendations on places we cover or you think that we ought to cover.

1. Why is this your preferred choice of budget travel guide?

   (Please tick as many as appropriate)

   a) the price ☐

   b) the cover ☐

   c) the content ☐

   d) other ______

2. What do you think of:

   a) the cover design ______

   b) the design and layout styles within the book ______

   ______

   c) the content ______

   ______

   d) the maps ______

3. Please tell us about any features that in your opinion could be changed, improved or added in future editions of the book, or any other comments you would like to make concerning this book ______

   ______

   ______

   ______

   ______

4. What is the single most useful/helpful aspect of this book? ______

   ______

cut along the dotted line

5. Have you purchased other *Independent Travellers* Guides in the series?

a) yes ☐

b) no ☐

If Yes, please specify which titles ____________________

6. Would you purchase other *Independent Travellers* Guides?

a) yes ☐

b) no ☐

If No, please specify why not ____________________

7. What other titles would you like to see in this series?

____

____

Your age category: ☐ under 21 ☐ 21–30 ☐ 31–40 ☐ 41–50 ☐ 51+

Mr/Mrs/Miss/Ms/Other

Surname ____________________ Initials ____________

Full address: (Please include postal or zip code) ____________________

____

____

Daytime telephone number: ____________________

E-mail address: ____________________

Please detach this page and send it to: The Series Editor,
***Independent Travellers* Guides, Thomas Cook Publishing, PO Box 227,**
The Thomas Cook Business Park, Units 15–16, Coningsby Road,
Peterborough PE3 8SB, United Kingdom.

Alternatively, you can e-mail us at: *books@thomascook.com*

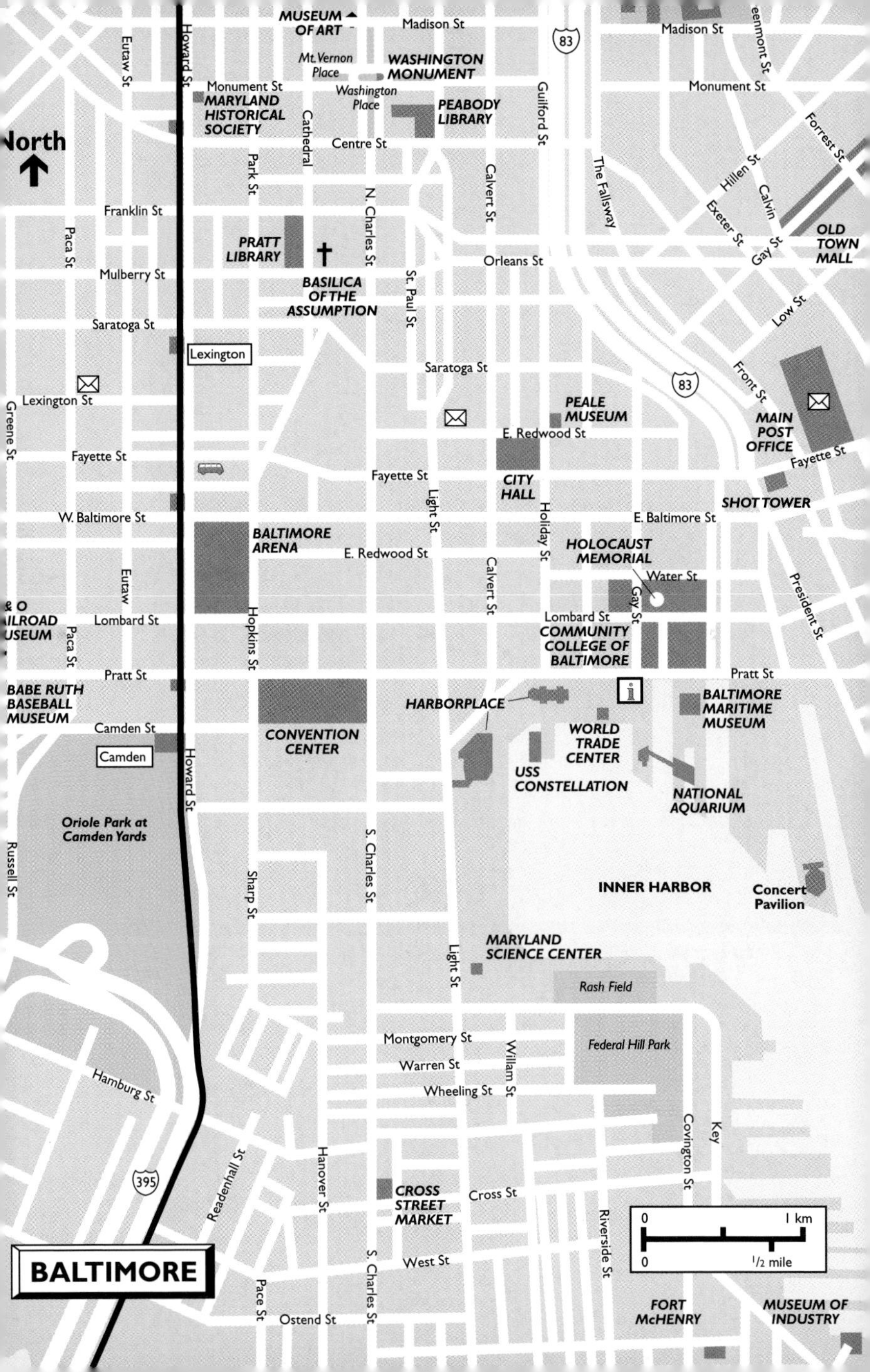

BALTIMORE
North
MUSEUM OF ART
WASHINGTON MONUMENT
Mt. Vernon Place
Washington Place
MARYLAND HISTORICAL SOCIETY
PEABODY LIBRARY
PRATT LIBRARY
BASILICA OF THE ASSUMPTION
OLD TOWN MALL
Lexington
PEALE MUSEUM
MAIN POST OFFICE
CITY HALL
SHOT TOWER
BALTIMORE ARENA
HOLOCAUST MEMORIAL
B & O RAILROAD MUSEUM
COMMUNITY COLLEGE OF BALTIMORE
BABE RUTH BASEBALL MUSEUM
HARBORPLACE
BALTIMORE MARITIME MUSEUM
Camden
CONVENTION CENTER
WORLD TRADE CENTER
USS CONSTELLATION
NATIONAL AQUARIUM
Oriole Park at Camden Yards
INNER HARBOR
Concert Pavilion
MARYLAND SCIENCE CENTER
Rash Field
Federal Hill Park
CROSS STREET MARKET
FORT McHENRY
MUSEUM OF INDUSTRY
Madison St
Monument St
Centre St
Franklin St
Mulberry St
Saratoga St
Orleans St
Lexington St
Fayette St
E. Redwood St
W. Baltimore St
E. Baltimore St
Water St
Lombard St
Pratt St
Camden St
Montgomery St
Warren St
Wheeling St
Hamburg St
Cross St
West St
Ostend St
Eutaw St
Howard St
Cathedral
Park St
N. Charles St
St. Paul St
Calvert St
Guilford St
The Fallsway
Hillen St
Calvin
Exeter St
Gay St
Forrest St
Low St
Front St
Paca St
Greene St
Light St
Holiday St
President St
Hopkins St
Sharp St
S. Charles St
Russell St
Willam St
Covington St
Key
Riverside St
Hanover St
Readenhall St
Pace St
83
395
0
1 km
1/2 mile

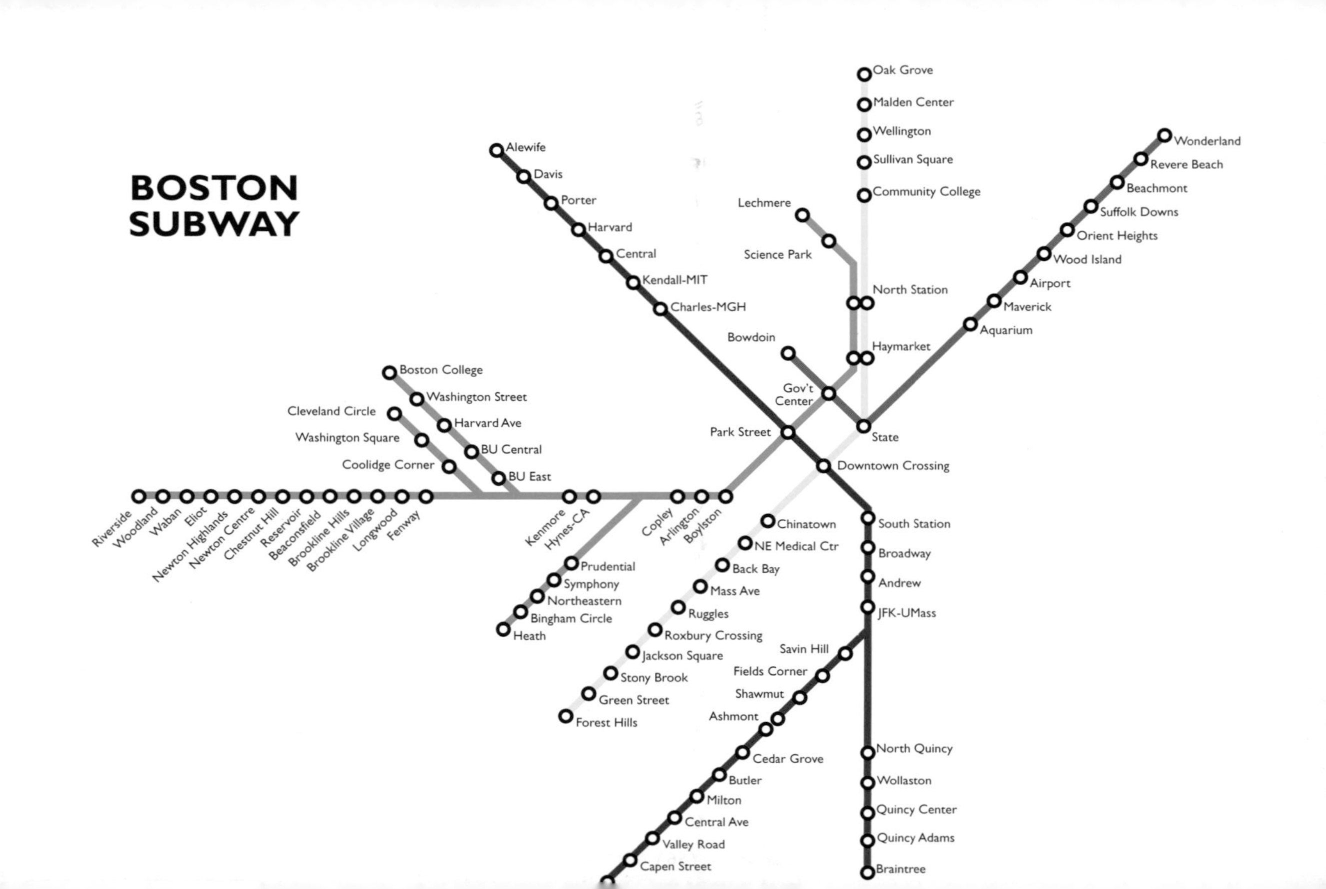
BOSTON SUBWAY
Alewife
Davis
Porter
Harvard
Central
Kendall-MIT
Charles-MGH
Park Street
Downtown Crossing
South Station
Broadway
Andrew
JFK-UMass
North Quincy
Wollaston
Quincy Center
Quincy Adams
Braintree
Savin Hill
Fields Corner
Shawmut
Ashmont
Cedar Grove
Butler
Milton
Central Ave
Valley Road
Capen Street
Oak Grove
Malden Center
Wellington
Sullivan Square
Community College
North Station
Haymarket
State
Chinatown
NE Medical Ctr
Back Bay
Mass Ave
Ruggles
Roxbury Crossing
Jackson Square
Stony Brook
Green Street
Forest Hills
Wonderland
Revere Beach
Beachmont
Suffolk Downs
Orient Heights
Wood Island
Airport
Maverick
Aquarium
Gov't Center
Bowdoin
Lechmere
Science Park
Boylston
Arlington
Copley
Hynes-CA
Kenmore
Prudential
Symphony
Northeastern
Bingham Circle
Heath
Boston College
Washington Street
Harvard Ave
BU Central
BU East
Cleveland Circle
Washington Square
Coolidge Corner
Fenway
Longwood
Brookline Village
Brookline Hills
Beaconsfield
Reservoir
Chestnut Hill
Newton Centre
Newton Highlands
Eliot
Waban
Woodland
Riverside

NEWYORK DISTRICT
North
NEWARK
NEW JERSEY
NEWARK INTERNATIONAL AIRPORT
JERSEY CITY
ELLIS ISLAND
STATUE OF LIBERTY
STATEN ISLAND
Verrazano Narrows Bridge
BROOKLYN
MANHATTAN
PORT AUTHORITY BUS TERMINAL
PENN STATION
CENTRAL PARK
HUDSON
George Washington Bridge
NEWYORK BOTANICAL GARDENS
LA GUARDIA AIRPORT
QUEENS
EAST
NEW YORK
JAMAICA BAY
JOHN F. KENNEDY INTERNATIONAL AIRPORT
GATEWAY NATIONAL RECREATION AREA
Garden State Parkway
New Jersey Turnpike
Pulaski Skyway
Cross Island Parkway
Inter Boro Parkway
Belt Parkway
Ocean Parkway
0 10 kms
0 5 miles

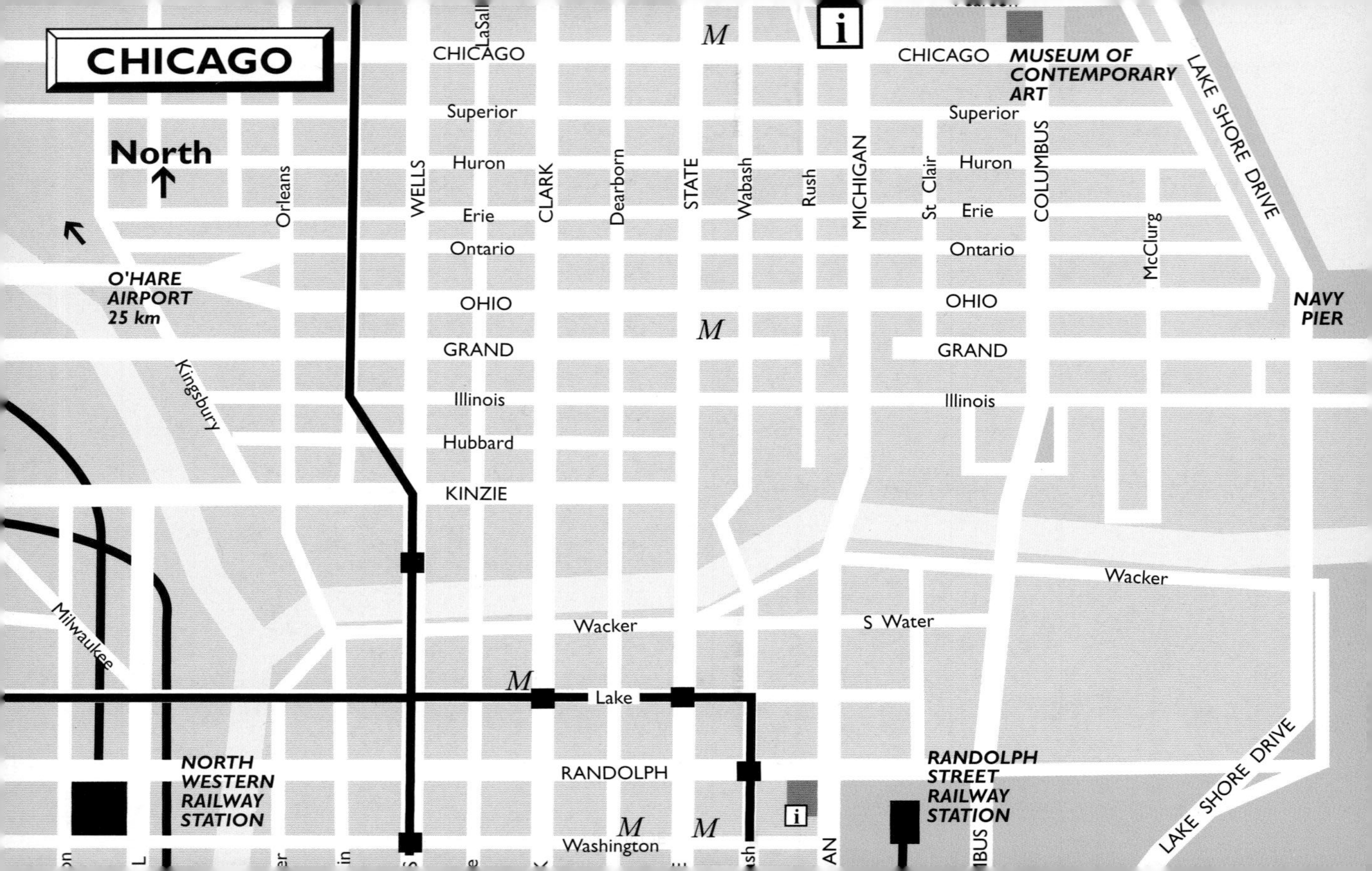
CHICAGO
North
O'HARE AIRPORT 25 km
Orleans
Kingsbury
Milwaukee
WELLS
CLARK
Dearborn
STATE
Wabash
Rush
MICHIGAN
St Clair
COLUMBUS
McClurg
CHICAGO
Superior
Huron
Erie
Ontario
OHIO
GRAND
Illinois
Hubbard
KINZIE
Wacker
S Water
Lake
RANDOLPH
Washington
MUSEUM OF CONTEMPORARY ART
LAKE SHORE DRIVE
NAVY PIER
NORTH WESTERN RAILWAY STATION
RANDOLPH STREET RAILWAY STATION

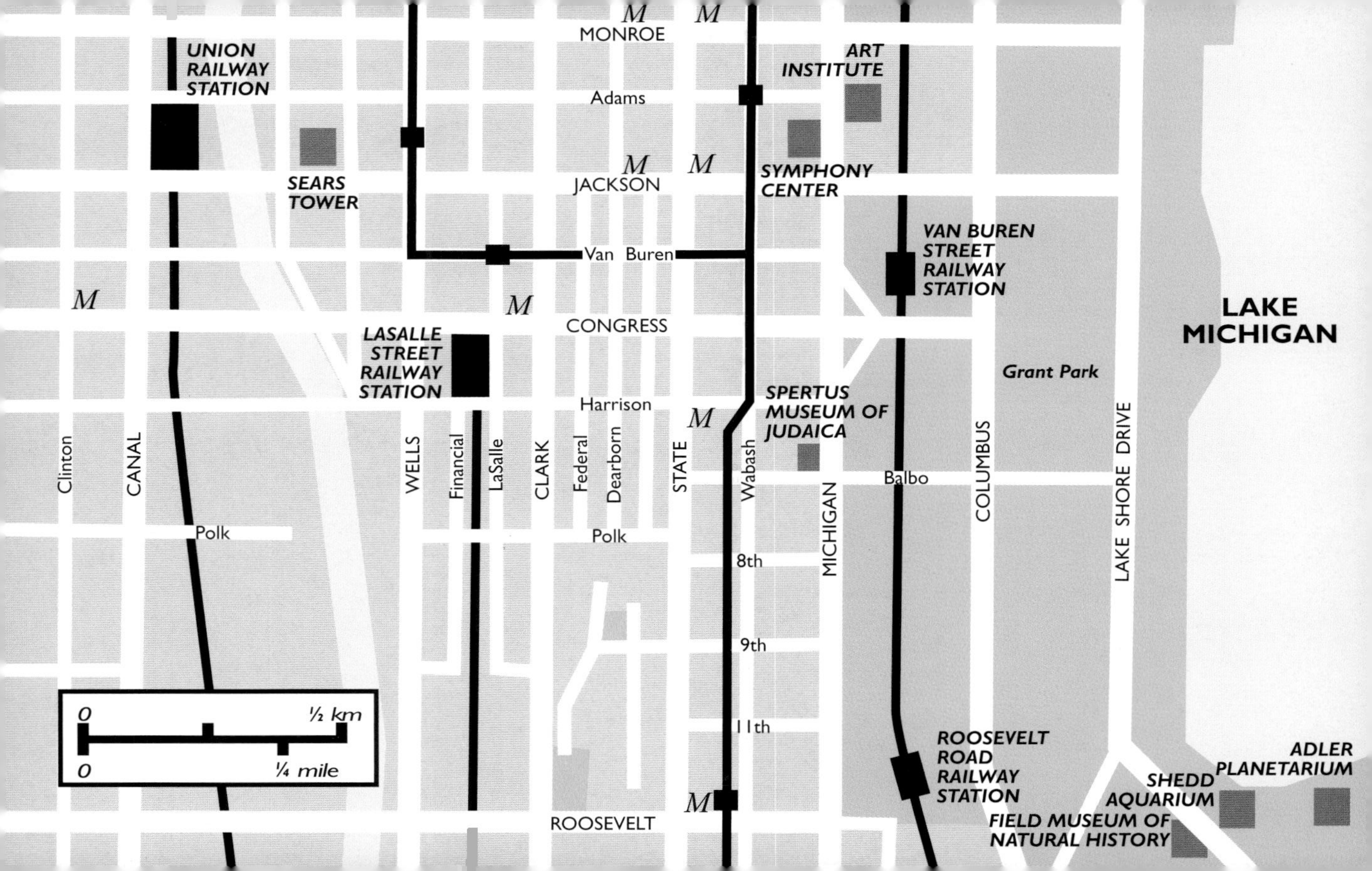
LAKE MICHIGAN
UNION RAILWAY STATION
SEARS TOWER
LASALLE STREET RAILWAY STATION
ART INSTITUTE
SYMPHONY CENTER
VAN BUREN STREET RAILWAY STATION
Grant Park
SPERTUS MUSEUM OF JUDAICA
ROOSEVELT ROAD RAILWAY STATION
ADLER PLANETARIUM
SHEDD AQUARIUM
FIELD MUSEUM OF NATURAL HISTORY
MONROE
Adams
JACKSON
Van Buren
CONGRESS
Harrison
Polk
Balbo
8th
9th
11th
ROOSEVELT
Clinton
CANAL
WELLS
Financial
LaSalle
CLARK
Federal
Dearborn
STATE
Wabash
MICHIGAN
COLUMBUS
LAKE SHORE DRIVE
M
0
½ km
0
¼ mile

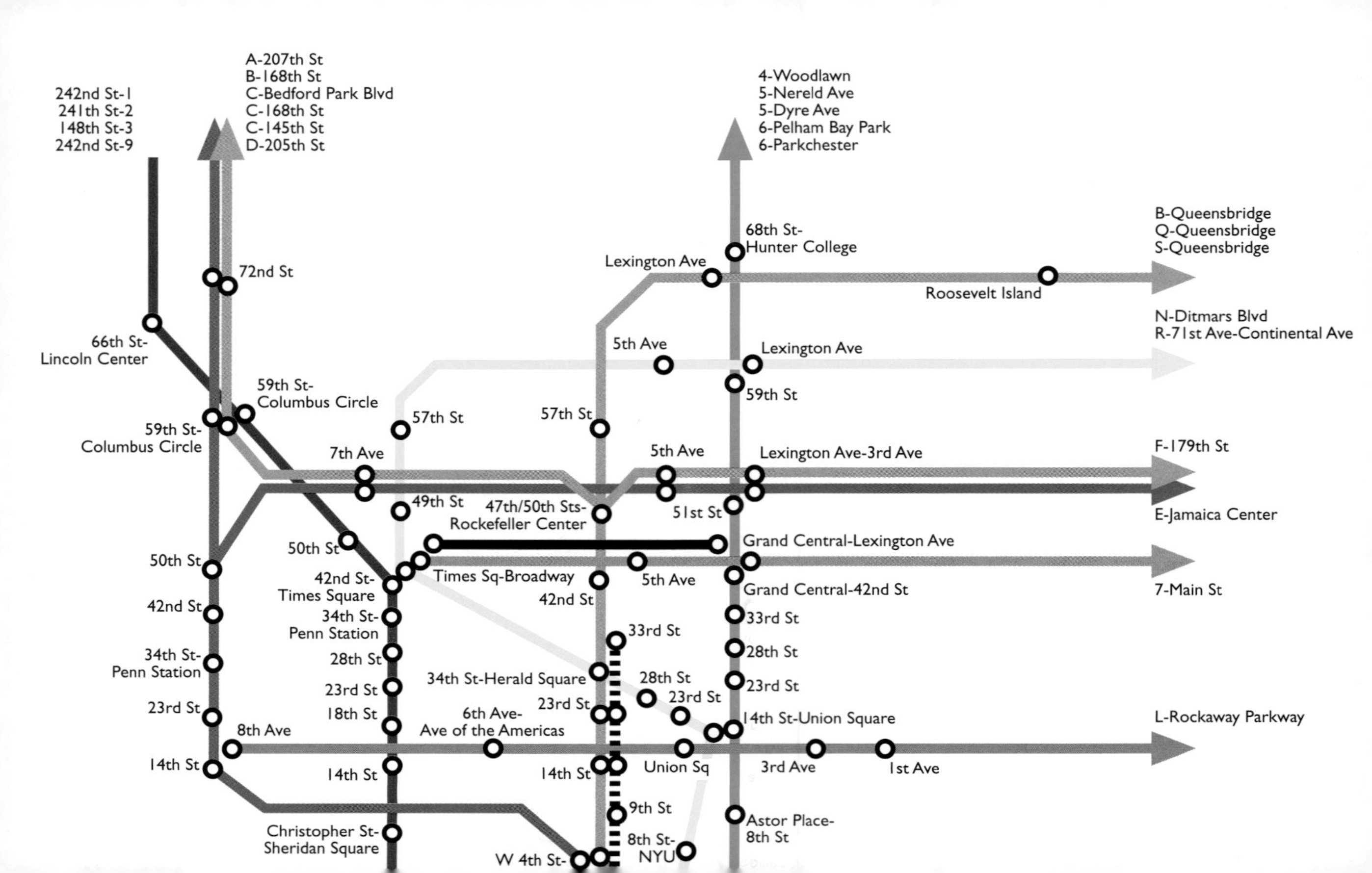
242nd St-1
241th St-2
148th St-3
242nd St-9
A-207th St
B-168th St
C-Bedford Park Blvd
C-168th St
C-145th St
D-205th St
4-Woodlawn
5-Nereld Ave
5-Dyre Ave
6-Pelham Bay Park
6-Parkchester
B-Queensbridge
Q-Queensbridge
S-Queensbridge
68th St-
Hunter College
Lexington Ave
Roosevelt Island
72nd St
66th St-
Lincoln Center
N-Ditmars Blvd
R-71st Ave-Continental Ave
5th Ave
Lexington Ave
59th St
59th St-
Columbus Circle
59th St-
Columbus Circle
57th St
57th St
7th Ave
5th Ave
Lexington Ave-3rd Ave
F-179th St
49th St
47th/50th Sts-
Rockefeller Center
51st St
E-Jamaica Center
50th St
Grand Central-Lexington Ave
50th St
Times Sq-Broadway
42nd St-
Times Square
42nd St
5th Ave
Grand Central-42nd St
7-Main St
42nd St
34th St-
Penn Station
33rd St
33rd St
34th St-
Penn Station
28th St
34th St-Herald Square
28th St
28th St
23rd St
23rd St
23rd St
23rd St
23rd St
18th St
6th Ave-
Ave of the Americas
14th St-Union Square
L-Rockaway Parkway
8th Ave
14th St
14th St
14th St
Union Sq
3rd Ave
1st Ave
9th St
Astor Place-
8th St
Christopher St-
Sheridan Square
8th St-
NYU
W 4th St-

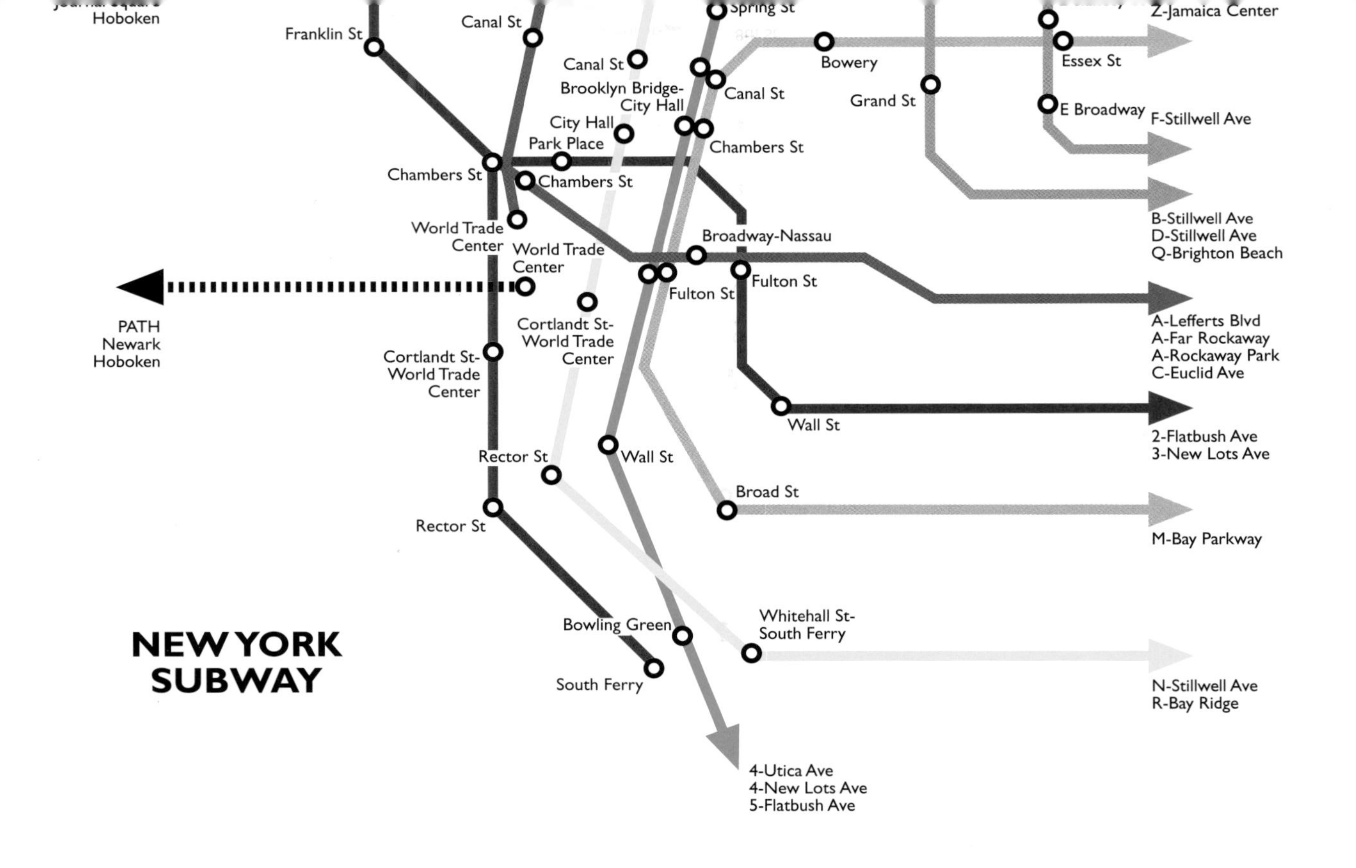
Hoboken
Franklin St
Canal St
Canal St
Brooklyn Bridge-
City Hall
City Hall
Park Place
Chambers St
Chambers St
Chambers St
World Trade
Center
World Trade
Center
Spring St
Canal St
Bowery
Grand St
Essex St
E Broadway
Z-Jamaica Center
F-Stillwell Ave
B-Stillwell Ave
D-Stillwell Ave
Q-Brighton Beach
Broadway-Nassau
Fulton St
Fulton St
A-Lefferts Blvd
A-Far Rockaway
A-Rockaway Park
C-Euclid Ave
PATH
Newark
Hoboken
Cortlandt St-
World Trade
Center
Cortlandt St-
World Trade
Center
Wall St
2-Flatbush Ave
3-New Lots Ave
Rector St
Wall St
Rector St
Broad St
M-Bay Parkway
Bowling Green
Whitehall St-
South Ferry
South Ferry
N-Stillwell Ave
R-Bay Ridge
4-Utica Ave
4-New Lots Ave
5-Flatbush Ave
NEW YORK
SUBWAY

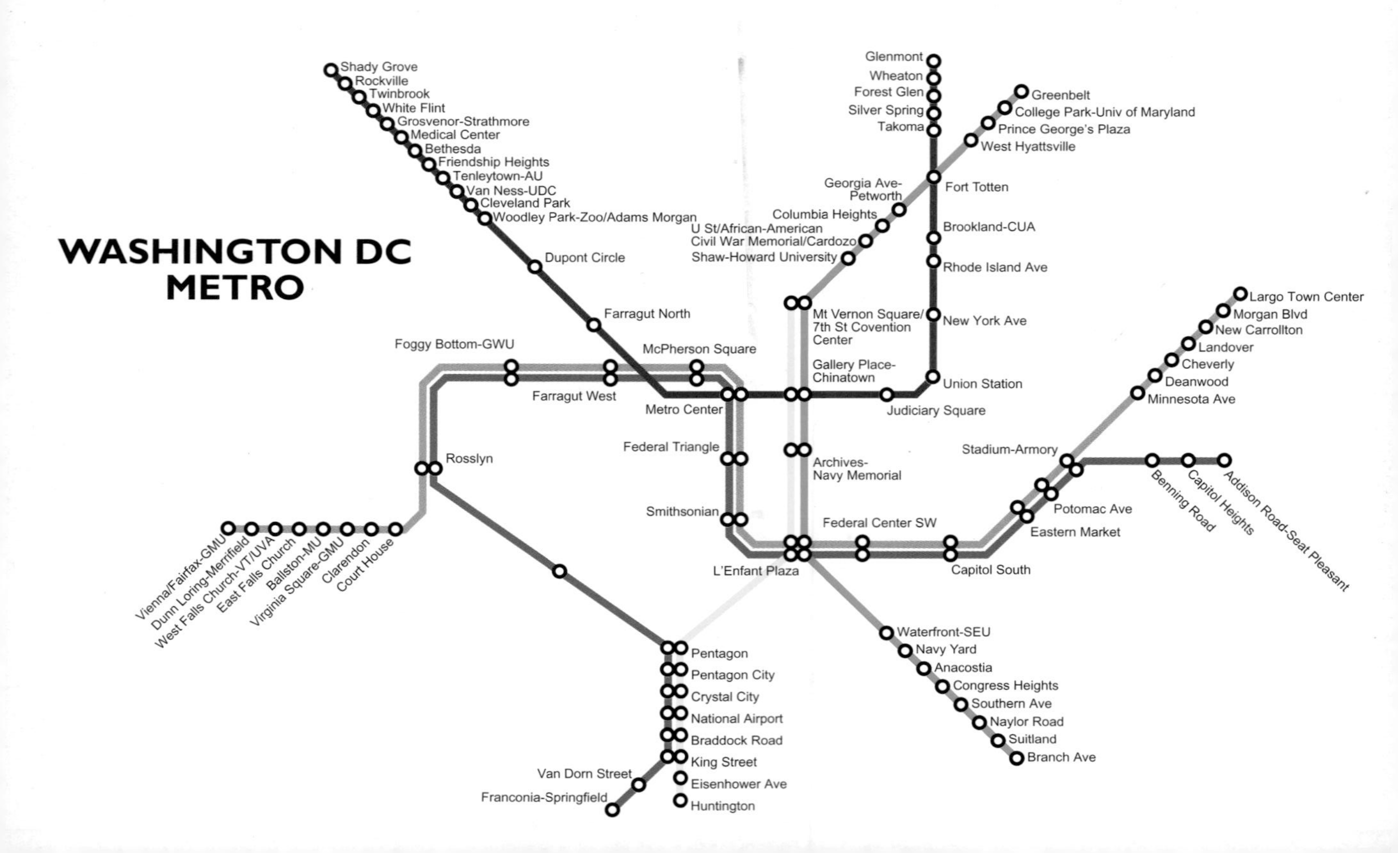

WASHINGTON DC METRO
Shady Grove
Rockville
Twinbrook
White Flint
Grosvenor-Strathmore
Medical Center
Bethesda
Friendship Heights
Tenleytown-AU
Van Ness-UDC
Cleveland Park
Woodley Park-Zoo/Adams Morgan
Dupont Circle
Farragut North
Glenmont
Wheaton
Forest Glen
Silver Spring
Takoma
Greenbelt
College Park-Univ of Maryland
Prince George's Plaza
West Hyattsville
Fort Totten
Georgia Ave-Petworth
Columbia Heights
U St/African-American Civil War Memorial/Cardozo
Shaw-Howard University
Brookland-CUA
Rhode Island Ave
Mt Vernon Square/7th St Covention Center
New York Ave
Gallery Place-Chinatown
Union Station
Judiciary Square
Foggy Bottom-GWU
McPherson Square
Farragut West
Metro Center
Federal Triangle
Archives-Navy Memorial
Smithsonian
L'Enfant Plaza
Federal Center SW
Capitol South
Eastern Market
Potomac Ave
Stadium-Armory
Minnesota Ave
Deanwood
Cheverly
Landover
New Carrollton
Morgan Blvd
Largo Town Center
Benning Road
Capitol Heights
Addison Road-Seat Pleasant
Rosslyn
Vienna/Fairfax-GMU
Dunn Loring-Merrifield
West Falls Church-VT/UVA
East Falls Church
Ballston-MU
Virginia Square-GMU
Clarendon
Court House
Pentagon
Pentagon City
Crystal City
National Airport
Braddock Road
King Street
Eisenhower Ave
Huntington
Van Dorn Street
Franconia-Springfield
Waterfront-SEU
Navy Yard
Anacostia
Congress Heights
Southern Ave
Naylor Road
Suitland
Branch Ave